LEGEND

TRANSPORT FEATURES

AIR
- ✈ Airport
- ✛ Airfield

ROAD
- Expressway
- Expressway (U/C)
- Major Street
- Secondary Road
- Large Minor Street
- Small Minor Road
- Footpath

RAILWAY
- JR Shinkansen lines
- JR railway line
- Other railways line

GENERAL TRANSPORT FEATURES
- Bus Terminal
- ℗ Car Park
- Gate
- → One-way Arrow
- Petrol Station
- ⑯ National Highway Route
- ㉘ Prefecture Route

WATER
- 4 hours Ferry Route and Travel Time
- Ferry Terminal
- ⚓ Harbor

BUILDINGS
- Building with Known Shape
- ▲ General Building

RECREATIONAL FEATURES

DINING & ACCOMMODATION
- Ⓗ Hotel
- Ⓡ Restaurant
- Ⓕ Food Center

ENVIRONMENTAL AMENITIES
- Nature Reserve
- Park/Open Space

RECREATIONAL AMENITIES
- Beach
- ⋒ Cave
- ♨ Hot Spring/ Onsen
- Monument
- 🏛 Museum
- ★ Place of Interest
- ⓘ Tourist Information
- ◉ World Heritage Site
- Waterfall
- Cinema
- Travel Agent/Airline Office

SHOPPING
- Ⓜ Market
- ⊖ Shop/ Shopping

SPORTS AMENITIES
- Diving
- Golf Corse
- Sea Sport Center
- Stadium
- Surfing
- Snorkeling
- Ski Area

PHYSICAL FEATURES
- + Elevation Point
- Lake/Sea
- Sand
- Swamp
- River

GENERAL FEATURES

BOUNDARIES
- International Border
- Prefecture Border

DIPLOMATIC MISSIONS
- Embassy/Consulate

EDUCATION
- School
- ▪ Higher Education

PLACES OF WORSHIP
- ⛩ Sinto Shrine
- Temple
- † Church
- ☾ Mosque

PUBLIC AMENITIES
- Ⓑ Bank
- ✚ Hospital
- ✶ Police
- ✉ Post Office

STRUCTURES
- — Dam
- Lighthouse/ Tower

URBAN AREA ZONE
- Built-up Area
- Park/ Garden
- Other Area

LOCALITIES

CITY PLANS
- GINZA Town Name
- Ebisucho Village Name

MEDIUM SCALES
- MIYAZU Town Name
- Nakatsu Village Name

AREA MAPS
- ■ Large City
- ▣ City
- ◉ Large Town
- ◎ Medium Town
- ○ Small Town
- ○ Village

Front cover photo:
© Sean Pavone/123rf.com

GLOSSARY

JAPANESE	ENGLISH	DEUTSCH	FRANÇAIS	NEDERLANDS
Daigaku	University	Universitat	Universite	Universiteit
Doro	Street	Straße	Rue	Weg/Straat
Gakko	School	Schule	Ecole	School
Gawa	River	Fluß	Rivière	Rivier
Gu/ Jingu/ Jinja	Shrine	Schrein	Tombeau	Heiligdom
Hama	Beach	Badestrand	Plage	Strand
Hanto	Peninsula	Halbinsel	Péninsule	Schiereiland
Hondo	Main Hall	Haupthalle	Hall Principal	Grote zaal
Hyakkaten	Dep't Store	Kaufhaus	Grand magasin	Warenhuis
Ichiba	Market	Markt	Marché	Markt
Ji/ Do/ Dera/ Tera	Temple	Tempel	Temple	Tempel
Jo	Castle	Schloss	Château	Kasteel
Kaikan	Hall/ Building	Gebäude	Bâtiment	Gebouw
Kaikyo	Strait	Meerenge	Détroit	Zeestraat
Ko	Lake	See	Lac	Meer
Koen	Park	Parkanlage	Jardins	Tuinen
Ku	Ward	Mündel	Quartier	Afdeling
Mon/ Torii	Gate	Tor	Porte	Gate
Oka	Hill	Hügel	Colline	Heuvel
Onsen	Hot Spring	Therme	Source chaude	Hot Spring
Ryokan	Inn	Gasthaus	Auberge	Herberg
Shima/ Jima/ To	Island	Insel	Île	Eiland
Shoto	Archipelago	Archipel	Archipel	Archipel
Teien	Garden	Garten	Jardin	Park/Tuinen
Wan	Bay	Bucht	Bai	Baai
Yama/ Zan	Mountain	Berg	Montagne	Berg

Japan
Travel Atlas

Published By Tuttle Publishing,
an imprint of Periplus Editions (HK) Ltd.
www.tuttlepublishing.com

© 2014 Periplus Editions (HK) Ltd.
First Edition
All Rights Reserved
ISBN 978-4-8053-0966-7

Distributors:
North America, Latin America & Europe
Tuttle Publishing
364 Innovation Drive
North Clarendon, VT 05759-9436, USA
Tel: 1 (802) 773 8930
Fax: 1 (802) 773 6993
info@tuttlepublishing.com
www.tuttlepublishing.com

Japan
Tuttle Publishing
Yaekari Bldg. 3rd Floor
5-4-12 Osaki Shinagawa-ku,
Tokyo 141-0032 Japan
Tel: (81) 3 5437 0171
Fax: (81) 3 5437 0755
sales@tuttle.co.jp
www.tuttle.co.jp

Asia Pacific
Berkeley Books Pte Ltd
61 Tai Seng Avenue #02-12
Singapore 534167
Tel: (65) 6280 1330
Fax: (65) 6280 6290
inquiries@periplus.com.sg
www.periplus.com

Indonesia
PT Java Books Indonesia
Jl. Rawa Gelam IV No. 9
Kawasan Industri Pulogadung
Jakarta Timur 13930 Indonesia
Tel: 62 (021) 4682 1088
Fax: 62 (021) 461 0206
crm@periplus.co.id
www.periplus.com

Printed in Singapore   1404CP
16 15 14   1 2 3 4 5
TUTTLE PUBLISHING ® is a registered
trademark of Tuttle Publishing,
a division of Periplus Editions (HK) Ltd.

HOW TO USE THIS TRAVEL ATLAS

The maps in *Travel Atlas Japan* are organized into eleven chapters, each one covering a major region of the country. Each of the 148 detailed maps in this atlas is presented in a logical, easy-to-follow manner, with emphasis given to covering the most frequently-visited areas. All cities, towns, villages, and tourist sites including nature reserves are indexed for quick reference.

Each chapter begins with an overview map of the region covered. Blue boxes indicate the insets which follow on subsequent pages, allowing user to go directly to the desired pages.

The contents page of this atlas shows a key map of Japan. This map has color-coded boxes indicating the respective regions covered by each chapter. All maps, where possible, are arranged so that towns and cities are shown adjacent to a regional map of the area, allowing the user to locate nearby points of interest and find out how to travel from one area to another.

The index at the end of the atlas lists all names of cities, towns and tourist sites that appear on the various maps. These listings give the page number and inset map where they are located to help users find the place quickly.

TUTTLE Publishing

Tokyo | Rutland, Vermont | Singapore

CONTENTS

TOKYO

Greater Tokyo 4 – 5
Imperial Palace & Tokyo Station 6 – 7
Ginza, Tsukiji & Tokyo Tower 8 – 9
Asakusa, Ueno & Akihabara 10 – 11
Roppongi, Shibuya, Omotesando,
Harajuku & Meiji Shrine 12 – 13
Shinjuku 14 – 15
Ikebukuro 16 – 17
Meguro & Shinagawa 18 – 19
Odaiba 20 – 21

MT. FUJI & AROUND TOKYO

Izu Islands 22
Ogasawara Islands 22
Mt. Fuji & Around Tokyo 22 – 23
Yokohama Area 23
Yokohama 24 – 25
Kawasaki 25
Kamakura 26 – 27
Mt. Fuji 28
Hakone 29
Hakone Town 29
Lake Kawaguchi 29
Izu Peninsula 30
Kozu-shima & Nii-jima 30
Miyake-jima 30
Atami 31
Shimoda 31
Oshima 31
Hachijo-jima 31
Chichi-jima 31
Haha-jima 31
Nikko Area 32 – 33
Nikko Town 32
Kawagoe - Little Edo 32
Narita 33

CENTRAL HONSHU

Central Honshu 34
Shirakawa-go & Gokayama 34
Nagoya Area 35
Central Nagoya 36 – 37
Inuyama 37
Kanazawa 38
Takayama 39
Noto Peninsula 39
Gujo Hachiman 39
Nagano & Matsumoto Areas 40
Nagano 41
Lake Suwa 41
Matsumoto 41
Shizouka 41

KYOTO

Kyoto 42
Central & Eastern Kyoto 43
Kawaramachi & Gion 44 – 45
Northern Kyoto 46 – 47
Western Kyoto 48 – 49
Southern Kyoto 50 – 51
Fushimi Area 50
Kurama Village 52
Takao Village 52
Enryaku-ji & Mt. Hiei 52
Ohara Village 53
Uji Town 53

KANSAI

Kansai Area 54
Osaka Area 55
Greater Osaka 56 – 57
Osaka Station 58 – 59
Osaka Namba 60 – 61
Kobe 62 – 63
Around Nara 64
Nara 64 – 65
Mt. Koya 64
Asuka 65
Yoshino 65
Himeji Castle 66
Kinosaki 66
Amano Hashidate 66
Hikone Castle 66
Hongu Onsens 66
Lake Biwa 67

HIROSHIMA & WESTERN HONSHU

Hiroshima & Western Honshu 68 – 69
Shodo Island 68
Hiroshima 70 – 71
Hagi 72
Shimonoseki 72
Tsuwano 73
Miyajima 73
Iwami Ginzan 73
Yamaguchi 73
Iwakuni 73
Matsue 74
Onomichi 74
Tottori 75
Okayama 75
Kurashiki 75

NORTHERN HONSHU

Shirakami Mountains 76
Hirosaki 76
Aomori 76 – 77
Lake Towada 76 – 77
Northern Honshu 77
Akita 78
Kakunodate 78
Lake Tazawa 78 – 79
Hanamaki 78 – 79
Hiraizumi & Ichinoseki 79
Aizu, Inawashiro & Ura-bandai 80
Sado-ga Island 80
Sendai 81
Matsushima 81
Dewa Sanzen 81
Zao Onsen 81

HOKKAIDO

Daisetsuzan National Park 82
Niseko & Lake Toya 82
Kushiro National Park 82
Hokkaido 82 – 83
Rishiri-Rebun-Sarobetsu National Park 83
Akan National Park 83
Shiretoko National Park 83
Otaru 84
Hakodate 84
Sapporo 85

Yaeyama Islands   Miyako Is

SHIKOKU

Shimanami Kaido 86
Uwajima 86
Shikoku 86 – 87
Iya Valley 87
Kochi 86 – 87
Seto-ohashi Bridge 87
Matsuyama 88 – 89
Kotohira 88
Tokushima 88 – 89
Takamatsu 89

KYUSHU

Kyushu 90
Kagoshima 90 – 91
Miyazaki 91
Beppu Area 91
Central Beppu 91
Kannawa Hells Area 91
Aso Area 90 – 91
Yufuin 91
Nagasaki 92
Shimabara 92
Fukuoka 92 – 93
Kumamoto 92 – 93
Takachiho 93

Rebun-to
Rishiri-to

HOKKAIDO
Shiretoko Nat. Park
Daisetsuzan Nat. Park
Akan Nat. Park
Otaru
Sapporo

Hakodate

Aomori
Hirosaki
Towada Lake
Akita
Kakunodate

NORTHERN HONSHU
Dewa Sanzan
Sendai
Yamagata
Shado-ga-shima
Niigata

Noto Peninsula
Nagano
Kanazawa
Matsumoto
Nikko
Mito

Oki Islands

CENTRAL HONSHU
TOKYO
Inuyama
Mt. Fuji ▲
Narita
Yokohama

HIROSHIMA & WESTERN HONSHU
Matsue
Tottori
Kinosaki
Kyoto ○
Nara
Nagoya
Shizuoka
Izu Peninsula

MT. FUJI & AROUND TOKYO

Tsu-shima
Hagi
Hiroshima
Okayama
Himeji
Kobe
Osaka
Hongu Onsens
KANSAI

JAPAN

Shimanoseki
Matsuyama
Takamatsu
Kochi
SHIKOKU
Uwajima
Fukuoka
Beppu
Shimabara
Nagasaki
KYUSHU
Miyazaki
Kagoshima

Yakushima

Amami Oshima

OKINAWA & THE SOUTHWEST ISLANDS

Okinawa Honto
Naha

OKINAWA & THE SOUTHWEST ISLANDS

Naha 94
Okinawa & The Southwest Islands 94 – 95
Okinawa-honto 95
Shuri Castle 95
Yaeyama Islands 96 – 97
Ishigaki City 96
Yakushima 96 – 97
Amami Oshima 97
Miyako Islands 97
Miyako-jima 97

INDEX 98 – 128

TOKYO

4

NERIMA

to Omiya
Oyama
Central Circular Route
Takinogawa
Shimo-itabashi
Itabashi
Nishi-Sugamo
Toei Mita (Line)

IKEBUKURO 16-17

TOSHIMA

Fuji H'way
Takanodai
Shakujii-koen
Seibu Ikebukuro Line
Koyama
Nerima-Takanodai
Nukui
Nerima Ward Art Museum
Fujimidai
Mejiro-dori
Toshima-en Amusement Park
Toshimaen
Nerima
Culture Center
Kotake-Mukaihara
Oyaguchi
Senkawa
Kanamecho
Kanamecho

Shakujii Park
Chihiro Art Museum
Kyu Waseda-dori
Minami-tanaka
Nakamura-bashi
Nakamura
Eharacho Shinogota
Toei Oedo Line
Sakuradai
Toyotama-kami
Toyotama-dori
Shin-Sakuradai
Kotakecho
Ekoda
Asahigaoka
Chiaya
Higashi-Nagasaki
Ikebukuro
Senkawa
Kami-Ikebukuro

Shimo-shakuji
Kami-Igusa
Igusha
Shimo-Igusa
Shin-Oume H'way
Seibu Shinjuku Line
Saginomiya
Toritsukasei
Nogata
NAKANO WARD
Museum of History & Folklore
Egota
Shin-Oume H'way
Numabukuro
Matsugaoka
TETSUGAKUDO PARK
Minami-nagasaki
Nagasaki
Mejiro-dori
Shinamachi
Minami-Ikebukuro
Philatelic Museum
Mejiro

Waseda-dori
Imagawa
Shimo-igusa
Shirasagi
HEIWANOMORI PARK
Araiyakushi-mae
Arai
Nakai
Shimo-Ochiai
Naka-ochiai
Kami-ochiai
Shin Mejiro-dori
Ochiai
Takadanobaba
Takada
Mejirodai
Zoshigaya-koen
Waseda

Momoi
Shimizu
Kamiogi
Suginami Science Museum
Hon-amanuma
Yamatocho
NAKANO
Koenjikita
Numabukuro
Kami-takada
Ryukuincho
Nishi-waseda
Edogawabashi
Sekiguchi

Nishiogi-kita
Nishi-Ogikubo
JR Chuo Line (Local Train)
Asagaya
Koenji
Nakano
Higashi-nakano
Kita-shinjuku
Okubo-dori
Haiku Literary Museum
Okubo
Tozai Line
Waseda
Tozai Line
Kagurazaka

JR Chuo Line (Rapid Service)
Ogikubo
Asagayakita
Minami-Asagaya
Shin-Koenji
Higashi-Koenji
Nakano-Sakaue
Nishi-Shinjuku
Seibu-Shinjuku
Kabukicho Golden Gai
TOYAMA HEIGHTS
Wakamatsu-cho
Ushigome-Yanagicho
Ushigome-Kagurazaka

SHINJUKU 14-15

Minami-ogikubo
SUGINAMI
Koenji
Marunouchi Line
Shin-nakano
Honcho
Nakano-Shimbashi
Honan-dori
Yayoicho
Shinjuku-gochome
SHINJUKU
Shinjuku-sanchome
Toei Shinjuku Line
Akebonobashi
Yochomachi
Kawadacho
Katamachi

Inokashira-dori
Miyamae
Kugayama
Hitomo H'way
Fujimigaoka
ZENPUKUJI RIVER GREEN PARK
Toyotama
Matsunoki
Horinouchi
WADABORI PARK
Omiya
Suginami Ward Folk Museum
Nakano-Fujimicho
Minamidai
Honancho
Honmachi
Tochomae
Nishi-shinjuku-gochome
Shinjuku-gyoen Garden
Yotsuya Sanchome
Marunouchi Line
Wakaba
New Otani Art Museum

Takaido-nishi
Takaido
Takaido-higashi
Keio Inokashira Line
Hamadayama
Nishi-Eifuku
Izumi
Wada
Hatagaya
Honan
Honancho
Hatsudai
Sangubashi
Meiji-Jingu Shrine
Shinanomachi
Sendagaya
Shinanomachi
Geihinkan (State Guesthouse)

TSUKAYAMA PARK
Shimo-takaido
Eifukucho
Eifuku
Hatagaya
Hatsudai
Nishihara
Yoyogi
Yoyogi-uehara
Yoyogi-koen
Meiji Jingu Outer Garden
Meiji Shrine
Yoyogi Park
HARAJUKU
Aoyama-Itchome
Nogizaka
Hanzomon Line
Akasaka

to Chofu
Kita-karasuyama
Rokakoen
Yawatayama
Kami-Kitazawa
Keio Line
Sakurajosui
Shimo-Takaido
Hanegi
Higashi-Kitazawa
Shin-Daida Shopping Town
Inokashira-dori
KOMABA PARK
SHIBUYA
Tomigaya
Jinnan
Watari-Um Museum
Meiji-jingu-mae
Jingu-mae
Omotesando
Meiji Aoyama
Gaien-mae
Tessenkai Noh Theater
Nezu Museum
National Art Center
Roppongi

Chitose-Karasuyama
Kasuya
Hachimanyama
Setagaya Literary Museum
Kagawa Archives & Resource Center (Matsuzawa Church)
Akatsutsumi
Higashi-Matsubara
Shimo-kitazawa
Shimokitazawa
Shinsen
Shoto
Former Marquis Maeda's House
Hachiko Statue
Shibuya Shopping
Nishi-azabu
Roppongi Hills
Moto Azabu

ROKA KOSHIN-EN PARK
Chitosedai
Matsubara
Daida
HANEGI (PARK)
Setagaya-Daida
Ikenoue
Daizawa
Komaba Todai-mae
Komaba
SHIBUYA
Higashi
Azabu Juban Shopping Town

ROPPONGI, SHIBUYA, OMOTESANDO, HARAJUKU & MEIJI SHRINE 12-1

SOSHIGAYA PARK
Soshigaya
Funabashi
Kyodo
Kyodo
Gotokuji
Miyasaka
Umegaoka
Mishuku
Ohashi
Aobadai
Ikejiri-Ohashi
Daikanyama
Hiro-o
ARISUGAWA-NOMIYA-KOEN (PARK)
MINATO

Seijo-Gakuen-mae
Chitose-Funabashi
Odakyu Line
Kamimachi
Shoin Jinja-mae
Setagaya
Wakabayashi
Nishi-Taishido
Taishido
Ikejiri
Higashiyama
SETAGAYA PARK
Ebisu
Ebisu Garden Place
Shirokane
Shirokane-Takanawa

Soshigaya-Okura
Kinuta
SETAGAYA
BAJI-KOEN PARK
Setagaya Ward Folk Museum
Kamiuma
Sangenjaya
Shimouma
Nozawa
Gohongi
Yutenji
Komazawa-Daigaku
Nakacho
Mita
Naka-Meguro
Institute for Nature Study
Takanawadai

Okura
Kinutakoen
Setagaya Art Museum
KINUTA PARK
Kami-yoga
Yoga
Sakura-Shinmachi
Hasegawa Machiko Museum
Sakura-shinmachi
Higashi-gaoka
HIMONYA PARK
Gakugei-Daigaku
Chuocho
MEGURO
Shimo-meguro
Meguro-honcho
Fudomae
Takanawa
Hara Museum of Contemporary Art

Okamoto
Matsumoto Memorial Museum
Seikado Bunko Art Museum
Yoga
Seta
Shinmachi
KOMAZAWA OLYMPIC PARK
Kakinokizaka
Takaban
RINSHINOMORI PARK
Musashi-Koyama
Togoshi-Ginza
Gotanda
Osaki-Hirokoji
Osaki

to Hakone
Kamata
Tama Tsutsumi-dori
Komazawa-dori
Yakumo
Nakane
Minami
Ebara
Senzoku
Nishi-shinagawa
Hiromachi

Unane
Kuji
Tamagawa
Todoroki
Tokyu Oimachi Line
Midorigaoka
Oyama
Senzoku
Kita-Senzoku
Minami-senzoku
Ebara-Nakanobu
Togoshi-koen
Togoshi Shinkoten
Shimo-Shinmei
Oi

Fuchu H'way
Mizonokuchi
Atsugi H'way
Seta
Suwa
Tamagawa-den'enchofu Memorial Art Museum
Jiyugaoka
Midorigaoka
Okayama
Okusawa
Okusawa
Senzoku-ike Park
Nakahara H'way
Nagahara
Hatanodai
Yutakacho
Nishi-Oi

Nombu Line
Tsudayama
Takatsu
Kan-Pachi-dori
Noge
Kami-noge
Todoroki
Omayadai
Kuhonbutsu
Omiya-dori
Miyamoto Saburo den'enchofu
Ebaramachi
Nishi-shinagawa

MEGURO & SHINAGAWA 18-19

Tama River
Tamagawa River

Scale 1 : 70,000

1km   0.5mile

Cross-reference boxes:
- ASAKUSA, UENO & AKIHABARA 10-11
- IMPERIAL PALACE & TOKYO STATION 6-7
- GINZA, TSUKIJI & TOKYO TOWER 8-9
- ODAIBA 20-21

District names:
KATSUSHIKA · SUMIDA · ARAKAWA · BUNKYO · TAITO · ASAKUSA · CHIYODA · EDOGAWA · KOTO · SHINAGAWA · ODAIBA · CHUO

Selected labels:

Kumano-mae · Yanagihara · Senju-hakaicho · Kita-Senju · Ushida · Ohanajaya · Keisei Main line · Keisei-Takasago · Hosoda · to Misato · Horikiri-Shobuen · Horikiri Iris Garden · Horikiri-bashi · Horikiri · Takaramachi · Tateishi · Keisei-Tateishi · Okudo H'way · Okudo · Hi-gahara · Kami-Nakazato · Tohoku-Joetsu Shinkansen · Machiya · Machiya-ekimae · Keisei Main line · Senju-Ohashi · Bokutei-dori · Senju-akebonocho · Keiseiseikiya · Keisei Oshiage Line · Yotsugi · Higashi-yotsugi · Heiwabashi-dori · Okudo H'way · Furukawa-bashi · Nakazato Line · Tabata Shako-mae · Higashi-Ogu Sanchome · Arakawa Line · Shin-Mikawashima · Arakawa Kuyakusho-mae · Arakawa-itchumae · Minami-senju · Yotsugi-bashi · Higashi-shinkoiwa · Kuramae-hashi-dori · Sobu Line · Higashi-shinkoiwa · Hon-isshiki · Edogawa Culture Center · Yamanote Line · Tabata Bunshimura Memorial Museum · Tabata · Nishi-Nippori · Mikawashima · Minowabashi · Minami-senju · Tobu Isezaki Line · Kanegafuchi · Higashi-sumida · Nishi-shinkoiwa · Shin-Koiwa · Chiba H'way · Matsushima · Nambudu Line · Yanaka Ginza · Nippori · Jaban Line · Higashi-nippori · Minowa · Jokan-ji (Geisha Burials) · Kiyokawa · Shirahige-bashi · Mukojima · Yahiro · Meiji-dori · Keisei-Hikifune · Kyojima · Hiraiyohashi · Hirai · Matsushima · Higashi-Komatsugawa-machi · Rikugi-en Garden · Sensoku · Komagome · Hongo-dori · Hakusan · Sendagi · Yanaka · Uguisudani · Iriya · Senzoku · Imado · Sumidagawa River · Tobu Kameido Line · Kameido · Kameido Central Park · Keiyo Rd · Nishi-Komatsugawa-machi · Aoki Konyo Monument · Mukogaoka · Yayoi · Todai-mae · Ueno Park · Ace World Bag & Luggage Museum · Oshiage-Hanzomon Line · Omurai · Tachibana · to Narita International Airport · Asakura Sculpture Museum and Garden · Ueno · Higashi-Ueno · Kotatoidori · Nishi-Asakusa · Senso-ji · Tokyo Sky Tree & Tokyo Solamachi · Honjo · Yokokawa · Asakusa-dori · Higashi-azuma · Keiyo Rd · Matsue · BUNKYO · Nishikata · Koishikawa · Kasuga · Hongo · Tokyo Univ. Museum · Ikenohata · Inaricho · Tawaramachi · Ginza Line · Narihirabashi · Honjoazubashi · Ishiwara · Tachibana · Chuo · Keiyo Rd 14 · Hakusan · Tokyo Wonder Site Hongo · Ueno-hirokoji · Shin-okachimachi · Edo-Tokyo Museum · KINSHI PARK · Kameido · Keiyo Rd · Matsue · to International Airport · Kogeikan (Crafts Gallery) · Korakuen · Suehirocho · Toei Asakusa Line · Kuramae · Sobu Line · Kinshicho · Kotobashi · Higashi-Ojima · Komatsugawa · Koiwa Iris Garden · OJIMA-KOMATSUGAWA PARK · Higashi-Komatsugawa · La Qua · Tokyo Dome (Big Egg) · Suidobashi · Akihabara Electric Town · Akihabara · Asakusabashi · Ryogoku-bashi · Ryogoku · Metropolitan Expressway No.7 Komatsugama Route · Nishi-Ojima · Ojima · Nakagawa Funa Bansho Museum · EDOGAWA · Fujimi · Yasukuni Shrine · Ochanomizu · Nikolai Cathedral · Iwamotocho · Midori · Sarue · Kikukawa · Sumiyoshi · Tiara Koto Hall · Sarue · Shin-Shinjuku Line · Funabori · Higashi-Ojima · Kudanshita · Jimbocho · Awajicho · Kanda · Higashi-nihon-bashi · Kodenmacho · Hamacho · Chitose · Morishita · Sumiyoshi · Higashisuna · Funabori · Ninoecho · Kogeikan · National Museum of Modern Art · Ogawacho · Kanda · Bakuroyokoyama · Kiyosumi Teien (Garden) · Kiyosumi-Shirakawa · Senda · Umibe · Kitasuna · Maruhachi-dori · Kita-kasai · Imperial East Gardens · Otemachi · Shinnihonbashi · Nihonbashi · Ningyocho · Tokyo Metropolitan Museum of Modern Arts · Minamisuna · Ukitacho · Kasai · Imperial Palace · Otemachi · TOKYO STATION · Yaesu · Kayabacho · Eitai-bashi · Toyo · Kasai-bashi · GYOSEN-KOEN (PARK) · Nishi-kasai · Kannana-dori · Parliamentary Museum · Marunouchi/My Plaza · Tokyo Int'l Forum · National Film Center · Hatchobori · Tomioka · KIBA PARK · Kiba · Toyocho · Kasaibashi-dori · Natural Zoo · Kasai · CHIYODA · Kokkai Gijido National Diet Bldg · Hibiya Park · Hibiya · Ginza · Minato · Monzen-Nakacho · Minamisuna · Nishi-kasai · Kasumigaseki · Hibiya · Ginza Noh Theater · Higashi-ginza · Chuo · Kabuki-za Theater · Tsukiji · Metropolitan Expressway No.9 Fukagawa Route · Minato · Metropolitan Expressway Central Circular Route · TORANOMON · Kami-yacho · Atago · Shiba · Onarimon Toei Mita Line · Shimbashi · Ginza Line · Tsukiji-shijo · Kachidoki · Yurakucho Line · Shin-kiba · Tozai Line · Nishi-Kasai · Kasai · Tokyo Tower · Onarimon · Shio Sight · Shiba Daimon · Tsukiji Fish Market · Tsukiji Kachidoki Bridge Museum · Tsukishima · Shiohama · Shin-306 · Keiyo Line · Shinsuna Tennis Court · Seishincho · Minami-kasai · Vita Italia · Kachidoki · Tsukuda · Tsukishima · Monzen-Nakacho · Kiba · Toyo · Shinonome · Shin-kiba · Zojo-ji · Daimon · Shiba Rikyu Garden · Hama Rikyu Garden · KidZania · Toyosu · Yumenoshima Tropical Greenhouse Dome · Yumenoshima · Kasai-Rinkai-Koen · kabanebashi · Shiba · Mita · Takeshiba · Hinode · Harumi · Urban Dock Lalaport Toyosu · YUMENOSHIMA PARK · Yumenoshima · Rinkaicho · Kasai-Rinkai-Koen Park · Mita · GINZA, TSUKIJI & TOKYO TOWER 8-9 · Tatsumi · KOTO · Metropolitan Expressway Bayshore Route · to Ciba · Tamachi · Shibaura · Kaigan · Tokyo Bay · Ariake Tennis-no-mori · Shinkiba · Shin-kiba · Nishi Nagisa · Keiyo Line · SHINAGAWA · Shibaura-futo · Rainbow Bridge · Metropolitan E'way No.11 Daiba Route · Ariake Tennis-no-mori Park · Kokusi Tenjio · Ariake · Higashi Nagisa · SHINAGAWA · Odaiba Kaihin koen · Tokyoteleport · Daiba · Kokusai Tenjio · Tokyo International Exhibition Hall (Tokyo Big Sight) · Sunamachi-minami-unga · Konan Museum of Fishery Sciences · Statue of Liberty · ODAIBA · Rinkai-shinkotsu Line · Tokyoteleport · Fune-no-kagakukan · Kokusai-Tenjijo-Seimon · Port of Tokyo · WAKASU GOLF LINKS · Wakasu · Disney Resort Line · Disneyland · Temponzume · Museum of Maritime Science · Aomi · FUNENO-KAGAKUKAN · Shin-Shimbashi Line · Tokyo-ko Tunnel · Telecomcenter · ODAIBA 20-21 · Metropolitan Expressway No.11 Haneda Route · 357 · Shinagawa Seaside · Aomi · Tokyo Gate Bridge · Metropolitan Expressway No.11 Haneda Route · Keikyu Line · Samezu · Katsushima · Yashio · Tokai · to Tokyo International Airport · to Yokohama · Tokyo Monorail

Port of Tokyo

Arakawa River · Kyu-naka-gawa · Tokyo Bay

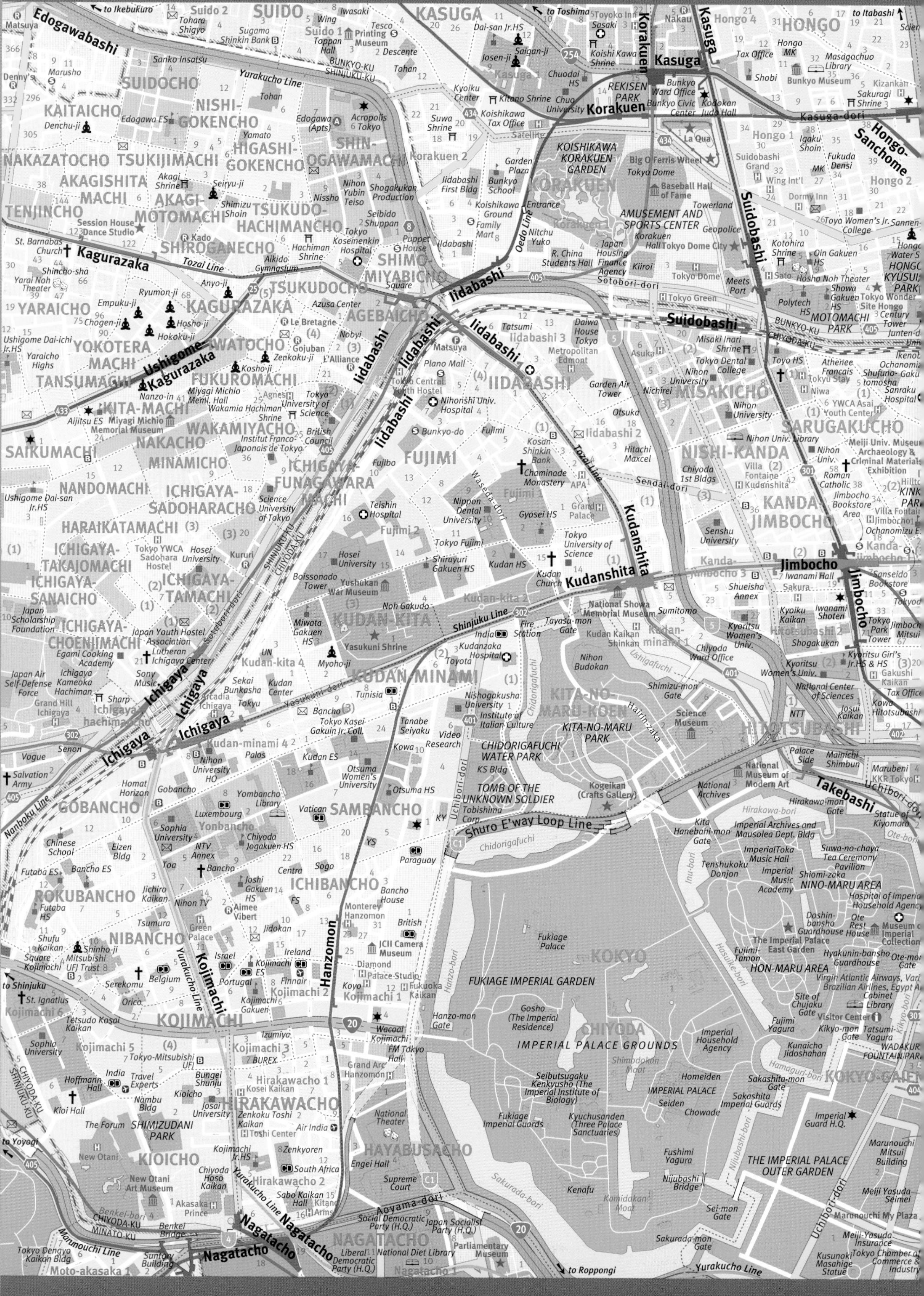

to Ikebukuro
Edogawabashi
SUIDO
KASUGA
to Toshima
Korakuen
Kasuga
HONGO
to Itabashi
SUIDOCHO
NISHI-GOKENCHO
KAITAICHO
Yurakucho Line
Kasuga-dori
Hongo-Sanchome
NAKAZATOCHO
TSUKIJIMACHI
HIGASHI-GOKENCHO
SHIN-OGAWAMACHI
KOISHIKAWA KORAKUEN GARDEN
Tokyo Dome
AKAGISHITA MACHI
AKAGI-MOTOMACHI
TENJINCHO
TSUKUDO-HACHIMANCHO
KORAKUEN
AMUSEMENT AND SPORTS CENTER
Suidobashi
SHIROGANECHO
Kagurazaka
Tozai Line
SHIMO-MIYABICHO
Iidabashi
Sotobori-dori
TSUKUDOCHO
KAGURAZAKA
YARAICHO
AGEBACHO
YOKOTERA MACHI
IWATOCHO
Ushigome Kagurazaka
TANSUMACHI
FUKUROMACHI
IIDABASHI
MISAKICHO
KITA-MACHI
WAKAMIYACHO
SARUGAKUCHO
SAIKUMACHI
NAKACHO
MINAMICHO
FUJIMI
NISHI-KANDA
NANDOMACHI
ICHIGAYA-FUNAGAWARA MACHI
ICHIGAYA-SADOHARACHO
Sendai-dori
KANDA JIMBOCHO
HARAIKATAMACHI
Kudanshita
Jimbocho
ICHIGAYA-TAKAJOMACHI
ICHIGAYA-SANAICHO
ICHIGAYA-TAMACHI
KUDAN-KITA
Shinjuku Line
ICHIGAYA-CHOENJIMACHI
Yasukuni Shrine
KUDAN-MINAMI
KITA-NO-MARU-KOEN
KITA-NO-MARU PARK
HITOTSUBASHI
Ichigaya
CHIDORIGAFUCHI WATER PARK
Takebashi
GOBANCHO
SAMBANCHO
TOMB OF THE UNKNOWN SOLDIER
Shuto E'way Loop Line
ROKUBANCHO
ICHIBANCHO
NINO-MARU AREA
NIBANCHO
Kojimachi
Hanzomon
KOKYO
FUKIAGE IMPERIAL GARDEN
HON-MARU AREA
to Shinjuku
KOJIMACHI
CHIYODA
IMPERIAL PALACE GROUNDS
HIRAKAWACHO
IMPERIAL PALACE
KOKYO-GAIEN
to Yoyogi
SHIMIZUDANI PARK
KIOICHO
HAYABUSACHO
THE IMPERIAL PALACE OUTER GARDEN
Nagatacho
NAGATACHO
Marunouchi Line
to Roppongi
Yurakucho Line
Moto-akasaka 1

Scale 1 : 15,000 | 200m | 500ft

Ueno-Okachimachi
Ueno-Hirokoji
Okachimachi
Naka-Okachimachi
Shin-Okachimachi
Yushima
Hongo-Sanchome
UENO
YUSHIMA
MOTO-ASAKUSA
KOTOBUKI
KOJIMA
MISUJI
KURAMAE
TAITO
TORIGOE
SOTO-KANDA
Suehirocho
Ochanomizu
Shin-Ochanomizu
SURUGADAI
Akihabara
KANDA-IZUMICHO
KANDA-SAKUMACHO
ASAKUSA-BASHI
YANAGIBASHI
Asakusabashi
Kuramae
HIGASHI-KANDA
KANDA SUDACHO
Iwamotocho
IWAMOTOCHO
Awajicho
Ogawamachi
KANDA-OGAWAMACHI
Kanda
KAJICHO
UCHI-KANDA
Bakurocho
NIHOMBASHI-BAKUROCHO
Bakuro-Yokoyama
Higashi-Nihombashi
HIGASHI-NIHOMBASHI
Kodenmacho
NIHOMBASHI-KODENMACHO
NIHOMBASHI-ODENMACHO
Shin-Nihombashi
NIHOMBASHI-HONCHO
NIHOMBASHI-HONGOKUCHO
Mitsukoshi-mae
NIHOMBASHI-MUROMACHI
Otemachi
Ningyocho
NIHOMBASHI-NINGYOCHO
Hamacho
NIHOMBASHI HAMACHO
Suitengu-mae
NIHOMBASHI KAKIGARACHO
NIHOMBASHI NAKASU
Nihombashi
NIHOMBASHI KABUTOCHO
Kayabacho
KAYABACHO
HAKOZAKICHO
Tokyo
TOKYO STATION
Nijubashi-mae
Shuto Expressway No.1 Ueno Line
Shuto Expressway No.9 Fukagawa Line
Yamanote Line
Sobu Line
Hibiya Line
Tozai Line
Hanzomon Line
Ginza Line
Chiyoda Line
Mita Line
Shinjuku Line
Asakusa Line
Sumidagawa River
to Ueno
to Asakusa
to Horikiri
to Edogawa
to Narita Int'l Airport
to Koto, Ciba
to Tsukiji
to Shinagawa

Tokyo Bay

Scale 1 : 15,000 — 200m — 500ft

to Akihabara (2) · to Chiyoda · Shuto Expressway No.9 Fukagawa Line · Hanzomon Line

Districts and areas:
KYOBASHI · HATCHOBORI · SHINKAWA · SAGA · FUKUZUMI · FUKAGAWA · EITAI · MONZEN-NAKACHO · BOTAN · SINTOMI · IRIFUNE · MINATO · AKASHICHO · TSUKIJI · TSUKUDA · OKAWABATA · ETCHUJIMA · TSUKISHIMA · TSUKISHIMA ISLAND · KACHIDOKI · HARUMI · TOYOSU · TOYOMICHO

Notable places (selection):
Pacific Century · Iowa Yaesu · Bridgestone Museum of Art · Kitaoji · Toda Corp. · Yaesu Book Center · Four Seasons Marunouchi · Meidi-ya · Mitsui Sumitomo Insurance · Uchida Yoko · Yamagata-ya · Ajinomoto (H.O.) · Kyobashi Kensetsu Hall · Villa Fontaine Kayabacho · IBM Hakozaki · Home Center Kohnan · Meiji Dai-ichi Seika Seimei · Shimizu Construction · Kanematsu · Hokke Inn · Kyoka Square · Kitin Brewery · Meisho ES · Kayabacho Tower · Toyoko Inn · Shibusawa City Place Eitai · Rinkai ES · Tokyo Mitsubishi UFJ

Police Museum · National Film Center · Ginza Saison · Ginza Yu · Ginza Aster · Sotetsu Fresa Inn · Kajibashi-dori · Tsukiboshi Bldg · Dormy Inn · Kyobashi Medical Clinic · Mercure Ginza · WINS Ginza · Ginza Blossom · Ginza Tower · Atox · Fuji Fire & Marine Insurance · Sankyo Bldg · Lietocourt Arx Tower · Century Park Tower

Magazine House · Kabuki-za Theater · Yamato City Transport (HQ) · Chuo City Hall · Kyobashi Tax Office · Tsukiji Police Station · Nichirei Bldg · River Point Tower · Sky Light Tower · East Towers II · RIVER CITY 21 · East Tower · OKAWABATA · Tsukudashima Lighthouse · Old Fishermen's Quarter · Tsukuda ES · Tsukuda Jr.HS · IHI Tokyo Hospital · River City 21 · The Crest Tower · Kosha Tower

Atami-so · Dentsu · Togeki · Ginza Capital · Ginza Capital Annex · Kashiwabara Soko · Nichirei · Tsukuda-Ohashi · Sumiyoshi Shrine · Ozaki Namiyoke Shrine · Lions Tower · Aioi-ohashi · Tokyo University of Marine Science and Technology · Fukagawa Dai-san Jr.HS

ADK Shochiku Square · Kyobashi Tsukiji · Sagawa Insatsu · MF · Nikkan Sports New · St. Luke's College of Nursing · Dr. Henry Faulds Monument · Asahi Soko · Nana · TSUKUDA · Etchujima ES

Shimbashi Embujo Theater · Togeki · Ginza Marunouchi · Presso Inn · Tsukiji Hongan-ji · Nikkan Sports Insatsu · Mikiji · St. Luke's International Hospital · St. Luke's Residences Tower · New Hankyu Tsukiji · AKATSUKI GARDEN · DUTCH LEARNING AREA · Sumiyoshi Shrine · TSUKISHIMA · Etchujima 2 · Tokyo Sports Shinbun

Int'l Cancer Center Central Hospital · Tokyu Stay Higashi Ginza · Toto Suisan · Hoko-ji · Hahsui · Sui Shrine · Zenrin-ji · Hakkaido Gyoren · Cradle of Modern Japanese Culture Marker · Apa Hotel · Chuo Samaria Hospital · Gekkeikan · Tsukiji Suisan · Sky City Toyosu Bayside Tower · Canal Wharf Towers · Dai-San Comm. HS

Outer Market · Yoshinoya · Park · HATOBA PARK · Nichirei · Mizuho Bank · NR Bldg · Aji-no Hamato · Tokyo Ace Lane · Sun City Bldg · Jonathan's · Hompi-ji · Library · Santa Corporation · Harumien · Toyosu 1 · Nihon Unisys, Ltd. Headquarters · Shibaura Institute of Technology Univ. Toyosu Campus

Johoku Shinkin Bank · Namiyoke Inari Shrine · Kachidoki-bashi · Kachidoki Bridge Museum · Plaza Kachidoki · Arakawamaru · Plaza Tower Kachidoki · Denny's Kachidoki · Kachidoki Public Hall · Harumisogo HS · Anglican-Episcopal Church · Tokyo Metropolitan University Harumi Campus · IHI Headquarters · The Toyosu Tower · Royal Parks

Inner Market · Tsukiji Central Wholesale Market · Tokyo Ichiba Reizo · Cerurean Homes Kachidoki · Kachidoki-dai-ni ES · Tsukishima-dai-ichi ES · Tsukishima Dai-ichi ES · Harumi View Tower · SHIN-TSUKISHIMA PARK · Park City Toyosu · KidZania · Ukiyo-e Tokyo Museum · Toyosu Center Building (NTT DATA Headquarters) · Toyosu Center Building Annex

Toichi Reizoko · Forefront Tower 2 · Forefront Tower 1 · Kachidoki BUK · Kachidoki View Tower · Tokyo BUK · Kachidoki-2 · Triton View Tower · Tsukishima-dai-san ES · Urban Dock Lalaport Toyosu · Annex

Water Bus Pier · Crest City Residence · Office Tower Z · Dai-ichi Seimei Hall · HARUMI ISLAND TRITON SQUARE · Office Tower Y · Office Tower X · Skylink Tower · Moon Tower · Tokyo Kalin Kaikan · Toyosu CIEL Tower · Shin-Toyosu

The Tokyo Towers Mid Tower · The Tokyo Towers Sea Tower · Toyomi ES · TOYOMI SPORTS PARK · Marines' Court · Chuo Incineration Plant · Tokyo International Trade Fair Center · Tokyo Gas Science Museum · TEPCO Toyosu

Sea-bus Terminal · HARUMI FUTO PARK · Harumi Passenger Terminal · Harumi Wharf · Harumi Ohashi · Road Proposed

Rivers and lines: Nihombashi River · Great Sumida · Sumidagawa River · Tozai Line · Oedo Line · Yurakucho Line · KOTO-KU / CHUO-KU · Eitai-bashi · Eitai-dori · Kiyosumi-dori · Harumi-dori

YANAKA
NEGISHI
MUKOGAOKA
UENO-SAKURAGI
SHITAYA
NEZU
YAYOI
NISHI-KATA
UENO-KOEN
KITA-UENO
HIGASHI-UENO
IKENOHATA
HONGO
MOTO-ASAKUSA
UENO
YUSHIMA
KOJIMA
TAITO
TORIGOE
SOTO-KANDA
SARUGAKUCHO
KANDA-IZUMICHO
ASAKUSABASHI
KANDA-SAKUMACHO
KANDA-JIMBOCHO
KANDA-AWAJICHO
KANDA-SUDACHO
HIGASHI-KANDA
KANDA-OGAWAMACHI
IWAMOTOCHO
NIHOMBASHI-BAKUROCHO
KANDA-SUKASAMACHI
KANDA-TACHO
Sendagi
Todai-mae
Nezu
Yushima
Hongo-Sanchome
Ueno-Hirokoji
Ueno-Okachimachi
Naka-Okachimachi
Okachimachi
Shin-Okachimachi
Ueno
UENO STATION
Inaricho
Uguisudani
Iriya
Akihabara
Ochanomizu
Shin-Ochanomizu
Suehirocho
Awajicho
Ogawamachi
Jimbocho
Iwamotocho
Kanda
Bakurocho
Suidobashi
YANAKA CEMETERY
KAN'E-JI CEMETERY
TOKYO NATIONAL MUSEUM COMPLEX
UENO ZOOLOGICAL GARDENS
Higashien
Nishien
Boto-ike
Shinobazu-ike
TOKYO UNIVERSITY
Kyu Iwasaki-tei House & Gardens
Tokyo Metropolitan Art Museum
National Science Museum
National Museum of Western Art
Tokyo Metropolitan Festival Hall
Shitamachi Museum
Ameyoko Shopping Street
Akihabara Electric Town
Kanda Myojin
Yushima Seido
Nikolai Cathedral
Hibiya Line
Chiyoda Line
Ginza Line
Keisei Line
Yamanote Line
Oedo Line
Shinjuku Line
Hanzomon Line
Namboku Line
Marunouchi Line
Shuto Expressway
Hongo-dori
Kasuga-dori
Kototoi-dori
Shinobazu-dori
Chuo-dori
Showa-dori
Kuramae-bashi-dori
Yasukuni-dori
to Itabashi
to Toshima
to Koto
to Chuo

Scale 1 : 15,000 — 200m — 500ft

to Adachi
to Misato
to Katsushita

HASHIBA
HIGASHI-ASAKUSA
HIGASHI-MUKOJIMA
SENZOKU
ASAKUSA
IMADO
MATSUGAYA
NISHI-ASAKUSA
HANAKAWADO
MUKOJIMA
OSHIAGE
RIYA
Iriya 1
KAMINARI MON
TAWARAMACHI
AZUMABASHI
NARIHIRA
KOTOBUKI
KOMAGATA
HIGASHI-KOMAGATA
HONJO
YOKOKAWA
KURAMAE
MISUJI
ISHIWARA
TAIHEI
YANAGIBASHI
YOKOAMI
KAMEZAWA
KINSHI
ASAKUSABASHI
RYOGOKU
MIDORI
KOTOBASHI
HIGASHI-NIHOMBASHI

Senzoku 4, Senzoku 3, Senzoku 2, Senzoku 1
Kiyokawa 1, Hashiba 1
Higashi-asakusa 2, Higashi-asakusa 1
Imado 2, Imado 1
Asakusa 4, Asakusa 5, Asakusa 6, Asakusa 7, Asakusa 3
Iriya 2, Iriya 1
Matsugaya 4, Matsugaya 3
Mukojima 5, Mukojima 4, Mukojima 3, Mukojima 2
Higashi-mukojima 1, Higashi-mukojima 2
Oshiage 2, Oshiage 1
Kuramae 4, Kuramae 3, Kuramae 1
Misuji 2, Misuji 1
Honjo 1, Honjo 2, Honjo 3, Honjo 4
Narihira 1
Azumabashi 3
Yokokawa 1
Ishiwara 1, Ishiwara 2
Taihei
Kinshi 1
Kamezawa 1, Kamezawa 2
Yokoami 2, Yokoami 1
Yanagibashi 1
Ryogoku 2, Ryogoku 3
Midori 1, Midori 2, Midori 3

Otori Shrine, Taito Hospital, Yoshiwara Benzaiten
Soho Asakusa, Kanko
Asakusa Hospital, Renso-ji, Shoun-ji, Koraku-ji, Ansho-ji, Shofuku-ji
Shobo-ji, Imado Shrine, Asakusa HS
Shirahige Shrine, Tsutsumi-dori 1
Dai-ichi-terajima ES, Sumidagawa, Akiba Shrine
Shoku-ji, Keiyozen-ji, Honryu-ji, Honryu-in, Matsuchiyama Shoten, Choko-in
Sakurabashi Jr.HS, Banryu-ji, Kototoi ES
Chomei-ji, Kofuku-ji
Sumida Jr.HS, Honjo HS
Senzoku ES, Fuji ES
Edo Shitamachi Traditional Crafts Museum
Kinryu ES, Toyoko-Inn
Sakura Ryokan, Senzoku 1
Honnen-ji, Banryu-ji
Sogen-ji, Kaizen-ji
Tengaku-ji, Nichirin-ji
Asakusa View, WINS Asakusa
Hanayashiki Amusement Park
Senso-ji (Asakusa Kannon Temple)
Asakusa Shrine, Kaminari Gorogoro Kaikan
Five Storey Pagoda, Hozomon Gate, Nitenmon Gate
Denpo-in, Asakusa Engie Hall
Nakamise-dori Shopping Street
Kaminarimon-dori, Kaminarimon Gate
Asakusa PO
Kappabashi Plastic Food and Cooking Utensil Shopping Street
Kototoi-dori
Sumida City Museum, Koume ES
Mimeguri Shrine
Ushijima Shrine, Hongyo-ji, Josen-ji
Entsu-ji
Sumida Ward Office, Water-bus Station
Asahi Breweries (Super Dry Hall), Life Tower
Tokyo Sky Tree, Tokyo Solamachi
Oshiagee-kimae Post Office
Tax Office, Narihira 1
JT Nihon Tabako, Yokokawa 1
Narihira Elementary School
Yokokawa ES
Honjo Jr.HS, Honjo Health Center
Toppan Printing
Kegon-ji, Genko-ji
Sumida Park Studio Kura
Kasuga-dori
Honjo Fire Station
Kuramaebashi-dori
Yamada Memorial Hospital
Kinshi Jr.HS
NTT
Toshin Kogyo
Kuramae Shrine
Tax Office
Power Plant
Sewage Bureau
Kuramae Technical HS, NTT Bronze Plaque
Asakusa Jr.HS
Sakaki Shrine
Kinshi Elementary School
Ewatari
Sumida Triphony Hall
Arca West, Arca Central, Arca East, ARCA TOWERS, Arca Kit
Tobu Hotel Levant Tokyo
Olinas Tower
KINSHI PARK
Kinshicho Marui Dept. Store
EARTHQUAKE MEMORIAL PARK
Tokyo Memorial Hall
KYU-YASUDA GARDENS
Yasuda Gakuen
Doai Kinen Hospital
Earthquake Memorial Open-air Gallery
Ryogoku Public Hall
Dai-ichi Hotel
Docomo History Square
Futaba ES
Kokugikan Hall
Sumo Stadium, Sumo Museum
Edo-Tokyo Museum
Ryogoku Jr.HS
Tatekawa Jr.HS
Lord Kira's Villa Site
Eko-in
Theater X
Miyoshi Sekken Seizo
Midori ES
Ryogoku HS
Keiyo-doro
Keiyo-dori
Sobu Line
Kuramaebashi-dori
Asakusa Line
Asakusa-dori
Mito Kaido
Oedo Line
Toei No.7 Mukojima Line
Sumidagawa River
Shuro Expressway No.7 Komatsugawa Line
Tobu Sky Tree Line
Kaminari-dori
Kinshicho
Yatsume-dori
Kinshicho

to Chuo
to Edogawa

Keio Line
to Chofu

HATSUDAI
Hatashiro ES
Hatsudai 1
Hatsudai 2
Shibuya Ward Sports Center
Park Grandy Yoyogi
Naruman

YOYOGI
Yoyogi 5
Yoyogi 46

Odakyu Line
Sangubashi

MEIJI INNER GARDEN
Tokyo Yoyogi Youth Hostel
Central Africa Republic
St. Joseph Nursery School
Electrical Safety & Environment Tech. Lab.
Brazil
Bulgaria
Vietnam

National Olympics Memorial Youth Center

Meiji Shrine
Misogiba
Higashi-ike

Kita Sando
Kita-Sando
Adachi House
WDI Bldg
Sendagaya 3
Fukutoshin Line
Meiji Jingu Kaikan Hall

NISHIHARA
Nishihara ES
Nishihara 1
Nishihara 2
Nishihara 3
Afghanistan

MOTO-YOYOGICHO
Yoyogi Church
Yoyogi Hachiman Shrine
Fukusen-ji

YOYOGI-KAMIZONOCHO
IRIS GARDEN
South Water Lily Pond
Meiji Jingu Goen
Meiji Jingu Bunkakan
O-torii
Shamusho
Shansui-den

HARAJUKU
Harajuku-Gaien
Shibuya Ward Central Library
Takeshita-dori Shopping Street
Takeshita-dori
Togo Memorial Hall
Togo Shrine
Beams F

Yoyogi-Uehara
Uehara 1
Tomigaya ES
Inoue Hospital

Yoyogi-Hachiman
Yoyogi-Koen
Chiyoda Line

YOYOGI PARK
Chuo Hiroba
Bird Sanctuary
Minami-ike

Jingu-mae Entrance
Harajuku Quest
YM Square
La Foret
Zara
Soho's
Earth Music

Jingu-mae 1
Beams
H&M
KDDI
Ota Museum of Ukiyo-e Prints

UEHARA
Uehara 3
Uehara ES
Uehara 2

TOMIGAYA
Tomigaya 1
Bethel Church
Tokyo Church of Christ

YOYOGI SPORTS CENTER
Football Field
Athletic Field

MINAMI
JINAN
Jinan 2
Gymnasium (No.2)
Olympic Commemoration Hall
National Yoyogi Gymnasium (No.1)
NHK Hall
Kishi Memorial Gymnasium
Koen-dori
Kuwasawa Design School

Kirin Brewery
Chosen-ji
Audi Diamond FBI
Paul Smith
United Arrows
Burberry (Black Label)

Jingu-mae 6
Base Station
Jingu-mae 5
Dior
Louis Vuitton
Kita Aoyama
Aoyama Hospital

Tokyo University, Komaba II Campus
Museum of Modern Japanese Literature

KOMABA PARK
Former Marquis Maeda's House
Japan Folk Crafts Museum

Baseball Ground
Rugby Field
Arts Faculty of Tokyo Univ.
Tokyo University, Komaba I Campus
Komaba ES

Tokai Univ. Affiliated HS
Cote d' Ivoire
Tokai Univ. Yoyogi Campus
NTT Yoyogi Bldg
Tomigaya 2

KAMIYAMACHO
New Zealand
Mongolia
Jordan

New Washington
Nihon Amway
NHK Broadcasting Center
Video Studio
Zarigani

Shibuya Tax Office
C.C. Lemon Hall
Shibuya Ward Office
Tobacco and Salt Museum
Jinnan Common Gov't Bldg
Shibuya Fire Station
Shibuya HS

Margaret Howell
Jinnan ES
Gold Rush
Apple Store
Marui City
Redwood
Tower Records
Cassina
Tomorrowland
Aoyama Park Tower

SHIBUYA
Shibuya 1
Aoyama Book Ctr
Cosmo
National Children's Castle
Aoyama Theater

Shoto Jr.HS
Kanze Noh Theater
Shoto 1
Orchard Hall
Les Deux Magots
Cocoon Theater
The Museum
Tokyu

Tokyu Hands
Shibuya Parco 3
Parco 2
Parco 1
Seibu B
Loft
Disney

MIYASHITA PARK
Metro Plaza
Pola
Kaleido

Aoyama Society Flower Japan
Wild Bird
H & S

Teguri Museum of Art
SHOTO
Shoto 2
Goldwin
Central Hospital
Shoto Art Museum
Josho Kai-ji

Quattro
H&M
Zara
Forever 21
Tsutaya
Seibu A
109
Shibuya Cine Tower

SHIBUYA CROSSING
Tokyu
Bic Camera
Shibuya Inn
Miyamasuzaka Building
Shionogi Building
Shibuya Cross Tower

Komaba-Todai-mae
Keio Inokashira Line

KOMABANO PARK
KOMABA
Komaba 2
Komaba ES

Shotaku-ji
Nihon Kogyodai Komaba HS
Komabara Agora Theater
Komaba 1

Kokusai HS
Kokai HS
Nat. Center for Univ. Entrance Exam.
Fuji Jr.HS

Dogenzaka
Shibuya
Shunju
Shibuya Mark City
Love Hill
Yachiyo
109
Hachiko Statue

SHIBUYA STATION
Shibuya Excel Tokyu
Shibuya Plaza
Shibuya Hikarie

Meiji-dori
Tokyu Toyoko Line
Labour Bank
Shibuya 3
Episcopal Church of Japan
WINS Shibuya
Tofuku-ji
Kinno Shrine

DAI-ZAWA
Dai-zawa 1
Komaba Gakuen HS

Tsukuba University Affiliated Komaba Jr.HS
Komaba Toho Jr.HS

SHINSENCHO
Shinsen
Pororoca
Tokyu Stay Shibuya

MARUYAMACHO
Mark City
Legato
Dogenzaka 1

Cerulean Tower
Cerulean Tower Tokyu
Sumitomo Seimei
Sukiya
Tokyo Inst. of Tech.
Yamaha Electone
Shibuya Infoss Tower

Co-op Plaza
Sowaya Shinkin Bank
Mets Shibuya
Life

Shibuya Property Tokyu
COMS
Shibuya Garbage Disposal Facilities

IKEJIRI
Ikejiri 4
Ikejiri 3
Ikejiri-Ohashi
Tamagawa-dori
to Yamato

OHASHI
Toho University Hospital
Hikawa Shrine
Taishin

OHASHI
MEGURO-KU SETAGAYA-KU
Furuhata Hospital
Ohashi 1
246
Suave

Fukudaya
JT Nihon Tabako
Philippines
NANPEIDAICHO
U.A.E.
Miki Takeo Memorial Museum

SAKURAGAOKACHO
Hachiyama Jr.HS

UGUISUDANICHO

Aobadai 4
Aobadai Hills
Daikyo-ji
Aobadai 2
Aobadai 3
AOBADAI
Sugekari ES
Aobadai 1
Meguro Community Center
Aoba Int'l School

Malaysia
Guinea
Uganda
NTT Tower
HACHIYAMACHO
Baptist
Sarugaku ES
Honda Memorial Church
SARUGAKUCHO
Ogawaken
Libya
Seijyo Ishii
Subway

Egypt
Denmark
Senegal
Ristorante ASO
MEGURO-KU SHIBUYA-KU
Dai-ichi High School of Commerce
La Fuente Daikanyama
Hillside Terrace

DAIKAN YAMACHO
Met. Shibuya Higashi 2-chome Apts.
Daikanyama Address
Daikanyama CA Bldg
Daimari Peacock
Paul Smith

EBISU-NISHI
Ebisu-nishi 2
Nagayato ES
Ebisu-nishi 1
EBISU STATION

HIGASHIYAMA
Higashiyama 3
Higashiyama 1
ASA

Daikanyama
Kami-meguro
Yamate-dori

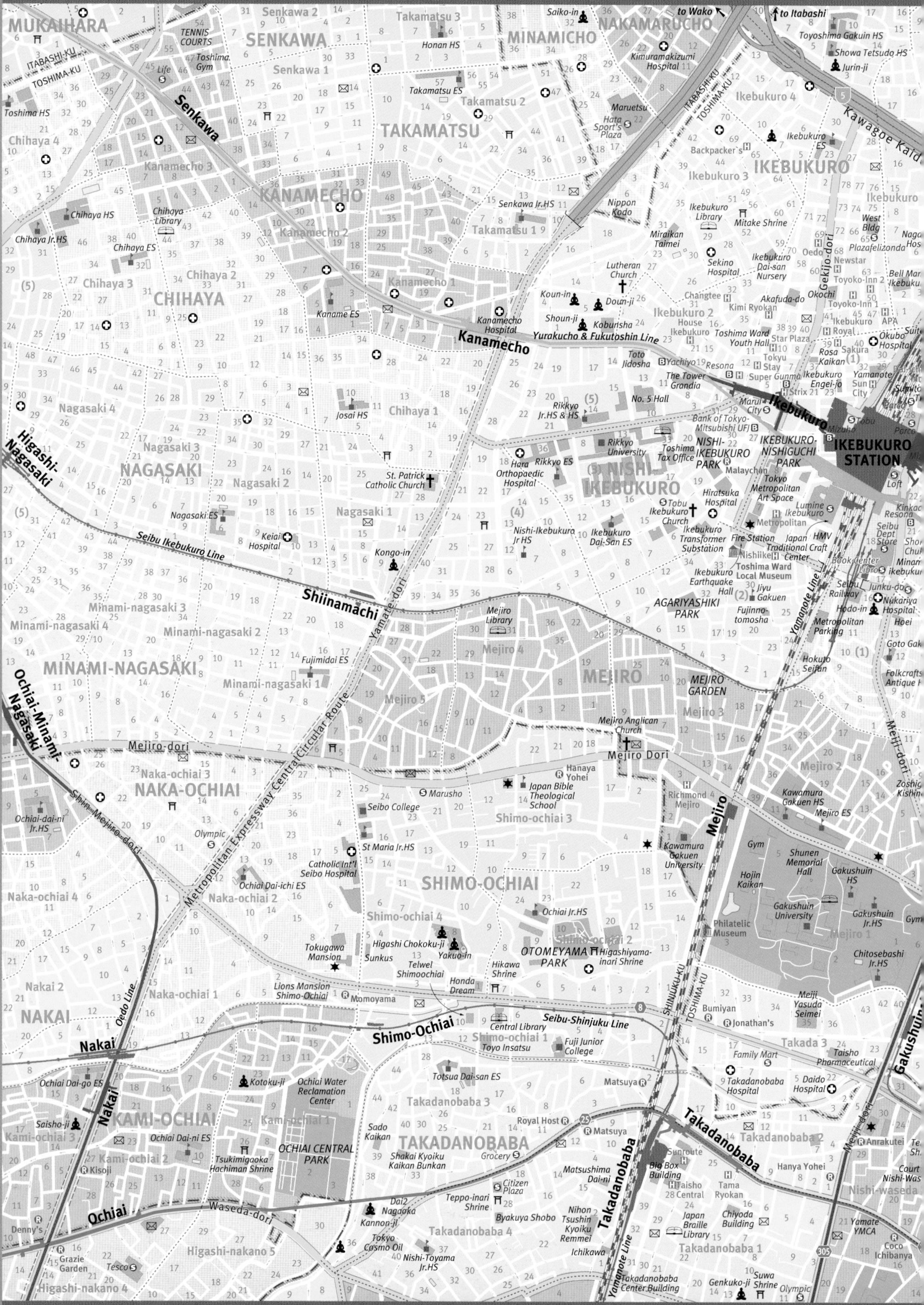

MUKAIHARA
TENNIS COURTS
Toshima Gym
Life
ITABASHI-KU
TOSHIMA-KU
Toshima HS
SENKAWA
Senkawa 2
Senkawa 1
Senkawa
Takamatsu 3
Honan HS
Takamatsu ES
Takamatsu 2
TAKAMATSU
MINAMICHO
Saiko-in
to Wako
NAKAMARUCHO
Kimuramakizumi Hospital
Maruetsu
Hata Sport's Plaza
to Itabashi
Toyoshima Gakuin HS
Showa Tetsudo HS
Jurin-ji
Ikebukuro 4
Kawagoe Kaido
Backpacker's
Ikebukuro ES
IKEBUKURO
Ikebukuro 3
Ikebukuro
Chihaya 4
Kanamecho 3
KANAMECHO
Kanamecho 2
Kanamecho 1
Chihaya HS
Chihaya Library
Chihaya Jr.HS
Chihaya ES
Chihaya 3
Chihaya 2
CHIHAYA
Senkawa Jr.HS
Takamatsu 1
Nippon Kodo
Ikebukuro Library
Mitake Shrine
West Bldg
Miraikan Taimei
Sekino Hospital
Ikebukuro Dai-san Nursery
Plazafelizonda
Newstar
Toyoko-Inn 2
Toyoko-Inn 1
Bell Mar Ikebuku
Gekijo-dori
Oedo
Lutheran Church
Koun-in
Doun-ji
Shoun-ji
Koburisha
Changtee
Kimi Ryokan
Akafuda-do
Okochi
Ikebukuro 2
Ikebukuro House
APA
Royal
Kaname ES
Kanamecho Hospital
Yurakucho & Fukutoshin Line
Kanamecho
Toshima Ward Youth Hall
Star Plaza
Okubo Hospital
Toto Jidosha
Yachiyo
Resona
Tokyu Stay
Rosa Kaikan
Sakura
Super Gunma
Ikebukuro Engei-jo
Yamanote Sun City
The Tower Grandia
No. 5 Hall
Strix
Nagasaki 4
Josai HS
Chihaya 1
Rikkyo Jr.HS & HS
Marui City
Bank of Tokyo-Mitsubishi UFJ
Ikebukuro
Tobu
Mizuho
Parco
Higashi-Nagasaki
Nagasaki 3
NAGASAKI
Nagasaki 2
St. Patrick Catholic Church
Hara Orthopaedic Hospital
Rikkyo ES
Rikkyo University
NISHI-IKEBUKURO
Toshima Tax Office
NISHI-IKEBUKURO PARK
IKEBUKURO-NISHIGUCHI PARK
IKEBUKURO STATION
Malaychan
Tokyo Metropolitan Art Space
Loft
Nagasaki ES
Nagasaki 1
Keiai Hospital
Nishi-Ikebukuro Jr HS
Ikebukuro Dai-San ES
Tobu Ikebukuro Church
Hiratsuka Hospital
Lumine Ikebukuro
Metropolitan
Kinkac
Resona
Seibu Dept Store
Ikebukuro Transformer Substation
Fire Station
Japan Traditional Craft Center
HMV
Nishiike
Book Center
Kongo-in
Seibu Ikebukuro Line
Toshima Ward Ikebukuro Local Museum
Ikebukuro Earthquake Hall
Jiyu Gakuen
Seibu Railway
Junku-do
Ikebukuro
Nukariya Hospital
Hodo-in
Hoei
Shiinamachi
Minami-nagasaki 3
Minami-nagasaki 4
Minami-nagasaki 2
Yamate-dori
Mejiro Library
AGARIYASHIKI PARK
Fujinnotomosha
Metropolitan Parking
Yamanote Line
Goto Gak
MINAMI-NAGASAKI
Fujimidai ES
Minami-nagasaki 1
Mejiro 4
MEJIRO
MEJIRO GARDEN
Hokuto Seifun
Folkcrafts Antique
Mejiro 5
Mejiro 3
Ochiai-Minami-Nagasaki
Metropolitan Expressway Central Circular Route
Mejiro-dori
Mejiro Anglican Church
Mejiro Dori
Meiji-dori
Mejiro 2
Naka-ochiai 3
NAKA-OCHIAI
Shin-Mejiro-dori
Marusho
Hanaya Yohei
Japan Bible Theological School
Richmond Mejiro
Kawamura Gakuen HS
Mejiro ES
Zoshig Kishin
Ochiai-dai-ni Jr.HS
Seibo College
Shimo-ochiai 3
Mejiro
Olympic
St Maria Jr.HS
Catholic Int'l Seibo Hospital
Kawamura Gakuen University
Gym
Shunen Memorial Hall
Hojin Kaikan
Gakushuin HS
Naka-ochiai 4
Ochiai Dai-ichi ES
Naka-ochiai 2
SHIMO-OCHIAI
Gakushuin University
Gakushuin Jr.HS
Gym
Shimo-ochiai 4
Ochiai Jr.HS
Philatelic Museum
Mejiro 1
Tokugawa Mansion
Higashi Chokoku-ji
Yakuo-in
Sunkus
OTOMEYAMA PARK
Higashiyama-inari Shrine
Shimo-ochiai 2
Chitosebashi Jr.HS
Nakai 2
Naka-ochiai 1
Telwel Shimoochiai
Hikawa Shrine
Lions Mansion Shimo-Ochiai
Honda Dream
SHINJUKU-KU
TOSHIMA-KU
Meiji Yasuda Seimei
Oedo Line
NAKAI
Momoyama
Central Library
Seibu-Shinjuku Line
Bumiyan
Jonathan's
Gakushuin
Nakai
Shimo-Ochiai
Shimo-ochiai 1
Toyo Insatsu
Fuji Junior College
Takada 3
Taisho Pharmaceutical
Family Mart
Ochiai Dai-go ES
Kotoku-ji
Ochiai Water Reclamation Center
Totsuka Dai-san ES
Matsuya
Takadanobaba Hospital
Daido Hospital
Nakai
KAMI-OCHIAI
Kami-ochiai 1
Takadanobaba 3
Saisho-ji
Kami-ochiai 3
Ochiai Dai-ni ES
Sado Kaikan
TAKADANOBABA
Royal Host
Matsuya
Takadanobaba
Takadanobaba 2
Anrakutei
Kami-ochiai 2
Kisoji
Tsukimigaoka Hachiman Shrine
OCHIAI CENTRAL PARK
Shakai Kyoiku Kaikan Bunkan
Grocery
Sunroute
Big Box Building
Hanya Yohei
Court Nishi-Was
Matsushima Dai-ni
Citizen Plaza
Taisho Central
Tama Ryokan
Nishi-waseda
Ochiai
Waseda-dori
Teppo-inari Shrine
Dai2 Nagaoka
Kannon-ji
Byakuya Shobo
Nihon Tsushin Kyoiku Remmei
Takadanobaba
Japan Braille Library
Chiyoda Building
Yamate YMCA
Coco Ichibanya
Denny's
Takadanobaba 4
Takadanobaba 1
Grazie Garden
Tesco
Higashi-nakano 5
Tokyo Cosmo Oil
Nishi-Toyama Jr.HS
Ichikawa
Yamanote Line
Takadanobaba Center Building
Genkuko-ji
Suwa Shrine
Olympic
Higashi-nakano 4

ale 1 : 15,000   200m   500ft

to Itabashi

Sainen-ji
ukuro Dai-ni ES
KITA-KU
TOSHIMA-KU
Toko-an
Shukutoku Sugamo HS
Sugamo Hospital
Sugamo-kita Jr.HS
Sugamo 5
Asahi ES
to Akihabara

Kami-ikebukuro 4
Nishi-sugamo 2
Hofuku-ji
Jigen-ji
Komagome 7
Shorin-ji
Hojo-ji
Hommyo-ji
Renge-ji
Senshu-in
Komagome 6
Kami-ikebukuro 3
Myokyo-ji
NISHI-SUGAMO
Nishi-sugamo 1
Taiso-ji
Somei-inari
KOMAGOME
Kami-ikebukuro Library
Myoho-ji
SOMEI CEMETERY
Komagome 5
Hongo Gyoko ES Jr.HS & HS
Momiji Kindergarten

KAMI-IKEBUKURO
Kami-ikebukuro 1
Yamaguchi Hospital
Nishisugamo ES
Sugamo 4
Toshima Wholesale Market
Zenko-ji
Komagome 4
Komagome Jr.HS

Toshima Central Hospital
Maruetsu
Peacock
Hojo-ji
Tokyo Metropolitan Otsuka ES & Chuo Jr.HS
Kozan-ji (Togenuki Jizo)
Bunkyo Gakuin University

Koyasu Inari Shrine
Sugamo 2
Hosei ES
Bunkyo HS
Seiwa ES
SUGAMO
Sugamo Library
Kamogawa Inn
Sugamo 3
Sugamo 2
Hon-komagome 6

Toshima Garbage Incineration Plant
Yamanote Line
McDonalds
Sugamo
Sugamo

Meiji-dori
Kita-otsuka 2
Otsuka Town
Kita-otsuka 1
Jumonji HS
Sugamo 1

Yachiyo
Teikyo Heisei University
Kita-otsuka 3
KITA-OTSUKA
Otsuka Sun-First
R&B
Toyoko Inn 6
R&B

Meiji Yasuda Seimei
Toshima City Office
Tokyo Electric Power Co.
Otsuka
Otsuka City
Tofuku-ji
Sengoku 4

HIGASHI-IKEBUKURO
Tokyo Electronics College
Wing Int'l
Toyo Girl's HS
Sengoku Library

Toshima Public Hall
Toshima Civic Center
Vanguard Tower
City Tower Ikebukuro
Okamoto Hospital
Tenso Shrine
Otsuka City Otsuka Sun-First
Sugamo ES
Toyo

Grand City
St.Tropez
Ark
Mandarake
Daihatsu Tokyo
Minami-otsuka 3
Minami-otsuka 1

Ikebukuro Hospital
Urbannet Ikebukuro
Nissan
MINAMI-OTSUKA
Sengoku 3
SENGOKU
Sengoku 1

Tokyu Hands
Sunshine 60-dori
Sunshine 60
Sunshine City Prince Hotel
Sunshine Int'l Aquarium
Bunka Senta (Culture Center)
Minami-otsuka 2
Sengoku 2
Hayashicho ES
Dai-ju Jr.HS

Toyota Auto Salon Amlux
Toshimagaoka-joshi Gakuen
Sunshine City Alpa
Planetarium
Ancient Orient Museum
Nishisugamo Jr.HS
Yamakawa Hospital
Ommyo-ji
Metr. Otsuka Hospital
Life

Keio Presso Inn Ikebukuro
Namco Namja Town
Sunshine Theater
Mint Bureau Tokyo Branch
Toden Arakawa Line
Marunouchi Line
Shin-Otsuka
Kasuga-dori

INAMI-BUKURO PARK
Former site of Sugamo Prison
Kampo Health Plaza Tokyo
Seiyu
Owl Tower
Mitsubishi Air Rise Tower
Higashi-ikebukuro
Otsuka 6
TOSHIMA-KU BUNKYO-KU
Tokyo Kenkei Hospital
Chiko-ji
Hikawa Shrine

Honryu-ji
Sengyo-ji
Resol Ikebukuro
Travelland
Honkyo-ji
Kanju-in
Otsuka ES
University of Tokyo Museum Koishikawa Annex

Seitai-ji
Homyo-ji
Higashi-ikebukuro
Honjo-ji
Kenshin-ji
Toho College of Music
Otsuka 4
Koishikawa Hospital
Honden-ji
I Affiliated ES
Otsuka 3
KOISHIKAWA BOTANICAL GARDEN

MINAMI-IKEBUKURO
ZOSHIGAYA CEMETERY
TOSHIMAGAOKA CEMETERY
Fukiage-inari Shrine
Fire Sta.

Toshima Shinjo-in Mimizuku Museum
Tokyo Music College
Susodo
Kokyo-ji
Enjo-ji
OTSUKA
Gokoku-ji
Gokokuji Hombonai Butsuden
Kogen-in
Bunkyo Sports Center
Kubomachi ES
Koishikawa 5

Otori Shrine
Hojo-ji
Seiryu-in
Aoyagi ES
Yurakucho Line
Otsuka 5
Nichidai-Buzan HS
Affiliated Jr.HS
Affiliated HS
The University of The Air

Kishibojin-mae
ZOSHIGAYA
Zoshigaya 1
Zoshigaya Missionary Museum
Honjo-ji
Otowa 2
Affiliated ES
Kodansha
Ochanomizu Women's University
Meikei Kaikan Bldg
Koishikawa Library
Dai-ichi Jr.HS
Koishikawa 5

Zoshigaya 2
Park Bldg
Shinobazu-dori
St. Dominics Monastery
Gokokuji
Shuro Expressway No.5
Otsuka 1
Atomi Gakuen HS
Teisei Gakuen HS
Harimazako Seiso Jigyosho
Eisai Tekahaya

MEJIRODAI
Nihon Women's University
Mejirodai 3
Otowa Jr.HS
Tsukuba University Affiliated Jr.HS & HS
Rinsen-ji
Tokun-ji
Shinko-ji
Koishikawa 4

Konjo-in
Mejirodai 2
Keirin-ji
Royal House
Takushoku University
Demmei-ji
Zennin-ji

Nanzo-in-ji
Nihonjoshi Univ. Homei ES
MEJIRODAI ATHLETIC PARK
Kodansha Noma Memorial Museum
Sekiguchi 3
Tokyo St. Marys Cathedral
Tokyoon Univ. HS
Kohinata 3
Kohinata 2
KOISHIKAWA

Takada 1
Eisei Bunko Museum
SHIN-EDOGAWA PARK
Renko-ji
Dokkyo HS
Daien-ji
Kohinata-dai-machi
Meidai Jr.HS
Takehaya ES & Jr.HS

Tokyo Somei-monogatari Museum
Four Seasons Tokyo Chinzan-so
Hatoyama Hall
KOHINATA
Kohinata-dai ES
Densei Kosei Kikin Kaikan

KANSENEN PARK
Mizu-inari Shrine
SEKIGUCHI
Imamiya Shrine
Kohinata 1
Shosai-ji
Tafuin-ji

Waseda
Sui Shrine
Power Plant
Daisen-ji
Genkuko-ji
Mizuho Ginko ES
Shomyo-ji
Kanatomi
Ryukan-ji
SUIDO

International Conference Center
Tokyo Metropolitan Waseda (Apts)
Kinusui
Sekiguchi 1
Hachiman Shrine
Eisen-ji
Doei-ji
Kobinata Shrine
Fukusho-ji
Suidobata Library
Suido 1
Iwasaki

SHI-WASEDA
Tozai Line
Chuo Library
Theater Museum
Kannon-ji Waseda University
Okuma Hall
Okuma Kodo
OKUMA GARDEN
Shin Mejiro Bldg
EDOGAWA PARK
Sekiguchi 1
Matsuya
Edogawabashi
to Chiyoda
Hoshlai Hospital
Tohara Shigyo
Sugamo Shinkin Bank
Wing Toppan Hall
Suido 1
Tesco
Descente
Alfresa
to Akihabara

to Itabashi   Hakusan-dori   Sugamo 5

Shin-mejiro-dori

BUNKYO-KU SHINJUKU-KU

Yamate-dori
Kami-meguro 1
Komazawa-dori
Nagayato ES
Ebisu-nishi 1
Excellent
Ebisu 19
Ebisu 1
EBISU
Metropolitan Hiro-o Hospital
Keio Yochisa ES
New San

Ebisu Business Tower
Subaru Car Dearship
Zest
Ebisu 2
Community Center
Toyoyama Church
Shirokane

Autobacs Car Service
Ebisu Grand Bowl
Ebisu Neonate
305
Ebisu 4
Konkoyko Shrine
Mansion Franco-Japonaise
Ebisu 3

Naka-Meguro
Tokyu
417
Matsuzakaya Store
Seito Church
Calpis Food
EBISU-MINAMI
Ebisu-minami 1
Yebisu Beer Museum
Kakeizuka ES
Shirokane 6

Naka-Meguro Atlas Tower
Meguro Gakuin HS
Ebisu-minami 3
Semmyo-ji
Beer Station
Mitsukoshi
Sapporo Breweries (H.Q.)
Shinno

Naka-Meguro GT
Naka-meguro 1
SHIBUYA-KU MEGURO-KU
Yebisu Garden Place Tower
YEBISU GARDEN PLACE
Xinhua News Agency (Shin-kasha)
Shirokane 6

Mizuho 6 Bank
Bals Store
Kawa-no Museum
Defense Agency Technical Research & Development Institute
Naka-meguro 2
Mita 1
Tokyo Metro Museum of Photography
Taillevent Robuchon
Court Annex
Shirokanedai 5

Kami-meguro 2
Shogaku-ji
Tokyo Kyosai Hospital
NAKA MEGURO PARK
Mita
Garden Hall
Garden Terrace Ichibankan
Westin Tokyo
Zimbabwe
Tokyo Univ. Medical Scien. Hospital

Meguro Ward Office
416
Naka-meguro 3
Self Defense Force
Kosei Chuo Hospital
Ebisu Garden Place Tower
Ebisu View Tower
Matsuoka Museum of Art

Hachiman Shrine
Naka-meguro ES
Stanley Denki
Poland
Algeria
Mita 2
Hinomaru Driving School
Kami-osaki 2
Institute for Nature Study
Cafe La Boheme Shirokane
Boschetta
Belarus

NAKA-MEGURO
Meguro Garbage Incineration Plant
Dendo ES
Princess Garden
Shirogane Church
Nihon Eiga Shinsa
Taipei Economic & Cultural Representative Office
Ozawa
Shirokanedai Welfare Hall

Yuten-ji
Urban Heights Naka-Meguro
Dendo Community Center
Meguro Civic Center
Metro Meguro Itchome Apts
Hinode Gakuen HS
IK Bldg
Meguro Plaza
Tokyo Metro Teien Art Museum
Former Residence of Prince Asaka
Shiro-Kanedai 5

Naka-meguro 5
Naka-meguro 4
Library Swimming Pool
Meguro Museum of Art
Tokyu Store
Wing
Kume Art Museum
Jonathan's
Meguro Tokyu Bldg
The Garden Shiba Shirokane
Naikan-
Koshu-ji
Saijo-ji

Nakacho 2
Meguro 1
Shimo-Meguro ES
International Mid Inf
Meguro Plaza
Meguro
Kofuku-ji
Shinsei
Fukuraya
KAMI-OSAKI
Hozo-ji
Seigan-ji
Ryuso-ji
Kaiho-ji
Hongan-ji

MEGURO
Morinaga Nyugyo Central Research Laboratory
Meguro 2
Tokyo Mitsubishi UFJ
Aben
Meguro
Atre 1
Kami-osaki 1
Dai-San Hino ES

NAKACHO
Bangladesh
Sekolah Republik Indonesia Tokyo
Meguro 3
Sakura Bank Building
Shimo meguro 1
Mizuho
Risona
Atre 2
Kami-osaki 3
Thailand
IKEDAYAMA PARK

Aburamen ES
Royal House
Otori Shrine
Daien-ji
Kami-osaki 4
Colombia
NTT East Kanto Hospital

Nakacho 1
Meguro 4
Meguro-dori
Oggi
Arco Tower
Meguro Gajoen
Indonesia

Shinsakae Church
Tamadai Meguro HS
Meguro San Jr.HS
Highness Meguro
Sugino Costume Museum
Mali
Higashi-gotanda 5

Clasca
Meguro Parasitological Museum
Shimo-meguro 5
Shimo-meguro 4
CUE Bldg
Meguro Gajoen
Sugino Fashion College
Microbial Chemistry Research Foundation
HIGASHI-GOTAND

Daiyon Jr.HS
Kyrgyzstan
Djibouti
SHIMO-MEGURO
Gohyaku Rakan-ji
SkyPerfecTelevision Meguro Media Center
Tokuzo-ji
DNP Gotanda
NTT
POLA
Tokyo Design Center

Shimo-meguro 6
Uzbekistan
Meguro-fudo
Jonan Hospital
Nishi Gotanda 3
Paraguay
Fuji Photo's Bldg
Der

Meguro Gakuen HS
Nat'l Inst. for Educational Research
Joju-in
MEGURO-KU SHINAGAWA-KU
Yamate-dori
DNP Logistics
IAPT Gotanda, ICHI Corporation
Keio Presso Inn
Tokyo Mitsubishi UFJ
Nishi-gotanda 1

Meguro-honcho 1
Fudou ES
Fudo-mae
Nishi-gotanda 4
NISHI-GOTANDA
Nishi-gotanda 2
Mitsubishi UFJ Trust
Tokyu Store

Meguro-Honcho 4
RINSHINOMORI PARK
Daiyonhino ES
Osaki Post Office
Jonan Shinkin (H.Q.)
Nissay Gotanda
Mizuho
Royal Oak

Koyamadai
Koyamadai Housing Complex
Nishi-gotanda 5
Anraku-ji
Book-off
Nishi-gotanda 8
Osaki-Hirokoji
Social Insurance Office

Meguro-Honcho 3
Koyamadai 1
Dai-ichi Hino ES
Gotanda Library
Nishi-gotanda 6
TOC
U-port
Rissho University
Osaki Tut Publishi

MEGURO-HONCHO
Koyamadai ES
Koyamadai HS
Kosakai Hospital
Koyama 1
Nishi-gotanda 7
Resona
Rissho HS

Meguro-honcho 5
Musashi-Koyama
Koyama 3
Zambia
Gotanda
Route Inn Gotanda
Irugi Shrine

Central Gym
Tokyo Mitsubishi UFJ
KOYAMA
Koyama 2
Hoshi University
Ebara 1
Ebara Dai-ichi Jr.HS
Osaki 4
Hosui ES
Osaki 3

Mukaihara ES
Tokyo Meguro Line
Koyama 4
Ebara 2
Togoshi-Ginza
Nishi-shinagawa

Haramachi 1
Koyama 5
Ebara 3
Ebara
Tokyo City Shiokin
Hiratsuka 1
Togoshi Jr. High School
Togoshi 1
Osaki Jr.HS

HARAMACHI
Nishi-Koyama
Ebara Dai-roku Jr.HS
Koyama ES
Ebara 4
Hiratsuka ES
Keiyo ES
HIRATSUKA
to Kawasaki
Togoshi
TOGOSHI

Scale 1 : 15,000 200m 500ft

to Shinjuku to Chiyoda↑ to Shinbashi→ to Shinbashi

MITA

Shuto Expressway No.2 Meguro Line

Hanamasa

Nishihara Hospital

Kitazato Infectious Disease Institution Hospital
Kitazato University

Shirokane 1

Shirokane 3

Asahi Jr.HS
Saiko-ji
Sanko ES

Hommyo-ji
Royal Shirokane Garden
Senshin-ji
Hikawa Shrine
Ryugyo-ji

SHIROKANE

Shirokane 4

Belarus

Shogen-ji

Chosu-ji

Shirokane 2

AXA Head Office
Shirokane Tower

Takanawa Tosei Bldg

Library

Takanawa 1

Tokaku-ji

Ryugen-ji
Daisho-ji
Hosho-in-ji
Furendo Gakuen HS
Kofuku-ji
Renjo-ji
Semisei

Mita Library

Mita

Dai-ichi
Botan
Yanase
Mitsubishi Motors
Morinaga Plaza
Tamachi Center Bldg

Mita 5
Gankai-ji
Kuwait
Daizo-ji
Mita 4
Jorin-ji
Ningan-ji
Jisso-ji
Tokyo International School
Mita Jr.HS

Zuino-ji

Shogaku-in-ji

Mita ES
Jokyo-ji

Mita Twin Building West (La Tour Mita)

TAMACHI

Minato Ward Sports Center

Tokyo Gas Laboratory
RQ Cafe
Asuka Seiyaku
Bridgestone
Tokyo Port Bowling
Tokai Kaiun
to Chuo

SHIBAURA

Granpark Tower
Shibaura 3
Shibaura Institute of Technology
Daily Foods
Nishihara
Nakano Kosan
Trest Inn
Azuma
NEC
Gorei Service
Coca Cola
Urban Wing Ocean Wing
Shibaura 2
Toshi Kosaido
Tokyo Bowling
Nisshin
Yasuda Soko
Mitsubishi Soko
Onward Kashiyama
Nittsu Koku

Takanawa

Shirokane-Takanawa

Nambokú & Mita Line

Takanawa Fire Station
Takamatsu Jr.HS

Mita 3
Yamaha Tokyo Branch
Mozambique

SHIROKANEDAI

HAPPO-EN GARDEN
Happoen Yokan
Meiji Gakuin University

Sheraton Miyako

Gakurin-ji
Kodai-in
Gensho-ji

Chosu-ji

Kogaku-ji

Meiji Gakuin HS
Shirokane ES

Sri Lanka
Hoan-ji

Tokai Univ. Takanawadai HS
Tokai University Sengaku-ji

Sengakuji

Songen-ji

Iraq

Mita M. Square
Nakau
Mita Avanti

NTT DATA Mita Bldg
Kokusai Kogyo/Mita

Takanawa Center Bldg

Asakusa Line

Okidenki Bisnis Center
Japan Times
Capital Mark Tower
Odenki Kogyo
MS Shibaura
Toyota
Shibaura Shimizu Bldg
Shibaura 4

KONAN

Shibaura Square
Sukiya
NEC
JEMIC
Amai
Kandenko Co. Ltd.
Dupre Shibaura
Shibaura ES

Glove Tower
Bloom Tower
Cape Tower
Shimbun Yuso
Nihon Shimbun Insatsu
NEC DSK Bldg

Fuji Express
Keihin Onward
Shibaura Island
Tokyo Labour Bureau Kaigan Government Bldg
Tokyo TetsukoTsui Kyoryo
Kenko Seihan

Wangan Koku
Yamada Soko Denkosha

Tokai Kisen

Shibaura Drainage Pump Station

TAKANAWA

Myofuku-ji
Obai-in
Jokyo-ji
Takanawadai ES
Seirin-ji
Koyasan Tokyo Betsu-in
Enpuku-ji
Tozen-ji

Graves of Lord Asano and the 47 Ronin
Takanawa High Mansion
Takanawa Shrine
Nomura Securities Training Center
Shogaku-ji

Legal Training Research Inst. Shirokane Annex

Shirokanedai 2

Bussho Ginenkai

Ajinomoto
TAKANAWA PARK
Takanawa Welfare Hall

Takanawa Residence Members of House

Healthcare Univ.

Int'l Convention Center Pamir
The Prince Sakura Tower
Lexus

Shibaura Sewage Disposal Center

Konan 1
Nippon Tsuun

Shibaura ES

Kambara Shoji
Konan 3
Library

Bay Crest Tower

Yurikamome Line

Tokyo Water Police Station

Minato Incineration Plant

Hokuren

Konan 5
Konan Shika

JA Zenno Meet Foods
Hochi Shimbun Sha
Aqua Tower

NTT Docomo
NTT Shinagawa Twins Data
NTT Shinagawa Twins Annex
Sony Shinagawa (H.Q.)

NTT Shinagawa Twins Office
NTT Data Shinagawa Building
Tokyo Mitsubishi UFJ

SHINAGAWA STATION

Kokuyo & Showroom
Tokyo (Chunichi) Newspapers

City Tower Shinagawa
Konan ES

Konan-ohashi

Sempo Takanawa Hospital

Takanawa 3

Shinagawa Tax Office
Pacific Tokyo
Singapore Seafood Republic

Strings Tokyo Intercontinental
Shinagawa Intercity Tower A
Taiyo Seimei Shinagawa Building
Shinagawa East One Tower
Shinagawa Grand Central Tower
Shinagawa Intercity Tower B
Mitsubishi Heavy Industries Building
Canon S Tower
Shinagawa Intercity Tower C

Takanawa-mon Checkpoint
Wing Takanawa Takanawa Tobu
Takanawa Keikyu

Keihin Annex Aqua Tower

EPSON Aqua Stadium

Tennis Center

Shinagawa Prince

Bowling Center

Sony Kaikan
Iceland

Brunei

Sony No.8
No.7
No.6

Sony No.10
Sony Historical Museum

Sony No.1
Sony No.4
Sony NS
Sony No.2

Kita-shinagawa 6
CATS Theater

Takanawa Park Tower

Oval Court Osaki

Sony No.5
Sony No.3

Takanawa Club
Kaito-kaku
Tokyo American Club

Goten'yama Mori

Serbia & Montenegro

Goten'yama Tower
Laforet Tokyo

Hara Museum of Contemporary Art

KITA-SHINAGAWA

Keio Shinagawa Building
Strata Shinagawa
Shinagawa V Tower
Kita-Shinagawa
Shinagawa Funasei
Toshin Tennozu Bldg
Nittsu Warehouse

Shinagawa Girls Academy HS

Zempuku-ji

Hozen-ji

Isshin-ji

Shotoku-ji

Higashi-shinagawa 1
Daiba ES
TV Tokyo Studio
Pana Plaza Tokyo
Matsushita Denki Bldg
Art Corp
Terada Warehouse
Shinagawa Central Tower

Terada Warehouse

Shinfokai-bashi

Sanko Bldg

Sphere Tower Tennozu
Tennozu 1st Tower
Tennozu Yusen Bldg
Tennozu Park Side Bldg
Tennozu View Tower

Dai-ichi City Group Center
Tennozu Central Tower

Crystal Yacht Club

BMW Tokyo Tennozu Service Center

Tennozu-Isle

TENNOZU

Shinagawa Thermoelectric Power Plant

Higashi-shinagawa 2

Japan Airlines (H.Q.)
Sanshin Warehouse

Wakashio-bashi

HIGASHI-SHINAGAWA

Oi Thermoelectric Power Plant

KONAN PARK

Museum of Fishery Sciences

Tokyo Univ. of Marine Science and Technology

Tower Face
Tokyo Met. Meat Market
Meisan Takahama Bldg

Museum of Logistics
Trade Representative of Russia

Garden Takanawa

Seisen University

Higashi-gotanda 3
Abe Hospital

Sunroute Gotanda

Higashi-gotanda 4

Sakurada-dori

Jusho-ji

Honryu-ji

Grand Prince Shin-Takanawa

Museum of Logistics

Shinagawa Ward Gymnasium
New Otani Inn
OSAKI NEW CITY
Mizuho

OSAKI

West Tower

GATE CITY OSAKI
Osaki MT Bldg
Patagonia

Tower Think Park
Sony

Osaki

Parks Tower Tokyo South

City Towers

Art Village Osaki

Gochome Apts

Kita-shinagawa 5

Osaki Hospital Heart Center

Mauritania

Myanmar

Mid Southern Residence Gotenyama

Hino Jr.HS

Cine Aki IMAGICA

Hanamasa

Osaki 1

Mitsui ES

Osaki 2 Central Towers

CHILDREN'S FOREST PARK

Shinagawa Shrine
Jonan Jr.HS
Kita-shinagawa
Shinagawa ES
Seitoku-ji

Shinbaba

Shunu-ji

Dai-ichi Sankyo Labo.

NISHI-SHINAGAWA

Hiromachi 1

Shinagawa Sport Center
Shinagawa Library

Minami-shinagawa 4
Seiko-ji
to Ota
Hongaku-ji

Minami-shinagawa 1
Jonan Dai-ni ES
to Yokohama

Yokosuka Line & Tokaido Shinkansen

357

Yamate-dori

Tennozu-dori

Daisho-ji
Furendo
Gakuen HS
Tokyo International School
Kuwait
Mita Jr. HS
Mita Twin Building West (La Tour Mita)
Tokyo
Yamaha Tokyo Branch
Mita 3
Mozambique
Mita Avanti
Kokusai Kogyo Mita
to Shinbashi
Mita Library
Renjo-ji
Semisei
Tamachi Center Bldg
Sumitomo
Granpark Tower
Nishihara
Villa Fontaine Yokogawa
Japan Times
Capital Mark Tower
Odenki Kogyo
Shibaura Square
Sukiya
Toyota
Shibaura Shimizu Bldg
Kandenko Co. Ltd.
Dupre Shibaura
Shibaura ES
Shimbun Yuso
Kanto Denki Hoan Kyokai
Nihon Shimbun Insatsu

Mita
Dai-Ichi Tamachi Mitsubishi Motors
Botan
Yanase
to Chuo
Hinode Pier

Morinaga Plaza
Minato Ward Sports Center
Tokyo Tech High School of Science and Technology
Katsu
Gracery
Shibaura Institute of Technology
Daily Foods
Trest Inn
Nakano Kosan
Yoshinoya
JAL City Tamachi
Toppan Insatsu
Hirano
MS Shibaura
Amai
NEC
JEMIC
Tokyo Tetsukotsu Kyozyu
Fuji Express
Cape Tower

SHIBAURA
Tokyo Port Bowling
Tokyo Gas Laboratory
Asuka Seiyaku
Bridgestone
Coca Cola
Urban Wing
Ocean Wing
Kosaido
Toshi
Tamachi Bowling
Azuma
NEC
Gorei Service
Yasuda Soko
Shubaura Air Tower
Nisshin
Daimaru Peacock
Onward Kashiyama

Shibaura 2
Yamu Yamu
FOTO PARK
Mitsubishi Soko

Shibaura 3
Okidenki Bisnis Center
Shibaura 4
MS Shibaura
Glove Tower
Bloom Tower
Shibaura Island
Tokyo Labour Bureau Kaigan Government Bldg
Keihin
Onward
Yamada Soko
Denkosha
NEC DSK Bldg
Tokai Kisen
Kenko Seihan
Shibaura Drainage Pump Station

Shibaura-Futo
Piasis
Yasuda Soko
Pia City
Yamatane
IBM
Toko Denki
Itokin
Naibo San-go Soko
Naibo Ichi-go Uwaya
Naibo Ni-go Uwaya
Shibaura Pier
Fuji Soko Unyu
Yokoso Rainbow Tower
Yasuda Soko
Wangan Shokudo
Nittsu Koku

Kaigan 3
BARAQUE Shibaura
Terada Soko
RQ Cafe
Takai Kaiun
NGRA
KAIGAN
Hinode Pier

Tokyo Bay

Shibaura Sewage Disposal Center
Konan 1
NTT Docomo
NTT Shinagawa Twins Data
NTT Shinagawa Twins Annex
Sony Shinagawa (H.Q.)
NTT Shinagawa Twins Office
NTT Data Shinagawa Building
Tokyo (Chunichi) Newspapers

KONAN
Kambara Shoji
Nippon Tsuun
Konan 3
Library
Konan Jr. HS
Bay Crest Tower
Bureau Shinagawa
Saizeriya
Rivage Shinagawa
City Tower Shinagawa
Konan ES
Konan-ohashi

Konan 5
Hokuren
Konan Shiko
Oji Butsuryu
Konan Bldg
Tokyo Regional Immigration Bureau
Oji Butsuryu
Yokohama Soko
Terada Soko
Nichirei
Nippon Tsuun

Tokyo Water Police Station
Minato Incineration Plant
Shinagawa Wharf

DAI-ROKU DAIBA

Konan 4
Museum of Fishery Sciences
Tokyo Univ. of Marine Science and Technology
Shinagawa Intercity Tower A
Shinagawa East One Tower
Shinagawa Intercity Tower B
Tokyo Met. Meat Market
Tower Face
Shinagawa Intercity Tower C
Meisan Takahama Bldg
Kita-Shinagawa
Shinagawa Funasei
Kita-shinagawa 1
Toshin Tennozu Bldg
Pana Plaza Tokyo
Higashi-shinagawa 1
Nittsu Warehouse
Matsushita Denki Bldg
Art Corp
Daiba ES
TV Tokyo Studio
Kagata Shrine
Shinfokai-bashi
Sanko Bldg
Hozen-ji
Isshin-ji
Kita-shinagawa 2
Shotoku-ji

KONAN PARK
MINATO-KU
SHINAGAWA-KU
Tennozu 1st Tower
Sphere Tower
Tennozu Central Tower
Tennozu Yusen Bldg
Tennozu View Tower
Terada Warehouse
Metro Apartments
Shinanen Canal Side Bldg
Sanshin Warehouse

World City Towers
Hochi Shimbun Sha
Aqua Tower
Boathouse
Meijiyasuda Seimei Shinagawa Konan Bldg
Daiichi Tokyo Seafort
City Group Center
Tennoz Galaxy Theatre
Center Bldg
JTB Bldg
Crystal Yacht Club
Shinagawa Park Side Bldg
Tennozu-Isle
Japan Airlines (H.Q.)
Wakashio-bashi

Star Zen
Tokyo Teion
JA Zenno Meet Foods
BMW Tokyo Tennozu Service Center

Higashi-shinagawa 5
Nippon Tsuun
Shinagawa Futo-bashi
Shinagawa Thermoelectric Power Plant

Shinbaba
Shinagawa Library
Kaitoku-ji
Jonan Dai-ni ES
Minami-shinagawa 1
Hozen-ji
Hongaku-ji
to Ota
HIGASHI-SHINAGAWA
Higashi-shinagawa 2
Higashi-shinagawa 3
to Yokohama

Shuto Expressway No.11 Daiba Line
Rainbow Bridge
Shuto Expressway No.1 Haneda Line
Yurikamome Line
Tokyo Monorail
Asakusa Line
Old Kaigan-dori
Kaigan-dori
Yamate-dori
Tennozu-dori
Konan-dori
Rinkai Line

Ocean Dining, Sushi Tachibana
Nikko Tokyo
Grand Pacific Le Daiba
Verre et La
SHIOKAZE PARK
NORTH COAST DECK
SOUTH COAST DECK
HIGASHI-YASHIO
YASHIO
Oi Thermoelectric Power Plant
Yashio 1
Tokyo-ko Tunnel
to Haneda Airport

Scale 1 : 15,000

200m

500ft

Harumi
Passenger
Terminal

CHUO-KU
KOTO-KU

Shinonome 1

Shijio-mae

Toyosu 6

SHINONOME

ShinonomeES

SHINONOME
PARK

Tanome ES

Shinonome 2

Galleria
Grande

CORNES

Kaetsu Ariake

to Chiba

Ariake Tennis-no-mori

Differ
Ariake

Ariake 1

Ariake
Coliseum

The Tokyo Rinkai
Disaster Prevention Park

Shuto Expressway Wangan Line

Kokusai-Tenjijo Ariake

Cancer Institute
Hospital

Ariake 2

Ariake Tennis-
no-mori Park

Kimura-ya
Sohonten

Yamato
Unyu

DAI-SAN
DAIBA
HISTORICAL
PARK

Searea Odaiba
Ichiban-gai

Tomin Tower
Ichiban-gai

Ariake Sports
Center

Ariake
Incineration
Plant

Panasonic
Center
Panasonic Digital
Network Museum
(Risupia)

Tokyo Bay Ariake
Washington

Ariake
Park
Bldg

East Exhibition
Hall

Sunroute
Ariake

Tomin Tower
Sanban-gai

Searea Odaiba
Sanban-gai

TOC Ariake

ARIAKE

Saizeriya
Ariake
Frontier

Ariake Central
Tower

Tokyo International
Exhibition Hall
(Tokyo Big Sight)

DAIBA

ODAIBA BEACH
PARK

Seaside Mall

Odaiba-
Kaihinkoen

The Towers
Daiba

Suntory

Ariake
Center Bldg

Tokyo Water Science
Museum

Tokyo
Fashion
Town

Wanza Ariake

IDC Otsuka
kagu

Nippon Steel

Hawaian
Restaurant Kula

Daiba
Frontier
Bldg

Sukiya

Conference
Tower

Kokusai-Tenjijo-
Seimon

West Exhibition
Hall

Sea-Bus Terminal

Decks Tokyo
Beach

Island
Mall

Saizeriya

Tokyo
Baycourt Club

Partire
Tokyo Bay
Wedding
Village

Sea-bus
Terminal

Yurikamome
Train Base

The Oven-American
Buffet, Gonpachi

Joyopolis

Trade Pier
Odaiba

Trusty Tokyo
Bayside

Statue of
Liberty

Daiba 1

Yume-no-ohashi
Bridge
(Dream Bridge)

Yurikamome
Train Base

Aqua City

Aomi-bashi

Tokyo Waterfront
New Transit
Yurikamome
HQ

Joyopolis

Fuji TV

Daiba 2

Ariake 3

Tokyo Teleport

CENTER PROMENADE

Telecom Bridge

Bamiyan

The Sky
Wheel

Tokyo
Leisure
Land

Rinkai-shinkotsu Line

Akemi-ohashi

Sumitomo Steel

History
Garage

Palette
Town

Mega
Web

Zepp
Tokyo

Ariake TSS
Kanri Center

Iino
Enterprise

Aomi

Nihon Seisi
Batsuryu

Nippon
Paper

PROMENADE
PARK

Venus Fort

Aomi 1

Tokyo Met
Ichi-go Uwaya

Daio Paper's
Warehouse

AOMI
PARKING

Tokyo
Kokusai Futo

Dai1 Go

Mitsubishi
Soko

Fune-no-
kagakukan

AOMI

AOMI CHUO
FUTO PARK

Gaibo
Teikisen
Wharf

Tokyo Met
Ni-go Uwaya

FERRY FUTO
PARK

Museum of
Maritime
Science

Tokyo International
Exchange Center

Fuji TV
Studio

Daito Corp. New
International Universal
Distribution Center

Tokyo Met
San-go Uwaya

Ariake 4

Soya

National Museum of
Emerging Science and
Innovation

Yotei-maru

AIST Tokyo
Waterfront

Bio IT Yugo
Kenkyuta

Aomi
Frontier

Tokyo
Kokusai
Futo

Telecomcenter

TELECOM
Center

Sea-bus
Terminal

Tokyo
Ferry
Terminal

Tokyo
Customhouse

Odaiba Hot Spring Theme Park
(Oedo-Onsen Monogatari Spa)

Mt. Fuji & Around Tokyo

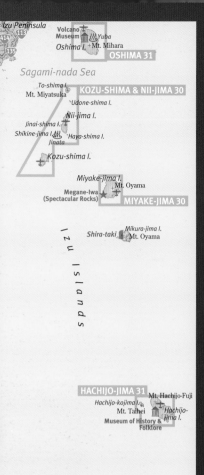

Izu Islands

Ogasawara Islands

Yokohama Area

Scale 1 : 200,000

5km

2miles

Yokohama

Scale 1 : 15,000   200m   500ft

YOKOHAMA STATION

Major areas and labels:

KITA-KARUIZAWA DAI-NI PARK, SHAKAI FUKUSHI-KAIKAN PUBLIC HALL, SAWATARI CHUO PARK, Dai-machi, Old Tokaido, to Kawasaki, KANAGAWA PARK, Hamakei, Bay West, Bay East, COTTON TOWER, Hashimotocho

to Kohoku, KITA-KARUIZAWA PARK, Kangyo-ji, Pola Yokohama Research Institute, Nibankan, Old Tokaido, Tokyu-Toyoko Line, Miki Bldg, Kanagawa Miyamae, KANAGAWA PARK, Kogaya Community Center, Sakaecho, Three F, Seikabu, See West, Cotton Harbor Club

Shinden Kempo Kaikan, Familymart, Asahi Bldg, Tsuruyacho, Keihin Kyuko Line, Tobu Bldg, Urban Square, Toyota, Plaza Eiko Seisenkan, The Yokohama Towers, See East

Kusunokicho, Volvo, Daily Yamazaki, Camelot, Yoshinoya, Kanagawa Bank, Kanagawa Institute of Information Security, Yodobashi Camera, Sukiya, Yokohama Creation Square, Ichibankan, Mitsubishi Jyuko Port Side Bldg, Genuine Yokohama Central Wholesale Market, Yamanouchicho

Starbucks, GM21, Plumm, Taisei, 7 Eleven, Citibank, Bank of Yokohama, Yokohama CIAL, Yokohama Plaza, Onocho, Art Grace Port Side Villa, PORT SIDE PARK, Yokohama Shijo Reizo, Yokohama Reito, Suisambutsubu, Shijo Center Bldg

Kita-saiwai, NTT Data, Vivre, Kokusai, McDonalds, Sotetsu Joinus, Takashimaya, Sotetsu Joinus, Sogo, Sogo Museum of Art, Minatomirai Grand Bridge, JR Freight Line

Tsurumi Clinic, Minami Saiwai Orime, Dalei, Yokohama Central PO, Porta Underground Shopping Mall, Lumine, Sky Bldg, Nissan Motor, YOKOHAMA MINATOMIRAI SPORTS PARK, Keihin Port & Harbor Office

Toyoko Inn, Taiso Okanocho Bldg, Minami-saiwai, Tokyu Hands, Tokyu Honda Theater, Kitagawa Shoji, First Place Yokohama, Tsukiji Bridge, Fuji Xerox R&D Square

Nikko Bldg, Shinnyoen, Okano, Nishi Chiku Center, Katabira-gawa River, YSC Yokohama Swimming Center, Yokohama Dai-ichi Hospital, Shin-Takashima, Gento Yokohama, TAKASHIMA CENTRAL PARK, Ocean Twr, Tide Containing Pond

Okano Jr. HS & HS, Yokohama Hiranuma HS, Lawson, Toyu Yokohama Club, Nissan, 109 Cinemas, Jonathan's, Blitz, Suzukake-dori, Jackmall East, MM Towers, SEASIDE PARK (RINKO PARK)

Hiranuma, Yokohama Ocean Bldg, JR Negishi Line, INAX Yokohama Showroom, Cosmo World, Jackmall West, Foresis L, Foresis R, Pacifico Yokohama Exhibition Hall

Yokohama Towering Square, Tokyo Gas Kanagawa Pipeline Network Center, 7 Eleven, Kanachu Bldg, Super Autobacs, Otsuka Kagu, Leaf Minatomirai, Tsutaya, Keiyu Hospital, Daily Yamazaki, Shop Minato Fureai, National Convention Hall

Soleado Homes, Sky Court, PC Depot, Anpanman Children's Museum, Home Center Sekichu, Minatomirai Center Bldg, Yokohama Minato Mirai Hall, Pier 21, Yokohama Grand InterContinental

Tobe Police Station, Public Bath, Toden Doso Denki, Kisoji, Icho-dori, Mitsubishi Minatomirai Industrial Museum, Yokohama Museum of Art, GRAN MALL PARK, Tower C, East QUEEN'S SQUARE, Pan Pacific Yokohama Bay

Sakuragicho, Tobehoncho, Sunkus Matsushima Hospital, Kobai-dori, TOYOTA JOY PARK, Mitsubishi, Landmark Plaza, Tower B, atl 1st, Yokohama Cosmoworld, Japanese Oversea Migration Museum

Sunkus, Kameda Hospital, Sony Yokohama NS Center Bldg, Ganki Yokocho, Bank of Yokohama, Landmark Tower, Tower A, Sirius, Monument Moku-Moku Waku-Waku, Yokohama Yo-Yo Hard Rock, Dockyard Garden, Ferris Wheel / Yokohama Cosmo World Amusement Park, JICA Yokohama Center

Goshoyamacho, GOSHO-YAMA PARK, Myosho-ji, Hanasakicho, Viamare, Royal Park, Kids Carnival Zone, Warner Mycal Cinemas, KFC, McDonalds

KFC, Public Bath, Nishi-mae ES, Nishi Ward Office, KAMON-YAMA PARK, Noh Theater, Kanagawa Pref. Library, Kanagawa Youth Hostel, Nisseki Yokohama Bldg, Nippon-maru (Sail Training Ship), Yokohama Port Museum, Navios, Bankoku-bashi Bridge, Dai-ichi Kou Government B

Chuo, Hamamatsucho, Nishi Jr. HS, Tobe ES, Tobecho, Myogen-ji, Seishonen Center, Terrace, Hoko-ji, New Otani Inn, Naka-naka Bridge, Kita-nakadori, Nippon Yusen Navigati Museum, Kaigandori

Nishi-maecho, Gansho-ji, Watanabe Clinic, Iseyama Kotai Jingu Shrine, Honcho ES, Momijigaoka, Ongaku-dori, Minato Mirai 21, Sakuragicho, Yokohama Island Tower, Bashamichi, Honcho

Fujidanacho, Inaridai ES, Nishi-tobecho, Sumeya Bldg, Isecho, Shiju Kaikan Public Hall, Miyazakicho, Nigiwai-za Theater, Suigyodo, Gyoza-no Ohsho, Yokohama Government Office Building No. 2, Kaigandori, Kaigancho, Nippon Yusen, am pm

Oimatsucho, Kawamoto Clinic, Nogeyama Fudoson, Shokuhinkan Aoba, Hanasakicho, Downbeat Bay, Breeze, am pm, Benten-bashi Bridge, Toyoko Inn, Oya Machi, Heiwa Plaza, Kanagawa Prefectural Museum of Cultural History

Keihin Kyuko Line, Mandarin, Noge Chiku Center, Nogecho, Basil, Marutani, Legend, Hiyoshi Bldg, Kamome Live Matters, Route Inn Bashamichi, Bentendori, Minatomirai Line

Kasumigaoka, Nogeyama Zoo, Yokohama City Chuo Library, Miyagawacho, Onoecho, Yoshidamachi, Gusto, Richmond, Underground Drug Store, Autocom Japan Inc., Otamachi, Port Open, Takiwacho, Kannai Hall

Dobutsuen Office, Nogeyamaso, Seishonen Koryu Center, Oimatsu, Fukutomicho, Nishidori, Higashidori, Curry Museum, Kannai, Nakadori, Comfort Kannai, Minami-nakador, Aioicho, Toyoko Inn

Fushimicho, Sakainotani, NOGEYAMA PARK, Three F, Azumagaoka, Matsuya, Nogecho, Fukutomicho, Isezakicho, Yurin-do Bookshop, KFC Mohan, Apaiser Town, Yokohama Chuo YMCA, YOKOHAMA PARK

Miharudai, Saikyo-ji, Shinzenko-ji, Toko-ji, Myoon-ji, Tofuku-ji, Azuma ES, Ne Shrine, Akamoncho, Hinodecho, Pachinko Goraku Wakusei Concorde, Chojamachi, 7 Eleven, Circle K, Ohana Shoten, Yokohama Chuo YMCA, Yokohama City Hall, Minatocho, Yokohama Stadium, McDonalds

Hanabusacho, Kantogakuin ES, Kantogakuin HS, Fumon-in, Ota ES, Hatsunecho, Ikuaikai Clinic, Three F, Hinatsu Sakurai, Sueyoshicho, Wakabacho, Itsukishima Shrine, Horaicho, Grand States, Bandaicho, Yokohamakoen, Wing Int'l, Bankei

Nishi-nakacho, Shimizugaoka Hospital, Renge-ji, Yakuo-ji, Maesatocho, Koganecho, Keganecho, Shiroganecho, Akebonocho, Yoshinoya, Livemax, Yayoicho, Gyomu Super, Yokosuka Kaido, Furocho, Okinacho, Yokohama Cultural Gymnasium, OGMACHI PARK, Ogicho, Kotobukiche

Kanoedai, Mystays, Weekly Mansion, 7 Eleven, Yokohama Naka, Isezaki Police Station, Fujimicho, Fujimi Jr. HS, Akebonocho, Municipal Subway Line, to Yokosuka, Isezakicho Jamachi, HINODEGAWA PARK, Weekly Mansion, Kannai Mall 3, Matsukagecho, Zen, to Hodogaya

to Fujisawa, JR Tokaido Line, Tokai-do, Yokohama-eki Negishi dori, Fujidana Urafune-dori, Hinodecho, Keihin Kyuko Line, Blue Line, Metropolitan E'way K1 Yokohama Route, Onoecho-dori, JR Negishi Line

to Ebara
to Fuchu
TAMAGAWA GREEN
to Shinagawa

Kawaramachi
7 Eleven

Shinmeicho
Minamigawara ES
LogementK
Saiwaicho ES
Enshin-ji
Toshiba Building

NORTH DOCK
Mizuhocho

MINAMIGAWARA PARK
to Yokohama
Miyakocho
Public Bath
Saiwaicho

Tama River
Fuchu Highway
JR Tokaido Line
Keihin-Kyuko Line
Rokugo Bridge

Kawasaki Saiwai Hospital
Naka-saiwaicho
7 Eleven

Keikyu Daishi Line
Asahicho Heights Apartment

7 Eleven
7 Eleven
Kawasaki Technopia
Solid Square Building
Kanto ES

Minami-gawara Jr.HS
River South Kawasaki
Lawson
Family Mart
Lazona Plaza
Lazona Kawasaki Residence
Toyoko Inn
Ekimae-honcho
Sun Royal
Honcho
Shimpuku-ji
Horinouchicho
to Kawasaki Daishi Heiken-ji
Kawasaki Racetrack

Canon
Urbane Bio Apartment
Omiyacho
Muza Symphony Hall
McDonald's
7 Eleven
Mets
Kawasaki
Horikawacho
Yodabashi Camera
Nikko Marui
Cube Kawasaki
Le Front
More's
Keikyu-Kawasaki
Sosan-ji
Sosan-ji
Kawasaki Park
Dice
Toyoko Inn
Miyamotocho
Kawasaki City Office
Toyoko Inn
Sunroute
Grand
Inage Shrine
Rexio
La Vita City Condominium
Prefectural Government Office Building
Gymnasium
Dai-ichi-Keihin
Enokicho

Saikaya
Vivace
Daiwa Roynet
Kawasaki Ward Office
Kawasaki Central
Miyamae ES
Kawasaki Library
to Tokyo Bay
Fujimi Jr.HS

NTT
Ota General Hospital
Toshiba Information System
Ogawacho
La Cittadella
Kawasaki River
Isago
Higashidacho
Miyamaecho
Myoon-ji
Kawasaki Grand Bowl
Shinkawadori
Kawasaki Stadium

Sunsquare
Pirkastyle
Pearl
Kawasaki City Hospital
Sakaimachi

Tsutsumine
Century Plaza
Turtle Hills
Aoki Garden
Aisle Inn
Minami-machi
Sky Court
Fire Station
Lawson
Kaizuka Catholic Church
Kaizuka
Public Bath
Lawson

Nisshincho
Sun Flower
7 Eleven
Kawasaki ES
7 Eleven
Hasegawa Kiko Building
Lawson
7 Eleven

Kawasaki Jr.HS
Kawasaki Police Station
Family Mart
Nisshin Apartment
Lawson
Motogi
Watarida
7 Eleven
Family Mart

Nishimatsu Store
WATARIDA-SHINCHO PARK
Dai-ichi Clinic
Public Bath

Shimo-namiki
Ikeda
JR Nambu Line
Wincastle
Shincho ES
Watarida-shincho
Watarida Jr.HS
Tajima ES
7 Eleven

to Yokohama
Hachonawate
Dai-ichi-Keihin

Yokohama Harbor

SHINKO PIER
Yokohama Coast Guard Office
Japan Coast Guard Museum Yokohama Branch

Red Brick Park
Akarenga Soko Shopping Mall
AKA RENGA PARK

OSANBASHI PIER

Yokohama International Passenger Terminal

ZONOHANA PARK
Yokohama Customs Office
Osambashi Kokusai Kyakusen Terminal

to Tokyo
International Airport

YAMASHITA PIER

HONMOKU PIER A

Metropolitan E'way Bayshore Route

Nippon-Odori
Japan Newspaper Museum
Yokohamasuijo Police Station
Yokohama Archives of History
Port Opening Square
Rest House
Shin-Yamashita

Yokohama-Minato Continental
Silk Center & Museum
Center for Int'l Commerce and Industry
Urban History Museum
Akaikutsu Haiteta Onnanoko Statue
Kanagawa Kenmin Hall (Civic Hall)
Fountain "Goddes of Waters"
Girl Scout Monument
Hikawa Maru Ocean Liner
Yamashita-koen Terminal
Yamashita Park
Sekai-no-Hiroba

Minatomirai Line
Nihon-Odori
Yaka Ward Office
Jai City
Silk-dori
Mizumachi-dori
Yamashita-koen-dori
Monterey
Toda Peace Mem. Hall
Meidi-Ya
New Grand
Yokohama Marine Tower

Kaiko-michi
Heichinro Honten
Kagacho Police Station
Kanton-dori
Rose
Star
McDonalds
Yokohama Doll Museum

Super Kannai
North Gate
NTT
Zenrin-mon Gate
Teisan Kannai
Chukagai-Odori
Shanhai-ro
Maruetsu Petit
Mielparque
Barneys New York

Yoshimoto Ryusen
Chinatown
Dai-sekai
Familymart
Yokohama Joint Government Office Building
French Hill

Windjammer Bar Minatosogo HS
West Gate
Kantei-Byo Shrine
Yamasitacho
South Gate
Three F
Metropolitan E'way K3 Kariba Route

Yokohama Central Hospital
7 Eleven
Chuzan-ro
Ichiba-dori
Motomachi Plaza
Motomachi
Motomachi Shopping Area
Gaikokujin Cemetery
Shin-Yamashita
Harbor View Park (Minato No Mieru Oka Koen)

Park Square Yokohama
Ishikawacho
Iwasaki Museum
Yamate Jyuban-kan
Yamate Museum
British House
Yokohama Int'l School
Osaragi Jiro Memorial Museum
Kanagawa Museum of Modern Literature
Suwacho
McDonalds
to Yokosuka

Ishikawacho
Nakamura River
to Honmoku
to Yokohama

Hon-fujisawa
to Yamato
Shirahata
to Yokohama
Eiko Gakuen
Jr.HS & HS

Inari
Fujisawa HS
Fujisawa Bypass
Dai-giri
Dai-giri ES
7 Eleven
Shiromeguri
Ueki

Saizeriya
Oshimizu Jr.HS
Family Mart
KS Denki
Seisen Jogakuin HS

Misono Jogakuin HS
Shonan Choju-en Hospital
Shonan
Ringer Hut

Misono Jogakuin Jr.HS
Hananoki
Nishi-tomi
Karasawa
Tostem
Luana
Tamanawa kindergarten

Fujisawa Civic Hospital
Ryusho-in
Niki Golf
UGC
Konan Ofuna
Tamanawa Jr.HS

Fujisawa-Honmachi
Torei Gakuen Fujisawa Jr.HS
Watauchi
Ofuna Botanical Garden

to Oiso
Fujisawa Bypass
Fujisawa
Tsutaya
Honcho
Tengaku-in
Shonan Kamakura General Hospital

Mercian Corporation
Kuratomo
Fujigaoka
Fujigaoka Jr.HS
Olympic
Takaya ES
Takeda Yakuhin Shonan Research Institution

Trial
Fujisawa ES
Muraoka-higashi
JR Tokaido Line
Kotsuka

Hatori Jr.HS
Dai-ichi Jr.HS
7 Eleven
Grand Hotel Shonan
7 Eleven
Coco's
Tsutaya
Kami-machiya

Hatori
Kanagawa Shonan HS
FUJISAWA Business
Saikaya
Asahicho
7 Eleven
D2
Create
Mizuno Tennis Plaza

Lexus
Nihon Seiko
Tennis Court
Toyoko Inn
Fujisawa
Fujisawa City Hall
Beppu Hospital
Mirokuji
Muraoka Jr.HS
Miya-mae
Kobelco

Mr Max
Kujo-ji
Hosho-ji
Kugenuma-shinmei
Lumine
Muraoka ES
Goryo Shrine

Sony
Fill
JR Tokaido Line
Fumon-ji
Odakyu
Yamauchi Hospital
The Shonan Fujisawa
Takaya
JR EAST KAMAKURA TRAIN BASE

Kugenuma ES
Iris
Hokke Club
Fujisawa Plaza
Kugenuma-higashi
Jonathan's
Shonan Fukasawa

Hon-kugenuma
Lawson
Fujisawa Civic Hall
Victoria Golf
Hard Off
Fukasawa

NAGAKUBO URBAN GREENING BOTANICAL GARDEN
Shonan New Way
Kugenuma Jr.HS
Daiso
Driving Range
AOKI
Kamakura Tebiro Post Office
Create

Hon-Kugenuma
Kugenuma
Shimbayashi ES
Kawana
Fukazawa HS
Tebiro

Tsujido-taiheidai
Kugenuma-sakuragaoka
Ishigami
Minebea
Shimbayashi Park
Jinko-ji
Power Plant
Shonan Memorial Hospital

Honshin-ji
7 Eleven
Yanagikoji
Denny's
Shoren-ji

Kugenuma Athletic Park
Koyo ES
Fuji
Yamaka Fresh Mart
Tebiro Jr.HS
Nishi Kamakura ES

Circle K
Shonan Gakuen ES
Kugenuma-fujigaya
Kataseyama
Katase Jr.HS
Nishi-kamakura
Kamakurayama

Fuji
Shonan Gakuen HS
Kugenuma-matsugaoka
Katase ES
Coop
Royal Host
NTT

Kugenuma Shrine
Kugenuma Kaigan
Katase
Shonan Shirayuri Gakuen HS
Kataseyama
Tennis Court
Family Mart

Kugenuma-kaigan
Laguna
7 Eleven
Katase-mejiroyama
Tsu-nishi
Ryukomyo Shrine

to Hiratsuka
SHONAN KAIGAN PARK
Lillet
Africa
Odakyu Enoshima Line
Mejiro-Yamashita
Koshigoe ES
7 Eleven
Gusto
Munakata Print Museum

Enoshima Electric Railway
Katase River
Shonan-Kaigan-Koen
Shonan Monorail
Nissan
Create
Sichirigahama ES

Red Lobster
Saito Pierre
Shonan Enoshima
Hozen-in
Koshigoe Jr.HS
Tsu
Reiko-ji

Shin-Enoshima Aquarium
La Mer
Katase Enoshima
ENOSHIMA
Enoshima
Ryuko-ji
Nichiren & The Kamakura Execution Grounds
Hongyo-ji
Myoden-ji
Kamakura HS
Sichirigahama
Kamakura Sichirigahama Post Office

Katasekaigan
KKR Enoshima
New Koyo
Koshigoe
St. Theresa Hospital
Keifu-en Gastrointestinal Hospital
Kensho-ji
Sichirigahama HS

Katase Nishi-hama (West Beach)
Sea Road
Ishinasa
Kinokuniya Inn
Mampuku-ji
Sichirigahama-higashi

Katase Bridge
Katase Higashi-hama (East Beach)
Koyurugi Shrine
7 Eleven
Banquet Hall Shichirigahama
Kamakura Prince
Endoden Line

Benten-bashi
Shichirigahama

Enoshima Spa
Shonan Harbor

Enoshima Samuel Cocking Garden
Ebisuya
Iwamotoro
Enoshima Shrine

Observation Lighthouse
Okutsu-no-miya
Love Bell
Enoshima
Enoshima Dai-shi
ENOSHIMA ISLAND

Dai-ichi Cave (Benten Cave)
Dai-ni Cave (Dragon Cave)

Sagami Bay

scale 1 : 30,000

400m

1000 feet

Sagami Bay

to Yokohama
to Yokohama
Kami-nocho
Katsuradai-naka
Yokohama Kamigo Post Office
Katsuradai-nishi
Inuyamacho
Katsuradai-higashi
Katsuradai-minami
Katsuradai ES
Noshichiri

Toshiba Design Center
Shiseido Kamakura Factory
Ohi Plaza
Iwase
Ito Yokado
to Yokohama
Sakae Seijin-kai Hospital
Kuden ES
Kudencho

Ofuna Kannon-ji
Ofuna
Lumine
Dila
Kamakura Women's University
7 Eleven
Sainen-ji

OFUNA
Kamakura Performing Art Center
Ofuna Central Hospital

Kamakura Okamoto Post Office
Tamanawa
Tamanawa ES
Tamanawa Library
Dai
Ofuna ES
Family Mart
Hakusan Shrine
Sakae Ward
Kamakura City

kamoto
Denka
Mitsubishi Electric
Ofuna Jr. HS
Iwase Jr. HS

Fujimicho
Fuji
Kamakuradai Post Office
302
301
Kobukuroya
Create
21
Kita-Kamakura Museum
Tamon-in
Imaizumi ES
Imaizumi

Yamazaki
Osaka ES
Ofuna HS
Imaizumidai

itsubishi ectric
Takano
23
Kamakura CC
Yokohama Cemetery

Shonan Machiya
tsuka ES
Terabun
Kohachi Shrine
HANA Guest House Kamakura
Kamakura Kosaka Post Office
Yakumo Shrine
Shozoku-in
Sanzaigaike Forest Park

Yamasaki Elementary School
Villa Kita Kamakura
Engaku-ji
Kamakura Old Pottery Museum

Kamakura Central Park
Kita Kamakura Joshi Gakuen
Toshimaya
Tokei-ji
Meigetsuyo
Fuka
Grave of Hojo Tokiyori

Kajiwara
Matsu-ga-oka Bunko
Hachinoki Yo Shomei Museum
Jochi-ji
Tachibana
Meigetsu-in
Kencho-ji Hanso-bo
Nishi-mikado

Fukasawa Jr. HS
Kamakura Kajiwara Post Office
Kyoraian
Kamakura Gozan
Tengen-in
Kencho-ji Zen
Kaishun-in
Kakuon-ji

Grave of Hino Toshimoto
Kaizo-ji
Choju-ji
Binya Coffee
Kamakura Gakuen HS
Hachinoki
Dokei-in
Grave of Yoritomo

Kuzuharagaoka Shrine
Geniyama Park
Yakuo-ji
21
Enno-ji
Daisho Kangiten
Raiko-ji
Zuisen-ji

Hojo Clan Tokiwa-tei Ruin
Zeniarai Benten Shrine
Jokomyo-ji
Myoden-ji
Pref. Modern Art Museum Kamakura Annex
Yagumo Shrine
Egara Tenjin Shrine
Kamakura-gu Shrine

Sasuke Inari Shrine
Grave of Hojo Masako
Jufuku-ji
Yukinoshita
Tsurugaoka Hachiman-gu Shrine
Kamakura Museum of National Treasures
Nikaido

Yagumo Shrine
Enkyu-ji
Daibutsuzaka Hiking Course
Zenirai Benten Shrine
The Museum of Modern Art, Kamakura & Hayama
Yabusame Baba
Dai-ni ES
Jomyo-ji

eda
Komori Shrine
Daibutsu Kiritoshi
Minowa
Kaburagi Kiyokata Memorial Art Museum
Tatsumi Shrine
Mikawaya
Azumaya
Beniya
Hokai-ji
Sugimoto-dera

Rinkan Hospital
Sengen Shrine
Fukudori
Suwa Shrine
Tsurugaoka Kaikan
Kiyokawa Hospital
Kamakuraori-Kaikan
Dai-ni Jr.HS
Kamakura Jomyo-ji Post Office

Sasuke
Kamakura City Hall
21
Myoryu-ji
Hokkoku-ji
Juniso

Kamakura Daibutsu (Great Buddha)
Kamakura Otani Memorial Art Museum
Onari ES
KAMAKURA
Daigyo-ji
Ruin of Hojo Tokimasa's Residence
Kamakura Tennis School

32
Sotatsu
Izumi
Hongakuji-ji
Myohon-ji
Taniguchiya
Myohon-ji

Kotoku-in
Sankaido Amanawa Shrine
Kamakura Museum of Literature
Onarimachi
Omachi
Komachien
Joel-ji
Yagumo
Daiho-ji
Kamakura Zushi City

Toshimaya
Kaseiro
Yohira
HASE
Yuigahama
Sasamemachi
Hyakuen
Okuni
An-yo-ji
Motokids
Myoho-ji
Kamakura Kindergarten

Kosoku-ji
Ishibashi
Kamakura Orgoldo
Hase-dera
Rental Cycle
Kamakura Iogakuin HS
Jogyo-ji
311
Takenoya
Hisagi Oike Park

Goryo Shrine
Jashumon
Hase YH
Wadazuka
Enoshima Line
Mita Memorial Gymnasium
Kamakura Gymnasium
Honko-ji
Keiun-ji
Nukada Memorial Hospital
Ankokuron-ji
Zushi Highland Post Office

Inamuragasaki ES
Gokuraku-ji
Chikaramochiya
Joju-in
Kaihinso Kamakura
Sea Front
Denny's
KKR Kamakura Wakamiya
Kofuku-ji
Myocho-ji
Chosho-ji
Myoko-ji

Gokurakuji
Sakanoshita
Hase
Kamakura Municipal Inasegawa Nursery School
21
Toraji Sarah
Kuhon-ji
Raiko-ji
Gosho Shrine
Hossho-ji

amuragasaki
Kamakura Park
Ajisaido
Yuigahama
Zaimokuza
134
Fudaraku-ji
Kuhon-ji
Komyo-ji
Ganden-ji
Hisagi Jr.HS

134
Kamakura Kaihin Park
7 Eleven
Zaimokuza
Kotsubo
311
Myoko-ji
Hisagi ES
Seiwa Gakuin HS
Hisagi
Yamanone

Family Mart
Kindergarten
205
Family Mart
to Yokosuka

Shokaku-ji
Kotsubo ES
Riviera Zushi Marina
Zushi Kotsubo PO
KKR Zushi Shoteien
Shinjuku
Zushi

Hiroyama Park
CB Surfers
Marine Box 100
Zushi Kaisei Jr.HS & HS
7 Eleven
24

Kotsubo Marina
Osaki Park
Koyo-ji
134
Shin-Zushi

to Hayama

to Nagano
to Tokyo
Chuo E'way
140
305
312

FUEFUKI CITY
Iisso-ji
Kamikurailsana
Bypass
Fukkoen-ji
Kofu Kokusai
Country Club
137
36
Misaka-michi
JR Chuo Line

OTSUKI CITY
Magi Onsen
Ryokan
510
Hanasaki
Country Club
Otsuki
to Tokyo
Hinode
Kosen
20

Archeological
Museum
308
Sakaigawa
Country Club
Woodstock
Country Club
Kamui Misaka
Ski Area

Enraku-ji
Goten-taki

YAMANASHI

705
Chuo Tsuru
Country Club
Kaiseido Hospital
Fujikyu Otsuki Line
World Ace
Country Club
712
Yamamotodor
City Hospital
Tsuru-shi
35
Star Land

Mt Shakagatake
LAKE KAWAGUCHI 29
Mt Kuredake
137

Nishi Tokyo
Golf Club
Take 1
Country Club
Shoka Museum
Museum Tsuru
Tsuru
Country Club
Miyako
Museum
Seserag

113
Mt Settogatake
Mt Kanayama
Mt Kenashi

Sunnide
Resort
Kubota Itchiku
Museum
Hoto Fudo
Fuji Viewing
Platform
New
Century

NISHI-KATSURA TOWN
Mt Kinpu
Fuji-michi
718
Chuo E'way Tsurubunka
Dat-Gaku-Mae
Fuji Kyuko Line Tsurubunka

TSURU CITY
Tsuru Bunka
Univ. ES

Shoji
Blueline
358
Ashiwada
Minshuku
Kazu
Lake
Kawaguchi
Fuji Lake
Kachi Kachi Yama
Ropeway
Fuji
Yoshida
Matsuya
Michael's American Pub

MITSUTOGE CITY

O-dake
1623m
Saiko-Iyashi-
no-sato Nenba
Fuji Kawaguchiko
Town Office
Kawaguchiko
Sanrokuen
Regina
Fuji Visitor
Center
Kawaguchiko
Golf Course
Kawaguchiko
Fujikyu
Highland
Fujisan
139
City
Hospital

Murahamaso
Shoji Lake
Lake
Shoji
FUJI KAWAGUCHIKO TOWN
Koyo-dai
Lookout
SAIKOYACHO
NOMORI PARK
Lake Saiko
139
Taikokuya

Eboshi-san
Lookout
Mt Eboshi
300
Fugaku Fuketsu
(Wind Cave)
Narusawa
Hyoketsu
(Ice Cave)
139
Fujizakura
Country Club
Health Science
University
Kawaguchiko
Motor Museum
Sengen
Shrine
FUJIYOSHIDA CITY
Oshino-hakkai
Fuji Yusui-no
Sato Aquarium
Mt Ishiwari
1413m
413

Lake
Motosu
Hanamizuki
Aokigahara
Ocean of Trees
Forest Narusawa
Golf & Country Club
NARUSAWA VILLAGE
Fuji Lakeside
Country Club
FUJI-HOKUROKU PARK
Higashi Fuji Goko Rd
OSHINO VILLAGE
Inn Fujitomito
Mt Ohira
Mt Fuji
Yamanakako
Pheasant
Yamanakako
Hitanoya
Ryokan

Mt Ryugatake
1485m
Fuji Motosuko Resort
Motosu Fuketsu
(Wind Cave)
Mt Omuro
1468m
Fuji Fuketsu
(Wind Cave)
729
Fuji Minaha
Lake Yamanaka
Marino-dori
Auberge Fontaine
Bleau
Santa Claus
Museum

Fuji Classic
Fujiten
Snow Resort
Kawaguchi-ko Route
Mt Fuji Toll Rd
Nakano-chaya
Self Defense
Force
Abarth Car
Museum
Paueru
Yamanakako
YAMANAKAKO VILLAGE
Mt Mikuni
147

Asagiri
Country Club
Fuji Classic
71
Kawaguchi-ko
Yoshida-guchi
5th Station
Nyonin
Tenjo
Komitake
Shrine
Sengen
Shrine
Mt Obora

Tokyo University of
Agriculture Fuji Farm
Okuniwa
Nature Park
Gogoen
Okuniwa-so
Oniwa Nature Park
138
Taiyo
Golf Course
Fuji-kogen
Golf Course
Fuji Oyama
Golf Course

Asagiri Kogen
Green Park
75
FUJI-HAKONE-IZU NATIONAL PARK
Komitake
Shrine
Omuro Sengen
Shrine
Subashiri Route
Sengen
Shrine
Murodo
Museum
Higashi Fuji
Golf Course
OYAMA TOWN

Asagiri Jamboree
Country Club
MT. FUJI
3776m
Fujisan
Subashiri
New 5th
Station
Fuji-heigen
Golf Course
151
Fuji-kokusai
Golf Course
150

New
Fuji
Odakyu Nishi Fuji
Golf Course
Hoei-san
2693m
Gotemba
5th Station
138
Green
Plaza Fuji

Shizuokafuji
Hospital
Shiraito
The National
Golf Course
Fujinomiya/
Mishima
5th Station
23
Gotemba Route
Mt Fuji Skyline
246
Hakoneura Hwry
to Kanagawa

Nishi-fuji
Library
Shiraito-no-taki
139
72
152
JSDF FIELD
Gotembakogen
Hospital
Tobu Hospital
GOTEMBA CITY
Select Inn Fujisan
Gotemba

Taiseki-ji
Kiseki Museum of
World Stones
Mt Fuji Skyline
180
Fujinomiya / Mishima Route
Snow Town Yeti
Grinpa
Amusement Parks
Bindi
Golf Park
Fuji Manyo
Botanical Garden
Garden
Taiheiyo
Golf Course
Jinbayama
Shrine
469

469
Sagittarius
Country Club
Jurigi
Country Club
Fujisan Museum
to Kanagaw

FUJINOMIYA CITY
Minami-fuji
Hospital
184
Mt. Fuji
Children's
World
Fuji Safari Park
Bellevue Nagao
Golf Course
Koyamafukusei
Hospital
394
Tomei E'way
Gotemba Line

414
158
469
72
Minami-fuji
Country Club
Marubi Shizen-kan
Museum
Mt Kurodake
469
Susono
Country Club

182
Wakanomiya
Sengen Shrine
Fujinomiya
Shin-fuji
Hospital
Echizen-ga-take
1507m
SUSONO CITY

Fuji Chisan
Country Club
Minobu Line
Ofuji
Hospital
Seimei
Hospital
24
Mt Otake
Susono
Golf Course
337

Tachibana
Fujinomiya GC
Nishi-Fuji Rd
FUJI CITY
Takaoka
Hospital
to Suraga Bay
Dai-fuji Gjo
Fuji Tokoha
University
Mt Ashitaka
1187m
Odana-no-taki
Mishima
Golf Course
Five Hundred
Country Club
Fuji Ace
Golf Course
24
Tomeisusono
Hospital
to Mishima

Mt. Fuji

Scale 1 : 200,000
5km
2miles

169
to Nagoya
360
Tanaka
Imai
166
Ide
165
Tokai University
Ashitaka Golf Club
Tokaido Shinkansen
Shin-numazu Golf Club
to Tokyo
Nagaizumi Town Office
83
Mishima Golf Club
Grand Field Golf Club
Yamanaka Castle Ruins Park
MANAZURU
to Tokyo
Yugawara
YUGAWARA
Manazuru
102
Manazuru Seaport
Manazuru-misaki Point

Toya
165
City Sawadacho Hospital
Numazusenbon Hospital
NUMAZU
Mishima City Office
Mishima-taisha Shrine
SUNTO DISTRICT
1
Mishima
Kannami Golf Club
Jukkoku Toge Peak
20
Yugawara
Kannami Spring Golf Club
Himenosawa Park
Izusan Shrine
Japanizumu Art Museum
Miyako Yugawara Yoshihama

Numazu Central Hospital
Numazu City Office
Graduate University for Advanced Studies
Pasadena Art Museum
Mt Takanosu
Tokaido Shinkansen
Karuisawa
Atami Golf Club
MOA Museum of Art
Izusan
Atami Hospital

Suruga Bay

Wakayama Bokusui Memorial Museum
Ganyudo
Museum of History & Folklore
165
SHIMIZU
Mt Kanuki
139
Kam zawa
Kannami Town Office
Hatake
Nitta
TAGATA DISTRICT
Tanna Rift Park
Mt Kurotake 2621m
ATAMI 31
ATAMI
Atami Ropeway
Akane-zaki Point

Sagami Bay

Shige
Togo
414
Mt Ohira
129
Izu Hakone Suzu Line
Tabi
Daisen
Mt Daisen
Fuji Hakone Country Club
Kodai Shrine
Picture Book Museum of Art
Kamitaga
Nagahama

134
Hanasaka
Awashima Aquarium
Izu Mito Sea Paradise
Awa-shima Island Mitohama
132
Izu Nagaoka
Izunokuni City Office
Izunokuni Panorama Park Ropeway
IZUNOKUNI
Izu Nirayama Golf Club
Izu Skyline
Ikeda Masuo Museum
Ajiro
Ajiro
Hatsu-shima Island

Ose
Nishi-uranashi
Nishi-urakachibo
Rakoro Sun
17
Uchiuramoto
Shuzenji
Mt Asama
Taharano
Izu Ohito Golf Club
Amagibanrai Botanical Garden
Mt Sukumo
O-zaki Point
Usami
135

Ita
Izu Tropicalium Park
Mifuku
OHITO
Kumasaka
19
Japan Cycle Sports Center
Usami

Deai-mizaki Point
Heda Shipbuilding Museum
Mt Sanagi
Shuzen-ji Niji-no-sato Amusement Park
Yagyu no Sho
Shuzenji
18
Mt Kinkan
Izu Kokusai Golf Club
Shuzenji
Izu City Office
Kadono
Sano
80
Izu Sky Line Golf Club
Matsubara
Itohama

Mihama-mizaki Pt.
Mihama
HEDA
Shuzen-ji Oku-no-in
Laforet Shuzenji Golf Club
Shuzen-ji Shuzenji
12
Inoue Memorial Museum
Shuzenji Country Club
Umegi
Izu Sky Line
Itoshimin Hospital
Ito City Office
Kawana

17
127
Mt Garan
Shin Amagi Nikkatsu Golf Club
136
349
Kamifunabara
Izu Funabara Golf Club
Funabara
Waratbo
59
Hiekawa
Ito Golf Club
Okunaga
351
Ikeda 20th Century Art Museum
Yoshida
Izu Green Park
Kawana
Kawana Golf Club
Kawana

Odoi
Ivory Art Museum
Toi
410
Mochikoshi
Yoshino
Ikadaba
Izu Golf Club
Matsukawa Lake
Oita
Izu Shaboten Park
Marchen Forest Museum
Tsukino Usagi

Toihama
136
Yagisawa
411
Izu Yugashima Golf Club
Yugashima
Harvest
Mt Yahazu
Mt Omuro 1903m
Futo
109

Saifukuji Museum
Koshimoda
Joren-no-taki
Amagi Kogen Golf Club
Mt Togasa
Le-Nessa Agazawa
Nichiren-zaki Point
Izu Ocean Park
Izukogen Togasaki
112
Izu Ocean Park

Kogane-zaki Point
Koganezaki Crystal Park
KAMO
410
Mt Saru
Neginohata
Mt Amagi 4613m
Mt Hokigi
Ningyo-no-Museum Soleil
Ukiyama
Akazawa

Mt Ima
136
NISHI-IZU
59
Ebi-Daru
Shoke-Daru
Kawazu Nanadaru Onsen-kyo
Sagano Auto Camp
Mt Misuji
Inatori Golf Club
Izu-Okawa
Okawa
Hokkawa
Hokkawa

Tago-jima Island
Tago
Osori
Mt Saru
Deai-Daru & Oh-Daru
Kawazu Auto Camp
Mt Asama
Izu Inatori Sports Villa
Izu-Okawa
Naramoto
Atagawa
Atagawa
Izu-Atagawa

Futo
Ran-no-sato Dogashima Orchid Resort
Dogashima New Ginsui
Nishina
Kadono
Mt Chokuro
Onabe
115
Mt Omine
Shiki-no-kura Annex COCORO
Izu Animal Kingdom
Kawazukataba
Higashi-izu
Atagawa Tropical & Alligator Garden
Shirada
Katase
Izu Inatori

Nishi-izu Town Office
Sanya-so Youth Hostel
Osawa
Ikeshiro
KAMO DISTRICT
Mt Basara
Mine Daifunto Park Hot Spring Tower
Mine Kawazu Town Office
Izu-Inatori
Inatori-so
Tomoro-misaki Point

Matsuzaki Town Office
Iwachi
MATSUZAKI
Chohachi Museum
Suhaga
Mt Ohira
Kawazu Bagatelle Park
14
Imaizo
Izu-Imaihama Tokyu Resort
Imaihama

Mt Eboshi
Ishibu
Kumomi
Senganmon Rock Gate
121
Uehara Museum of Buddhism Art
Mitsukuri
Izukyu Line
Mt Tenrei
Kawasu
Kanaya

Izu Shinan
136
Yokokawa
Kanaya
Nawaji
Takome
Rendaiji
135

Matsuzaki Line
Ihama
Koura
119
MINAMI-IZU
Ichinese
Ichijo
Izukyu Shimoda
Mt Takane
Shirahama Chuo
Shirahama-ohama

Hagachi-zaki Point
Koura Mera Bay
Mera
Jaishi
Tenjimbara Botanical Garden
Chinese Garden
Ogamo
SHIMODA
Osawa
118
Rendaiji
Izukyu
SHIMODA 31
Tsumeki-zaki Pt.

Mt Nijurokuya
SHIZUOKA
Izu Shimoda Golf Club
Iruma
Nakaji
Nijo
Shimogamo Tropical Garden
Ernest House
Minato
116
Shimoda Yamatokan
Marine Aquarium Shimoda
Sotoura

Mitsuishi-misaki Point
16
Shitari
Minatoyu
Tarai-misaki Point
Yumigahama
Sand Ski
Toji
Ohama
Ebisu

Hirizo
Aloe Center
O-ne Island
Iro-saki Point

Sagami-nada Sea

Izu Peninsula
Scale 1 : 275,000   5km   2miles

Kozu-shima I.
Nakumi Bay
Mt Kobe
Nagahama
Kozu-shima Onsen Recreation Complex
Sawajiri
Mt Tenjo
Fiesta
Folk Museum
Kozu-shima Port
Maehama
Kozu-shima Village Office
Tako Bay
Takohama
Tadanae-jima I.
Saruga-saki Pt.
Tako Bay Port

Sagami-nada Sea

Kozu-shima & Nii-jima
Scale 1 : 300,000   5km   2miles

To-shima Port
To-shima Village Off.
Hachiman Shrine
Mt Miyatsuka
To-shima I.
Oyama Koyama Shrine
Minami-ga-yama Park

Udone-shima I.

Nebu-saki Pt.
Wakago
Maehama
Wakago Port
Domaru-saki Pt.
Mt Miyatsuka
Mt Azuchi
Wadahama
Habushi Port
Nii-jima Museum
Nii-jima
Nii-jima Port
Nii-jima Village Office
Habushiura Park
Jinai-shima I.
Yunohama Roten
Grand
Mamashita
Sculptures Promenade
Nii-jima I.
Glass Art Center
Hanado-saki Pt.
Mt O-mine
Shiromama Cliff

Tomari Port
Nobushi
Mt Tango
Shikine-jima I.
Ashizuki
Ashitsuki Port
Haya-shima I.
Mikawa Bay
Jinata

Izu-misaki Pt.
Okubohama
Yunohama
Akon-saki Pt.
Kamanoshi
Igaya Port
Ofunato Bay
Miyake
Miyake-jima I.
Megane-iwa (Spectacular Rocks)
Mt Oyama
Furusato Relaxation Village
Fureaino-Yu
Ako Port
Miike
Tairo-ike Lake
Sabigahama
Miyake-jima Nature Center
Tsurune-saki Pt.
Chotaro-ike

Miyake-jima
Scale 1 : 300,000   2km   1mile

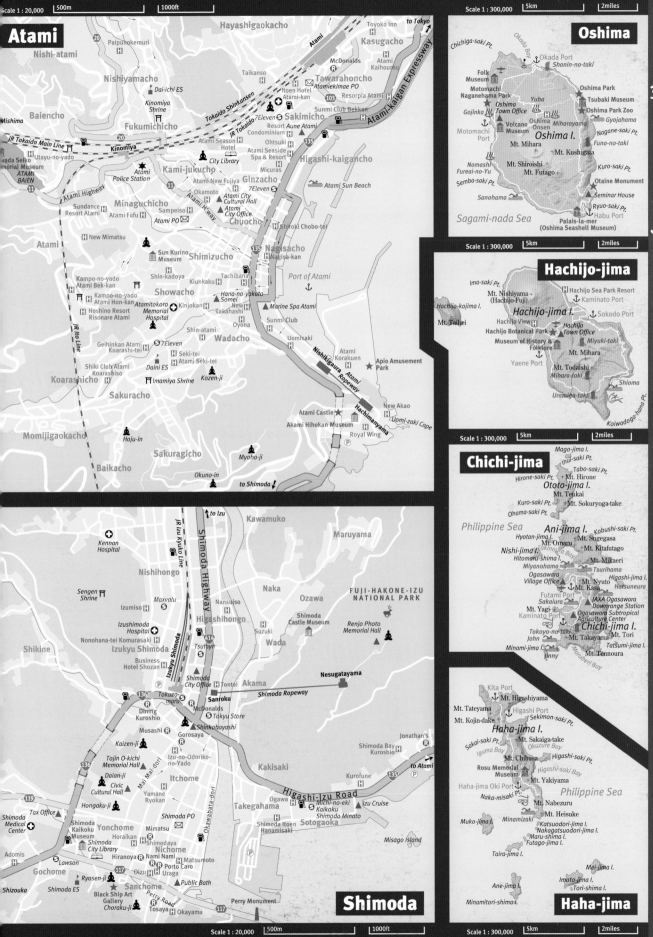

Nikko Area

Scale 1 : 85,000   1km   0.5mile

Onsen-ji
Yumoto
Nikko Yumoto Ski Area
Kyukamura
Nikko Yumoto
to Katashiana
Mt. Maeshirane
Lake Yuno-ko
Mt. To
Yu-taki
Iori-taki
Mt. Nyoho
Akana-taki
Nana-taki
Oshika-taki
Kuroiwa-taki
Kotoku Farm
Nikko Astraea
Mitsunori
Bonji-taki
Mt. Omanago
KOTOKU MARSH
Miyako-taki
Senjogahara Plateau
Senjogahara Monument
Fufushika-taki
Yumihari Pass
Odashirogahara Plateau
Akanuma Chaya
Jiran-no-taki
Mt. Taka
Mt. Nantai
Hatsune-no-taki
Hybrid Bus Sevice
120
Urami-no-taki
Ryuzu-no-taki
Nikko Prince
Shobugahama
Sakana-to-mori-no Kansatsu-en Park
Chuzenji Kanaya
Oku-Nikko Shikisai
Hannya-no-taki
Hoto-no-taki
Mt. Tanze
Nikko Futarasan Shrine Treasure Museum
Irohazaka (Steep Drive Way)
Nikko Toyokawa Inari Shrine
Furukawa Denko
Senjugahara
Senjugahara-mako Terminal
Shobuga-hama
Senjuga-hama
Lake Saino-ko
Mt. Naka
Nihon Romantic Highway
Chugushi
Nippon Research Institute
Restel Kinnami
Lake Chuzenji
Asian Garden
Lake Garden
Hana An
Petit
Lake Side Chuzenji
Shirakumo-no-taki
Agon-no-taki
Akechidaira Ropeway
Kiyotaki
Fami
Kegon-no-taki
Natural Science Museum
Akechidaira Plateau
Kiyotaki
Chuzen-ji
Fuga
Chanokidaira
Dai-ni Irohazaka (Steep Drive Way)
120
122
Hosho Dome Park
Mt. Kurobi-dake
Italian Embassy Villa Memorial Park
Chanokidaira Plateau
to Kiryu

Nikko Town

Scale 1 : 30,000   500m   1000 feet

Nikko Kirifuri Country Club
Hajime-no-ippo
to Kurobe Dam
169
MINOHARA SHINRIN PARK
Maple Reef
Poco a poco
One More Time
to Takino Shrine
Inari River
Weekend
Mori-no-yado Tasuke Junior
Takio Shrine
Takio Kotokusui Shrine
Narusawa Camp Site
Duet
Hampty Dumpty
Yama-no-ie
Shiraito-no-taki
Lambchop
Ogurayama Sanso
Resort Inn Kirifuri Plaza
Hakuba
169
Hangakimen
Nikko Kirifuri Ice Arena
L'escale
Kisugeso
Kitano Shrine
Ryuko-in
FUTARASAN SHRINE
TOSHO-GU
Mominoki
Casual Euro
Euro City
Rinno-ji Taiyu-in
Jigen-do
Honji-do
Yomei-mon Gate
Toshogu Museum
Nemuri-neko (Sleeping Cat)
Shin-kyusha (Holy Stable)
Gyoshintei Tokapso
Umeyashiki
Kosho
Nikko Woodcarving Center
Park Lodge
Narusawa Lodge
Seiryu Shrine
Tosho-gu Treasure House
Seikeen
Five Storey Pagoda
Kosugi Hoan Museum of Art
Nikko Woodcarving Center Annex
Urushi Museum
Rindo-no-ie
Pension Logette Sanbois
RINNO-JI
Honco
Nikko Senhime Monogatari
Kaze-no-hibiki
Nikkori-so Backpackers
Sabo Office
OGURAYAMA SHINRIN PARK
Green Hotel Natsukashiya Fuwari
Hachiman Shrine
Takumicho
Koun-do
Rinno-ji Homotsu-den (Treasure House)
Iroha
Shin-kyo
Tokinoyu
Hippari Dako
Daiyagawa YH
Hanabusa
Hanaishicho
TAMOZAWA IMPERIAL VILLA MEMORIAL PARK
120
Kami-hatsuishimachi
Johsyu-ya
Daiya River
Kanaya Hotel
Hoshino Yado
Onoya
247
Turtle Inn Nikko
Annex Turtle Hotori-An
Yuzawaya
Suzuki
Gusto
Hi-no-Kuruma
Nihon Romantic Highway
Hoteiya
Tobunikko
to Kiyoto
Botanical Garden
Shimo-hatsuishimachi
Gokomachi
Inarimachi
169
247
Bonten
Yoshinoya
Viva
Classic
to Kiyotaki
Ishiyamachi
Yoshinaya Ryokan
Nikko-Utsunomiya Rd
to Utsunomiya
to Tochigi
Matsubaracho

Kawagoe - Little Edo

Scale 1 : 20,000   500m   1000ft

to Kawajima
Ishiwaramachi
Tomyo-ji
Yaoko Kawagoe Museum
to A
Shitamachi
12
District Court
7 Eleven
Hikawa Shrine
Sakado
Jeans Mate
Hon'o-ji
Kosai-ji
Miyashitamachi
Sunkus
39
Dairen-ji
Hatsukari Jr.HS
Kawagoe City Museum
Kannon-ji
Kitamachi
Motomachi
Takazawa-dori
Osawa Family House
Kawagoe City Hall
Former Kawagoe Castle Site
HAT-KA PAI
Ranzan Memorial Art Gallery
Kagoe Matsuri-kaikan Museum
Museum of Kura-zukuri
Matsumuraya
Kawagoe Jr.HS
Yoju-in
Toki-no-kane Bell Tower
Kanetsuki-dori
Kuruwamachi
Fujimiyagura-ato
Choki-in
Gyoden-ji
Saiwaicho
Folklore Museum
Kappo Sakuma
Kawagoe Civic Hall
Kawagoe Ichi ES
Nakacho
Yamazaki Art Museum
City Chuo Library
Ukishima-inari Shrine
7 Eleven
51
Matsuecho
Kubomachi
Naritasan Betsu-in Temple
Kumano Shrine
Kawagoe Histo Museum
to Hidaka
Renkei-ji
City Plaza Kawagoe
Kosenbamach
Renjakucho
Hie Shrine
Kita Monzen-C
Mitsui Hospital
Saitama Hospital
Sanko
Kita-in
266
Hirose Hospital
229
Chuo ES
Nakaharamachi
Nishi-kosenbamachi
Tosho-gu Shrine
7 Eleven
15
Kawagoe Jr.HS
Seibu Hon Kawagoe PePe
KAWAGOE
Family Mart
Naka-in
Toshogu Nakan-dori
Wakatake Central
Prince
Taisho-Roman-Yume-dori
Family Mart
Kawag Sogo
Saiun-ji
Torimachi
Kawagoe Dai-ichi Jr.HS
Tobu Tojo Line
Kawagoe Technical High School
Hachiman-dori
Maruhiro Department Store
Kawagoe Tobu
Belc
Modi
Yamaguchi Hospital
Minami-torimachi
Seibu Shinjuku Line
Acacia-dori
Nihon Romantic Highway
Senbamachi
JR Kawagoe Line
Atre Maruhiro
City Library Branch
7 Eleven
to Ag
Lawson
to Sayama
Lumine
Kawagoe Dai-ichi
Kawagoe
Wakita-honcho
Wakitamachi
to Takashina
to Sayama

Nagoya Area

Scale 1 : 250,000

GIFU CITY
Sanko Art Museum
The Nawa Insect Museum
Mt Nishi
Enku Museum
Mt Kinka
Mt Miune
to Kanazawa, Noto Peninsula
SAKAHOGI TOWN
Mino-Ota
Minokawai
Akechi
to Kanazawa, Takayama
Shin-Kani
KANI CITY
Kogaya OGM Cherikuriku GC

Nishi-Gifu
Meitetsu Gifu
seum of Fine Art of Gifu
Kano-Tou
Castle Ruins
Nagamori
Hosobata
KAGAMIHARA CITY
Kagamigahara
Gifu CC
Kamigahara CC
Sakahogi
Nagoya Hills GC
Shin-Kani
Nishi-Kani
Nihon Line GC
Akechi Ruins
Toyozo Museum
Tsukigata Daitobo Art Museum
to Nagano, Matsumoto

GINAN CITY
Aqua Toto Gifu Aquarium
FUSO TOWN
Kisosansen Park
Naito Museum
INUYAMA 37
INUYAMA CITY
Little World
Token Shuga GC
Mt Hasso
Inuyama GC
Meiji Mura
Iruka Reservoir
Mt Mikosha
Kani Folk Museum
Kids Land Kodomo Toki Museum
Springfield GC
Tajimi
Mino Toji Historical Museum
TOKI CITY

INAZAWA CITY
KONAN CITY
OGUCHI TOWN
NIWA DISTRICT
Kashiwamori
Gakuden
Haguro
Funabashi Musical Instrument Museum
KOMAKI CITY
Mt Hongu
Mt Doju
Suwa Museum
Chuo Expressway
Tajimi Mino Pottery Museum
Ceramic Park Mino
TAJIMI CITY
Mt Miyama

Ise Bay

to Central Japan Inter'l Airport
to Tokyo

CENTRAL HONSHU

to Biwa-ko Lake, Kyoto

Biwajima · Higashi-biwajima · Minoji · Biwajima Sports Center · Yoshidzuya
Yoneda Hospital · Meijodai Fuzoku HS · Hokei-ji · Meisei
Tsuchie Shrine · Shiokecho · Meitetsu Hospital · Sakou · Sakou ES · Fujinomiyatori
Kikusen-ji · Sakocho · Business Asahi · Aichi Pref. Saiseikai Hospital
7 Eleven · Dainichicho · Chiharacho · Yonedacho · Momonokicho
Chihara Building · Public Bath Juocho · Oise Jr.HS · Noritake Head Quarter · Noritake Museum, Craft Center
Uniqlo · Sakomaecho · Aoi Engineering Mori Bldg · Nissan · Ibukacho · Kondo Bldg
Higashiyama Line · Honda · Lawson · Matsuya · Honjin · Kameshima · Sanuki Seimen · Felice · Mansion Freebell
Matsubaracho · Nakamura Holiday Medical Clinic · Mazda · Sasanabe Hospital · Ushijimacho · Kamejima · Meitetsu Inn
Oakicho Vocational School · Segan-ji · Hachimansha Shrine · Cosmo · Super · Lucent Tower · Shell
Hiyishicho · Kakuen-ji · Toei Bldg · Yoshinoya · Chisun Inn · Matsuzakaya · Mont Blanc · Palina
Daimoncho · Honda · Noritake Bldg · Matsumura Ryokan · Sunkus · Dainagoya Building
Nakajimacho · Noritake-hondori · Noritake · Nagoyakatei Miyoshi · Astria · Bic Camera · Le West · ESCA
Hakuo-ji · Wakamiyacho · Hyakugo Bank · Sato · Meitetsu New Grand · Central · Toyoko Inn
Ukai Rehabilitation Hospital · Taiko-dori · Nakamura Ward Office · Makino ES · Dai Star · Denny's
Daily Yamazaki · Nakamura Kuyakusho · Yoshikawa Clinic · Eco Flower · Idemitsu · Nakamura Police Station · Mizutani Bldg
Taiko · Daijo-ji · Makinocho · Aeon · Aoyama Bldg · Sasashimacho
Kami-komenocho · Shinsho-ji · Hosen-ji · Daikichi · Oise · Nagoya Central Hospital · Shimo-hiroicho
Gomaecho · Komeno Clinic · Gansho-ji · Palace · Zempuku-ji · Zepp Nagoya · JICA
Sennaritori · Circle K · Zenjo-ji · Gongentori · 7 Eleven · Komeno ES · Hiraikecho
Shirakocho · Kogane Jr.HS · Shofuku-ji · Taishocho · Chosho-ji
Kumanocho · Circle K · Fukakawacho · Empuku-ji · Shimo-komenocho
Kyodencho · Toyokuni Jr.HS · Kanayama Shrine · Nagatoicho · Nikkyohan · Ungacho · Ungatori
Kitahatacho · Kogahedori · Kogane · Satsukitori · Konohoecho · Fukuzumicho · Tsukishimacho · Hirosumicho
to Kuwana · Mitsuicho · Aonami Line · Satsuki-minamitori · Matsubacho · Hoseicho · Heiwado · Aichi ES · Kaisei Hospital
Nagaracho · Norikoshicho · Hosei-ji · Shoren-ji · Kitakansen · Craft · Yokoboricho
Minami-wakicho · Mannen-ji · Saya H'way · Chukyo-minamidori · Yanagishimacho · Sumiikecho · Nakagawaunga · Oisecho
Hirokawacho · Kannon-ji · Tsuyuhashicho · Hosen-ji · Maenamicho · Tsuyuhashi ES · Funatocho

Kikunoo Odori · Enoki ES · Tokai Print Sha · Oshikiri · Sengen · Kaifuku-ji · Hoshu-ji
Nagoyanishi HS · Saiho-ji · Tenjinyama Jr.HS · Nishi Ward Library
Sugikura Bldg · Nishi Police Station · Shotoku-ji · Nishi Ward Office
Hananoki · Tenjinyamacho · Miyasuzume · Saiko-ji · Ono Clinic · Chuden Kogyo · Drug Sugiyama
Tokuen-ji · Circle K · Kikui · Hoso-ji · Miura Bldg · Saigan-ji · Habashita ES · City Tours
Minamioshikiri ES · Aibi Gakuen Keimeigakkan HS · Kikui Jr.HS · Shogaku-ji · Ashikari Clinic
Jizo-in · NORITAKE GARDEN · Enishi ES · Aichi Shinkin Bank · 7 Eleven
Noritakecho · Noritake Museum, Craft Center · Gifu Shinkin Bank · Tokusei-ji
Sotobori-dori · Ogaki Kyoritsu Bank · Aichi Bank · Shinmichi · Habashita
Riuge Clinic · Idota Clinic · Aichi Sosai Bank · Circle K · Enton-ji
Meieki · Nagano ES · Kimiya Ryokan · Nagono · Masuda · Aiko Bldg
Sunroute Plaza Nagoya · Nagoya Prime Central Tower · Saiyu-ji · Imazu Clinic
Mercure Nagoya Cypress · Familymart · Mobil · Nagoya International Center Building · Hills Riverside
Ekimae · Resol Nagoya · Kokusai Center · Shisei-in-ji · Kirix Nagoya Building
JR Central Towers · Associa · Nisshin Building · Komya-in-ji · Hijieagata Shrine
NAGOYA STATION · Nagoya Marriott · Castle Plaza · Jiko-ji · Joshin-ji
Takashimaya · Palina · Sasashima ES · Pachinko Daitokai · Rolen · Tiger · Misono ES
Sanko Inn · Midland Square · Higashiyama Line · Sunkus · Aisan Bldg · Toyota · Aqua Town
Meitetsu & Kintetsu · Mode Gakuen Spiral Towers · Kanihonke · Richmond · Nakau · Mizuho Bank
McDonalds · Daiwa Roynet · Mizutani Clinic · Sumitomo Life Insurance Nagoya Building · Hilton Nagoya
Nippon Tsuun · Choen-ji · Yomiuri Shimbun · Kawabata Clinic · Circle K
Chuden Meieki Minami Building · Aichi-ken Seinen-kaikan · Noka Sports Center · Lions
Toko-ji · Shoko Bldg · Meieki Yutaka Building · Kuga Building · Bussho-ji · Iida Clinic · Hiide Shrine
Corona · Narita Hospital · Josho-ji · Seian-ji · Daiko-in-ji
Sakai Clinic · Kakomachi Building · Osu ES · Hosho-ji
Meieki-minami · Taiho · Yakushi-ji · Matsubara
Nishi-hioki · NTT Nishinihontokai Hospital · Honen-ji · Hosho-in
Matsushigecho · Higashi-shisen · Ensho-ji · Yanagiboricho
Aichicho · Zengyo-ji · Higashi-shisen · Sanno Onsen
Sanno-dori · Kannon-ji · Hosen-ji · Sanno · Sanno Jr.HS · Masaki · Masaki ES · Zensho-ji
Maenamicho · NAGOYA BASEBALL PARK · to Shizuoka Tokyo · Don Quijote · to Minato · Furuwataricho · to Atsuta

to Kiyosu · Myodo-ji · Sukiyacho · Josho-ji · MEIJO PARK
Nishi Ward Library · Nagoya Nishi Church · Meijo Bunsho
Emman-ji · Sato Senko · Meijo Park Flower Plaza
Horibatacho · Josai ES · Westin Nagoya Castle · Nagoya Castle · Honmaru
Hinokuchicho · Ofukaimaru Museum · NINOMARU GARDEN · Ni-no-Maru-Satei
Jutoku-ji · Miwata Clinic · Circle K · Ninomaru · Kishimen-tei
Hirano Bldg · Shogaku-ji · Shiro · Nagoya Noh Theater · Aichi Prefectural Gymnasium
McDonalds · Mazda · Sannomaru · Dekimachi-dori · Aichi Prefectural Local Autonomy Hall
Nagoya High Court · Meijo Hospital · KKR · Nagoya City Hall
Kyoraka Ryokan · Kyoya Ryokan · Aichi Prefectural Library · Aichi Peace Memorial Museum
Chunichi Shimbun Co., Ltd. · Aichi Gokoku Shrine · Aichi Prefectural Government
Habashita · Sakakura Clinic · CoCo Ichibanya · Keiei-ji · Token Corp. · Nakono Shrine · Najo ES
Toyoko Inn · Yoshinoya · Marunouchi · Tokuzen-ji · Noshin Bldg · Chunichi Hospital
Nagono · Marunouchi Alpine Tower · Eneos · Ono Yak · Nak
Mobil · Shisei-in-ji · Sanden Bldg · APA · 7 Eleven · Circle K · Ansei-ji · Sampo
Sakura Odori · Sakura-dori Line · Cosmo · Wing · Livemax
Bank of Japan · Nagoya International · Marubeni Bldg · Grace Inn · Nagoya Sakae
Familymart · 7 Eleven · Byo Bank · Trusty · Monan-ji · Sun
Kokusai Center · Castle Plaza · Jozuji-ji · Garden Palace · Daichi
Nishiki · Circle K · Shizuoka Bank · Fushimi · Circle K
Shimozono Park · Ebisuya · Kokusai International · Nagoya Tokyu Inn
The Shin Nagoya Musical Theatre · Hilton Nagoya · Misonoza · ZXA · The Electricity Museum
Hamilton Hotel Black · Washington · Sun · Genzu · APA · Sakae
Shirakawa Hall · Princess Garden · Nagoya City Science Museum
Nadya Park Business Center Building · Nagoya City Art Museum
SHIRAKAWA PARK · Sakae Center Bldg Design Center Building
Mitsubishi UFJ Lease · Sakae ES · Susaki Shrine · Wakamiya Hachimansha · Seishu-ji
Nagoya Expressway No. 2 Higashiyama Route
Gokuraku-ji · Daiko-in-ji · Miwa Sh · Yoshu-ji · Nakau
Oi Bldg · Soken-ji · Osu · Ohsu Plaza · Osso Brasil
Monzencho · Kami-mae · Tsurumai Line · Kinsen-ji · Ryuun-ji · Shudai-ji
Manpuku-ji · Zenko-ji · Tachibana ES · Choei-ji · Eikoku-ji
Aichisangyodai Technical HS · Higashibetsuin · Higashi-Betsuin · Masaki · Iseyama

Meijo Line · Shinkawa-dori · Meijo Park

Inuyama

CENTRAL HONSHU

Scale 1 : 20,000
500m
1000ft

to Takaoka, Toyama
to Takaoka
to Minam

Filtration Plant
Yasue Sumiyoshi Shrine
KFC
Hokutetsu Asanogawa Line
Naruwa Jr. HS
Naruwa
Public Bath
Ohimachi
Izumo Shrine
Sainen-ji
Saikyo-ji
Komeya Drugstore
Nanatsuyamachi
Otomarumachi
Johoku SC
Kanazawa Sakuragaok HS
Sainen
Enkyu-ji
Umezawamachi
Kasugamachi
Yosho-ji
Yusen-ji
EKINISHI CENTRAL PARK
Eki-nishi-hommachi
Shangria
Nishi-horikawamachi
Kyomachi
Johoku Hospital
Asanomachi ES
Kanazawa-higashi Police Station
Jinguji
Econo Higashi-Kanazawa
Naruwamachi
Naruwada
Manten Hotel Ekimae
Hirooka
Komeya Drugstore
Daiwa Roynet
R&B
Nanatsuya
Kyusho-ji
Yonezawa Hospital
Showa Odori
Asano-honmachi
Koganemachi
Motomachi
Jokyo-ji
Joko-ji
Yamanouemachi
Nagatamachi
Horikawamachi
Kosei-ji
Shoeimachi
McDonalds
Zendo-ji
Kokaku-ji
Kosaka Shrine
Hokutetsu Bicycle Rental
Rafflesia
Hokutetsu Bus Company
Castle Inn
Asano Shrine
Moriyamamachi ES
Joko-ji
Honpo-ji
Samegaicho
Nagatamachi ES
Dormy Inn Central
Yasue-hachimangu Shrine
Kasaichimachi
Kobashimachi
Moriyama
Jogyo-ji
Zensho-ji
Higashiyama
Apa
Crowne Plaza Ana
Econo
Nishi Betsu-in
Hyotanmachi
Public Bath
Myokoku-ji
Sampo-ji
Ryokoku-ji
Hirooka
Ishikawa Concert Hall
Namaste
Konohanamachi
Shoryu-ji
Enryu-ji
Myotai-ji
Shinjo-ji
Hiyoshimachi
Route Inn
Meisei ES
Honkaku-ji
Baba ES
Gemmon-ji
Saiyo-ji
Utatsumachi
Nakabashimachi
Nikko
Hommachi
Higashi Betsu-in
Hikosomachi
Jokei-ji
Kazuemachi
Mifuku
Yasue Gold Leaf Museum
Sakuda Gold Leaf Company
Soryu-ji
Uguisumachi
Mt. Utatsu
Nagata-honmachi
Rifare
Kawaguchi
Yasuecho
Kofuku-ji
Kikunoya Kizuya
Higashiyama Higashi Traditional Town
Izumi Kyoka Memorial Museum
Jukyo-ji
Kaikaro
Utatsu Shrine
Jiyuken
Ginmatsu
Yamanoo
Utatsu Craft Workshop
UTATSUYAMA PARK
Motogikucho
City Inn
Hayashi Hospital
Kinjo Hospital
Fukuromachi
Owaricho
Kanazawa Phonograph Museum
Hyakumangoku Odori
Kannon-in
Namikimachi
Kinjo-ro
Tokuda Shusei Memorial Museum
Koraimachi
Kakurin-ji
IRIS GARDEN
Zemyo-ji
Showamachi
Musashiga-tsuji Bus Stop
Meitetsu M'Za Sky Plaza
Kanazawa Sky
Kanazawa City
Hosai
Sanjamachi
Rokumaimachi
Kanazawa City
Musashimachi
Omicho Ichiba-kan
Citizen's Culture Museum
Bakuromachi
Matsumoto
Mr. Kurando
Terashima's House
Zempuku-ji
Ohi Pottery Museum
Hashibacho
Higashi-mikagemachi
Hokoku Shrine
Kanazawa XH
Circle K
Tamagawacho
Resol Trinity
Nishicho-sanbancho
Ikkenmachi
KKR
Ozaki Shrine
Ohori Odori
Utatsuyama-koen-dori
Performing Square
Public Bath
Tamagawa Children's Library
City Tamagawa Library
TAMAGAWA-KOEN
Kenrokusou
Marunouchi
Koike Hospital
Hakuchoro
Zaimokucho ES
Zaimokucho
Tokiwamachi
Zensho Bo
Nagadohe
Mitani Sangyo Co., Ltd.
Takaokamachi
New Grand Annex
Oyama Shrine
Kanazawa Castle Park
Oyamacho
Otemachi
Zaimoku-motomachi
Misokuracho ES
Nagamachi
Kanazawa City Cultural Hall
Chuo ES
New Grand
Hishi-yagura Watch Tower
Ishikawa-mon Gate
Kanko Bussankan
Kenrokumachi
Yokoyamamachi
Akatsukimachi
Nagamachi Yuzen-kan
Seirei Hospital
Minamicho
Takada Samurai House Site
Daiwa Dept. Store
KANAZAWA-JO PARK
Koshomachi Jr. HS
Kaga Yuzen Traditional Industry Center
Sakuramachi
Mikagemachi
Toyoko Inn
Nagamachi Samurai House Site
Chuo-dori
Murakami
Kanazawa Kutani Museum
Atrio Shopping Plaza
Gyokusen-en Garden
Kenroku-motomachi
Koshomachi
Kenroku Odori
Hosen-ji
Saigawa Shrine
Maeda Tosanokami Samurai House Site
Korinbo
Excel
Hirosaka
Janome-sushi Honten
21st Century Museum of Contemporary Art
KENROKU-EN GARDEN
Ishikawa Pref. Museum of Traditional Products & Crafts
Youfuku-ji
Ogimachi
Kanazawa Munehiro Hospital
Taimach
Chuodorimachi
Shuko-ji
Kanazawa Shinise Memorial Hall
Korinbo 109
Kanazawa Noh Museum
Ishikawa Prefectural Art Museum
Seison-kaku Daimyo Residence
Kanazawa Medical Center
Hoen-ji
Tenjinmachi
Nakamuramachi
Nakamura Museum
Ishino Hospital
Katamachi
Apa Villa
Legian
Muro Saisei Memorial Museum
Kanazawa City Hall
Higashi-kenrokuenmachi
Nakamura Memorial Museum
Hokuriku Gakuin HS
Kanazawa Medical HS
Shimo-ishibikimachi
Ishikawa Pref. Noh Theatre
Kakurin-ji
Nakamuramachi ES
Shiragikucho
Osteria del Campagne
Econo
Acty
Shimo-kakinokibatake
Great People of Kanazawa Memorial Museum
Prefectural Library
Suzuki Daisetsu Museum
Ishikawa Historical Museum
Honda-no-mori Hall
Shikindai Jr. HS
Kanazawa Folklore Museum
Ishikawa Prefectural Noh Theater
Kasuga Shrine
Apita
Sennichimachi
Tamazushi Smile
Murataya Ryokan
Kinokibatake
Oden Miyuki Honten
Shimo-Dewamachi
Nakamura Memorial Museum
Matsubara Hospital
Takaramachi
Kanazawadai Hospital
Kanazawa College of Art
Daikumachi
Shimmei-gu Shrine
Dairen-ji
Ankan-ji
Kanazawa Police Station
Kotatsu
Kanazawa Wanaka Memorial Museum
Tatemachi
Kanazawa University
Kanazawa University
Masuizumi
Aburaguruma
Jusangenmachi
Nakacho
Ibaragicho
Ikedamachi
Tatecho
Urokomachi
Gobancho
Hongyo-ji
Togaku-ji
Yuinen-ji
Myokei-ji
Ito Hospital
Prefectural Tech. HS
Hondamachi
Kanazawa Church
Kanazawadai Hospital
Nishi Chaya Museum
Gannen-ji
Stained Glass Museum
Mizutamemachi
Shin-tatemachi ES
Yugakkan HS
Ishibiki
Kyoo-ji
Kanazawa Commercial H
Nomachi
Tsudakoma Corp.
Apa
Myoryu-ji (Ninjadera)
Naka-kawayokemachi
Edamachi
Saiwaimachi
Ionan-dori
Tentoku-in
Hokutetsu Ishikawa Line
Public Bath
Kawakita Hospital
Fushimi-ji
Kawagishimachi
Honin-ji
Kiyokawamachi
Kasamai
Shiragikucho
Shorin-ji
Kotoku-ji
Daien-ji
Ryuzo-ji
Yuya Ruru Saisai
Kikugawa
Daigan-ji
Kodatsuno
Minami Avenue
Izumi
Honjo-ji
Honaku-ji
Kio-ji
Myoho-ji
Teramachi
Kikugawacho ES
Monkyo-ji
Nomachi ES
Yayoi
Yayoi ES
Honze-ji
Genko-in
Suzuki Ladies Hospital
Keigan-ji
Jonan
Kanazawa College of Art
Nensai-ji
Keigan-ji
Izumi Jr. HS
Izumino Sakuragi Shrine
Circle K
Kincharyo
Hoshu-ji
Kokuzo Shrine
Izumigaoka
Izuminomachi
Ryusho-ji
Juichiya ES
Hoshimamachi
Noda JHS
Kasamai-honmachi
Shoping Town Palatte
McDonalds
Albis
to Hakusan
to Toyama
Hashimotoya
Jonan-dori

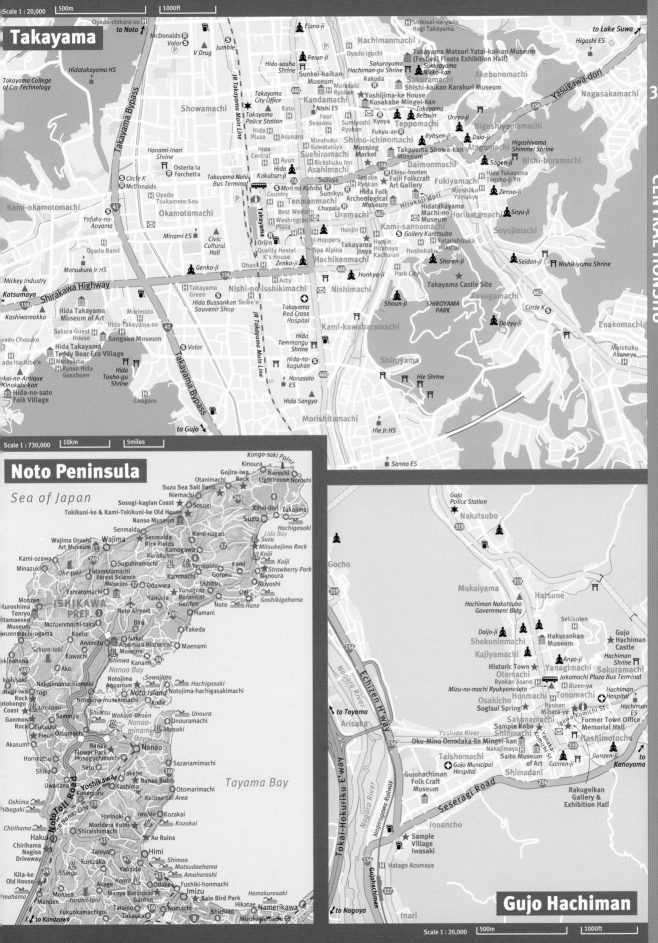

Takayama

Scale 1 : 20,000
500m
1000ft

to Noto ↑
Oyado-chikara-so
McDonalds
Valor
Jumble
V Drug
Hidatakayama HS
Takayama College of Car Technology
Takayama Bypass
JR Takayama Main Line
Showamachi
Hida-sosha Shrine
Eijana-ji
Reiun-ji
Hachimanmachi
Shikisai-no-yado Hagi Takayama
Oyado Iguchi
Takayama Matsuri Yatai-kaikan Museum (Festival Floats Exhibition Hall)
Nikko-kan
Sakurayama Hachiman-gu Shrine
Higashi ES
to Lake Suwa →
Yasugawa-dori
Akebonomachi
Nagasakamachi
39

Sunkei-kaikan Museum
Kandamachi
Murasaki
Rakuda
Shishi-kaikan Karakuri Museum
Sakuramachi
Nishi ES
Four Seasons
Kato
Yoshijima-ke House
Kusakabe Mingei-kan
Takayama Betsuin
Takayama City Office
Takayama Police Station
Hida Plaza
Asunaro
Sumiyoshi Ryokan
Kyoya
Fukyu-an
Shimo-ichinomachi
Takayama Showa-kan
Unryu-ji
Ryosen-ji
Daio-ji
Higashiyamamachi
Atagomachi
Higashiyama Shimmei Shrine
Nishi-boramachi

Hida Central
Suehiromachi
Morning Market
Kuwataniya
Rickshuku Inn
Teppomachi
Asahimachi
Daimonmachi
Sogen-ji
Nishi-boramachi

Kami-okamotomachi
Honami-Inari Shrine
Circle K
McDonalds
Osteria la Forchetta
Oyado Tsukamoto Sou
Hida Kokubun-ji
Takayama Nohi Bus Terminal
41
Suzuya
Tanabe
Ebisu-honten
Tabane
Fujii Folkcraft Art Gallery
Fukiyamachi
Hida Folk Archeological Museum
Hida Takayama Tensho-ji YH
Minshuku Yamakyu
Zenno-ji
Hidatakayama Machi-no Museum
Horibatamachi
Soyujimachi
Haku'un
Seidan-ji

Yofuku-no-Aoyama
Okamotomachi
Minami ES
Civic Cultural Hall
Genko-ji
Mori no Kotoba
Country
Best Western Washington Plaza
Orijin
Quality Hostel
K's House
Ohan
Tenmanmachi
Chapala
Uramachi
Honjin
Takayama Jinya
Spa Alpina
J-Hoppers
Hachikenmachi
Gallery Kuratsubo
Honkyo-ji
Park City
Shoren-ji
Kami-sannomachi
Honjin Hiranoya Kadho-an
Hoshokaku
Futarishizuka
Futarishizuka
Seidan-ji
Nishikiyama Shrine

Matsukura Jr.HS
Mickey Industry
Katsumaya
Shirakawa Highway
Kashiwamokko
Hida Takayama Museum of Art
Morimoto
Hida-Takayama-so
Sakura Guest House
Sangaku Museum
Hida Takayama Teddy Bear Eco Village
Murayama
Ryoso Hida Gosshoen
Hida Tosho-gu Shrine
Chogoro
Takayama Green
Hida Bussankan Seibe'e
Souvenir Shop
Hida Takayama-so
Valor
Hanasato
Hida Sangyo
Acty
Nishi-no-isshikimachi
Takayama Red Cross Hospital
Kami-kawaharamachi
Hida Temmangu Shrine
Hida-no-kagukan
Nishimachi
Shoun-ji
SHIROYAMA PARK
Takayama Castle Site
Kasugamachi
Circle K
Dairyu-ji
Enakomachi
Minshuku Asanoya
Shiroyama
Hie Shrine
Hie Jr.HS
Sanno ES
to Gujo ↓
Morishitamachi

CENTRAL HONSHU

Noto Peninsula

Scale 1 : 730,000
10km
5miles

Sea of Japan
Kongo-saki Point
Kinoura
Gojira-iwa Rock
Noroshi Lighthouse Noroshi
Otanimachi
Suzu Sea Salt Farm
Niemachi
Sosogi-kagian Coast
Sosogi
Kihei-dori
Takojima
Tokikuni-ke & Kami-Tokikuni-ke Old House
Nanso Museum
Suzu
Hachigasaki
Iida Bay
Mitsukejima Rock
Wajima Urushi Art Museum
Wajima
Senmaida Rice Fields
Kami-nagao
Koiji
Koiji
Strawberry Park
Kami-ozawa
Minazuki
Oke-taki
Suguhiramachi
Kamogawa
Yanagida
Kurokawa
Kami
Goroku
Nunoura
Akiyoshi
Monzen
Kuroshima
Tenryo
Tamaesen Museum
nzenmachi-ogama
Futamatamachi Forest Science Museum
Yamatomachi
Odawara
Yamada
Odanimachi
Ushitsu
Yanagida Botanical Garden
Ogi
Noto
Hane
Goshikigahama
ISHIKAWA PREF.
Noto Airport
Bira
Koeto
Monzenmachi-taira
Takeda
Maenami
Sakura-taki
kinohana
Anamizu
Anamizu Historical Museum
Kawachi
Shinwa
Kanami
atagi-iwa Rock
Togi
Nakajimamachiomaki
Sowajiara
Hachigasaki
Notojima Aquarium
Notojima-hachigasakimachi
Ganmon Rock
Fukuura
Shiotsu
Wakura-Onsen
Nanao-minami Bay
Unoura
Unouramachi
Akusaki
kaihisaki
Urukami
Otokongo Coast
Sampiyo
Noto Island
Koda
Akasumi
Fleuri
Otsumachi
Nanao
Nanao Flower Park
Hosoguchimachi
Seto
Sazanamimachi
Horimatsu
Shika
Uwadana
Yoshikawa
Kanemaru
Takebe
Nanao Ruins
Otomarimachi
Oshima
hibagaki
Chirihama
Chirihama Nagisa Driveway
Kita-ke Old House
Menden
mahama
Fukuokamachigo
Shingu
Yanaida
Akage
Kojiru
Odake
Fushiki-honmachi
Shimao
Matsudaehama
Amaharashi
Hamakurosaki
Furezaka
Taniya
Manyo Botanical Garden
Imizu
Kaio Bird Park
Taraino
Nomachi
Shichimi
Namerikawa
Mizuhashimachi
Tarumi-taki
Takaoka
to Kanazawa
Moridera Ruins
Iwado
Kozakai
Kozaka
Shiraishimachi
Himi
Harinoki
Kurosa Ski Area
Nanao Bay
Tayama Bay
Hakui
Nototoll Road
JR Nanao Line
Kashima

Gujo Hachiman

Scale 1 : 20,000
500m
1000ft

Gujo Police Station
Nakatsubo
Gujo
Mukaiyama
Hatsune
Hachiman Nakatsubo Government Bldg
Sekisuien
Gujo Hachiman Castle
Hachiman Shrine
Gocho
Daijo-ji
Shokuninmachi
Hakurankan Museum
Anyo-ji
Yanagimachi
Kajiyamachi
Hachiman ES
Historic Town
Otemachi
Jokamachi Plaza Bus Terminal
Bizen-ya
Sakuramachi
Ryokan Asano
Honmachi
Tonomachi
Hachiman Hospital
Osakicho
Sogisui Spring
Mizu-no-machi Ryukyonosato
Ryokan Mihara-ya
Yanaka Museum
Sakanamachi
Shinmachi
Igawa Komichi St
Former Town Office Memorial Hall
Hashimotocho
Sample Kobo
Oku-Mino Omodaka-ke Mingei-kan
Nakajimaya
Jionzen-ji
Ganzen-ji
to Kanayama →
Taishomachi
Gujo Municipal Hospital
Saito Museum of Art
Shimadani
Arisaka
Echizen H'way
Yoshida River
Tokai-Hokuriku E-way
Nagara River
Nagaragawa Railway
to Toyama ↓
Gujohachiman Folk Craft Museum
Jonancho
Rakugeikan Gallery & Exhibition Hall
Sample Village Iwasaki
Hatago Azumaya
to Gujohachiman
Seseragi Road
to Nagoya ↓
Inari

Kurobe · Funami Fureai

to Itoigawa
to Joetsu

13 · 125

Ikenotaira · 399

Otari · Atsuyu · Atsuyu

Kurohime Kogen Ski Area · Mt. Madar

Kareisawa Shinrin Park ★ · Unazuki · Unazaki Onsen

Kudarise

Ongonyu · Buno · Kurohime Dowa-no-mori Museum · 504 · 96 · 97

Mt. Asahi · Mt. Kazafuki

13

Mt. Sogadake ★ · Mt. Yukikura · Mt. Nonkura · Mt. Takatsuma · Nojiri-ko · 18 · 119

Mt. Korenge · Hakuba Cortina · Happo-one Ski Resort · Mt. Togakushi · Ninpo Museum · 60

132 · Mt. Shirouma · Tsugaike Natural Garden · Togakushi Ski Area · 37 · 18

Mt. Asahi · Tsugaike Kogen Ski Area · Kagami Pond ★ · Mt. Iizuna · Iizuna Resort Ski Area · Iizuna App Museum · 505

Mt. Kekachi ★ · Mt. Yarigatake · Hakuba Iwatake · Kids Ninja Village · JR Shin-etsu Main Line · 368

333 · Photograph Gallery · Hakuba Art Museum · Happoone · Mt. Karamatsu · Hakuba · Tomita Memorial Museum · 37

Mt. Ikenodaira · Takenoyu · 406 · 406 · 18

Senninyu · Hakuba 47 Winter Sports Park · Snow Harp · Mt. Mushikura · 86 · 406

Mt. Tsurugi · Mt. Kashima-Yarigatake · Hakuba Goryu Ski Resort · San Alpina Hakuba Sanosaka · 406 · Nagano · NAGANO 41 · Kitano Art Museum

Mt. Jiigatake · Hakuba Cross Country Field · Yanaba Snow & Green Park · Ogawa · Big Hat · M-Wave

Tateyama Snow Corridor · Murodo · Mt. Narasawa · Kashimayari Sports Village · Aoki-ko · 324 · 31 · 401 · Chausuyama Botanical Garden · White Ring · 403 · Rendai

6 · Tateyama Sangaku Ski Area · Kurobe Dam · Kizaki-ko · 148 · 497 · 384 · Olympic Stadium · Seisui-ji · 34 · Hoshi

Tateyama Ropeway & Kurobe Cablecar · Kizakiko · 31 · Miasa · Fudo · 70 · Kizankan · Kiyo-daki

Mt. Harinoki · Omachi · Alps Hot Spring Museum · 394 · NAGANO PREF. · 395 · 35

Mt. Washigatake · Mt. Kitakuzu · Shiki Theater Museum · Sangaku Museum · Chikuma · 390 · 18 · 77

Mt. Etchuzawa · Kuzu · Energy Museum · Omachi · 12 · 403

Mt. Fudo · Mt. Minamisawa · Nanakura Dam · Fotk Museum · 55 · Furusaka · Mt. Hijiri · Omi · Toguro Kamiyamada

Mt. Yakushi · Takase Dam · Mt. Karasawa · Matsuzawa · Yunosawa · 882 · 403 · 55

Takamagahara · Mt. Akaushi · Mt. Mitsudake · Mt. Gaki · Nakayama · Chikuhoku · 160 · 77

Mt. Kitanomata · Mt. Suisho · Mt. Nugochi-Goro · 147 · 19 · Ikeda · Ikusaka · 12 · Kusayu · 35 · to Fujio

CHUBU SANGAKU NATIONAL PARK · 306 · 273 · Ueda

Mt. Kurobegoro · Mt. Washiba · Mt. Tsubakuro · Nakabusa · 277 · 143 · 65 · 186

Mt. Mitsumata-Renge · Jigoku · Ariake · Mt. Ariake · Ariake Art Museum · 143 · Tazawa

Mt. Sugoroku · 327 · Hotaka · Ehon Museum · Rokuzan Art Museum · JR Shinonoi Line · 303 · Bessho · 12

Mt. Yariga 3108m · Mt. Higashi-Tenjo · 302 · 161

Mt. Kasagadake · Mt. Nakadake · Mt. Akaiwa · Azumino Herb Square ★ · Hotaka Togei-kaikan Iinuma Museum · 19 · 143 · Kakeyu · 254 · Oshio

Shin-Hotaka Mt. Hotaka 3190m+ · Kamikochi Resort · Mt. Jonen · Hodaka Togei-kaikan · Azumino · 302 · Yubuku-no-Satoyu

Mt. Shakujo ★ · Mt. Mae-Hodaka · Mt. Chogatake · 314 · 147 · Asama · 284 · Utsukushi-ga-hara · Utsukushi-ga-hara Kogen Museum · 464

Shin-Hotaka Ropeway · Kamikochi · Mt. Otaki · 319 · Matsumoto City Open Air Architectural Museum · Matsumoto · MATSUMOTO 41 · Mt. Chausu

to Toyama · Hida Shizen-kan Museum · Takezawa Marsh · 24 · Kamikochi · 25 · 278 · Iriyamabe

Bear Park ★ · Fukuchi · Taisho Pond · 295 · Tobira · 67 · 178

Mt. Terashiyama · Mt. Yake-dake · Mt. Kasumizawa · Nakanoyu · 158 · 494 · 48 · Yamagata · Matsumoto Airport · 63 · 67 · 142

158 · Hitayu · Mt. Hachibuse · Gakenoyu · 194

to Takayama · 84 · Mt. Jikkoku · 158 · Kiyomizu Ski Area · Asahi · 293 · Kita-kumai Ruins ★ · 142

Shirahone · Bandokoro-Otaki · Awanoyu · 291 · Matoo-no-Yu · 292 · Asahi Prime · Shiojiri · 19

Sambon-daki · Nagawada Dam · Shimosuwa · Suwa-taisha Shrine · 40 · Matsumoto Electric Rail

Mt. Norikura 3026m · Zengoro-no-taki & Ushidome Pond · Nagawa Museum of History & Folklore · Hirade Museum · 19 · 20 · Okaya · 297

Nokikura-kogen · 39 · 26 · Mt. Hachimori · Nagawa · LAKE SUWA 41 · Lake Suwa · Takashima Castle · Suwa · Kunisawa

to Nagoya · to Tokyo · JR Chuo Main Line · Chuo Expressway

Nagano & Matsumoto Areas

Scale 1 : 400,000 · 5km · 2miles

Inset (right):

Kita-Matsumoto · JR Shinonoi · Shiraita · to Takayama · Welton · Nagisa · Haba · Vega X Vega · Honda Cars · to Azumino · 143 · Kamada E · 19 · Kamada · 297 · to Shio

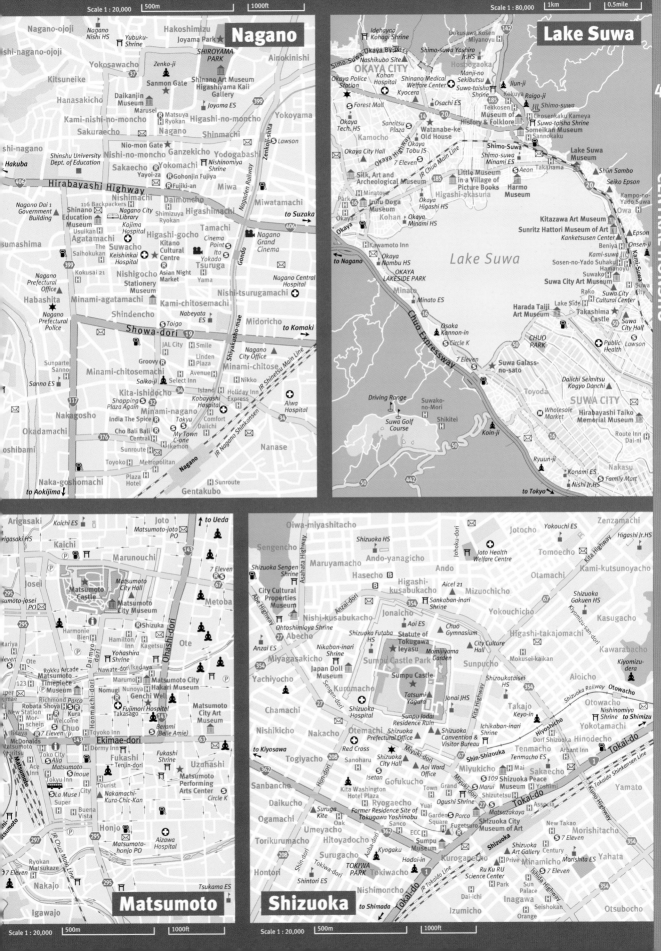

Nagano

Scale 1 : 20,000

500m
1000ft

Nagano-ojoji
Nagano Nishi HS
Hakoshimizu
shi-nagano-ojoji
Nagano Park
Joyama Park
Yubuku-Shrine
SHIROYAMA PARK
Ainokinishi
Yokosawacho
Zenko-ji
Kitsuneike
Sanmon Gate
Higashiyama Kaii Gallery
Hanasakicho
Daikanjin Museum
Shinano Art Museum
Joyama ES
Marusei
399
Kami-nishi-no-moncho
Matsuya Ryokan
Higashi-no-moncho
Yokoyama
Sakuraecho
Nagano
Shinmachi
Nio-mon Gate
Ganzeicho
Yodogabashi
shi-nagano
Shinshu University Dept. of Education
Nishi-no-moncho
Yokomachi
Nishinomiya Shrine
Miwatamachi
Hakuba
Sakaecho
Yayoi-za
Miwa
406
Gohonjin Fujiya
Fujiki-an
Miwatamachi
Hirabayashi Highway
Nishimachi
Daimoncho
Higashimachi
to Suzaka
Nagano Dai 1 Government Building
Shinano Education Museum
116 Backpackers
Nagano City Library
Shimizuya Ryokan
Tamachi
Higashi-gocho
sumashima
Agatamachi
Usuikan
Kojima Hospital
Kitano Cultural Centre
Cinema Point Ito Yokado
Nagano Grand Cinema
Suwacho
Saihokukan
Keishinkai Hospital
Tsuruga
Habashita
Kokusai 21
Nishigocho
Stationery Museum
Asian Night Market
Yama
Nagano Central Hospital
Nagano Prefectural Office
Minami-agatamachi
Kami-chitosemachi
Nishi-tsurugamachi
Nagano Prefectural Police
Shindencho
Nabeyata ES
Midoricho
Showa-dori
Toigo
to Komaki
19
Sunparte Sanno
JAL City
Smile
Groovy
Linden Plaza
Nagano City Office
Shiyakusho-mae
Minami-chitosemachi
Saiko-ji
Avenue
Select Inn
Istand
Nikko
Minami-chitose
Sanno ES
117
Kita-ishidocho
34
Kobayashi Hospital
Holiday Inn Express
Aiwa Hospital
Nakagosho
Shopping Plaza Again
India The Spice
32
Minami-nagano
Tokyu Daichi
Okadamachi
376
Cho Bali Bali Central
My Town C-one
Ikemon
oshibami
Sunroute
Toyoko
Metropolitan
Naka-goshomachi
Plaza Hotel
Sunroute
to Aokijima
Nagano
Gentakubo
Nanase

Lake Suwa

Scale 1 : 80,000

1km
0.5mile

41

CENTRAL HONSHU

Idehayao
Dokusawa Kosen Miyanoyu
142
Shimo-suwa Okaya By-Pass
Nashikubo Site
Shimo-suwa Yashiro Jr.HS
Hosbogaoka
OKAYA CITY
Kohan Hospital
Shinano Medical Welfare Center
Manji-no Sekibutsu
Suwa-taisha Shrine
Jiun-ji
Kokuya
Raigo-ji
Okaya Police Station
Kyocera
Osachi ES
185
Forest Mall
Tekkosen
Shimo-suwa
Okaya Tech. HS
Sanritsu Plaza
Museum of History & Folklore
Chosenkaku Kameya
Kamocho
Watanabe-ke Old House
Someikan Museum
Sannokaku
Okaya City Hall
Okaya Tobu JS
Shimo-Suwa
Lake Suwa Museum
7 Eleven
Okaya Higashi HS
Shimo-suwa Minami ES
Aeon
Takahama
Shiin Sambo
Silk, Art and Archeological Museum
185
Higashi-akasuna
Seiko Epson
Minatoya
Urufu Doga Museum
Little Museum in a Village of Picture Books
Harmo Museum
Kono-yado Suwa
Owa
16
Park
Okaya Higashi HS
20
to Nagano
Okaya
Kohan
Okaya Minami HS
Kitazawa Art Museum
Epson
Kawamoto Inn
Sunritz Hattori Museum of Art
Onsen-ji
Okaya Nambu HS
Kanketsusen Center
Beniya
OKAYA LAKESIDE PARK
Kami-suwa
Hamanoyu
Lake Suwa
Sosen-no-Yado Suhaku
Suwako
Minato
Minato ES
Suwa City Art Museum
Rako
Suwa
Harada Taiji Art Museum
Lake Side
Cultural Center
Osaka Kannon-in
50
Takashima Castle
Suwa City Hall
Circle K
56
Chuo Expressway
CHUO PARK
50
7 Eleven
Public Health
Lawson
Suwa Galass-no-sato
Daiichi Seimitsu Kogyo Danchi
SUWA CITY
Driving Range
Suwako-no-Mori
Toyoda
Hirabayashi Taiko Memorial Museum
Suwa Golf Course
Shikitei
Wholesale Market
Koin-ji
50
Route Inn Dai-ni
442
Ryuun-ji
16
Nakasu
Konami ES
Family Mart
to Tokyo
Nishi Jr.HS

Matsumoto

Scale 1 : 20,000

500m
1000ft

Arigasaki
Kaichi ES
Joto
to Ueda
Zenzamachi
rigasaki HS
Matsumoto-joto PO
Kaichi
143
Higashi Jr.HS
Marunouchi
7 Eleven
67
Josei
Matsumoto City Hall
Metoba
295
Matsumoto Castle
Matsumoto City Museum
sumoto-josei PO
Harmonie Bien
Ohashi-dori
Ote
Hamilton Inn
Kagetsu
Shizuka
mariya
Ote
Rokku Arcade
Yohashira Shrine
Nawate-dori Ikedaya
leven
123
Matsumoto Timepiece Museum
Marumo
Matsumoto City
Daimyo-dori
Honmachi-dori
Richmond Parco
Nomugi Nunoya
Takari Museum
New Station
Robata Shoya
Kura
Genchi Well
Matsumoto City Art Museum
iper
Mor-schein
Welcome
Fujimori Hospital
Chuo
7 Eleven
Takasago
Benami (Belle Amie)
Iidaya
Toyoko Inn
Ekimae-dori
63
McDonalds
Alio
297
143
Fukashi
Uzuhashi
sumoto
Toko City
Matsumoto
Tenjin-dori
Matsumoto Performing Arts Center
Ace Inn
Tokyu Inn
Fukashi Shrine
Inoue
La Muse I
City
Nakamachi-Kura-Chic-Kan
Circle K
Honjo
295
Buena Vista
Aizawa Hospital
Ryokan Matsukaze
Matsumoto-honjo PO
7 Eleven
295
Tsukama ES
Nakajo
Igawajo

Shizuoka

Scale 1 : 20,000

500m
1000ft

Oiwa-miyashitacho
Johoku-dori
Jotocho
Yokouchi ES
Zenzamachi
Oiwa-miyashitacho
Shizuoka HS
Joto Health Welfare Centre
Tomoecho
Higashi Jr.HS
Sengencho
Maruyamacho
Ando-yanagicho
Ando
Kami-kutsunoyacho
Shizuoka Sengen Shrine
Hasecho
Higashi-kusabukacho
Aicel 21
Mizochicho
Shizuoka Gakuen HS
City Cultural Properties Museum
354
Sankaban-inari Shrine
Kasugacho
Nishi-kusabukacho
Ohtoshimiya Shrine
27
Jonaicho
Aoi ES
Chuo Gymnasium
Yokouchicho
67
Abecho
Shizuoka Futaba HS
City Culture Hall
Higashi-takajomachi
Anzai ES
Nikaban-inari Shrine
Statue of Tokugawa Ieyasu
Kawarabacho
Miyagasakicho
Aoi Shrine
Momijiyama Garden
Mokusei-kaikan
Kiyomizu-dera
Japan Doll Museum
Sumpu Castle Park
Aioicho
Yachiyocho
Kurumacho
Sumpu Castle
Shizuokataisei HS
354
Chamachi
27
Shizuoka Hospital
Jonai JHS
Takajo
Keyo-in
Shizuoka Railway
Otowacho
Nishikicho
Nakacho
Otemachi
Sunpu Jodai Residence Ruin
Takajo
Hiyoshicho
Nishinomiya Shrine
to Shimizu
Yokotamachi
Togiyacho
Miyuki-dori
Ichiban-inari Shrine
Dorf Shizuoka HS
354
to Kiyosawa
362
Sanoharu
Shizuoka Convention & Visitor Bureau
67
Shin-Shizuoka
Tenmacho
Tenmacho ES
Tokai-do
Sanbancho
Isetan
Aoi Ward Office
Shizuoka Prefectural Office
Gofukucho
Miyukicho
Grand
Shizuoka Peace Museum
Sakaecho
Daikucho
Red Cross
Shizuoka City Hall
Marui
109 Shizuoka
Yoshimi
Tokaido Shinkansen Line
Ryogaecho
Town
Shizutetsu
Yamato
Ogamachi
Suruga Kite
Yuai
Garden Square
Parco
Ogushi Shrine
Fugetsuro
Shizuoka City Museum of Art
Umeyacho
Former Residence Site of Tokugawa Yoshinobu
Sanco
Matsuzakaya
Associa
New Takao
Morishitacho
Torikurumacho
362
Oak
Kita Washington Hotel Plaza
ECC
Shizuoka Art Gallery
7 Eleven
354
Hitoyadocho
Aoba-dori
Sumpu Museum
Prive
Century
Marishita ES
Yahata
Surugacho
Kyogaku
Hodai-in
Kurogane-do
Shizuoka Art Gallery
Minamicho
Hontori
Shin-dori
Tokiwa-dori
1
TOKIWA PARK
Ru Ku RU Science Center
Park
Sun Palace
Ishida Highway
Nishimoncho
Tokiwacho
H
Dai-ichi
Inagawa
Izumicho
Otsubocho
Nishimoncho
Tokai-do
JR Tokaido Line
to Shimada
354
Seishokan
Orange

KYOTO

Kyoto

Scale 1 : 115,000
2km
1mile

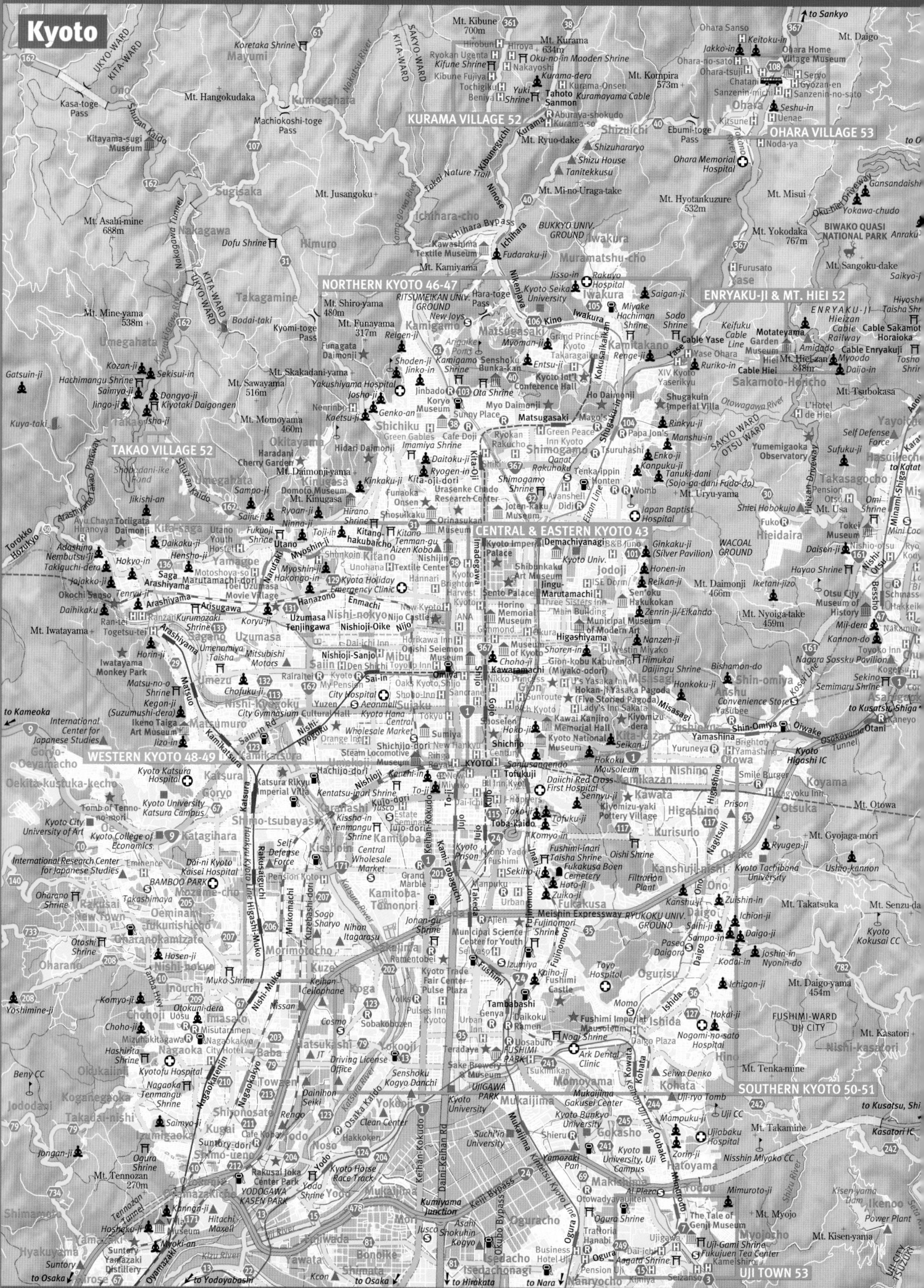

NORTHERN KYOTO 46-47
KURAMA VILLAGE 52
OHARA VILLAGE 53
ENRYAKU-JI & MT. HIEI 52
TAKAO VILLAGE 52
CENTRAL & EASTERN KYOTO 43
WESTERN KYOTO 48-49
SOUTHERN KYOTO 50-51
UJI TOWN 53

KITA-WARD
UKYO-WARD
SAKYO-WARD
SAKYO WARD
FUSHIMI-WARD
UJI CITY

Mt. Kibune 700m
Mt. Kurama +634m
Kurama-dera
Mt. Kompira 573m
Mt. Daigo
BIWAKO QUASI NATIONAL PARK
Mt. Yokodaka 767m
Mt. Sangoku-dake

Mt. Hangokudaka
Mt. Asahi-mine 688m
Mt. Jusangoku +
Mt. Mine-yama 538m
Mt. Shiro-yama 480m
Mt. Funayama 317m
Mt. Skakadani-yama 516m
Mt. Sawayama 516m
Mt. Momoyama 460m
Mt. Daimonji-yama +
Mt. Kinugasa
Mt. Iwatayama +
Mt. Daimonji 466m
Mt. Nyoiga-take 459m

Kasa-toge Pass
Machiokoshi-toge Pass
Kibune Shrine
Kurama-Onsen
Ohara Sanso
Jakko-ji
Keitoku-in
Seryo
Gyozan-no-sato
Seshu-in
Ohara Memorial Hospital
Ohara Home Village Museum

Kurama-dera Kuramaguchi Cable
Kibune Fujiya
Tochigiku
Tahoto Sanmon

Takao Village 52
Adashino Nembutsu-ji
Takiguchi-dera
Daihikaku
Okochi Sanso
Tenryu-ji
Arashiyama
Sagano
Iwatayama Monkey Park

Arashiyama
Togetsu-kyo
Ran-tei
Matsu-no-o Taisha

International Center for Japanese Studies
International Research Center for Japanese Studies

Kyoto University Katsura Campus
Kyoto College of Art
Kyoto City University of Art

Katsura Rikyu Imperial Villa
BAMBOO PARK
Rakusai New Town

Kyoto Imperial Palace
Kyoto Univ.
Ginkaku-ji (Silver Pavilion)
Honen-in
Nanzen-ji
Heian Jingu
Municipal Museum of Modern Art
Kyoto National Museum
Sanjusangendo
Tofuku-ji
Kyoto Station / KYOTO
To-ji
Nijo Castle
Kinkaku-ji
Ryoan-ji
Ninna-ji
Myoshin-ji

Fushimi-inari Taisha Shrine
Fushimi Castle
Fushimi Imperial Mausoleum
Daigo-ji
Mt. Daigo-yama 454m
Mt. Takatsuka
Mt. Senzu-dai

Daidatsu-mine
UJIGAWA PARK
Kyoto University
Kyoto Bunkyo University
Uji-ryo Tomb
Mampuku-ji
Uji CC
to Kusatsu, Shiga

The Tale of Genji Museum
Uji-Gami Shrine
Agata Shrine
UJI TOWN 53

Mt. Tennozan 270m
Suntory Yamazaki Distillery
YODOGAWA KASEN PARK
Kyoto Horse Race Track

to Osaka
to Yodoyabashi
to Hirakata
to Nara

Katsura River
Kamo River
Takano River
Uji River
Kizu River

to Kameoka
to Sankyo

Central & Eastern Kyoto

Scale 1 : 22,500

500m

1000ft

KAWARAMACHI & GION 44-45

to Hanazono · to Kyoto Shinkin Bank · Umeyacho · Lawson · 7Eleven · Shiga Bank · McDonald's · to Izumoji · Sakaimachigomon Gate · KAMIGYO-WARD · to Shimogamo · ampm

Marutamachi-dori · NAKAGYO-WARD · 187

Nakanocho · Tanakacho · Oicho · Sanbongicho · Sakamotocho · Yonchome · Funayacho · Shintomicho · Bikkuri Donkey · Konami Sports Club · Komanocho

Nishi-takeyacho · Takeyacho-dori · Kagamiyacho · Takeyacho-dori · Kyoto District Court · Uayocho · Takeyacho-dori · The Screen · WAK Japan · Iseyama · Daimojicho

Hashimotocho · Bishamoncho · Benzaitencho · Kyoto Chamber of Commerce & Industry · Fukuyacho · Goshominami ES · Jokei-ji · Umenokicho · Circle K

Myozen-ji · Yakushicho · Yakushi-ji-dori · Reisencho · Shoshicho · Matsuyacho · Kannoncho · Nijo-dori · Seimeicho · Hoteiyacho · Fujikicho · Hokodencho

Kusuriyacho · Yawatacho · Nijo-dori · Kawaranocho · Tojicho · Tachibanacho · Enokicho · Kamikorikicho

Karasuma-Oike · Karasuma-Oike · Oike-dori · Kyoto-Shiyakusho-mae

to Nishinokyo · Shimonnojimaecho · Shimomaruyacho

Shijo-dori · Karasuma · Kawaramachi · Shijo-ohashi

to Kyoto Station · to Fukakusa · to Fukuine

Kamo River · SHIMOGYO-WARD · HIGASHIYAMA-WARD · Kita-gomoncho · Nishi-gomoncho · Yamadacho

Scale 1 : 10,000   200m   500ft

to Takano
to Shugakuin

Marutamachi-dori

Quatre Saisons
Family Mart   Kuretake
Kumano Shrine
Tax Office
Kyoto Handicraft Center
Waraku-an GH
Okazaki Iriecho
Okazaki Hangan-ji
Komada Bldg
Okazaki Shrine
Seicho-no-le
Heiannomori   Higashi-tennocho
Marutamachi-dori

Lawson 100
imo-Tsutsumicho
Lawson
Family Mart   Ishida
Shichifukuya
Hyakunentofu
Torin
Byoko-ike
Soryu-ike
Sta Maria
Lawson
Okazaki Tsuruya
Okazaki Higashi-tennocho

Higashi-takeyacho
Kumano Dormitory
Shogoin Sannocho
Kyu Butokuden
Three Sisters Inn Annex
Grill Kodakara
Okazaki Jr. HS
Shishigatani Takagishicho

Water and Sewerage Control Center
Ebisugawa Dam
Nursery
Waterworks Dept. Sosui Office
Kumano Bridge
Kyoryori Rokusei
Rokuseichaya
HEIAN JINGU SHRINE
Jidai Matsuri Festival Oct. 22
Kansai Bijutsuin
Okunian
Kampo Museum
Okazaki Tennocho
Reisen-dori
Rakuyo-so
Eikando Nishimachi

Reisen-dori
Shogoin-rengezocho
Okazaki-tokuseicho
Kawamura Seifun
Tokusei Bridge
Okazaki Nishi-tennocho
Zohiko
Raisen Bridge
Otemmon
Heian Jingu Kaikan
Tsukemono Daiyasu
Mangan-ji
Okazaki Minami-goshocho
Yamamotomenzo
Mizen
Gontaro Okazaki
Seiryutei

imonjicho
Akitsukicho
Sugimotocho
in-pontocho
Vocational School
Jusco
Daion-ji
Karoko
Hosomi Art Museum
Kyoto Kaikan Hall
Bunka Shiminkyoku
Municipal Museum of Art Annex
OKAZAKI PARK
Municipal Museum of Art
Nijo-dori
Rakufuso
Stamford Nihon Center
Okazaki Hoshojicho

Kashiracho
Kensho-ji
Saisho-ji
Saiho-ji
Myoden-ji
Nijo-dori
Traditional Crafts Museum
Miyako Messe (Kyoto National Industrial Hall)
Kyoto Pref. Library
Municipal Zoo (Dobutsu-en)
Shinshin-an
Nanzenji Kusagawacho

CHOMYO-JI
Honryu-in
Daiju-in
Shinto ES
Sennen-ji
Honsho-ji
Dairen-ji
Kyoan-ji
Shonen-ji
Daiko-ji
Sensho-ji
Hommyo-ji
Kyoto Kaikan Hall
Municipal Museum of Modern Art
Hiromichi Bridge
Niomon-dori
Biwako Sosui Memorial Museum
Toriyasu
Shishigatani-dori
NANZEN-JI

oun-in
Shogan-in
Shin-tomi-no-koji
Jakuko-ji
Shogyo-ji
Ryumon
Niomon-dori
Gimmondo
MURINAN GARDEN
Yudofu Junsei
Kugetsuso
Bokugo-an-jв
Konchi-in

Okazaki-Enshojicho
Fire Station
Yurinkan Museum
Seven Eleven
Traveler's Inn
Hyotei
International Community House
Reflet's
Tairyu Sanso
Yachiyo
TARYUSANSO PARK

Wakaoku
Shoren-ji
Lawson
Kyoto Kanze Kaikan Hall
Kyoto Bunkyo HS
SANKYO-WARD
Yunokicho
Johojicho
Chapel Cinderella
Ryoriya Ryokan kikusui
Power Plant

Sanchujicho
Wakokucho
Tender House
Maruyamacho
Kitano-ya
HIGASHIYAMA-WARD
Koumeikan Guest House
Demian
Agonshu
Takeshigero
Risshokoseikai
Imamichicho

Masuya
Sunset Inn
Yoho-ji
Hongyo-in
Kango-ji
Ebisucho
Tawarayayoshitomi
Higashicho

agobashi-dori
Matsuba
Shinko-ji
New Nissho
Higashiyama Sanjo
Kotai-ji
McDonald's
Furukawacho
Higashiyama
Lawson
Asuka
Sanjo-dori
Higashi-bunkicho
Taniqawacho

Pig & Whistle
Kagoshin
Takematsu
Kyoto Chuo Shinkin
Bamboo
Big Week
Tozai Line
Bukko-ji
WESTIN MIYAKO

Sanjo Keihan
Ichi-ban
Nichome
Sanchome
Daishogun Shrine
Joan-ji
Minami-saikaishicho
Yado-Haruya
Gokencho
Shirakawa ES
Ryoon-ji
Awadaguchi Kajicho
Awadaguchi Kachocho
Kease

Kyouen
Chaimon Iroha
Sanjo Fukushi Center
Rentaku-ji
Tsutsumicho
Umemiyacho
Awadaguchi Sanjobocho
Awatasanso
Awata Shrine
Awadaguchi Awatayama-kitacho
Water Treatment Plant
Higashi-komonozacho

Wakamatsu-dori
Wakamatsucho
ihan Sanjo nami igetsu yo
Sanjo Community Center
Family Mart
Miyoshicho
Kyonoyado
Shirakawa Kita-dori Kyoto
Jomyo-ji
Kotoku-in
Shoren-in
Sonsho-in
Awadaguchi Awatayama-minamicho

Furumonzen-dori
Konjaku Nishimura
Shirakawa Minami-dori
Kinpyo
Bijutsu Club
A-yado
Shin-monzen-dori
Shinbashi to-masu
Kachojoshi HS
Shorenin Kyu Karigosho
Ryosho-in
CHION-IN
Kohojo
Awadaguchi Kachoyamacho

Yoshijima
Nishinocho
Shinmonso
Mume
Re-ru kurabu
Kosho-in
Jodoshu Shumucho
Saishido
Ohojo
Awadaguchi Kachoyamacho

Yang Wan
Seven Eleven
Shirakawa Minami-dori
Motosan
Semmonten
Rinkactio
Genko-in
Shinju-in Yoshimizukai-in
Sotai-in
Amida-do
Meido
Isshin-in

Kanki Shrine
Gion District
Shiraume
Hakubai
Ozawa
Umemotocho
Kiyomotocho
Heian Yoikun
Sammon
YAMASHINA-WARD
Hinookaebisudanicho

Tominagacho
Gael
m Pub
Bar Recoba
Tominagacho-dori
Issen Yoshoku
Minami Koji
Nakasueyoshicho
Gionmachi kitagawa
Kabitsukan Museum of Contemporary Art
Ochatsubo-dochu / Parade of Tea Jars
Tobu Koen Kanri Jimusho
Kyoto Yoshimizu Kanri Jimusho
Kichu-an
Awadaguchi Awatayama-minamicho

Meyami-jizo
Yamatocho
Gael
Gionmachi kitagawa
Yasaka Kaikan
Toju
Wajun Kaikan
MARUYAMA PARK
Ryotei Saami
Salon Haraguchi Tenseian
Awadaguchi Chorakuji-yamacho

Ikuokaya
Ichiryukutei
Yayoi-koji
Kyoto Gion
Lawson
Gyoza no Osho
Yume kitagawa
Yuzuya
Yasaka Shrine
Yama bokokan
Senraku
Maruyamacho
Kichu-an
Shogunzuka
to Misasagi

Yamatocho
Joko-in
Ikuokaya
Kamerin
Kikkume
Ishida
Tokiwa Minami Shiden romon Oil Lamp Museum
Chorakukan
Ryuchi Kaikan
Otani Sobyo
Yoshinoya
Bochi Jimusho
Choraku-ji
Tembodai
Shoren-in Shogunzuka Dainichido

Seiju-in
Hatsune-koji
Mametora
Higashiyama
Tsukumicho
Yamashita
Gion Hatanaka
Karaku
Maruyama Ongakudo
Sorin-ji
Korin-in
Kikunoi-in
Higashi-Otani Cemetery
Shogunzuka

meicho
Eigen-in
Donguri-dori
Koun-an
Kyoryori hanasaki
Kyoto Guest Palace Maifukan
Gion Sano
Sakanoue
Hamasaku
Ryokan Motonago
Uemura
Gesshin-ji
Entoku-in
KODAI-JI
Awadaguchi Higashiotani-yamacho

KENNIN-JI
Shimichi Jidokan
Daichu-in
Gion-Kobu Kaburan-jo
Yasuikitamon-dori
Kyoto
Pukuya
Inaka-tei
Ishibe Alley
Sakura
Tamahan
Rikiya
KODAIJI PARK
Gokoku Shrine

Yasaka-dori
Yasaka Endo
NTT
Rokudo Chinno-ji
Sunday Brunch
Shimokawara Azuki
Ryozen-Uemura
Homotsuden
Saikan
HIGASHIYAMA SANGHO PARK

Hishiroku
Seven Eleven
Kyoto Shinkin
Hisago
Ryokan Shikige
Kodaiji-minami-monzen-dori
Omen Kodai-ji
Ryozen Historical Museum
Reimei Shrine
Awadaguchi Kodaiji-yamacho

Komatsucho
Daito-ji
Kenjin Sodo
Raigen-ji
Family Mart
Shichikannon-ji
Bar Main Higashiyama
Hokan-ji Yasaka Pagoda (Five Stories Pagoda)
The Sodoh
Shoho-ji
Yasaka minamimachi

Saifuku-ji
Yasaka GH Annex
Gojo Tosho Frere
Bank of Kyoto
Uedacho
Ninen-zaka
Maiko Studio Shiki
Doi
B&B GH
Ryozen

Rukorocho
Matsubara-dori
Shoentei
Shinkaku-ji
Daizen-ji
Hoshinocho
Kasagi-ya
Saiko-ji
Ladies Inn Sakata
Kashogama Pottery School
Oblio
Seikanji Ryozancho

Happy Rokuhara
Zenryu-ji
Nittai-ji
Higashiyama Ward Office
Higashiyama 4-chome
Kiyomizu ES
Higashiyamaso
Shirakawa
Kiyomizu Sannenzaka Museum

Tamoncho
Rokuhara-ji
Rokuhara Inn
SUN Ikushikan
Higashiyama Fire Station
Amenity
Prince
Kiyomizu-zaka
Shichimiya
Kosho-ji

Rokuharamitsu-ji
Uramon-dori
Circle K
Uchiwa
Saiko-ji
Kiyomizu 4-chome

Kasamatsu
Hinotani
to Kumogahata
Nakajimagawaracho
Shimo-shodacho
Mt. Kami
Koyama
Nikenyac

Mt. Shiro 452m
Nishi-ninosaka
Eboshiiwa
Nakajimacho
KAMIGAMO PARK
Akira Ak

Nishiyama
Kami-shodacho
Ritsumeikan University Hiiragino Ground
Ibaradanicho
Kyoto Sangyo University International House
Institute for Glo Environmental Rese

Hagiwara
Hinoguchicho
Hiiragidanicho
Maedacho
Rokudandacho
Nishi-gotocho
Akaocho
New Joys
Aoidencho

Nishi-hagiwara
Inokuchicho
Keanaicho
Tsunokunicho
Higashi-gotocho
Kyoto Sangyo University
Kami-jinbaracho
7 Eleven

Ninosaka
Marumine
Oyanagicho
Meotoiwacho
Nishi-uenodancho
Circle K
Itchoguichicho
Bingodencho

Myokendo
Nishigamo JHS
Kanigasakacho
Hiragino ES
Higashi-uenodancho
Shimo-jimbaracho

Mt. Funayama 292m
Kita-kawakamicho
Aomori
Nakayamacho
Yone Kiyoshi Ozeki
Tanaka
Naka-nosakacho
Kamigamo Golf Course

to Sugisaka
NISHIGAMO
Umanomecho
Funatsukicho
Aniga-ike Pond

Iwamon
Naka-kawamakicho
Nishigawaracho

Akibasan
Funagata Daimonji Fire Festival Characters
Kawakamicho
Yamanomoricho
MK Bowl Kamigamo Homuvira Clinic
Kazan
Mt. Maruyama 149m
Mt. Komaruyama 137m
Ko-ike Pond

Nagasaka
Funeyama
Funayama Golf Course
Imaharacho
Minami-kawakamicho
7 Eleven
Okui
Sankusu
Asatsuyugaharacho

Mt. Shakadani 273m
Bishamonyama
Odoguchicho
Mizugakicho
Kakinokicho
Kanoshitacho
Aomomoricho
Mt. Jinguji 137m

Ichinosaka
Shoden-ji
Kita-chinjuancho
Okuricho
Bonoushirocho
Noriaki Maru Silk
Emujishoppu
Fuji
Children's Clinic
Kamo-wake-ikazuchi Shrine (Kamigamo Shrine)
Ota Shrine
Okamotocho

Momoyama
Kusayama
NISHIGAMO GARDEN
Obukecho
Harinokicho
Yasuko Tsukamoto Clinic
Aoi House
Futabainari Shrine
Kita-ojicho
Azekura
Kyoto Senso Bunka-kan

Shakuhachi-ike Pond
Chinjuancho
Marukawacho
Jinko-in
Ri-ibon
Yamamotocho
Yamashita Hiroshi Sakae Hall
Fujinokicho
Umegatsujicho

Shakadani
Yakushiyama Hospital
Seiho-ji
Jinkoincho
Omiya ES
Wanwan
Mukaiumecho
103
Kyoto

Nishi-somonguchicho
Misono
Nakanoyashirocho
Minami-tajiricho
Jinba Do
Ikedonoho
Eboshi-ga-kakiuchicho
Semi-ga-kakiuichich

Kita-yamanomaecho
Damon
7 Eleven
Kyoto Chuo Shinkin Bank
Misono
Kamigamo ES
Minami-ojicho
Tsuchikadocho

Josho-ji
Kumo Tsuki
Ichiyo-in
Lawson
Honjin
Fukunaga
Rozannu
BBA
Carlton Terrace
Emujisho
Ishikazuch

Genko-an
Shakadani
Instant Noodles
Nishi Onoboricho
Takenouchi
Minami-tsubakiharacho
Kameya
Shobuencho

Nenrinbo
Takagamine ES
Ichinoicho
OMIYA TRAFFIC PARK
Kami-takedanocho
Koryo Museum
Kamogawa JHS
Takanawatecho
KAMIGAMO

Koetsu-ji
Gentakukita-higashicho
Kitahakonoicho
Kita-daimoncho
Kyosushizen
Kyonagano
Shichiku ES
Shimo-nagamecho
Kafesaro

Ginsho-ji
Koetsucho
TAKAGAMINE
Minami-hakonoicho
Gen-I-dori
Kyonagano
Inokuma-dori
Kami-kosaicho
Week Building

Washiminecho
Tsuchitenjocho
Pateisuri Mimura
SHICHIKU
Shimo-kosaicho
Jinroku-ch

Driving Range
Fujibayashicho
Nishinoyamacho
Seihokucho
Cafe Doji
Kitayama-dori

Haradani-inuicho
Mt. Washiga-mine
SHOZAN
Kyoto Takagamine PO
7 Eleven
Kitayama-dori
Shimo-midoricho
Honda Cars
Motomachi
KYOTO BOTANICAL GARDENS

OKITAYAMA
Shozan Bowl
Nishi-rendainocho
Uenocho
Taihou ES
Ushiwakacho
Shichiku-kita-dori
Uekawa

Circle K
Mt. Daimonji-yama 231m
Tanpopo
Sendocho
Takanawacho
Nishi-takanawacho
Shichiku-minami-dori

Hasecho
Hidari Daimonji Fire Festival Characters
Kyudoicho
Higashi-rendainocho
Imamiya Shrine
Seinancho
Shimo-umenokicho
Hananokicho
KIX SAKYO WARD

Namikiri Fudo-ji
Fumon-ji
Himurocho
Hirakicho
Nagomi-an
Imamiya-dori
Imamiya Minami-dori
Hirakawa Fugetsudo
Kyoto Keisatsu Hospital
KOYAMA

Bukkyo University
Murasakino HS
Daisen-in
Sangen-in
Bon GH
Kami-sekiryucho
Otani University
Kita-kamifusacho

KINUGASA
Nishi-hirakicho
Kyoto Seieikai
Sanjo Tenno Imperial Mausoleum (Kitayama-no-misasagi)
Koto-in
DAITOKU-JI
Zuiho-in
Tani House
Ryogen-in
7 Eleven
Sekiryucho
Murasakino-dori
Minami-onocho

Friends World College
Himuro-michi
Kami-mikoshicho
Koho-an
Nishinocho
Kita-Oji-dori
Kita Ward Office
Higashi-goshodencho

Ritsumeikan University
Rokuon-ji Garden
ROKUON-JI (Kinkaku-ji)
Golden Pavilion House
7 Eleven
Family Mart
MURASAKINO
Shimo-tsukiyamacho
Nagomi GH
Unrinincho
Kayamacho

RYOAN-JI
Babacho
Minami-hananobocho
Shingon-in
Jobon Rendai-ji
Mt. Funaoka 112m
FUNAOKA PARK
Kenkun-dori
KITA-WARD
KAMIGYO-WARD
Shimo-seizoguchicho

Ryoan-ji Hojo Stone Garden
Tegaki Kobo Bireishin
Gonoue-cho
Funaoka-minami-dori
Miyanishicho
Craftsman GH
Saraca
Shincho
Kamigoryo Shri
Kotokuicho

Ritsumeikan Univ. (Kinugasa Campus)
Kaidocho
Kuramaguchi-dori
Minami-funaokacho
Funaoka Onsen
Kanei
Kahodo
Shinmachi-dori
Kamigoryo-mae-dori
Jisho-in

KITA-WARD UKYO-WARD
Domoto Museum
Somon-cho
Wara-tenjin
Rozanji-dori
Rozan-ji-dori
Nishi-yashirocho
Kosho-ji
Honpo-ji
Urasenke Chado Research Center
Jotenkai Museum

Mt. Kinugasa 200m
Yamacho
Tenjinmoricho
Injo-ji
Idacho
Shoshikaku-ji
Myorenjimaecho
Doshocho
Myoken-ji
Seni Gijutsu Center

HIRANO
Kinukeke-no-michi
Teranouchi-dori
Naka-kashiwanocho
Teranouchi-dori
Lady's Hotel Nishijin
Myoren-ji
Anrakukojicho
Hoon-ji
Shokoku-

Kami-yanagicho
Family Mart
Kyoto Museum for World Peace
Miyakitacho
McDonalds
Kyoto Coop
Shimo-kashiwanogho
Shakuzo-ji
Shosuikaku-ji
Papa Jon's

Goryonoshitacho
Kitamachi
Chrysantheme
HIRANO SHRINE PARK
Hirano Shrine
Senbon Shakado (Daihoon-ji)
Mizomaecho
Oimatsucho
Kashiwa-kiyomoricho
Kamidachiuri-dori
Orinasu-kan
NISHIJIN
Monyacho
Kyogashi Museum
Zuishoin

Toji-ji
Kami-yanagicho
Oimatsucho
Ichigoichie
Kyoto City
Globetrotters
Doshisha University
Uratsukiujicho

Scale 1 : 22,500

500m 1000ft

Kurama
Niken-Chaya
zuoka
o Chuo
kin Bank
yoto Forestry
Association
Rakukita
Hospital

Jitsuso-in
Iwakura
Hospital
Rakuyou
Hospital
Former Residence
of Iwakura Tomomi
Taikaku Bunko
Museum
Nishijima
Chuzaijicho
Nagatanicho
Saigan-ji

Kitamura
Clinic
Kyoto Seikadai-mae
Nakashima
Kyoto Seika
University
Kinocho
Kyoto Mingei
Museum
Meitoku ES
Aguracho
Circle K
Coop Coop
Iwakura Brach Office
Kyoto City Iwakura Library
Nakamachi
Nakamachi
Hanazonocho

Shimo-zaijicho
Kyoto Chuo
Shinkin Bank
Ekopu
Kiraku
Ichijoji
Ataka
Osho
Hiei
Hospital

Hokuryo HS
Mac's
House
Refureru
Mutou
Yume Hachi
Circle K
Ma Minamikaze
Shatoreze Sakyo
Iwakura
Saifuku-ji
Rakuhoku
JHS
Eizan Kurama Line
Tabata
Yasushi
Mama
Driving
Range
Saimyojiyama
Yofuku-ji
to Ohara

Nagashiro River
Minami-hiraokacho
Tax Office
Doshisha ES
IWAKURA
Mori Dentist
Iwakura-minami ES
Higashi-miyatacho
Osagicho
Miyakecho
Niwa Clinic
Miyakehachiman
Miyake Hachiman Shrine
Daimyojincho
Sudo
Shrine
Higashiyama

ra Cafe
otoyama
Entsu-ji
Sohonzan
Myoman-ji
7 Eleven
Goto Clinic
Futoshi-sen
Nishi-miyatacho
Minami-yonnotsubocho
Bookshop
Doshisha HS
Barubu
Minami-miyakecho
Satsutacho
Kitatacho
Ikenouchicho
Onocho
Kawaracho
Renge-ji
Seiken-ji
Suishacho
Xiv Kyoto
Yaserikyu
Ai Wa
Higashiyam

Hataedacho
Akoruamiti
Kita-ikedacho
Nishi-godacho
Kyoto Chuo
Shinkin Bank
De Plus
Towang
Higashi-godacho
Konan
Lawson
Midori
McDonalds
Morokicho
Mutsumi Association
Naito Clinic
Silk
Kurumajicho
Inaricho
Uenocho
Guchikomoricho
Higashidacho

Komura Shop
Coop
Minami-ikedacho
Shinyo-in
Takaragaike
Shop
Nakaosagicho
Jun Sai
La Rishesu
Fukadacho
Kana
Konan
Rinkocho
Maedacho
Hodo-ji
Kamonhayashicho
Boyama
Teradani

Villa
Yamazaki
Keshiyama
Kyoto
Equestrian
Club
Kyoto Hakurai-kai
Hospital
Grand Prince
Nenegayama
Kyoto International
Conference Center
TAKARAGAIKE
PARK
Ishidacho
Don's Steak
Purukogi
Circle K
Kami-takano ES
KAMITAKANO
Shuzenan

Eucalyptus Village
Nursing Home
Hazamacho
Enomigashiba
Takayama
Takaraga-ike
Pond
TAKARAGAIKE
PARK
Jogatani
Yamanohashicho
Nishi-himurocho
Nagaredacho
Furukawacho
Sawabuchicho
Kyoto Kami-takano PO
Higashi-himurocho
Teraechigo
Teraechigo
Hinokitogecho
Kaikonbocho

oroikecho
amotoguchicho
vodacho
vekachicho
Ikebatacho
Nishiyama
Mizodoi-ike
Pond
Aquatic Plants
Community
Kurama Animal
ital
Midoroikebata
Mt. Nishi
Matuko
Kitsunesaka
Takaragaike
Garden
Sasagatani
Kitoracho
Mt. Higashiyama
157m
Okimicho
Yamabana
Heihachi Jaya
Idegahanacho
Senmandacho
Kita-fukecho
Kinokuniya
Babawakicho
Sekizan-zen-in
Shugakuin Rikyu
Imperial Villa
Kyusuitei
Muromachi
Miyanomae

Lawson
tsumoto-cho
ra-ga-kakiuchicho
hare Royal
House
ny Place
ek
Kita-chonokicho
Minakuchicho
Sakami
Kitano-
nogamicho
Myo Daimonji
Fire Festival Characters
Takaragaike
Sports Park
Sosakucho
Children's Sports
Takaragaike
Driving School
Nishimachi
Hayashiyama
Matsugasaki ES
Myoen-ji
Goshonouchicho
Ho Daimonji
Fire Festival Characters
Takigahanacho
Morimotocho
Izumidonocho
Yabusoe
Matsumotocho
Otowadani
Rinkyu-ji
Rinuntei

Kitayama
Ining '23
Papa Jon's
Syntax
Tamusabai
Green Peace
Inn Kyoto
Kyoto Prefectural
Library and Archives
Notre
Dame
University
Shibamotocho
MATSUGASAKI
Art and Crafts
Museum
Shodencho
Kowakicho
Kawaradacho
Inuzukacho
SHUGAKUIN
Tsubeocho
Saginomori
Shrine
Gatsurinjicho
Kansai
Seminar
House
Manshu-in

Kyoto
Concert Hall
Kyoto
Pref.University
Kodonocho
Friend Food
Kitaizumi-dori
Kyoto Greece
Roman Museum
Sakyo
Ward Office
Kyoto Institute
of Technology
Kotakeyabucho
Fresco
Speakeasy
Ikari
Papa Jon's
Nakabayashicho
Hazamacho
Mizugakecho
Takeda
Botanical
Garden

iigaka
uchicho
AMO
Kitazonocho
Perfectural
University
Rakucho
angicho
Fujiwara
Clinic
Kitaizumi-dori
Family Mart
Izumigawacho
Kudocho
Yobikaericho
Sosui-dori
Sosui-bunyu River
Tamaokacho
Izumicho
Hatsuda
Kawaharacho
Family Mart
Kokusai
Condominium
YAMABANA
Mukaibatacho
Hayamacho
Enko-ji
Horikiri
Otani

angicho
SHIMOGAMO
Perfectural
University
Rakuhoku HS
CoCollchibanya
Aoi ES
7 Eleven
Sakuragicho
Kyoto Coop
Takagicho
Kamitakeyacho
Manjuin-dori
Minami-
omarucho
ICHIJOJI
Tsuruhashi
Tentenyu
Kita-
Takayasu
Motokame
Aojoicho
Shimizucho
Miyanohigashicho
Shakadocho
TSUJIIDO
PARK
Deguchicho
Shisen-do
Hongan-ji Kitayama-betsuin
Konpuku-ji
Tanuki-dani
(Sojo-ga-dani
Fudo-do)

Fujiwara
Clinic
Shibamotocho
Kashiwabecho
Kibunecho
kagawaracho
dori
Shimogamo Hospital
Morigamaecho
Tadekuracho
Tadekuracho
Shimogamo
JHS
TAKANO
Nishi-birakicho
Takeyacho
Shirakawa Sosui-dori
Sakyo-ku
PO Bank of
Kyoto
Kanto
Clinic
Nakamura
Clinic
Koshoinnobuaki
Daishinkaicho
Kitaoji-dori
Honda
Nissan
Saizeriya
Honda
Garamumasara
Iorinocho
Womb
Bell Chateau
Saikatacho
Matsuharacho
Driving
Range
Yomogigadanicho

Kyoto
Shinkin Bank
Shimamotocho
NTT
Izumiya
Qanat
Rakuhoku
Kojima
Nakau
Kawabata-dori
Shimogamo
Naka-dori
Shimogamo
Hon-dori
Higashi Kurama-
guchi-dori
Shimogamo ES
Shimogamo
Shrine
Kawabata-dori
Takano
Nakau
Daihatsu
Wakenyaku
Suzuki
Tenka-ippin
Honten
Gyoza-no Ohsho
7 Eleven
Circle K
Tsukamotocho
Kitashirakawa
Uryuzancho
Kamihate
cho
Kitashirakawa
Church
Mt. Uryu-yama
Kiyozawaguchicho

Izumoji-
tawaracho
Avanshell
Sato Senkocho
Ota Jusenma
Chayama
Nishi-
takaharacho
Nishi-ioricho
Kyoto University
of Art and Design
Nakayamacho

Shimogamoryo-cho
ichi-dori
dori
Miyazakicho
Norakuro
Kamo-mioya Shrine
Myosei-cho
Family Mart
Sakyo Library
Higashi-kuramaguchi-dori
Harunacho
Ioricho
Rakuda
Senauchicho
Yamadacho
KITASHIRAKAWA
Daidocho

Komyo-ji
Aoi-Matsuri
Festival
(May 15)
Izumigawacho
Shimizucho
Kawai Shrine
Tadeharacho
Nishiuracho
Okubocho
Higashi-
hinokuichicho
Hiragana-kan
Kitashirakawa
Church
Japan Baptist
Hospital
to Mt. Hiei

Amidajimaechu
Junen-ji
Homman-ji
Mikage-dori
Miyakawacho
Kyoto
Family Court
Kami-
yanagicho
Kyoto
Saryou
Shimogamo
TANAKA
Kami-Yosei ES
KAMOGAWA
PARK
Asukaicho
Mikage-dori
KYOTO UNIV.
GROUND
Science Dept.
Ogurocho
Donome-
cho
Tonryu
Kami-ikadacho
Maruyamacho
Pension
Kitashirakawa
Equibalance
Michael's
Shigaoge-michi
Mikage-dori

Fukataniicho

to Takao
Matsumotocho
Saga Hosp

Jikishi-an
Tomb of
Saga-tenno-ryo
Sanocho
Kitanodancho
Naginatazakacho
Udanotani

KITA-SAGA
Akasakacho
Minshuku
Warabinosato
Rengei-ji
Utano
Hospital
Myoraku-in
LeBlanc Per

Kibishacho
Nakoshocho

Okazakicho
Horanouchicho
Rokudaishibacho
Inuicho
SOLO
SAGRADO
KIOTO
Nishicho
Utano Youth
Hostel
Senju-ji
Ondoyamacho

Ikkahyocho
Sennocho
SAGA-KANKUJI
Daikaku-ji
Myozuicho
Sagaosawacho
Osawaike
Pond
Hachijocho
Ippongicho
Goryodencho
Nakayamacho
Fujinoki
YAMAGOE
Mizuhoc

Adashina
Nembutsu-ji
Daikoku
Kyokai
Kanku-ji
Kan'non-do
Kakusho-in
Kitasagai HS
Osawa-
ochikubocho
Chigo
Shrine
Hirosawaike
Pond
Tomb of
Montoku-tenno
Tamura-no-misasagi
Montokuike
Harukicho
Omron Sogyo
Memorial Museum
Hisagasonocho

Rokutancho
Torii gata Daimonji
Fire Festival Characters
Kubodencho
Noboricho
Tsuridohocho
BUKYO UNIV.
GROUND
HORIKAWA
HIGH SCHOOL
GROUND
Goryodencho
Kyoto Seikyo
Ukyo Shibu
Tokiwa T

Adashinocho
SAGA-TORIIMOTO
Kitadaicho
Nakasujicho
Chikurin
Rokudocho
SAGA-DAIKAKUJI-
MONZEN
Osawaiggata
Iwaido
Nishiuracho
Nishiuracho
Saga JHS
Hensho-ji
Kita-gebanocho
Horiikecho
Higashicho
Coop
Motoshoya-c

Kozakacho
Butsushodenocho
SAGA-NISON'IN-
MONZEN
Ikkyu
Saga JHS
Shingucho
Hirosawa ES
SAGA-HIROSAWA
Hoan Hoan
Marutamachi-dori

Gio-ji
Seiryo-ji
Nodomaecho
Miyanoshitacho
Shinucho
Goshonouchicho
Saga Grace
MG
Sagano HS

Takiguchi-dera
Komichi
Enri-an
Hokyo-in
Daimoncho
Itocho
Shikenocho
Gourmet
City
Maruta-machi-dori
Keiyo D2
Sagano-danmachi

Ojoincho
Adashino
Minami-chuincho
Hinomyojincho
SAGA-SHAKADO-
MONZEN
Setogawacho
Wakamiyacho
Kachuan Takeuchiseiho
Memorial Museum
Tomb of
Kabutozakai-kofun
Hoju-ji
Miyanomaecho
Aokigaharacho

Chojincho
Nison-in
Rakushisha
Donomaecho
Urayanagicho
Setogawacho
Saga
Arashiyama
Aburakakecho
Inuicho
Umazakacho
Hachiokach

Jojakko-ji
Yamamotocho
Nonomiyacho
Kyoto Arashiyama
Orgel Museum
Tsujimura
Hirokawa
Kisha Poppo
Shiinocho
Noshimizucho
Uzumasa

Saga-ogurayamacho
BAMBOO
FOREST
Saganoarashiyama
Kurumamichicho
SAGA-TENRYUJI
Imahoricho
Oritocho
Kariwacho

Taochinocho
Torokko
Arashiyama
Bamboo St.
Yojiya
Matatabian
Nekoya
Fresco
Kurumazakijinja
Sentoku-ji
Hachigaoka
JHS
Tarumiyamacho
Toei City
Studio Par

Okochi
Sanso
Arashiyama
Bamboo Grove
Tenryu-ji North Gate
Kongo-in
Randensaga
Rokuo-in
Kitaboricho
Kurumazaki Shrine
Arisugawacho
Arisugawa
Hirakicho
Katabira-
no-tsuji

Senko-ji
Hoshinoya
BAMBOO FOREST
Hogon-in
TENRYU-JI
Sanshu-in
Gyate
Arashiyama
Suminokuracho
Nakadoricho
Nakayamacho
Asahicho
Shojo-in
Arashiyama Main Line
Bola Bola GH
Taiyo
Shochiku Kyoto
Movie Studio
Katsuragicho

Saga-kamemachi
Kameyama-
koen
Susuki-no-babacho
Yomei-in
Tsukurimichicho
Rinsen-ji
Hananoe
Tokurin-ji
Sanjo-dori
SAGA
Myojocho
Fuki
Wakatake
Akikaidocho

Yudofu Sagano
Rantei
Kitao
Yoshida-ya
Mikazuki
Sanjo-dori
K-yard
Tayabucho
Uzumasa
Sagano
JHS

Kameyama ya
Benkei
Arashiyama
Yoshimura
Kamikawaracho
Arashiyamakan
Sanjo-dori
Arashiyama ES
Kyoto Saga
University of Art
Sagano ES
Nishinocho
UZUMASA

Boat Rental Stall
Togetsu-kyo
Bridge
ARASHIYAMA PARK
Higashi-
ichikawacho
Ishigatsubocho
Chiyonomichicho
Omokagecho
Tanamorich

Hanaikada
Togetsutei
Musubi Cafe
Nishi-ichikawacho
Chajiricho
SAGANO
Kitanocho
Shibanocho
Tsuchimotoch

Horin-ji
Toriichi
Arashiyama
Nakaoshitacho
Arashiyama
Hinokamicho
Higashi-kaidocho
ARASHIYAMA
HIGASHI
PARK
Takadacho
Rokutandacho
Hakamadacho
Yurigamotocho

Matsumuro-kita-matsuoyama
Arashiyama
Monkey Park
Iwatayama
Kongo-ji
Yamadacho
Minami-uracho
Umezu ES
Kita-gawacho
Hirakicho
Kawadokorocho

Kyotoarashiyama
Post Office
Furonohashicho
Fushiharacho
Hayashikuchicho
Kitauracho
Uedacho
Gotocho

Tanigatsujikocho
Morinomaecho
Umenomiya Taisha
Maedacho
Nishimuracho
Shijo-dori
Kitamachi
Kamaekichicho

Uchidacho
Genrokuzancho
Asatsuicho
UMEZU
Chofuku-ji
Kitamachi
Minamimachi

Yakushishitacho
Uchida
Hospital
Onawabacho
Umezu ES
Minamimachi

Miyanokitacho
Miyamachi
Matsu
JHS
Shirimizocho
Nakamuracho

Matsu-no-o
Shrine
Miyamaocho
Kawaracho
Katsura River
UKYO-WARD
NISHIKYO-WARD

Oiagecho
Nakamizocho
Matsuo
JHS
MATSUMURO
Hinokuchicho
Imaicho
Kitacho
Katsuragawa Hwy

Tsukiyomi
Shrine
Ogidacho
Kitakawaracho
Araboricho
Atagamicho
Nishicho
Shindench

Shimo-yamada
kami-sono'ocho
Yamazocho
Tanakacho
Suzukawacho
Katsuragawa
ES
Minamicho

Yamada-minami-
matsuoyama
Jikeyama
Kegon-ji
(Suzumushi-dera)
Jikecho
Mangokucho
Matsuo
Dairicho
Kinosocho
KATSURAKAMINO

SAIHO-JI
(Koke-dera)
Ikeno Taiga
Art Museum
Idocho
MATSUO
Aoyama Music
Memorial Hall
Onocho
Higashicho

Jingatanicho
Genchu-in
Nishiicho
KAMIKATSURA

Uenoyacho
Jizo-in
Kamikatsura
Tokudaijicho

Goryo-kita-oyamacho
Shimo-yamada-
chozukacho
Hamurocho
Morikamicho
Mitsubishi Kyoto
Hospital
Keituk

Joju-in
Sakuratanicho
Goshocho

Oe JHS
Minegado
YAMADA
Uenocho
Katsura JHS
Sannomiyacho
Morishitacho
to Oe
Ikejiricho

Katsusaka
ES
Goryo-oeyamacho 3
Minamicho
Kitayamadacho
Honda Cars
Nishikyo
Ward Office
Ushitoracho

Goryo-oeyamacho 2
Minegadocho 1
Minegadocho 4
Hakozakicho
Shinotsubocho

Scale 1 : 22,500   500m   1000ft

OMURO · Yomeibunko · Okubo-ji · Yamatacho · Goryonoshitacho · **RYOANJI** · Kitamachi · **KOMATSUBARA** · Hirano Shrine · **NISHIJIN** · Monyacho · Kyoto Municipal Archaeological Museum

NARUTAKI · Reizan-ji · NINNA- JI · Renge-ji · Nishimachi · Miyamothocho · Kitano Tenman-gu · **KITANO** · Itsu-tsuji-dori · Higashimachi

UTANO · Omuro-Ninnaji · Toji-in · Ryoanji · **TANIGUCHI** · Nishi-hakubaicho · Kitano-hakubaicho · Imadegawa-dori

KIWA · **HANAZONO** · MYOSHIN-JI · **TAISHOGUN** · Higashi-takatsukasacho · Prefectural Gymnasium · Ninnaji Kaido · **NISHIJIN**

UZUMASA-YASUI · Hanazono University · JR Sagano Line · Enmachi · **JURAKUMAWARI** · **NISHINOKYO** · NIJO-JO CASTLE · Ninomaru Palace

YAMANOUCHI · Keifuku Arashiyama Line · Nishioji-Oike · Oike-dori · Sanjo-dori · Nijo-jo-mae · SHINSEN-EN GARDEN

SAIIN · Sai-in · Shijo-dori · Omiya · **MIBU** · Mibudera · **CHUDOJI** · JR Sanin Main Line (Sagano Line)

NISHI-KYOGOKU · Hankyu Kyoto Line · WAKASA STADIUM KYOTO · KYOTO AQUA ARENA · **SUJAKU** · **NISHI-SHICHIJO** · Central Wholesale Market · **SHIMABARA** · HONGAN-JI (Nishi-Hongan-ji)

SHICHIJO GOSHONOUCHI · Shichijo-dori · **UMEKOJI** · Umekoji Steam Locomotive Museum · UMEKOJI PARK · Ryukoku University

KATSURA

Aoki Children's Hospital
Kogaku-ji
7 Eleven
Nishikyogoku ES
Nishioji ES
Nishioji
TONODACHO
UMEKOJI
Umekoji Steam Locomotive Museum
Umekoji Park
Rihga Royal
APA
BIC Camera
Isetan
KY STA

Katsura-Rikyu Imperial Villa Temple Cafe Collection
Dragonfly
Hachijo-dori
Terakoya
Lawson
KCI Gallery
Toji Rakunan Inn
Seifuen
Grocery Store
Sunkus
Shin Miyako
Godo Insatsu
Jr Nishihonn

United Church of Christ Church
KATSURA
Tanimura Clinic
Ryuheisoba
Bamboo Pavilion
Hachijo JHS
Rokusonno Shrine
Rokunan HS
Hachijo-dori
HACHIJO
KYO'OGOKOKU (To-ji)
Kanchi-in
Toji Gekijo Hall
Fukuden-ji
Fushimi-inari Otabi-sho
Nursery Ichiban
Family Mar

Kyoto Katsura PO
Family Mart
Katsura Azuma
Mc Donald's
KISSHOIN
Kentatsu Inari Shrine
KARAHASHI
Kyotoku Technical HS
Karahashi ES
Dainiadachi Hospital
Ruin of Rajo-mon Gate
Shindo
Nawa Clinic
Five-Storied Pagoda
Toji
Kannon-ji
Kujo MID Bldg
Nanto Bank
Kujo Law
Dai-i

Katsura Higashi ES
Orthopedic Tachiiri
Katsuragawa JHS
Kawaokahigashi ES
Circle K
Sukiya
Momo Jirou
Kujo Church
Estate
Rakunan
Hospital
Kojin Hospital
Circle K
Nursery
Shimizu Clinic
TONODA
PARK
7 Eleven
Kinoshita Shoten
Higashiku

Nishiyama Betsuin
Kawaoka ES
Iori Katsura Azuma Studio Shop
Katsura JHS
Shouhou ES
Sanuki Seimen
Nishioji-dori
Kujo-dori
Postal Seminar
Yubani
Saizeriya
Pioneer
Minami Ward Office
NTT
Public Bath
NISHIKUJO
Kawamura
HIGASHIKU

Uematsu Clinic
Aoya Dentist
All Soya Clinic
Joyful Store
Sasaki Dental Clinic
Kawase Dentist
Pierrot
Kisshoin Hospital
Kisshoan ES
Aeon
Rakunan JHS
Jujo Rehabilitation Hospital
Wako Giken
Toray Coatex
Otabe
7 Eleven
Daikin
Matsumoto Denki
Bamiyan

Dental Kimura
Diana
Marugameseimen
Kissho-in Tenmangu Shrine
Jujo-dori (Toba-dori)
Kyoto Seal Label
Maruta Kiki
Daido Maruta Senko
Jujo-dori (Toba-dori)
Kinden
Netz
Sunato Shoji
Seikatsu Kankyo Jimusho
KAMITOBA
Hakodate Ichiba
Mori Clinic
Driving Range
Miyamot Shik

Katsura HS
SHIMOTSUBAYASHI
USHIGASE
Aya Grilled Meat
KISSHOIN ATHLETIC PARK
KISSHOIN
Sansen-ji
Sekisui Chemical
Towa
Sagawa
Calliy
Benock
7 Eleven
Lawson
Sony
Able

GSDF Garrison
KUZE
Katsura Minami Shop
7 Eleven
Kisshoin Library
Selvac
JAF
Tikuson
Oke
Canon
Grand Marble
Yakult
Kawai
Murata Kikai
INDUSTRIAL AREA
Shimogawa

Medical Research Clinic Orthopedic
Daiei
Juju Karubi
Super Bowl Kisshoin
Shoei ES
Tonan HS
Hero's
Gain Corp.
Keihan Eng.
Otami
Chardonnay
Nissan
Hanshin Expressway No 8 Kyoto Line
Kyoto Prison

Rakusaiguchi
Iida Clinic
Nagai Clinic
Kuzebashi Dori
Kamitoba ES
Muten Kura-zushi
Wakita
Kamitoba-guchi
Kitamura
Kuinabashi
Takeda

MORIMOTOCHO
Kuze Nishi ES
Circle K
Oyabu ES
KAMONDEN
Central Wholesale Market
Nomura Tsukudani
Isso-ji
Trendy
Jonan Medical
Kuze

Mukomachi Ekimae PO
Kuze JHS
UCC Foods
Yakiniku Ogura Yuko
Toen-tei
Nishimatsuya
Nitori
Gyoza no Osho
7 Eleven
Kyoto Jonan Clinic
Taked

Higashimuko
Life City
KAMITOBA TOMONORI
Filtration Plant
Asuka Foods
Kanahara Pile Industry
Toho
Cafe Hana
McDonald's
Yoshinoya
TAKEDA
Aruforuno Italian
Kyoto Chuo Shinkin Bank
Yamamo Orthopaed Surge
7Elev
Taked

Fushimi Area

Kanidoraku
Pizza Hut
Kawano Clinic
to Kyoto
Nara-Kaido Road
Kyoto Immanuel Church
Sumizome Church
Eishun-ji
Ueno Dentist
Kaiho-ji
TONOMORI PARK
Ruins of Tobarikyu Park
Guest of Honor House
Jonanen (Chinese Restaurant)

to Kyoto
Seahorse Seafood
Kita-hatacho
Tobamachi
Shimo-shinsenencho
Dai-ni Akebono Nursery
Nakamocho
Ho Tange
Mogamicho
Ruins of Toba Imperial Villa
to Osaka
Circle K
Rakurin
NAKAJIMA
Kyoto Trade Fair Center (Pulse Plaza)

Lawson
Miyawaki Bookstore
Dental Kinoshita
Enokicho
Circle K
Yamatocho
Sumiyoshi ES
Sumiyoshi Nursery
Nakayama Orthopaedic
Momoyama Jr.HS
Tsuji Clinic
Azuma Ban Clinic
K's Denki
Chuo Shinkin Bank
Kinta
Pizza Hu
Kani-doraku
Kawano Clin

Prinsesu in Kyoto
Moricho
Butaicho
Nihon Sanmo Senshoku
Kajiyamachi
Fuji Stress Clinic
Honjo-ji
Minamimachi
Wind Virtue Committee
Kyotokyoiku Univ.
Tenrikyo Church
Sunks
Higashi Dental Clinic
HIGASHITSUME PARK
Seahorse Seafood
Ginkaku Ramen
Miyawaki Bookstore
Shimia Hospit

Jibucho
7 Eleven
Kyoto Chuo Shinkin Bank
Kinsho
Sakurai Tofu
Shonen-ji
Fushimi Itahashi ES
Kuretake Culture Center
Fushimi Jr HS
Tambabashi
Kyoto Municipal School
Minamimachi
Nishimachi
Momoyama HS
Kappa-zushi
Tonkatsu Katsuaji
Taniguchi Clinic
Dental Kinoshita
Nihon Sanmo Senshoku

Yofuku in Aoyama
Nets TOYOTA
Jurakumachi
Washoku Sato
Mishima Clinic
Kyoto Okago PO
Daikoku-ji
Shoryu-ji
Ishihara Gynecology
Mikawa
Kamikawa Clinic
Volkswagen
Shimotoba ES
SHIMOTOBA
Sakurai Tofu
Kinsho
Washoku Sato

Ducks
Kotobuki Foods
Dobashicho
Toiyamachi
Fushimi Ward Office
Fushimi Central Library
Genya
Nakamachi
KOGA
7 Eleven
Soup Shokudo
Takara
Yofuku in Aoyama
Ducks

Saint Marc
Seimen Kobo Kamakura Pasta
Nishimachi
Gekkei-kan
Saiko-ji
Hello Work Fushimi
Nanbumachi
Saiho-ji
Sampo-ji
Zenko-ji
Furuya Clinic
Co-op Momoyama
Haruyama Blue Label
Daily Yamazaki
Saint Marc
Hofuku-ji

Health Screening Clinic Asada Toba
MISU PARK
Obiyacho
Kawayacho
Goko-no-Miya Shrine
Shimpuku-ji
Fushimi Police
Udon Tokutoku
Soseikai General Hospital
Kafe Terasuean
Health Screening Clinic Asada Toba

Otesuji-dori
Misudoromachi-atocho
Kyotoohashi General Hospital
Todo Clinic
Aeon
Fushimi-Momoyama
Momoyama-Gonyo-mae
Cafe 'fragrance'
Tenrikyo Church
Gyoza no Osho
Akiyama Clinic
Kite Shop
Bikkuri Donkey
Coconut Club
Pharmacy
Nichirin
KOJIMA
7 Eleven

Bally
Yamazakicho
Kizakura Kappa Country
Hirose Women's Clinic
Momoyama Dental Clinic
Toryo Apartment Complex
Saiun-ji
YOKOOJI
Yakult Yokooji Center
Yoshinoya
Kyotoohashi General Hospit

Teradaya
Kita-hamacho
Gekkeikan Okura Memorial Sake & Brewery Museum
Family Mart
Choken-ji
Fushimi Minamihama ES
FUSHIMI PARK
Toba Pubs
Yoda Clinic
Toryo Catholic Church
Yokooji ES
Galaxy
Royal Home Center
Kyoto Outer Loop Route
McDonald's
Coconut Club

Tsujidocho
Shimo-nakacho
Kami-nakacho
Hirakawa
Tenrikyo Church
ENT Clinic
Myofuku-ji
Toryocho
Kangetsukyo
Kyotoyokooji PO
Kyoto Yokooozi Shop Workman
Dairen-ji
Tenrikyo Church
Hirakawa
ENT Clinic

Misucho 3 Chome
Dairen-ji
Misu Clinic
Keihan Uji Line
Chushojima
Yaguracho
Harbin Tenrikyo Church
Echigo R
Nambu Chemicals
SHIMOMISU
FUSHIMI AREA 50
Keihan Line
Chushojima
Nakamura Sabou
Fushimi Harbour Sport Center

Nakacho
Outer Loop Highway
Sunflowers
Sugano Clinic
to Joyo
to Katano

Fushimi Area

Scale 1 : 22,500

500m   1000ft

to Katano

Scale 1 : 30,000   500m   1000ft

IMAGUMANO

NISHINO

KAWATA

HONMACHI

SENNYUJI

FUKANE

HIGASHINO

KURISUNO

NISHINOYAMA

FUKAKUSA

Kanshuji-nishi

ONO

DAIGO

OKAYACHO

OKAMEDANI

OGURISU

ISHIDA

DAIGO-JI

KOHATA

MOMOYAMA

FUSHIMI PARK

Kyoto Dai-ni Tower

HIKARI PARK

KITAIWAMOTO PARK

Takahashi Chuko
Hinoya
Imakumano Shrine
Joshin-ji
Korai-ji
Tsurugi Shrine
Sokuju-in
Kaiko-ji
Shinzenko-ji
Imakumano Kannon-ji
Reiga-in
Kyoto Daiichi Red Cross Hospital
Tsukinowa Jr.HS
Cocohana
Doju-in
Shinsho-den Treasure House
Ryugin-an
Unryu-in
Sennyu-ji
Funda-In
TOFUKU-JI
Sesshu-ji
Komyo-in
International Jr.HS

Funeral Hall
Higashiyama Tunnel
Rokusho Shrine
Taikodaira Country Club
Yamashinakawata PO
Kiyomizu-yaki Pottery Village
Dodo ES
Higashiyama Football Park & Tennis Club
7 Eleven

Yamashina Library
Anshoji JHS
Yamashina PO
Sankai ES
Seiyu
Kato Yamashina Hospital
Tokai-do
Tokaido Shinkansen Line
Yamashina Affairs Ltd.
Sankaiminami ES
Yamashina Community Gymnasium
Sonnomiya
Yamashina Jr.HS
Tobu Cultural Hall
Prison

Hanshin Expressway Route 8

Gokuraku-ji
Oishi-jinja
K Cross
Yamashina Shrine

Yamashina Ward Office
Katorea
Yamashina Hospital
Kanshu-ji
Nagitsuji PO
Sato
Fresco
Grace Bible Church
Kanshu Jr.HS
Ono ES
Kanshu-ji
Zuishin-in

Kuno Hospital
Inari ES
7Eleven
Osaki
Daily
Fushimi-inari Shrine
Sekiho-ji
Hoto-ji
Nishikawa Dental Clinic
Kansai Association
Kobayashi Dental Clinic
Fushimi Catholic Church
Junior HS
Seibogakuin ES
Fukakusa Jr.HS
Ritsumeikan HS

Meishin Expressway (Toll Road)

Nanshi-in
Kyoto Daigo-kita PO
Paseo Daigoro
Daigo
Al Plaza
Touryou HS
Sampo-in

Soeda Clinic
Fushimi Tech. H S
McDonald's
Annie's
Police Academy
Ryukoku University
Family Mart
Takeda Coffee Shop
Matsuda Clinic
Tsuji Clinic
7Eleven
Family Mart
Kansai Urban Banking
Daiei
Kyoto Municipal Science Center for Youth
Fujinomori Jr.HS
Nishikawa Dental Clinic
Maruyama Dentist
Hayashi Orthopedic Clinic
Fujinomori Shrine
Kyoto University of Education
Kimoto Clinic
Matsumoto Clinic
Fujinomori Clinic
Kuroda Clinic
Sumizome Church
Kono Dental Clinic
Nishimura Clinic
7 Eleven

Pubs
Bank of Kyoto
Oishi Internal Medicine Clinic
Doutor Coffee
Ninmyo Tenno Fukakusa-ryo Imperial Mausoleum
Fuji Ramen
Lawson
Glass House
Rehabilitation Clinic
Tenrikyo Church
Christian Church of God Salvation
Driving Range

Ogurisu-miyayama ES
Ikeda ES
Ritsuryo Jr.HS
Ikedahigashi ES
Ichigon-ji
Ogurisu ES
Kyoto Coop
Saizeria
Royal
Ogurisu JHS
Ishida ES
Ishida
Kyotoishida PO
Kasugano
Kasugaoka JHS
Mori Pediatric Clinic
Yoshikawa Dental Clinic
Kyoto City Daigo Library
Takeda General Hospital
Sushicho
Momo
Joshin
Rokuji zo Hospital
Ito Yokado
Daigo Hospital
Nagomi-no-Sato Hospital
Hokai-ji

Christ Gospel Church
Kyoto Univ. of Education HS
Itou Clinic
Circle K
Fujii Clinic
Ochiai Clinic
Fushimi PO
Kyoto Immanuel
Pizard
Nakagawa Dental Clinic
Sumizome Church
Kaiho-ji
Nakayama Orthopaedic
Momoyama Jr.HS
Sumiyoshi Nursery
Kyoto Kyoiku Univ. Momoyama ES
Fujishiro ES
Kammu Tenno-ryo Imperial Mausoleum
Fushimi-Momoyama Castle
Meiji Tenno Fushimi Momoyama-ryo Imperial Mausoleum
Kyoto Toyo Hospita
Ogurisu ES

Daiichi Okamoto Hospital
Fujii Stress Clinic
Ishihara Gynecology
Zenko-ji
Furuya Clinic
Shimpuku-ji
Nogi Shrine
Kyoto Tachibana HS
Minami Dental Clinic
Tazato Clinic
Momomine Nursery
Izumiya Rokujizo Store
Orthodontic Kanagawa
Rokujizo
Kohata ES
Carmelite Monastery
Hoju-ji
Driving School

Fushimi Ward Office
Fushimi Central Library
Genya
Aeon
Momoyama-Goryo-mae
Goko-no-Miya Shrine
Torya Apartment Complex
Cafe 'fragrance'
Momoyama Catholic Church
Saiun-ji
Oshima Hospital
Ryugen-ji
Momoyama HS
Jibu Ike Pond
Mori Pediatric Clinic
Gyoza-no-Osho
Fushimi Fire Department
Yoshikawa Dental Clinic
Messiah Christian Church
Takamisawa
Momoyama Minami-guchi
Ogawa Clinic
Ikeda Gynecology Clinic
Momoyama Eiko Church
Kusuri Kirin-do Kowataike
Ujiogurayama PO
Kohata ES
Okurayama ES

Yoda Clinic
Gekkeikan Okura Sake Memorial Sake Brewery Museum
FUSHIMI
Minamihama ES
Toryo HS
yofuku-ji
Herbin Tenrikyo Church
Kintetsu Kyoto Line
Circle K
Mukaijima ES
Mukaijima Minami ES
Toji ENT Clinic
Iwai Dental Clinic
Furukawa Clinic
Sancho Division
Soka Gakkai Fushimi Heiwa Kaikan
Momoyama Kyoto Minami ES
Morita Otolaryngology
Unitika Kyoto Family Shopping Center
Kowata Jr.HS
McDonald's
Family Mart
Ujikowata PO
Kowata
Higashiuji HS

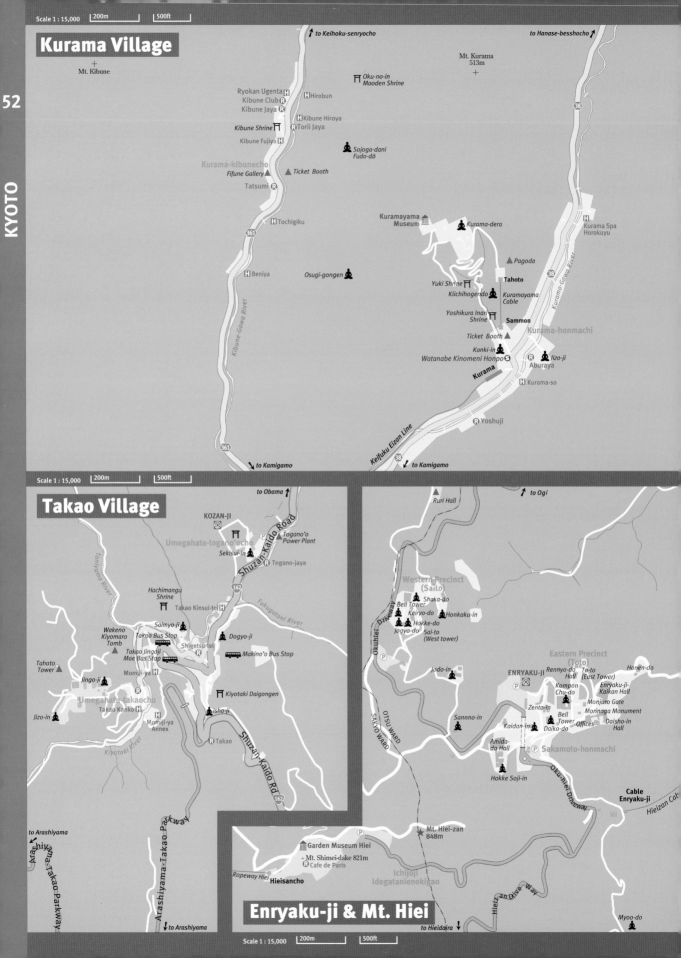

Scale 1 : 15,000 200m 500ft

Kurama Village

to Keihoku-senryocho →
to Hanase-besshocho →

Mt. Kibune

Mt. Kurama 513m

Oku-no-in Maoden Shrine

38

Ryokan Ugenta
Kibune Club
Kibune Jaya
Hirobun
Kibune Hiroya
Kibune Shrine Torii Jaya
Kibune Fujiya

Sojoga-dani Fudo-dō

Kurama-kibunecho

Fifune Gallery Ticket Booth

Tatsumi

Kuramayama Museum Kurama-dera

Kurama Spa Horokuyu

361 Tochigiku

Pagoda

Yuki Shrine Tahoto

Kiichihogendo Kuramayama Cable

Beniya Osugi-gongen

Yoshikura Inari Shrine Sammon

Ticket Booth

Kanki-in Kurama-honmachi

Watanabe Kinomeni Honpo Jizo-ji
Aburaya

Kurama Kurama-so

Yoshuji

Keifuku Eizan Line

Kibune-Gawa River

Kurama-Gawa River

← to Kamigamo
← to Kamigamo 38

Scale 1 : 15,000 200m 500ft

Takao Village

to Obama ↑

KOZAN-JI

Togano'o Power Plant

Umegahata-togano'ocho

Sekisui-in Togano-jaya

Shuzan-Kaido Road

Hachimangu Shrine

162

Takao Kinsui-tei

Fukugatani River

Wakeno Kiyomaro Tomb
Saimyo-ji
Takao Bus Stop
Dogyo-ji

Tamayama River

Shigetsu-tei

Tahoto Tower
Takao Jingoji Mae Bus Stop
Makino'o Bus Stop

Jingo-ji Momiji-ya

Umegahata-takaocho

Kiyotaki Daigongen

Jizo-in Takao Kanko
Momiji-ya Annex
Isho-ji

Takao

Shuzan-Kaido Rd

162

Kiyotaki River

Arashiyama-Takao Parkway

to Arashiyama

↓ to Arashiyama

Enryaku-ji & Mt. Hiei

Ruri Hall to Ogi ↑

Western Precinct (Saito)

Shaka-do
Bell Tower
Keiryo-do Honkaku-in
Hokke-do
Jogyo-do Sai-to (West tower)

Okuhiei Driveway

Jodo-in

Eastern Precinct (Toto)

ENRYAKU-JI Honen-do

Rennyo-do Hall To-to (East Tower)

Kompon Chu-do Enryaku-ji-Kaikan Hall

Zento-in Monjuro Gate Moringa Monument

Sannno-in Bell Tower Daisho-in Hall
Kaidan-in Daiko-do Offices

OTSU WARD
SAKYO WARD

Amida-do Hall Sakamoto-honmachi

Hokke Soji-in

Okuhiei Driveway

Cable Enryaku-ji

Hieizan Cab

Garden Museum Hiei
Mt. Shimei-dake 821m
Cafe de Paris

Mt. Hiei-zan 848m

Ropeway Hiei Hieisancho

Ichijoji Idegatanienokigao

Hiei an Drive Way

to Hieidaira

Myoo-do

to Jakko-in

Ohara Sanso
Iketani-jaya
Ohara-no-sato
Ohara-tsuji
Keitoku-in
Kumoi-jaya
Ohara-kusaocho
Kusao-Gawa River
Kissa Natsume
Kusakizome-an Ohara-kobo

108

to Bomura

367

Shorin-in
(Mondodera)

Hosen-in

Ohara Jr.HS

**Ohara Home
Village Museum**
Jikko-in
Rokawa-jaya
Sanzenin-no-sato
Shibakyu

Juntoku Tenno-ryo
(Imperial Mausoleum)
Ohara-shorin'incho
Sanzen-in

Tamba-jaya
Roritsu-jaya
Sabo Rokawa
Sawada
Roso Chatani

Seryo
Gyozan-en
Ono-sanso

Jorenge-in

Raigo-in

Ohara Kobo
Takano-Gawa River
Ohara-raikoncho
Yamashiro
Ohara PO

Cafe Terrace Irori

108
Ohara-nomuracho

Sanzenin-michi
Kobo ai-no-yakata

Ohara-onagasecho

Seshu-in
Ohara Gokosui

Ohara sato-no-eki
Ohara-uenocho
367
Nomura-sanso
Hanji
JA
Family Mart

Tsujishiba-honpo

Joraku-do

Kissa Uenae

Kyoto Kusakizome-kobo

Uenae

Kitsune

40

Komatsu Hitoshi
Art Museum

Oharaidecho

to Central Kyoto

Oshima

to Central Kyoto

Monguchi
Ujitodo PO
Deguchi
Nishinaka
Otani

Kurumada

Yakitori
Daikichi

Yabusato
Nakasuji
Kahara

Johachi Shrine
Shigatani

Kitauchi

Joyce Pot

Mimuroto-ji

Ohata
Uji River
Todo

Den Den
Tanisagari
Monmae

Nenbutsu-ji
Tadakawa

241
MAKISHIMA
PARK
Ohata

Mimurodo
Happy
Rokuhara
Bank of
Kyoto
Nishimura
Dental Clinic

Enba

Ohata

Seicho-ji
Uji-no-waki-iratsuko-no-miko
Mausoleum
Fresco
Taniguti Internal
Medicine Clinic

Okunoike
Hojo-in

Tsukiyo

Tire Select

Uji Unyu

Harada Internal
Medicine Clinic

Tanaka

Izumiya
Liquor Store
Mimurodo ES

Okadani

Tobai
Chaho
Yell
Engineering

Nakatoku
Mokuzai

Kinki Sangyo
Nozomi Nursery

Otsukata

Aramaki

7

Doi Medicine

Ikeyama

Myojoen

Yamada

Nintendo

Daiichi
Kotsu
Lawson

Ogaito
Tokura
Hospital

Myoken

MYOJOCHO

Hinojiri

Kozakura Nursery

Maruyama

Kamanariya

Gusto

UJI

The Tale of Genji Museum

Kozakura

Kamiya
Gynecology

Nishiyamada

Iwatani
Gas

Kissa Hanachirusato

Koshu

Konan

Unitika
Fibers

Uji Shiminkaikan

Hashiderahojo-in
Shogaku-in

Matsuri
DAIKICHIYAMA
FUCHI PARK

Yaochi

Uji Takeda Hospital

Ujibashi PO

Seizeriya

Renge

Uji Bridge

Shokuhin-kan
Apuro

Catholic
Church

Keihan Uji
Sanatorium

UJIGAMI SHRINE

Yamada

Unitika Fitness Club

Shoda Clinic

Uji Daiichi
Bank of
Kyoto

Ujigawa
Hashihime
Shrine

Tachibana
Bridge

247
Uji Shrine

Tonouchi

Uji

7 Eleven

Kinki Rodo
Kinko Bank

Circle K

Morikawa
Clinic

Tchikuro

Asagiri
Bridge

Saisho-in

Kannondo

Eshin-in
Kosho-ji

Kosai

Motomura
Clinic

7 Eleven

246

Jodo-in

Fukujuen
Tea Center

Maruka
Delivery
Service

Wakamori

Family Mart

JR Nara Line

Umonji

Kyoto
Shinkin

Myoraku

BYODO-IN
Hoshunen
Hosho-kan

UJI PARK
Tourism
Center
Fukuya

Tozen-in

Kameishiro

Uji City Office

15

Tenrikyo
Church

Agata
Shrine

3

Tomi-jaya

Uji Jr.HS

Ichiban

Kunitsuru

Hanayashiki
Ukifune-en

Komesaka

Uji-ichiban PO

Sanno

Niban

to Osaka

Todo ES

Hozo Shrine

Sea of Japan

10miles

500ft

KINOSAKI 66
AMANO HASHIDATE 66
LAKE BIWA 67
HIMEJI CASTLE 66
OSAKA AREA 55
AROUND NARA 64
HONGU ONSENS 66

Cities: Fukui, Tottori, Gifu, Kyoto, Otsu, Tsu, Kobe, Osaka, Nara, Himeji, Wakayama, Tokushima

Katsuyama, Eiheiji, Mt Johoji, Echizen, Sabae, Ono, Mt Dais, Tsuruga, Obama, Maizuru, Ayabe, Fukuchiyama, Toyooka, Yabu, Asago, Tanba, Sasayama, Nantan, Kameoka, Nagaokakyo, Takatsuki, Nishinomiya, Takarazuka, Minoo, Kadoma, Higashi-Osaka, Yao, Fujidera, Sakurai, Yoshino, Koya, Hashimoto, Gojo, Kinokawa, Kainan, Arida, Tanabe, Shirahama, Kushimoto

Awaji-shima Island, Shodo-shima Island, Kii Oshima Island

Kansai International Airport, Kobe Airport, Tokushima Airport, Nanki Shirahama Airport, Fukui Airport

Lake Biwa, Hikone Castle, Hikone

Osaka Bay, Wakasa Bay, Ise Bay, Sea of Kumano-nada

Kumano Kodo Kohechi, Kumano Kodo Iseji, Kumano Kodo Nakahechi, Kumano Kodo Kiiji, Kumano Kodo Ohechi, Omine Okugake-michi

KUMANO HAYATAMA-TAISHA SHRINE, SEIGANTO-JI, KUMANO NACHI-TAISHA SHRINE, FODARAKUSAN-JI, Kumano Sanzen, NACHI PRIMEVAL FOREST, NACHI-OTAKI

Kumano Hongu Taisha, Shingu, Nachi-Katsu'ura, Taiji Whale Museum, Kiho, Kumano, Owase, Kihoku

PACIFIC OCEAN

to Kanazawa, to Agano, to Tsuyama, to Okayama, to Takamatsu, to Matsuyama, to Tokyo, to Miyazaki

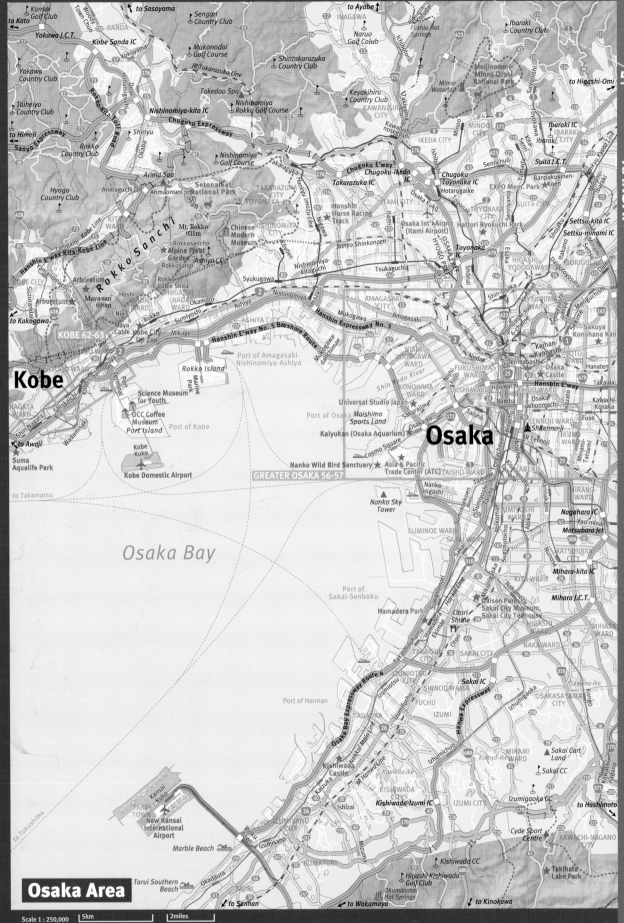

AMAGASAKI CITY

Inabaso
Inaba-motomachi
Oshima ES
Oshima
to Nishinomiya
National Highway Road No 2
Osho-Kita
Osho-nishimachi
Osho-naka-dori
Osho-nishimachi
Kotouracho
Nakiriyamacho
Amagasaki Kyotei Stadium (Motorboat Racecourse)
Mukogawa
Mukogawacho
to Nishinomiya
Nishi ES
Motohamacho
Wakaba ES
Furukawa Electric
Takasucho
Higashi-naniocho
Marushimacho
Ohamacho
Kizaemon-shinden
Matabee
Nishi
Suehirocho
to Kobe
Higashi-Kaigancho
Higashi-Kaigancho
Funade
Higashi-Kaigancho

Amagasaki City Hall
Amagasakiimakita PO
Oshokita Jr. HS
Hamada ES
Hamadacho
Naniwacho
Naniwa ES
Yomogawacho
Kanda-kitadori
Kanda-minamidori
Miyauchicho
Tateyacho
Deyashiki
Sakuragicho
Higashi-hakuragicho
Kaimeicho
Nakazaikecho
Higashi-mukojima-nishinocho
Higashi-mukojima-higashi-nocho
Tsukiji
Matsushimacho
Hatsushimacho
Kita-hatsushimacho
Higashi-takasucho
Higashi-hamacho
Otakasucho
Nishijima
Nakajima
Kubota
Nakajima PA

Nisshin Jr. HS
Nanatsumatsucho
Kitaniwa ES
Baika ES
Amagasaki Central
Amagasaki Main Line
Hanshin Main Line
Dojcho
Amagasaki Center Pool-mae
Mukojimacho
Smumitomo Metals Steel Tube Works
Kawakita ES
Nakajima
Nakajimagawa River
Amagasaki Higashikaigan Ramp

Hopinn
Aming
Hama
Hama ES
Wakakusa Jr. HS
AMAGASAKI MUNICIPAL MEMORIAL PARK
Fusocho
Nagasucho
Kinrakujicho
Showa-minamidori
New Archaic
Amagasaki
JR Tokaido (Kobe) Line
Odaminami Jr. HS
Hopinn Hotel F
Hopinn Hotel D
Seiwa ES
Kinrakuji ES
Nagasu-nishi-dori
Nagasu-naka-dori
Nagasu-hondori
Nagasu ES
Kita-daimotsucho
Showa-dori
Higashi-daimotsucho
Higashi-daimotsucho
Misonocho
Daimotsucho
Jonai
Higashi-honmachi
Higashi-matsushimacho
Higashi-hatsushimacho
Nakajima

NISHIYODOGAWA WARD

Hama ES
Amagasaki
Kanzaki Technica HS
Nagasu-higashi-dori
Jokoji
Imafuku
Kuise ES
Kuise-kitashinmachi
Kuise-honmachi
Kuise-minamishinmachi
Kuise
Kajigashima
Tsukida Jr. HS
Tsukuda-nishi ES
Tsukuda-minami ES
Tsukuda
Chibune
Kobun Gakuen Joshi HS
Dekijima
Dekijima
Dekijima ES
Yodogawa Steel Works
Owada
Owada ES
Higashi Yodo Jr. HS
Nishi-yodo Jr. HS
Himesato Shrine
Himejima Shrine
Ono
Fuku
Fuku ES
Fukumachi
Fukumachi
Hyakushima
Himejima ES
Himejima
Takami
Takami ES
Denpo ES
Denpo
Shinkanjima ES
Asahi
Shikanjima
Torishima ES
Torishima
Konohana Ward Office
Kasugade-kita
Baika Jr. HS
Konohana PO
Baika ES
Sakuya-konohana HS
Kasudaenaka
KasuKade Jr. HS
Kasugade-minami

to Osaka Int'l Airport
Oshimaco
Kaguhashi Shrine
JR Sanyo Shinkansen
Kashima
Juso-suji
Takejima
Kashima ES
Mitsushima Jr. HS
The Ezaki Memorial Hall
Mitsuya-kita
Mitsuya
Mitsuyanaka
Mitsuya-minami
Tagawa-kita
Tagawa
Juso-honma
Juso-moto-imaz
Tsukamoto
Shin-kit
Utajima
Nishi-Yodogawa Ward Office
Nozato
Nozato ES
Kashiwazato ES
Hanakawa
Kashiwazato
Ebie-nishi ES
Yasaka-kita
Yasaka Shrine
Sagisu
Ebie
Ohiraki
Fukushima Ward Office
Yoshino ES
Nishi-noda Koka HS
Noda
Noda ES
Nishi-Kujo
Nishi-kujo
Kawaguc
Kujo
Ajigawa

KONOHANA WARD

Hokko Yacht harbor
Tsuneyoshi
Maishima Heliport
Maishima Sludge Center
Barbecue Garden
Autocamp Site
Hokuko-ryokuchi
Amity Maishima
Maishima Pottery Village
Lodge Maishima
MAISHIMA SPORTS LAND
Maishima Arena
Maishima Incineration Plant
Tennis Court
Maishima Seaside Promenade
Maishima Baseball Stadium
Hokuko-shiratsu
Yumeshima-naka
Yumenai Ohashi (Movable Bridge)
Port of Osaka
Yumeshima-Higashi

YUMESHIMA ISLAND

Hokko Junction
Hokko-Nishi Ramp
Hokko
Sakurajima
Umemachi
Sakurajima
Shimaya ES
Shimaya
Hokko-dori
Simple Heart
Sumitomo Metals Osaka Steel Works
Ajikawa-guchi
JR Yumesaki Line
Universal City Walk
Kintetsu
Universal City
Nikko Bayside
Universal Studio Japan
Universal City Walk
Universal Port
Modern Transportation Museum
Benten
Bay Tower Osaka
Ishida
Benten ES
Minato Library
Ichioka Jr. HS
Tanaka
Tanaka ES
Isoji
Isoji ES
Yunagi
Ichioka
Ichioka ES
Mitsu Shrine
Minato-dori
Minato Ward Office
Osaka Pool
Asashiobashi

MINATO WARD

Tempozan Big Ferris Wheel
Rosei
Osaka Aquarium (Kaiyukan)
Market Place
Kaigan-dori
Osaka-ko
Seagull Tempozan Osaka
Suntory Museum
Minato-dori
Tempozan Junction
Nat'l Trade Fair Exhibition Hall
Minato Sumiyoshi Shrine
Chikko
Misaki
Ikejima
Kosei ES
Yahataya
Yahataya
Kosei
Fukuzaki

TAISHO WARD

Osaka Port (Int'l Ferry Terminal)
Cosmo Square
SEASIDE COSMO
Fureai Minato Kan
Cosmo Square
Morinomiya University of Medical Sciences
Wine Museum
Kongo Gakuen HS
Maritime Museum
Osaka Food's Outlet
ATC Green Eco Plaza
Grande Center Mae
Sportology Gallery
ATC Town Outlet Mare
WTC Cosmo Tower
ATC (Asia & Pacific Trade Center)
Intex Osaka
O's
SOAI University
Hyatt Regency Osaka
Nanko-kita Jr. HS
Nanko-kita ES
Nanko Wild Bird Sanctuary
Nanko-sakura ES
Nakafuto
Nanko-minami Jr. HS
Port Town Nishi
Port Town Higashi
Nanko-minami ES
Nanko Port Town Line
Nanko-midori ES
Nanko-nagisa ES
NANKO CHUO PARK
Nankonaka
to Kansai Int'l Airport

Tsuruhama
Tsuruhama-nishi
IKEA Tsuruhama
Taisho-kita HS
Kobayashi-nishi
Kobayashi
Hirao-ES
Hirao
Taisho-nishi Jr. HS
Taishi-tsurumachi PO
Taishi-tsurumachi
Taisho-dori
Minami-Okajima
Funamachi

Kujo-minami
Kujo-Minami
Minami-Ichioka
Sangenya higash'
Sangenya-nishi
Izu-kita ES
Izuo
Naka-izuo ES
Izuo-higashi ES
Kitamura
Kita-okajima ES
Kobayashi
Chishima
CHISHIMA PARK
Hirao

to Amagasaki
to Takamatsu
to Tokushima

Shin Yodo River
Kizugawa River

Scale 1 : 50,000

OSAKA STATION 58-59

OSAKA NAMBA 60-61

Wards: YODOGAWA WARD, KITA WARD, MIYAKOJIMA WARD, ASAHI WARD, FUKUSHIMA WARD, JOTO WARD, NISHI WARD, CHUO WARD, HIGASHINARI WARD, NANIWA WARD, TENNOJI WARD, IKUNO WARD, NISHINARI WARD, ABENO WARD

Shin Yodo River

Yodo River

OGIMACHI PARK, OSAKA BUSINESS PARK, OSAKA-JO PARK, NAKANOSHIMA PARK, UTSUBO PARK, TENNOJI PARK, JOHOKU PARK, NAIWA-NO-MIYA-ATO PARK, Tsurumiryokuchi Expo '90 Commemorative Park, KYUHOJI RYOKUCHI PARK

Osaka Castle, Osaka Historical Museum, Osaka Prefectural Government Office, Osaka International Peace Center, Hokoku Shrine

Tsutenkaku Tower, Shitenno-ji, Tennoji Zoo, Spa World, Osaka Municipal Museum of Art

to Suita, to Moriguchi, to Shijonawate, to Nara, to Matsubara, to Sakai, to Sakai

Hanshin Expressway Moriguchi Line, Hanshin Expressway Matsubara Route, Midosuji Line, Tanimachi Line, Sakaisuji Line, Imazatosuji Line, JR Osaka Loop Line, Keihan Line, JR Tozai Line, Kintetsu Nara Osaka Line, Nankai Koya Line, Nankai Main Line, Inner Loop Route, JR Katamachi (Gakkentoshi) Line, JR Kansai (Yamatoji) Line, Osaka Higashi Line

New Osaka, JR Osaka, JR Namba, Kintetsu Nipponbashi, Namba, Kyobashi, Tsuruhashi, Imazato, JR Tennoji, Abeno, Tengachaya, Fuse

Route markers: 2, 8, 13, 25, 26, 29, 30, 41, 43, 159, 163, 168, 172, 173, 308, 423, 479, 702, 5

to Osaka Int'l Airport
YODOGAWA RIVERSIDE PARK
to Toyonaka
Mido-suji
Gallery Namban
Nakatsu 7
Juso Bypass
Nakatsu 6
Nakatsu-roku PO
Nippon Tsuun
Mitsubishi
Saiseikai Nakatsu Hospital
176
Kisyu Tetsudo JR West
New H
Kashiwazato 1
Yodogawa
Nobuhara Soko
Oyodo-Kita 1
Nakatsu-minami ES
Umeda Dormitory
Osaka Parcel Post Office
Nakatsu 5
Shibata 2
Saizen-ji 1
Yayoi Kaikan
Shoko Chukin
Oyodo Haisuijo
Nobuhara Soko
OYODO KITA PARK
Koman-ji
Umeda Sky Bldg
Germany
Shin-Umeda City
Landmark Umeda
New Hanky
Hanshin Expressway No. 11 Ikeda Route
JR Kobe Line
Nihon Paint HQ
Manyo
Meiji Sangyo
Toppan
Tohan
Oyodo-naka 2
Vocational School
Resona Trust
Yodobashi Camera
Oyodo-naka 3
The Westin Osaka
Kamotsu Station
Ofukacho
NISHI-YODOGAWA-WARD
FUKUSHIMA-WARD
Marudai Foods
OYODO-NAKA
Oyoda Jr. HS
KITA-WARD
FUKUSHIMA-WARD
JR Umeda Freight Train Station
Visitors Informati
Gare Osaka
Acty Osaka
OSAKA STATION
YODOGAWA RIVERSIDE PARK
Oyodo-naka 5
Oyodo-naka 4
Oyodo ES
Fuji Jidosha
Osaka Tower
Daimaru
Umeda
Hanshin
JAL
Riverside Sagisu Apts
Shoraku-ji
Oyodo-minami 3
Oyodo-minami 2
Symphony Hall
Nippon Tsuun
Osaka Central PO
Hilton Plaza
Daiko
Umeda 3
Osaka Shiki Theater
Umeda 2
Nishi-Umeda
Ebie 3
Sagisu 6
Yasaka Jr. HS
URAE PARK
Ensho-ji
Gusto
Monterey Daiwa House
Hello H
Sagisu 5
Kinrakai HS
KM Nishi-umeda
Osaka Central Hospital
Meiji Yasuda Seimei
Herbis
Breeze Tower
The Ritz Carlton
Sakurabashi
Sakurabashi
Ekimae Da Ichi Bldg
Nankei-ji
Ebie 4
Ebiehigashi ES
Shionogi Central Laboratories
Sagisu ES
Myoju-ji
YM
Mainichi Newspapers
TKP Gate Tower
Second Inn
AX
Toyo
Kita-Shinchi
Ebie 5
Yasaka Shrine
Ebie PO
JR Kobe Line
Mansei Denki
Shoten Kyotoku-in
KAMI-FUKUSHIMA PARK
Vista Premi
Sonezaki
Ebienishi
ES
Dainippon Pharma
Sagisu 2
Shotenmae PO
Kami-Fukushima
Mister Donut
Dojima 2
Sonezaki-shinchi
Sonezaki shinchi
DOJIMA
Ebie 2
Ebie 5
Matsumoto Hospital
Wiste
Senko-ji
Kido
Toyota
FUKUSHIMA PARK
Daihatsu
Joyu-ji
Dojima 3
NTT Telepark Dojima
Shin Fujita
Dentsu
Fujita Toyobo
Dojima 2
Keihan
Kintetsu
Dojima
Mizuho
Ebie 8
Ebie 5
Ebie 7
Hanshin Main Line
Fukushima 8
Kosho-ji
Shin-Fukushima
Fukushima
Fukushima Tenmangu Shrine
The Teppet Osaka
Toyobo
Suntory
Axis
Denmark
to Nishinomiya
National Line Highway Route No. 2
Ebie
Noda-Hanshin
Noda
Sagisu 3
Fukusen-ji
Lawson
Fukushima 2
Public Prosecutor's Office
Nakanoshima-dori
Watanabebashi
Dai Bldg
Asahi Shimbun
Mit Bu Festival Hall
Nishi-noda Koka HS
Fukushima PO
Yoshino 1
Vocational School
Hongu-ji
Fukushima ES
Kansai Electric Power Hospital
Asahi Broadcasting
Dojimagawa
NAKANOSHIMA
Kansai Electric Power
Nakanoshima 4
Asahi
Apa
Ohiraki 1
Ohiraki ES
Yoshino 2
Fujita Hospital
Honda
Tamagawa ES
Osaka Koseinenkin Hospital
SHIMO-FUKUSHIMA PARK
Saizen-ji
Community Plaza
NAKANOSHIMA
N4 Tower
NTT
National Museum of Art
Nakanoshima
Yamabun
Ohiraki 2
Fukushima Police Office
Yoshino PO
Yoshino ES
Teshima Hospital
Yazaki Sogyo
Osaka Science Museum
Kincho Tosabori
Osaka Church
Tosabori 1
Nippon Koa
Sompo
Pacific Life
Yoshino 3
Shin-Namiwasuji
Shimo-fukushima Pool
Honjo-ji
King Mansion
Dojimagawa
Grancub Osaka
Rehga Royal
Tosabori
In Bldg
Sanyo
Seven Eleven
Super
Risso
Center Bldg
Tamagawa
Noda
Yoshino 4
New Matsugae
Tamagawa 4
Shimo-fukushima Jr. HS
NEC Fielding
Sumitomo Hospital
Fuji Xerox
Edobori Center
Nishi-senba ES
Edobori 1
Kyomachibori 2
NISHISENBA PARK
Yoshinoya
Noda Jr. HS
Subway Sennichimae Line
Tamagawa 3
Max
Ajinomoto
Nakanoshima Center Building
NCB
Nakanoshima 6
NTT
Family Inn
Edobori 2
Tenshin
Kinki
Myojo
OSTEC
(Osaka Science & Technology Center)
JR Osaka Loop Line
Noda 3
Tamagawa 3
NCB
Fujikura Shoji
Hananoi Jr. HS
Edobori-dori
EDOBORI NAKA PARK
Itachibori 2
Kyomachibori-dori
Utsubo Tennis Center
UTSUBO PARK
Noda Jr. HS
Noda ES
Noda 2
Furudsu Bashi
Kamishinaru Bashi
Minami
Bashi
Super Edobori 1
Tennenonsen
EDOBORI NISHI PARK
Tanigaki
Utsubohonmachi 2
IBM Japan
Shinanobasi Mitsui
Noda 5
Noda 1
Osaka Central Wholesale Market
Showa-Bashi
Chida
Enokojima 2
Mazda Kidoriya
Yamanashi Hospital
China
CPC
UTSUBO PARK
City Route Yanase
Park Hotel
Okazaki
172
Nishi-kujo 1
Noda 6
Noda 4
Sumitomo Soko
Look
Honmachi-dori
Kizugawa-Bashi
Okuuci
Sun Life
New Oriental
Nishi-honmachi 2
Tachibana Eletech
Nishi-honmachi
Kanda
Tatsuno
Fuso
Ajigawa 1
Ajigawa
Kawaguchi 2
Nishi Police Office
Enokojima 1
Honden ES
Osaka-nishi PO
Awaza
Chuo-Odori
Inaba Denki
Awaza 2
Toyopet
NTT
Anglers
Awaza 1
Park Bldg
Honden 4
Kujo 3
Kawaguchi 3
Kawaguchi 1
172
16
Osaka Port Route
Yokohama Tire
Nankyoku
Sumitomo Mitsui
Dai-ichi Kogyo
Meiji ES
Shohin Torihikijo
Shokuryo
Itachibori 1
Higashi Shink
Honden 3
Honden 2
Hanshin Expressway No. 16 Osaka Port Route
Kizugawa-Ohashi
Nissei Hospital
SHIMAZU PARK
Oin-ji
Shofuku-ji
AWAZA MINAMI PARK
Yamazen
Itachibori 3
Sanko Industry
Olix Theater
Kawata
Dais
Ajiwara 1
Honden PO
Owatari-Bashi
Nishi Indoor Pool
Inoue Byora Kogyo
Monsada
Kogyo
Chiyoda Seiki
Dunlop Falken
Renown
Fusen Usagi
SHINMACHI PARK
Daiwa Roynet
to Tenpozan
Osaka Kisaikai Hospital
Honden 1
Itachibori 5
Itachibori 6
Konkokyo
VW
to Sakai
Shinmachi 3
Shinmachi
DG
ISS

N

to Minotani ↑ Tennodani-higashifuku

Tennodani-
higashifukuyama

HIYODORI
VIEW PARK

Karasuhara-chosuichi
Reservoir

Tennocho

Myoho-ji

HIRANODAI
VIEW PARK

Hiranocho

Family
Mart

Hiyodorigoesuji

Tachie-ji

Gyoshu-ji

Chidoricho

Sannocho

Namiyatoyamacho

Spa Minatoyama

Gion Shrine

Shofuku-ji

Koyamacho

Kitayamacho

Tsuyunocho

Kami-sanjocho

Kami-gioncho

Shimizucho

Ishiicho

Takiyamacho

Kumanocho

Komyo-ji

Daidocho

Reizan-ji

Minatoyama ES

Jizo-in
Myokan-ji

Gonomiyacho

Umemotocho

Chofuku-ji

Kumano Shrine

Yuki-no-goshocho

Tofuku-ji

Kobe-gonomiya
PO

Kobe Water
Science

Kobe Yam
Coll

Hiyodorigoe ES

Hirano ES

Kobe Koyukai
Clinic

Yumenocho

Shimo-sanjocho

Shimo-gioncho

Myoso-ji

Myoko-ji

Yabecho

Kusudanicho

Futatabisujiche

Kobe-hiyodorigoe PO

Yui
Hospital

KIKUSUI
PARK

Minato
JHS

Lawson

Joko-ji

Kandacho

Yamamoto-

Minatogawacho

Minatogawa
Hospital

Kikusuicho

Prison

Aishin
Gakuen

Yamanote ES

Kobe Ch
Dobun Sch

Kobe-minatogawa PO

Family Court

Babacho

Sonko-ji

Kumano Shrine

Kobe Immigration
Head office

Chinese Mouse
(Kanteibyo)

Shorin-ji

Kikusuicho

Arata ES

HYOGO WARD

Tokusho-ji

Kobe Marines
Kosei Hospital

Hoon-ji

Higashiyama ES

Zensho-ji

Myogo-ji

Butsuryu-ji

Kobe
Tamon

Municipal Medical
College Hospital

OKURAYAMA
PARK

Kobe Chuo
Municipal Library

Community
Plaza

Seven
Eleven

EGEYAMA
PARK

Zenko-ji

Kobe Gakuin
HS

Higashi
Hangan-ji

Kobe Arata PO

Mariner's
Hall

Seven
Eleven

Kobe Church
(Protestant)

Hanakumacho

Omoikecho

Hampo-ji

Egeyamacho

Oi-dori

Kawasaki

Seven
Eleven

Public Bath

Keitoku-ji

Kogan-ji

Apartment

Kobe
Medical
College

Escale
Kobe

Honju-ji

Fukutoku-ji
Toyofuku

Matsumoto-dori

Hokke-ji

Kusunoki HS

Hyogo
Ward Office

Daie

Ohara
Hospital

Minato Shonan
Jr.HS

Kobe-shimo-yamate PO

Kobe Gajoen

Hokke-ji

Kobe Bunka Hall

Shimo-yamate-dori

Greenclub

Minatogawa
ES

MINATOGAWA
PARK

Minatogawa-
tamon ES

Kusunokicho

Modern-dera
Temple

Kuma
Hospital

Inoue
Hospital

Egeyama ES

Seishin-Yamate Line

Kobe Kosoku

Hanakuma

Kamisawa-dori

Kobekamisawa PO

Bowling
Center

Tōyoko
Inn

Casabella Inn

Kargto
Clinic

Municipal
Gymnasium

The Kobe Bar
Association Hall

Motomachi-d

Daily
Yamazaki

Circle K

District
Court

District Legal
Affairs Bureau

Nishi
Motomachi

Motomachi Cake

Mina
Moton

Tozan-ji

Jotoku-ji

Shimosawa-dori

Kobe Water
Works Dept.

Kobe-
tachibana
PO

Sakaemachi-dori

Funeral Hall

Family Mart

Fukusen-ji

Pachinko

Tachibana-dori

Minatogawa
Shrine

am pm

Kobe-nakamichi PO

Nakamichi-dori

Mizuki-dori

Kadoya Ryokan

Pasto

Nakamichidori

Mizukami

Hikosaka
Hospital

Tamon-dori

Friendly
NTT Kobe

Central
Post Office

Nakao

Round One

Clio

Kosoku-Kobe

Urban

Life

Yoshinoya

Seven
Eleven

Bentencho

to Akashi

Tax Office

Shinkaichi

Funeral Hall

Nakamachi-dori

Chisun Hotel

HDC

Kobe Crystal
Tower

Le Suite K

Harborlan

Daikai

Kobe Kosoku

Manekiya

Hyogo PO

Winbell
Magic

Asahi
Capsule &
Sauna

Shinkaichi

Kominato-dori

Kobi

Duo Kobe

Kobe
Gas Light

Kamomeria
(Naka Pier
Central Muse
Terminal)

Daikai-dori

Hyogo
Daikai ES

Gril Kimpura

Kobe Hamate Byr

Kobe
Sishu-G

Daiya
Parking

Kohnan

Port To

Tsukamoto-dori

Gomyo
Clinic

Itsukushima
Shrine

Eizawacho

KAVC Hall

Aioicho

Crown Plaza

Promena
Kobe

HaRe

Daiya
Parking

South Mall

Harborland

Meijiya Kobe Chuo-tei
Queen Rokko
Terminal

Sky Lounge

Naka Pie
Termina

Gokuraku-ji

Kobe-tsukamoto PO

Hyogo
JHS

Dolf
Kobe

Largo
TN

Tsukemen Shinki

Familio

Culmeni

Mosaic Mall

Joei-ji

Luminous

Hasaka-dori

Hachio-ji

Mikawaguchicho

Ebara

Maya Hyogo HS

Mason View
Harborland

Kobe
Education
Center

Rengasako

Syliphide Arrivals
& Departures

Hyogo

Shopping U

Sunkus

Fukukai-ji

Kuon-ji

Minato
Hachiman
Shrine

Kosho-ji

Kyoshu
Temple

Blind

Minato ES

Kobe Anpanman Kodomo
Museum & Mall

Mosaic Garden
Amusement Park

McDonald's

am pm

Nishi-yanagiwaracho

Fukugon-ji

Hyogocho

Sabiecho

Higashi-kawasakicho

Family Mart

Kobe Sea Bus Port Tours
Arrivals & Departures

Seven
Eleven

Hamasaki-dori

Monguchicho

Erin-ji

Saiko-ji

Fujino-Tera

Nishidemachi

HIGASHI
KAWASAKI
PARK

Site of the
old Kobe
Port Signal

Ekiminami-dori

Public Bath

Hanshin Expressway Kobe Line

Kobe-honmachi PO

Higashidemachi

Nishi-miyauchicho

Higashi-yanagiwaracho

Honmachi

McDonald's

Shichinomiya
Shrine

Matsuo-inari
Shrine

Higashide PO

to Akashi

Sunkus

Irie-dori

Nishi-nakamachi

Business Inn
Yutaka

Kawanishi Soko

Kawasaki Jukogyo

Meishin ES

Ogawa-dori

Nofuku-ji

am pm

Kajiyacho

Family Mart

Susano-dori

Minami-sakasegawacho

Shimagamicho

Shichinomiyacho

Matsubara-dori

Ogiharamisaki
Hospital

Isonocho

Kobematsubara PO

Susano JHS

Kiretocho

Funadaikucho

Toa Gaigyo

Ashihara-dori

Shinko-ji

489

Central Wholesale
Market

Seven
Eleven

Auto Bachs

Nakanoshima

Chuoichibamae

Yakusen-ji

Dezaikecho

Tsukijicho

le 1 : 15,000 200m 500ft

Mt. Dotoku

Kuchienkobo

Kyonoo

Sanroku By-pass

Sanyo Shinkansen

Sanroku By-pass

Nunobikio-daki

Higashiyama

Meoto-daki

Nunobikyuenchi

Tokuka-in-ji Kobe Ichi HS

Fukiaicho

Nunobikiyama

Umadome

Kobeko-jikata

Kuchijchiriyama

SHIROYAMA TEMBO PARK

Shinkobe Tunnel

Nunobikime-daki

NUNOBIKI PARK

Nunobiki Jr.HS

be Yamate Women's JHS

+ Mt. Suwa

Futatabi Driveway

Venus Bridge

Suwa Shrine

SUWAYAMA PARK

wayamacho

Kazamidori-no-Yakata

Moegi-no-Yakata

Former of Panama Consulate

Yamate Hachiban-kan,
Uroko-no-ie,
Uroko Museum

Kitano Tenman Shrine

Shin-Kobe Ropeway

Kitano Foreigners Association

Kitano Club Soda

Herb-en
Sanroku

Shin-Kobe

Sun Members HS

Hosai-ji

Isago

Kumochicho

Shin-Kobe Oriental Theater

Oriental Avenue

Kobe Nadaman Crowne Plaza

Shin-Kobe

Kobe Geijutsu Center

Unchu ES

Fukiai JHS

Kitanocho

Original Holand House

Kobe Kitano Museum

Former of Chinese Consulate

Platon
Decorative Art Museum

Grand Vista

Yoshinoya

Kumochibashi-dori

American Teddy Museum

Jewish Center

Jofuku-ji

Rhine House

England House

Ben's House

Green Hill Kobe

Holliday Inn Express Shin-Kobe

Kozen-ji

Kobe Club

Roteroze

Kitano Street

Yamamoto-dori

Koson-ji

Grasiani

Starbucks

Yokan Nagaya

Green Hill Urban

Union Church (Protestant)

Seven Eleven

Ninomiyach

Chapel Suite

Chueke House

Asshu

Indian Consulate General

Ijinkan Street (Yamamoto St)

Kobe Baptist Church

Kitano Rokko-so

Daisen-ji

Piena Kobe

Chuo ES

Meiho Hospital

Kamiwaka-dori

Shinko HS

Pearl Street

Kitano Meister Garden

Hunter Zaka

Catholic Kobe Central Church

Kobe Kita No-Saka

New Kobe

Ninomiya ES

Kobe Kur Haus

Grand Chariot

Shozen-ji

Saiho-ji

Totenkaku

Hyogo Kyosai Kaikan

Kobe Women's University

Seven Eleven

Fudo-Zaka

Yuzuson-ji

Tofuku-ji

Arakuma-inari Shrine

Ueda-ji

Nakayamate-dori

Sorakuen Hall

SORAKUEN GARDEN

Kobe ES

Kobe Yamamotodori PO

St. Michal's Int'l School

NHK

Korean Consulate

Sannomiyat

Marutakachukasoba

Kunika-dori

Kasuganomichi

Michael's athedral

Hyogo Prefectural Govt. Office

Rasse Hall

Pato

Nakayamate Street

Ikuta Fire Station

Seishin-Yamate Line

Ninomiya Shrine

Ninomiya Ryokan

Wakana-dori

Shinonome-dori

Kobe-kasugano PO

Kenchomae

Eiko (Protestant)

Tor Road

Monterey Amalie

Area One

Ramen Taro

Kitagami Annex

Seven Eleven

Shoo-ji

Prefectural Police HQ

Tor Road

Ikuta Shrine

Higashimon Gai

Tokyu Hands

Business Tomoe

Sansei Hospital

Hankyu-Kobe Line

JR Kobe Line

Higashi Kobe Clinic

Ks Maison Sylphide

Prefectural GH

Shinkaku-ji

Sunkus

Kobe Hand

am pm

Asahi-dori

Sannomiya

Higure-dori

Yagumo-dori

Ogihara Orthopedic

Kita-nagasa-dori

Kobe Ikuta JHS

Palmore Hospital

Kokawa Avenue

Kadomoku

Sannomiya

Kobe Sauna

Business Hotel Sanyo

Sannomiya Terminal

Suncity Kat

Hanshin Line

Azuma-dori

Lawson

AKUMA k

Motomachi

Motomachi-koka-dori

Kobe Kosoku

Seven Eleven

Sannomiya

Sun City

M-Int Kobe

Marutaka

Kumoi-dori

Suzume

Toyoko Inn Kobe Sannomiya

Seven Eleven

Family Mart

Fukiai PO

to Osaka

Motomachi Shopping-dori

Smile

Kobe Plaza

Center Plaza West

Center Plaza

Sun Plaza

Marui

Sogo Dept. Store

Tokyu Inn

Kobe Int'I Inn

Labor

Sansaido

Nat'l Highway Route 2

BMW

NTT Nishi-H

Toyoko Inn Kobe Sannomiya

Kita-honmachi-dori

Kasuganomichi

Sakaemachi-dori

R&B Kobe Motomachi

Assiette

Kobe Bal

Tsutaya

Sanchika Plaza

Sonnomiya

Hanadokei-mae

Kobe Int'l Hall

APA

Daiwa Roynet

Goko-dori

Sannomiya Union

Onoe-dori

Minami-honmachi-dori

Nankin-Machi (China Town)

Vega

Kyu-Kyoryuchi Daimaru-mae

Sannomachi

Akashimachi

Daimaru Kobe

Tokyu Bizfort

Trusty Kobe

Edomachi

Kobe City Hall

Ipsx East

Isogami-dori

Masago-dori

Kobe Hakuai

Kobe Kakyo Historical Museum

Naniwamachi

Itomachi

ISOGAMI PARK

1-2-3 Kobe

to Osaka

Nishimachi

Maemachi

Shosen Mitsui

Taiwa Bldg

Via Mare Kobe

Hachiman-dori

Sunroute Sopia Kobe

WAKINOHAMA PARK

Nagisa ES

Wakinohama-kaigan-dori

Yusen Bldg

Shinko Bldg

Oriental

Kyomachi

Kyomachisui

Kobe Lamp Museum

Flower Clock

Seven Eleven

Hamame-dori

HAT YUME PARK

to Osaka

atobacho

Cafe Fish

Fish Dance Hall

Mitsui Bldg

Charterd Bldg

Bank of Japan

Kobe City Museum

HIGASHI YUENCHI PARK

Earthquake Memorial Monument

City Ground

Urban View Kobe Sannomiya

am pm

Isobe-dori

Boeki Center

Hamame-dori

Circle K

Marine Observatory

Kobe Red Cross Hospital

be Kaiyo Museum

KOBEKO SHINSAI MEMORIAL PARK

Higashimachi

Kansai Electric Co.

Kobe Sanbo Hall

Trade Center

Kobe Kaigan

Onohamacho

Port of Kobe

Kobe Sea Bus Arrivals Departure

eriken Park

Meriken Pier

Pier 1

Port of Kobe

Kobe Customs

Onohamacho

MINATO-NO-MORI PARK

Hanshin Expressway Kobe Line

to Osaka

Pier 3

Shin Port Ferry Terminal

Design Creative Center Kobe

Mitsui Soko

Fuji Film Logistics

Mevius Co.,Ltd

su, Osaka

Osaka Bay

Port Terminal

to Port Island, Kobe Airport

Scale 1 : 17,500   200m   500ft

Konoike Ballpark Baseball Stadium
Konoike Athletic Track & Field Stadium
Nara Prison   Prison
Nara YH
Handabirakicho
Kozenincho
to Kasagi
Nakamura Sangyo
Mikasa Hot Spring
Mikasa
Heijo
Nataokuyama Drive Way

Mureshikaso
Horensahoyama
Dai-ni Budojo
City Central Gymnasium
Konoike
Meteorological Observatory
Budo Gymnasium
Tamon-jo Castle Site
District Weather Bureau
Jofuku-ji
Higashi-nosaka
Koren-ji
Kawakamicho
Goko-in
Kita-mikadocho
Jukkokudai

Chokei-ji
Konbu-in
Paket
44
Shomutenno-ryo (Mausoleum)
Imperial Mausoleum of Empress Komyo
Tamatetsu-inari Shrine
Kawakamicho
369
Zoshicho
Pension Nara Club
Kukai-ji
Chisoku-in
Ryusho-in
Jiho-in
Hogen-in

YH Nara Seishonen Kaikan
Kasuganoso
Hatakeyama
Ichijo-dori
104
Sahogawa Tenmangu Shrine
104
Tegari-mon Gate
Tsuzaka ES
Ryuzo-in
Kaizando
Hoju-in
Nigatsu-do

Horencho
Saho ES
Hide Iku HS
Horencho
Hide Iku ES
Kita-fukurocho
Higashi-kanenagacho
Higashi-sasabokocho
Imakojicho
Daibutsuike
TODAI-JI
Zoshicho
Shunjodo
Shigatsu-do
Sammaido
Sangatsu-do

Nishi-shinzakikecho
Yaomata Sawai Hospital
Nara Perfectural University
Nishi-sasabokocho
Naka-mikadocho
Seiryo-in
Kaidan-in
Soji-in
Chu-mon Gate
Daibutsu-den (Great Buddha Hall)
Shoro Belfry
Karakuni Shrine
Tamukeyama Hachimangu Shrine
NAGI FOREST

Komugiko
Kitakojicho
Daily Yamazaki
Nashiharacho
Nara Women's University
Gotocho
Kawakubocho
Tamaru
Shingon-in
Ruin of Saito (West Tower)
Nagami ike
Ruin of Toto (East Tower)
Kannon-in
Kasugano Inn
NAGI

Miyako Sushi
Coop
Shobuikecho
Mameyamacho
Nabeyacho
Yamato
NHK
Yurugicho
Suimoncho
Jizo-in
Nandai-mon Gate
Todai-ji
Todai-ji Library
Kasugano Inn
Matsu-no-ya Inn
Mikasa

Okushibacho
Rencho-ji
Takamaichicho
Yashima Shrine
Nara Public Procurator's Office
Nara Hakushika-so Inn
Green Hotel Ashibi
Nara District Court
Noborioicho
Nara Prefectural Cultural Hall
Nara Library
Prefectural Museum
Nara Police Sta.
Neiraku Museum
NARA KOEN (NARA PARK)
ISUIEN GARDEN
Nara Park Silk Road Exchange Hall
Musashino Inn
Sugimoto
NARA PARK
Mizuyagawa

369
Saiho-ji
Imperial Mausoleum of Emperor Kaika
Kangoku Shrine
Nara Prefectural Office
369
Shizuka
Kankoso
Himuro Shrine
Sanshutei
Prefectural Public Hall
Miharu-tei
Fuun Shrine
Hitokotonushi Shrine
Tsukihitei
Mizuya Shrine
Motomiya Shrine

Noborioji Avenue
Hayashi Shrine
Hanako michi
Tenpyo-inn
Noborioji Kasuga
Fluke Cafe
Hokuendo
Three Storied Pagoda
Honbo Main Hall
KOFUKU-JI
Nara Int'l Seminar House
Nara National Museum
Nara National Museum Annex
Hiranojaya
Turunojaya
Kasuga Taisha Kamizono
Kasuga Taisha Homotsu-den
KAZUGA TAISHA SHRINE
Kasuga Taisha Homotsu-den Trasure House
Mt. Mikasa-yama 293m

Imperial Mausoleum of Emperor Kaika Asyl
Washington
Nara Japanese Language School
Nanto
Vivre
Mellow
Hiranoya
Coco
Hakubo
Five Storied Pagoda
Daibutsukan
Kikusuiin
Eizan-ji
Edo-san Inn
Asajigahara
Manyo Botanical Garden
Ni-no-Torii
Second Torii Gate
Wakamiya Shrine
Kinryu Shrine

Sanjo Nara
New Iroha
Super Hotel JR Naraekimae
Kitamukicho
Isagawa Shrine
Denko-ji
Kyoso-An
Ayura Cafe
Tenpyo
NARA
Sanjo-dori
Kaeruen
Sunkus
Kitamukicho
Ogawacho
Tsubakishou
Nishi-jodocho
Hiraso
Yoshino Inn
Yoshidaya
Yamatoji
Sarusawaso
Asukaso
Koto Inn
Koto Inn
Matsumae
Nara Hotel
Suntoute
ROKUEN (DEER PARK)
Kataoka
Tobuhino
Ukimi-do
Sagiike
KKR Nara Mikasa-so
Munakata Shrine
Kii Shrine

Super Hotel Lohas JR Nara-eki
Oku-komoricho
Nara-Kotsu Bus Center
Comfort
Tokigan-ji
Raigo-ji
Nakata B&B
Tera Machi
Mimatsu
Uosa
Nara-machi (Nara Old Town)
Furuichi
Fushigata-
Araike
Takahata
Shiga Naoya Former House

Komachi GH
Minami-jodocho
Kitamurocho Tempura Asuka
Sugioka Calligraphy Museum
Harishin
GANGO-JI (Gokuraku-bo)
Rahotsu
Welness Asukaji
Magatama No le
754
Suruga-machi
Minami-uoyacho
Shimo-mikadocho
Yuan
Naramachi Monogatari-kan
Naramachi Museum
Kosode
Gen
Fukuchi-in
80
Takabatakecho
Shin-Yakushi-ji
Nara University of Educational
Nara City Museum of Photography

Hiden-in
Saiko-in
Jurin'in-hatamachi
Juriinhatamachi
Zuto
Omoricho
Minami-shinmachi
Anyo-in
Sakuraya
Kidaeracho
Hiki Shrine
Asuka Jr.HS

Seibi ES
Nabara
Jaguar
Tokuyu-ji
Seiko-in
Saiko-ji
Mars Lapin
Rakuyo
Asuka ES
169

Higashi-kitsujicho
Seikan-so
Naramachi Koushi-no-le
Kawanokamicho
Tsujinouchicho
Asuka ES
80

Bu Ke
Kasuga Jr.HS
Nishi-kitsujicho
Nagai Clinic
Matsukura Hospital
Inouecho
Kawaradocho
Naramachi
Nara Shinkin Bank
Renjo-ji
to Tenri
Narajoshidai Fuzoku HS
Gakusei Kaikan

Scale 1 : 60,000   1km   0.5mile

Asuka

Okubo Machizukuri-kan
Okubo Kita ES
Okwa
Shimoyatsuchiro
to Nara
Nara Research Inst. for Cultural Properties
Amanokaguyama
Minamiurocho

Okubocho
Hidacho
Archaeological Institute
Unebigoryomae
Motoyakushi-ji Ruins
161
Kamihidacho
Amanoiwato Shrine
Kaigecho
Kashihara City Insectarium
Minamiyamacho

Unebicho
125
Kashihara Kanko
Polytechnic
Tanakacho
Kiduki Shrine
Daikandai-ji Ruins
Jofuku-ji
Yamada-dera Ruins

Eiwacho
Kashihara Shrine
Gobocho
Unebi Jr.HS
Koyama
206
Asuka Historical Museum
Higashi Otani Himemikoto Shrine

Kumecho
Royal
Ikatsuchi
124
214
Yatsuri
Asuka Nimasu Shrine
Higashiyama

Kashiharajingumae
Wadacho
Toyoura
Amakashi HILL
Asuka
Manyo Culture Complex
Asuka Oohara
Asuka Folk Museum

207
Unebi Higashi ES
Shobucho
Gojonocho
ASUKA REKISHI PARK AMAKASHIOKA AREA
Kawahara-dera
Asuka Town Office
Haruta Shrine
Oka-dera

Shirakashi Kita ES
Unebi Minami ES
Ogarucho
Misono
Asuka School for the Disabled
Kawahara
Asuka ES
Oka

Okadera
169
Noguchi
Tomb of Temmu-tenno
205
Tachibana-tenno
Tachibana
Shimasho
Jogo
155

Shirakashi Minami ES
Minamiyohojicho
Asuka Historical Park Museum
Hirata
Takamatsuzuka Hekiga-kan
Yasaka Shrine
Ishibutai Tomb
Iwaido

to Koya-Ryujin
Asuka Koshi
Tomb of Marukoyama
Mayumi
Misono
Saiho-ji
210
Takamatsuzuka Tomb
to Yoshino
Takanatsuka
Asuka Inabuchi Palace Ruins
Sakada

Scale 1 : 60,000   1km   0.5mile

Yoshino

Senbonguchi
to Oyodo
Tomb of Murakami Yoshiteru
Yoshinoyama
37

Ryokan Kato
Sakoya
Tatsumiya
YOSHIMIZU SHRINE
Mt. Funaoka

JIKUSAN FOREST PARK
Mausoleum of Kukai
KIMPUSEN-JI
YOSHINOYAMA
Yoshino Onsen Motoyu
Ebisukan
Nyoirin-ji

Mt. Tenjiku 918m
Toro-do Hall
15
Yoshino Onsen Motoyu
Kamimachi

Okuno-in
Gokusho Offering Hall
Katte Shrine
Kizo-in
MT. YOSHINO

Naka-no-hashi Bridge
Chikurinin Gumpoen
257
Chikurin-in
Kami-sembon

to Hashimoto
Oku-no-in-mae Bus Stop
371
YOSHINO-MIKURI SHRINE
Komori

Nakanohashi
371
257
to Shimoichi
Tonode
SAITANI
Naka
KIMPU SHRINE

Tamagawa
Tini
48
Saisho-ji
Iwakura

to Koya-Ryujin
to Tenkawa
to Ominesan-ji

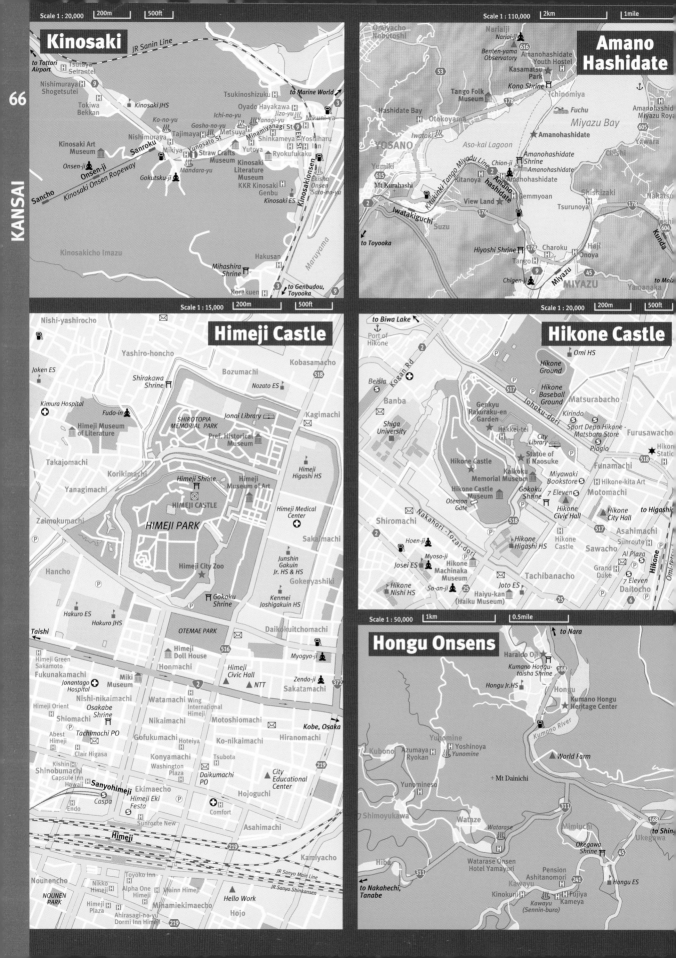

Scale 1 : 300,000

5km

2miles

Lake Biwa

Lake Biwa

HIKONE CASTLE 66

to Noto Peninsula, Kanazawa

to Nagoya

to Osaka

to Nagoya

to Kyoto

Sea of Japan

Tottori
TOTTORI 75

Matsue
MATSUE 74

Izumo

Yonago

Kurayoshi

Tsuyama

Niimi

Miyoshi

Okayama
OKAYAMA 75

Kurashiki
KURASHIKI 75

Takamatsu

Onomichi
ONOMICHI 74

SHODO ISLAND 68

Osaka Bay

Harima-nada Sea

Fukuyama

Higashi-hiroshima

Hiroshima Airport

Takehara

Marugame

Tokushima

Niihama

Imabari

Hiuchi-nada Sea

Matsuyama

to Kochi

to Osaka

to Kobe

to Himeji

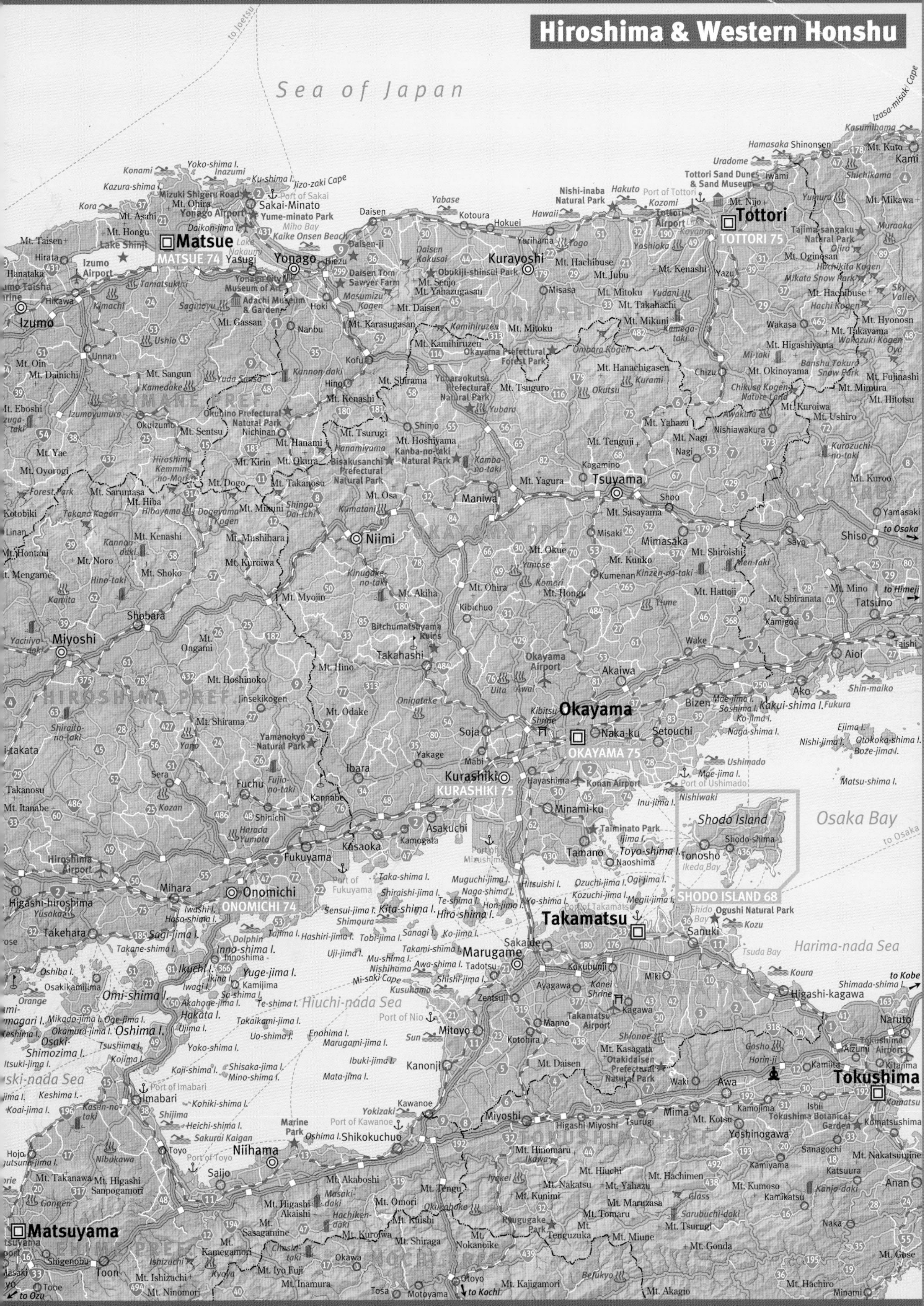

to Ozuka

Taiyu-in

Ryuocho

to Oshiba

Misasa Shrine
Koseido Nagasaki Hospital
JR Kabe Line
7 Eleven

Kasunokicho

183

JR Sanyo Main Line

Yokogawaeki

Kabe Kaido

Johoku-dori

Misasa Bridge

34

Poplar
7 Eleven

Yamatecho

JR Sanyo Shinkansen Line

Hiroshima City Nishi Kumin Bunka Center

Yokogawacho

7 Eleven

Setouchi Kanko

Sanyo Marunako

NISHI WARD

Koi-higashi

Hiroshima Ongaku HS

Notre Dame Seishin HS

Expressway No. 4

Nakahiromachi

Kojinkai Makidonojun Memorial Hospital

Yokogawa-shinmachi

Vocational School

7 Eleven

Yokogawa Line

Yokogawa Itchome

Yokogawa Shinbashi Bridge

Public Bath

P

Koi-naka

Ota River

JR Sanyo Main Line

Power Plant

Jonan-dori

7 Eleven

Nakahiro HS

Family Mart

Nakahiro-dori

Hiroshima International House

Betsuinmae

183

Jisso-ji
Kyojun-ji
Hongan-ji
Hiroshima Betsuin
Joman-ji
Kofuku-ji
Josen-ji
Tokuo-ji
Koen-ji
Joko-ji

Teramachi

Motomachi

Motomachi Shopping Centr

Motomachi E

Hosen Bo
Zensho Bo
Enryu-ji
Shozen Bo
Ganjo-ji
Chosen-ji

Hirose-kitamachi

Hirose ES

Lawson

265

Subaru Technical Center

Tema-gawa

Hirosemachi

Harada Hospital

Shinko-ji

Karazaya Bridge

Jonan-dori

CENTRAL PARK

Hiroshima Prefectural Sports Center (Green Arena)

Jonan-do

Ogawachimachi

Kosho-ji

Public Bath

265

Saizen-ji

Kami-tenmacho

7 Eleven

Family Mart
Hotel Provence 21 Hiroshima

Fresta

Tema ES

Nishi-tokaichimachi

7 Eleven

Aioi-dori

Tokaichimachi

Sorasaya Inao Shrine

Honkawacho

Daily Yamazaki
Hoen-ji
Shimizu
Seiju-ji
Wada
Sunkus

Children's Museum of Science

Kodomo Library

Hiroshim Central Libra

Rihga Roya

Sogo Anne

NTT

Aioi-dori

265

Kojinkai Kajikawa Hospital

Enomachi

7 Eleven

Teramachi-dori

Tokaichimachi

Chamber of Commerce & Industry

Hiroshima Municipal Stadium

Fukushimacho

Heiwa-odori

Myoren-ji

Miyakomachi

7 Eleven

Tenmacho

265

Aioi-dori

7 Eleven

Eba Line

Honkawa Kinen Hospital

Masaoka Hospital

Organza

Business H

Honkawa E.S. Peace Museum

HIROSHIMA PEACE MEMORIAL

Genbaku-Dome Mae

Aioi Bridge

Honkawa ES (Gembaku Dome)

Mielparque

Hiroshima Inn Aioi

AC

Sogo

7 Eleven

Shinkoi-bashi Bridge

Daily Yamazaki

Fukushima Seikyo Hospital

7 Eleven

Tenmacho

Tram Line 2

Koamicho

Dobashi

HONKAWA PARK

Korean Atomic Bomb Memorial

Children's Peace Monument

Kamiyacho-Nish

Deo Deo

Kawamura Hospital

Zucchini

Sun Mall

Vocational School

Nishi Ward Office

Nishikanonmachi

Kanonmachi

Koamicho

Business Ryokan Sansui
J-Hoppers Hiroshima

Teramachi-dori

Dohashicho

Peace Memorial Park

PEACE PARK

Cenotaph for Atomic Bomb Victims

Hiroshima National Peace Memorial Hall for the Atomic Bomb Victim

Appare

Sanuki

Sairen-ji

Hondori

Cha Cha Ni Moon

Park Side

Vocational School

P

Nishi-kannonmachi

Kanon ES

7 Eleven

Akebonokai Shimura Hospital

Ilkawa Ryokan

Ikedaya Annex

International Conference Center Hiroshima

Higashi-kan

Peace Memorial Museum

Tsuchiya General Hospital

Heiwa-Odori

Suisan Kaikan

Hok

Kuko-dori

Kanon-honmachi

7 Eleven

Higashi-kannonmachi

Public Bath

Sainen-ji

Aurora

Clio

Funairimachi

Funairimachi

Kawaramachi

Hon-kawa

Heiwa-Odori

Ristorante Mario

Charl

Heiwa-Ohashi Bridge

NHK

Ryuko-ji

7 Eleven

Shinkamisha

Million City

Crow Plaza A

Dormy I

Kannon Koko Tennis Court

to Nishi-ku

Minami-kannonmachi

Kanon JHS

2

Sunkus

7 Eleven

Fukuma Surgical Hospital

Vocational School

Lawson

Petit Bebefit

Silkroad
Two in One
Nikkou
To You

Lawson

Kouzaki ES

Hiroshima City Bunka Koryu Kaikan

Nakajimacho

Joen-ji

Chuden Hospital

Joon-ji

Comfort Hotel Hiroshima

Chuden-ma

Joonji Building

Jonen-ji

Ryuko-ji

Johoji

Ujina Line

Daiwa Royne

Kokutaiji

Ichinose Hospital

Public Bath

Kyosai-ji

Higashi-kannonmachi

Nishihiroshima Bypass

2

Funairihonmachi

Hiroshima Kanon HS

Hiroshima City Funairi Hospital

7 Eleven

Sunkus

Orutokai Hamawaki Orthopaedic Hospital

Kakomachi

Nakajima ES

Aster Plaza International Youth House

Otemachi Commercial HS

Honkyoji Building

Matsumura Building

Otemachi

Naka Ward Office

Hiroshima City Office

NTT Medi Supply

262

Minami-kannon

Kyosai-ji

Family Mart

Nishi-kawaguchicho

Funairi-nakamachi

Eiko-ji

Reikoku Data Bank

Shinmeji Bridge

7 Eleven

JA Building

2

Chokyu-ji

Harima

Fresta

Kokutaijimachi

Sunkus Gusto

Funairitsuiwaicho

Eba Line

Funairi-honmachi

Fuji Hospital

Funairi-saiwaicho

Sumiyoshi Shrine

Yoshijima-dori

Ryushin-ji

Nakamura Clinic

Salon Cinema

Cocostore

Takanohashi Central Hospital

7 Eleven

Shimamur

Funairi-dori

Hoon-ji

Sumiyoshicho

Sumiyoshicho

NAKA WARD

7 Eleven

Izawa

Takanobashi

Ujina Line

245

Joshin-ji

Vocational School

Abas Higashisenda

Clarion

Vocational School

Poplar

Funairi-kawaguchicho

Public Bath

Yoshijimacho

Driving Range

P

Lawson

City Plaza

Banana
France

City Fire Department

2001

Hiroshima Red Cross Atomic Bomb Survivors Hospital

Shakai Fukushi Center

Sendamachi

Joshin-ji

Nissaki-gyoin-mae

Royal Host

Hiroshim Universi

ale 1 : 15,000

200m

500ft

to Ushita

Hakushima

Astram Line

Aioi Shimo

JR San-yo Main Line

Hakushima-nakamachi

Ushita-honmachi

Ushita-naka

Ushita-higashi

Renson-ji

HIGASHI WARD

Hakushima-kitamachi

7 Eleven

Kanda Bridge

Anraku-ji

Ushitayama

USHITA GREEN SPACE

Hiroshima-toshogu Shrine

Alliance

Tomon-ji

7 Eleven

Nishi-hakushimacho

Johoku

Hakushima ES

Motomachi HS

Hiroshima ES

KKR

Sunkus

Enko-ji

Tokou-ji

Myofu-ji

Hakushima

Nigitsu Shrine

Myojo-in

Tsuruhane Shrine

Hakarigaoka

Hiroshima Railway Hospital

Kokuzen-ji

Shoko-ji

Hakushima Line

Tokiwa Bridge

Futabanosato

Johoku-dori

Futaba-dori

Futaba Jr.HS

Onaga ES

shima Castle

Hiroshima Teishin Hospital

Kami-osugacho

Senko-ji

264

shima Castle Ruins

Hiroshima Supreme Court

Prison

Chuo-dori

Kyobashi-gawa

Tanada

Hiroshima-toshogu Shrine

7 Eleven

oku Shrine

Tax office

Shukkei-en Garden

JR San-yo Main Line

New Matsuo

Granvia

Futaba-dori

Marvalu EX

Makitsubo Hospital

Lawson

NTT Tower

Hatchobori Chanter

Shukkei-en Path and Bridges

Sakae-bashi Bridge

New Hiroden

Sheraton

Active Inter City Hiroshima

New Tachibana

Hiroshima Garden Palace

shima seum of Art

Hiroshima Prefectural Art Museum

Noboricho HS

7 Eleven

Unizo

Jonan-dori

Hiroshima Jogakuin HS

Viainn Hiroshima

Hiroshima

Urbain Hiroshima Executive

Yorimoto

Hiroshima Municipal Hospital

Japan Housing Finance Agency

Nobori Kaikan

Pacific

Konoike Building

JAL City

Flex

7 Eleven Ekimae

Green Hotel

Hiroshima

Asse

Green Rich

Makusacho

Atagomachi

Hiroshima Business Tower

Ogawa Building

Jonan-dori

Noboricho ES

Apa

Yale Yale A

Hiroshima Kankoku Kaikan

Akebono-dori

7 Eleven

Higashi-kaniyacho

Akebono-dori

Poplar

Sumitomo Seimei

Cube

Chokaku-ji

7 Eleven

Fukuya

Matsuya

Matsubaracho

Joko-ji

Hiroshima City Higashi Ward Office

Chuden Motomachi

Fred

Tsuchimoto Hospital

Genko-in

Tenryu

Ark Hotel

70

JR Sanyo Shinkansen Line

Hiroshima Prefecture Government

7 Eleven

Chuo-dori

Nagarekawa-dori

Elizabeth University of Music

Hiroshima Grand Intelligent

7 Eleven

Century 21

Intelligent

7 Eleven

Lawson

JR San-yo Main Line

Tokyu Hands

Masui

Yagenbori-dori

Kojaku-ji

Senryu-ji

Toyoko Inn

Wins Hiroshima

Enkobashicho

Kojinmachi

Higashi-kojinmachi

Nishi-kaniya

JR San-yo Main Line

niyacho-Nishi

Tatemachi

Aioi-dori

Hatchobori

Ebisucho

Chisan

Active

Kaki-tei

Inari-bashi Bridge

Aioi-dori

Dai-ichi Seimei OS

Matobacho

Vessel Inn

Hiroshima Ekimae

Best Electronics

Kojinmachi ES

Mazda Stadium

Nomura Fudosan

Sukiya

Godo Bank

San-In

Tram Line 2

Kanayamacho

7 Eleven

Inarimachi

Lawson

K's House Hiroshima

Nippon Tsuun

Spicy Bar Lal's

Yamashita

Mitsukoshi

Ebisu-dori

Fuji Sky

Chugoku Rodo Kinko

Sawasaki Clinic

NTT

164

Suishin

Maruzen

Kuro-sawa

Pao

Intelligent Hotel Annex

Jonen-ji

Yoshizaki Hospital

Fuji Butsuryu

Wada

Hon-dori Arcade

Lawson

Chugoku Shoten

Akuse

Okonomi-mura

Poplar

Nawanai

Yukariya

Yamago Building

Danbara ES

Kyoei

Hosokawa

Minami-kaniya

Fukuromachi ES

Ninjo Ganko Yatai

Tokuei-ji

7 Eleven

Myoei-ji

Minami Line

Momiji

Kodama Clinic

Zentsu-ji

7 Eleven

Momiji Bank

Sera Bekkan

Nagarekawa-dori

Yagenbori-dori

Danbara Itchome

Mitsuru-dori

Myosen-ji

Ozu Dori

Lawson

Kameman

Koba

Lotus

Shanti

Vegan Cafe

Hiroshima-Shi Credit Cooperative

Higashi-Hiroshima-bashi Bridge

Kawahori Hospital

Taiyo

Coco's

Lawson

Sukiya

Hotoku-ji

Namiki

Ehime Bank

Hiroshima Town

Hiroshima Shogin

Jutaku Seikyo Hijiyama

Dambara Medical Building

7 Eleven

Mitsui Garden

Lawson

Kozen-ji

Hiroshima Shogin

Tosho

Lawson

iwa-Odori

Tokyu Inn

Daiwa

Hotel 28 Oriental

Kompira-Shrine

Junkyo-ji

Mantoku

Chosho-in

Manga Library

Tenri Kyokai

Pachinko Texas

Nakanishi Clinic

7 Eleven

en-ji

Honsho-ji

Heiwa-Odori

Hiroshima Shinkin

Super Hotel

Denso

Toyoko Inn

Heiando Umetsubo

Hiroshima Shinkin

Moriippoen

Sunkus

Danbara-hinode 1

Emmei-ji

Nakau

Essor

Fukuyama Tsuun

The Hiroshima City Museum of Contemporary Art

Lawson

Hijiyama Hospital

Kinryuzen-ji

Shika Ishi Kaikan

Asano Kensetsu

Zenkyo-ji

Warner Mycal Cinemas

Takagi

Hiroshima Bank

Danbara Jr.HS

Hijiyama ES

7 Eleven

Fuji Grand

Ekimae-dori

RGB

Higashi Hogan-ji

Takeya ES

Morita

Inagaki Clinic

Tanaka Clinic

nrin-ji

Izo-Dori

Mantoku

Takaramachi

Chugoku Shimbun Service Center

Tsurumicho

Hijiyama Park

Danbara-minami

Danbara-yamasaki

Shinonome

Takeyacho

Shinyo Kumiai Kaikan

Hiroshima Dambara Shopping Center

MINAMI WARD

Saisho-ji

Miyuki-bashi Bridge

Nishizume-dori

Hachiman

7 Eleven

Momiji

Hibari

Butsuryu-ji

Sugihime-inari Shrine

Poplar

Shinonome-honmachi

Chugoku Denryoku

Hiroshima Sanikugakuin ES

Meruken Baby Center

Shoryu-ji

Hiroshima Gas

Fudosan Kaikan

Danto

Radiation Effect Research Foundation

Okada Clinic

Police Academy

Nishihiroshima Bypass

Dempuku-ji

Hirano-bashi Bridge

Hiyama-bashi Bridge

Hijiyamahonmachi

Minami Kuyashomae

Fujicolor

Hiroshima University

nami-takeyacho

Hiranomachi

Showamachi

Hijiyamabashi

Fujicolor

Force

GASHISENDA PARK

Togi Clinic

Mitsubishi

Toshiba Tech

Chudenko

Kenko Fukushi Center

Hiroshima Industry Culture Center

Hiroshima Industrial Hall to Deshio

NTT West Chugoku Health Care Center

Shin Deshio Hospital

Senda ES

Denryoku Rodo Kaikan

487

2

Hiroden Bowling Alley

NTT Data Hijimaya

HIROSHIMA & WESTERN HONSHU

Sea of Japan

Oze-bana Point
Shizuki-yama 143m
Tsumemaru Ruins
SHIZUKI PARK
Mangan-ji Ruins
Shizukiyama Shrine
Hanano-e Tea House
Ruins of Hagi Castle
SEKICHO PARK
Nishinohama
Tenshukaku Ruins
Hagiyaki Museum
Hagi Historical Museum
Asa Mori House
Hagi-jo Kiln
Kikugahama
Senshunraku
Hagi-ichirin
Haginohama
Hagi Youth Hostel
People's Hotel Facilities Joen
Senshunraku Bekkan Mirakutei
Watch Tower
Midoriya Farm
Hokumon Yashiki
Hagi Seminar House
Hagi Joshi Road
Hermitage
Hagi Museum
Kubota House
Horiuchi
Hagi HS
Haginishi Jr. HS
Gofukumachi
Kikuya House
Tamaki Hospital
Minami-katakawamachi
Minami-furuhagimachi
Nishi-tamachi
Kannon-in
Kurae
Tokiwa-ohashi Bridge
Kasuga Shrine
Hagi Hospital
Ajiro
Hotori Tei
Ensei-ji
Heian Bridge
Ishii Teabowl Museum
CENTRAL PARK
Hagi City Library
Tamaeura Kan-i PO
Yamada
Zenshinkai Hospital
Hiyakomachi
Heian-ji
Mangyo-ji
Hagi Uragami Museum
Meirin ES
Kitaura H'way
Hagi Civic Hall
Hagi City Office
Daini Government Building
Hagi PO
McDonald's
Tamae
Tamaeura
Hagi-yako PO
Anyo-ji
Hagi Comm. & Tech. HS
Aiba Waterway
Inoue Kenkabo Birthplace
Tokurin-ji
Kusaka Genzui Birthplace
Fusho-ji
Emukai
Omotomachi
Hagi Police Station
Tamae Shrine
Tamae Bridge
7 Eleven
Citrus Park
Shingyo-ji
HAGI CITY
Driving School
Hashimotomachi
Yamagata Aritomo Birthplace
Hagihashimoto PO
Aiba Waterway
Hagi Oukan H'way
Tomita
Driving Range
to Misuminaka
Kazoe River Park
Kozoe
Rensho-in
Zempuku-ji
Tsubaki Bridge
Zoshikicho
Kanaya
7 Eleven
Kawashima
Katsura Taro Old Residence
Yukawa Family Old Residence
Aibagawa Canal
Hagi Civic Hospital
Oomi
Gymnasium
Chinzei ES
Kanaya Temmangu Shrine
Tsubaki
to Akiragi
Hagi

Hamasakimachi
Higashi-hamasakicho
Shinkawanishi
Shinkawa-higa
Fujita Ryokan
Yamanaka Family Old Residence
Old Hagi Domain Boathouse
Hagishinkawa PO
Shinkawa-nina
Sumiyoshi Shrine
Hagi-hamasaki PO
Hamasaki-shincho
Onnadaiba (Women's Mound)
Howaso
Hagi no Yado Tomoe
Kita-furuhagimachi
Ima-uonotanamachi
Taruyacho
Kumaya Museum of Art
Kotoku-ji
Hagi Murata Hospital
Abugawa
Minshuku Hagi-no-le
Hagi Grand
Don Don Udonya
Hagi Shinkai
Hijufmi
Ganjima-bashi Bridge
Kitaura H'way
JR San-in Line
Hagi-bashi Bridge
Hagi Royal Intelligence
Riverside
Petit Clanvert
Hagi Rainbow Cycles
Teramachi
Shioyacho
Choji-ji
Tsumoricho
Jonen-ji
Maru
Hagi Travel Inn
Orange Mutagaha
Saikumachi
Kami-gokenmachi
Komeyacho
Higashi-tamachi
Ima-furuhagimachi
Yoshidacho
Shimo-gokenmachi
Nakamura
Maebara Issei Old Residence
People's Facilities Hagiura-
Jokmachi
Kawaramachi
Fujitaya
Hagi-tamachi PO
Hagi Koen Gakuin HS
Hagi-higashi Jr. HS
Cafe Tikal
Yamaguchi Municipal Court
Hagi Bus Center
New Takadai
Sunlive
Karahimachi
Yubi-kan
Hijiwara
Hagi Police Station
Zenshinkai

Scale 1 : 20,000
200m
500ft

Kaian-ji
7 Eleven
Izakicho
Nagasakicho
Yamatecho
to Hatabu
Sanren-ji
Myoren-ji
Shinchicho
Hosho-in
Kanseicho
Imauracho
Entsu-ji
Uejocho
Daigan-ji
Shimonoseki Rehabilitation Hospital
Hikoshima-amanogocho
Kansei-honmachi
Sumire Ryokan
Prince
Wing Int'l
Nagatomachi
Nagasaki-chuocho
Washington
7 Eleven
Green Mall (Little Busan)
Station
Shimonoseki
Takezakicho
Sasayamacho
Nishio Hospital
Via Inn
Daimaru
Fukusen-ji
Yabure Kabure
Buzendacho
Tofuku-ji
Kokumin Ryokan Tenkai
Shimonoseki Sakuraza Theater Zero
Sea Mall
Tokyu Inn
Fine
7 Eleven
7 Eleven
Toyoko Inn
Hosoecho
Nishi-iriecho
Iriecho
International Ferry Terminal
Shimonoseki Police Station
Higashi-yamatomachi
Dormy Inn Premium
Kaikyo Yume Tower
Hananocho
Kowan Government Bldg
Hosoe-shinmachi
Plaza
Port of Shimonoseki
Mitsubishi Heavy Industries

SHIMONOSEKI
Saiwaimachi
Tanakamachi
Honmachi
Yoji ES
Meichi ES
Lawson
Public Bath
Chuzan-ji
Kozen-ji
Tennis Court
Oe ES
Business
Yufuku
Shimonoseki City Office
Yamagin Data Museum
Sennen-ji
Yamachi
Akamacho
Sunkus
Arukapoto
Arka Port
Karatocho
Keikyo-kan Marine Science Museum
Karato Pier
Sanyo Expressway
Kanmon Strait
to Kokura
to Kyushu
Honmachi
Moriyama Hospital
Miyadamachi
Lawson
Karato Central
Hongyo-ji
Kyoho-ji
Akita Co.
Tokyo Daiichi
7 Eleven
Former British Consulate
Injo-ji
Fujiwara Yoshie Memorial Museum
Akama Shrine
Gokuraku-ji
Amidaijicho
Dannouracho
Family Lodge
Kanmon Wharf
Karato Ichiba
Grand
Shunpanro

Scale 1 : 20,000
200m
500ft

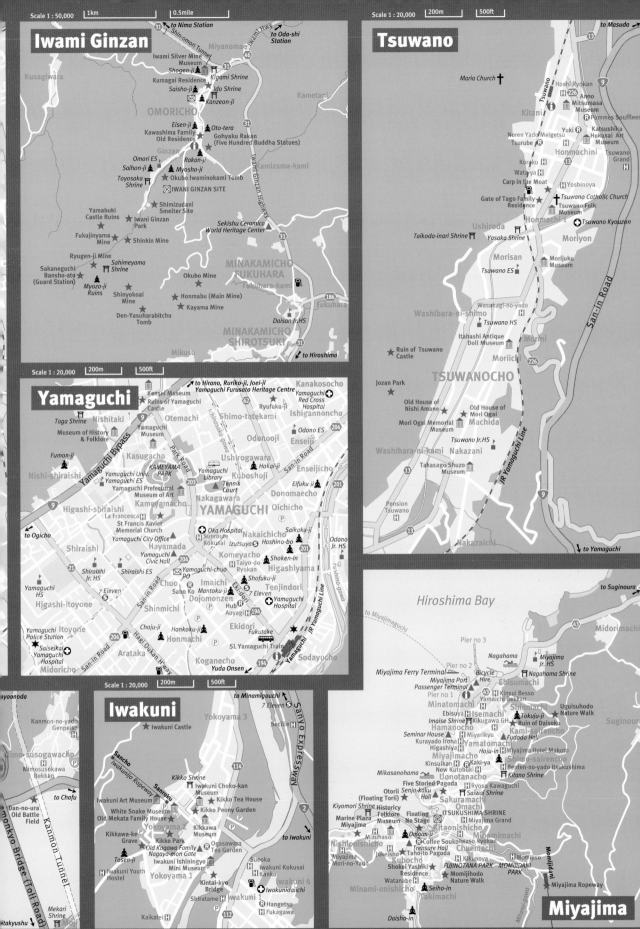

Iwami Ginzan

Scale 1 : 50,000

to Nima Station
Shin-omori Tunnel
Miyanomae
Iwami Hwy
to Oda-shi Station
Iwami Silver Mine Museum
Shogen-ji
Kumagai Residence
Kigami Shrine
Saisho-ji
Ido Shrine
Kanzeon-ji
OMORICHO
Kametani
Kamizama-kami
Kusagiwara
Eisen-ji
Oto-tera
Kawashima Family Old Residence
Gohyaku Rakan (Five Hundred Buddha Statues)
Ginzan
Omori ES
Rakan-ji
Saihon-ji
Myosho-ji
Omori Iwaminokami Tomb
Toyosaka Shrine
Okubo Iwaminokami Tomb
IWANI GINZAN SITE
Iwami Ginzan Highway
Yamabuki Castle Ruins
Iwani Ginzan Park
Shimizudani Smelter Site
Fukujinyama Mine
Shinkin Mine
Sekishu Ceramica World Heritage Center
Ryugen-ji Mine
Sahimeyama Shrine
Sakaneguchi Bansho-ato (Guard Station)
Myozo-ji Ruins
Shinyokoai Mine
Okubo Mine
Fukuhara-kami
MINAKAMICHO FUKUHARA
Honmabu (Main Mine)
Kayama Mine
Fukuhara
186
Den-Yasuharabitchu Tomb
Daisan Jr.HS
MINAKAMICHO SHIROTSUKI
Mikusu
to Hiroshima

Tsuwano

Scale 1 : 20,000

to Masuda
Maria Church
Tsuwano
Hoshi Ryokan
Anno
Mitsumasa Museum
Kitani
Pommes Soufflees
Katsushika Hokusai Art Museum
Noren Yado Meigetsu
Tsurube
Yuki
Honmachini
Tsuwano Grand
Koraku
Wataya
Yoshinoya
Carp in the Moat
Gate of Tago Family Residence
Tsuwano Catholic Church
Tsuwano Folk Museum
Honmachi
Ushiroda
Tsuwano Kyouzon
Taikoda-inari Shrine
Yasaka Shrine
Moriyon
Morisan
Morijuku Museum
Tsuwano ES
San-in Road
Washibara-ni-shimo
Morii
Wasakagi-no-yado
Tsuwano HS
Itahashi Antique Doll Museum
Moriichi
Ruin of Tsuwano Castle
TSUWANOCHO
Jozan Park
Old House of Nishi Amane
Old House of Mori Ogai
Mori Ogai Memorial Museum
Machida
Tsuwano Jr.HS
Washibara-ni-kami
Nakazani
Takasago Shuzo Museum
Pension Tsuwano
JR Yamaguchi Line
Nakazaichi
to Yamaguchi

Yamaguchi

Scale 1 : 20,000

to Hirano, Ruriko-ji, Joei-ji
Yamaguchi Furusato Heritage Centre
Kanakosocho
Kensei Museum
Ruins of Yamaguchi Castle
Yamaguchi Red Cross Hospital
Ishigannoncho
Taga Shrine
Nishitaki
Shimo-tatekami
Ryufuku-ji
Otemachi
Yamaguchi Museum
Odono ES
Odonooji
204
Enseiji
Museum of History & Folklore
Fumon-ji
Kasugacho
Enseijicho
Nishi-shiraishi
Yamaguchi Bypass
KAMEYAMA PARK
Hokai-ji
Ushirogawara
Kuboshoji
Yamaguchi Univ. ES
Yamaguchi Library
Eifuku-ji
Donomaecho
Yamaguchi Prefectural Museum of Art
Tennis Court
Nakagawara
YAMAGUCHI
Oichicho
Higashi-shiraishi
La Francesca
St Francis Xavier Memorial Church
Oka Hospital
Suproure
Nakaichicho
Saikaku-ji
Odono Jr. HS
Kokusai
Izutsuya
Hashino-bo
Shiraishi
Yamaguchi City Office
Hayamada
Komeyacho
Shoken-in
Higashiyama
Shiraishi Jr.HS
Yamaguchi Civic Hall
Shiraishi ES
Taiyo-do Ryokan
Yamaguchi HS
Shofuku-ji
Tenjindori
Chuo
Yamaguchi-chuo PO
Imaichi
Mantoku-ji
Higashi-itoyone
San-in Road
Sabo Ko
Dojomonzen
7 Eleven
Yamaguchi Hospital
Hub
Shinmichi
Aoyagi
Choju-ji
Honkoku-ji
Ekidori
Fukutake
Yamaguchi Itoyone Police Station
Honmachi
SL Yamaguchi Train
Saiseikai Yamaguchi Hospital
Midoricho
Arataka
Hagi Oukan Hwy
Koganecho
Yuda Onsen
Sodayucho
JR Yamaguchi Line

Iwakuni

Scale 1 : 20,000

to Minamigouchi
7 Eleven
Yokoyama 3
Sanyo Expressway
Iwakuni Castle
Secile
Sancho
Iwakunijo Ropeway
Kikko Shrine
Kanmon-no-yado Genpeiso
Iwakuni Choko-kan Museum
Sanroku
Iwakuni Art Museum
Kikko Tea House
White Snake Museum
Kikko Peony Garden
Old Mekata Family House
Yokoyama 2
Kikkawa Museum
Kikkawa-ke Grave
Kikko Park
Old Kagawa Family Nagaya-mon Gate
114
Ogasawara Tea Garden
to Iwakuni
Tosen-ji
Iwakuni Ishiningyo Mini Museum
Sueoka
Iwakuni Kokusai Kanko
Iwakuni 4
Iwakuni Youth Hostel
Kintai-kyo Bridge
Shiratame
Iwakuni
Iwakunidaiichi
Yokoyama 1
112
Kaikatei
Hangetsu
Fukagawa

Dan-no-ura Old Battle Field
Kanmon Bridge (Toll Road)
Kanmon Tunnel
Mimosusokawa Bekkan
to Chofu
Shimo-susogawacho
Mekari Shrine
itakyushu

Miyajima

Scale 1 : 20,000

Hiroshima Bay
to Suginoura
Midorimachi
to Miyajimaguchi
Pier no 3
Nagahama
Miyajima Jr. HS
43
Miyajima Ferry Terminal
Pier no 2
Bicycle Hire
Kinsui Besso
Nagaoka Shrine
Suginoura
Miyajima Port Passenger Terminal
Pier no 1
Yamaichi Bekkan
Ebisumachi
Minatomachi
Kikugawa GH
Tokuju-ji
Shinmachi
Uguisuhodo Nature Walk
Ebisuya
Isemachi
Miyarikyu
Ruin of Daisoku
Hamanocho
Imaise Shrine
Fudoda Hall
Seminar House
Kami-sairencho
Kurayado Iroha
Miyarikyu
Hoju-in
Yamatomachi
Hagishiya
Miyajima Hotel Makoto
Miyajimacho
Kaki-ya
Shimo-sairencho
Kinsuikan
New Kutobuki
Benten-no-yado Itsukushima
Mikasanohama
Uonotacho
Kitano Shrine
Otori
Senjo-kaku
Ryoso Kawaguchi
Five Storied Pagoda
Saiwai Shrine
Sakuramachi
Kiyomori Shrine
(Floating Torii)
Histority Folklore Museum
Floating No Stage
ITSUKUSHIMA SHRINE
Omachi
Marine Plaza Miyajima
Mizuhaso
Daigan-ji
Miyajima Grand
Kitaonishicho
Minamimachi
Nishinonishicho
Miyajima Mori-no-Yado
Taho-in Pagoda
Treasure Hall
Coffee Souko Iwaso Ryokan
Chuemachi
Kubochi
Jukeishon
Kikunoya
Shokei Yashiki Residence
Momijihodo Nature Walk
FUJINOTANA PARK
Momijiso
MOMIJIDANI PARK
Watanabe
Momijidani
Minami-onishicho
Seiho-ji
Miyajima Ropeway
Takimachi
Daisho-in

Scale 1 : 20,000

73

HIROSHIMA & WESTERN HONSHU

Matsue

Scale 1 : 20,000 200m 500ft

to Shimane Town
to Shimane Town
to Sakai Port

Kurodacho
Okudanicho
Senju-in
Dairincho
Reikan-ji
Lawson

Koizimi Yakumo (Lafcadio Hearn) Memorial Museum
Ishibashicho
Shimane Univ. affiliated ES
Shimane Univ. affiliated Jr.HS
Rainbow Plaza

Ryuun-ji
Matsuekita HS
Junko-ji
Matsue Public Health

Koizumi Yakumo (Lafcadio Hearn) Old Residence
Tanabe Art Museum
Yakumo-an
Horo ES
Lawson

Horikawa-yuransen Boat Trip
Buke Yashiki Samurai Residence

RAKUZAN PARK

Kitahori Museum Arts Cultural Hall
Jozan-inari Shrine
Kitahoricho
Kita-tamachi
Rakuzan Kiln

Caspal
MATSUE JOZAN PARK
Fumon-in
Nishiocho

Tennis Court
Matsue History Museum
Tonomachi
Matsue Red Cross Baby Home
Lawson
to Yatsuka Town

Forest Office
Matsue Castle
Matsue Shrine
Horikawa Sightseeing Boat
Vocational School
City General Gymnasium
Family Mart

Sunagocho
Matsue Kyodo-kan
Shimane Library
Yonagomachi
Minami-tamachi
KITA PARK
Gakuenminami

Uchi-nakabara ES
Shimane Prefectural Office
Sunrapport Murakumo
Matsue Red Cross Hospital
Jisho-in
Kunibiki Messe

Dai-ichi Jr.HS
Shimane International Centre
Karakoro Art Studios
Lawson
Matsue Taxation
Mukojimacho

Soto-nakabaracho
Tsufumaru
Ark Hotel

Arawai Shrine
Matsue City Hotel Horikan
Nakria
Minamikan
Route Inn
Kunibiki Ohashi

Suetsugucho
Matsue New Urban Hotel Annex
Naniwa
Kawa-kyo
Cafe Bar EAD
Shin Ohashi

Daio-ji
Omachi
Matsue City Office
Hachikenyacho
Tanaka-ya
Notsu
Mazda Rent-a-Car

Nakabaracho
Matsue Shinjiko Onsen
Hot Spring Foot Bath
Mefu Shrine
Otesenbacho
Alpha-one
Tokyu Inn
Urban

Ichibata
Shirakata-honmachi
Isemiyacho
Ichibata
Ekimae Universal
Lake Shinji Pleasure Boat "Hakucho"
Daisan Jr.HS Ground

Kita-Matsue Line
Yukei Kohan Suitenkaku
Chidoricho
Uomachi
Zendo-ji
Ryusho-ji
Teramachi
Toyoko Inn Matsuekan
Lawson
Matsue
Aeon
JR San'in Main Line

Naniwa Issui
Souvenir Center
Matsue Shinjiko
Nadamachi
Green Rich Hotel Matsue
Alpha-one Matsue
Higashi-asahimachi

to Matsue English Garden
SHIRAKATA PARK
Jokyo-ji
Tenjinmachi
Seigan-ji
Universal
Matsue Plaza
Vocational School
Daisan Jr.HS
Lawson

Shirakata Shrine
Terazuya
Ninjinkata
Taishocho
Chuo ES
Lawson

Shimane Art Museum
Shingyo-ji
Hongocho
Shin-saikamachi
Tsudacho
Funeral Hall
to Mats Po

Shogen-ji
Business Hotel Lake Inn
Tsuda Highway
Zempuku-ji

Saiwaimachi
Tsuda Highway
Lawson
Tsuda Highway

Lake Shinji (Shinjiko)
Tsuda Highway
9

Honsei-ji
Saikamachi
UFO
Nishitsuda
City Library
Nishi-tsuda

Matsue Police Station
Enjo-ji
Yokobamacho
Saika ES
Bodai-ji
Joki-ji

to Izumo Airport
Shinmachi
Toko-ji
Matsue City Culture Center
Driving School

to Matsue General Sports Park

Onomichi

Scale 1 : 20,000 200m 500ft

to Miyosi
to Fukuyama
Kotobuki

Aoyama Hospital
Kurihara-higashi 2
Onomichi Minami HS
Saikoku-ji
Shintakayama 1
Mitsui Outlet Park Kurashiki

Nagae ES
Kongo-in
Nishi-kubocho
Onomichi Higashi HS
Kurashiki Mirai Park

Vocational School
Misode-tenmangu Shrine
Jizen-in
Kubo ES
Sun Pl
Iwamicho

Sakuramachi
Kurihara-higashi
Taisan-ji
Shonen-ji
Josen-ji
Higashi-kubocho
Saigo-ji
Kaitoku-ji
JR Hakubi Line
White Ine
Yamadaya

Shiomicho
Fukusen-ji
Nagae
Kasai Hospital
City Chuo Library
Jodo-ji
Kairyu-ji
to Fukuyama
JR Sanyo Main Line
Iwamicho

SENKOJI PARK
Viewing Platform
Senko-ji
Onomichi Historical Museum
Shirakaba Art Museum
Jodo-ji Garden
429

Nakata Museum of Art
City Art Museum
Ropeway
Maneki Neko Art Museum
Kubo
Ozaki-honmachi
Onomichi-ohashi Bridge
Shiseikai Akamatsu Hospital

Saiho-ji
Senkoji Sanso
Higashi-tsuchidocho
Tennei-ji
Shukaen
Nishiyama Honkan
Takeruマya
Ryotei Uonobu
Matsumoto Hospital
to Fukuyama
123

Kurihara-nishi
Shingyo-ji
Komyo-ji
Hodo-ji
Onomichi City Office
Onomichi Cinema Museum
Oimatsuch

Hibisaki ES
View Hotel Seizan
Jiko-ji
Keifuku-ji
Onomichi Royal
Hitachi
Sunkus

Aeon
Deodeo
Tsuchido ES
7 Eleven
JR Sanyo Line
Tsuchido
Kaneda
Matsumoto
Omatsu ES

Sangenyacho
Higashi-goshocho
Onomichi
Kurashikiheisei Hospital

Tenmacho
Alpha-one
Taishoen
Minatoya
Cinema Onomichi
Mt. Iwaya
Happy H

Fukuyama Shimanami Kouryuukan
Teatro Shell-rune
Green Hill
Nishi Seto E'way

to Mihara, Hiroshima Airport
Miyako
Sato
Onomichi Daiichi
Kono Onsen
Okajima
JFE
Yuho
to Innoshima Island
Sato Gastroenteric and Surgical Hospital

Nishi-goshocho
Mukaishimacho
McDonalds

Tottori

Scale 1 : 20,000 200m 500ft

KYUSHO PARK

en-ji
Sendai River
Tottori Loop Rd
Tashima
Omori Shrine
Aioicho
to Tottori Airport, Toyooka, Sand Dunes
Nishi-honji
Shomyo-ji
Tottori-jouhoku HS
Yakushimachi
Zaimokucho
Kita Jr.HS
Wakasa Highway
Higashimachi
Watanabe Hospital
Tottori Prefectural Museum
Ruins of Tottori Castle
Nagata Shrine
Minami-yasunaga
Family Mart
Sendaigawa-ryokuchi Park
Fuso Gymnasium
Shin-honjicho
Genchu-ji
Nishi Jr.HS
Kotobukicho
Genkocho
Jumpu ES
Nishimachi
Jinpukaku Mansion
Nishi HS
Kyusho ES
Kozen-ji
Midorigaoka
Tennis Court
Fuso ES
Chamachi
Warabekan (Toy Museum)
Ueta Hospital
Keiai HS
Honmachi
Family Mart
Tottori Pref. Office
Daini
Nichiko-ji
Dairin-ji
Hoshin-ji
Kuritanicho
Honji-in
Myokensan
Kanryu-in
Furumi
JR San'in Line
Jonin-ji
Minamimachi
Motouomachi
Senkyo ES
Chuden Fureai Hall
Tottori Red Cross Hospital
City Hall
Civic Hall
Myoen-ji
Uemachi
Tottori City Historical Museum
Jigen-ji
Imamachi
Hijiri Shrine
Kawaramachi
Shinkyo-ji
Ichigyo-ji
Komyo-ji
Keian-ji
Hongan-ji
Myoyo-ji
Kakuo-ji
Kannon-in
Kannon-in Garden
Am's
TOSC
Gyotoku
Meitoku ES
Yamazaki
Sakaemachi
Yayoicho
Tottori City
Lawson
Super Hotel Kiktaguchi
Green Hotel
New Otani
Kirinoya
Morris
Resh
Ekimani Dori
Hinomaru Hot Springs
Nisshin ES
Baio-ji
Saiwaicho
Higashihonjicho
Dalmaru
Alpha One
Jujuan
Tottori-ya
Rent-a-Cycle
National
Monarch
Matsuya-so
Kyushokaku
Daiun-in
Sanyo Seishi
Shan Shan Festival
Tottori
Eirakuonsencho
Washington
Marumo
Hope Star
Kansuitei
Kozeniya
Kodomo Science Museum
Cultural Hall
Tachikawacho
Shohei-ji
Aeon
Wei City
Tenjincho
Super Hotel
Toyoko Inn
Tottori Hot Springs
Apa Tottori Ekimae
Yayoikan
Union Plaza
Funeral Hall
Tottori Shinwa Church
Tottori Higashi HS
Shuritsu ES
Furuichi
Konankaku
Taisuikaku
Minamiyoshikata
Cosmo
Yoshikata
Sanyo Denki
Lawson
Shobu
Nenhou-ji
Furuichi Shrine
Saint Marc
Minami Jr.HS
Konancho
Sanyo Denki
Power Plant
Family Mart
Fire Department
Nishimatsuya
Family Mart
to Chizu
Wakasa H'way

Kurashiki

Scale 1 : 20,000 200m 500ft

to Okayama
Hinodecho 1
7 Eleven
Marunako
Achi 1
Tenmaya
Showa 2
Matsuba Hospital
Business Hotel Airport
Kurashiki Station
Kurashiki Central Hospital
Tsurugata 1
7 Eleven
Bios Arcade (Senta-gai)
Ebisu Inn
Toyoko Inn
Yoshii
Kurashikihigashi ES
Tsurugata 2
Kanryu-ji
Achi 2
Seigan-ji
Tsurugata Shrine
Honei-ji
Kurishiki-no-Yado Higashimachi
Jizo-in
Achi 3
Old Ohara Family Residence
Nikko
Resol
Dormy Inn
Ohara Museum of Art
Kurashiki Character Banks Museum
Choren-ji
Minamimachi
Astronical Observatory
Oyama University
Kurashiki-shi Geibunkan
Kyozen-ji
Kurashiki YH
Bakurocho
Royal Host
Kurashiki Commercial HS
7 Eleven
Funaguracho

Okayama

Scale 1 : 20,000 200m 500ft

to Airport, Tottori
Okayama Business
High Court
Legal Government Office
Hama
Yumeji Art Museum
Plaza
Prefectural Museum
Okayama Saiseikai Hospital
Tondacho
Yuminocho
Okayama-chuo ES
Izushicho
Korakuen-dori
Yuka Shrine
Hokancho
Iwatacho
Sun Peach
Okayama-chuo Jr.HS
Tenjincho
Okayama Korakuen Garden
Ekimaecho
Nodayacho
Prefectural Museum of Art
Okayama-korakuen Jr.HS
Okayama Ekimae
Banzancho
Orient Museum
Higashiyama Line
Excell Okayama
Okayama Castle
Ujo Park
Momotaro Odori
Togiyacho
Shiroshita
Comfort
Shinzoboyo Center Sakakibara
Honmachi
Maira
Kencho-dori
Tori-soba
Hayashibara Museum of Art
Marunouchi
Okayama Library
Saiwaicho
Castle
Central Post Office
Tenmaya
Ota
Okayama Prefectural Office
Renaiss Hall
Furugyocho
Sankoso Atoriumu Hall
Library
Tamachi
Akura-dori
Kawasaki
Bee Wing 2
Uchisange
Civic Cultural Hall
to Himeji
Shimoishii
Yanagimachi
Haru
Omotecho
Kyobashicho
Chunagoncho
Chuocho
Okayama Universal
to Tamano, Kurashiki
Kokuseji-ji
Kobashicho

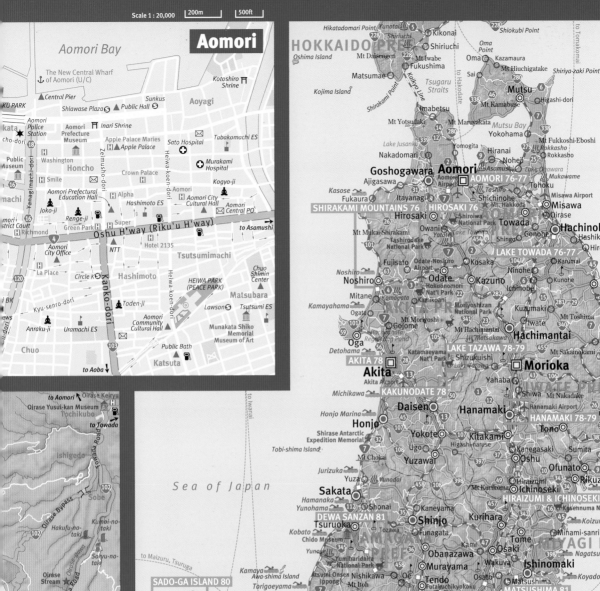

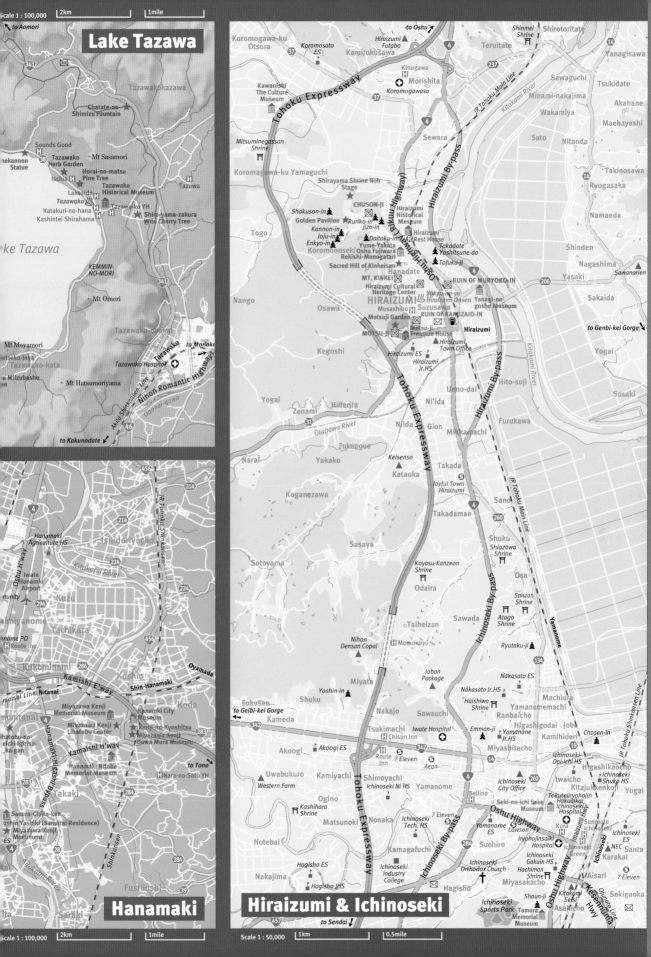

Sado-ga Island

Scale 1 : 600,000
10km
5miles

Sea of Japan

Futatsu-game Rock
Hajiki-zaki Point
Ono-game Rock
Washisaki
Sotokaifu
Iwayaguchi
Sotokaifu YH
Sandogura
Seki-zaki Point
Mt Bunagahira
Mt Dantoku
Mourazaki Park
Mt Matsukura
Sado Range
Ryotsu Bay
to Niigata
Aikawa Hiranezaki
Ageshima Aquarium
Mt Kinpoku
Hime-saki Point
Belle Mer YH
Kusuga-zaki Point
Mt Myoken
Hakuundai
Ryotsu Port
Ryotsu
Tassha
Osado Skyline Drive
Seaside
Tokaei
Sumiyoshi
Historic Relic Sado
Gold Mine
Green Village
Michi-no-eki Geino-to-toki-no-sato
Aikawa
Sado Kinzan (Gold Mine)
Kanai
Uryuya
Mt Osumi
Katano
O-sado
Sado
Myosho-ji
Konpon-ji
Mt Kunimi
Meoto
Sado Museum
Inakujira
Sawada
Shimmachi
Myosen-ji
Rekishi-Densetsu-kan
Mt Kigane
Mano Bay
Mano
Mt Ogami
Mano-Go-yu (Imperial Mausoleum)
Nishi-mikawa Gold Park
Mt Kyozuka
Tsubakio
Matsugasaki
Kua Terme Sado
Cultopia
Sobama
Sado Folk Museum
Minshuku Sakaya
Hamochi
Akadomori
Shiobaya Cape
Ogi
Hamochi Port
Shukunegi
to Naoetsu
to Teradomari

Mt Oshirabu
Odaira
Goshiki
Mt Kabuto
Tsunagi
Mt Ogasa
Mt Zaza
Sunamori
Namegawa
Ainowatari
Shirabu
Odaira
Tsuga-mori
Mt Minowa
Mt Takakura
Kotobachi
Tengendai Kogen
Mt Higashi-Daiten
Mt Dainichi
Mt Tobachi
Ubayu
Mt Legata
Mt Nishi-Agatsuma
Mt Eboshi
Mt Yahazu
Mt Nishi-Daiten
Jododaira Astronomical Observatory
Ko-daki
Mt Naka-Azuma
Kagoyama Inari-Shrine
O-daki
Hibara Historical Museum
Mt Jinkuro
Grandeco Snow Resort
Maku-daki
Mt Yanabe
Fudo-daki
Grandeco
Akayu
Makukawa
Lake Hibara
URA-BANDAI AREA
Comfort Ura-bandai
Onogawa-ko
Bandai-Azuma Lake Line
Ura-bandai Royal
Mt Idemori
Goshiki-numa (Five-colored Lake)
Banda-san Volcanic Memorial Museum
Lake Akimoto-ko
Sengan-sanso
Mt Takamori
Minowa
Bandai Hinohara-kohan
Hoshi-no shizuku
Ura-bandai Kogen
Wakamiya
Mt Shirabu
Takamori
Hoshino Resort
Banso
Kawakami
Mt Sayanoki
Shiraiti-no-daki
to Nihonm
Ura-bandai Highland
Ura-bandai
Shobu-en
Mt Yake
Numajiri
Ura-bandai Nekoma
Oguni-numa
Nakanoyu
Tsuchiyuzawa
Tatsusawa-fudo-daki
to Kitakata
Oguni-numa March Plant Community
Mt Kushiga-mine
Nakanosawa
Mt Nunomori
Mt Hitaki
Fudo-daki
Chosiga-da
Mt Mayatake
Mt Bandai
Family Snow Park Bandai x2
Inawashiro
Alts Bandai
Mt Akahani
Ryugasawa Yusui Spring
Bandaisan Onsen
Showa-no-mori Park
Mt Ichinono
Mt Kawageta
Mt Otaki
Ohara Site
Enichi-ji Kondo
Ottate
Inawashiro Resort
Mine-no-oishi Rock
Listel Ski Fantasia
Mt Tengusumotori
Fukusawa
Higashi-Nagahara
Serashina
INAWASHIRO AREA
Suwamae
Iwasato
Yahata
Listel Inawashiro Honkan
Nishita-mo
to Kitakata
Sekimori
Ura-Bandai
Inawashiro
Oghi-shima
JR Banetsusai Line
Mitsuta
Ban-etsu Expressway
Osada
Inawashiro Swan Wintering Place
Kawageta
Mt Ideko
Motomi
Iwane
Inawashiro Beer Hall
Noguchi Hideyo Memorial Hall
Naka-komatsu
Kaneda
Mt Mizunashi
Mt Muso
to Tam
to Niigata
Nakaji
Minami-aga-oka Farm
Okinazawa
Ogishima Marina
Kobiragata-temmangu Shrine
Kawasaki
Mt Narisawa
Echigo Highway
Ban-etsu Expressway
Ban-etsu Expressway
AIZU-WAKAMATSU
Mt Nagura
Okina-shima Island
Tsuboyo
Mt Kurate
Nakayama-juku
Bandai Atami
to Tam
Kanemagari Bypass
Kita-takizawa
Ugimachi
Aizu-Wakamatsu
Mt Eboshi
Yashiki
Joko
BANDAI ATAMI AREA
Suehiro Brewery
Route 118 Aizuwakamatsu
Lake Inawashiro
Karuisawabu
Koriyama
Aizu Sake Museum
Tsuruga Castle
Oyakuen Garden
Aizu Bukeyashiki
Nakadahama
Sakikawahama
Kitamachigagoya
Bandai Atami
Onyado Toho
Fukushima Museum
Higashiyama
Oyado Higashima
Nakada
Sangi-daki
Higashiyama Grand
AIZU-WAKAMATSU CITY
Mt Hitaidori
Maeyama
Sekiba
Yokosawahama
Yashiki
Aizu Railway
Ryokan Sasakubo
Shineo
Higashiyama Grand
Seishohama
Fukushima
Mondenmachi
Mt Katahira
Takasaka
Hidama
Oish
Mt Awaji
Mt Fukiya
to Shirakawa
Arai
Otomachi
Mt Otakamori
Mt Kayano
Houra
Tobu-Gawa River
Otomachi Kami-miyori Omameda
Mt Futaedaira
Tashiro
Mt Takatsubari
to Shirakawa
Yasumiishi
Yokosa

Aizu, Inawashiro & Ura-bandai

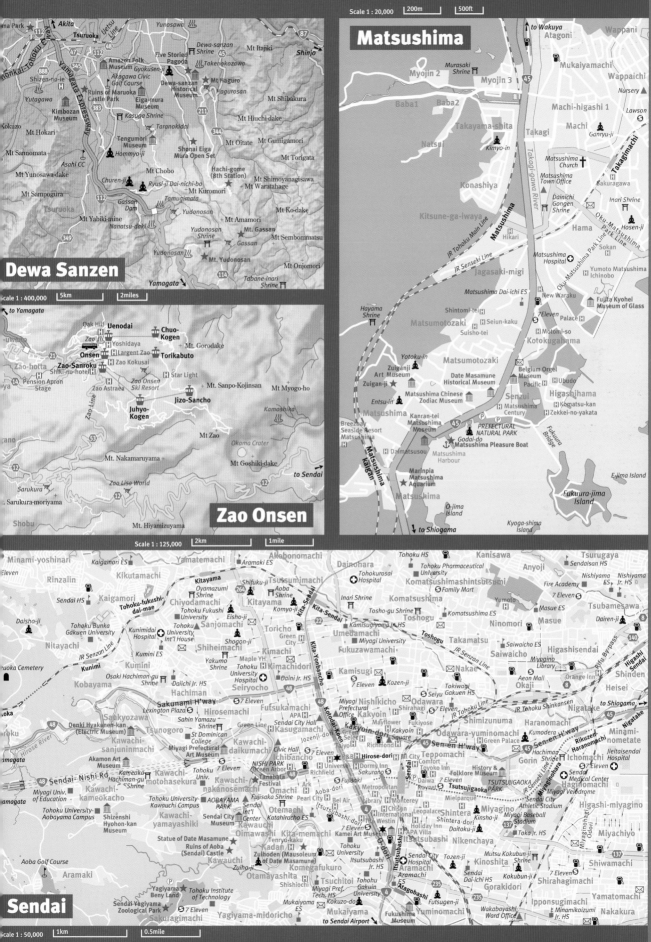

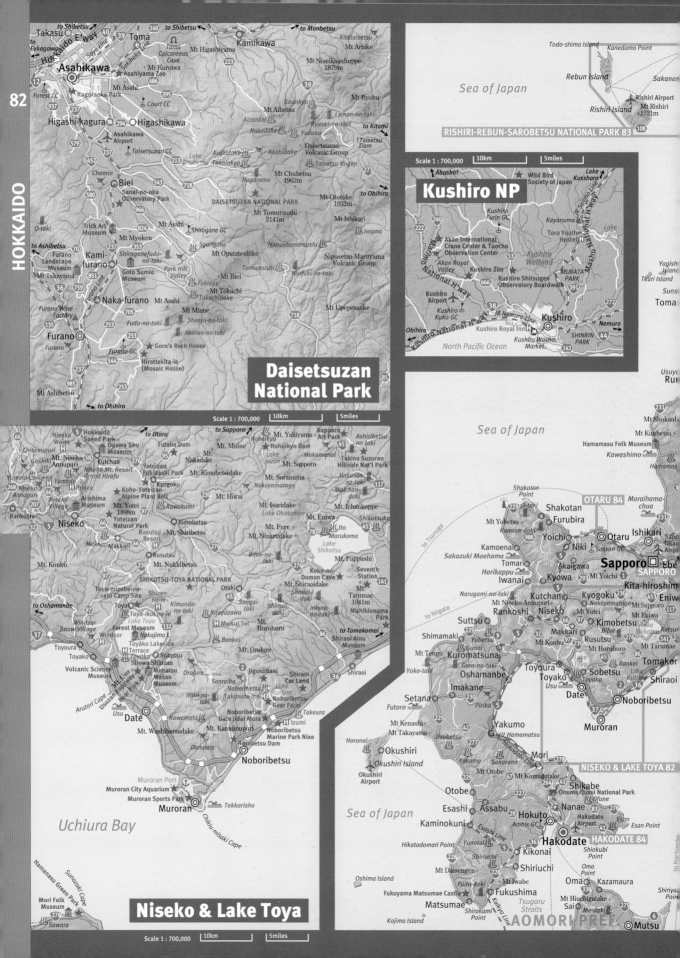

Rishiri-Rebun-Sarobetsu NP

Scale 1 : 700,000

Soya Bay
Soya Point
The Northern end of Japan Monument
Toyoiwa Site
Sea of Okhotsk

kkanai
Wakkanai
Sarufutsu
Sarufutsu Park
138

Ik Museum
Mt Poroshiri
84
Hama-tonbetsu

otomi
Mt Sutchosa CC
Sarobetsu CC
Kotobuki
Naka-tonbetsu
Mikasayama
238

Horonobe
shio
Mt Pinneshiri
120
Esashi
Omu
12

Museum Mt Panke
40
Pinneshiri
238
Nakagawa
238

betsu
119
Otoireppu
238
Okoppe

Saito Mokichi Monument
Mt Hakodake
120
Bifuka
40
60
49

118
40
Mt Kuroiwa
Ohotsuku
Omu

olk Museum
Shosanbetsu
Bifuka
275
Nayoro
239
49

Mt Pisshiri
Mt Piyashiri
Nishiokoppe
Monbetsu

boro
275
Shumanai
Nayoro Shirakabo CC
273
Oyama
Monbetsu Airport

oal-no
239
40
Shimokawa
Takinoue

aeological
Kenbuchi
101
Shibetsu
242
Lake Saroma

eum
126
Wassamu
Mt Shokotsu
137
Engaru
Saroma
103

ra
Horotachi
48
Shiokari
101
Mt Teshio
Luck Valley
76
Boshiiwa

t Poroshiri
99
Shiokari
101
Mt Chitokaniushi
Ikotoiya
Lake Notoro

ala
275
72
Pippu
333
Kamikawa
242
Kitami
7

Sea of Okhotsk

Abashiri
Museum of Abashiri Prison
104
Ozora
Shari

ISETSUZAN NATIONAL PARK 82

mata
Chippubetsu
12
Asahikawa
Sounkyo
39
Kitami
102

uryu
Fukagawa
237
Higashikawa
Asahikawa Airport
213
Mt Daisetsu
Oketo
143
Bihoro
Koshimizu
Kiyosato

ikawa Akabira
452
Eiei
966
Mt Tomuraushi
Kanoko
51
240
Mt Shari
244

agawa
36
70
237
Kamifurano
Tomuraushi
Mt Higashi-Mikuni
Tsubetsu
Sharidake National Park

usu
115
Kami-sunagawa
135
Nakafurano
Niposetsu-Maruyama Volcanic Group
88
Ginga-no-Mori Astronomical Observatory
Mt Shibetsu Nakasibetsu Airport
150
Shibetsu

12
Naie
452
Furano
Nukabira Gonsenkyo
Meto
Mt Oakan
241
Mashu
150
Naka-shibetsu

al
Mikasa
Furano GC
Shinada
Mt Meakan
Akankosi
664
Teshikaga
13

wamizawa
237
Kami-shihoro
Lake Shikaribetsu
Meakan
240
Shibecha

uriyama
38
Minami-furano
Arisuto GC
Ashoro
Mt Ukotakinupuri
Tsurui
Shibecha

Yubari
136
Shintoku
274
Shihoro
88
143
O-taki
Lake Toro
272

Yuni
Shimukappu
36
Shikaoi
Honbetsu
392
Akan Royal Valley
391
44

rose
Chitose CC
274
Shimizu
36
Otofuke
Kushiro Airport
44
142

Atsuma
131
Memuro
56
Obihiro
Ikeda
Akkeshi

235
10
59
Makubetsu
Urahoro
Shiranuka
Kushiro
KUSHIRO NATIONAL PARK 82

kawa
Biggusugi GC
Mt Nukkibetsu
Toyokoro
Tokachi-Obihiro Airport

ukawa
Biratori
80
Mt Daisen
Mt Kamui-Ekunchikaushi
Sarabetsu
336

Hidaka
111
Mt Betegari
Mt Kamui
Haluugindai

Niikappu
Shinhidaka
235
Mt Pirika-Nupuri
Taiki
Bansei

Urakawa
Baji Museum
Mt Rakko
Fumbe-no-taki
336
Hiroo

Samani
Mt Pinneshiri
336
Mt Toyoni

Erimo
34
Cape Erimo

NORTH PACIFIC OCEAN

Rishiri-Rebun-Sarobetsu NP

Rebun Airport (closed)
Field Inn
Seikan-so
Funadomari

RISHIRI REBUN SOROBETSU NATIONAL PARK
Nisshoku Kansoku Monument
Mt Rebun-dake

Rebun Island

Hanashin
Hana Rebun
Momoiwa-so
Rebun

Kachan Yado

Green Hill
Rishiri-fuji
Rishiri Airport
Rishiri Fuji
Fuji Kanko
Hokuroku

Kutsugata Misaki
Mt Chokan
Ponyama
Rishiri
Rishiri Island
Mt Rishiri Zan
Rosoku-iwa (Candle Rock)

RISHIRI REBUN SOROBETSU NATIONAL PARK
108

Municipal Museum
Rishiri Island Folk Museum
Mt Senhoshi-ponyama

Sea of Japan

Rebun Suido

Rishiri Suido

Noshappu-misaki
Saihate Ryokan
Anma
to Wakkanai Airport
Wakkanai Moshiriana
Wakkanai
Hokuroku Kyampu-jo Island Inn
40
Sakanoshita

Harp Seal Viewing
Bakkai Port
to Sarobetsu Genya

RISHIRI REBUN SAROBETSU NATIONAL PARK
106

Shiretoko NP

Scale 1 : 700,000

Shiretoko-misaki Cape
Bunkichi Bay
Me-daki
Oi-daki

Sea of Okhotsk

Mt Poromoi
Mt Shiretoko
Shiretoko Nat'l Park
1254m
Kashuni-no-taki
Seseki
Seseki-no-taki

SHIRETOKO NATIONAL PARK
Kamuiwakkayu-no-taki
Mt Tokkarimui
Aidomari

Shiretoko Five Lakes
Kamuiwakkayu-no-taki
Mt Io
Mt Chienbetsu
Furepe-no-taki
Shiretoko Grand
Iwaobetsu
Mt Sashirui
Port of Chiembetsu-gyoko

Utoro
Shiretoko Nature Center
Mt Rausu 1660m
Port of Okkabake-gyoko

Mie-no-taki
Lake-O
Rausu
Minsyuku Honma

Chinishibetsu
Kumagoe-no-taki
334
Rausu
Port of Rausu-gyoko

Mt Onnebetsu
335
to Shibetsu
Nemuro Straits

SHIRETOKO NATIONAL PARK 83

Mt Shiretoko
O-daki
Seseki
57
Iwaobetsu
Mt Chienbetsu
334
Mt Rausu
Rausu

Kunashiri Island

Shiretoko Museum
334
Mt Onnebetsu
335

Mt Unabetsu
Kanayama
Kanayama Athletic Park

Sea of Okhotsk

Shikotan Island

391
Mt Shibetsu Nakasibetsu Airport
150
Shibetsu
950
Notsuke Bay

Habomai Islands
Nosappu Point

Betsukai
Bekkai
Nemuro GC
55
Nemuro

AKAN NATIONAL PARK 83
44
Lake Furen
Yururi Island

Tonden Kaitaku Memorial Museum
272
Sakai-tsutsuji

Hamanaka
Kojima Island

Akkeshi
Seabird Habitat

NORTH PACIFIC OCEAN

Akan National Park

Scale 1 : 700,000

to Bihoro
Mt Mokoto
to Abashiri
Ojika-no-taki
Shandake Natural Park
Mt Shibetsu

27
Tsubetsu
243
Furuume Dam
Misono
391
Cottage Loghouse Kawayu
Mt Yoroushi

Bihorotoge Pass
Nibushi
Nibushi-no-sato
Nakajima I.
Mt Iozan
Kawayu
Kawayu Eco Museum

Tsubetsu
Kussharo
Prince
Lake Kussharo
Ikenoyu
Kotan
102
52
Kageyama
Observation Point Deck 3
Mt Onsen Fuji

651
240
Mt Samakkarinupuri
Wakoto Museum
Wakoto
Kotan-ainu
Minzoku
Nonkisha
Kamuinupuri (Mashudake)
Lake Mashu
150

Mt Kotominupuri
Mt Samakkenupuri
Shiryokan
Marukibune
Observation Point Deck 1
Mashu Kanko Bunka Center
885

Mt Kikindake
Mt Ahorodake
Lake Pankoro
Mt Yukimi
Teshikaga (Mashu)
243
13

Mt Iyudaninupuri
Shirafuji-no-taki
Mt Oakan
New Akan
Mt Nishibetsudake
Mt Omonai

Nonaka Onsen
Akanko
New Akan Kohan
Oshima I.
Akan Kohan Eco Museum
241
53

Meakan
Kokusetsu Akan Kohan
Akan Kohan
240
Mt Meakan 1499m
Mt Akan-fuji
to Kushiro
664
Mt Onneto

Hokkaido

Scale 1 : 2,000,000   50km   20miles

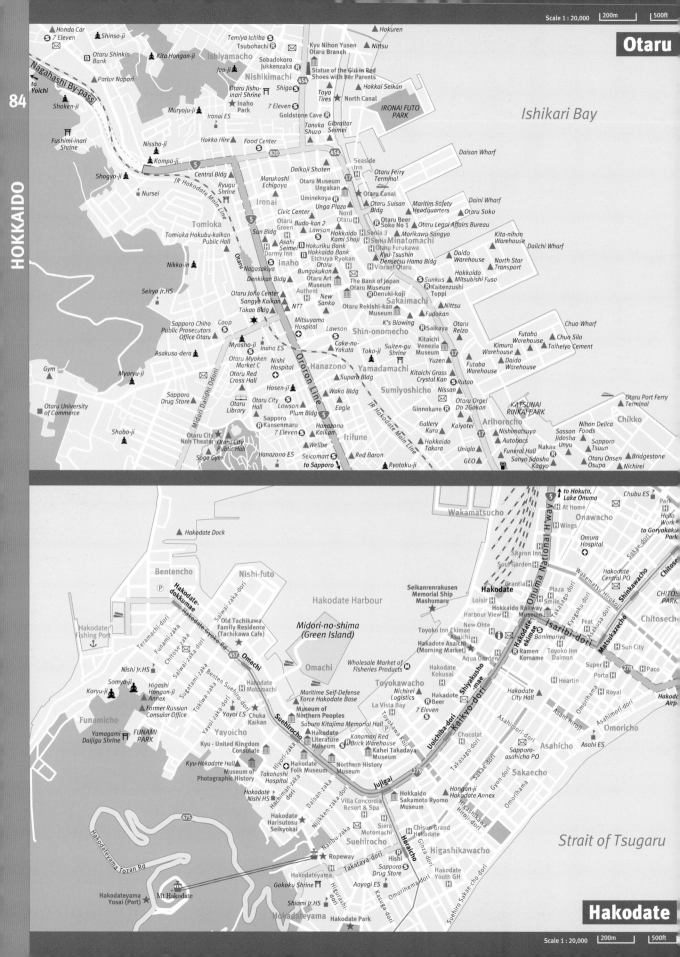

Sapporo

Scale 1 : 20,000   200m   500ft

SETO-OHASHI BRIDGE 87

TAKAMATSU 89

KOTOHIRA 88

KOTOHIRA 88

TOKUSHIMA 88-89

IYA VALLEY 87

KOCHI 86-87

PACIFIC OCEAN

Tosa Bay

Seto-ohashi Bridge

Scale 1 : 300,000   2km   1mile

Iya Valley

Scale 1 : 300,000   5km   2miles

5mile

Matsuyama

Scale 1 : 20,000   200m   500ft

to Mitsufuto ↑
to Horie ↑

Kinuyama
Entsu-ji
Kinuyama
Palty Fuji Kinuyama
Sanimato Kinuyama Store
Yamagoemachi
Kiyacho
Misawa
Rokkenyacho
Kayamachi 6-chome
Honmachi 6-chome
Kiyacho
Takasagocho
Johoku Park
Miyuki-dera
Senshu Zenji
Gokoku Shrine
Yuzuki
Matsuyama University
Dogo-himata
Bunkyocho
Dogo-kitash
Inari Shrine
Katsuyama Jr. HS
Shimizu ES
Iyotetsu Takahama Line
Matsuyama Memorial Hospital
JR Yosan Line
Myogen-ji
Hoto-ji
Shinko-ji
Asami
Aikocho
Asahigaoka
Miyanishi
Vocational School
Misake ES
Komachi
Kayamachi
Honmachi 5-chome
Honmachi 4-chome
Shimizumachi
Takasagomachi
Shimizumachi
Teppocho
Matsuyama University
Ehime University
Higashi Jr. HS
Matsuyama-kita HS
Matsuyama Red Cross Hospital
Midorimachi
Sekijuji-byoin-mae
Heiwadori 1-chome
Heiwadori
Dogo-ichima
Islan
Anumi Shrine
Millennia
Honmachi 3-chome
Teppocho
Taihei Annex
Taihei
Heiwa-dori
Sun Garden
Nishi-ichimanmachi
Midorimachi
Marunoumachi
Kami-ichiman
ABC
Showma
Kita-moch
Fuji Grand Matsuyama
Dairin-ji
Koshin-an Garden
Matsuyama Castle
Osugi Shrine
Matsuyama Castle Ropeway
GH Matsuyama
Matsuyama Shinnome HS
Okaido
Kachimachi
Kiyomachi
Minami mochidam
Mitakarama
Myogen
Miyatacho
Matsuyama Central Park
Fukusen-ji
Tsujimachi
Sunroute
Crown Hills
City
Matsuyama Ekimae
Iyo Takahama Line
Public Bath
Shiroyama Park
Ninomaru Historical Garden
Gudabutsuan House
Saka-no-ue-no-kumo Museum
District Public Prosecutor's Office
Tokyu Inn
International
Abis Inn
Iyotetsu Jonan Line
Katsuyamacho
Ichibancho
Toyoko Inn
Nibancho
Washington
Azalea
Matsuyama Comm. HS
Asahima
Asahi Hachiman Shrine
Taiho-ji
Yamauchi Shrine
Minamiedo
Miyatamachi
Mont Blanc
New Kajiwara
Otemachi Ekimae
Nishihoribata
Mitsukoshi
Gondola
Cafe Bleu
Cafe Jumelle
Check Inn Matsuyama
Yasaka Shrine
Tengu no Kakurega
Minamiedo
to Airport ←
Otsuka Clinic
Sky
JAL City
Dai Ichi
Domestic Courts
Citizen Hall
Prefectural Museum of Art
Ehime Prefectural Office
Kencho-mae
Shiyakusho-mae
Abis
Ana
New Grand
Sanbancho
Goshiki Somen Morikawa
No. 1 Matsuyama
Minami-Horibata
Prefectural Library
Matsuyama City Hall
Okaido
Ana H
Filtration Plant
Seven Stars Minamiedo Store
Chifunemachi
Hanazonomachi
Iyo Takahama Line
Matsuyama-shi Ekimae
Chifunemachi
Minatomachi
Cinaema Lunatic Minatomachi
Josei JHS
Business Hotel Clark
Indoor Pool
Gym
City Library
Aratama ES
Saibi HS
Camelia Hall
Matsuyama Sogo Community Center
Iyotetsu Takashimaya Kita
Fujiwara Bekkan
Matsuyama-shi
St. Catherine Girl HS
Shiki-do Museum
Matsuyama University
Lec Tokyo Legal Mind
Minatomachi
Nakanokawa-dori
Nakatsuya
Ikushimachi
Takewaramachi
Ana
Fujiwaramachi
Dobashi
Yugun ES
Masagocho
to Shiki-Do, Uwajima ↓
Matsuyama Technical HS
Suehiromachi
Matsuyama-minami HS
Yanaimachi
Kawaramachi
Public Bath
Nakamura
Prefectural Central Hospital
Tachibana Wakamiya Shrine
Yakushi-ji

Kotohira

Scale 1 : 20,000   200m   500ft

Kamino-murayama
to Tadotsu →
JR Dosan Line
Umatate
Yanaginohana
Obashi-higashi
Osacho
Homei
Yokoze
Fukuijo-ji
Kotoden Kotohira Line
Kitahataoka
Kotoden Kotohira Line
Enai
Obashinishi
Shinmichi
Minami-hataoka
208
Kitanomachi
Onishi Hospital
Nishinoki Shrine
Nishinaka
Kotohira
Kuranaka
Higashi-naka
Shinraku-ji
Shijo
Awa Betsu Highway
Kotohira Highway
282
Shinmeicho
Kayaba-shimo
Takara-ya
Takadoro (Lantern Tower)
Kobaitei
Kotohira Town Office
Ekimae
Iwasa Hospital
Rokuhigashi
Rokunishi
Enai
Enai ES
Enai Park
Honnaka
Kagawa Prefectural Nogyo University
Onishiyama
Kotohira PO
Kotosankaku
207
Asahimachi
Kotohira Riverside
Sunwell Kotohira
Honjo
Keino
Yumoto Yachiyo
Tsuruya Ryokan
Sakaemachi
Sushikoma Ryokan
Minamishinmachi
Kotohira Jr. HS
Honmura
Kinryo-no-Sato (Sake Museum)
Kotohira-gu Library
Kotobuki Ryokan
Kotohira HS
Uchimachi
Museum of History
Awachokita
Ryusho-ji
190
Kompira-san Inner Shrine
Marine Museum
Fudanomae
New Wataya
Koshindo
Tokiwa Shrine
Toramaru Ryokan
Sakuranosho Kotohira Grand
Awachokami
JR Dosan Line
Takahashi Yuichi Museum
Kanamaru-za Theater
Kawakita-higashi
Ichinosaka
Homotsu-kan (Treasure House)
Kotohira Kadan
Kawamukai
to Ayagawa →
Kotohira-gu Shrine
Hongu (Main Hall)
Shoin
Kamitsubaki
Okagomi
Kotohira Jidosha Seibi Kyogyo-kumiai
Ema-do (Ema Pavilion)
Asahino Yashiro
Tanigawa
Sugawara Shrine
Kotohira Park
319
Minamidoricho
Filtration Plan
32
Atagomachi
Teppan-yaki Tanakaya
Gojo-wakui
Lawson
208
Kaita
to Toyohama ↙
to Miyoshi ↓

Tokushima

Scale 1 : 20,000   200m   500ft

P
Naka-maegawach
Kitasako
Ichibancho
P
Sako
JR Kotoku Line
Kyoeu
Dekijima-hone
DEKIJ
Eigetsu
Fukuzo-ji
to Mima ←
Iyo Highway
Vocational School
Sunshine
Sako Nibancho
Lawson
Sako Ichibancho
Myoho-ji
McDonalds
Iwase Clinic
Seisui-ji
Rinko-ji
Awagin
Suwa Shrine
Rissho-ji
Mishima Shrine
Nishi-daikumachi
Kyodai-ji
Teramac
Jisen-ji
Anju-ji
Ganjo-ji
Toso-in
Bizancho
Choon-J
Kasuga Shrine
Yasaka Shrine
Zengak
Honka-ji
Honkaku-ji
Kunitamahik
Otakiyama
Bizan Ropeway
Sanroku
Awa Odori Museum
Tsurugiyama Shrine
Shinmachi ES
Higashi-yamatecho
Zuigan-ji
Mosukegahara
Sancho
Pagoda Peace Memorial Tower
Yumihi
Kunitamahik Shrine
Grand

KYUSHU

Hibiki-nada Sea
Genkai-nada Sea
Suo-nada Sea
Iyo-nada Sea

Shunan
Kudamatsu
Sanyo-Onoda
Hofu
Hikari
Tabus
Yoshimo
Yasuoka
Shimonoseki
Munakata
Kiwa
Tanoura
Murozumi
Ushi-jima I.
Nakanourd
Waita
Kira
Shiratsuchi
Kita-Kyushu
Ube Port
Yamaguchi
Ube Airport
Koiwai-jima I.
Iwai-jima I.
Uwa-jima I.
O-shima I.
Jino-shima I.
Chikuzen
Kitakyushu Airport
Okagaki
Onga
Nakama
Kanda
Hime-jima I.
Himeshima
Mukata
Satobama
Komizuhama
Iki I.
Tsutsukihama
Miyajima-cho
Ano-oshima I.
Munakata
Nogata
Miyako
Yukuhashi
Shirasuna
Iki Airport
Mt Tsujiyama
Koga
Miyawaka
Tagawa
Aka
Chikujo
Buzen
Kunisaki
Kunisaki Cape Natural Park
Kitsuki

Azuchi O-shima I.
Taku-shima I.
Ikitsuki I.
Kakara-shima I.
Madara-shima I.
Mukou-jima I.
Kuro-shima I.
Taka-shima I.
Hime-jima I.
Shingu
Hisayama
Iizuka
Fukuoka
FUKUOKA 92-93
Umi
Dazaifu
Kama
Mt Kunimi
Usa
Oita Airport
Mt Omure
Kozaki

Hirado
Matsuura
Genkai
Karatsu
Nakagawa
Kiyama
Tosu
Asakura
Ukiha
Hita
Kusu
Yufu
YUFUIN 91
Beppu
BEPPU AREA 91
Oita

Saza
Sasebo
Imari
Taku
Kanzaki
Kurume
Kamimine
Hirokawa
Kamimine
Usuki

Hasami
Kawatana
Takeo
Saga
Yanagawa
Chikugo
Miyama
Yamaga
Minami-Oguni
Aso
Taketa
Bungo-Ono
Saiki
Tsukumi

Kashima
Omachi
Omuta
Arao
Tamana
Nagomi
Kikuchi
ASO AREA 90-91
Ubuyama
Takamori

Isahaya
Unzen
NAGASAKI 92
Nagasaki
SHIMABARA 92
Shimabara
Kumamoto
KUMAMOTO 92-93
Koshi
Ozu
Kikuyo
Nishihara
TAKACHIHO 93
Takachiho
Hinokage
Nobeoka

Reihoku
Amakusa
Yatsushiro
Hikawa
Uto
Uki
Kosa
Gokase
Morotsuka
Kadogawa
Hyuuga

Minamata
Nagashima
Ashikita
Kuma
Yamae
Sagara
Taragi
Misato
Tsuno
Kawaminami
Saito
Shintomi

Izumi
Akune
Ebino
Kobayashi
Yusui
Takaharu
MIYAZAKI 91
Miyazaki

Satsuma-Sendai
Satsuma
Kirishima
Miyakonojo
Mimata
Nichinan

Ichiki-Kushikino
Hioki
Soo
Kushima

KAGOSHIMA 90-91
Kagoshima
Tarumizu
Shibushi
Higashikushira

Minami-Satsuma
Minami-Kyushu
Kanoya
Kimotsuki
Kinko

Makurazaki
Ibusuki
Minami Osumi

Cape Sata

Kyushu
Scale 1 : 1,500,000
20km
10miles

Aso Area
Scale 1 : 400,000

KAGOSHIMA

Beppu Area

↑ to Yufuin
to Kunisaki, Peninsula, Usa

Oita Expressway
Beppu Medical Center
Kamegawa
↑ to Yufuin
to Kunisaki, Peninsula, Usa
Chinoike Jigoku (Blood Pond Hell)
Shibaseki
10
Beppu Keirin-Jo (Velodrome)
KANNAWA HELLS AREA
Oni-ishi Bozu Jigoku
Kannon-ji
Hyotan Onsen
Kannawa
645
Shonin-ga-hama Park
Beppu Art Museum
Bozu Jigoku
Kyushu - Odan Rd
Beppu University
Beppu-Daigaku
Shonin-ga-hama Sand Bath
218
Kannawa
Kita-ishigaki
500
to Matsuyama, Osaka
Shin-Beppu National Hospital
JISSOJI CHUO PARK
Sun Valley
Obatake
Beppu Traditional Bamboo Craft
645
Kyushu Univ. Advanced Medical Center
Beppu International Port Ferry Terminal
Nishi-Beppu National Hospital
Tsurumioka HS
JR Nippo Line
10
Fujikan
Self Defense Force
MINAMI-TATEISHI PARK
Beppu Aoyama HS
Kitahama Termas
Spa Kitahama Termas
White Rose
Aqua Beat Indoor Pool
Suginoi Bowl
Beppu City Office
Fujimi-dori
Fuyo Club
Horita
Suginoi Palace
Suginoi
Ojisan-no-mori Children's Library
Kyushu-Odan Rd
Aso-Oita
Kannon
Zen-ji
Ryochiku
BEPPU PARK
Kei Sato Art Museum
52
Beppu
Mt Funabaru
Rakutenchi Amusement Park
Beppu Arena
52
Beppu
Cable Car
Hamawaki
CENTRAL BEPPU
to Oita, Usuki
to Oita

Kannawa Hells Area

Kannawa-kami
Kita-kannawa
Kifune Castle
Sakura Tei
218
Onsen Oni-yama Jigoku (Demon Mountain Hell)
Iyashi-no-Yado Iroha
Kannawa Mushi-yu
Kamado Jigoku (Boiling Hell)
Ida
Kannawa-higashi
Daikanyamacho
Yama Jigoku (Mountain Hell)
Saifuku-ji
Fujiya
Umi Jigoku (Sea/Ocean Hell)
Marugamiya
Miyuki
7Eleven
Yokoso
Furomoto
Akai Jigoku
Kannawaen
Umi
Miyuki-zaka
Kinryu
Eifuku-ji
Futabaso
Marashi-kan
Miharu Museum
Beppu Yukemuri Lookout
Oni-ishi Bozu Jigoku (Oni-ishi Monk's Hell)
Shira-ike Jigoku (White Pond Hell)
Hyotan
Fugetsu Hammond
OTANI PARK
Zuiko-ji
Kannawa
NAFCO Tsurumi
500
Kitaju
Tsurumi
Marushoku
Kamihiratacho
Beppu Rehabilitation Center
Spa Yume-tamatebako Yunosato
Autobacs
Honomecho Public Hall
Beppu City Branch Office
Kannawa PO
Nishi
Matsuya
Kamefuku
to Myoban
Goody
Fire Station
Kitajucho Public Hall
Best Denki
Parlor Diamond
Daichan Land
Joyfull
Asahi Jr.HS
Kanpo-no-yado Beppu
Koyasan Soen-in
7Eleven
Beppu Hyogu Center
Ishigaki Hospital
500
Hono'o Honome Shrine
Nursery
Jisso-ji
Asahi ES
Shin-beppu Public Hall
Shin-beppu
Asahi Ohirayama Chiku Public Hall
Tokusho-ji
to Beppu Bay
Lawson
Oyado Yunooka
Kyukofuku Beppu Rest Center
218
Tsuruni Market
Asahigaokacho
Nursery
Cosmos
Marumiya
Jissoji

Yufuin

to Hita
Ubuyama
45
Daikanbo Lookout
El Patio Ranch
Ichinoyama
Shiroyama Lookout
Plaza
Aso City Office
213
to Oita
to Usa
Art Museum
Wazanho
Yuyado Kurabi
Shoya-no-yakata
Sadohara
Sanso Murata
Watakushi Art Museum
110
57
Miyai
JR Kyushu
Yufu Riverside
Sagiritei
Hoshifuruyado
Yufu Yume Art Museum
Kutsurogino
Nakashima
Aso Shrine
Cuddly Dominion
Aso Azelea 21
Zoo
Kango-no-Yado
Aso Kodai-no-sato Museum
214
Ryoso Kikuya
Kahorino Sato
Yado Nanakawa
Santokan
217
Hinohara
Hanamura
Tsuka Kirinko
Kamenoi Besso
Kijima Volcano useum
265
Sensui Gorge
Yufuin Club
Tatsumi
Yufuin
Kotobuki
Jonoyu
Norman Rockwell Museum
Sueda Art Museum
Tsue
Mt. Aso
Mt. Neko
Naka-dake Crater
135
Takamori Onsenkan
Yuri
Hananosho
Sansuikan
Yufuin
Shuhokan
Stained Art
Tsuenosho
Hikari-no-ie
Nanairono Kaze
Aso Nat'l Park
218
Kyukamura Minami-Aso
Mikadoya
Sanso
Tanaka
Glass Museum
Miyajiri
to Beppu
Cable Car
Blue Grass
Suigetsuso
Yufuin Kosei Nenkin Hospital
Fukinoya
Mebaeso
Unagihime Shrine
Yufu-no-go Saigakuan
Takamori Town Office
319
151
YH Murataya
212
Yamano Hotel
Musoen
Yamashiro
Mihoshi
Nishi-ishimatsu
to Oita
to Nobeoka
325

Central Beppu

Community Center
Sakaigawa ES
Atio
to Kitsuki
Beppu
Kami-noguchicho
Noguchi
Wakakusacho
Nippo Line
Joyfull
Beppu-chuo ES
Oita International Bldg
Aoyama ES
City Fire Department
Worker's Athletic Center
Tenma Shrine
Saiwaimachi
Kokura Highway
645
Kaimonji Noguchi Cemetery
Bansho-ji
Takeshi Hospital
Kyomachi
Fujimicho
Kitahama Onsen Termas
Beppu Municipal Water Bureau
Aoyamacho-dori
Sanyo Sangyo
Fujimi Seihyo Kojo
Beppu Bay
Citizen Gym
Sawacho-dori
Tenmancho
Beppu-saiwai PO
645
Marushoku
Beppu Chuo Hospital
Fujimi-dori
MATOGAHAMA PARK
Noguchi-hara
Beppu City Office
Oita Bank
Beppu Noguchi Fureai
Kitamoto Bldg
Spa Beach
Fujimi-dori
Beppu Health Center
Oita-dori
Minami-matogahamacho
Beppu Convention Center
Ojisan-no-mori Children's Library
Hommon-ji
Beppu Church
Koryu Center
Shinzenko-ji
Nishi-noguchicho
Family Mart
Bekai
Umne
Yamanote Junior HS
BEPPU PARK
Shiragiku
Noguchi Fureai
Family Mart
Zensho-ji
10
Seaside
Mimatsu Oetei
Kamiharucho
Aoyama-dori
Matsukaze
Seisei Hospital
Hangan-ji
Kai Bldg
Yamada Besso
New Matsumi
Koraku
Miyajidake Shrine
Aoyama ES
Hanabeppu
Daiichi
Sansenkaku
Seifu
Joyfull
Sato Kei Art Museum
Beppu Arena
Star
Ekimae-honmachi
Fujiyoshii
Nishitetsu Resort Inn
Hanabishi
Haramachi
Nagarekawa-dori
Vocational School
7Eleven
Sea Wave
Ekimae-PO
kitahama PO
Ureshii-ya
Ekimae-dori
Arthur
Tokiwa
Royal Host
New Tsuruta
Haramachi
Beppu Nakashima PO
Momiya
Civic Hall
Furocho
Saiho-ji
Okajima Clinic
Takeya
Kamadaha Chukei Pumping Station
Kami-tanoyumachi
Hasenso
Kamenoi
Kami-tanoyumachi
Akiba Shrine
Nagarekawa-dori
Lawson
Nakamura Hospital
Marushoku
You Me Town
Nakashimacho
Hata Hospital
7Eleven
Beppu Church
Mos Burger
Hikarimachi
Nishi ES
Yamamoto Hospital
Akiba-dori
Lawson
Kemenoyu
Kojil Good Inn
Asami Shrine
Yamazaki
Uchida-dori
Beppu
Funeral Hall
Beppu Matsubara Post Office
Sky Resort
Asami Hospital
Ichiriki Ryokan
Tatsutacho
10
to Oita

Kagoshima

HIROYAMA PARK
oyama Observatory
to Aira
10
Reimeikan
Nishimuta
Okinawa Seishonen Kaikan
Shirayamacho
Yasuicho
Shiroyama Kanko
Keitenkaku
Kagoshima Library
District Court
Meizan ES
Modern Literature
Manshu
Kagoshima City Office
Sakura-jima Pier Ferry Terminal
Io World Kagoshima Aquarium
Kagoshima Kanko
City Museum of Art
240
Lawson
Mishima Town Office
North Pier Passenger Terminal
Saigo Takamori Statue
Houzan Hall
Yozan
Brand Shop
NHK
Archaeological
Nishi-Hongan-ji
Hon-koshin-
Aqua Garden
Board Walk
kukini Bunko
Nanshu
Asahi-dori
machi
Dolphin Port
Richmond
Meizancho
South Pier Passenger Terminal
CHUO PARK
Prefectural
Museum
Tenyukan Central Park
Kagoshima Harbor Government Office
Fukiage
7Eleven
Izumicho
Yamagataya
Izuro
Sumiyoshicho
Imamura Hospital
Xavier Church
Besso
Miami-dori
214
Fast Ship Passenger Terminal
Village Vanguard
igen-ryu the Art
Sunflex
Gofukumachi
Kagoshima Port
of War Museum
Terukuni-dori
Tenmonkan-dori
Higashi Hongan-ji
Gate In Kagoshima
Dormy Inn
Cent
Kyoo-ji
Family Mart
Blue Wave
Kagoshima Fish Market
Hokke Club
Lexton
Nishino
Horiecho
Tennokan
Perth-dori
Hagiwara-dori
216
Matsubaracho
Kajimicho
Sagara Hospital
Koto
Perth-dori
Daimonjicho
Kinko-dori
Siena
XYZ
Kagoshima Chuo HS
Sameshima Hospital
Tennokan-dori
Kyushu
City Hospital
Shin-yashikicho
Santorini
Ministry of Land
Kagoshima Women's Junior College
7Eleven
Nanrinjicho
Kagoshima Chuo Police Station
Shinsaki
Jonan-dori
Iwao Hospital
Lawson
20
to Ibusuki

Miyazaki

Hanadonocho
to Saito
Shimoharacho
Nursery
Nishiike ES
Ehira ES
Victoria
Miyazaki Daiichi
2Eleven
JR Kyushu
Shimohara Cemetery
Wachigawara
Nishiike
Ehiracho
Lawson
Miyazaki-nishi
Garden Terrace
Aobacho
Nakatsusecho
Miyazaki Police Station
Funeral Hall
Ohashi
Oe Orthopaedic Hospital
Nishi-ikecho
26
Marushimacho
Rugby Ground
Miyazaki-eki-higashi
Nishikimachi
NAFCO
Shimizu
Green
KFC
10
Miyazaki Eye Hospital
Lawson
Funeral Hall
Nichinan-dori
Takachihodori
Miyazaki Prefectural Gymnasium
to Kobayashi
Daiku
Odo ES
Jal City
Marix Lagoon
Route Inn
7Eleven
Carino
Family Mart
Sky Tower
Bus Center
Maxvalu
26
Air Line
Miyazaki City
Yamakataya
Toyoko Inn
Richmond
Chigusacho
Takachiho-dori
JR Miyazaki
Miyazaki Municipal General Gymnasium
Five Oaks
Miyazaki Prefectural Hospital
Manix
Bonberuta
25
Miyazaki
Oimatsu
Tachibanadori-higashi
Ichibangai Arcade
Plum
Bosco
Jazz Club
Science Museum
New Wel
Chuodori
Togakushi
Grandy
Lifetime
7Eleven
MIYAZAKI CENTRAL PARK
Kita-takamatsucho
Miyazaki Medical Center Hospital
Merieges
Beppucho
Lawson Plus
Jodoecho
Nishi-takamatsucho
Tachibanadori-nishi
Rissho-ji
Yakata
Wakakusa
Hachimangu
Miyazaki Gakuen HS
Tachibanadori
Motomiyacho
Planet Cafe Sports
Super
Odo-so
7Eleven
Showacho
269
Matsubashi
Kaminomachi
Miyazaki
Prefectural
Police
Prefectural Office
Miyazaki Showa PO
Suehiro
Daisan Government Bldg
Kusunoki-dori
Family Mart
Horikawacho
Tsurunoshima
Togakushi
Pref. Exhibition Hall
Crane
Miyazaki Kencho
Sunflower
Miyazaki Police
Nagano
Asahi
Himawari-so
Asahi-dori
Ueno Cho-dori
Miyazaki City Office
Green Rich
Ogura
Hirakucho
Oyodo River
Kawaramachi
341
Segashira Shrine
to Miyazaki
220
to Miyakonojo
Miyazaki Kanko
Matsuyama
Segashiracho
11
Miyazaki
Jr.HS

Kagoshima

Miyazaki

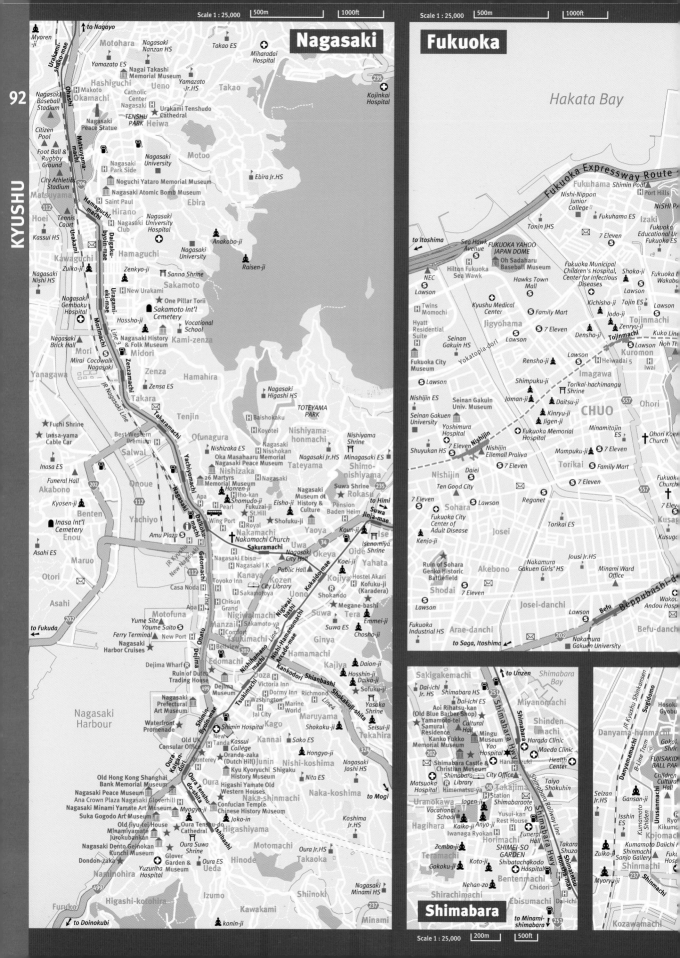

Naha

Scale 1 : 25,000
500m
1000ft

Port of Naha-shinko
Tomari Fish Market
to Aguni, Tonaki, Zamami, Tokashiki

to Onna
Tenkudai Hospital
Ekka
Ameku Ryubo
Sports
Kokusai HS
Mekaru ES
Family Mart
AMEKU PARK
Shin-toshin Mekaru City Hall
Ryukyu Shimpo Hall
Naha City Hall
McDonald's
SHIN-TOSHIN PARK
to Urasoe
Seigen-ji
Uenoya
Ameku-gu Shrine
Omoromachi Medical Center
Apple Town
Prefectural Museum & Art Museum
Shoe
Butsuryu-ji
Tomari HS
Sea Pappa GH fo Women
Family Mart
Omoromachi Main Place
Sanei Naha
Toyoko Inn
Bank of Japan
Hokke Club
Libre Garden
Cocostore
Tomari International Cemetery
Paradise Club
Vocational School
City Front Harumi YH
Lawson
Avanti Urban Stay Omoro
Mizu-no-shiryokan Museum
DFS Galleria
Yui Railway
Makabi ES
Okinawa Senin Kaikan
Tomarin Port Terminal
Family Mart
Dai-ni Office Complex
Sun Plaza
Makabi ES
Sen'in Kaikan
Peace Land
Smile
Family Mart
Tomari ES
The Naha Terrace
Daiwa Roynet
Vocational School
Maejima
Wakasa ES
Lawson
Oriental
Yoshida
Family Mart
Itokazu Hospital
Toyoko Inn
Asato Catholic Church
Nozato Bldg
Naminoue
Maejima
City Court
Richmond
Family Mart
Sogenji-dori
Church of Jesus Christ of latter-day Saints
Asato
Spirit of Jesus Church
Wakasa Library
Naha Jr. HS
Maejima ES
Dai-ichi Seimei
Sun Plaza
Medical Plaza Daido Chuo
Okinawa
Naminoue Shrine
Lawson
Route Inn
Shintoku-ji
Family Mart
Gokoku-ji
Urashima
Suncoral
Rasso
Narumi Gekko-so
MaxValu
Royal Orion
Daido Central Hospital
Daido ES
Ryusei Hospital
Salad Bowl
Tsushimaru Museum
Wakasa
Solvita
GRG
Family Mart
Central
Nansei Kanko
Sun Ocean
Daido Odori
The Spiral
Kume Shiseibyo
Matsuyama
Toyoko Inn
Lawson
Family Mart
Sakaemachi-dori
Continental
Washington
MATSUYAMA PARK
Airway
Kumoji ES
Kokusai-dori
Ryubo
Daido ES
Western
Tsuji
Naha Comm. HS Captains
Hana
Apa
Yamaichi
Mitsukoshi
Tsuboya ES
Bingo
Ryotei
Fukushu-en
MIDORIGAOKE PARK
Yamanouchi McDonald's
Traditional Arts & Crafts Center
Castle Nozaki
Kume
Lawson
Daiten-ji
Sun Palace
Plaza
Kumoji
Jal City
Naha Opa
Dai-ichi Makishi Public Market
Sakurazaka Theatre
Shinkyo-ji
Minshuku Hikarinoie
Nishitetsu Sun Resort Inn
Sanwa
Family Mart Lawson
Grand
Hakuseiso
Stella Resort
Makishi
Tsuboya Pottery Museum
Naha
Marine West
Ryukyu
Sun Royal
Kariyushi
Family Mart Comfort
Rocore
New Okinawa
Minshuku
Getto
Chitose Shotengai Bldg
Pachinko Sunshine
Gallery Gunjo
Mihara St. Paul Church
Family Mart
Higashimachi
Izumizaki
Okinawa Pref. Office
Chura Ryukyu
Naha HS
Matsuo
Tsuboya
Kamihara ES
McDonald's
Mawashi Jr. HS
Hilton
Ryukyu Kowa
Minshuku Minatoso
Kainan ES
Rainbow
Higawa
Kamihara Jr. HS
Soba Takeya
Nakahara Bldg
Tondocho
Route Inn
Lawson
Family Mart
Kainan Hon-dori
YOGI PARK
Okinawa Pref. Library
Ohara Hospital
Naha Port Ferry Terminal
Naha Crown Plaza
Kainan Catholic Church
City Chuo Library
Yorimiya Bldg
Bank of Ryukyus
Mawashi ES
Port of Naha
Okiden Naha Bldg
Southern Plaza Kaiho
Biztort
Harborview
District Court
Shimin Kaikan-dori
Civic Hall
Naha-byoin-dori
Family Mart
Asahibashi
Asahimachi
Vocational School
Family Mart
Sobe
Bank of Ryukyus
Joyfull
Dai-ichi Chiho Gov. Bldg
Shimin Kaikan-dori
Okinawa Red Cross Hospital
Bank of Okinawa
Nagata
Yorimiya Jr HS
Bunyan Town
Kokusai YH
Mercure
Ryukyu Ginko Kempo Kaikan
Yamada Kensetsu
Okinawa Kaiho Bank
Jogaku ES
Yogi ES
Okinawa Prefectural College of Nursing
Yorimiya
Family Mart
Okinawa Cellular Stadium Naha
Onoyama Athletic Field
Okinawa Postal Museum
Zamami Bldg
Lawson
Tsubogawa
Town Plaza Kanehide
Yogi
Kokuba
ONOYAMA PARK
Swimming Complex
Gokoku Shrine
JA Bldg
Yogi Chapel
Kanehide
Yamashita-Kakinohana Rd
Yuai Sports Center
Kakinohana ES
Kawahira Hospital
Kohagura
Lawson
Kokura Bldg
Kanehide
Kokuba Riubo
Yambaru Shokudo
Yamasitacho
MANKO PARK
Lawson
Kohagura Mutsumi Kaikan
Chuo Fire Station Kokuba
Okinawa-shogaku HS
Oroku HS
Yui Railway
Naha Inner Loop Route
Okinawa Kaiho Bank
MANKO PARK
Family Mart
to Madanbashi
to Nishihara

Okinawa & The Southwest Islands

Yokote-jima I.
Wanjo
Okino-Erabu-jima
Yoron-jima I.
Iheya-jima I.
Izena-jima I.
Ie-jima I.
Okinawa-honto
Nago
Uruma
Okinawa
Aguni-jima I.
Hatenohama
Idesuna I.
Kume-jima I.
Shinri
Ara
O-jima
Tonaki-jima I.
Zamami-jima I.
Aka-jima I.
Naha
Kudaka I.
Tokashiki-jima I.
Nanjo
OKINAWA-HONTO 95

Kuba-jima I.
Uotori-jima I.
Kitako-jima I.
Minami Ko-jima I.

PACIFIC OCEAN

MIYAKO ISLANDS 97
Irabu-jima I.
Hirara
Minna-jima
Tori-ike
Miyako-jima
Tarama-jima

Ayamihabiru-kan
Yonaguni-jima I.
Yonaguni Submarine Ruins
Iriomote Onsen
Urauchi-gawa River
Trip Pier
Iriomote-jima I.
Ishigaki-jima I.
Ishigaki
Nakanougan-jima I.
YAEYAMA ISLANDS 96
Hateruma-jima I.

How to use this Index

The index lists towns, cities and districts within cities on any of the maps in the atlas as well as points of interest, national parks, temples and other landmarks. Each entry in the index is followed by a page number and the name of the map in which that item appears. If an entry appears on more than one map—for example an area map and also a more detailed map—only the page reference and name of the more detailed map are given.

21_21 Design Sight Museum 13 Roppongi, Shibuya, Omotesando, Harajuku & Meiji Shrine
21st Century Museum of Contemporary Art 38 Kanazawa
26 Martyrs Memorial Museum 92 Nagasaki
3D Uchu Kyoryu-kan Museum 33 Nikko Area
A Factory 76 Aomori
Abarth Car Museum 28 Mt. Fuji
Abashiri 83 Hokaido
Abecho 41 Shizuoka
Abeno 55 Osaka Area
Abeno Motomachi 57 Greater Osaka
Abeno Ward 57 Greater Osaka
Abenosuji 57 Greater Osaka
Abiko 23 Mt. Fuji & Around Tokyo
Abu 68 Hiroshima & Western Honshu
Aburaguruma 38 Kanazawa
Aburakakecho 48 Western Kyoto
Ace World Bag & Luggage Museum 11 Asakusa, Ueno & Akihabara
Achi 75 Kurashiki
Achi Shrine 75 Kurashiki
Ada 95 Okinawa-honto
Adachi Museum & Garden 69 Hiroshima & Western Honshu
Adashinocho 48 Western Kyoto
Adventure World Zoo 54 Kansai Area
Advertising Museum of Tokyo 8 Ginza, Tsukiji & Tokyo Tower
Agano 77 Northern Honshu
Agariya 37 Inuyama
Agatamachi 41 Nagano
Agebaicho 6 Imperial Palace & Tokyo Station
Ageshima Aquarium 80 Sado-ga Island
Agon-no-taki 32 Nikko Area
Agriculture Research Center 78 Hanamaki
Agui 55 Kansai
Aguracho 47 Northern Kyoto
Aha 95 Okinawa-honto
Ai Chikyuhaku Memorial Park 35 Nagoya Area
Aiaicho 49 Western Kyoto
Aibagawa Canal 72 Hagi
Aibetsu 83 Hokaido
Aichi Ceramic Museum 35 Nagoya Area
Aichi District 67 Lake Biwa
Aichi Peace Memorial Museum 36 Central Nagoya
Aichi Pref. 34 Central Honshu
Aichi Pref. Art Museum 37 Central Nagoya
Aichi Pref. Forest Park 35 Nagoya Area
Aichicho 36 Central Nagoya
Aidomari Hot Spring 83 Shiretoko National Park
Aikawa 80 Sado-ga Island
Aikawa Hiranezaki Hot Spring 80 Sado-ga Island
Aikocho 88 Matsuyama
Ainai 76 Shirakami Mountains
Ainan 86 Shikoku
Aino 78 Kakunodate
Ainokinishi 41 Nagano
Ainokura Folk Museum 34 Shirakawa-go & Gokayama
Ainokura Traditional Farmhouses 34 Shirakawa-go & Gokayama
Ainu Ruins 83 Hokaido
Aioi 37 Inuyama
Aioi 54 Kansai Area
Aioi-dori 57 Greater Osaka
Aioichi 37 Central Nagoya
Aioicho 24 Yokohama
Aioicho 32 Nikko Town
Aioicho 41 Shizuoka
Aioicho 62 Kobe
Aioicho 74 Matsue
Aioicho 75 Tottori
Airasan-ryo Imperial Mausoleum 93 Takachiho
Aisai 54 Kansai Area
Aisari 79 Hiraizumi & Ichinoseki
Aisho 54 Kansai Area
Aizankei Hot Spring 82 Daisetsuzan National Park
Aizome-en Munakata Shiko Museum 34 Central Honshu
Aizu Bukeyashiki 80 Aizu, Inawashiro & Ura-Bandai
Aizu Kogen Nango 77 Northern Honshu
Aizu Sake Museum 80 Aizu, Inawashiro & Ura-Bandai
Aizu-wakamatsu 80 Aizu, Inawashiro & Ura-bandai

Aizu-wakamatsu Castle 77 Northern Honshu
Aizu-wakamatsu City 80 Aizu, Inawashiro & Ura-bandai
Aizumi 69 Hiroshima & Western Honshu
Aizumicho 15 Shinjuku
Ajigasawa 77 Northern Honshu
Ajigaura 23 Mt. Fuji & Around Tokyo
Ajigawa 56 Greater Osaka
Ajihara-honmachi 61 Osaka Namba
Ajiharacho 61 Osaka Namba
Ajiro 30 Izu Peninsula
Ajiro 57 Greater Osaka
Ajiro-kita 57 Greater Osaka
Ajiro-minami 57 Greater Osaka
Ajiro-shinmachi 57 Greater Osaka
Aka 90 Kyusu
Aka-daki 64 Around Nara
Akabira 83 Hokaido
Akabono 92 Nagasaki
Akabori 22 Mt. Fuji & Around Tokyo
Akada Beach 68 Hiroshima & Western Honshu
Akadomori 80 Sado-ga Island
Akagawa 57 Greater Osaka
Akage 39 Noto Peninsula
Akagi 22 Mt. Fuji & Around Tokyo
Akagi-motomachi 6 Imperial Palace & Tokyo Station
Akagishitamachi 6 Imperial Palace & Tokyo Station
Akahane 79 Hiraizumi & Ichinoseki
Akai Jigoku Hot Spring 91 Kannawa Hells Area
Akaigawa 82 Hokaido
Akaikutsu Haiteta Onnanoko Statue 25 Kawasaki
Akaishi-gawa Stream 76 Shirakami Mountains
Akaiwa 69 Hiroshima & Western Honshu
Akaiwa-no-taki 82 Daisetsuzan National Park
Akama 31 Shimoda
Akama Shrine 72 Shimonoseki
Akama-bairin (Plume Grove) 22 Mt. Fuji & Around Tokyo
Akamacho 72 Shimonoseki
Akame Hot Spring 54 Kansai Area
Akami Hihokan Museum 31 Atami
Akamon Art Museum 81 Sendai
Akamoncho 24 Yokohama
Akan International Crane Center & Tancho Observation Center 82 Kushiro National Park
Akan Kohan Eco Museum 83 Akan National Park
Akan National Park 83 Akan National Park
Akan Royal Valley Ski Area 82 Kushiro National Park
Akana-taki 32 Nikko Area
Akanabe 37 Inuyama
Akanko Hot Spring 83 Akan National Park
Akanuma Chaya 32 Nikko Area
Akaocho 46 Northern Kyoto
Akarenga Kyodokan Museum 78 Akita
Akasaka 13 Roppongi, Shibuya, Omotesando, Harajuku & Meiji Shrine
Akasaka 93 Fukuoka
Akasakacho 48 Western Kyoto
Akasaki Hot Spring 39 Noto Peninsula
Akashi 54 Kansai Area
Akashi-Kaikyo-Ohashi Bridge 54 Kansai Area
Akashicho 9 Ginza, Tsukiji & Tokyo Tower
Akashimachi 63 Kobe
Akasumi 39 Noto Peninsula
Akatsukacho 37 Central Nagoya
Akatsukimachi 38 Kanazawa
Akatsutsumi 4 Greater Tokyo
Akayu Hot Spring 80 Aizu, Inawashiro & Ura-Bandai
Akazawa 30 Izu Peninsula
Akazawa Beach 30 Izu Peninsula
Akebono 92 Fukuoka
Akebonocho 24 Yokohama
Akebonocho 86 Uwajima
Akebonomachi 39 Takayama
Akebonomachi 81 Sendai
Akechi 34 Central Honshu
Akechi Ruins 35 Nagoya Area
Akechidaira Plateau 32 Nikko Area
Akechidaira Ropeway 32 Nikko Area
Aki 87 Shikoku
Aki-takata 69 Hiroshima & Western Honshu
Akibasan 46 Northern Kyoto
Akihabara 5 Greater Tokyo
Akihabara Electric Town 7 Imperial Palace & Tokyo Station

Akikaidocho 48 Western Kyoto
Akiota 68 Hiroshima & Western Honshu
Akishima 22 Mt. Fuji & Around Tokyo
Akita 77 Northern Honshu
Akita Airport 77 Northern Honshu
Akita City Folklore and Performing Art Center 78 Akita
Akita Co. 72 Shimonoseki
Akita Literature Museum 78 Akita
Akita Pref. 77 Northern Honshu
Akita Prefectural Museum of Art 78 Akita
Akita University Museum 78 Akita
Akitsukicho 45 Kawaramachi & Gion
Akiyoshi 39 Noto Peninsula
Akiyoshi-do Limestone Cave 68 Hiroshima & Western Honshu
Akkeshi 83 Hokaido
Ako 39 Noto Peninsula
Ako 54 Kansai Area
Akoogi 79 Hiraizumi & Ichinoseki
Akoyama Ski Area 67 Lake Biwa
Akune 90 Kyusu
Aloe Center 30 Izu Peninsula
Alpen Rose Ski Area 54 Kansai Area
Alpine Plant Garden 55 Osaka Area
Alps Hot Spring Museum 40 Nagano & Matsumoto Areas
Alts Bandai 80 Aizu, Inawashiro & Ura-Bandai
Ama District 35 Nagoya Area
Ama Kaigan Beach 87 Shikoku
Ama Ward 35 Nagoya Area
Amadani Hot Spring 34 Central Honshu
Amadomari Hot Spring 95 Okinawa & The Southwest Islands
Amagasaki City 56 Greater Osaka
Amagasaki Kyotei Stadium (Motorboat Race-course) 56 Greater Osaka
Amagataki Park 86 Shikoku
Amagibanrai Botanical Garden 30 Izu Peninsula
Amagiri-no-taki 87 Shikoku
Amago-iwa Rock 76 Shirakami Mountains
Amaharashi Beach 39 Noto Peninsula
Amakashi Hill 65 Asuka
Amakusa 90 Kyusu
Amakusa Airport 90 Kyusu
Amami Airport 97 Amami Oshima
Amami City Museum 97 Amami Oshima
Amami Island Botanical Garden 97 Amami Oshima
Amami Marine Museum 97 Amami Oshima
Amami Park 97 Amami Oshima
Amamizu Historical Museum 39 Noto Peninsula
Amanai 76 Shirakami Mountains
Amanawa Shrine 27 Kamakura
Amano-Iwato Legendry Cave 54 Kansai Area
Amanohashidate 66 Amano Hashidate
Amanoiwato Hot Spring 93 Takachiho
Amanoiwato Shrine 93 Takachiho
Amanomanai Spring Water 93 Takachiho
Amanuma 4 Greater Tokyo
Amazon Folk Museum 81 Dewa Sanzen
Amenomori Hoshu-an 67 Lake Biwa
American Teddy Museum 63 Kobe
Ameyoko Shopping Street 7 Imperial Palace & Tokyo Station
Amidagaminecho 43 Central & Eastern Kyoto
Amidaijicho 72 Shimonoseki
Amidajimaecho 47 Northern Kyoto
Amijimacho 59 Osaka Station
Ammon Hot Spring 76 Shirakami Mountains
Ammon-no-taki 76 Shirakami Mountains
Amuse Museum 11 Asakusa, Ueno & Akihabara
An-yo-ji 27 Kamakura
Anamizu 39 Noto Peninsula
Anan 34 Central Honshu
Anan 87 Shikoku
Anbo 97 Yakushima
Ancient Orient Museum 17 Ikebukuro
Ando 41 Shizuoka
Ando 54 Kansai Area
Ando Residence 78 Kakunodate
Ando Town 64 Around Nara
Ando-yanagicho 41 Shizuoka
Andojimachi 61 Osaka Namba
Anjo City 35 Nagoya Area
Anjo Okazaki 34 Central Honshu
Ankokuron-ji 27 Kamakura
Annaka 22 Mt. Fuji & Around Tokyo
Anno Mitsumasa Museum 73 Tsuwano
Anpanman Children's Museum 24 Yokohama
Anraku Hot Spring 90 Kyusu

Anrakukojicho 46 Northern Kyoto
Anshu 42 Kyoto
Anyobo 47 Northern Kyoto
Anyoji 81 Sendai
Ao Ruins 39 Noto Peninsula
Aobacho 91 Miyazaki
Aobadai 12 Roppongi, Shibuya, Omotesando, Harajuku & Meiji Shrine
Aoi 34 Central Honshu
Aoi 37 Central Nagoya
Aoi Rihatsu-kan (Old Blue Barber Shop) 92 Shimabara
Aoi-Matsuri Festival (May 15) 47 Northern Kyoto
Aoichi 30 Izu Peninsula
Aoidencho 46 Northern Kyoto
Aoinomoricho 46 Northern Kyoto
Aojoicho 47 Northern Kyoto
Aoki Hot Spring 34 Central Honshu
Aoki Konyo Monument 5 Greater Tokyo
Aokigahara Ocean Of Trees 28 Mt. Fuji
Aokigaharacho 48 Western Kyoto
Aomi 21 Odaiba
Aomori 77 Northern Honshu
Aomori Airport 77 Northern Honshu
Aomori Bank Memorial Hall 76 Hirosaki
Aomori Pref. 77 Northern Honshu
Aomori Prefecture Museum 77 Aomori
Aomori Prefecture Tourist Information Counter 76 Aomori
Aoyagi 77 Aomori
Aoyagi Samurai Manor Museum 78 Kakunodate
Aoyagihama Beach 67 Lake Biwa
Aoyama 13 Roppongi, Shibuya, Omotesando, Harajuku & Meiji Shrine
Aoyama Music Memorial Hall 48 Western Kyoto
Apio Amusement Park 31 Atami
Aqua Beat Indoor Pool 91 Beppu Area
Aqua City 21 Odaiba
Aqua Green Village Anmon 76 Shirakami Mountains
Aqua Park Kan 33 Nikko Area
Aqua Toto Gifu Aquarium 35 Nagoya Area
Aquabus Pier 59 Osaka Station
Aquamarine Fukushima 77 Northern Honshu
Aquarium 8 Ginza, Tsukiji & Tokyo Tower
Aquatic Plants Community 47 Northern Kyoto
Aquatic Zoo 10 Asakusa, Ueno & Akihabara
Ara 94 Okinawa & The Southwest Islands
Araboricho 48 Western Kyoto
Arae-danchi 92 Fukuoka
Aragusuku Beach 97 Miyako Islands
Arai 30 Izu Peninsula
Arai 4 Greater Tokyo
Arai 80 Aizu, Inawashiro & Ura-bandai
Arakawa 5 Greater Tokyo
Arakawa 57 Greater Osaka
Arakawa 95 Okinawa-honto
Arakawa 96 Ishigaki City
Arakawa Beach 77 Northern Honshu
Arakawa Starting Point 97 Yakushima
Araki Hot Spring 68 Hiroshima & Western Honshu
Arakicho 15 Shinjuku
Arakogawa-koen Garden Plaza 35 Nagoya Area
Arakura Horinuki Site Museum 29 Lake Kawaguchi
Aramachi 81 Sendai
Aramaki 53 Uji Town
Aramaki 81 Sendai
Arao 90 Kyusu
Arashiyama 48 Western Kyoto
Arashiyama Bamboo Grove 48 Western Kyoto
Arashiyama Monkey Park Iwatayama 48 Western Kyoto
Aratacho 62 Kobe
Arataka 73 Yamaguchi
Aratsu 93 Fukuoka
Araya 29 Lake Kawaguchi
Archaeological Museum 76 Hirosaki
Archaeological 91 Kagoshima
Archaeological Museum 83 Hokaido
Archeological Museum 28 Mt. Fuji
Ariake 21 Odaiba
Ariake Art Museum 40 Nagano & Matsumoto Areas
Ariake Coliseum 21 Odaiba
Ariake Hot Spring 40 Nagano & Matsumoto Areas
Ariake Tennis-no-mori Park 21 Odaiba
Arida 54 Kansai Area

Arida Hot Spring 54 Kansai Area
Aridagawa 54 Kansai Area
Arifuku Hot Spring 68 Hiroshima & Western Honshu
Arigasaki 41 Matsumoto
Arihorocho 84 Otaru
Arima Hot Spring 55 Osaka Area
Arisaka 39 Gujo Hachiman
Arishima Museum 82 Sado-ga Island
Arisugawacho 48 Western Kyoto
Arkopia Ski Area 34 Central Honshu
Art and Crafts Museum 47 Northern Kyoto
Art Gallery 14 Shinjuku
Art Museum 91 Yufuin
Art Tower Mito 23 Mt. Fuji & Around Tokyo
Arukapoto 72 Shimonoseki
Arume 95 Okinawa-honto
Asa Mori House 72 Hagi
Asadacho 43 Central & Eastern Kyoto
Asagayakita 4 Greater Tokyo
Asagiri Kogen Green Park 28 Mt. Fuji
Asago 54 Kansai Area
Asagogunzan Natural Park 54 Kansai Area
Asahi 29 Lake Kawaguchi
Asahi 40 Nagano & Matsumoto Areas
Asahi 57 Greater Osaka
Asahi 77 Northern Honshu
Asahi 91 Miyazaki
Asahi 92 Nagasaki
Asahi Hot Spring 68 Hiroshima & Western Honshu
Asahi Prime Ski Area 40 Nagano & Matsumoto Areas
Asahi Tengusuton Ski Area 68 Hiroshima & Western Honshu
Asahi Ward 64 Around Nara
Asahi-dori 63 Kobe
Asahicho 26 Kamakura
Asahicho 48 Western Kyoto
Asahicho 76 Aomori
Asahicho 79 Hiraizumi & Ichinoseki
Asahicho 84 Hakodate
Asahidake Hot Spring 82 Daisetsuzan National Park
Asahidake Ski Area 82 Daisetsuzan National Park
Asahigaoka 4 Greater Tokyo
Asahigaoka 42 Kyoto
Asahigaoka 88 Matsuyama
Asahigaokacho 91 Kannawa Hells Area
Asahikawa 82 Daisetsuzan National Park
Asahikawa Airport 82 Daisetsuzan National Park
Asahimachi 39 Takayama
Asahimachi 61 Osaka Namba
Asahimachi 66 Hikone Castle
Asahimachi 66 Himeji Castle
Asahimachi 86 Uwajima
Asahimachi 88 Kotohira
Asahimachi 88 Matsuyama
Asahimachi 94 Naha
Asahino Yashiro 88 Kotohira
Asahiyama Zoo 82 Daisetsuzan National Park
Asajigahara 65 Nara
Asaka 22 Mt. Fuji & Around Tokyo
Asaki 90 Kyusu
Asakita-ku 68 Hiroshima & Western Honshu
Asakuchi 69 Hiroshima & Western Honshu
Asakura 90 Kyusu
Asakura Sculpture Museum and Garden 5 Greater Tokyo
Asakusa 11 Asakusa, Ueno & Akihabara
Asakusa-bashi 10 Asakusa, Ueno & Akihabara
Asama Hot Spring 40 Nagano & Matsumoto Areas
Asami 88 Matsuyama
Asaminami-ku 68 Hiroshima & Western Honshu
Asamushi Hot Spring 77 Northern Honshu
Asari Beach 68 Hiroshima & Western Honshu
Asato 94 Naha
Asatsukicho 48 Western Kyoto
Asatsuyugaharacho 46 Northern Kyoto
Asazawa 78 Hanamaki
Asazumacho 44 Kawaramachi & Gion
Ashibetsu 83 Hokaido
Ashihara 57 Greater Osaka
Ashihara-dori 62 Kobe
Ashikaga 22 Mt. Fuji & Around Tokyo
Ashikita 90 Kyusu
Ashikita Coast Natural Park 90 Kyusu
Ashikura 34 Shirakawa-go & Gokayama
Ashinoko Hot Spring 29 Hakone
Ashinoyu Hot Spring 29 Hakone
Ashiribetsu-no-taki 82 Sado-ga Island
Ashiya 54 Kansai Area

Ashiya City 55 Osaka Area
Ashiyasu Hot Spring 34 Central Honshu
Ashizuki Hot Spring 30 Kozu-shima & Nii-jima
Ashizuri Kaiteikan Museum 86 Shikoku
Ashizuri Kaiyokan Aquarium 86 Shikoku
Ashoro 83 Hokaido
Ashoro Hot Spring 83 Hokaido
Aso 23 Mt. Fuji & Around Tokyo
Aso 91 Aso Area
Aso District 91 Aso Area
Aso Kodai-no-sato Museum 91 Aso Area
Aso Nat'l Park 91 Aso Area
Aso Panorama Line 90 Aso Area
Aso Volcano Museum 91 Aso Area
Asobara Hot Spring 40 Nagano & Matsumoto Areas
Assabu 82 Hokaido
Astronical Observatory 75 Kurashiki
Astronomical Observatory 90 Kyusu
Asuka 65 Asuka
Asuka Folk Museum 65 Asuka
Asuka Historical Museum 65 Asuka
Asuka Historical Park Museum 65 Asuka
Asuka Inabuchi Palace Ruins 65 Asuka
Asuka Village 64 Around Nara
Asukaicho 43 Central & Eastern Kyoto
Atagamicho 48 Western Kyoto
Atagawa 30 Izu Peninsula
Atagawa Hot Spring 30 Izu Peninsula
Atagawa Tropical & Alligator Garden 30 Izu Peninsula
Atago 37 Inuyama
Atago 8 Ginza, Tsukiji & Tokyo Tower
Atagocho 86 Uwajima
Atagomachi 39 Takayama
Atagomachi 71 Hiroshima
Atagomachi 88 Kotohira
Atagoni 81 Matsushima
Atami 31 Atami
Atami Castle 31 Atami
Atami Ropeway 30 Izu Peninsula
Atami Sun Beach 31 Atami
Atarashiya 34 Shirakawa-go & Gokayama
Atehama 68 Shodo Island
Athletic Park 83 Hokaido
Atomic Energy Center 23 Mt. Fuji & Around Tokyo
Atsugi 22 Mt. Fuji & Around Tokyo
Atsuma 83 Hokaido
Atsumi Onsen Ippongi 77 Northern Honshu
Atsumi Peninsula 34 Central Honshu
Atsuta Ward 35 Nagoya Area
Atsuta-jingu Shrine 35 Nagoya Area
Atsuyu Hot Spring 40 Nagano & Matsumoto Areas
Autocamp Site 56 Greater Osaka
Awa 87 Shikoku
Awa Ikeda 87 Iya Valley
Awa Odori Museum 88 Tokushima
Awachokami 88 Kotohira
Awachokita 88 Kotohira
Awadaguchi 43 Central & Eastern Kyoto
Awadaguchi Awatayama-kitacho 45 Kawaramachi & Gion
Awadaguchi Awatayama-minamicho 45 Kawaramachi & Gion
Awadaguchi Chorakuji-yamacho 45 Kawaramachi & Gion
Awadaguchi Higashiotani-yamacho 45 Kawaramachi & Gion
Awadaguchi Kachocho 45 Kawaramachi & Gion
Awadaguchi Kachoyamacho 45 Kawaramachi & Gion
Awadaguchi Kajicho 45 Kawaramachi & Gion
Awadaguchi Kodaiji-yamacho 45 Kawaramachi & Gion
Awadaguchi Sanjobocho 45 Kawaramachi & Gion
Awadaguchi Toriicho 45 Kawaramachi & Gion
Awai Hot Spring 69 Hiroshima & Western Honshu
Awaji 87 Shikoku
Awaji World Park Onokoro 87 Shikoku
Awajimachi 59 Osaka Station
Awakura Hot Spring 69 Hiroshima & Western Honshu
Awano 22 Mt. Fuji & Around Tokyo
Awanoyu Hot Spring 40 Nagano & Matsumoto Areas
Awara 34 Central Honshu
Awashima Aquarium 30 Izu Peninsula
Awashima Beach 82 Sado-ga Island
Awashima Marine Park 22 Mt. Fuji & Around Tokyo
Awaza 57 Greater Osaka
Aya 90 Kyusu

Aya-zaimokucho 44 Kawaramachi & Gion
Ayabe 54 Kansai Area
Ayagawa 87 Shikoku
Ayamihabiru-kan 94 Okinawa & The Southwest Islands
Ayaomiyacho 49 Western Kyoto
Ayugaeshi Waterfall 90 Kyusu
Ayukawa Beach 34 Central Honshu
Azabu Juban Shopping Town 13 Roppongi, Shibuya, Omotesando, Harajuku & Meiji Shrine
Azabu-juban 13 Roppongi, Shibuya, Omote-sando, Harajuku & Meiji Shrine
Azabu-mamianacho 8 Ginza, Tsukiji & Tokyo Tower
Azabu-nagasakacho 13 Roppongi, Shibuya, Omotesando, Harajuku & Meiji Shrine
Azabudai 8 Ginza, Tsukiji & Tokyo Tower
Azagawa 29 Lake Kawaguchi
Azama Sun Sun Beach Beach 95 Okinawa-Honto
Azekachicho 47 Northern Kyoto
Azekatsucho 49 Western Kyoto
Azimuno Herb Square 40 Nagano & Matsumoto Areas
Azuchi Castle Archaeological 67 Lake Biwa
Azuchi Ruins 67 Lake Biwa
Azuchimachi 59 Osaka Station
Azukiyuhara Beach 68 Hiroshima & Western Honshu
Azuma 22 Mt. Fuji & Around Tokyo
Azuma-dori 63 Kobe
Azumabashi 11 Asakusa, Ueno & Akihabara
Azumagaoka 24 Yokohama
Azumino 40 Nagano & Matsumoto Areas
B1 Kadoza Theater 61 Osaka Namba
Baba 33 Narita
Baba 42 Kyoto
Baba 81 Matsushima
Baba 91 Kannawa Hells Area
Baba-shitacho 15 Shinjuku
Babacho 49 Western Kyoto
Babacho 57 Greater Osaka
Babacho 62 Kobe
Babadani Hot Spring 40 Nagano & Matsumoto Areas
Babawakicho 47 Northern Kyoto
Baiencho 31 Atami
Baika 56 Greater Osaka
Baikaicho 31 Atami
Baikoen-danchi 93 Fukuoka
Bainan 57 Greater Osaka
Baji Museum 83 Hokaido
Bakurocho 49 Western Kyoto
Bakurocho 75 Kurashiki
Bakuromachi 38 Kanazawa
Bakuromachi 57 Greater Osaka
Banba 66 Hikone Castle
Banbacho 43 Central & Eastern Kyoto
Banbacho 59 Osaka Station
Bancho 89 Takamatsu
Banda-san Volcanic Memorial Museum 80 Aizu, Inawashiro & Ura-Bandai
Bandai 80 Aizu, Inawashiro & Ura-bandai
Bandai Atami Area 80 Aizu, Inawashiro & Ura-bandai
Bandai Atami Hot Spring 80 Aizu, Inawashiro & Ura-Bandai
Bandaicho 24 Yokohama
Bandaimachi 80 Aizu, Inawashiro & Ura-bandai
Bando 22 Mt. Fuji & Around Tokyo
Bandokoro Park 90 Kyusu
Bandokoro-Otaki 40 Nagano & Matsumoto Areas
Bankei Hot Spring 82 Sado-ga Island
Bansho-ga-hara Ski Area 40 Nagano & Matsu-moto Areas
Banshu Tokura Snow Park 69 Hiroshima & Western Honshu
Banso Hot Spring 80 Aizu, Inawashiro & Ura-Bandai
Bantoyacho 44 Kawaramachi & Gion
Banzaicho 59 Osaka Station
Banzancho 75 Okamaya
Barasu-to 96 Yaeyama Islands
Barbecue Garden 56 Greater Osaka
Base Gallery 7 Imperial Palace & Tokyo Station
Baseball Hall of Fame 6 Imperial Palace & Tokyo Station
Bay Quarter 24 Yokohama
Bear Park 40 Nagano & Matsumoto Areas
Bear Park 82 Sado-ga Island
Befu-danchi 92 Fukuoka
Befukyo Hot Spring 87 Shikoku
Bekkai Hot Spring 83 Hokaido
Belgium Orgel Museum 81 Matsushima

Bella Beach 95 Okinawa & The Southwest Islands
Benten 56 Greater Osaka
Benten 92 Nagasaki
Bentencho 15 Shinjuku
Bentencho 62 Kobe
Bentencho 84 Hakodate
Bentendori 24 Yokohama
Bentendori 64 Mt. Koya
Bentenmachi 92 Shimabara
Benzaiten-daki 64 Around Nara
Benzaitencho 44 Kawaramachi & Gion
Beppu Art Museum 91 Beppu Area
Beppu Traditional Bamboo Craft Centre 91 Beppu Area
Beppu Yukemuri Lookout 91 Kannawa Hells Area
Beppucho 91 Miyazaki
Bessho Hot Spring 40 Nagano & Matsumoto Areas
Besshocho 65 Asuka
Betsukai 83 Hokaido
Betsuso 37 Inuyama
Bibai 83 Hokaido
Bibi Beach 95 Okinawa-Honto
Biei 82 Daisetsuzan National Park
Bifue-no-taki 82 Sado-ga Island
Bifuka 83 Hokaido
Bifuka 83 Hokaido
Big Hat 40 Nagano & Matsumoto Areas
Big O Ferris Wheel 6 Imperial Palace & Tokyo Station
Bihoro 83 Hokaido
Bihorotoge Pass 83 Akan National Park
Bingo Athletic Park 86 Shimanami Kaido
Bingodencho 46 Northern Kyoto
Bingomachi 57 Greater Osaka
Bira 39 Noto Peninsula
Biratori 83 Hokaido
BiribetsuWaterfall 83 Hokaido
Bisai Museum of History & Folklore 35 Nagoya Area
Bisakusanchi Prefectural Natural Park 69 Hiroshima & Western Honshu
Bishamoncho 44 Kawaramachi & Gion
Bishamonyama 46 Northern Kyoto
Bishoen 57 Greater Osaka
Bitchumatsuyama Ruins 69 Hiroshima & Western Honshu
Biwa-no-taki 87 Iya Valley
Biwajima 36 Central Nagoya
Biwako Kantaku Museum 67 Lake Biwa
Biwako Sosui Memorial Museum 45 Kawaramachi & Gion
Biwako Valley Ski Area 67 Lake Biwa
Bizan Ropeway 88 Tokushima
Bizancho 88 Tokushima
Bizen 69 Hiroshima & Western Honshu
Black Ship Art Gallery 31 Shimoda
Blue Sun 35 Nagoya Area
Board Walk 91 Kagoshima
Boat Dock 87 Iya Valley
Boat Rental Stall 48 Western Kyoto
Bodai-taki 42 Kyoto
Bonji-taki 32 Nikko Area
Bonoike 42 Kyoto
Bonoma Natural Park 90 Kyusu
Bonoushirocho 46 Northern Kyoto
Boshiiwa 83 Hokaido
Botan 9 Ginza, Tsukiji & Tokyo Tower
Botanical Garden 32 Nikko Town
Boyama 47 Northern Kyoto
Boyashikicho 65 Nara
Bozumachi 66 Himeji Castle
BridgestoneMuseum of Art 7 Imperial Palace & Tokyo Station
British House 25 Kawasaki
Buheicho 37 Central Nagoya
Buke Yashiki Samurai Residence 74 Matsue
Bukkoji-higashimachi 44 Kawaramachi & Gion
Bungo-ono 90 Kyusu
Bungo-takada 90 Kyusu
Bungosido Natural Park 90 Kyusu
Bunka Gakuen Costume Museum 14 Shinjuku
Bunkadori 64 Mt. Koya
Bunkyo 5 Greater Tokyo
Bunkyo Museum 10 Asakusa, Ueno & Akihabara
Bunkyocho 88 Matsuyama
Buno Hot Spring 40 Nagano & Matsumoto Areas
Butaino 50 Fushimi Area
Butsushodencho 48 Western Kyoto
Buzen 90 Kyusu
Buzendacho 72 Shimonoseki
Byobu-iwa Rock 67 Lake Biwa

Byobu-iwa Rock 76 Shirakami Mountains
Byobuga-taki 67 Lake Biwa
Byobugaura (Scenic Rocky Coast) 23 Mt. Fuji & Around Tokyo
Byodo-in 53 Uji Town
Cable Car 91 Aso Area
Calligraphy Museum 10 Asakusa, Ueno & Akihabara
Calligraphy Museum 33 Narita
Canal City 93 Fukuoka
Carp in the Moat 73 Tsuwano
Cedar Avenue Park 33 Nikko Area
Cenotaph for Atomic Bomb Victims 70 Hiroshima
Central Japan Int'l Airport 34 Central Honshu
Ceramic Park Mino 35 Nagoya Area
Chagama-taki 34 Central Honshu
Chajiricho 48 Western Kyoto
Chamachi 41 Shizuoka
Chamachi 75 Tottori
Chanokidaira 32 Nikko Area
Chanokidaira Plateau 32 Nikko Area
Chatate-no-Shimizu Fountain 79 Lake Tazawa
Chausuyama Botanical Garden 40 Nagano & Matsumoto Areas
Chausuyama Burial Mound 61 Osaka Namba
Chausuyamacho 61 Osaka Namba
Chayamachi 59 Osaka Station
Cherry Blossom Tunnel 78 Kakunodate
Chiba 23 Mt. Fuji & Around Tokyo
Chiba Flower & Plant Center 33 Narita
Chiba Kids Dom 23 Mt. Fuji & Around Tokyo
Chiba Pref. 23 Mt. Fuji & Around Tokyo
Chibune 56 Greater Osaka
Chichibu 22 Mt. Fuji & Around Tokyo
Chichibu Muse Park 22 Mt. Fuji & Around Tokyo
Chichibu-tama-kai National Park 22 Mt. Fuji & Around Tokyo
Chido Museum 77 Northern Honshu
Chidoricho 62 Kobe
Chidoricho 74 Matsue
Chifunemachi 88 Matsuyama
Chigasaki 22 Mt. Fuji & Around Tokyo
Chigiriyacho 44 Kawaramachi & Gion
Chigusacho 91 Miyazaki
Chiharacho 36 Central Nagoya
Chihaya 16 Ikebukuro
Chihaya-akasaka 54 Kansai Area
Chihaya-akasaka Village 64 Around Nara
Chihiro Art Museum 4 Greater Tokyo
Chiiori House 87 Iya Valley
Chika Dam Museum 97 Miyako Islands
Chikaramachi 37 Central Nagoya
Chikko 56 Greater Osaka
Chikko 84 Otaru
Chikko-honmachi 93 Fukuoka
Chikubu-shima Island 67 Lake Biwa
Chikugo 90 Kyusu
Chikuhoku 40 Nagano & Matsumoto Areas
Chikujo 90 Kyusu
Chikuma 40 Nagano & Matsumoto Areas
Chikura 23 Mt. Fuji & Around Tokyo
Chikusa Kogen Nature Land Ski Area 69 Hiroshima & Western Honshu
Chikusa Ward 35 Nagoya Area
Chikusei 77 Northern Honshu
Chikuzen 90 Kyusu
Chikuzen Textile Museum 90 Kyusu
Children's Amusement Park 23 Yokohama Area
Children's Museum of Science 70 Hiroshima
Children's Peace Monument 70 Hiroshima
Children's Science & Culture Center 93 Fukuoka
Children's Science Museum 35 Nagoya Area
Children's Zoo 10 Asakusa, Ueno & Akihabara
China Town 23 Yokohama Area
China Town 80 25 Kawasaki
Chinatown 25 Kawasaki
Chinen 95 Okinawa-honto
Chinese Modern Museum 55 Osaka Area
Chinjuancho 46 Northern Kyoto
Chino 34 Central Honshu
Chinoike Jigoku (Blood Pond Hell) 91 Beppu Area
Chippubetsu 83 Hokaido
Chirihama Beach 39 Noto Peninsula
Chirihama Nagisa Driveway 39 Noto Peninsula
Chiryu 34 Central Honshu
Chiryu City 35 Nagoya Area
Chisenupuri Ski Area 82 Sado-ga Island
Chishi 66 Amano Hashidate
Chisuji-no-taki 29 Hakone Town
Chita 34 Central Honshu
Chita City 35 Nagoya Area
Chitose 23 Mt. Fuji & Around Tokyo
Chitose 5 Greater Tokyo

Chitose 7 Imperial Palace & Tokyo Station
Chitose 83 Hokaido
Chitosecho 84 Hakodate
Chitosedai 4 Greater Tokyo
Chitosetsuru Museum Annex 85 Sapporo
Chitosetsuru Sake Museum 85 Sapporo
Chiyo 93 Fukuoka
Chiyoda 23 Mt. Fuji & Around Tokyo
Chiyoda 37 Central Nagoya
Chiyoda 7 Imperial Palace & Tokyo Station
Chiyodamachi 81 Sendai
Chiyonomichicho 48 Western Kyoto
Chiyozaki 57 Greater Osaka
Chizu 69 Hiroshima & Western Honshu
Cho-ji-taki 33 Nikko Area
Chochinyamacho 43 Central & Eastern Kyoto
Chodo 57 Greater Osaka
Choeiji 57 Greater Osaka
Chogatsubo 37 Inuyama
Chohachi Museum 30 Izu Peninsula
Chohoji 42 Kyoto
Chojamachi 24 Yokohama
Chojincho 48 Western Kyoto
Choki-in 32 Kawagoe-Little Edo
Chomin Ski Area 82 Daisetsuzan National Park
Chomonkyo Hot Spring 68 Hiroshima & Western Honshu
Choshi 23 Mt. Fuji & Around Tokyo
Choshi O-taki 77 Lake Towada
Choshi-kei Wild Monkey Park 68 Shodo Island
Choshi-no-taki 76 Lake Towada
Choshi-no-taki 86 Shikoku
Choshi-taki 86 Shikoku
Chosho-ji 27 Kamakura
Chosiga-daki 80 Aizu, Inawashiro & Ura-Bandai
Chosiga-taki 67 Lake Biwa
Chotaro-ike Beach 30 Miyake-jima
Choyo 90 Aso Area
Chubu Sangaku National Park 40 Nagano & Matsumoto Areas
Chudoji 49 Western Kyoto
Chuemachi 73 Miyajima
Chugushi 32 Nikko Area
Chuka Kaikan 84 Hakodate
Chukyo-minamidori 36 Central Nagoya
Chunagoncho 75 Okamaya
Chuo 14 Shinjuku
Chuo 24 Yokohama
Chuo 34 Central Honshu
Chuo 41 Matsumoto
Chuo 42 Kyoto
Chuo 57 Greater Osaka
Chuo 73 Yamaguchi
Chuo 77 Aomori
Chuo 92 Fukuoka
Chuo Ward 57 Greater Osaka
Chuocho 31 Atami
Chuocho 4 Greater Tokyo
Chuocho 75 Okamaya
Chuocho 86 Uwajima
Chuocho 89 Takamatsu
Chuocho 90 Kagoshima
Chuodori 91 Miyazaki
Chuodorimachi 38 Kanazawa
Chuson-Ji 79 Hiraizumi & Ichinoseki
Chuwa 76 Shirakami Mountains
Chuzaijicho 47 Northern Kyoto
Citizen's Culture Museum 38 Kanazawa
Citrus Park 72 Hagi
Citrus Park 86 Shimanami Kaido
City Art Museum 74 Onomichi
City Art Museum 75 Kurashiki
City Cultural Properties Museum 41 Shizuoka
City Ground 63 Kobe
City Hyakkokucho Museum 76 Hirosaki
City Modern Literature 91 Kagoshima
City Museum 59 Osaka Station
City Museum of Art 91 Kagoshima
Civic Art Museum 87 Seto-ohasi Bridge
Clock Tower 85 Sapporo
Coiffure Museum 45 Kawaramachi & Gion
Communications Museum 7 Imperial Palace & Tokyo Station
Confucian Temple Chinese History Museum 92 Nagasaki
Cormorant-fishing Pier 37 Inuyama
Cosmo Square 56 Greater Osaka
Cruising Lake Ashinoko (Attraction) 29 Hakone
Cuddly Dominion Zoo 91 Aso Area
Cultopia Beach 80 Sado-ga Island
Cultural Hall 75 Tottori
Culture Center 4 Greater Tokyo
CurrencyMuseum 7 Imperial Palace & Tokyo Station
Curry Museum 24 Yokohama
Dado-kitamachi 57 Greater Osaka

Dado-minamimachi 57 Greater Osaka
Dado-nishi 57 Greater Osaka
Dai 27 Kamakura
Dai 78 Hanamaki
Dai-giri 26 Kamakura
Dai-ichi Cave (Benten Cave) 26 Kamakura
Dai-ichi Makishi Public Market 94 Naha
Dai-machi 24 Yokohama
Dai-ni Cave (Dragon Cave) 26 Kamakura
Dai-ni Irohazaka (Steep Drive Way) 32 Nikko Area
Dai-to 64 Mt. Koya
Dai-zawa 12 Roppongi, Shibuya, Omotesando, Harajuku & Meiji Shrine
Daiba 21 Odaiba
Daibutsu-den (Great Buddha Hall) 65 Nara
Daida 4 Greater Tokyo
Daido 61 Osaka Namba
Daidocho 47 Northern Kyoto
Daidocho 62 Kobe
Daigo 23 Mt. Fuji & Around Tokyo
Daigo 51 Southern Kyoto
Daigo-ji 51 Southern Kyoto
Daigyo-ji 27 Kamakura
Daikai-dori 62 Kobe
Daikanbo Lookout 91 Aso Area
Daikancho 37 Central Nagoya
Daikancho 76 Hirosaki
Daikanjin Museum 41 Nagano
Daikanyamacho 12 Roppongi, Shibuya, Omotesando, Harajuku & Meiji Shrine
Daikanyamacho 91 Kannawa Hells Area
Daiki 54 Kansai Area
Daikoku 60 Osaka Namba
Daikokucho 44 Kawaramachi & Gion
Daikokuitchomachi 66 Himeji Castle
Daiku 91 Miyazaki
Daikucho 49 Western Kyoto
Daikucho 76 Hirosaki
Daikumachi 38 Kanazawa
Daikyocho 15 Shinjuku
Daimaru Museum 58 Osaka Station
Daimojicho 44 Kawaramachi & Gion
Daimon-chubu 64 Mt. Koya
Daimoncho 36 Central Nagoya
Daimoncho 41 Nagano
Daimoncho 48 Western Kyoto
Daimonjicho 45 Kawaramachi & Gion
Daimonmachi 39 Takayama
Daimontobu 64 Mt. Koya
Daimotsucho 56 Greater Osaka
Daimyo 93 Fukuoka
Daimyo Tokei Clock Museum 10 Asakusa, Ueno & Akihabara
Daimyojincho 47 Northern Kyoto
Dainichicho 36 Central Nagoya
Dainichiyamacho 43 Central & Eastern Kyoto
Dainohara 81 Sendai
Daionjicho 44 Kawaramachi & Gion
Daiozaki 55 Kansai
Dairicho 48 Western Kyoto
Dairincho 74 Matsue
Daisen 69 Hiroshima & Western Honshu
Daisen 77 Northern Honshu
Daisen Kokusai Ski Area 69 Hiroshima & Western Honshu
Daisen Park, Sakai City Museum, Sakai City Teahouse 55 Osaka Area
Daisen Tom Sawyer Farm 69 Hiroshima & Western Honshu
Daisen-ji 69 Hiroshima & Western Honshu
Daisetsuzan National Park 82 Daisetsuzan National Park
Daishinkaicho 47 Northern Kyoto
Daito 64 Around Nara
Daitocho 57 Greater Osaka
Daitocho 66 Hikone Castle
Daitokujicho 46 Northern Kyoto
Daiwa Hot Spring 95 Okinawa & The Southwest Islands
Daiyahama Beach 34 Central Honshu
Daizawa 4 Greater Tokyo
Dam Memorial Museum 35 Nagoya Area
Dam Museum 95 Okinawa-Honto
Dampara Ski Area 82 Sado-ga Island
Dan-no-ura Old Battle Field 73 Shimonoseki
Danbara-hinode 71 Hiroshima
Danbara-minami 71 Hiroshima
Danbara-yamasaki 71 Hiroshima
Danicho 48 Western Kyoto
Danmachi 49 Western Kyoto
Dannouracho 72 Shimonoseki
Danyama-honmachi 92 Kumamoto
Date 77 Northern Honshu
Date 82 Sado-ga Island

Date Masamune Historical Museum 81 Matsushima
Date Museum 86 Uwajima
Dazaifu 90 Kyusu
Dazaifu Tenman-gu Shrine 90 Kyusu
Deai-daru & Oh-daru 30 Izu Peninsula
Decks Tokyo Beach 21 Odaiba
Deguchi 53 Uji Town
Deguchicho 47 Northern Kyoto
Dejima 23 Mt. Fuji & Around Tokyo
Dejima Museum 92 Nagasaki
Dekijima 56 Greater Osaka
Dekijima-honcho 88 Tokushima
Dekimachi 37 Central Nagoya
Demizucho 43 Central & Eastern Kyoto
Den-Yasuharabitchu Tomb 73 Iwami Ginzan
Denki Hyakunen-kan (Electric Museum) 81 Sendai
Denpo 56 Greater Osaka
Deshiro 57 Greater Osaka
Design Museum 36 Central Nagoya
Detohama Beach 77 Northern Honshu
Dewa-sanzan Historical Museum 81 Dewa Sanzen
Dewamachi 38 Kanazawa
Dezaikecho 62 Kobe
Dinosaur Museum 34 Central Honshu
Disneyland 5 Greater Tokyo
Dobashicho 50 Fushimi Area
Dobuku Festival Museum 34 Shirakawa-go & Gokayama
Docomo History Square 11 Asakusa, Ueno & Akihabara
Dodora-taki 87 Shikoku
Dodoro-taki 87 Iya Valley
Dogashia Hot Spring 29 Hakone
Dogashiba 57 Greater Osaka
Dogashima 30 Izu Peninsula
Dogashima Hot Spring 29 Hakone Town
Dogenzaka 12 Roppongi, Shibuya, Omotesando, Harajuku & Meiji Shrine
Dogo Giyaman Museum of Glass 89 Matsuyama
Dogo Onsen Honkan 89 Matsuyama
Dogo-himata 88 Matsuyama
Dogo-himezuka 89 Matsuyama
Dogo-ichiman 88 Matsuyama
Dogo-imaichi 88 Matsuyama
Dogo-kitamachi 89 Matsuyama
Dogo-kitashiro 88 Matsuyama
Dogo-machi 89 Matsuyama
Dogo-midoridai 89 Matsuyama
Dogo-sagidanicho 89 Matsuyama
Dogo-takocho 89 Matsuyama
Dogo-yunomachi 89 Matsuyama
Dogo-yuzukuricho 89 Matsuyama
Dogoyama Kogen Ski Area 69 Hiroshima & Western Honshu
Dohashicho 70 Hiroshima
Doicho 56 Greater Osaka
Doigahama Beach 68 Hiroshima & Western Honshu
Doinouchicho 49 Western Kyoto
Dojima 58 Osaka Station
Dojimahama 57 Greater Osaka
Dojomonzen 73 Yamaguchi
Doketsu-no-taki 34 Central Honshu
Doll Town & Toy Town 7 Imperial Palace & Tokyo Station
Doll Town Pleasure District 5 Greater Tokyo
Dolphin Beach 69 Hiroshima & Western Honshu
Domoto Museum 46 Northern Kyoto
Dondon-zaka 92 Nagasaki
Donno In Saikachi Museum 29 Hakone
Donomae-cho 47 Northern Kyoto
Donomaecho 48 Western Kyoto
Donomaecho 73 Yamaguchi
Doshi 22 Mt. Fuji & Around Tokyo
Doshin 57 Greater Osaka
Doshin Yashiki (Samurai Residence) 79 Hanamaki
Doshocho 46 Northern Kyoto
Doshomachi 59 Osaka Station
Doshomachi Pharmaceutical 59 Osaka Station
Dotemachi 76 Hirosaki
Dotonbori 57 Greater Osaka
Doyamachi 76 Hirosaki
Doyamacho 59 Osaka Station
Doza 92 Nagasaki
Dynaland Ski Area 34 Central Honshu
Earth Wall of Nagasaki 68 Shodo Island
Earthquake Memorial Monument 63 Kobe
Eastern Precinct (Toto) 52 Enryaku-ji & Mt. Hiei
Ebara 18 Meguro & Shinagawa
Ebesu 33 Narita
Ebetsu 82 Hokaido
Ebi-daru 30 Izu Peninsula

Ebie 56 Greater Osaka
Ebina 22 Mt. Fuji & Around Tokyo
Ebino 90 Kyusu
Ebino Highland 90 Kyusu
Ebira 92 Nagasaki
Ebisu 18 Meguro & Shinagawa
Ebisu Garden Place 4 Greater Tokyo
Ebisu-higashi 61 Osaka Namba
Ebisu-honmachi 61 Osaka Namba
Ebisu-minami 18 Meguro & Shinagawa
Ebisu-nishi 12 Roppongi, Shibuya, Omotesando, Harajuku & Meiji Shrine
Ebisu-nishi 61 Osaka Namba
Ebisubashi Bridge 61 Osaka Namba
Ebisucho 44 Kawaramachi & Gion
Ebisudanicho 43 Central & Eastern Kyoto
Ebisumachi 73 Miyajima
Ebisumachi 92 Shimabara
Ebisunobanbacho 49 Western Kyoto
Ebisunocho 44 Kawaramachi & Gion
Eboshi-ga-kakiuchicho 46 Northern Kyoto
Eboshi-san Lookout 28 Mt. Fuji
Eboshiiwa 46 Northern Kyoto
Eboshiyacho 44 Kawaramachi & Gion
Echizen 34 Central Honshu
Eda-jima 68 Hiroshima & Western Honshu
Edamachi 38 Kanazawa
Edamatsu 89 Matsuyama
Edo Shitamachi Traditional Crafts Museum 11 Asakusa, Ueno & Akihabara
Edo Wonderland Nikko Edomura 33 Nikko Area
Edo-Tokyo Museum 5 Greater Tokyo
Edobori 57 Greater Osaka
Edogawa 5 Greater Tokyo
Edogawa Culture Center 5 Greater Tokyo
Edomachi 63 Kobe
Edomachi 92 Nagasaki
Egara Tenjin Shrine 27 Kamakura
Egeyamacho 62 Kobe
Egota 4 Greater Tokyo
Eguchi Yoshi Memorial Museum 34 Central Honshu
Eharacho 4 Greater Tokyo
Ehime Pref. 90 Kyusu
Ehiracho 91 Miyazaki
Ehon Museum 40 Nagano & Matsumoto Areas
Eidaimachi 88 Matsuyama
Eiei 83 Hokaido
Eifuku 4 Greater Tokyo
Eiga-mura Museum 81 Dewa Sanzen
Eihei-ji 34 Central Honshu
Eiheiji 34 Central Honshu
Eikando Nishimachi 45 Kawaramachi & Gion
Eikandocho 43 Central & Eastern Kyoto
Eirakucho 91 Miyazaki
Eirakuonsencho 75 Tottori
Eisei Bunko Museum 17 Ikebukuro
Eitai 9 Ginza, Tsukiji & Tokyo Tower
Eiwa 57 Greater Osaka
Eiwacho 65 Asuka
Eizawacho 62 Kobe
Eki-nishi-hommachi 38 Kanazawa
Ekidori 73 Yamaguchi
Ekimae 76 Hirosaki
Ekimae 88 Kotohira
Ekimae-honcho 25 Kawasaki
Ekimae-honmachi 91 Central Beppu
Ekimaecho 66 Himeji Castle
Ekimaecho 75 Okamaya
Ekimaecho 76 Hirosaki
Ekiminami-dori 62 Kobe
Ekisha Onsen Sato-no-yu 66 Kinosaki
Ema-do (Ema Pavilion) 88 Kotohira
Emerald Beach 95 Okinawa-Honto
Emukai 72 Hagi
Ena 34 Central Honshu
Enai 88 Kotohira
Enakomachi 39 Takayama
Enba 53 Uji Town
Enbetsu 83 Hokaido
Energy Museum 40 Nagano & Matsumoto Areas
Engaku-ji 27 Kamakura
Engaru 83 Hokaido
Enichi-ji Kondo 80 Aizu, Inawashiro & Ura-Bandai
Eniwa 82 Hokaido
Enjukaigan Natural Park 54 Kansai Area
Enku Museum 35 Nagoya Area
Enmachi 49 Western Kyoto
Enokicho 15 Shinjuku
Enokicho 25 Kawasaki
Enokicho 44 Kawaramachi & Gion
Enokicho 50 Fushimi Area
Enokojima 57 Greater Osaka
Enomachi 70 Hiroshima

Enomigashiba 47 Northern Kyoto
Enoshima 26 Kamakura
Enoshima Dai-shi 26 Kamakura
Enoshima Samuel Cocking Garden 26 Kamakura
Enoshima Shrine 26 Kamakura
Enoshima Spa 26 Kamakura
Enou 92 Nagasaki
Enryaku-ji 52 Enryaku-ji & Mt. Hiei
Enseiji 73 Yamaguchi
Enseijicho 73 Yamaguchi
Enshojicho 43 Central & Eastern Kyoto
Enzan 22 Mt. Fuji & Around Tokyo
Epson Aqua Stadium 15 Meguro & Shinagawa
Erimo 83 Hokaido
Esan Hot Spring 82 Hokaido
Esashi 83 Hokaido
Esashimachi 61 Osaka Namba
Etchujima 9 Ginza, Tsukiji & Tokyo Tower
EXPO Mem. Park 55 Osaka Area
Family Snow Park Bandai x2 80 Aizu, Inawashiro & Ura-Bandai
Ferris Wheel 59 Osaka Station
Ferris Wheel/ Yokohama Cosmo World Amusement Park 24 Yokohama Area
Festival City Auga 76 Aomori
Fishing Center 86 Shimanami Kaido
Five Storey Pagoda 32 Nikko Town
Five Storied Pagoda 50 Southern Kyoto
Five Storied Pagoda 65 Nara
Five Storied Pagoda 73 Miyajima
Five Storied Pagoda 81 Dewa Sanzen
Fleuri 39 Noto Peninsula
Floating No Stage 73 Miyajima
Flower Centre 35 Nagoya Area
Flower Clock 63 Kobe
Folk Historical Museum 97 Amami Oshima
Folk Museum & Saltpeter Museum 34 Shirakawa-go & Gokayama
Folk Museum 30 Kozu-shima & Nii-jima
Folk Museum 31 Oshima
Folk Museum 34 Central Honshu
Folk Museum 40 Nagano & Matsumoto Areas
Folk Museum 76 Shirakami Mountains
Folk Museum 83 Hokaido
Folk Museum 86 Shimanami Kaido
Folk Toy Museum 34 Central Honshu
Folklore Museum 32 Kawagoe-Little Edo
Foreign Cemetery 55 Osaka Area
Forest Museum 82 Sado-ga Island
Forest Park Ski Area 69 Hiroshima & Western Honshu
Forest Science Museum 39 Noto Peninsula
Former British Consulate 72 Shimonoseki
Former Ishiguro (Kei) Residence 78 Kakunodate
Former Kawagoe Castle Site 32 Kawagoe-Little Edo
Former Marquis Maeda's House 12 Roppongi, Shibuya, Omotesando, Harajuku & Meiji Shrine
Former Osaka Guesthouse 59 Osaka Station
Former Residence of Iwakura Tomomi Taikaku Bunko Museum 47 Northern Kyoto
Former Town Office Memorial Hall 39 Gujo Hachiman
Fountain "Goddes of Waters" 25 Kawasaki
Free Observatory 14 Shinjuku
Fuchi Shrine 92 Nagasaki
Fuchidacho 49 Western Kyoto
Fuchizaki 68 Shodo Island
Fuchu 22 Mt. Fuji & Around Tokyo
Fuchu 55 Osaka Area
Fuchu 69 Hiroshima & Western Honshu
Fuchu Beach 66 Amano Hashidate
Fudai 77 Northern Honshu
Fudanomae 88 Kotohira
Fudaraku-ji 27 Kamakura
Fudarakusan-Ji 54 Kansai Area
Fudegasakicho 61 Osaka Namba
Fudo Hot Spring 40 Nagano & Matsumoto Areas
Fudo-daki 80 Aizu, Inawashiro & Ura-Bandai
Fudo-daki 82 Hokaido
Fudo-no-taki 82 Daisetsuzan National Park
Fudo-no-taki 83 Hokaido
Fudo-taki 34 Central Honshu
Fudo-taki 64 Around Nara
Fudo-taki 76 Shirakami Mountains
Fudocho 44 Kawaramachi & Gion
Fudogaoka 33 Narita
Fueda 27 Kamakura
Fuefuki City 28 Mt. Fuji
Fufushika-taki 32 Nikko Area
Fugaku Fuketsu (Wind Cave) 28 Mt. Fuji
Fuji 22 Mt. Fuji & Around Tokyo

Fuji 34 Central Honshu
Fuji City 28 Mt. Fuji
Fuji Film Square 13 Roppongi, Shibuya, Omotesando, Harajuku & Meiji Shrine
Fuji Fuketsu (Wind Cave) 28 Mt. Fuji
Fuji Kawaguchiko Town 28 Mt. Fuji
Fuji Manyo Botanical Garden 28 Mt. Fuji
Fuji Motosuko Resort 28 Mt. Fuji
Fuji Museum 29 Lake Kawaguchi
Fuji Photo Salon Osaka 59 Osaka Station
Fuji Safari Park 28 Mt. Fuji
Fuji Viewing Platform 29 Lake Kawaguchi
Fuji Visitor Center 29 Lake Kawaguchi
Fuji Yusui-no Sato Aquarium 28 Mt. Fuji
Fuji-hakone-izu National Park 28 Mt. Fuji
Fuji-Q Highland Amusement Park 29 Lake Kawaguchi
Fuji'Idera City 64 Around Nara
Fujibayashicho 46 Northern Kyoto
Fujidanacho 24 Yokohama
Fujidera 54 Kansai Area
Fujieda 34 Central Honshu
Fujigaoka 26 Kamakura
Fujii Folkcraft Art Gallery 39 Takayama
Fujikicho 44 Kawaramachi & Gion
Fujiko F. Fujio (Doraemon) Museum 23 Yokohama Area
Fujikoto 76 Shirakami Mountains
Fujimi 22 Mt. Fuji & Around Tokyo
Fujimi 34 Central Honshu
Fujimi 6 Imperial Palace & Tokyo Station
Fujimicho 24 Yokohama
Fujimicho 37 Central Nagoya
Fujimicho 37 Inuyama
Fujimicho 91 Central Beppu
Fujinokicho 48 Western Kyoto
Fujinomiya City 28 Mt. Fuji
Fujinomiyatori 36 Central Nagoya
Fujio-no-taki 69 Hiroshima & Western Honshu
Fujioka 22 Mt. Fuji & Around Tokyo
Fujisaki Mokushi Historical Museum 33 Narita
Fujisan Museum 28 Mt. Fuji
Fujisan Shizuoka Airport 34 Central Honshu
Fujisato 76 Shirakami Mountains
Fujisawa 23 Yokohama Area
Fujisawa 26 Kamakura
Fujita Kyohei Museum of Glass 81 Matsushima
Fujita Museum of Art 59 Osaka Station
Fujiten Snow Resort 28 Mt. Fuji
Fujitsukacho 89 Takamatsu
Fujiwada 42 Kyoto
Fujiwara Yoshie Memorial Museum 72 Shimonoseki
Fujiwaramachi 88 Matsuyama
Fujiyoshida 22 Mt. Fuji & Around Tokyo
Fujiyoshida City 28 Mt. Fuji
Fuka Matekata Beach 68 Hiroshima & Western Honshu
Fukabuchi Natural Park 87 Iya Valley
Fukadacho 47 Northern Kyoto
Fukae-kita 57 Greater Osaka
Fukae-minami 57 Greater Osaka
Fukagawa 83 Hokaido
Fukagawa 9 Ginza, Tsukiji & Tokyo Tower
Fukakawacho 36 Central Nagoya
Fukakusa 51 Southern Kyoto
Fukamachi 86 Shimanami Kaido
Fukasawa 4 Greater Tokyo
Fukashi 41 Matsumoto
Fukatanicho 48 Western Kyoto
Fukaura 76 Shirakami Mountains
Fukaya 22 Mt. Fuji & Around Tokyo
Fukenoue 79 Hiraizumi & Ichinoseki
Fuki-no-mori Hot Spring 34 Central Honshu
Fukiage Hot Spring 82 Daisetsuzan National Park
Fukiage Hot Spring 90 Kyusu
Fukiagehama Park 90 Kyusu
Fukiaicho 63 Kobe
Fukiyamachi 39 Takayama
Fukuchi Hot Spring 40 Nagano & Matsumoto Areas
Fukuchicho 43 Central & Eastern Kyoto
Fukuchiyama 54 Kansai Area
Fukuda 68 Shodo Island
Fukudacho 86 Shimanami Kaido
Fukue 37 Central Nagoya
Fukuhama 92 Fukuoka
Fukuhara 73 Iwami Ginzan
Fukuhara-kami 73 Iwami Ginzan
Fukui 34 Central Honshu
Fukui Airport 34 Central Honshu
Fukui Pref. 34 Central Honshu
Fukuiizumi Ski Area 54 Kansai Area
Fukuine 51 Southern Kyoto
Fukujinyama Mine 73 Iwami Ginzan

Fukumachi 56 Greater Osaka
Fukumichicho 31 Atami
Fukunakamachi 66 Himeji Castle
Fukuojicho 49 Western Kyoto
Fukuoka 90 Kyusu
Fukuoka Art Museum 93 Fukuoka
Fukuoka Asian Art Museum 93 Fukuoka
Fukuoka City Museum 92 Fukuoka
Fukuoka Municipal Zoo and Botanical Gaeden 93 Fukuoka
Fukuoka Pref. 90 Kyusu
Fukuokamachigoi 39 Noto Peninsula
Fukura Beach 69 Hiroshima & Western Honshu
Fukuroi 34 Central Honshu
Fukuromachi 38 Kanazawa
Fukuromachi 6 Imperial Palace & Tokyo Station
Fukusaki 54 Kansai Area
Fukusawa 80 Aizu, Inawashiro & Ura-bandai
Fukusen 79 Hiraizumi & Ichinoseki
Fukushima 57 Greater Osaka
Fukushima 58 Osaka Station
Fukushima 80 Aizu, Inawashiro & Ura-bandai
Fukushima 82 Hokaido
Fukushima Airport 77 Northern Honshu
Fukushima Museum 80 Aizu, Inawashiro & Ura-Bandai
Fukushima Museum 81 Sendai
Fukushima Pref. 77 Northern Honshu
Fukushima Ward 57 Greater Osaka
Fukushimacho 70 Hiroshima
Fukushu-en 94 Naha
Fukutomicho Higashidori 24 Yokohama
Fukutomicho Nakadori 24 Yokohama
Fukutomicho Nishidori 24 Yokohama
Fukuura 39 Noto Peninsula
Fukuyacho 44 Kawaramachi & Gion
Fukuyama 69 Hiroshima & Western Honshu
Fukuyama Castle 86 Shikoku
Fukuyama Matsumae Castle 82 Hokaido
Fukuzai-ji 92 Nagasaki
Fukuzaki 56 Greater Osaka
Fukuzawamachi 81 Sendai
Fukuzumi 9 Ginza, Tsukiji & Tokyo Tower
Fukuzumicho 36 Central Nagoya
Fumbe-no-taki 83 Hokaido
Fuminosato 57 Greater Osaka
Funabara Hot Spring 30 Izu Peninsula
Funabashi 23 Mt. Fuji & Around Tokyo
Funabashi 4 Greater Tokyo
Funabashi Musical Instrument Museum 35 Nagoya Area
Funabori 5 Greater Tokyo
Funadaikucho 62 Kobe
Funade 56 Greater Osaka
Funado Beach 77 Northern Honshu
Funagata 77 Northern Honshu
Funagata Daimonji Fire Festival Characters 46 Northern Kyoto
Funaguracho 75 Kurashiki
Funahirayama Ski Area 68 Hiroshima & Western Honshu
Funairi-honmachi 70 Hiroshima
Funairi-kawaguchicho 70 Hiroshima
Funairi-nakamachi 70 Hiroshima
Funairi-saiwaicho 70 Hiroshima
Funairimachi 70 Hiroshima
Funakoshi Beach 68 Hiroshima & Western Honshu
Funakoshi Beach 97 Amami Oshima
Funakoshicho 59 Osaka Station
Funamachi 15 Shinjuku
Funamachi 56 Greater Osaka
Funamachi 66 Hikone Castle
Funami Fureai Hot Spring 40 Nagano & Matsumoto Areas
Funamicho 84 Hakodate
Funaoka Onsen 46 Northern Kyoto
Funatocho 36 Central Nagoya
Funatsu 29 Lake Kawaguchi
Funatsukicho 46 Northern Kyoto
Funayacho 44 Kawaramachi & Gion
Funazakacho 49 Western Kyoto
Funeyama 46 Northern Kyoto
Funo-no-taki 31 Oshima
Furano 82 Daisetsuzan National Park
Furano Landscape Museum 82 Daisetsuzan National Park
Furano Ski Area 82 Daisetsuzan National Park
Fureai Minato Kan 56 Greater Osaka
Fureai-kan Kyoto Museum of Traditional Crafts. 43 Central & Eastern Kyoto
Fureaino-yu Hot Spring 30 Miyake-jima
Furepe-no-taki 83 Shiretoko National Park
Furezaka 39 Noto Peninsula
Furocho 24 Yokohama
Furomoto 91 Kannawa Hells Area

INDEX

Furonohashicho 48 Western Kyoto
Furu-ishiba 9 Ginza, Tsukiji & Tokyo Tower
Furu-kogarasumachi 93 Fukuoka
Furubira 82 Hokaido
Furudono 77 Northern Honshu
Furue 68 Shodo Island
Furugoshocho 49 Western Kyoto
Furugyocho 75 Okamaya
Furuhagimachi 72 Hagi
Furuhamacho 49 Western Kyoto
Furuichi 57 Greater Osaka
Furuichi 75 Tottori
Furukawa 76 Aomori
Furukawa 79 Hiraizumi & Ichinoseki
Furukawa Art Museum 35 Nagoya Area
Furukawa Garden 5 Greater Tokyo
Furukawacho 47 Northern Kyoto
Furuko 92 Nagasaki
Furukyomachi 93 Kumamoto
Furumi 75 Tottori
Furunishicho 45 Kawaramachi & Gion
Furusaka Hot Spring 40 Nagano & Matsumoto Areas
Furusato Historical Museum 67 Lake Biwa
Furusato Relaxation Village 30 Miyake-jima
Furusato-mura Camp Site 68 Shodo Island
Furusawacho 66 Hikone Castle
Furushirocho 44 Kawaramachi & Gion
Furuume Dam 83 Akan National Park
Furuwataricho 36 Central Nagoya
Fusaki Beach 96 Yaeyama Islands
Fuseishicho 89 Takamatsu
Fushigata-sujicho 65 Nara
Fushiharacho 48 Western Kyoto
Fushiki-honmachi 39 Noto Peninsula
Fushimi-inari Shrine 51 Southern Kyoto
Fushimi-Momoyama Castle 51 Southern Kyoto
Fushimicho 24 Yokohama
Fushimimachi 59 Osaka Station
Fushio Hot Spring 55 Osaka Area
Fushiushi 79 Hanamaki
Fuso Town 35 Nagoya Area
Fusocho 56 Greater Osaka
Futaba 77 Northern Honshu
Futaba Dam 82 Sado-ga Island
Futabacho 41 Shizuoka
Futabanosato 71 Hiroshima
Futagojima National Park 77 Northern Honshu
Futakuchikyokoku National Park 77 Northern Honshu
Futamatamachi 39 Noto Peninsula
Futami Ruins 64 Around Nara
Futami Sea Paradise 34 Central Honshu
Futaomote 68 Shodo Island
Futarasan Shrine 32 Nikko Town
Futatabishicho 36 Central Nagoya
Futatsubashicho 62 Kobe
Futatsu-game Rock 80 Sado-ga Island
Futatsuimachi 76 Shirakami Mountains
Futenma 95 Okinawa-honto
Futenma Airbase 95 Okinawa-Honto
Futo 30 Izu Peninsula
Futo Beach 30 Izu Peninsula
Futo Beach 90 Kyusu
Futomi 23 Mt. Fuji & Around Tokyo
Futomi Flower Centre 23 Mt. Fuji & Around Tokyo
Futoro Beach 82 Hokaido
Futsukamachi 81 Sendai
Futtsu Park 22 Mt. Fuji & Around Tokyo
Gakenoyu Hot Spring 40 Nagano & Matsumoto Areas
Gakuenminami 74 Matsue
Gallery Namban 58 Osaka Station
Gamagori 34 Central Honshu
Gamo District 67 Lake Biwa
Gamonsaki 37 Inuyama
Gamou 57 Greater Osaka
Gangara Cave 76 Shirakami Mountains
Gango-Ji (Gokuraku-Bo) 65 Nara
Ganmon Rock 39 Noto Peninsula
Ganyudo 30 Izu Peninsula
Ganzekicho 41 Nagano
Garden Museum Hiei 52 Enryaku-ji & Mt. Hiei
Gashitakadacho 49 Western Kyoto
Gassan Ski Area 81 Dewa Sanzen
Gate of Tago Family Residence 73 Tsuwano
Gatsurinjicho 47 Northern Kyoto
Gebu Hot Spring 34 Central Honshu
Geihinkan (State Guesthouse) 4 Greater Tokyo
Geihinkan (Statue Guest Houses) 15 Shinjuku
Geihoku Bunka Land Ski Area 68 Hiroshima & Western Honshu
Geisei 87 Shikoku
Gekkeikan Okura Memorial Sake & Brewery Museum 50 Fushimi Area

Genchi Well 41 Lake Suwa
Genjigaoka 57 Greater Osaka
Genkai 90 Kyusu
Genko Historical Museum 93 Fukuoka
Genkocho 75 Tottori
Genkyu Rakuraku-en Garden 66 Hikone Castle
Genrokuzancho 48 Western Kyoto
Gentakubo 41 Nagano
Gentakukita-higashicho 46 Western Kyoto
Gero 34 Central Honshu
Gifu 34 Central Honshu
Gifu City 35 Nagoya Area
Gifu Pref. 34 Central Honshu
Ginan City 35 Nagoya Area
Ginga-no Mori Astronomical Observatory 83 Hokaido
Ginkakujicho 43 Central & Eastern Kyoto
Ginowan 95 Okinawa-honto
Ginoza 95 Okinawa-honto
Ginya 92 Nagasaki
Ginyu Hot Spring 90 Kyusu
Ginza 8 Ginza, Tsukiji & Tokyo Tower
Ginza 89 Tokushima
Ginza High-fashion District 8 Ginza, Tsukiji & Tokyo Tower
Ginza Noh Theater 8 Ginza, Tsukiji & Tokyo Tower
Ginzacho 31 Atami
Ginzan 31 Iwami Ginzan
Ginzan 76 Lake Towada
Gion 45 Kawaramachi & Gion
Gion 79 Hiraizumi & Ichinoseki
Gion District 45 Kawaramachi & Gion
Gion-odori 45 Kawaramachi & Gion
Gionmachi 93 Fukuoka
Gionmachi-kitagawa 45 Kawaramachi & Gion
Gionmachi-minamigawa 45 Kawaramachi & Gion
Girl Scout Monument 25 Kawasaki
Glass Art Center 30 Kozu-shima & Nii-jima
Glass Ski Area 87 Shikoku
Glover Garden & Museum 92 Nagasaki
Gobancho 6 Imperial Palace & Tokyo Station
Gobo 54 Kansai Area
Gobocho 65 Asuka
Gobu 33 Narita
Gocho 39 Gujo Hachiman
Gochome 31 Shimoda
Gochome 44 Kawaramachi & Gion
Gofukucho 41 Shizuoka
Gofukumachi 66 Himeji Castle
Gofukumachi 72 Hagi
Gofukumachi 91 Kagoshima
Gohomatsu 78 Kakunodate
Gohongi 4 Greater Tokyo
Gohyaku Rakan (Five Hundred Buddha Statues) 73 Iwami Ginzan
Goi 23 Mt. Fuji & Around Tokyo
Gojikkokumachi 76 Hirosaki
Gojinka Hot Spring 31 Oshima
Gojira-iwa Rock 39 Noto Peninsula
Gojo 54 Kansai Area
Gojo City 64 Around Nara
Gojo-wakui 88 Kotohira
Gojohashi-higashi 43 Central & Eastern Kyoto
Gojome 77 Northern Honshu
Gojonocho 65 Asuka
Goju-no-to (Five-story Pagoda) 64 Around Nara
Gokanosho Heike-no-sato Museum 90 Kyusu
Gokase 90 Kyusu
Gokasho 42 Kyoto
Gokayama Hot Spring 34 Shirakawa-go & Gokayama
Gokayama Suganuma Traditional Farmhouses 34 Shirakawa-go & Gokayama
Gokencho 44 Kawaramachi & Gion
Gokenyashiki 66 Himeji Castle
Gokiso 37 Central Nagoya
Gokisocho 37 Central Nagoya
Goko-dori 63 Kobe
Gokomachi 32 Nikko Town
Goku 86 Uwajima
Gokuraku-ji 27 Kamakura
Gokurakuji 27 Kamakura
Gokurakuyu Sapporo Yayoi Hot Spring 85 Sapporo
Gokusho Offering Hall 65 Mt. Koya
Golden Gai 15 Shinjuku
Golden Pavilion 79 Hiraizumi & Ichinoseki
Gomaecho 36 Central Nagoya
Gongen Hot Spring 86 Shikoku
Gongen-daki 54 Kansai Area
Gongentori 36 Central Nagoya
Gonohe 77 Northern Honshu
Gonomiyacho 62 Kobe

Gonomuro 64 Mt. Koya
GonoueCho 46 Northern Kyoto
Gora 29 Hakone Town
Gorakidori 81 Sendai
Goricho 49 Western Kyoto
Gorin 81 Sendai
Goro-no-taki 82 Hokaido
Goro's Rock House 82 Daisetsuzan National Park
Goroku 39 Noto Peninsula
Goroku 81 Sendai
Goryo 42 Kyoto
Goryo Shrine 27 Kamakura
Goryo-kita-oeyamacho 48 Western Kyoto
Goryo-no-taki 77 Lake Towada
Goryo-oeyamacho 42 Kyoto
Goryocho 43 Central & Eastern Kyoto
Goryodencho 48 Western Kyoto
Goryonoshitacho 49 Western Kyoto
Gose 54 Kansai Area
Gose City 64 Around Nara
Gosen 77 Northern Honshu
Goshiki Hot Spring 80 Aizu, Inawashiro & Ura-Bandai
Goshiki Hot Spring 82 Sado-ga Island
Goshiki-numa (Five-colored Lake) 80 Aizu, Inawashiro & Ura-Bandai
Goshikigahama Beach 39 Noto Peninsula
Goshikihama Beach 87 Shikoku
Gosho Hot Spring 87 Shikoku
Gosho-no-yu 66 Kinosaki
Goshocho 48 Western Kyoto
Goshodencho 46 Northern Kyoto
Goshogadani 93 Fukuoka
Goshogawara 77 Northern Honshu
Goshonouchicho 48 Western Kyoto
Goshoyamacho 24 Yokohama
Gotemba City 28 Mt. Fuji
Goten-taki 28 Mt. Fuji
Gotenba 22 Mt. Fuji & Around Tokyo
Gotenmachi 86 Uwajima
Goto Art Museum 4 Greater Tokyo
Goto Sumio Museum 82 Daisetsuzan National Park
Gotocho 48 Western Kyoto
Gotocho 65 Nara
Gotsu 68 Hiroshima & Western Honshu
Gozaishi Hot Spring 34 Central Honshu
Gozen'yama 23 Mt. Fuji & Around Tokyo
Grandeco Snow Resort Ski Area 80 Aizu, Inawashiro & Ura-Bandai
Great People of Kanazawa Memorial Museum 38 Kanazawa
Green Mall (Little Busan) 72 Shimonoseki
Grinpa Amusement Parks 28 Mt. Fuji
Group Statue for Peace 68 Shodo Island
Guchikomoricho 47 Northern Kyoto
Gudabutsuan House 88 Matsuyama
Gujo 34 Central Honshu
Gujo Hachiman Castle 39 Gujo Hachiman
Gujohachiman Folk Craft Museum 39 Gujo Hachiman
Gumma 22 Mt. Fuji & Around Tokyo
Gumma No Mori Art Museum and History Museum 22 Mt. Fuji & Around Tokyo
Gumma Safari World 22 Mt. Fuji & Around Tokyo
Gunai Hot Spring 82 Hokaido
Gunkan-jima (Battle Ship Island) 90 Kyusu
Gunma Pref. 22 Mt. Fuji & Around Tokyo
Gushikawa 95 Okinawa-honto
Gusukube Athletic Park 97 Miyako Islands
Gyojahama Beach 31 Oshima
Gyokuren-taki 33 Nikko Area
Gyokuseikan Memorial Art Museum 87 Shikoku
Gyokusen-en Garden 38 Kanazawa
Gyokuto 90 Kyusu
Gyotoku 75 Tottori
Habashita 36 Central Nagoya
Habashita 41 Nagano
Habaue 40 Matsumoto
Habikino City 64 Around Nara
Haboro 83 Hokaido
Habu-minato 22 Mt. Fuji & Around Tokyo
Habushiura Park 30 Kozu-shima & Nii-jima
Hachi Kogen Ski Area 69 Hiroshima & Western Honshu
Hachi-gome (8th Station) 81 Dewa Sanzen
Hachigasaki Beach 39 Noto Peninsula
Hachijo 50 Southern Kyoto
Hachijo Botanical Park 31 Hachijo-jima
Hachijocho 48 Western Kyoto
Hachiken-daki 86 Shikoku
Hachikencho 48 Western Kyoto
Hachikenmachi 39 Takayama
Hachikenyacho 74 Matsue

Hachikita Kogen Ski Area 69 Hiroshima & Western Honshu
Hachio Statue 12 Roppongi, Shibuya, Omotesando, Harajuku & Meiji Shrine
Hachiman 81 Sendai
Hachiman-dori 63 Kobe
Hachimanmachi 39 Takayama
Hachimantai 77 Northern Honshu
Hachimanyama 4 Greater Tokyo
Hachinohe 77 Northern Honshu
Hachioji 22 Mt. Fuji & Around Tokyo
Hachiokacho 48 Western Kyoto
Hachiyamacho 12 Roppongi, Shibuya, Omotesando, Harajuku & Meiji Shrine
Hadano 22 Mt. Fuji & Around Tokyo
Haebaru 95 Okinawa-honto
Haga 23 Mt. Fuji & Around Tokyo
Hagi 68 Hiroshima & Western Honshu
Hagi Historical Museum 72 Hagi
Hagi Museum 72 Hagi
Hagi Uragami Museum 72 Hagi
Hagigaka Kiuchicho 47 Northern Kyoto
Hagihara 92 Shimabara
Hagino-chaya 61 Osaka Namba
Haginomachi 81 Sendai
Hagisho 79 Hiraizumi & Ichinoseki
Hagiwara 46 Northern Kyoto
Hagiyaki Museum 72 Hagi
Hagoromo 82 Daisetsuzan National Park
Hagoromo-taki 33 Nikko Area
Hagurosan Ski Area 81 Dewa Sanzen
Haguro-taki 33 Nikko Area
Haijima 22 Mt. Fuji & Around Tokyo
Haiku Literary Museum 14 Shinjuku
Haiyu-kan (Haiku Museum) 66 Hikone Castle
Haizawa Hot Spring 34 Central Honshu
Haji 66 Amano Hashidate
Hakadote Asaichi (Morning Market) 84 Hakodate
Hakamadacho 48 Western Kyoto
Hakarigaoka 71 Hiroshima
Hakata Beach 86 Shimanami Kaido
Hakata Machiya Furusato-kan 93 Fukuoka
Hakata Riverain 93 Fukuoka
Hakata-za Theater 93 Fukuoka
Hakatacho 45 Kawaramachi & Gion
Hakataekichuogai 93 Fukuoka
Hakkatoge Viewpoint 76 Lake Towada
Hakodate 82 Hokaido
Hakodate Airport 82 Hokaido
Hakodate Folk Museum 84 Hakodate
Hakodate Harisutosu Seikyokai 84 Hakodate
Hakodate Literature Museum 84 Hakodate
Hakodate Park 84 Hakodate
Hakodateyama Ski Area 67 Lake Biwa
Hakodateyama Yosai (Port) 84 Hakodate
Hakone 22 Mt. Fuji & Around Tokyo
Hakone Barrier Museum 29 Hakone
Hakone Botanical Garden Of Wetlands 29 Hakone
Hakone Garden Museum 29 Hakone
Hakone Meissen Antique Museum 29 Hakone Town
Hakone Museum of Art 29 Hakone Town
Hakone Open Air Museum 29 Hakone Town
Hakone Outdoor Sculpture Museum 22 Mt. Fuji & Around Tokyo
Hakone Sekisho-ato (Site of Barrier) 29 Hakone
Hakone-en Garden 29 Hakone
Hakone-machi 29 Hakone
Hakoshimizu 41 Nagano
Hakozakicho 7 Imperial Palace & Tokyo Station
Hakozukacho 48 Western Kyoto
Hakuba 40 Nagano & Matsumoto Areas
Hakuba 47 Winter Sports Parl 40 Nagano & Matsumoto Areas
Hakuba Cortina Ski Area 40 Nagano & Matsumoto Areas
Hakuba Cross Country Field 40 Nagano & Matsumoto Areas
Hakuba Goryu Ski Resort 40 Nagano & Matsumoto Areas
Hakuba Goryu Ski Area 40 Nagano & Matsumoto Areas
Hakuba Iwatake Ski Area 40 Nagano & Matsumoto Areas
Hakufu-no-taki 77 Lake Towada
Hakugindai Ski Area 83 Hokaido
Hakui 39 Noto Peninsula
Hakurakucho 49 Western Kyoto
Hakurankan Museum 39 Gujo Hachiman
Hakuryo-no-taki 86 Shikoku
Hakusan 34 Central Honshu
Hakusan 5 Greater Tokyo
Hakusan National Park 34 Central Honshu
Hakusanbira 37 Inuyama
Hakusason-so Garden & Museum 43 Central & Eastern Kyoto

Hakusen-no-taki 82 Sado-ga Island
Hakushima-kitamachi 71 Hiroshima
Hakushima-nakamachi 71 Hiroshima
Hakusui 91 Aso Area
Hakusui Hot Spring 91 Aso Area
Hakuto Beach 69 Hiroshima & Western Honshu
Hakutsuru Fine Art Museum 55 Osaka Area
Hakuundai 80 Sado-ga Island
Hakuuntei Viewpoint 76 Lake Towada
Hama 56 Greater Osaka
Hama 75 Okamaya
Hama 81 Matsushima
Hama Rikyu Garden 8 Ginza, Tsukiji & Tokyo Tower
Hama-tonbetsu 83 Hokaido
Hamabe-dori 63 Kobe
Hamada 68 Hiroshima & Western Honshu
Hamada Beach 90 Kyusu
Hamadacho 56 Greater Osaka
Hamadakaigan Prefectural Natural Park 68 Hiroshima & Western Honshu
Hamadayama 4 Greater Tokyo
Hamadera Park 55 Osaka Area
Hamaguchi 92 Nagasaki
Hamahira 92 Nagasaki
Hamakanaya 22 Mt. Fuji & Around Tokyo
Hamakurosaki Beach 39 Noto Peninsula
Hamamachi 92 Nagasaki
Hamamasu Folk Museum 82 Hokaido
Hamamasu Hot Spring 82 Hokaido
Hamamatsu 34 Central Honshu
Hamamatsu Hot Spring 82 Hokaido
Hamamatsucho 24 Yokohama
Hamamatsucho 8 Ginza, Tsukiji & Tokyo Tower
Hamanaka 83 Hokaido
Hamanaka Beach 77 Northern Honshu
Hamanasu Green Park 82 Sado-ga Island
Hamani 39 Noto Peninsula
Hamanocho 73 Miyajima
Hamanocho 89 Takamatsu
Hamanomotocho 49 Western Kyoto
Hamarikyu-teien 8 Ginza, Tsukiji & Tokyo Tower
Hamasaka Beach 69 Hiroshima & Western Honshu
Hamasaki-dori 62 Kobe
Hamasaki-shincho 72 Hagi
Hamasakicho 96 Ishigaki City
Hamasakimachi 72 Hagi
Hamawaki Hot Spring 91 Beppu Area
Hamochi 80 Sado-ga Island
Hamurocho 48 Western Kyoto
Hanabusacho 24 Yokohama
Hanadacho 37 Central Nagoya
Hanadate 79 Hiraizumi & Ichinoseki
Hanadonocho 91 Miyazaki
Hanaguri Beach 68 Hiroshima & Western Honshu
Hanaichicho 33 Nikko Area
Hanaishicho 32 Nikko Town
Hanakawa 56 Greater Osaka
Hanakawado 11 Asakusa, Ueno & Akihabara
Hanakumacho 62 Kobe
Hanakura Hot Spring 68 Hiroshima & Western Honshu
Hanamaki Airport 77 Northern Honshu
Hanamaki City Cultural Hall 78 Hanamaki
Hanamaki Hot Spring 78 Hanamaki
Hanamaki Nitobe Memorial Museum 79 Hanamaki
Hanamiyama Ski Area 69 Hiroshima & Western Honshu
Hanamki City Museum 79 Hanamaki
Hanano-e Tea House 72 Hagi
Hananocho 72 Shimonoseki
Hananoki 26 Kamakura
Hananoki 36 Central Nagoya
Hananokicho 46 Northern Kyoto
Hananomiyacho 89 Takamatsu
Hanasaka 30 Izu Peninsula
Hanasakicho 24 Yokohama
Hanasakicho 41 Nagano
Hanashiki Hot Spring 22 Mt. Fuji & Around Tokyo
Hanaten-higashi 57 Greater Osaka
Hanaten-nishi 57 Greater Osaka
Hanawa 22 Mt. Fuji & Around Tokyo
Hanazono 49 Western Kyoto
Hanazono 84 Otaru
Hanazono-kita 61 Osaka Namba
Hanazonocho 47 Northern Kyoto
Hanazonocho 89 Takamatsu
Hanazonomachi 88 Matsuyama
Hancho 66 Himeji Castle
Handa 34 Central Honshu
Handa City 35 Nagoya Area
Handa-cho 87 Iya Valley

Handabirakicho 65 Nara
Hane Beach 39 Noto Peninsula
Hane Beach 68 Hiroshima & Western Honshu
Hanegi 4 Greater Tokyo
Hanga Museum 83 Hokaido
Hangakimean 33 Nikko Area
Hangakimen 32 Nikko Town
Hangicho 47 Northern Kyoto
Hannan 54 Kansai Area
Hannancho 57 Greater Osaka
Hanno 22 Mt. Fuji & Around Tokyo
Hannya-no-taki 32 Nikko Area
Hanshin HorseRacingTrack 55 Osaka Area
Hanyu 22 Mt. Fuji & Around Tokyo
Happo 76 Shirakami Mountains
Happo-one Ski Resort 40 Nagano & Matsumoto Areas
Happoone Ski Area 40 Nagano & Matsumoto Areas
Happy Raft 87 Iya Valley
Hara 30 Izu Peninsula
Hara 34 Central Honshu
Hara 97 Yakushima
Hara Museum 23 Yokohama Area
Hara Museum of Contemporary Art 15 Meguro & Shinagawa
Hara Museum of Contemporary Art 22 Mt. Fuji & Around Tokyo
Harada Taiji Art Museum 41 Lake Suwa
Harada Yumoto Hot Spring 69 Hiroshima & Western Honshu
Haradani Cherry Garden 42 Kyoto
Haradani-inuicho 46 Northern Kyoto
Haragamaobama Beach 77 Northern Honshu
Haraido Oji 66 Hongu Onsens
Haraigawa Hot Spring 86 Shikoku
Haraikatamachi 6 Imperial Palace & Tokyo Station
Harainotocho 47 Northern Kyoto
Harajuku 12 Roppongi, Shibuya, Omotesando, Harajuku & Meiji Shrine
Harajuku 33 Nikko Area
Harajuku Shopping District 12 Roppongi, Shibuya, Omotesando, Harajuku & Meiji Shrine
Haramachi 15 Shinjuku
Haramachi 49 Western Kyoto
Haramachi 91 Central Beppu
Haranomachi 81 Sendai
Harazuru Hot Spring 90 Kyusu
Harbor View Park (Minato No Mieru Oka Koen) 25 Kawasaki
Harborland 62 Kobe
Harima 54 Kansai Area
Harimamachi 63 Kobe
Harinoki 39 Noto Peninsula
Harinokicho 46 Northern Kyoto
Harmo Museum of Art 41 Lake Suwa
Harp Seal Viewing 83 Rishiri-rebun-sarobetsu National Park
Haruhi Museum of Art 35 Nagoya Area
Harukicho 48 Western Kyoto
Harumaki Village 97 Yakushima
Harumi 9 Ginza, Tsukiji & Tokyo Tower
Harunacho 47 Northern Honshu
Harutahama Beach 97 Yakushima
Haruyoshi 93 Fukuoka
Hasaka-dori 62 Kobe
Hasami 90 Kyusu
Hase 27 Kamakura
Hase-dera 27 Kamakura
Hasecho 41 Shizuoka
Hasecho 46 Northern Kyoto
Hasedera Hot Spring 64 Around Nara
Hasegawa Machiko Museum 4 Greater Tokyo
Hashi Beach 68 Hiroshima & Western Honshu
Hashiba 11 Asakusa, Ueno & Akihabara
Hashibacho 38 Kanazawa
Hashiguchi 92 Nagasaki
Hashikaidai 33 Narita
Hashikami 77 Northern Honshu
Hashikurasan Ropeway 87 Iya Valley
Hashima 34 Central Honshu
Hashimoto 54 Kansai Area
Hashimoto 77 Aomori
Hashimoto City 64 Around Nara
Hashimotocho 24 Yokohama
Hashimotocho 39 Gujo Hachiman
Hashimotocho 44 Kawaramachi & Gion
Hashimotocho 57 Greater Osaka
Hashimotomachi 27 Hagi
Hashiuracho 44 Kawaramachi & Gion
Hasseiden Folk Museum 23 Yokohama Area
Hasuikecho 42 Kyoto
Hataedacho 47 Northern Kyoto
Hatagaya 14 Shinjuku

Hatagi-iwa Rock 39 Noto Peninsula
Hatake Hot Spring 30 Izu Peninsula
Hatakeda 33 Narita
Hataketa 80 Aizu, Inawashiro & Ura-bandai
Hatakeyama Memorial Museum 15 Meguro & Shinagawa
Hatamachi 47 Northern Kyoto
Hatatsuka-dori 63 Kobe
Hatayama Hot Spring 87 Shikoku
Hatchobori 9 Ginza, Tsukiji & Tokyo Tower
Hatenohama 94 Okinawa & The Southwest Islands
Hatobacho 63 Kobe
Hatogayu Hot Spring 34 Central Honshu
Hatori 26 Kamakura
Hatotani 34 Shirakawa-go & Gokayama
Hatoyama 42 Kyoto
Hatoyama Hall 17 Ikebukuro
Hatsudai 12 Roppongi, Shibuya, Omotesando, Harajuku & Meiji Shrine
Hatsukaichi 68 Hiroshima & Western Honshu
Hatsukashi 42 Kyoto
Hatsune 39 Gujo Hachiman
Hatsune-no-taki 32 Nikko Area
Hatsunecho 24 Yokohama
Hatsuneura Beach 31 Chichi-jima
Hatsushimacho 56 Greater Osaka
Hattachi Beach 77 Northern Honshu
Hattori Ryokuchi Park 55 Osaka Area
Hawaii Beach 69 Hiroshima & Western Honshu
Hayabusacho 6 Imperial Palace & Tokyo Station
Hayakawa 34 Central Honshu
Hayama 23 Yokohama Area
Hayamacho 47 Northern Kyoto
Hayamada 73 Yamaguchi
Hayashibara Museum of Art 75 Okamaya
Hayashigoakocho 31 Atami
Hayashiji 57 Greater Osaka
Hayashikuchicho 48 Western Kyoto
Hayashima 69 Hiroshima & Western Honshu
Hayashiyama 47 Northern Kyoto
Hazaki 23 Mt. Fuji & Around Tokyo
Hazamacho 37 Central Nagoya
Hazamacho 47 Northern Kyoto
Hazawa 4 Greater Tokyo
Heavens Sonohara Snow World 34 Central Honshu
Hebino 78 Akita
Heda 30 Izu Peninsula
Heda Shipbuilding Museum 30 Izu Peninsula
Hedo 95 Okinawa-honto
Heguri Town 64 Around Nara
Heijo Palace Site 64 Around Nara
Heike Castle 95 Okinawa & The Southwest Islands
Heike Clan Folk Museum 87 Iya Valley
Heike Historical Village 77 Northern Honshu
Heisei 81 Sendai
Heisei-kan 10 Asakusa, Ueno & Akihabara
Heishu Memorial Museum 35 Nagoya Area
Heiwa 37 Central Nagoya
Heiwa 92 Nagasaki
Heiwadori 88 Matsuyama
Hiba 66 Hongu Onsens
Hibara 80 Aizu, Inawashiro & Ura-bandai
Hibara Historical Museum 80 Aizu, Inawashiro & Ura-Bandai
Hibayama Hot Spring 69 Hiroshima & Western Honshu
Hibiya Park 8 Ginza, Tsukiji & Tokyo Tower
Hibiya-koen 8 Ginza, Tsukiji & Tokyo Tower
Hida 34 Central Honshu
Hida Folk Archeological Museum 39 Takayama
Hida Nagareha Ski Area 34 Central Honshu
Hida Shizen-kan Museum 40 Nagano & Matsu-moto Areas
Hida Takayama Museum of Art 39 Takayama
Hida Takayama Teddy Bear Eco Village 39 Takayama
Hida-no-sato Folk Village 39 Takayama
Hidacho 65 Asuka
Hidaka 54 Kansai Area
Hidaka 83 Hokaido
Hidaka 86 Shikoku
Hidaka Kokusai Ski Area 83 Hokaido
Hidaka-gawa 54 Kansai Area
Hidama 80 Aizu, Inawashiro & Ura-bandai
Hidari Daimonji Fire Festival Characters 46 Northern Kyoto
Hidatakayama Machi-no Museum 39 Takayama
Hiden'in-cho 61 Osaka Namba
Hidericho 49 Western Kyoto
Hiderita 79 Hiraizumi & Ichinoseki
Hieidaira 42 Kyoto
Hiekawa 30 Izu Peninsula

Hiezu 69 Hiroshima & Western Honshu
Higashi 13 Roppongi, Shibuya, Omotesando, Harajuku & Meiji Shrine
Higashi Iya Folk Museum 87 Iya Valley
Higashi Nada Ward 55 Osaka Area
Higashi Ward 35 Nagoya Area
Higashi Ward 64 Around Nara
Higashi Ward 71 Hiroshima
Higashi Yamate Old Western Houses 92 Nagasaki
Higashi-agatsuma 22 Mt. Fuji & Around Tokyo
Higashi-akasuna 41 Lake Suwa
Higashi-asahimachi 74 Matsue
Higashi-asakusa 11 Asakusa, Ueno & Akihabara
Higashi-azabu 8 Ginza, Tsukiji & Tokyo Tower
Higashi-bunkicho 45 Kawaramachi & Gion
Higashi-chichibu 22 Mt. Fuji & Around Tokyo
Higashi-daimotsucho 56 Greater Osaka
Higashi-dekijimacho 89 Tokushima
Higashi-dori 57 Greater Osaka
Higashi-dori 77 Northern Honshu
Higashi-dori-kannonmae 78 Akita
Higashi-dori-nakamachi 78 Akita
Higashi-enokicho 15 Shinjuku
Higashi-gaoka 4 Greater Tokyo
Higashi-gekkocho 49 Western Honshu
Higashi-gocho 41 Nagano
Higashi-godacho 47 Northern Kyoto
Higashi-gokencho 6 Imperial Palace & Tokyo Station
Higashi-goshocho 74 Onomichi
Higashi-goshodencho 46 Northern Kyoto
Higashi-gotanda 18 Meguro & Shinagawa
Higashi-gotocho 46 Northern Kyoto
Higashi-hachiokacho 49 Western Kyoto
Higashi-hakuragicho 56 Greater Osaka
Higashi-hakushimacho 71 Hiroshima
Higashi-hamacho 56 Greater Osaka
Higashi-hamasakicho 72 Hagi
Higashi-hata 37 Inuyama
Higashi-hatsushimacho 56 Greater Osaka
Higashi-himurocho 47 Northern Kyoto
Higashi-hinokuchicho 47 Northern Kyoto
Higashi-hiroshima 69 Hiroshima & Western Honshu
Higashi-honmachi 56 Greater Osaka
Higashi-ichikawacho 48 Western Kyoto
Higashi-ikebukuro 17 Ikebukuro
Higashi-ikedacho 49 Western Kyoto
Higashi-imazato 57 Greater Osaka
Higashi-itoyone 73 Yamaguchi
Higashi-izu 30 Izu Peninsula
Higashi-junnaincho 49 Western Kyoto
Higashi-kagawa 87 Shikoku
Higashi-kagura 82 Daisetsuzan National Park
Higashi-kaidocho 48 Western Kyoto
Higashi-kaigancho 31 Atami
Higashi-kaigancho 56 Greater Osaka
Higashi-kaigawacho 49 Western Kyoto
Higashi-kanayama 33 Narita
Higashi-kanda 7 Imperial Palace & Tokyo Station
Higashi-kanenagacho 65 Nara
Higashi-kaniyacho 71 Hiroshima
Higashi-kannonmachi 70 Hiroshima
Higashi-kawaracho 43 Central & Eastern Kyoto
Higashi-kawasakicho 62 Kobe
Higashi-kenrokuenmachi 38 Kanazawa
Higashi-kitsujicho 65 Nara
Higashi-koen 93 Fukuoka
Higashi-kojimacho 37 Inuyama
Higashi-kojinmachi 71 Hiroshima
Higashi-koken 37 Inuyama
Higashi-komagata 11 Asakusa, Ueno & Akihabara
Higashi-komatsugawa 5 Greater Tokyo
Higashi-komonozacho 45 Kawaramachi & Gion
Higashi-koraibashi 59 Osaka Station
Higashi-kotohira 92 Nagasaki
Higashi-kozucho 61 Osaka Namba
Higashi-kubocho 74 Onomichi
Higashi-kusabukacho 41 Shizuoka
Higashi-matsushimacho 56 Greater Osaka
Higashi-matsuyama 22 Mt. Fuji & Around Tokyo
Higashi-mikagemachi 38 Kanazawa
Higashi-miyagino 81 Sendai
Higashi-miyatacho 47 Northern Kyoto
Higashi-miyoshi 87 Shikoku
Higashi-monzencho 45 Kawaramachi & Gion
Higashi-mukojima 11 Asakusa, Ueno & Akihabara
Higashi-mukojima--nishinocho 56 Greater Osaka

Higashi-mukojima-higashi-nocho 56 Greater Osaka
Higashi-nagamachi 76 Hirosaki
Higashi-naka 88 Kotohira
Higashi-nakahama 57 Greater Osaka
Higashi-nakajima 57 Greater Osaka
Higashi-nakamoto 57 Greater Osaka
Higashi-nakano 14 Shinjuku
Higashi-nakasone 97 Miyakojima
Higashi-naniwacho 56 Greater Osaka
Higashi-naruocho 56 Greater Osaka
Higashi-naruse 77 Northern Honshu
Higashi-nihombashi 7 Imperial Palace & Tokyo Station
Higashi-nippori 5 Greater Tokyo
Higashi-no-moncho 41 Nagano
Higashi-nodamachi 57 Greater Osaka
Higashi-obase 57 Greater Osaka
Higashi-odawara 64 Mt. Koya
Higashi-ogu 5 Greater Tokyo
Higashi-omi 54 Kansai Area
Higashi-omi City 67 Lake Biwa
Higashi-osaka 54 Kansai Area
Higashi-osaka City 64 Around Nara
Higashi-osaka Folk Museum 64 Around Nara
Higashi-osugicho 37 Central Nagoya
Higashi-ozonecho 37 Central Nagoya
Higashi-rendainocho 46 Northern Kyoto
Higashi-sakuracho 43 Central & Eastern Kyoto
Higashi-sanrizuka 33 Narita
Higashi-sasabokocho 65 Nara
Higashi-sengokucho 91 Kagoshima
Higashi-shimbashi 8 Ginza, Tsukiji & Tokyo Tower
Higashi-shinagawa 15 Meguro & Shinagawa
Higashi-shincho 37 Central Nagoya
Higashi-shinkoiwa 5 Greater Tokyo
Higashi-shinsaibashi 61 Osaka Namba
Higashi-shiraishi 73 Yamaguchi
Higashi-shisen 36 Central Nagoya
Higashi-sonogi 90 Kyusu
Higashi-sotoboricho 37 Central Nagoya
Higashi-sumida 5 Greater Tokyo
Higashi-takajomachi 41 Shizuoka
Higashi-takasucho 56 Greater Osaka
Higashi-takatsukasacho 49 Western Kyoto
Higashi-takeyacho 45 Kawaramachi & Gion
Higashi-tamachi 72 Hagi
Higashi-tenma 57 Greater Osaka
Higashi-tsuchidocho 74 Onomichi
Higashi-ueno 10 Asakusa, Ueno & Akihabara
Higashi-uenodancho 46 Northern Kyoto
Higashi-uoyacho 44 Kawaramachi & Gion
Higashi-uracho 47 Northern Kyoto
Higashi-watokumachi 76 Hirosaki
Higashi-yamatecho 88 Tokushima
Higashi-yamatomachi 72 Shimonoseki
Higashi-yanagiwaracho 62 Kobe
Higashi-yashio 20 Odaiba
Higashi-yodogawa 55 Osaka Area
Higashi-yoshino 54 Kansai Area
Higashi-yoshinocho 89 Tokushima
Higashi-yotsugi 5 Greater Tokyo
Higashi-yozaka 37 Inuyama
Higashicho 45 Kawaramachi & Gion
Higashidacho 25 Kawasaki
Higashidacho 47 Northern Kyoto
Higashidacho 89 Takamatsu
Higashidemachi 62 Kobe
Higashidori 78 Akita
Higashigodai 79 Hiraizumi & Ichinoseki
Higashihama 81 Matsushima
Higashihongo 31 Shimoda
Higashihonjicho 75 Tottori
Higashikaocho 79 Hiraizumi & Ichinoseki
Higashikawa 82 Daisetsuzan National Park
Higashikawacho 84 Hakodate
Higashikujo 50 Southern Kyoto
Higashikushira 90 Kyusu
Higashimachi 41 Nagano
Higashimachi 49 Western Kyoto
Higashimachi 63 Kobe
Higashimachi 75 Tottori
Higashimachi 94 Naha
Higashinari Ward 64 Around Nara
Higashino 51 Southern Kyoto
Higashinocho 43 Central & Eastern Kyoto
Higashisendai 81 Sendai
Higashisuna 5 Greater Tokyo
Higashiura Town 35 Nagoya Area
Higashiyama 12 Roppongi, Shibuya, Omote-sando, Harajuku & Meiji Shrine
Higashiyama 38 Kanazawa
Higashiyama 47 Northern Kyoto
Higashiyama 63 Kobe
Higashiyama 73 Yamaguchi

Higashiyama 92 Nagasaki
Higashiyama Higashi Traditional Town 38 Kanazawa
Higashiyama Hot Spring 80 Aizu, Inawashiro & Ura-Bandai
Higashiyama Kaii Setouchi Museum of Art 87 Seto-ohasi Bridge
Higashiyama-ohara 65 Asuka
Higashiyamacho 62 Kobe
Higashiyamamachi 39 Takayama
Higata 23 Mt. Fuji & Around Tokyo
Higawa 94 Naha
Higucicho 44 Kawaramachi & Gion
Higure-dori 63 Kobe
Hiikekaigan Beach 54 Kansai Area
Hiiragidanicho 46 Northern Kyoto
Hiji 90 Kyusu
Hiji O-taki 95 Okinawa-Honto
Hijiri-no-taki 82 Sado-ga Island
Hijiwara 72 Hagi
Hijiyama Park 71 Hiroshima
Hijiyamahonmachi 71 Hiroshima
Hikari 68 Hiroshima & Western Honshu
Hikarimachi 91 Central Beppu
Hikatae 39 Noto Peninsula
Hikawa 69 Hiroshima & Western Honshu
Hikawa 90 Kyusu
Hikawa Maru Ocean Liner 25 Kawasaki
Hikone 54 Kansai Area
Hikone Castle 66 Hikone Castle
Hikone Castle Museum 66 Hikone Castle
Hikone City 67 Lake Biwa
Hikone Machinaka Museum 66 Hikone Castle
Hikoshima-amanogocho 72 Shimonoseki
Hikosomachi 38 Kanazawa
Himeji 54 Kansai Area
Himeji Castle 66 Himeji Castle
Himeji City Zoo 66 Himeji Castle
Himeji Doll House 66 Himeji Castle
Himeji Museum of Art 66 Himeji Castle
Himeji Museum of Literature 66 Himeji Castle
Himejima 56 Greater Osaka
Himekannon Statue 79 Lake Tazawa
Himenosawa Park 30 Izu Peninsula
Himeshima 90 Kyusu
Himi 39 Noto Peninsula
Himon'ya 4 Greater Tokyo
Himuro 42 Kyoto
Himurocho 46 Northern Kyoto
Hino 42 Kyoto
Hino 54 Kansai Area
Hino 69 Hiroshima & Western Honshu
Hino Town 67 Lake Biwa
Hino-taki 69 Hiroshima & Western Honshu
Hinode 92 Nagasaki
Hinodecho 24 Yokohama
Hinodecho 41 Shizuoka
Hinodecho 75 Kurashiki
Hinodemachi 89 Matsuyama
Hinoecho 47 Northern Kyoto
Hinoemata 77 Northern Honshu
Hinoguchicho 46 Northern Kyoto
Hinohara Tomin-no-mori Park 22 Mt. Fuji & Around Tokyo
Hinojiri 53 Uji Town
Hinokage 90 Kyusu
Hinokamicho 48 Western Kyoto
Hinokicho 49 Western Kyoto
Hinokimachi 64 Nara
Hinokitogecho 47 Northern Kyoto
Hinokuchicho 36 Central Nagoya
Hinokuchicho 48 Western Kyoto
Hinokuchicho 59 Osaka Station
Hinomaru Hot Spring 75 Tottori
Hinomyojincho 48 Western Kyoto
Hinooka 43 Central & Eastern Kyoto
Hinookaebisudanicho 45 Kawaramachi & Gion
Hinotani 46 Northern Kyoto
Hinotori Hot Spring 90 Aso Area
Hioki 90 Kyusu
Hira Art Museum 67 Lake Biwa
Hirabayashi Taiko Memorial Museum 41 Lake Suwa
Hirade Museum 40 Nagano & Matsumoto Areas
Hirado 90 Kyusu
Hirafuku Memorial Art Museum 78 Kakunodate
Hiragishi Folk Museum 85 Sapporo
Hiragishi-ichijo 85 Sapporo
Hiragishi-nijo 85 Sapporo
Hirai 5 Greater Tokyo
Hiraikecho 36 Central Nagoya
Hiraizumi 77 Northern Honshu
Hiraizumi Cultural Heritage Center 79 Hiraizumi & Ichinoseki
Hiraizumi Historical Meseum 79 Hiraizumi & Ichinoseki

Hiraka 76 Lake Towada
Hirakawacho 6 Imperial Palace & Tokyo Station
Hirakicho 48 Western Kyoto
Hiramachi 49 Western Kyoto
Hiranai 77 Northern Honshu
Hirano 46 Northern Kyoto
Hirano 92 Nagasaki
Hirano Ward 64 Around Nara
Hirano-baba 57 Greater Osaka
Hirano-ichimachi 57 Greater Osaka
Hirano-kita 57 Greater Osaka
Hirano-machi 59 Osaka Station
Hirano-miyamachi 57 Greater Osaka
Hirano-motomachi 57 Greater Osaka
Hirano-ward 55 Osaka Area
Hiranocho 62 Kobe
Hiranocho 90 Kagoshima
Hiranomachi 66 Himeji Castle
Hiranomachi 71 Hiroshima
Hiranuma 24 Yokohama
Hirao 56 Greater Osaka
Hirao 68 Hiroshima & Western Honshu
Hirao 93 Fukuoka
Hirao-josuimachi 93 Fukuoka
Hiraokamachi 93 Fukuoka
Hirara 97 Miyakojima
Hirata 65 Asuka
Hirata 69 Hiroshima & Western Honshu
Hirata 77 Northern Honshu
Hiratsuka 18 Meguro & Shinagawa
Hiratsuka 22 Mt. Fuji & Around Tokyo
HirauchiKaichuOnsen 96 Yakushima
Hiraya 34 Central Honshu
Hirayama Hot Spring 90 Kyusu
Hirayama Ikuo Art Museum 86 Shimanami Kaido
Hirayu Hot Spring 40 Nagano & Matsumoto Areas
Hirizo Beach 30 Izu Peninsula
Hiro-o 13 Roppongi, Shibuya, Omotesando, Harajuku & Meiji Shrine
Hirogawa 54 Kansai Area
Hirokawa 90 Kyusu
Hirokawacho 36 Central Nagoya
Hiromachi 4 Greater Tokyo
Hirono 77 Northern Honshu
Hiroo 83 Hokaido
Hirooka 38 Kanazawa
Hiroomote 78 Akita
Hirosaka 38 Kanazawa
Hirosaki 77 Northern Honshu
Hirosaki City Museum 76 Hirosaki
Hirosaki Cultural Center 76 Hirosaki
Hirosaki-jo Castle 76 Hirosaki
Hirose 42 Kyoto
Hirose-kitamachi 70 Hiroshima
Hirosemachi 70 Hiroshima
Hirosemachi 81 Sendai
Hiroshima 68 Hiroshima & Western Honshu
Hiroshima Airport 69 Hiroshima & Western Honshu
Hiroshima Castle 71 Hiroshima
Hiroshima Castle Ruins 71 Hiroshima
Hiroshima Kemmin-no-Mori Ski Area 69 Hiro-shima & Western Honshu
Hiroshima Museum of Art 71 Hiroshima
Hiroshima National Peace Memorial Hall for the Atomic Bomb Victim 70 Hiroshima
Hiroshima Peace Memorial (Gembaku Dome) 70 Hiroshima
Hiroshima Pref. 69 Hiroshima & Western Honshu
Hiroshima Prefectural Art Museum 71 Hiroshima
Hiroshima-Nishi Airport 68 Hiroshima & Western Honshu
Hirosumicho 36 Central Nagoya
Hirotai Beach 77 Northern Honshu
Hirottekita-ie (Mosaic House) 82 Daisetsuzan National Park
Hisada 76 Shirakami Mountains
Hisagi 27 Kamakura
Hisakatacho 49 Western Kyoto
Hisamatsu Five Brave Monument Honoring 97 Miyako Islands
Hisayama 90 Kyusu
Hishi-yagura Watch Tower 38 Kanazawa
Hishio Beach 86 Shimanami Kaido
Hishiyacho 44 Kawaramachi & Gion
Historic Relic Sado Gold Mine 80 Sado-ga Island
Historic Town 39 Gujo Hachiman
Historical And Folk Museum 87 Shikoku
Historical Museum 23 Yokohama Area
HistoricyFolklore Museum 73 Miyajima
History & Folklore Museum 81 Sendai

History Garage 21 Odaiba
Hita 90 Kyusu
Hitachi 77 Northern Honshu
Hitachi-omiya 23 Mt. Fuji & Around Tokyo
Hitachinaka 23 Mt. Fuji & Around Tokyo
Hitachiota 77 Northern Honshu
Hito-suji 79 Hiraizumi & Ichinoseki
Hitomi Museum 67 Lake Biwa
Hitotsubashi 6 Imperial Palace & Tokyo Station
Hitoyadocho 41 Shizuoka
Hitoyama 68 Shodo Island
Hitoyama Rural Kabuki Stage 68 Shodo Island
Hitoyosi 90 Kyusu
Hiyakomachi 72 Hagi
Hiyishicho 36 Central Nagoya
Hiyodorigoecho 62 Kobe
Hiyodorigoesuji 62 Kobe
Hiyoshicho 57 Greater Osaka
Hiyoshidai 33 Narita
Hiyoshikura 33 Narita
Hiyoshimachi 38 Kanazawa
Ho Daimonji Fire Festival Characters 47 Northern Kyoto
Ho Tange 50 Fushimi Area
Hoanjicho 49 Western Kyoto
Hodaka Togei-kaikan 40 Nagano & Matsumoto Areas
Hodogawa 23 Yokohama Area
Hodono-haranomachi 78 Akita
Hodono-kanasamachi 78 Akita
Hodono-nakacho 78 Akita
Hodono-ohatacho 78 Akita
Hodono-sakuramachi 78 Akita
Hodono-suwacho 78 Akita
Hodono-torimachi 78 Akita
Hodosan Zoo 22 Mt. Fuji & Around Tokyo
Hoei 92 Nagasaki
Hoenzaka 57 Greater Osaka
Hofu 68 Hiroshima & Western Honshu
Hoheikyo Dam 82 Sado-ga Island
Hoheikyo Hot Spring 82 Sado-ga Island
Hojo 66 Himeji Castle
Hojo 69 Hiroshima & Western Honshu
Hojo 86 Shikoku
Hojoguchi 66 Himeji Castle
Hoki 69 Hiroshima & Western Honshu
Hokkaido Ainu Association 85 Sapporo
Hokkaido Museum of Literature 85 Sapporo
Hokkaido Museum of Modern Art 85 Sapporo
Hokkaido Pref. 83 Hokaido
Hokkaido Railway Museum 84 Hakodate
Hokkaido Sakamoto Ryomo Museum 84 Hakodate
Hokkaido Speed Park 82 Sado-ga Island
Hokkaido Univ. Botanical Garden 85 Sapporo
Hokkaido Univ. Museum 85 Sapporo
Hokkaido University 85 Sapporo
Hokkawa Hot Spring 30 Izu Peninsula
Hokki-Ji 64 Around Nara
Hokko 56 Greater Osaka
Hokko Yacht harbor 56 Greater Osaka
Hokko-ji 27 Kamakura
Hokodencho 44 Kawaramachi & Gion
Hokudan Murotsu Beach 54 Kansai Area
Hokuei 69 Hiroshima & Western Honshu
Hokuko-ryokuchi 56 Greater Osaka
Hokuko-shiratsu 56 Greater Osaka
Hokuonomori National Park 77 Northern Honshu
Hokuryu 83 Hokaido
Hokuto 34 Central Honshu
Hokuto 82 Hokaido
Homa 80 Aizu, Inawashiro & Ura-bandai
Homei 88 Kotohira
Homma Art Museum 29 Hakone
Homotsu-kan (Treasure House) 88 Kotohira
Hon-amanuma 4 Greater Tokyo
Hon-dori Arcade 71 Hiroshima
Hon-fujisawa 26 Kamakura
Hon-isshiki 5 Greater Tokyo
Hon-komagome 6 17 Ikebukuro
Hon-koshin-machi 91 Kagoshima
Hon-kugenuma 26 Kamakura
Hon-sanrizuka 33 Narita
Honan 4 Greater Tokyo
Honbetsu 83 Hokaido
Honbo Main Hall 65 Nara
Honcho 14 Shinjuku
Honcho 24 Yokohama
Honcho 25 Kawasaki
Honcho 26 Kamakura

Honcho 76 Hirosaki
Honcho 77 Aomori
Honco 32 Nikko Town
Honda 23 Mt. Fuji & Around Tokyo
Hondamachi 38 Kanazawa
Honden 56 Greater Osaka
Honencho 37 Central Nagoya
Honenincho 43 Central & Eastern Kyoto
Hongakuji-ji 27 Kamakura
Hongan-ji (Nishi-Hongan-ji) 49 Western Kyoto
Hongo 10 Asakusa, Ueno & Akihabara
Hongocho 74 Matsue
Hongu (Main Hall) 88 Kotohira
Hongu 66 Hongu Onsens
Honimbo Shusaku Igo Memorial Museum 86 Shimanami Kaido
Honjo 11 Asakusa, Ueno & Akihabara
Honjo 33 Narita
Honjo 41 Matsumoto
Honjo 77 Northern Honshu
Honjo 88 Kotohira
Honjo Marina Beach 77 Northern Honshu
Honjo-higashi 57 Greater Osaka
Honjo-nishi 57 Greater Osaka
Honjohama Beach 54 Kansai Area
Honkan Japanese Art Museum 10 Asakusa, Ueno & Akihabara
Honkawa E.S. Peace Museum 70 Hiroshima
Honkawacho 70 Hiroshima
Honmabu (Main Mine) 73 Iwami Ginzan
Honmachi 14 Shinjuku
Honmachi 38 Kanazawa
Honmachi 39 Gujo Hachiman
Honmachi 51 Southern Kyoto
Honmachi 59 Osaka Station
Honmachi 62 Kobe
Honmachi 65 Nara
Honmachi 66 Himeji Castle
Honmachi 72 Shimonoseki
Honmachi 73 Tsuwano
Honmachi 73 Yamaguchi
Honmachi 75 Okamaya
Honmachi 75 Tottori
Honmachi-bashi 59 Osaka Station
Honmachini 73 Tsuwano
Honmaru 36 Central Nagoya
Honmaru 93 Kumamoto
Honmura 88 Kotohira
Honome 91 Kannawa Hells Area
Honryusuicho 44 Kawaramachi & Gion
Honshiocho 15 Shinjuku
Hontori 41 Shizuoka
Hopparacho 43 Central & Eastern Kyoto
Hoppo Hot Spring 22 Mt. Fuji & Around Tokyo
Horai-no-matsu Pine Tree 79 Lake Tazawa
Horaicho 24 Yokohama
Horanouchicho 48 Western Kyoto
Horencho 65 Nara
Horensahoyama 65 Nara
Horibatacho 36 Central Nagoya
Horibatamachi 39 Takayama
Horie Beach 86 Shikoku
Horiecho 91 Kagoshima
Horiikecho 48 Western Kyoto
Horikappu Beach 82 Hokaido
Horikawa Sightseeing Boat 74 Matsue
Horikawacho 25 Kawasaki
Horikawacho 49 Western Kyoto
Horikawacho 91 Miyazaki
Horikawamachi 38 Kanazawa
Horikecho 45 Kawaramachi & Gion
Horikiri 47 Northern Kyoto
Horikiri 5 Greater Tokyo
Horikiri Iris Garden 5 Greater Tokyo
Horikoshi 68 Shodo Island
Horikoshicho 61 Osaka Namba
Horimachi 92 Shimabara
Horimatsu 39 Noto Peninsula
Horino Memorial Museum 44 Kawaramachi & Gion
Horinouchi 33 Narita
Horinouchi 37 Inuyama
Horinouchi 4 Greater Tokyo
Horinouchicho 25 Kawasaki
Horinouchicho 43 Central & Eastern Kyoto
Horita Hot Spring 91 Beppu Area
Horiuchi 72 Hagi
Horobetsu Dam 82 Sado-ga Island
Horokanai 83 Hokaido
Horomachi 74 Matsue
Horonai Hot Spring 82 Hokaido
Horonobe 83 Hokaido
Horotachi Ski Area 83 Hokaido
Horyu-Ji 64 Around Nara

Horyu-ji Treasures Museum 10 Asakusa, Ueno & Akihabara
Hosai 38 Kanazawa
Hosai Ozaki Memorial Hall 68 Shodo Island
Hoseicho 36 Central Nagoya
Hoshi-no-Museum 67 Lake Biwa
Hoshigaekecho 49 Western Kyoto
Hoshimamachi 38 Kanazawa
Hoshina Hot Spring 40 Nagano & Matsumoto Areas
Hoshinocho 45 Kawaramachi & Gion
Hoshisuna-no-hama Beach 96 Yaeyama Islands
Hoshogaoka 41 Lake Suwa
Hoshojicho 43 Central & Eastern Kyoto
Hosoda 5 Greater Tokyo
Hosoe-shinmachi 72 Shimonoseki
Hosoecho 72 Shimonoseki
Hosogoemachi 78 Kakunodate
Hosoguchimachi 39 Noto Peninsula
Hosomi Art Museum 45 Kawaramachi & Gion
Hot Spring Foot Bath 74 Matsue
Hotaka 40 Nagano & Matsumoto Areas
Hotaka Hot Spring 40 Nagano & Matsumoto Areas
Hoteiyacho 44 Kawaramachi & Gion
Hoto-no-taki 32 Nikko Area
Hozuicho 49 Western Kyoto
Huis Ten Bosch (Amusement Park) 90 Kyusu
Hukuba Art Museum 40 Nagano & Matsumoto Areas
Hyakkokumachi 76 Hirosaki
Hyakuna Beach 95 Okinawa-Honto
Hyakunicho 37 Central Nagoya
Hyakunincho 14 Shinjuku
Hyakushima 56 Greater Osaka
Hyakuyama 42 Kyoto
Hyogo Pref. 54 Kansai Area
Hyogo Ward 55 Osaka Area
Hyogocho 62 Kobe
Hyokeikan Archeological Museum 10 Asakusa, Ueno & Akihabara
Hyotan Hot Spring 91 Kannawa Hells Area
Hyotanmachi 38 Kanazawa
Hyuuga 90 Kyusu
Ibara 69 Hiroshima & Western Honshu
Ibaradanicho 46 Northern Kyoto
Ibaragicho 38 Kanazawa
Ibaraki 23 Mt. Fuji & Around Tokyo
Ibaraki City 55 Osaka Area
Ibaraki Pref. 23 Mt. Fuji & Around Tokyo
Ibaraki Prefectural Museum of History 77 Northern Honshu
Ibi Kogen Ski Area 34 Central Honshu
Ibigawa 34 Central Honshu
Ibigawa 54 Kansai Area
Ibukacho 36 Central Nagoya
Ibusuki 90 Kyusu
Ibusuki Hot Spring 90 Kyusu
Icchyu 87 Iya Valley
Ichi-no-hashi 64 Mt. Koya
Ichi-no-yu 66 Kinosaki
Ichiban 53 Uji Town
Ichibancho 49 Western Kyoto
Ichibancho 6 Imperial Palace & Tokyo Station
Ichibancho 76 Hirosaki
Ichibancho 81 Sendai
Ichibancho 88 Matsuyama
Ichibecho 49 Western Kyoto
Ichigaya-choenjimachi 6 Imperial Palace & Tokyo Station
Ichigaya-daimachi 15 Shinjuku
Ichigaya-funagawaramachi 6 Imperial Palace & Tokyo Station
Ichigaya-hachimancho 6 Imperial Palace & Tokyo Station
Ichigaya-honmuracho 15 Shinjuku
Ichigaya-kagacho 15 Shinjuku
Ichigaya-koracho 15 Shinjuku
Ichigaya-nakanocho 15 Shinjuku
Ichigaya-sadoharacho 6 Imperial Palace & Tokyo Station
Ichigaya-sanaicho 6 Imperial Palace & Tokyo Station
Ichigaya-takajomachi 6 Imperial Palace & Tokyo Station
Ichigaya-tamachi 6 Imperial Palace & Tokyo Station
Ichigaya-yakuojimachi 15 Shinjuku
Ichigaya-yamabushicho 15 Shinjuku
Ichigaya-yanagicho 15 Shinjuku
Ichihara 23 Mt. Fuji & Around Tokyo
Ichihara-cho 42 Kyoto
Ichijo 30 Izu Peninsula
Ichijocho 49 Western Kyoto
Ichijoji 47 Northern Kyoto

Ichijoji Idegatanienokigao 52 Enryaku-ji & Mt. Hiei
Ichikai 23 Mt. Fuji & Around Tokyo
Ichikannoncho 49 Western Kyoto
Ichikawa 22 Mt. Fuji & Around Tokyo
Ichikawa 54 Kansai Area
Ichikawa-misato 22 Mt. Fuji & Around Tokyo
Ichikawamisato 34 Central Honshu
Ichiki-kushikino 90 Kyusu
Ichimatsu-cho 43 Central & Eastern Kyoto
Ichinobe 77 Northern Honshu
Ichinocho 44 Kawaramachi & Gion
Ichinoicho 49 Western Kyoto
Ichinomata Keikoku Hot Spring 86 Shikoku
Ichinomiya 34 Central Honshu
Ichinomiya 66 Amano Hashidate
Ichinomiya Beach 23 Mt. Fuji & Around Tokyo
Ichinomiya City 35 Nagoya Area
Ichinomiya Hot Spring 91 Aso Area
Ichinosaka 46 Northern Kyoto
Ichinosaka 88 Kotohira
Ichinose 30 Izu Peninsula
Ichinoseki 77 Northern Honshu
Ichinoura Beach 90 Kyusu
Ichioka 56 Greater Osaka
Ichioka-motomachi 56 Greater Osaka
Ichomachi 81 Sendai
Ida 91 Kannawa Hells Area
Ida-no-hama Beach 96 Yaeyama Islands
Idacho 46 Northern Kyoto
Ide 30 Izu Peninsula
Ide 54 Kansai Area
Idegahanacho 47 Northern Kyoto
Idemitsu Museum of Arts 8 Ginza, Tsukiji & Tokyo Tower
Idocho 48 Western Kyoto
Ie 95 Okinawa-honto
Iga 34 Central Honshu
Iga 54 Kansai Area
Igaryu Ninja Museum 54 Kansai Area
Igawajo 41 Matsumoto
Igisue 68 Shodo Island
Igodai 33 Narita
Igusha 4 Greater Tokyo
Ihama 30 Izu Peninsula
Iidabashi 6 Imperial Palace & Tokyo Station
Iidacho 33 Narita
Iidamachi 37 Central Nagoya
Iijima 34 Central Honshu
Iijima 34 Shirakawa-go & Gokayama
Iino Castle Ruins 90 Kyusu
Iinuma Museum 40 Nagano & Matsumoto Areas
Iitate 77 Northern Honshu
Iiyama 34 Central Honshu
Iizuka 90 Kyusu
Iizuna Apple Museum 40 Nagano & Matsumoto Areas
Iizuna Resort Ski Area 40 Nagano & Matsumoto Areas
Ijino-shinden 33 Narita
Ikadaba 30 Izu Peninsula
Ikaho 22 Mt. Fuji & Around Tokyo
Ikaruga Town 64 Around Nara
Ikata 86 Shikoku
Ikatsuchi 65 Asuka
Ikawa Ski Area Kainayama 87 Iya Valley
Ikawa-cho 87 Iya Valley
Ike 30 Izu Peninsula
Ikebatacho 47 Northern Kyoto
Ikebukuro 16 Ikebukuro
Ikebukuro-honcho 4 Greater Tokyo
Ikeda 20th Century Art Museum 30 Izu Peninsula
Ikeda 25 Kawasaki
Ikeda 40 Nagano & Matsumoto Areas
Ikeda 54 Kansai Area
Ikeda 68 Shodo Island
Ikeda 83 Hokaido
Ikeda City 55 Osaka Area
Ikeda Masuo Museum 30 Izu Peninsula
Ikedacho 59 Osaka Station
Ikedamachi Tatecho 38 Kanazawa
Ikedonoho 46 Northern Kyoto
Ikego Museum 23 Yokohama Area
Ikeji Beach 95 Okinawa & The Southwest Islands
Ikejima 56 Greater Osaka
Ikejiri 12 Roppongi, Shibuya, Omotesando, Harajuku & Meiji Shrine
Ikejiricho 48 Western Kyoto
Ikeno Taiga Art Museum 48 Western Kyoto
Ikenohata 10 Asakusa, Ueno & Akihabara
Ikenoo 42 Kyoto

Ikenotaira Hot Spring 40 Nagano & Matsumoto Areas
Ikenouchicho 49 Western Kyoto
Ikenoyu Hot Spring 83 Akan National Park
Ikeshiro 30 Izu Peninsula
Ikeshitacho 48 Western Kyoto
Ikesucho 44 Kawaramachi & Gion
Iketsutsumicho 43 Central & Eastern Kyoto
Ikeyama 53 Uji Town
Iki 90 Kyusu
Iki Airport 90 Kyusu
Ikkahyocho 48 Western Kyoto
Ikoma City 64 Around Nara
Ikoma District 64 Around Nara
Ikotuiya 83 Hokaido
Ikue 57 Greater Osaka
Ikuno Korea Town 64 Around Nara
Ikuno Ward 64 Around Nara
Ikuno-higashi 57 Greater Osaka
Ikuno-nishi 57 Greater Osaka
Ikusaka 40 Nagano & Matsumoto Areas
Ikushimachi 88 Matsuyama
Ikuta Shrine 63 Kobe
Ikutacho 63 Kobe
Ikutama-maemachi 61 Osaka Namba
Ikutama-teramachi 61 Osaka Namba
Ikutamacho 61 Osaka Namba
Ima-furuhagimachi 72 Hagi
Ima-uonotanamachi 72 Hagi
Imabari 86 Shikoku
Imabari Castle 86 Shimanami Kaido
Imabashi 57 Greater Osaka
Imabayashi 57 Greater Osaka
Imabetsu 77 Northern Honshu
Imachi 49 Western Kyoto
Imado 11 Asakusa, Ueno & Akihabara
Imafuku 56 Greater Osaka
Imafuku-higashi 57 Greater Osaka
Imafuku-minami 57 Greater Osaka
Imafuku-nishi 57 Greater Osaka
Imagawa 4 Greater Tokyo
Imagawa 92 Fukuoka
Imagumano 43 Central & Eastern Kyoto
Imahama Beach 39 Noto Peninsula
Imaharocho 46 Northern Kyoto
Imahoricho 48 Western Kyoto
Imai 30 Izu Peninsula
Imaichi 57 Greater Osaka
Imaichi 73 Yamaguchi
Imaicho 48 Western Kyoto
Imaihama Beach 30 Izu Peninsula
Imaizumi 27 Kamakura
Imaizumi 80 Aizu, Inawashiro & Ura-bandai
Imaizumi 93 Fukuoka
Imaizumidai 27 Kamakura
Imajukuhama Beach 67 Lake Biwa
Imakane 82 Hokaido
Imakojicho 65 Nara
Imakura-shinden 33 Narita
Imakusuriyacho 43 Central & Eastern Kyoto
Imamachi 75 Tottori
Imamichicho 45 Kawaramachi & Gion
Imari 90 Kyusu
Imasato 42 Kyoto
Imashinza-ikenishicho 49 Western Kyoto
Imauracho 72 Shimonoseki
Imazatocho 89 Takamatsu
Imazu-minami 57 Greater Osaka
Imazu-naka 57 Greater Osaka
Imba 23 Mt. Fuji & Around Tokyo
Imizu 39 Noto Peninsula
Imoritai 76 Shirakami Mountains
Imperial East Gardens 5 Greater Tokyo
Imperial Mausoleum of Emperor Jinmu 65 Asuka
Imperial Mausoleum of Emperor Kaika 65 Nara
Imperial Mausoleum of Emperor Kogen 65 Asuka
Imperial Mausoleum of Emperor Temmu & Jito 65 Asuka
Imperial Mausoleum of Empress Bifukumon-in 64 Mt. Koya
Imperial Palace 5 Greater Tokyo
Imperial Theater 8 Ginza, Tsukiji & Tokyo Tower
Ina 34 Central Honshu
Inaba Cave 86 Shikoku
Inaba-motomachi 56 Greater Osaka
Inabacho 49 Western Kyoto
Inabadocho 44 Kawaramachi & Gion
Inabaso 56 Greater Osaka
Inaei Park 35 Nagoya Area
Inagawa 41 Shizuoka
Inagawa 55 Osaka Area
Inagwa 54 Kansai Area
Inaho 84 Otaru
Inaho Park 84 Otaru

Inakujira 80 Sado-ga Island
Inami 54 Kansai Area
Inari 26 Kamakura
Inari 39 Gujo Hachiman
Inari 60 Osaka Namba
Inaricho 44 Kawaramachi & Gion
Inarimachi 32 Nikko Town
Inarimachi 75 Kurashiki
Inariyama Hime-zuka Mausoleum 89 Taka-matsu
Inasa-no-Hama Beach 68 Hiroshima & Western Honshu
Inasa-yama Cable Car 92 Nagasaki
Inashiki 23 Mt. Fuji & Around Tokyo
Inawashiro 80 Aizu, Inawashiro & Ura-bandai
Inawashiro Area 80 Aizu, Inawashiro & Ura-bandai
Inawashiro Resort Ski Area 80 Aizu, Inawashiro & Ura-Bandai
Inawashiro Ski Area 80 Aizu, Inawashiro & Ura-Bandai
Inawashiro Swan Wintering Place 80 Aizu, Inawashiro & Ura-Bandai
Inazawa City 35 Nagoya Area
Inazumi Beach 69 Hiroshima & Western Honshu
Ine 54 Kansai Area
Information Bureau of Tokyo 14 Shinjuku
Inkura-no-taki 82 Sado-ga Island
Inno-shima Athletic Park 86 Shimanami Kaido
Inno-shima Flower Center 86 Shimanami Kaido
Innoshima 69 Hiroshima & Western Honshu
Ino 86 Shikoku
Inohana Beach 77 Northern Honshu
Inokecho 49 Western Kyoto
Inokuchicho 46 Northern Kyoto
Inosawa Hot Spring 87 Shikoku
Inotani 34 Shirakawa-go & Gokayama
Inotani 68 Shodo Island
Inouchi 42 Kyoto
Inoue Kenkabo Birthplace 72 Hagi
Inouecho 65 Nara
Institute For Nature Study 18 Meguro & Shinagawa
Int'l House (Belgium Flanders Museum) 61 Osaka Namba
Intermediatheque Museum 7 Imperial Palace & Tokyo Station
Intex Osaka 56 Greater Osaka
Inuicho 48 Western Kyoto
Inukami District 67 Lake Biwa
Inuyama 37 Inuyama
Inuyama Artifacts Museum 37 Inuyama
Inuyama Castle 37 Inuyama
Inuyama City 35 Nagoya Area
Inuyamacho 27 Kamakura
Inuzukacho 47 Northern Kyoto
Inzai 23 Mt. Fuji & Around Tokyo
Io Jigoku (Hell Of Sulfur) 29 Hakone
Io World Kagoshima Aquarium 91 Kagoshima
Iojimatodai Park 90 Kyusu
Iori-taki 32 Nikko Area
Ioricho 47 Northern Kyoto
Iorinocho 47 Northern Kyoto
Ippongicho 48 Western Kyoto
Ipponsugimachi 81 Sendai
Irago Beach 34 Central Honshu
Irie-dori 62 Kobe
Iriecho 72 Shimonoseki
Irifune 84 Otaru
Irifune 9 Ginza, Tsukiji & Tokyo Tower
Irigura 80 Aizu, Inawashiro & Ura-bandai
Irihi-no-taki 86 Shimanami Kaido
Iriomote Hot Spring 96 Yaeyama Islands
Iriya 11 Asakusa, Ueno & Akihabara
Iriyamabe Hot Spring 40 Nagano & Matsumoto Areas
Irohazaka (Steep Drive Way) 32 Nikko Area
Ironai 84 Otaru
Irozaki 30 Izu Peninsula
Irufu Doga Museum 41 Lake Suwa
Iruma 30 Izu Peninsula
Isago 25 Kawasaki
Isahaya 90 Kyusu
Isaka Memorial Museum 76 Shirakami Mountains
Isaniwa Shrine 89 Matsuyama
Ise 54 Kansai Area
Ise 92 Nagasaki
Ise-Jingu Shrine 54 Kansai Area
Isecho 24 Yokohama
Isedacho 42 Kyoto
Isedachonagi 42 Kyoto
Isehara 22 Mt. Fuji & Around Tokyo
Isemachi 73 Miyajima

Isemiyacho 74 Matsue
Isesaki 22 Mt. Fuji & Around Tokyo
Iseyacho 44 Kawaramachi & Gion
Iseyama 36 Central Nagoya
Isezakicho 24 Yokohama
Ishiba Family Old House 76 Hirosaki
Ishibashi 22 Mt. Fuji & Around Tokyo
Ishibashicho 74 Matsue
Ishibiki 38 Kanazawa
Ishibu 30 Izu Peninsula
Ishida 37 Inuyama
Ishida 51 Southern Kyoto
Ishida 56 Greater Osaka
Ishidacho 47 Northern Kyoto
Ishidoriyacho 79 Hanamaki
Ishigaki 96 Ishigaki City
Ishigaki Airport 96 Yaeyama Islands
Ishigaki Traditional Craftwork Center 96 Ishigaki City
Ishigaki Yaeyama Museum 96 Ishigaki City
Ishigannoncho 73 Yamaguchi
Ishigatsubocho 48 Western Kyoto
Ishigatsujicho 61 Osaka Namba
Ishige 23 Mt. Fuji & Around Tokyo
Ishigedo 77 Lake Towada
Ishihama Beach 77 Northern Honshu
Ishii 30 Izu Peninsula
Ishii 87 Shikoku
Ishii Teabowl Museum 72 Hagi
Ishiicho 49 Western Kyoto
Ishiicho 62 Kobe
Ishikakecho 47 Northern Kyoto
Ishikari 82 Hokaido
Ishikawa 95 Okinawa-honto
Ishikawa Beach 95 Okinawa-Honto
Ishikawa Historical Museum 38 Kanazawa
Ishikawa Pref. 39 Noto Peninsula
Ishikawa Pref. Museum of Traditional Products & Crafts 38 Kanazawa
Ishikawa Pref. Noh Theatre 38 Kanazawa
Ishikawa Prefectural Art Museum 38 Kanazawa
Ishikawa-mon Gate 38 Kanazawa
Ishikawacho 25 Yokohama
Ishikazucho 46 Northern Kyoto
Ishiki 30 Izu Peninsula
Ishinadacho 49 Western Kyoto
Ishinomaki 77 Northern Honshu
Ishioka 23 Mt. Fuji & Around Tokyo
Ishite-ji 89 Matsuyama
Ishiwara 11 Asakusa, Ueno & Akihabara
Ishiwaramachi 32 Kawagoe-little Edo
Ishiyamachi 32 Nikko Town
Ishiyamacho 84 Otaru
Ishizekicho 75 Okamaya
Ishizuchi Ski Area 86 Shikoku
Isobe-dori 63 Kobe
Isogami-dori 63 Kobe
Isogo 23 Yokohama Area
Isoji 56 Greater Osaka
Isonocho 62 Kobe
Isonoura Beach 54 Kansai Area
Isotake Beach 68 Hiroshima & Western Honshu
Issaikyodanicho 43 Central & Eastern Kyoto
Isshinji Theater Kura 61 Osaka Namba
Isshochi Hot Spring 90 Kyusu
Isso 96 Yakushima
Isso Beach 96 Yakushima
Isumi 23 Mt. Fuji & Around Tokyo
Ita Beach 30 Izu Peninsula
Itachibori 57 Greater Osaka
Itahashi Antique Doll Museum 73 Tsuwano
Itakura 22 Mt. Fuji & Around Tokyo
Italian Embassy Villa Memorial Park 32 Nikko Area
Itami City 55 Osaka Area
Itano 87 Shikoku
Itanyagi 77 Northern Honshu
Itcho-dencho 49 Western Kyoto
Itchoda 37 Inuyama
Itchome 31 Shimoda
Ito 30 Izu Peninsula
Ito Denzo Memorial Museum 78 Hanamaki
Ito District 64 Around Nara
Ito Hot Spring 82 Sado-ga Island
Itocho 48 Western Kyoto
Itohama Beach 30 Izu Peninsula
Itoigawa 34 Central Honshu
Itomachi 63 Kobe
Itoman 95 Okinawa-honto
Itoyacho 44 Kawaramachi & Gion
Itoyamachi 59 Osaka Station
Itoyone 73 Yamaguchi
Itsuki 90 Kyusu
Itsukigokanosho Natural Park 90 Kyusu
Itsukushima Shrine 73 Miyajima

Itsutsubashi 81 Sendai
Ittori-taki 76 Shirakami Mountains
Ivory Art Museum 30 Izu Peninsula
Iwa-ga-kakiuchicho 47 Northern Kyoto
Iwachi 30 Izu Peninsula
Iwachi Beach 30 Izu Peninsula
Iwadate 76 Shirakami Mountains
Iwade 54 Kansai Area
Iwafune Beach 77 Northern Honshu
Iwagami-higashi 93 Takachiho
Iwagatani 68 Shodo Island
Iwahashi Samurai Residence 78 Kakunodate
Iwaicho 79 Hiraizumi & Ichinoseki
Iwaido 65 Asuka
Iwaido Hot Spring 39 Noto Peninsula
Iwaimachi 57 Greater Osaka
Iwaizumi 77 Northern Honshu
Iwaki 77 Northern Honshu
Iwakuni 68 Hiroshima & Western Honshu
Iwakuni Art Museum 73 Iwakuni
Iwakuni Castle 73 Iwakuni
Iwakuni Choko-kan Museum 73 Iwakuni
Iwakuni Ishiningyo Mini Museum 73 Iwakuni
Iwakura 47 Northern Kyoto
Iwakura 65 Yoshina
Iwakura City 35 Nagoya Area
Iwama 23 Mt. Fuji & Around Tokyo
Iwama Hot Spring 82 Daisetsuzan National Park
Iwami 69 Hiroshima & Western Honshu
Iwami Airport 68 Hiroshima & Western Honshu
Iwami Silver Mine Museum 73 Iwami Ginzan
Iwamicho 74 Kurashiki
Iwamizawa 83 Hokaido
Iwamon 46 Northern Kyoto
Iwamotocho 7 Imperial Palace & Tokyo Station
Iwanai 82 Hokaido
Iwane 80 Aizu, Inawashiro & Ura-bandai
Iwani Ginzan Part 73 Iwami Ginzan
Iwani Ginzan Site 73 Iwami Ginzan
Iwanuma 77 Northern Honshu
Iwaobetsu Hot Spring 83 Shiretoko National Park
Iwasaki 76 Shirakami Mountains
Iwasaki Museum 25 Kawasaki
Iwasakimachi 89 Matsuyama
Iwasato 80 Aizu, Inawashiro & Ura-bandai
Iwase 27 Kamakura
Iwashiro Plum-grove Park 54 Kansai Area
Iwata 34 Central Honshu
Iwatacho 75 Okamaya
Iwate 77 Northern Honshu
Iwate Hanamaki Airport 79 Hanamaki
Iwate Pref. 77 Northern Honshu
Iwatocho 6 Imperial Palace & Tokyo Station
Iwatoyamacho 44 Kawaramachi & Gion
Iwatsuki 22 Mt. Fuji & Around Tokyo
Iwaya-no-taki 76 Shirakami Mountains
Iwayaguchi 80 Sado-ga Island
Iya Hot Spring 87 Iya Valley
Iya Kazura-bashi (Vine Suspension Bridge) 87 Iya Valley
Iya Valley 87 Iya Valley
Iya-guchi 87 Iya Valley
Iyakei Hot Spring 69 Hiroshima & Western Honshu
Iyo 86 Shikoku
Izaki 92 Fukuoka
Izakicho 72 Shimonoseki
Izu 30 Izu Peninsula
Izu Animal Kingdom 30 Izu Peninsula
Izu Green Park 30 Izu Peninsula
Izu Mito Sea Paradise 30 Izu Peninsula
Izu Nagaoka Hot Spring 30 Izu Peninsula
Izu Ocean Park 30 Izu Peninsula
Izu Shaboten Park 30 Izu Peninsula
Izu Shinan Beach 30 Izu Peninsula
Izu Tropicalium Park 30 Izu Peninsula
Izukyu Shimoda 31 Shimoda
Izumi 23 Yokohama Area
Izumi 37 Central Nagoya
Izumi 38 Kanazawa
Izumi 4 Greater Tokyo
Izumi 55 Osaka Area
Izumi 90 Kyusu
Izumi City 55 Osaka Area
Izumi Kyoka Memorial Museum 38 Kanazawa
Izumi-minami 78 Akita
Izumi-shikiocho 49 Western Kyoto
Izumicho 41 Shizuoka
Izumicho 47 Northern Kyoto
Izumicho 91 Kagoshima
Izumidonocho 43 Central & Eastern Kyoto
Izumigaoka 38 Kanazawa
Izumigaoka 42 Kyoto
Izumigawacho 47 Northern Kyoto
Izumimachi 57 Greater Osaka

Izuminomachi 38 Kanazawa
Izumiotsu City 55 Osaka Area
Izumisano City 55 Osaka Area
Izumizaki 94 Naha
Izumo 69 Hiroshima & Western Honshu
Izumo 92 Nagasaki
Izumo Airport 69 Hiroshima & Western Honshu
Izumo Taisha Shrine 69 Hiroshima & Western Honshu
Izumoji-tatemotocho 46 Northern Kyoto
Izumoji-tawaracho 47 Northern Kyoto
Izumoyumura Hot Spring 69 Hiroshima & Western Honshu
Izumozaki 77 Northern Honshu
Izunokuni 30 Izu Peninsula
Izunokuni Panorama Park Ropeway 30 Izu Peninsula
Izuo 56 Greater Osaka
Izusan 30 Izu Peninsula
Izushicho 75 Okamaya
Izutsuyacho 44 Kawaramachi & Gion
Jagasaki-migi 81 Matsushima
Jaishi 30 Izu Peninsula
Jakko-no-taki 33 Nikko Area
Janokuchino-taki 97 Yakushima
Japan Coast Guard Museum Yokohama Branch 25 Kawasaki
Japan Cycle Sports Center 30 Izu Peninsula
Japan Doll Museum 41 Shizuoka
Japan Folk Art Museum 61 Osaka Namba
Japan Folk Crafts Museum 12 Roppongi, Shibuya, Omotesando, Harajuku & Meiji Shrine
Japan Folk Crafts Museum 23 Yokohama Area
Japan Football Museum 7 Imperial Palace & Tokyo Station
Japan Monkey Park 37 Inuyama
Japan Newspaper Museum 25 Kawasaki
Japan Rural Toy Museum 75 Kurashiki
Japanese Overseas Migration Museum 24 Yokohama
Japanese Sword Museum 14 Shinjuku
Japanizumu Art Museum 30 Izu Peninsula
Jazz Club Lifetime 91 Miyazaki
JCII Camera Museum 6 Imperial Palace & Tokyo Station
Jibucho 50 Fushimi Area
Jidai Matsuri Festival Oct. 22 45 Kawaramachi & Gion
Jigen-ryu the Art of War Museum 91 Kagoshima
Jigoku Hot Spring 40 Nagano & Matsumoto Areas
Jigokudani 82 Sado-ga Island
Jigyohama 92 Fukuoka
Jikecho 48 Western Kyoto
Jikeyama 48 Western Kyoto
Jikkenmachi 38 Kanazawa
Jinan 12 Roppongi, Shibuya, Omotesando, Harajuku & Meiji Shrine
Jinata Hot Spring 30 Kozu-shima & Nii-jima
Jingatanicho 48 Western Kyoto
Jingu-mae 13 Roppongi, Shibuya, Omotesando, Harajuku & Meiji Shrine
Jinguji 38 Kanazawa
Jinkoincho 46 Northern Kyoto
Jinny Beach 31 Chichi-jima
Jinpukaku Mansion 75 Tottori
Jinsekikogen 69 Hiroshima & Western Honshu
Jiran-no-taki 32 Nikko Area
Jisho-ji (Ginkaku-ji, Silver Pavilion) 43 Central & Eastern Kyoto
Jison-Ji 64 Around Nara
Jissoji 91 Kannawa Hells Area
Jizo-yu 66 Kinosaki
Jizozaki 68 Shodo Island
Jo-an Teahouse 37 Inuyama
Jobo 79 Hiraizumi & Ichinoseki
Jochi-ji 27 Kamakura
Jodo-ji Garden 74 Onomichi
Jododaira Astronimical Observatory 80 Aizu, Inawashiro & Ura-Bandai
Jododani 42 Kyoto
Jodoecho 91 Miyazaki
Jodoji 43 Central & Eastern Kyoto
Joei-ji 27 Kamakura
Joetsu 77 Northern Honshu
Jogashima 22 Mt. Fuji & Around Tokyo
Jogatani 47 Northern Kyoto
Jogo 65 Asuka
Jogyo-ji 27 Kamakura
Johana 34 Central Honshu
John Beach 31 Chichi-jima
Johojicho 45 Kawaramachi & Gion
Johoku 23 Mt. Fuji & Around Tokyo
Joju-in 27 Kamakura
Jokan-ji (Geisha Burials) 5 Greater Tokyo

okmachi 72 Hagi
okoji 56 Greater Osaka
okomyo-ji 27 Kamakura
omon-sugi 97 Yakushima
omyo-ji 27 Kamakura
onai 56 Greater Osaka
onaicho 41 Shizuoka
onan 38 Kanazawa
onan-teramachi 61 Osaka Namba
onancho 39 Gujo Hachiman
oo-daki 86 Shimanami Kaido
oren-no-taki 30 Izu Peninsula
osei 41 Matsumoto
osei 90 Kagoshima
osei 92 Fukuoka
osei-danchi 92 Fukuoka
oshi 66 Amano Hashidate
oshin'etsu-kogen National Park 22 Mt. Fuji &
  Around Tokyo
osoidori 93 Fukuoka
otenkaku Museum 46 Northern Kyoto
oto 41 Matsumoto
oto Ward 64 Around Nara
otocho 41 Shizuoka
otomachi 93 Kumamoto
oyama Park 41 Nagano
oyopolis 21 Odaiba
ozan Park 73 Tsuwano
ufuku-ji 27 Kamakura
ukkoku Toge Peak 30 Izu Peninsula
umonjicho 44 Kawaramachi & Gion
unikencho 61 Osaka Namba
uniko Eco Museum Kokyokan 76 Shirakami
  Mountains
unin 92 Nagasaki
uniso 27 Kamakura
untoku Tenno-ryo (Imperial Mausoleum) 53
  Ohara Village
uocho 36 Central Nagoya
urakucho 49 Western Kyoto
urakumachi 50 Fushimi Area
urakumawari 49 Western Kyoto
uriinhatamachi 65 Nara
urinncho 65 Nara
urizuka Beach 77 Northern Honshu
usangenmachi Nakacho 38 Kanazawa
ushichi-nagare 78 Akita
uso-honmachi 56 Greater Osaka
uso-moto-imazato 56 Greater Osaka
Kabazaiku-denshokan Museum 78 Kakunodate
Kabira-wan Beach 96 Yaeyama Islands
Kabuki-za Theater 9 Ginza, Tsukiji & Tokyo
  Tower
Kabukicho 15 Shinjuku
Kaburagi Kiyokata Memorial Art Museum 27
  Kamakura
Kabutozukacho 48 Western Kyoto
Kachi Kachi Yama Ropeway 29 Lake Kawaguchi
Kachidoki 9 Ginza, Tsukiji & Tokyo Tower
Kachidoki Bridge Museum 9 Ginza, Tsukiji &
  Tokyo Tower
Kachimachi 88 Matsuyama
Kachocho 43 Central & Eastern Kyoto
Kachoyamacho 43 Central & Eastern Kyoto
Kachuan Takeuchiseiho Memorial Museum 48
  Western Kyoto
Kadan 81 Sendai
Kadena 95 Okinawa-honto
Kadena Airbase 95 Okinawa-Honto
Kadogawa 90 Kyusu
Kadoma 54 Kansai Area
Kadoma City 64 Around Nara
Kadono 30 Izu Peninsula
Kadonocho 49 Western Kyoto
Kaga 34 Central Honshu
Kaga Yuzen Traditional Industry Center 38
  Kanazawa
Kagami Pond 40 Nagano & Matsumoto Areas
Kagamihara City 35 Nagoya Area
Kagamiishicho 46 Northern Kyoto
Kagamino 69 Hiroshima & Western Honshu
Kagamiyacho 44 Kawaramachi & Gion
Kagawa 69 Hiroshima & Western Honshu
Kagawa Archives & Resource Center (Matsu-
  zawa Church) 4 Greater Tokyo
Kagawa Pref. 87 Shikoku
Kagawa University Museum 89 Takamatsu
Kagawazu 72 Hagi
Kagetsu Theater 59 Osaka Station
Kagimachi 66 Himeji Castle
Kago 92 Nagasaki
Kagoe Matsuri-kaikan Museum 32 Kawagoe-
  Little Edo
Kagoshima 90 Kyusu
Kagoshima Airport 90 Kyusu

Kagoshima Museum of Environment Planet
  Earth and Future 90 Kagoshima
Kagoshima Pref. 90 Kyusu
Kagoyamachi 89 Tokushima
Kaguraoka Park 82 Daisetsuzan
  National Park
Kagurazaka 6 Imperial Palace & Tokyo Station
Kahadakyo Natural Park 54 Kansai Area
Kahara 53 Uji Town
Kahei Takadaya Museum 84 Hakodate
Kahitsukan Museum of Contemporary Art 45
  Kawaramachi & Gion
Kai 34 Central Honshu
Kaichi 41 Matsumoto
Kaidocho 46 Northern Kyoto
Kaigake-dani Hon-shakunage Community 67
  Lake Biwa
Kaigamori 81 Sendai
Kaigan 8 Ginza, Tsukiji & Tokyo Tower
Kaigan-dori 56 Greater Osaka
Kaigancho 56 Greater Osaka
Kaigandori 24 Yokohama
Kaigata Hot Spring 90 Kyusu
Kaigecho 65 Asuka
Kaiho-kan Shell Museum 97 Miyako Islands
Kaikaro 38 Kanazawa
Kaike Onsen Beach Beach 69 Hiroshima &
  Western Honshu
Kaikoku Memorial Museum 66 Hikone Castle
Kaikonbocho 47 Northern Kyoto
Kaikyo Yume Tower 72 Shimonoseki
Kaimeicho 56 Greater Osaka
Kaimukura 34 Shirakawa-go & Gokayama
Kainan 54 Kansai Area
Kaio Bird Park 39 Noto Peninsula
Kairakuen 23 Mt. Fuji & Around Tokyo
Kaishojicho 49 Western Kyoto
Kaita 88 Kotohira
Kaitaicho 6 Imperial Palace & Tokyo Station
Kaitaku Museum 83 Hokaido
Kaiyo 87 Shikoku
Kaiyodo Figure Museum 67 Lake Biwa
Kaizo-ji 27 Kamakura
Kaizuka 25 Kawasaki
Kaizuka Museum 35 Nagoya Area
Kajicho 43 Central & Eastern Kyoto
Kajicho 7 Imperial Palace & Tokyo Station
Kajigahama Beach 86 Shikoku
Kajigashima 56 Greater Osaka
Kajiicho 43 Central & Eastern Kyoto
Kajimachi 76 Hirosaki
Kajiwara 27 Kamakura
Kajiya 92 Nagasaki
Kajiyacho 62 Kobe
Kajiyacho 91 Kagoshima
Kajiyamachi 39 Gujo Hachiman
Kajiyamachi 50 Fushimi Area
Kakamigahara 34 Central Honshu
Kakamigahara Aerospace Science Museum 35
  Nagoya Area
Kakegawa 34 Central Honshu
Kakeyu Hot Spring 40 Nagano & Matsumoto
  Areas
Kakimotocho 49 Western Kyoto
Kakinokibatake 38 Kanazawa
Kakinokicho 46 Northern Kyoto
Kakinokizaka 4 Greater Tokyo
Kakisaki 31 Shimoda
Kakiuchicho 49 Western Kyoto
Kakogawa 54 Kansai Area
Kakomachi 70 Hiroshima
Kakshiracho 43 Central & Eastern Kyoto
Kakudacho 59 Osaka Station
Kakunodate Onsen 78 Kakunodate
Kakunodate-no-Shidarezakura (Overhanging
  Cherry Blossoms) 78 Kakunodate
Kakunodatemachi 78 Kakunodate
Kakusencho 76 Hirosaki
Kakyoin 81 Sendai
Kaleidoscope Museum of Kyoto 44 Kawara-
  machi & Gion
Kama 90 Kyusu
Kama-daru 30 Izu Peninsula
Kamada 40 Matsumoto
Kamado Jigoku (Boiling Hell) 91 Kannawa
  Hells Area
Kamaekichicho 48 Western Kyoto
Kamagafuchi 79 Hiraizumi & Ichinoseki
Kamaishi 77 Northern Honshu
Kamakura 27 Kamakura
Kamakura Daibutsu (Great Buddha) 27
  Kamakura
Kamakura Museum of Literature 27 Kamakura
Kamakura Museum of National Treasures 27
  Kamakura
Kamakura Old Pottery Museum 27 Kamakura

Kamakura Otani Memorial Art Museum 27
  Kamakura
Kamakura Performing Art Center 27 Kamakura
Kamakura-gu Shrine 27 Kamakura
Kamakurabori Museum 23 Yokohama Area
Kamakurayama 26 Kamakura
Kamano 68 Shodo Island
Kamanoshiri Beach 30 Miyake-jima
Kamata 4 Greater Tokyo
Kamatsuchicho 47 Northern Kyoto
Kamaya Beach 77 Northern Honshu
Kamayahama Beach 77 Northern Honshu
Kamba-no-taki 69 Hiroshima & Western
  Honshu
Kambiray-no-taki 96 Yaeyama Islands
Kameda 79 Hiraizumi & Ichinoseki
Kamedake Hot Spring 69 Hiroshima & Western
  Honshu
Kamega-taki 69 Hiroshima & Western Honshu
Kamei Art Museum 81 Sendai
Kameicho 45 Kawaramachi & Gion
Kameido 5 Greater Tokyo
Kamejima 36 Central Nagoya
Kamenokomachi 76 Hirosaki
Kameoka 54 Kansai Area
Kameokacho 89 Takamatsu
Kametani 73 Iwami Ginzan
Kameyacho 44 Kawaramachi & Gion
Kameyama 54 Kansai Area
Kameyama-koen 48 Western Kyoto
Kameyamacho 73 Yamaguchi
Kamezawa 11 Asakusa, Ueno & Akihabara
Kami 39 Noto Peninsula
Kami 54 Kansai Area
Kami-adachicho 43 Central & Eastern Kyoto
Kami-banbacho 43 Central & Eastern Kyoto
Kami-chitosemachi 41 Nagano
Kami-furano 82 Daisetsuzan National Park
Kami-gioncho 62 Kobe
Kami-gokenmachi 72 Hagi
Kami-hatsuishimachi 32 Nikko Town
Kami-hidacho 65 Asuka
Kami-higashi 57 Greater Osaka
Kami-horitsumecho 43 Central & Eastern Kyoto
Kami-igusa 4 Greater Tokyo
Kami-ikadacho 43 Central & Eastern Kyoto
Kami-ikebukuro 17 Ikebukuro
Kami-jinbaracho 46 Northern Kyoto
Kami-jukucho 31 Atami
Kami-kaidocho 48 Western Kyoto
Kami-kawaharamachi 39 Takayama
Kami-kawanobori 93 Takachiho
Kami-kawarakecho 76 Hirosaki
Kami-kita 57 Greater Osaka
Kami-kitayama 54 Kansai Area
Kami-komenocho 36 Central Nagoya
Kami-komori 37 Inuyama
Kami-kosaicho 46 Northern Kyoto
Kami-kutsunoyacho 41 Shizuoka
Kami-machiya 26 Kamakura
Kami-maezu 36 Central Nagoya
Kami-mikoshicho 46 Northern Kyoto
Kami-nagao 39 Noto Peninsula
Kami-nakacho 50 Fushimi Area
Kami-neko 78 Hanamaki
Kami-nishi-no-moncho 41 Nagano
Kami-noguchicho 91 Central Beppu
Kami-ochiai 16 Ikebukuro
Kami-okamotomachi 39 Takayama
Kami-osaki 18 Meguro & Shinagawa
Kami-oshikata 93 Takachiho
Kami-osugacho 71 Hiroshima
Kami-ozawa 39 Noto Peninsula
Kami-sairencho 73 Miyajima
Kami-sanjocho 62 Kobe
Kami-sannomachi 39 Takayama
Kami-sekiryucho 46 Northern Kyoto
Kami-sembon 65 Yoshina
Kami-shihoro 83 Hokaido
Kami-shodacho 46 Northern Kyoto
Kami-shokakuji 57 Greater Osaka
Kami-sugasawa 78 Kakunodate
Kami-sunagawa 83 Hokaido
Kami-suwa Hot Spring 41 Lake Suwa
Kami-takada 4 Greater Tokyo
Kami-takedanocho 46 Northern Kyoto
Kami-tanoyumachi 91 Central Beppu
Kami-tatetsuginocho 37 Central Nagoya
Kami-tenjincho 89 Takamatsu
Kami-tenmacho 70 Hiroshima
Kami-tokihazama 37 Inuyama
Kami-tonda 54 Kansai Area
Kami-tsutsumicho 38 Kanazawa
Kami-yanagicho 46 Northern Kyoto
Kami-yoga 4 Greater Tokyo
Kami-zenza 92 Nagasaki

Kamifunabara 30 Izu Peninsula
Kamifurano 83 Hokaido
Kamifusacho 46 Northern Kyoto
Kamigamo 46 Northern Kyoto
Kamigata Ukiyoe 61 Osaka Namba
Kamigori 54 Kansai Area
Kamiharucho 91 Central Beppu
Kamihatecho 47 Northern Kyoto
Kamihideri 79 Hiraizumi & Ichinoseki
Kamihiratacho 91 Kannawa Hells Area
Kamihiruzen Ski Area 69 Hiroshima & Western
  Honshu
Kamiichi 89 Matsuyama
Kamiizumi 22 Mt. Fuji & Around Tokyo
Kamiji 57 Greater Osaka
Kamijima 86 Shikoku
Kamikatsu 87 Shikoku
Kamikatsura 48 Western Kyoto
Kamikawa 54 Kansai Area
Kamikawa 82 Daisetsuzan National Park
Kamikawaracho 48 Western Kyoto
Kamikazan 42 Kyoto
Kamikita-manchome 78 Hanamaki
Kamikoani 77 Northern Honshu
Kamikochi 40 Nagano & Matsumoto Areas
Kamikochi Hot Spring 34 Central Honshu
Kamikochi Resort 40 Nagano & Matsumoto
  Areas
Kamikorikicho 44 Kawaramachi & Gion
Kamikuroiwa Archaeological Museum 86
  Shikoku
Kamimachi 65 Yoshina
Kamimine 90 Kyusu
Kaminarimon 11 Asakusa, Ueno & Akihabara
Kaminashi 34 Shirakawa-go & Gokayama
Kamino-murayama 88 Kotohira
Kaminocho 27 Kamakura
Kaminocho 43 Central & Eastern Kyoto
Kaminocho 89 Takamatsu
Kaminokaya Castle 77 Northern Honshu
Kaminoki 37 Inuyama
Kaminokuni 82 Hokaido
Kaminomachi 91 Miyazaki
Kaminoseki 68 Hiroshima & Western Honshu
Kamiogi 4 Greater Tokyo
Kamisawa-dori 62 Kobe
Kamisho 68 Shodo Island
Kamisu 23 Mt. Fuji & Around Tokyo
Kamisucho 56 Greater Osaka
Kamisugi 81 Sendai
Kamisuwa Hot Spring 40 Nagano & Matsumoto
  Areas
Kamita Hot Spring 69 Hiroshima & Western
  Honshu
Kamitaga 30 Izu Peninsula
Kamitakano 47 Northern Kyoto
Kamitakeyacho 47 Northern Kyoto
Kamitoba 50 Southern Kyoto
Kamitoba Tomonori 50 Southern Kyoto
Kamitokusawa 79 Hiraizumi & Ichinoseki
Kamiuma 4 Greater Tokyo
Kamiumacho 43 Central & Eastern Kyoto
Kamiwaka-dori 63 Kobe
Kamiya Museum 35 Nagoya Area
Kamiyachi 79 Hiraizumi & Ichinoseki
Kamiyacho 66 Himeji Castle
Kamiyama 87 Shikoku
Kamiyama Power Plant Museum 87 Shikoku
Kamiyamachi 93 Fukuoka
Kamiyamacho 12 Roppongi, Shibuya, Omote-
  sando, Harajuku & Meiji Shrine
Kamiyamacho 59 Osaka Station
Kamiyanagicho 44 Kawaramachi & Gion
Kamizama-kami 73 Iwami Ginzan
Kamizawa 30 Izu Peninsula
Kammachi 39 Noto Peninsula
Kammu Tenno-ryo Imperial Mausoleum 51
  Southern Kyoto
Kamo 30 Izu Peninsula
Kamo 47 Northern Kyoto
Kamo District 30 Izu Peninsula
Kamo-mioya Shrine 47 Northern Kyoto
Kamo-wake-ikazuchi Shrine (Kamigamo Shrine)
  46 Northern Kyoto
Kamocho 41 Lake Suwa
Kamoenai 82 Hokaido
Kamogata 69 Hiroshima & Western Honshu
Kamogawa 23 Mt. Fuji & Around Tokyo
Kamogawa 39 Noto Peninsula
Kamogawa Sea World 23 Mt. Fuji & Around
  Tokyo
Kamogawa-odori 44 Kawaramachi & Gion
Kamojima 69 Hiroshima & Western Honshu
Kamonden 50 Southern Kyoto
Kamonhayashicho 47 Northern Kyoto

Kamoshika Hot Spring 81 Zao Onsen
Kamou 68 Shodo Island
Kampo Museum 45 Kawaramachi & Gion
Kamui Misaka Ski Area 28 Mt. Fuji
Kamuiwakkayu-no-taki 83 Shiretoko National Park
Kamuiwakkayu-no-taki Hot Spring 83 Shiretoko National Park
Kanagawa 23 Yokohama Area
Kanagawa Museum of Modern Literature 25 Kawasaki
Kanagawa Museum of Natural History 29 Hakone
Kanagawa Pref. 22 Mt. Fuji & Around Tokyo
Kanagawa Prefectural Museum of Cultural History 24 Yokohama
Kanai 80 Sado-ga Island
Kanakosocho 73 Yamaguchi
Kanamaru-za Theater 88 Kotohira
Kanamecho 16 Ikebukuro
Kanami 39 Noto Peninsula
Kanan Town 64 Around Nara
Kanaya 72 Hagi
Kanaya 78 Hanamaki
Kanaya 92 Nagasaki
Kanayama 83 Hokaido
Kanayama Castle Ruins 22 Mt. Fuji & Around Tokyo
Kanayama-shita 78 Kakunodate
Kanayamako Forest Park 83 Hokaido
Kanazawa 23 Yokohama Area
Kanazawa 34 Central Honshu
Kanazawa Castle Park 38 Kanazawa
Kanazawa Folklore Museum 38 Kanazawa
Kanazawa Kutani Museum 38 Kanazawa
Kanazawa Noh Museum 38 Kanazawa
Kanazawa Phonograph Museum 38 Kanazawa
Kanazawa Shinise Memorial Hall 38 Kanazawa
Kanazawa Zoological Garden 23 Yokohama Area
Kanba-no-taki Natural Park 69 Hiroshima & Western Honshu
Kanda 5 Greater Tokyo
Kanda 90 Kyusu
Kanda Higashi Matsushitacho 7 Imperial Palace & Tokyo Station
Kanda Kajicho 7 Imperial Palace & Tokyo Station
Kanda Kita-norimonocho 7 Imperial Palace & Tokyo Station
Kanda Kon'yacho 7 Imperial Palace & Tokyo Station
Kanda Mikuracho 7 Imperial Palace & Tokyo Station
Kanda Nishi-fukudacho 7 Imperial Palace & Tokyo Station
Kanda Sudacho 7 Imperial Palace & Tokyo Station
Kanda Tomiyamacho 7 Imperial Palace & Tokyo Station
Kanda-awajicho 7 Imperial Palace & Tokyo Station
Kanda-izumicho 7 Imperial Palace & Tokyo Station
Kanda-jimbocho 10 Asakusa, Ueno & Akihabara
Kanda-jimbocho 6 Imperial Palace & Tokyo Station
Kanda-kitadori 56 Greater Osaka
Kanda-minamidori 56 Greater Osaka
Kanda-nakadori 56 Greater Osaka
Kanda-nishi-kicho 7 Imperial Palace & Tokyo Station
Kanda-ogawamachi 7 Imperial Palace & Tokyo Station
Kanda-sakumacho 7 Imperial Palace & Tokyo Station
Kanda-sudacho 7 Imperial Palace & Tokyo Station
Kanda-surugadai 7 Imperial Palace & Tokyo Station
Kanda-tacho 7 Imperial Palace & Tokyo Station
Kanda-tsukasamachi 7 Imperial Palace & Tokyo Station
Kandacho 37 Central Nagoya
Kandacho 49 Western Kyoto
Kandacho 62 Kobe
Kandaijincho 44 Kawaramachi & Gion
Kandamachi 39 Takayama
Kaneda 80 Aizu, Inawashiro & Ura-bandai
Kanegahama Beach 90 Kyusu
Kanegasaki 77 Northern Honshu
Kanegasaki 79 Hiraizumi & Ichinoseki
Kaneicho 59 Osaka Station
Kanemaru 39 Noto Peninsula
Kaneshitacho 57 Greater Osaka
Kaneyama 77 Northern Honshu

Kangakuincho 49 Western Kyoto
Kani City 35 Nagoya Area
Kani Folk Museum 35 Nagoya Area
Kanie Historical Museum 35 Nagoya Area
Kanie Town 35 Nagoya Area
Kanigasakacho 46 Northern Kyoto
Kanisawa 81 Sendai
Kanjo-daki 87 Shikoku
Kankakedori 68 Shodo Island
Kankakei Gorge Ropeway 68 Shodo Island
Kankijicho 49 Western Kyoto
Kanko Fukko Memorial Museum 92 Shimabara
Kankodai 77 Lake Towada
Kankodai Viewpoint 77 Lake Towada
Kankodori 89 Takamatsu
Kanmaki Town 64 Around Nara
Kanna Beach 95 Okinawa-Honto
Kannabe 69 Hiroshima & Western Honshu
Kannai 92 Nagasaki
Kannawa 91 Kannawa Hells Area
Kannawa Mushi-yu 91 Kannawa Hells Area
Kannawa-higashi 91 Kannawa Hells Area
Kannawa-kami 91 Kannawa Hells Area
Kannon Hot Spring 30 Izu Peninsula
Kannon Waterfall 90 Kyusu
Kannon Zen-ji Hot Spring 91 Beppu Area
Kannon-daki 69 Hiroshima & Western Honshu
Kannon-daki 82 Hokaido
Kannon-honmachi 70 Hiroshima
Kannon-in Garden 75 Tottori
Kannon-ji Ruins 67 Lake Biwa
Kannoncho 44 Kawaramachi & Gion
Kano-jo Castle Ruins 35 Nagoya Area
Kanoedai 24 Yokohama
Kanoko Hot Spring 83 Hokaido
Kanonji 87 Shikoku
Kanoshitacho 46 Northern Kyoto
Kanoya 90 Kyusu
Kanpo Museum 43 Central & Eastern Kyoto
Kanra 22 Mt. Fuji & Around Tokyo
Kanran-tei Matsushima Museum 81 Matsushima
Kanrin 37 Inuyama
Kanrocho 44 Kawaramachi & Gion
Kansei-honmachi 72 Shimonoseki
Kanseicho 72 Shimonoseki
Kanshuji-nishi 51 Southern Kyoto
Kanuma 22 Mt. Fuji & Around Tokyo
Kanzaki 90 Kyusu
Kanzakicho 61 Osaka Namba
Kanzanji Hot Spring 34 Central Honshu
Karabe 33 Narita
Karahashi 50 Southern Kyoto
Karahimachi 72 Hagi
Karahori-dori Shopping Street 61 Osaka Namba
Karahoricho 61 Osaka Namba
Karaike 37 Inuyama
Karakai 79 Hiraizumi & Ichinoseki
Karakiyocho 61 Osaka Namba
Karakoro Art Studios 74 Matsue
Karakura 33 Nikko Area
Karakuri (Marionette) Museum 37 Inuyama
Karasawa 26 Kamakura
Karasudake 93 Takachiho
Karasugatsuji 61 Osaka Namba
Karasumarucho 47 Northern Kyoto
Karatocho 72 Shimonoseki
Karatsu 90 Kyusu
Kareisawa Shinrin Park 40 Nagano & Matsumoto Areas
Kariwa 77 Northern Honshu
Kariwawacho 48 Western Kyoto
Kariya 34 Central Honshu
Kariya City 35 Nagoya Area
Kariyushi Beach 95 Okinawa-Honto
Karuisawa 30 Izu Peninsula
Karuisawabu 80 Aizu, Inawashiro & Ura-bandai
Karuizawa 77 Northern Honshu
Karumai 77 Northern Honshu
Kasadonocho 49 Western Kyoto
Kasagataki 68 Shodo Island
Kasagi 54 Kansai Area
Kasagoe 33 Nikko Area
Kasai 54 Kansai Area
Kasai Rinkai-koen Park 5 Greater Tokyo
Kasaichimachi 38 Kanazawa
Kasakane 22 Mt. Fuji & Around Tokyo
Kasama 23 Mt. Fuji & Around Tokyo
Kasama 77 Northern Honshu
Kasamai 38 Kanazawa
Kasamai-honmachi 38 Kanazawa
Kasamatsu 46 Northern Kyoto
Kasamatsu Park 66 Amano Hashidate
Kasaoka 69 Hiroshima & Western Honshu

Kasen-no-taki 86 Shikoku
Kashiba City 64 Around Nara
Kashihara 54 Kansai Area
Kashihara City 64 Around Nara
Kashihara City Insectarium 65 Asuka
Kashima 23 Mt. Fuji & Around Tokyo
Kashima 39 Noto Peninsula
Kashima 56 Greater Osaka
Kashima 68 Shodo Island
Kashima 90 Kyusu
Kashima Beach 87 Shikoku
Kashimayari Sports Village 40 Nagano & Matsumoto Areas
Kashiracho 45 Kawaramachi & Gion
Kashita-honmachi 57 Greater Osaka
Kashita-nishi 57 Greater Osaka
Kashiwa 23 Mt. Fuji & Around Tokyo
Kashiwa-kiyomoricho 49 Western Kyoto
Kashiwabecho 47 Northern Kyoto
Kashiwara City 64 Around Nara
Kashiwazaki 77 Northern Honshu
Kashiwazato 56 Greater Osaka
Kashuni-no-taki 83 Shiretoko National Park
Kasori Shell Mound Beach 23 Mt. Fuji & Around Tokyo
Kasose Beach 77 Northern Honshu
Kasuga 6 Imperial Palace & Tokyo Station
Kasuga Taisha Homotsu-den Treasure House 65 Nara
Kasugacho 31 Atami
Kasugacho 41 Shizuoka
Kasugacho 49 Western Kyoto
Kasugacho 73 Yamaguchi
Kasugade-kita 56 Greater Osaka
Kasugade-minami 56 Greater Osaka
Kasugadenaka 56 Greater Osaka
Kasugai 34 Central Honshu
Kasugai City 35 Nagoya Area
Kasugamachi 38 Kanazawa
Kasugamachi 39 Takayama
Kasugamachi 81 Sendai
Kasuganocho 65 Nara
Kasugayama Primeval Forest 64 Around Nara
Kasukawa 22 Mt. Fuji & Around Tokyo
Kasumigaoka 24 Yokohama
Kasumigaokamachi 13 Roppongi, Shibuya, Omotesando, Harajuku & Meiji Shrine
Kasumigaseki 8 Ginza, Tsukiji & Tokyo Tower
Kasumihama Beach 69 Hiroshima & Western Honshu
Kasunokicho 70 Hiroshima
Kasuya 4 Greater Tokyo
Katagihara 42 Kyoto
Katajo 68 Shodo Island
Katakai Beach 23 Mt. Fuji & Around Tokyo
Katamachi 38 Kanazawa
Katamachi 4 Greater Tokyo
Katamaeyama National Park 77 Northern Honshu
Katano 54 Kansai Area
Katano 80 Sado-ga Island
Kataoka 65 Nara
Kataoka 79 Hiraizumi & Ichinoseki
Katase 26 Kamakura
Katase Higashi-hama (East Beach) 26 Kamakura
Katase Higashi-hama (West Beach) 26 Kamakura
Katase Hot Spring 30 Izu Peninsula
Katase-mejiroyama 26 Kamakura
Katasekaigan 26 Kamakura
Kataseyama 26 Kamakura
Katashina 22 Mt. Fuji & Around Tokyo
Kato 54 Kansai Area
Katoku Beach 97 Amami Oshima
Katsunuma 22 Mt. Fuji & Around Tokyo
Katsura 50 Southern Kyoto
Katsura Rikyu Imperial Villa 50 Southern Kyoto
Katsura Taro Old Residence 72 Hagi
Katsuradai-higashi 27 Kamakura
Katsuradai-minami 27 Kamakura
Katsuradai-naka 27 Kamakura
Katsuradai-nishi 27 Kamakura
Katsuragi 54 Kansai Area
Katsuragi City 64 Around Nara
Katsuragicho 48 Western Kyoto
Katsuragisan Ropeway 64 Around Nara
Katsurahama 87 Shikoku
Katsurakamino 48 Western Kyoto
Katsurao 77 Northern Honshu
Katsurazawa Ski Area 83 Hokaido
Katsuren 95 Okinawa-honto
Katsushika 5 Greater Tokyo
Katsushika Hokusai Art Museum 73 Tsuwano
Katsushima 5 Greater Tokyo
Katsuta 77 Aomori

Katsuura 23 Mt. Fuji & Around Tokyo
Katsuura 87 Shikoku
Katsuura Marine Harbor 23 Mt. Fuji & Around Tokyo
Katsuyama 29 Lake Kawaguchi
Katsuyama 61 Osaka Namba
Katsuyama-kita 57 Greater Osaka
Katsuyama-minami 57 Greater Osaka
Kawa-no Museum 18 Meguro & Shinagawa
Kawaba 22 Mt. Fuji & Around Tokyo
Kawabatacho 43 Central & Eastern Kyoto
Kawachi 39 Noto Peninsula
Kawachi-daikumachi 81 Sendai
Kawachi-kameokacho 81 Sendai
Kawachi-motohasekura 81 Sendai
Kawachi-nagano 54 Kansai Area
Kawachi-nagano City 64 Around Nara
Kawachi-nakanosemachi 81 Sendai
Kawachi-no-Kaza'ana Cave 67 Lake Biwa
Kawachi-sanjuninmachi 81 Sendai
Kawachi-yamayashiki 81 Sendai
Kawadacho 15 Shinjuku
Kawadokorocho 48 Western Kyoto
Kawageta 80 Aizu, Inawashiro & Ura-bandai
Kawagishimachi 38 Kanazawa
Kawagoe 32 Kawagoe-little Edo
Kawagoe 54 Kansai Area
Kawagoe City Museum 32 Kawagoe-Little Edo
Kawagoe History Museum 32 Kawagoe-Little Edo
Kawaguchi 29 Lake Kawaguchi
Kawaguchi 56 Greater Osaka
Kawaguchi 92 Nagasaki
Kawaguchi Music Forest 29 Lake Kawaguchi
Kawaguchi-ko Kitahara Museum 29 Lake Kawaguchi
Kawaguchi-ko Motor Museum 28 Mt. Fuji
Kawaguchi-ko Muse Museum 29 Lake Kawaguchi
Kawaguchi-ko Museum of Art 29 Lake Kawaguchi
Kawaguchiko 22 Mt. Fuji & Around Tokyo
Kawaguri 33 Narita
Kawahara 65 Asuka
Kawaharacho 47 Northern Kyoto
Kawai 54 Kansai Area
Kawai Kanjiro Memorial Hall 43 Central & Eastern Kyoto
Kawai Town 64 Around Nara
Kawajiricho 47 Northern Kyoto
Kawakami 33 Narita
Kawakami 34 Central Honshu
Kawakami 54 Kansai Area
Kawakami 92 Nagasaki
Kawakami Hot Spring 80 Aizu, Inawashiro & Ura-Bandai
Kawakami Hot Spring 82 Sado-ga Island
Kawakami Village 64 Around Nara
Kawakamicho 46 Northern Kyoto
Kawakamicho 65 Nara
Kawakita-higashi 88 Kotohira
Kawakubocho 65 Nara
Kawamata Hot Spring 82 Sado-ga Island
Kawamatsuri Museum 35 Nagoya Area
Kawaminami 90 Kyusu
Kawamoto 22 Mt. Fuji & Around Tokyo
Kawamoto 68 Hiroshima & Western Honshu
Kawamukai 27 Hakone Town
Kawamukai 88 Kotohira
Kawamuko 31 Shimoda
Kawamuro 33 Nikko Area
Kawana 26 Kamakura
Kawana 30 Izu Peninsula
Kawanishi 54 Kansai Area
Kawanishi 77 Northern Honshu
Kawanishi Beach 77 Northern Honshu
Kawanishi City 55 Osaka Area
Kawanishi The Culture Museum 79 Hiraizumi & Ichinoseki
Kawanishi Town 64 Around Nara
Kawanishimachi 75 Kurashiki
Kawanobori 93 Takachiho
Kawanoe 69 Hiroshima & Western Honshu
Kawanokamicho 65 Nara
Kawara Beach 90 Kyusu
Kawarabacho 41 Shizuoka
Kawaracho 48 Western Kyoto
Kawarada Samurai Residence 78 Kakunodate
Kawaradacho 47 Northern Kyoto
Kawaradocho 65 Nara
Kawaramachi 25 Kawasaki
Kawaramachi 57 Greater Osaka
Kawaramachi 70 Hiroshima
Kawaramachi 72 Hagi
Kawaramachi 75 Tottori
Kawaramachi 88 Matsuyama

Kawaramachi 91 Miyazaki
Kawaranocho 44 Kawaramachi & Gion
Kawarashicho 49 Western Kyoto
Kawaratai 76 Shirakami Mountains
Kawarayamachi 57 Greater Osaka
Kawarayu Hot Spring 22 Mt. Fuji & Around Tokyo
Kawasaki 23 Yokohama Area
Kawasaki 77 Northern Honshu
Kawasaki 80 Aizu, Inawashiro & Ura-bandai
Kawasaki City Museum 23 Yokohama Area
Kawasaki Racetrack 25 Kawasaki
Kawasakibun 80 Aizu, Inawashiro & Ura-bandai
Kawashima 72 Hagi
Kawashima Family Old Residence 73 Iwami Ginzan
Kawashima Textile Museum 42 Kyoto
Kawashimo Beach 82 Hokaido
Kawashiri Hot Spring 95 Okinawa & The Southwest Islands
Kawasu 30 Izu Peninsula
Kawasu 30 Izu Peninsula
Kawata 51 Southern Kyoto
Kawata Park 35 Nagoya Area
Kawatacho 49 Western Kyoto
Kawatana 90 Kyusu
Kawatana Hot Spring 68 Hiroshima & Western Honshu
Kawauchi 77 Northern Honshu
Kawauchi 81 Sendai
Kawauchi Oimawashi 81 Sendai
Kawayacho 50 Fushimi Area
Kawayu (Sennin-buro) Hot Spring 66 Hongu Onsens
Kawayu 66 Hongu Onsens
Kawayu Eco Museum 83 Akan National Park
Kawayu Hot Spring 83 Akan National Park
Kawazu 30 Izu Peninsula
Kawazu Auto Camp 30 Izu Peninsula
Kawazu Bagatelle Park 30 Izu Peninsula
Kawazu Nanadaru Onsen-kyo 30 Izu Peninsula
Kawazuikataba 30 Izu Peninsula
Kayaba 37 Central Nagoya
Kayaba-shimo 88 Kotohira
Kayabacho 7 Imperial Palace & Tokyo Station
Kayama Mine 73 Iwami Ginzan
Kayamachi 88 Matsuyama
Kayamacho 46 Northern Kyoto
Kayanuma Hot Spring 82 Kushiro National Park
Kayo 95 Okinawa-honto
Kayogoshocho 49 Western Kyoto
Kayona Museum of Antique 59 Osaka Station
Kazamatsuri 29 Hakone
Kazamaura 77 Northern Honshu
Kazamidori-no-Yakata 63 Kobe
Kaze-no Museum 86 Shikoku
Kaze-no-matsubara Windbreak 76 Shirakami Mountains
Kazoe River Park 72 Hagi
Kazuemachi 38 Kanazawa
Kazuga Taisha Shrine 65 Nara
Kazuno 76 Lake Towada
Kazuno 77 Northern Honshu
Kazura-bashi Camping Village 87 Iya Valley
Kazura-ya 87 Iya Valley
Kazurahara Beach 90 Kyusu
Kazurawara 93 Takachiho
Kazusa-ichinomiya 23 Mt. Fuji & Around Tokyo
Kazusa-nakano 23 Mt. Fuji & Around Tokyo
KCI Gallery 50 Southern Kyoto
Keanaicho 46 Northern Kyoto
Kegon-no-taki 32 Nikko Area
Kegoshi 79 Hiraizumi & Ichinoseki
Keihanhon-dori 57 Greater Osaka
Keikyo-kan Marine Science Museum 72 Shimonoseki
Keino 88 Kotohira
Keiryu Hot Spring 34 Central Honshu
Keitakuen Garden 61 Osaka Namba
Kemacho 57 Greater Osaka
Kempo-ji Ruins 34 Central Honshu
Kenbuchi 83 Hokaido
Kencho-ji Hanso-bo 27 Kamakura
Kencho-ji Zen 27 Kamakura
Kenji-no-Kyoshitsu 79 Hanamaki
Kenroku-motomachi 38 Kanazawa
Kenrokuen Garden 34 Central Honshu
Kenrokumachi 38 Kanazawa
Kensei Museum 73 Yamaguchi
Kesennuma National Park 77 Northern Honshu
Keshiyama 47 Northern Kyoto
Kibichuo 69 Hiroshima & Western Honshu
Kibishacho 48 Western Kyoto
Kibunecho 47 Northern Kyoto
Kichijoji 22 Mt. Fuji & Around Tokyo
Kideracho 65 Nara

Kidoike Hot Spring 22 Mt. Fuji & Around Tokyo
Kids Carnival Zone 24 Yokohama
Kids Land Kodomo Toki Museum 35 Nagoya Area
Kids Ninja Village 40 Nagano & Matsumoto Areas
Kids Plaza Osaka 59 Osaka Station
KidZania 9 Ginza, Tsukiji & Tokyo Tower
Kifune Castle 91 Kannawa Hells Area
Kiguramachi 38 Kanazawa
Kihei-dori 39 Noto Peninsula
Kiho 54 Kansai Area
Kihoku 54 Kansai Area
Kihoku 86 Shikoku
Kihoku Tenkyu-kan Planetarium 90 Kyusu
Kijishi Museum 67 Lake Biwa
Kijo 90 Kyusu
Kikawa-higashi 57 Greater Osaka
Kikawa-nishi 57 Greater Osaka
Kikkawa Museum 73 Iwakuni
Kikkawa-ke Grave 73 Iwakuni
Kikko Park 73 Iwakuni
Kikko Peony Garden 73 Iwakuni
Kikko Tea House 73 Iwakuni
Kikonai 82 Hokaido
Kikuchi 90 Kyusu
Kikugahama Beach 72 Hagi
Kikugawa 34 Central Honshu
Kikugawa 38 Kanazawa
Kikugawa Hot Spring 68 Hiroshima & Western Honshu
Kikui 36 Central Nagoya
Kikuicho 15 Shinjuku
Kikumasamune Sake Museum 55 Osaka Area
Kikusuicho 62 Kobe
Kikutamachi 81 Sendai
Kikuya House 72 Hagi
Kikuyo 90 Kyusu
Kimachi 81 Sendai
Kimachi Hot Spring 69 Hiroshima & Western Honshu
Kimachidori 81 Sendai
Kimbozan Museum 81 Dewa Sanzen
Kimino 54 Kansai Area
Kimitsu 22 Mt. Fuji & Around Tokyo
Kimobetsu 82 Sado-ga Island
Kimotsuki 90 Kyusu
Kimpu Shrine 65 Yoshina
Kimpusen-Ji 65 Yoshina
Kimundo-no-taki 82 Sado-ga Island
Kin 95 Okinawa-honto
Kinjo-cho Stone-paved Street 95 Shuri Castle
Kinko 90 Kyusu
Kinocho 47 Northern Kyoto
Kinoe Beach 86 Shikoku
Kinohatacho 46 Northern Kyoto
Kinokawa 54 Kansai Area
Kinoko Museum 33 Nikko Area
Kinomotocho 65 Asuka
Kinone 33 Narita
Kinosaki Art Museum 66 Kinosaki
Kinosaki Literature Museum 66 Kinosaki
Kinoshita 37 Inuyama
Kinoshita 81 Sendai
Kinoshitacho 44 Kawaramachi & Gion
Kinosho 68 Shodo Island
Kinosocho 48 Western Kyoto
Kinoura 39 Noto Peninsula
Kinrakujicho 56 Greater Osaka
Kinryo-no-Sato (Sake Museum) 88 Kotohira
Kinryu Jigoku Hot Spring 91 Kannawa Hells Area
Kinshi 11 Asakusa, Ueno & Akihabara
Kintai-kyo Bridge 73 Iwakuni
Kintoyokotocho 44 Kawaramachi & Gion
Kinugake-no-taki 69 Hiroshima & Western Honshu
Kinugasa 46 Northern Kyoto
Kinugawa Hot Spring 22 Mt. Fuji & Around Tokyo
Kinuta 4 Greater Tokyo
Kinutakoen 4 Greater Tokyo
Kinuyama 88 Matsuyama
Kinzen-no-taki 69 Hiroshima & Western Honshu
Kioicho 6 Imperial Palace & Tokyo Station
Kioroshi 23 Mt. Fuji & Around Tokyo
Kirara Beach 90 Kyusu
Kirara Beach Yakeno Beach 68 Hiroshima & Western Honshu
Kiretocho 62 Kobe
Kirifuki-no-taki 82 Daisetsuzan National Park
Kirifuri Kogen 33 Nikko Area
Kirifuri-no-taki 33 Nikko Area
Kirishima 90 Kyusu
Kiryu 77 Northern Honshu
Kisarazu 22 Mt. Fuji & Around Tokyo

Kiseki Museum of World Stones 28 Mt. Fuji
Kishimotocho 47 Northern Kyoto
Kishinosato 57 Greater Osaka
Kishiwada Castle 55 Osaka Area
Kishiwada City 55 Osaka Area
Kisomura 34 Central Honshu
Kisosansen Park 35 Nagoya Area
Kisshoin 50 Southern Kyoto
Kisugedaira Plateau 33 Nikko Area
Kita 55 Osaka Area
Kita Aoyama 4 Greater Tokyo
Kita Family Samurai House 87 Iya Valley
Kita Nakagusuku 95 Okinawa-honto
Kita Ward 35 Nagoya Area
Kita Ward 57 Greater Osaka
Kita-aoyama 13 Roppongi, Shibuya, Omote-sando, Harajuku & Meiji Shrine
Kita-batake 57 Greater Osaka
Kita-biraki 60 Osaka Namba
Kita-chikusa 37 Central Nagoya
Kita-chinjuancho 46 Northern Kyoto
Kita-chonokicho 47 Northern Kyoto
Kita-daicho 48 Western Kyoto
Kita-daimoncho 46 Northern Kyoto
Kita-daimotsucho 56 Greater Osaka
Kita-dori 57 Greater Osaka
Kita-fukecho 47 Northern Kyoto
Kita-fukurocho 65 Nara
Kita-furuhagimachi 72 Hagi
Kita-gawacho 48 Western Kyoto
Kita-gebanocho 48 Western Kyoto
Kita-gojo 85 Sapporo
Kita-gomoncho 44 Kawaramachi & Gion
Kita-goshocho 49 Western Kyoto
Kita-hakusanbira 37 Inuyama
Kita-hamacho 50 Fushimi Area
Kita-handa Nakamachi 65 Nara
Kita-hatacho 36 Central Nagoya
Kita-hatacho 50 Fushimi Area
Kita-hatsushimacho 56 Greater Osaka
Kita-hiroshima 68 Hiroshima & Western Honshu
Kita-hiroshima 82 Hokaido
Kita-honmachi-dori 63 Kobe
Kita-horie 57 Greater Osaka
Kita-ibaraki 77 Northern Honshu
Kita-ichijo 85 Sapporo
Kita-ikedacho 47 Northern Kyoto
Kita-in 32 Kawagoe-Little Edo
Kita-ishidocho 41 Nagano
Kita-ishigaki 91 Beppu Area
Kita-jonai 56 Greater Osaka
Kita-jujo 85 Sapporo
Kita-kamakura Museum 27 Kamakura
Kita-kamifusacho 46 Northern Kyoto
Kita-kanazawa 76 Aomori
Kita-kannawa 91 Kannawa Hells Area
Kita-karasuyama 4 Greater Tokyo
Kita-kasai 5 Greater Tokyo
Kita-katsuragi District 64 Around Nara
Kita-kawabe 22 Mt. Fuji & Around Tokyo
Kita-kawahoricho 61 Osaka Namba
Kita-kawakamicho 46 Northern Kyoto
Kita-kazan 42 Kyoto
Kita-ke Old House 39 Noto Peninsula
Kita-koromodecho 49 Western Kyoto
Kita-kosugi 37 Inuyama
Kita-kubizuka 37 Inuyama
Kita-kumai Ruins 40 Nagano & Matsumoto Areas
Kita-kyuhojimachi 59 Osaka Station
Kita-kyushu 90 Kyusu
Kita-machi 6 Imperial Palace & Tokyo Station
Kita-memachi 81 Sendai
Kita-mikadocho 65 Nara
Kita-mochida-machi 88 Matsuyama
Kita-monzencho 45 Kawaramachi & Gion
Kita-nagasa-dori 63 Kobe
Kita-nagoya City 35 Nagoya Area
Kita-nakadori 24 Yokohama
Kita-nijo 85 Sapporo
Kita-no-maru-koen 6 Imperial Palace & Tokyo Station
Kita-noharacho 46 Northern Kyoto
Kita-ojicho 46 Northern Kyoto
Kita-okajima 56 Greater Osaka
Kita-omuarucho 47 Northern Kyoto
Kita-otsuka 17 Ikebukuro
Kita-rokujo 85 Sapporo
Kita-saga 48 Western Kyoto
Kita-saiwai 24 Yokohama
Kita-sakasegawacho 62 Kobe
Kita-sasama 78 Hanamaki
Kita-shichijo 85 Sapporo
Kita-shijo 85 Sapporo
Kita-shinagawa 15 Meguro & Shinagawa

Kita-shinjuku 14 Shinjuku
Kita-shinmachi 59 Osaka Station
Kita-tachibana 22 Mt. Fuji & Around Tokyo
Kita-takamatsucho 91 Miyazaki
Kita-takizawa 80 Aizu, Inawashiro & Ura-bandai
Kita-tamachi 74 Matsue
Kita-tanabe 57 Greater Osaka
Kita-tsubakiharacho 46 Northern Kyoto
Kita-tsuboicho 49 Western Kyoto
Kita-tsumori 57 Greater Osaka
Kita-tsuru 22 Mt. Fuji & Around Tokyo
Kita-ueno 10 Asakusa, Ueno & Akihabara
Kita-uoya-nishimachi 65 Nara
Kita-yamabushicho 15 Shinjuku
Kita-yamanomaecho 46 Northern Kyoto
Kita-yamanomoricho 46 Northern Kyoto
Kitabetsuso 37 Inuyama
Kitaboricho 48 Western Kyoto
Kitacho 48 Western Kyoto
Kitagata 54 Kansai Area
Kitagawa 87 Shikoku
Kitago Hot Spring 90 Kyusu
Kitahakonoicho 46 Northern Kyoto
Kitahama 59 Osaka Station
Kitahama 91 Central Beppu
Kitahama Onsen Termas 91 Central Beppu
Kitahama-higashi 59 Osaka Station
Kitahamacho 89 Takamatsu
Kitahataoka 88 Kotohira
Kitahira Beach 67 Lake Biwa
Kitahori Museum Arts Cultural Hall 74 Matsue
Kitahoricho 74 Matsue
Kitaichi Venezia Museum 84 Otaru
Kitaigorocho 49 Western Kyoto
Kitajima 87 Shikoku
Kitaju 91 Kannawa Hells Area
Kitajukkenkoji 79 Hiraizumi & Ichinoseki
Kitakami 77 Northern Honshu
Kitakansen 36 Central Nagoya
Kitakata 77 Northern Honshu
Kitakawaracho 48 Western Kyoto
Kitakazan 43 Central & Eastern Kyoto
Kitakinutacho 49 Western Kyoto
Kitakojicho 65 Nara
Kitakomatsu Beach 67 Lake Biwa
Kitakyushu Airport 90 Kyusu
Kitamachi 32 Kawagoe-little Edo
Kitamachi 48 Western Kyoto
Kitamachigagoya 80 Aizu, Inawashiro & Ura-bandai
Kitami 83 Hokaido
Kitami Hot Spring 83 Hokaido
Kitamukicho 65 Nara
Kitamura 56 Greater Osaka
Kitamura Art Museum 43 Central & Eastern Kyoto
Kitamurocho 65 Nara
Kitani 73 Tsuwano
Kitano 49 Western Kyoto
Kitano 78 Kakunodate
Kitano Art Museum 40 Nagano & Matsumoto Areas
Kitano Cultural Centre 41 Nagano
Kitano Kaburenjo (Kitano Odori) 49 Western Kyoto
Kitano-nogamicho 47 Northern Kyoto
Kitanobocho 43 Central & Eastern Kyoto
Kitanocho 48 Western Kyoto
Kitanocho 63 Kobe
Kitanodancho 48 Western Kyoto
Kitanomachi 88 Kotohira
Kitaonishicho 73 Miyajima
Kitasako Ichibancho 88 Tokushima
Kitashirakawa 47 Northern Kyoto
Kitasuna 5 Greater Tokyo
Kitatacho 47 Northern Kyoto
Kitataisetsu Ski Area 82 Daisetsuzan National Park
Kitatenjin 37 Inuyama
Kitauchi 53 Uji Town
Kitaura 23 Mt. Fuji & Around Tokyo
Kitauracho 47 Northern Kyoto
Kitayama 54 Kansai Area
Kitayama 81 Sendai
Kitayama-sugi Museum 42 Kyoto
Kitayamacho 61 Osaka Namba
Kitayamacho 62 Kobe
Kitayamadacho 48 Western Kyoto
Kitayasue 38 Kanazawa
Kitayokocho 76 Hirosaki
Kitayuzawa Hot Spring 82 Sado-ga Island
Kitazawa 4 Greater Tokyo
Kitazawa Art Museum 41 Lake Suwa
Kitazonocho 47 Northern Kyoto
Kitchoan Museum 27 Kamakura

Kite Museum 67 Lake Biwa
Kite Museum 7 Imperial Palace & Tokyo Station
Kitorocho 47 Northern Kyoto
Kitsuki 90 Kyusu
Kitsune-ga-iwaya 81 Matsushima
Kitsuneike 41 Nagano
Kitsunesaka 47 Northern Kyoto
Kiwa Beach 68 Hiroshima & Western Honshu
Kiyacho 88 Matsuyama
Kiyama 90 Kyusu
Kiyan 95 Okinawa-honto
Kiyanocho 49 Western Kyoto
Kiyo-daki 40 Nagano & Matsumoto Areas
Kiyoichi 45 Kawaramachi & Gion
Kiyokawa 5 Greater Tokyo
Kiyokawa 93 Fukuoka
Kiyokawamachi 38 Kanazawa
Kiyomachi 88 Matsuyama
Kiyomizu 1-chome 43 Central & Eastern Kyoto
Kiyomizu 4-chome 45 Kawaramachi & Gion
Kiyomizu Sannenzaka Museum 45 Kawaramachi & Gion
Kiyomizu Ski Area Hot Spring 40 Nagano & Matsumoto Areas
Kiyomizu-dera 43 Central & Eastern Kyoto
Kiyomizu-yaki Pottery Village 51 Southern Kyoto
Kiyomotocho 45 Kawaramachi & Gion
Kiyosato 83 Hokaido
Kiyosu City 35 Nagoya Area
Kiyosumi 5 Greater Tokyo
Kiyosumi Teien (Garden) 5 Greater Tokyo
Kiyotaki 32 Nikko Area
Kiyotaki-arasawacho 33 Nikko Area
Kiyozawaguchicho 47 Northern Kyoto
Kizaemon-shinden 56 Greater Osaka
Kizakiko Hot Spring 40 Nagano & Matsumoto Areas
Kizankan 40 Nagano & Matsumoto Areas
Kizugawa 57 Greater Osaka
Kizugawa City 64 Around Nara
Kizuri 57 Greater Osaka
Ko-daki 80 Aizu, Inawashiro & Ura-Bandai
Ko-nikaimachi 66 Himeji Castle
Ko-no-yu 66 Kinosaki
Koamicho 70 Hiroshima
Koarashicho 31 Atami
Kobaicho 59 Osaka Station
Kobama Beach 54 Kansai Area
Kobama Beach 90 Kyusu
Kobasamacho 66 Himeji Castle
Kobashicho 75 Okamaya
Kobashimachi 38 Kanazawa
Kobato Beach 77 Northern Honshu
Kobayama 81 Sendai
Kobayashi 90 Kyusu
Kobayashi-higashi 56 Greater Osaka
Kobayashi-nishi 56 Greater Osaka
Kobe 55 Osaka Area
Kobe 68 Shodo Island
Kobe Airport 54 Kansai Area
Kobe Anpanman Kodomo Museum & Mall 62 Kobe
Kobe City 55 Osaka Area
Kobe City Museum 63 Kobe
Kobe Domestic Airport 55 Osaka Area
Kobe Kaiyo Museum 63 Kobe
Kobe Kakyo Historical Museum 63 Kobe
Kobe Kitano Museum 63 Kobe
Kobe Lamp Museum 63 Kobe
Kobe Municipal Oji Zoo 55 Osaka Area
Kobe MunicipalArboretum 55 Osaka Area
Kobe Water Science 62 Kobe
Kobeko-jikata 63 Kobe
Kobitomachi 78 Kakunodate
Koboke Gorge 87 Iya Valley
Kobukuroya 27 Kamakura
Kobuse Waterfall 90 Kyusu
Kobyaku 33 Nikko Area
Kochi 86 Shikoku
Kochi Pref. 69 Hiroshima & Western Honshu
Kochi Ryoma Airport 87 Shikoku
Kochinda 95 Okinawa-honto
Kochipref. 86 Shikoku
Koda 39 Noto Peninsula
Koda 79 Hanamaki
Kodachi 29 Lake Kawaguchi
Kodai-ji Sho Museum 45 Kawaramachi & Gion
Kodama 22 Mt. Fuji & Around Tokyo
Kodansha Noma Memorial Museum 17 Ikebukuro
Kodate 78 Kakunodate
Kodatsuno 38 Kanazawa
Kodeki 37 Central Nagoya
Kodomo Science Museum 75 Tottori

Kodomo-no-kuni (Children's Land) 22 Mt. Fuji & Around Tokyo
Kodono 93 Takachiho
Kodonocho 47 Northern Kyoto
Koenjikita 4 Greater Tokyo
Koeto 39 Noto Peninsula
Koetsucho 46 Northern Kyoto
Kofu 22 Mt. Fuji & Around Tokyo
Kofu 69 Hiroshima & Western Honshu
Kofuku-ji (Karadera) 92 Nagasaki
Kofuku-Ji 65 Nara
Koga 22 Mt. Fuji & Around Tokyo
Koga 50 Southern Kyoto
Koga 90 Kyusu
Koganecho 24 Yokohama
Koganecho 73 Yamaguchi
Koganedori 36 Central Nagoya
Koganegaoka 42 Kyoto
Koganei 22 Mt. Fuji & Around Tokyo
Koganei Park Outdoor Folk House Museum 22 Mt. Fuji & Around Tokyo
Koganemachi 38 Kanazawa
Koganezaki Crystal Park 30 Izu Peninsula
Koganezawa 79 Hiraizumi & Ichinoseki
Kogeikan (Crafts Gallery) 6 Imperial Palace & Tokyo Station
Kogurusu 34 Shirakawa-go & Gokayama
Kogushi Beach 68 Hiroshima & Western Honshu
Kohagura 94 Naha
Kohan 41 Lake Suwa
Kohata 51 Southern Kyoto
Kohinata 17 Ikebukuro
Koho-Yoteizan Alpine Plant Belt 82 Sado-ga Island
Kohoku 23 Yokohama Area
Koi-higashi 70 Hiroshima
Koi-naka 70 Hiroshima
Koiji Beach 39 Noto Peninsula
Koiji Hot Spring 39 Noto Peninsula
Koikehama Beach 95 Okinawa & The Southwest Islands
Koinaricho 43 Central & Eastern Kyoto
Koinokubo 64 Nara
Koinokubo-higashimachi 64 Nara
Koirigawa 76 Shirakami Mountains
Koishikawa 17 Ikebukuro
Koishikawa Korakuen Garden 5 Greater Tokyo
Koiwa Iris Garden 5 Greater Tokyo
Koizimi Yakumo (Lafcadio Hearn) Memorial Museum 74 Matsue
Koizumi Beach 77 Northern Honshu
Koizumi Yakumo (Lafcadio Hearn) Old Residence 74 Matsue
Koizumi Yakumo (Lafcadio Hern) Old House 93 Kumamoto
Koizumicho 44 Kawaramachi & Gion
Kojima 7 Imperial Palace & Tokyo Station
Kojima Torajiro Memorial Hall 75 Kurashiki
Kojimachi 6 Imperial Palace & Tokyo Station
Kojincho 44 Kawaramachi & Gion
Kojinmachi 71 Hiroshima
Kojirakawa 34 Shirakawa-go & Gokayama
Kojiro Hot Spring 39 Noto Peninsula
Kojiya 92 Nagasaki
Kojomachi 92 Kumamoto
Kokawacho 59 Osaka Station
Koke-no-Domon Cave 82 Sado-ga Island
Kokkai Giji-do (National Diet Bldg) 5 Greater Tokyo
Kokonoe 90 Kyusu
Kokonoecho 36 Central Nagoya
Kokuba 94 Naha
Kokubu Beach 68 Hiroshima & Western Honshu
Kokubucho 61 Osaka Namba
Kokubunji 22 Mt. Fuji & Around Tokyo
Kokubunji 59 Osaka Station
Kokubunji 69 Hiroshima & Western Honshu
Kokumachi 59 Osaka Station
Kokuraminami-ku 68 Hiroshima & Western Honshu
Kokusetsu Akan Kohan Ski Area 83 Akan National Park
Kokusetsu Osorakan Ski Area 68 Hiroshima & Western Honshu
Kokutaicho 75 Okamaya
Kokutaijimachi 70 Hiroshima
Kokyo 6 Imperial Palace & Tokyo Station
Kokyo-gaien 6 Imperial Palace & Tokyo Station
Komaba 12 Roppongi, Shibuya, Omotesando, Harajuku & Meiji Shrine
Komae 23 Yokohama Area
Komagane 34 Central Honshu
Komagata 11 Asakusa, Ueno & Akihabara
Komagata Hot Spring 76 Shirakami Mountains
Komagome 17 Ikebukuro

Komaino 33 Narita
Komaki 34 Central Honshu
Komaki City 35 Nagoya Area
Komanocho 44 Kawaramachi & Gion
Komatoritai 77 Lake Towada
Komatsu 34 Central Honshu
Komatsu 78 Kakunodate
Komatsu Airport 34 Central Honshu
Komatsu Beach 87 Shikoku
Komatsu Hitoshi Art Museum 53 Ohara Village
Komatsubara 49 Western Kyoto
Komatsubaracho 59 Osaka Station
Komatsucho 45 Kawaramachi & Gion
Komatsugawa 5 Greater Tokyo
Komatsushima 81 Sendai
Komatsushima 87 Shikoku
Komatsushimashintsutsumi 81 Sendai
Komazawa Olymic Park 23 Yokohama Area
Komegafukuro 81 Sendai
Komesaka 53 Uji Town
Komesu 95 Okinawa-honto
Komeyacho 72 Hagi
Komeyacho 73 Yamaguchi
Kominato-dori 62 Kobe
Komiyacho 61 Osaka Namba
Komizuhama Beach 90 Kyusu
Komochi 22 Mt. Fuji & Around Tokyo
Komomo 54 Kansai Area
Komomu 65 Yoshina
Komori Hot Spring 69 Hiroshima & Western Honshu
Komoro 34 Central Honshu
Komusubidanacho 44 Kawaramachi & Gion
Komyo-ji 27 Kamakura
Komyoincho 65 Nara
Konami Beach 69 Hiroshima & Western Honshu
Konan 15 Meguro & Shinagawa
Konan 23 Yokohama Area
Konan 34 Central Honshu
Konan 87 Shikoku
Konan Airport 69 Hiroshima & Western Honshu
Konan City 35 Nagoya Area
Konan City 67 Lake Biwa
Konancho 75 Tottori
Konashiya 81 Matsushima
Kondo 64 Mt. Koya
Kondoi Beach 96 Yaeyama Islands
Kongo Beach 34 Central Honshu
Kongobu-ji 64 Mt. Koya
Kongosan Ropeway 64 Around Nara
Kono Beach 34 Central Honshu
Konoecho 43 Central & Eastern Kyoto
Konohana Museum 29 Lake Kawaguchi
Konohana Ward 56 Greater Osaka
Konohanamachi 38 Kanazawa
Konohanamachi 89 Matsuyama
Konoura 68 Shodo Island
Konyacho 43 Central & Eastern Kyoto
Konyamachi 66 Himeji Castle
Kora 54 Kansai Area
Kora Beach 69 Hiroshima & Western Honshu
Kora Town 67 Lake Biwa
Koraibashi 57 Greater Osaka
Koraimachi 38 Kanazawa
Korakuen 6 Imperial Palace & Tokyo Station
Korean Atomic Bomb Memorial 70 Hiroshima
Korikimachi 66 Himeji Castle
Korinbo 38 Kanazawa
Koriyama 80 Aizu, Inawashiro & Ura-bandai
Korokan Museum 93 Fukuoka
Koromogawa-ku Yamaguchi 79 Hiraizumi & Ichinoseki
Koromodecho 49 Western Kyoto
Koromogawa-ku Otsura 79 Hiraizumi & Ichinoseki
Koromonoseki 79 Hiraizumi & Ichinoseki
Korosa Ski Area 39 Noto Peninsula
Koryo Museum 46 Northern Kyoto
Koryo Town 64 Around Nara
Kosa 90 Kyusu
Kosai 34 Central Honshu
Kosai 53 Uji Town
Kosaka 76 Lake Towada
Kosaka 77 Northern Honshu
Kosaka 89 Matsuyama
Kosakacho 49 Western Kyoto
Kose 68 Shodo Island
Koseda 97 Yakushima
Kosegawa 78 Hanamaki
Kosei 56 Greater Osaka
Kosenbamachi 32 Kawagoe-little Edo
Koseto Beach 68 Shodo Island
Koshi 65 Asuka
Koshi 90 Kyusu
Koshibami 41 Nagano

Koshima 97 Yakushima
Koshimizu 83 Hokaido
Koshimoda 30 Izu Peninsula
Koshin-an Garden 88 Matsuyama
Koshindo 88 Kotohira
Koshio 79 Hanamaki
Koshomachi 38 Kanazawa
Kosino Beach 34 Central Honshu
Kosoku-ji 27 Kamakura
Kosuge 33 Narita
Kosugi Hoan Museum of Art 32 Nikko Town
Kotakecho 4 Greater Tokyo
Kotakeyabucho 47 Northern Kyoto
Kotan Hot Spring 83 Akan National Park
Kotan-ainu Minzoku-shiryokan: Marukibune 83 Akan National Park
Kotesumicho 49 Western Kyoto
Koto 5 Greater Tokyo
Koto-no-taki 54 Kansai Area
Kotobashi 11 Asakusa, Ueno & Akihabara
Kotobuki 7 Imperial Palace & Tokyo Station
Kotobuki Ski Area 83 Hokaido
Kotobukicho 24 Yokohama
Kotobukicho 57 Greater Osaka
Kotobukicho 74 Kurashiki
Kotobukicho 75 Tottori
Kotogahama Beach 68 Hiroshima & Western Honshu
Kotohira 87 Shikoku
Kotohira-Gu Shrine 88 Kotohira
Kotokugahama 81 Matsushima
Kotokujicho 46 Northern Kyoto
Kotoura 69 Hiroshima & Western Honshu
Kotouracho 56 Greater Osaka
Kotsubo 27 Kamakura
Kotsuka 26 Kamakura
Koumagoe 68 Shodo Island
Koumi 22 Mt. Fuji & Around Tokyo
Koura 30 Izu Peninsula
Koura Beach 30 Izu Peninsula
Koura Beach 87 Shikoku
Kowakicho 47 Northern Kyoto
Kowakidani Hot Spring 29 Hakone Town
Koya 54 Kansai Area
Koya 81 Zao Onsen
Koya Town 64 Around Nara
Koya-imamachi 93 Kumamoto
Koyadocho 44 Kawaramachi & Gion
Koyadori Beach 77 Northern Honshu
Koyama 18 Meguro & Shinagawa
Koyama 46 Northern Kyoto
Koyama 65 Asuka
Koyamacho 49 Western Kyoto
Koyamacho 62 Kobe
Koyamadai 18 Meguro & Shinagawa
Koyasan 64 Mt. Koya
Koyo 37 Central Nagoya
Koyo-dai Lookout 28 Mt. Fuji
Kozagawa 54 Kansai Area
Kozakacho 48 Western Kyoto
Kozakai 39 Noto Peninsula
Kozakai Beach 39 Noto Peninsula
Kozaki Beach 90 Kyusu
Kozakura 53 Uji Town
Kozan Hot Spring 69 Hiroshima & Western Honshu
Kozan-ji 52 Takao Village
Kozawamachi 92 Kumamoto
Kozen 92 Nagasaki
Kozenincho 65 Nara
Kozoe 72 Hagi
Kozomi Beach 69 Hiroshima & Western Honshu
Kozu 57 Greater Osaka
Kozu Beach 87 Shikoku
Kozu-shima Onsen Recreation Complex 30 Kozu-shima & Nii-jima
Kozunomori 33 Narita
Kua Terme Sado Hot Spring 80 Sado-ga Island
Kubo 74 Onomichi
Kubocho 73 Miyajima
Kubodencho 48 Western Kyoto
Kubomachi 32 Kawagoe-little Edo
Kubomachi 49 Western Kyoto
Kubon-no-taki 67 Lake Biwa
Kubono 66 Hongu Onsens
Kuboshoji 73 Yamaguchi
Kubota House 72 Hagi
Kubota Itchiku Museum 29 Lake Kawaguchi
Kubote Museum 90 Kyusu
Kuboyoshi 60 Osaka Namba
Kuchienkobo 63 Kobe
Kuchiichiriyama 63 Kobe
Kudamatsu 68 Hiroshima & Western Honshu
Kudan-kita 6 Imperial Palace & Tokyo Station
Kudan-minami 6 Imperial Palace & Tokyo Station

Kudan-no-taki 77 Lake Towada
Kudarise Hot Spring 40 Nagano & Matsumoto Areas
Kudencho 27 Kamakura
Kudocho 47 Northern Kyoto
Kudoyama Town 64 Around Nara
Kugai 42 Kyoto
Kugai 97 Miyakojima
Kugenuma 26 Kamakura
Kugenuma-fujigaya 26 Kamakura
Kugenuma-higashi 26 Kamakura
Kugenuma-kaigan 26 Kamakura
Kugenuma-matsugaoka 26 Kamakura
Kugenuma-sakuragaoka 26 Kamakura
Kugenuma-shinmei 26 Kamakura
Kuhon-ji 27 Kamakura
Kuise-honmachi 56 Greater Osaka
Kuise-kitashinmachi 56 Greater Osaka
Kuise-minaminishimachi 56 Greater Osaka
Kuise-terajima 56 Greater Osaka
Kuji 4 Greater Tokyo
Kuji 77 Northern Honshu
Kujira Museum 87 Shikoku
Kujo 56 Greater Osaka
Kujo-minami 56 Greater Osaka
Kujukuri 23 Mt. Fuji & Around Tokyo
Kujukurihama Beach 23 Mt. Fuji & Around Tokyo
Kujukushima Islands 90 Kyusu
Kuki 22 Mt. Fuji & Around Tokyo
Kukisawa 76 Shirakami Mountains
Kukominami 79 Hanamaki
Kuma 90 Kyusu
Kumagai Residence 73 Iwami Ginzan
Kumagawa Beach 77 Northern Honshu
Kumagawajuku 67 Lake Biwa
Kumagayacho 72 Hagi
Kumagoe-no-taki 83 Shiretoko National Park
Kumakogen 86 Shikoku
Kumamoto 90 Kyusu
Kumamoto Airport 90 Kyusu
Kumamoto Castle Honmaru Palace 93 Kumamoto
Kumamoto Museum of Art 93 Kumamoto
Kumamoto Museum of Art Annex 93 Kumamoto
Kumamoto Pref. 90 Kyusu
Kumano 68 Hiroshima & Western Honshu
Kumano Beach 95 Okinawa & The Southwest Islands
Kumano Hayatama-Taisha Shrine 54 Kansai Area
Kumano Hongu Taisha 54 Kansai Area
Kumano Hongu-kan Heritage Center 66 Hongu Onsens
Kumano Hongu-Taisha Shrine 66 Hongu Onsens
Kumanocho 36 Central Nagoya
Kumanocho 62 Kobe
Kumanoyo Hot Spring 22 Mt. Fuji & Around Tokyo
Kumasaka 30 Izu Peninsula
Kumata 57 Greater Osaka
Kumatani Hot Spring 69 Hiroshima & Western Honshu
Kumatori 55 Osaka Area
Kumaya Museum of Art 72 Hagi
Kume 33 Narita
Kume 94 Naha
Kume Art Museum 18 Meguro & Shinagawa
Kume Shiseibyo 94 Naha
Kumecho 65 Asuka
Kumenan 69 Hiroshima & Western Honshu
Kumeno 33 Narita
Kumihama Hot Spring 54 Kansai Area
Kumini 81 Sendai
Kumochibashi-dori 63 Kobe
Kumochicho 63 Kobe
Kumogahata 42 Kyoto
Kumoi-dori 63 Kobe
Kumoi-no-taki 77 Lake Towada
Kumomi Hot Spring 30 Izu Peninsula
Kumonoue Hot Spring 64 Around Nara
Kunijima 57 Greater Osaka
Kunika-dori 63 Kobe
Kunimasa 37 Inuyama
Kunimi 77 Northern Honshu
Kunimidake Ski Area 54 Kansai Area
Kuninao Kaigan Beach 97 Amami Oshima
Kunisaki 90 Kyusu
Kunisaki Cape Natural Park 90 Kyusu
Kuniyoshi 76 Shirakami Mountains
Kuniyoshi Hot Spring 76 Shirakami Mountains
Kunizakai Kogen Snow Park 67 Lake Biwa
Kunneppu 83 Hokaido
Kuno 33 Narita
Kunohe 77 Northern Honshu

Kunoki Hot Spring 90 Aso Area
Kunuginome 78 Hanamaki
Kurabo Memorial Hall 75 Kurashiki
Kurae 72 Hagi
Kuragasaki 33 Nikko Area
Kurama-honmachi 52 Kurama Village
Kurama-kibunecho 52 Kurama Village
Kuramae 7 Imperial Palace & Tokyo Station
Kuramayama Museum 52 Kurama Village
Kurami Hot Spring 69 Hiroshima & Western Honshu
Kuranaka 88 Kotohira
Kuranushicho 76 Hirosaki
Kurasaki Beach 97 Amami Oshima
Kurashiki 69 Hiroshima & Western Honshu
Kurashiki Character Banks Museum 75 Kurashiki
Kurashiki Ivy Square 75 Kurashiki
Kurashiki Mirai Park 74 Kurashiki
Kurashiki Museum of Folk Craft 75 Kurashiki
Kurayoshi 69 Hiroshima & Western Honshu
Kurazukuri Zone (Traditional Architecture Zone) 22 Mt. Fuji & Around Tokyo
Kure 68 Hiroshima & Western Honshu
Kureon Hot Spring 90 Kyusu
Kurige 93 Takachiho
Kurihara 77 Northern Honshu
Kurihara-higashi 74 Onomichi
Kurihara-nishi 74 Onomichi
Kurihashi 22 Mt. Fuji & Around Tokyo
Kurimoto 23 Mt. Fuji & Around Tokyo
Kurio 96 Yakushima
Kuriohama Beach 96 Yakushima
Kurisawa Hot Spring 83 Hokaido
Kurisuno 51 Southern Kyoto
Kuritanicho 75 Tottori
Kuriyama 83 Hokaido
Kuro-taki 76 Shirakami Mountains
Kuro-taki 80 Sado-ga Island
Kuroba Hot Spring 34 Shirakawa-go & Gokayama
Kurobe 40 Nagano & Matsumoto Areas
Kurodacho 74 Matsue
Kurodanicho 43 Central & Eastern Kyoto
Kurogahama Beach 90 Kyusu
Kuroganecho 41 Shizuoka
Kurohime Dowa-no-mori Museum 40 Nagano & Matsumoto Areas
Kurohime Kogen Ski Area 40 Nagano & Matsu-moto Areas
Kurohone 22 Mt. Fuji & Around Tokyo
Kuroiwa 68 Shodo Island
Kuroiwa-taki 32 Nikko Area
Kurokawa Hot Spring 39 Noto Peninsula
Kuromatsu Beach 68 Hiroshima & Western Honshu
Kuromatsunai 82 Hokaido
Kuromon 92 Fukuoka
Kuromoncho 37 Central Nagoya
Kuromoncho 46 Northern Kyoto
Kurosaki 76 Shirakami Mountains
Kurosawa 76 Shirakami Mountains
Kurose 69 Hiroshima & Western Honshu
Kuroshima Tenryo Kitamaesen Museum 39 Noto Peninsula
Kuroshio 86 Shikoku
Kurotaki Village 64 Around Nara
Kurozakicho 59 Osaka Station
Kurozuchi-no-taki 69 Hiroshima & Western Honshu
Kurumacho 41 Shizuoka
Kurumada 53 Uji Town
Kurumajicho 47 Northern Kyoto
Kurumamichicho 37 Central Nagoya
Kurumamichicho 48 Western Kyoto
Kurume 90 Kyusu
Kurusu 34 Shirakawa-go & Gokayama
Kuruwamachi 32 Kawagoe-little Edo
Kusagae 92 Fukuoka
Kusagawacho 43 Central & Eastern Kyoto
Kusagiwara 73 Iwami Ginzan
Kusaka Genzui Birthplace 72 Hagi
Kusakabe 68 Shodo Island
Kusakabe Mingei-kan 39 Takayama
Kusasenri 91 Aso Area
Kusatsu 34 Central Honshu
Kusatsu 54 Kansai Area
Kusatsu City 67 Lake Biwa
Kusayama 46 Northern Kyoto
Kusayama Hot Spring 54 Kansai Area
Kusayu Hot Spring 40 Nagano & Matsumoto Areas
Kushi 95 Okinawa-honto
Kushida Shrine 93 Fukuoka
Kushigecho 49 Western Kyoto
Kushima 90 Kyusu

Kushimoto 54 Kansai Area
Kushimoto Marin Park 54 Kansai Area
Kushiro 82 Kushiro National Park
Kushiro Airport 82 Kushiro National Park
Kushiro Shitsugen Observatory Boardwalk 82 Kushiro National Park
Kushiro Zoo 82 Kushiro National Park
Kusu 90 Kyusu
Kusudanicho 62 Kobe
Kusugamicho 89 Takamatsu
Kusugawa 97 Yakushima
Kusugawa Hot Spring 97 Yakushima
Kushama Beach 87 Shikoku
Kusunoki Ruins 64 Around Nara
Kusunokicho 24 Yokohama
Kusunokicho 62 Kobe
Kusuriyacho 44 Kawaramachi & Gion
Kusushi 76 Aomori
Kutchan 82 Sado-ga Island
Kutsuki Ski Area 67 Lake Biwa
Kuwabara 89 Matsuyama
Kuwana 34 Central Honshu
Kuwana District 35 Nagoya Area
Kuwana Tennen Onsen Genkimura 35 Nagoya Area
Kuwazu 57 Greater Osaka
Kuya-taki 42 Kyoto
Kuze 50 Southern Kyoto
Kuzu 22 Mt. Fuji & Around Tokyo
Kuzu 79 Hanamaki
Kuzu Hot Spring 40 Nagano & Matsumoto Areas
Kuzuharagaoka Shrine 27 Kamakura
Kuzumaki 77 Northern Honshu
Kyo-odori 44 Kawaramachi & Gion
Kyo'ogoku-ji (To-ji) 50 Southern Kyoto
Kyobashi 9 Ginza, Tsukiji & Tokyo Tower
Kyobashicho 75 Okamaya
Kyoda 95 Okinawa-honto
Kyodencho 36 Central Nagoya
Kyodo 4 Greater Tokyo
Kyogamisaki 54 Kansai Area
Kyogashi Museum 46 Northern Kyoto
Kyogatani 47 Northern Kyoto
Kyogoku 82 Sado-ga Island
Kyoharacho 94 Naha
Kyojima 5 Greater Tokyo
Kyojo 87 Iya Valley
Kyokuho-ku Nishikimachi 78 Akita
Kyokuho-ku Teramachi 78 Akita
Kyokunan 78 Akita
Kyomachi 38 Kanazawa
Kyomachi 63 Kobe
Kyomachi 91 Central Beppu
Kyomachibori 58 Osaka Station
Kyonan 22 Mt. Fuji & Around Tokyo
Kyonoo 63 Kobe
Kyoritsu-dori 57 Greater Osaka
Kyotanabe 54 Kansai Area
Kyotanba 54 Kansai Area
Kyoto 54 Kansai Area
Kyoto Arashiyama Orgel Museum 48 Western Kyoto
Kyoto Art Center 44 Kawaramachi & Gion
Kyoto City Art Museum Annex 43 Central & Eastern Kyoto
Kyoto Cuisine & Maiko Evening 45 Kawara-machi & Gion
Kyoto Greece Roman Museum 47 Northern Kyoto
Kyoto Historical Museum 43 Central & Eastern Kyoto
Kyoto Imperial Palace 43 Central & Eastern Kyoto
Kyoto Imperial Palace Park 43 Central & Eastern Kyoto
Kyoto Int'l Manga Museum 44 Kawaramachi & Gion
Kyoto Mingei Museum 47 Northern Kyoto
Kyoto Municipal Archaeological Museum 49 Western Kyoto
Kyoto Municipal Science Center for Youth 51 Southern Kyoto
Kyoto Municipal Zoo 43 Central & Eastern Kyoto
Kyoto Museum for World Peace 46 Northern Kyoto
Kyoto National Museum 43 Central & Eastern Kyoto
Kyoto Pref. 54 Kansai Area
Kyoto Prefectural Library and Archives 47 Northern Kyoto
Kyoto Tower 43 Central & Eastern Kyoto
Kyoto Trade Fair Center (Pulse Plaza) 50 Southern Kyoto

Kyoto Univ. Museum 43 Central & Eastern Kyoto
Kyowa 82 Hokaido
Kyoya Hot Spring 86 Shikoku
Kyu Iwasaki-tei House & Gardens 7 Imperial Palace & Tokyo Station
Kyu Kyoryuchi Shigaku History Museum 92 Nagasaki
Kyu Nihon Yusen Otaru Branch 84 Otaru
Kyu-Fukuoka-ken Kokaido Kihinkan 93 Fukuoka
Kyu-Shurin-ji Garden 67 Lake Biwa
Kyu-United Kingdom Consulate 84 Hakodate
Kyudoicho 46 Northern Kyoto
Kyuhojimachi 57 Greater Osaka
Kyushu Energy Museum 93 Fukuoka
Kyutaromachi 57 Greater Osaka
La Cittadella 25 Kawasaki
La Qua 6 Imperial Palace & Tokyo Station
Laforet Museum 8 Ginza, Tsukiji & Tokyo Tower
Lake Biwa Museum 67 Lake Biwa
Lake Biwa-ko Cruise 67 Lake Biwa
Lake Juniko 76 Shirakami Mountains
Lake Shinji 69 Hiroshima & Western Honshu
Lake Shinji Pleasure Boat "Hakucho" 74 Matsue
Lake Suwa Museum 41 Lake Suwa
Lake Tazawa-ko 78 Lake Tazawa
Lalique Museum, Hakone 29 Hakone
Lapis Oboke Stone and Specter Museum 87 Iya Valley
Lida 34 Central Honshu
Lihatobu-no-fukeichi Igirisu-kaigan 79 Hanamaki
Linan 69 Hiroshima & Western Honshu
Listel Ski Fantasia 80 Aizu, Inawashiro & Ura-Bandai
Literature Stone Monuments 68 Shodo Island
Little Museum in a Village of Picture Books 41 Lake Suwa
Little World 35 Nagoya Area
Lock Valley Ski Area 83 Hokaido
Louvre Sculpture Museum 34 Central Honshu
Love Bell 26 Kamakura
Lumbini Art Museum 78 Hanamaki
Lyman-no-taki 82 Daisetsuzan National Park
M-Wave 40 Nagano & Matsumoto Areas
Mabi 69 Hiroshima & Western Honshu
Mabuni 95 Okinawa-honto
Machi 81 Matsushima
Machi-higashi 81 Matsushima
Machida 22 Mt. Fuji & Around Tokyo
Machida 73 Tsuwano
Machiura 79 Hiraizumi & Ichinoseki
Machiya 5 Greater Tokyo
Maebara Issei Old Residence 72 Hagi
Maebashi 77 Northern Honshu
Maebayashi 79 Hiraizumi & Ichinoseki
Maeda Tosanokami Samurai House Site 38 Kanazawa
Maedacho 48 Western Kyoto
Maehama Beach 30 Kozu-shima & Nii-jima
Maehama Beach 97 Miyako Islands
Maejima 94 Naha
Maemachi 63 Kobe
Maenami 39 Noto Peninsula
Maenamicho 36 Central Nagoya
Maesatocho 24 Yokohama
Maezato 96 Ishigaki City
Magawa 57 Greater Osaka
Magohashicho 45 Kawaramachi & Gion
Maguse Hot Spring 77 Northern Honshu
Maibara City 67 Lake Biwa
Maihara 34 Central Honshu
Maika 44 Kawaramachi & Gion
Maishima Pottery Village 56 Greater Osaka
Maishima Seaside Promenade 56 Greater Osaka
Maizuru 54 Kansai Area
Maizuru 93 Fukuoka
Makabe 23 Mt. Fuji & Around Tokyo
Maki 34 Shirakawa-go & Gokayama
Makigahara Children's Zoo 23 Yokohama Area
Makino Shiratani Hot Spring 67 Lake Biwa
Makinocho 36 Central Nagoya
Makinohara 34 Central Honshu
Makishi 94 Naha
Makishima 42 Kyoto
Makiyama Observatory 97 Miyako Islands
Makkari 82 Sado-ga Island
Makkari Hot Spring 82 Sado-ga Island
Makomanai Ski Area 82 Sado-ga Island
Maku-daki 80 Aizu, Inawashiro & Ura-Bandai
Makubetsu 83 Hokaido
Makukawa Hot Spring 80 Aizu, Inawashiro & Ura-Bandai

Makura-taki 33 Nikko Area
Makuracho 46 Northern Kyoto
Makurazaki 90 Kyusu
Makurazaki Airport 90 Kyusu
Mamako Waterfall 90 Kyusu
Mamashita Beach 30 Kozu-shima & Nii-jima
Mamedacho 49 Western Kyoto
Mameyamacho 65 Nara
Mampuku-ji 26 Kamakura
Manai-no-taki 93 Takachiho
Manazuru 29 Hakone
Manazuru 30 Izu Peninsula
Mandara-yu 66 Kinosaki
Maneki Neko Art Museum 74 Onomichi
Mangan-ji Ruins 72 Hagi
Mangokucho 48 Western Kyoto
Mangrove Park 97 Amami Oshima
Maniwa 69 Hiroshima & Western Honshu
Manjuji-nakanocho 44 Kawaramachi & Gion
Mannekin Pis 87 Iya Valley
Manno 69 Hiroshima & Western Honshu
Mano 80 Sado-ga Island
Mano-Go-ryo (Imperial Mausoleum) 80 Sado-ga Island
Manta Scramble 96 Yaeyama Islands
Manyo Botanical Garden 39 Noto Peninsula
Manyo Botanical Garden 65 Nara
Manyo Culture Complex 65 Asuka
Manzai 92 Nagasaki
Manzamo Cliff 95 Okinawa-Honto
Marble Beach 55 Osaka Area
Marchen Forest Museum 30 Izu Peninsula
Marine Aquarium Shimoda 30 Izu Peninsula
Marine Museum 88 Kotohira
Marine Park 86 Shikoku
Marine Plaza Miyajima 73 Miyajima
Marine Youth Center 86 Shimanami Kaido
Marinpia Matsushima Aquarium 81 Matsushima
Maritime Museum 56 Greater Osaka
Mariyudo-no-taki 96 Yaeyama Islands
Marounouchi 5 Greater Tokyo
Marubi Shizen-kan Museum 28 Mt. Fuji
Marugame 87 Shikoku
Marukawacho 46 Northern Kyoto
Marukin Soy Sauce Historical Museum 68 Shodo Island
Maruko 47 Northern Kyoto
Marukoma Hot Spring 82 Sado-ga Island
Marumine 46 Northern Kyoto
Marumori 77 Northern Honshu
Marunouchi 36 Central Nagoya
Marunouchi 38 Kanazawa
Marunouchi 41 Matsumoto
Marunouchi 7 Imperial Palace & Tokyo Station
Marunouchi 75 Okamaya
Marunouchi 89 Takamatsu
Marunouchi My Plaza 6 Imperial Palace & Tokyo Station
Marunoumachi 88 Matsuyama
Maruo 86 Uwajima
Maruo 92 Nagasaki
Maruou Bunka Kyoto
Marushimacho 56 Greater Osaka
Marushimacho 91 Miyazaki
Maruya 33 Nikko Area
Maruyama 92 Nagasaki
Maruyama 31 Shimoda
Maruyama 4 Greater Tokyo
Maruyama 53 Uji Town
Maruyama-dori 57 Greater Osaka
Maruyamacho 12 Roppongi, Shibuya, Omotesando, Harajuku & Meiji Shrine
Maruyamacho 41 Shizuoka
Maruyamacho 45 Kawaramachi & Gion
Masago-dori 63 Kobe
Masagocho 24 Yokohama
Masagocho 88 Matsuyama
Masaki 36 Central Nagoya
Masaki 86 Shikoku
Masaki-daki 86 Shikoku
Mashiko 23 Mt. Fuji & Around Tokyo
Mashu Hot Spring 83 Hokaido
Mashu Kanko Bunka Center 83 Akan National Park
Masuda 68 Hiroshima & Western Honshu
Masue 81 Sendai
Masugatacho 86 Uwajima
Masuizumi 38 Kanazawa
Masumizu Kogen Ski Area 69 Hiroshima & Western Honshu
Masuyacho 44 Kawaramachi & Gion
Masuzawa 76 Shirakami Mountains
Matabee 56 Greater Osaka
Mataburi 53 Uji Town
Matida Civic Theatre 97 Miyakojima

Matoo-no-Yu Hot Spring 40 Nagano & Matsumoto Areas
Matsu 57 Greater Osaka
Matsubacho 36 Central Nagoya
Matsubara 30 Izu Peninsula
Matsubara 36 Central Nagoya
Matsubara 4 Greater Tokyo
Matsubara 77 Aomori
Matsubara Beach 67 Lake Biwa
Matsubara Beach 86 Shimanami Kaido
Matsubara City 64 Around Nara
Matsubara-dori 62 Kobe
Matsubaracho 32 Nikko Town
Matsubaracho 36 Central Nagoya
Matsubaracho 45 Kawaramachi & Gion
Matsubaracho 71 Hiroshima
Matsubaracho 91 Kagoshima
Matsubashi 91 Miyazaki
Matsuda 22 Mt. Fuji & Around Tokyo
Matsudaehama Beach 39 Noto Peninsula
Matsuda 22 Mt. Fuji & Around Tokyo
Matsue 5 Greater Tokyo
Matsue 69 Hiroshima & Western Honshu
Matsue Castle 74 Matsue
Matsue History Museum 74 Matsue
Matsue Kyodo-kan 74 Matsue
Matsue Shinjiko 74 Matsue
Matsuecho 32 Kawagoe-little Edo
Matsugaecho 59 Osaka Station
Matsugahanacho 61 Osaka Namba
Matsugaoka 4 Greater Tokyo
Matsugasaki 47 Northern Kyoto
Matsugasaki Beach 80 Sado-ga Island
Matsugaya 11 Asakusa, Ueno & Akihabara
Matsuharacho 47 Northern Kyoto
Matsuicho 49 Western Kyoto
Matsuida 22 Mt. Fuji & Around Tokyo
Matsukagecho 24 Yokohama
Matsukami 76 Shirakami Mountains
Matsukawa 34 Central Honshu
Matsukawa Hot Spring 77 Northern Honshu
Matsumae 82 Hokaido
Matsumi-no-taki 76 Lake Towada
Matsumoto 34 Central Honshu
Matsumoto Castle 41 Lake Suwa
Matsumoto City Art Museum 41 Lake Suwa
Matsumoto City Hakari Museum 41 Lake Suwa
Matsumoto City Museum 41 Lake Suwa
Matsumoto City Open Air Architectural Museum 40 Nagano & Matsumoto Areas
Matsumoto Memorial Museum 4 Greater Tokyo
Matsumoto Memorial Music Guest House 23 Yokohama Area
Matsumoto Performing Arts Center 41 Lake Suwa
Matsumoto Samurai Residence 78 Kakunodate
Matsumoto Timepiece Museum 41 Lake Suwa
Matsumoto-cho 49 Western Kyoto
Matsumoto-dori 62 Kobe
Matsumotocho 37 Inuyama
Matsumotocho 44 Kawaramachi & Gion
Matsumotozaki 81 Matsushima
Matsumuro 48 Western Kyoto
Matsumuro-kita-matsuoyama 48 Western Kyoto
Matsumushi-dori 57 Greater Osaka
Matsunaga Memorial Museum 29 Hakone
Matsunase Beach 54 Kansai Area
Matsuno 86 Shikoku
Matsunoki 4 Greater Tokyo
Matsunoki 79 Hiraizumi & Ichinoseki
Matsunokicho 43 Central & Eastern Kyoto
Matsuo 48 Western Kyoto
Matsuo 94 Naha
Matsuodani-matsuoyamacho 48 Western Kyoto
Matsuogawa Dam 87 Iya Valley
Matsuoka Museum of Art 18 Meguro & Shinagawa
Matsurabacho 66 Hikone Castle
Matsusaka 54 Kansai Area
Matsushigecho 36 Central Nagoya
Matsushima 5 Greater Tokyo
Matsushima 81 Matsushima
Matsushima Chinese Zodiac Museum 81 Matsushima
Matsushima Pleasure Boat 81 Matsushima
Matsushimacho 56 Greater Osaka
Matsushitacho 57 Greater Osaka
Matsuura 90 Kyusu
Matsuya-machi 61 Osaka Namba
Matsuya-machi- Sumiyoshi 59 Osaka Station
Matsuyacho 44 Kawaramachi & Gion
Matsuyama 86 Shikoku
Matsuyama 91 Miyazaki
Matsuyama 92 Nagasaki
Matsuyama 94 Naha

Matsuyama Airport 86 Shikoku
Matsuyama Castle 88 Matsuyama
Matsuyama Castle Ropeway 88 Matsuyama
Matsuyama Historical Folk Museum 90 Kyusu
Matsuzaki 30 Izu Peninsula
Matsuzakicho 57 Greater Osaka
Matsuzawa Hot Spring 40 Nagano & Matsumoto Areas
Matsuzonocho 78 Hanamaki
Mausoleum of Kukai 65 Mt. Koya
Mausoleum of Takamatsuka 65 Asuka
Mausoluem of Tokugawa 64 Mt. Koya
Mayacho 76 Hirosaki
Mayumi 42 Kyoto
Mayumi 65 Asuka
Me-daki 83 Shiretoko National Park
Meakan Hot Spring 83 Akan National Park
Mega Web 21 Odaiba
Megahira Ski Area 68 Hiroshima & Western Honshu
Megane-bashi 92 Nagasaki
Megane-iwa (Spectacular Rocks) 30 Miyake-jima
Meguro 18 Meguro & Shinagawa
Meguro 23 Yokohama Area
Meguro Museum of Art 18 Meguro & Shinagawa
Meguro Parasitological Museum 18 Meguro & Shinagawa
Meguro Ward Art Museum 23 Yokohama Area
Meguro-honcho 18 Meguro & Shinagawa
Meieki 36 Central Nagoya
Meieki-minami 36 Central Nagoya
Meigetsu-in 27 Kamakura
Meiji Hot Spring 34 Central Honshu
Meiji Ishin Historical Museum 34 Central Honshu
Meiji Mura 35 Nagoya Area
Meiji Restoration Museum 91 Kagoshima
Meiji Shrine 12 Roppongi, Shibuya, Omotesando, Harajuku & Meiji Shrine
Meiji Shrine Outer Garden 4 Greater Tokyo
Meiji Tenno Fushimi Momoyama-ryo Imperial Mausoleum 51 Southern Kyoto
Meiji Univ. Museum Archaeology & Criminal Materials Exhibition 10 Asakusa, Ueno & Akihabara
Meiji-Jingu Shrine 4 Greater Tokyo
Meiji-no-mori-Minoo Quasi National Park 55 Osaka Area
Meirincho 37 Central Nagoya
Meisei 36 Central Nagoya
Meito Art Museum 35 Nagoya Area
Meito Ward 35 Nagoya Area
Meiwa 22 Mt. Fuji & Around Tokyo
Meiwa 54 Kansai Area
Meizancho 91 Kagoshima
Mejiro 16 Ikebukuro
Mejirodai 17 Ikebukuro
Memanbetsu Airport 83 Hokaido
Memuro 83 Hokaido
Men-taki 69 Hiroshima & Western Honshu
Menden 39 Noto Peninsula
Menuma 22 Mt. Fuji & Around Tokyo
Meoto-daki 63 Kobe
Meoto-iwa Hot Spring 34 Central Honshu
Meotoai-no Kane 83 Hokaido
Meotoiwacho 46 Northern Kyoto
Mera 30 Izu Peninsula
Meriken Park 63 Kobe
Meto Hot Spring 83 Hokaido
Metoba 41 Matsumoto
Meyohendori 64 Mt. Koya
Mi-taki 69 Hiroshima & Western Honshu
Miasa Hot Spring 40 Nagano & Matsumoto Areas
Mibu 49 Western Kyoto
Mibu 77 Northern Honshu
Michikawa Beach 77 Northern Honshu
Michinoku 76 Shirakami Mountains
Midaka 30 Izu Peninsula
Midodencho 49 Western Kyoto
Midori 11 Asakusa, Ueno & Akihabara
Midori 23 Yokohama Area
Midori 57 Greater Osaka
Midori 92 Nagasaki
Midori Ward 35 Nagoya Area
Midoricho 41 Nagano
Midoricho 73 Yamaguchi
Midoricho 76 Hirosaki
Midorigaoka 4 Greater Tokyo
Midorigaoka 75 Tottori
Midorimachi 57 Greater Osaka
Midorimachi 73 Miyajima
Midorimachi 88 Matsuyama
Midoroikebata 47 Northern Kyoto

Midoroikecho 47 Northern Kyoto
Mie Pref. 54 Kansai Area
Mie-no-taki 83 Shiretoko National Park
Mifuku 30 Izu Peninsula
Migishi Kotaro Art Museum 85 Sapporo
Migitahama Beach 77 Northern Honshu
Mihama 55 Kansai
Mihama Beach 30 Izu Peninsula
Mihara 86 Shimanami Kaido
Mihara 94 Naha
Mihara Athletic Park 86 Shimanami Kaido
Mihara City Historical and Folk Museum 86 Shimanami Kaido
Mihara Ward 64 Around Nara
Mihara-taki 31 Hachijo-jima
Miharayama Hot Spring 31 Oshima
Miharu Museum 91 Kannawa Hells Area
Miharudai 24 Yokohama
Miikehama Beach 30 Miyake-jima
Mikagemachi 38 Kanazawa
Mikagura Hot Spring 77 Northern Honshu
Mikamo-cho 87 Iya Valley
Mikasa 65 Nara
Mikasa 83 Hokaido
Mikasa Hot Spring 65 Nara
Mikasanohama Beach 73 Miyajima
Mikasayama Ski Area 83 Hokaido
Mikata Snow Park 69 Hiroshima & Western Honshu
Mikata-kaminaka District 67 Lake Biwa
Mikatagoko Lakes 67 Lake Biwa
Mikawa 50 Fushimi Area
Mikawaguchicho 62 Kobe
Miki 87 Shikoku
Miki Museum 66 Himeji Castle
Miki Takeo Memorial Museum 12 Roppongi, Shibuya, Omotesando, Harajuku & Meiji Shrine
Mikimoto Pearl Island 55 Kansai
Mikkamachi 79 Hiraizumi & Ichinoseki
Miko Beach 54 Kansai Area
Mikoshigaokacho 49 Western Kyoto
Mikuni-honmachi 57 Greater Osaka
Mikusu 73 Iwami Ginzan
Mima 87 Iya Valley
Mima District 87 Iya Valley
Mimasaka 69 Hiroshima & Western Honshu
Mimata 90 Kyusu
Mimatsu Masao Museum 82 Sado-ga Island
Mime 68 Shodo Island
Mimiuchi 66 Hongu Onsens
Mimo-susogawacho 73 Shimonoseki
Minabe 54 Kansai Area
Minabe Plum-grove Park 54 Kansai Area
Minakami 22 Mt. Fuji & Around Tokyo
Minakamicho Fukuhara 73 Iwami Ginzan
Minakamicho Shirotsuki 73 Iwami Ginzan
Minakuchi Joshi 34 Central Honshu
Minakuchicho 47 Northern Kyoto
Minamata 90 Kyusu
Minami 23 Yokohama Area
Minami 34 Central Honshu
Minami 38 Kanazawa
Minami 4 Greater Tokyo
Minami 57 Greater Osaka
Minami 87 Shikoku
Minami 92 Nagasaki
Minami Alps 34 Central Honshu
Minami Boso Q.N.P. 23 Mt. Fuji & Around Tokyo
Minami Chita Beach Land 34 Central Honshu
Minami Ward 35 Nagoya Area
Minami Ward 55 Osaka Area
Minami Ward 71 Hiroshima
Minami-agatamachi 41 Nagano
Minami-aiki 22 Mt. Fuji & Around Tokyo
Minami-aips National Park 34 Central Honshu
Minami-aizu 77 Northern Honshu
Minami-aoyama 13 Roppongi, Shibuya, Omotesando, Harajuku & Meiji Shrine
Minami-azabu 13 Roppongi, Shibuya, Omotesando, Harajuku & Meiji Shrine
Minami-biraki 60 Osaka Namba
Minami-chikura Beach 23 Mt. Fuji & Around Tokyo
Minami-chita 55 Kansai
Minami-chitose 41 Nagano
Minami-chitosemachi 41 Nagano
Minami-cho 48 Western Kyoto
Minami-chuincho 48 Western Kyoto
Minami-dacho 43 Central & Eastern Kyoto
Minami-dori 57 Greater Osaka
Minami-dori-kamenocho 78 Akita
Minami-dori-misonomachi 78 Akita
Minami-dori-miyata 78 Akita
Minami-dori-tsukiji 78 Akita

Minami-doricho 88 Kotohira
Minami-echizen 54 Kansai Area
Minami-edo 88 Matsuyama
Minami-ekimaecho 66 Himeji Castle
Minami-enokicho 15 Shinjuku
Minami-fukurocho 65 Nara
Minami-fukuromachi 76 Hirosaki
Minami-funaokacho 46 Northern Kyoto
Minami-furano 83 Hokaido
Minami-furuhagimachi 72 Hagi
Minami-ga-oka Farm 80 Aizu, Inawashiro &
    Ura-Bandai
Minami-ga-yama Park 30 Kozu-shima & Nii-jima
Minami-hakonoicho 46 Northern Kyoto
Minami-hananobocho 46 Northern Kyoto
Minami-hataoka 88 Kotohira
Minami-higashinocho 49 Western Kyoto
Minami-hiraokacho 47 Northern Kyoto
Minami-hirocho 49 Western Kyoto
Minami-honmachi 59 Osaka Station
Minami-honmachi-dori 63 Kobe
Minami-horie 57 Greater Osaka
Minami-ichijo 85 Sapporo
Minami-ichioka 56 Greater Osaka
Minami-ikebukuro 17 Ikebukuro
Minami-ikedacho 47 Northern Kyoto
Minami-imaharacho 46 Northern Kyoto
Minami-izu 30 Izu Peninsula
Minami-jodocho 65 Nara
Minami-juhachijo-nishi 85 Sapporo
Minami-juichijo 85 Sapporo
Minami-juichijo-nishi 85 Sapporo
Minami-junijo 85 Sapporo
Minami-jurokujo-nishi 85 Sapporo
Minami-jushichijo-nishi 85 Sapporo
Minami-kaniya 71 Hiroshima
Minami-kannon 70 Hiroshima
Minami-kannonmachi 70 Hiroshima
Minami-kasai 5 Greater Tokyo
Minami-katakawamachi 72 Hagi
Minami-kawabatacho 76 Hirosaki
Minami-kawachi 22 Mt. Fuji & Around Tokyo
Minami-kawachi District 64 Around Nara
Minami-kawahoricho 61 Osaka Namba
Minami-kawakamicho 46 Northern Kyoto
Minami-koen 93 Fukuoka
Minami-koken 37 Inuyama
Minami-kosugi 37 Inuyama
Minami-ku 69 Hiroshima & Western Honshu
Minami-kyuhojimachi 59 Osaka Station
Minami-kyujo 85 Sapporo
Minami-kyushu 90 Kyusu
Minami-machi 25 Kawasaki
Minami-machi 48 Western Kyoto
Minami-machi 50 Fushimi Area
Minami-machi 73 Miyajima
Minami-machi 75 Kurashiki
Minami-machi 75 Tottori
Minami-machi 80 Aizu, Inawashiro & Ura-
    bandai
Minami-machi 89 Matsuyama
Minami-matogahamacho 91 Central Beppu
Minami-minowa 34 Central Honshu
Minami-miyakecho 47 Northern Kyoto
Minami-mochidamachi 88 Matsuyama
Minami-morimachi 59 Osaka Station
Minami-motomachi 15 Shinjuku
Minami-myohojicho 65 Asuka
Minami-nagano 41 Nagano
Minami-nagasaki 16 Ikebukuro
Minami-nakadori 24 Yokohama
Minami-nakajima 79 Hiraizumi & Ichinoseki
Minami-nakanocho 49 Western Kyoto
Minami-nometate 81 Sendai
Minami-ogikubo 4 Greater Tokyo
Minami-ogimachi 59 Osaka Station
Minami-oguni 90 Kyusu
Minami-oimikadocho 49 Western Kyoto
Minami-ojicho 46 Northern Kyoto
Minami-okajima 56 Greater Osaka
Minami-omarucho 47 Northern Kyoto
Minami-onishicho 73 Miyajima
Minami-onocho 46 Northern Kyoto
Minami-osagicho 47 Northern Kyoto
Minami-osumi 90 Kyusu
Minami-otsuka 17 Ikebukuro
Minami-rokujo 85 Sapporo
Minami-saikaishicho 45 Kawaramachi & Gion
Minami-saiwai 24 Yokohama
Minami-sakasegawacho 62 Kobe
Minami-sanriku 77 Northern Honshu
Minami-sanrizuka 33 Narita
Minami-satsuma 90 Kyusu
Minami-senba 61 Osaka Namba
Minami-senju 5 Greater Tokyo
Minami-senzoku 4 Greater Tokyo

Minami-shimabara 90 Kyusu
Minami-shinagawa 15 Meguro & Shinagawa
Minami-shinmachi 59 Osaka Station
Minami-shinmachi 65 Nara
Minami-shinmachi 88 Kotohira
Minami-shiro 47 Northern Kyoto
Minami-soma 77 Northern Honshu
Minami-tajiricho 46 Northern Kyoto
Minami-takeyacho 71 Hiroshima
Minami-tamachi 74 Matsue
Minami-tanaka 4 Greater Tokyo
Minami-torimachi 32 Kawagoe-little Edo
Minami-tsubakiharacho 46 Northern Kyoto
Minami-tsuboimachi 93 Kumamoto
Minami-tsumori 57 Greater Osaka
Minami-uonuma 77 Northern Honshu
Minami-uoyacho 65 Nara
Minami-uracho 48 Western Kyoto
Minami-uracho 65 Asuka
Minami-wakicho 36 Central Nagoya
Minami-yamacho 65 Asuka
Minami-yamashiro 54 Kansai Area
Minami-yasunaga 75 Tottori
Minami-yokocho 76 Hirosaki
Minami-yonnotsubocho 47 Northern Kyoto
Minami-yoshikata 75 Tottori
Minami-yoshinari 81 Sendai
Minami-za Theater 45 Kawaramachi & Gion
Minamibetsuso 37 Inuyama
Minamicho 38 Kanazawa
Minamicho 41 Shizuoka
Minamicho 6 Imperial Palace & Tokyo Station
Minamidai 14 Shinjuku
Minamihama Beach 67 Lake Biwa
Minamikawara 22 Mt. Fuji & Around Tokyo
Minamisuna 5 Greater Tokyo
Minamiyama 37 Inuyama
Minamiyamate Jurokubankan 92 Nagasaki
Minamizaki Beach 31 Haha-jima
Minano 22 Mt. Fuji & Around Tokyo
Minato 23 Yokohama Area
Minato 30 Izu Peninsula
Minato 41 Lake Suwa
Minato 9 Ginza, Tsukiji & Tokyo Tower
Minato 93 Fukuoka
Minato Beach 68 Hiroshima & Western Honshu
Minato Mirai 21 24 Yokohama
Minato Ward 35 Nagoya Area
Minato Ward 56 Greater Osaka
Minatocho 24 Yokohama
Minatocho 62 Kobe
Minatogawacho 62 Kobe
Minatomachi 60 Osaka Namba
Minatomachi 73 Miyajima
Minatomachi 84 Otaru
Minatomachi 88 Matsuyama
Minatomirai 24 Yokohama
Minatoyu Hot Spring 30 Izu Peninsula
Minawa 87 Iya Valley
Minazuki 39 Noto Peninsula
Mine 68 Hiroshima & Western Honshu
Mine Daifunto Park Hot Spring Tower 30 Izu
    Peninsula
Mine Hot Spring 30 Izu Peninsula
Mine-no-oishi Rock 80 Aizu, Inawashiro &
    Ura-Bandai
Minedayama Park 97 Amami Oshima
Minegado 48 Western Kyoto
Minegadocho 48 Western Kyoto
Mingu Museum 92 Shimabara
Minna-no-mori Auto Camp Site 91 Aso Area
Mino 34 Central Honshu
Mino Toji Historical Museum 35 Nagoya Area
Mino-cho 87 Iya Valley
Mino-shima Beach 90 Kyusu
Mino'o-no-taki 55 Osaka Area
Minobu 22 Mt. Fuji & Around Tokyo
Minoo 54 Kansai Area
Minoo City 55 Osaka Area
Minoshima 93 Fukuoka
Minowa 34 Central Honshu
Minowa 80 Aizu, Inawashiro & Ura-Bandai
Mint Museum 59 Osaka Station
Mirokuji 26 Kamakura
Misaki 56 Greater Osaka
Misaki no Bunkyojo (Branch School) 68 Shodo
    Island
Misakicho 6 Imperial Palace & Tokyo Station
Misakicho 96 Ishigaki City
Misasa 69 Hiroshima & Western Honshu
Misasagi 42 Kyoto
Misato 22 Mt. Fuji & Around Tokyo
Misato 68 Hiroshima & Western Honshu
Misato 90 Kyusu
Misatodai 33 Narita
Misawa 77 Northern Honshu

Misawa 88 Matsuyama
Misawa Airport 77 Northern Honshu
Mise 42 Kyoto
Misecho 65 Asuka
Mishima 30 Izu Peninsula
Mishimacho 49 Western Kyoto
Mishuku 4 Greater Tokyo
Misono 65 Asuka
Misonocho 56 Greater Osaka
Misucho 3-chome 50 Fushimi Area
Misudoromachi-atocho 50 Fushimi Area
Misuji 7 Imperial Palace & Tokyo Station
Mita 8 Ginza, Tsukiji & Tokyo Tower
Mitakaramachi 88 Matsuyama
Mitake Valley 22 Mt. Fuji & Around Tokyo
Mitane 77 Northern Honshu
Mitejima 56 Greater Osaka
Mito 23 Mt. Fuji & Around Tokyo
Mitohama Beach 30 Izu Peninsula
Mitoyo 87 Shikoku
Mitsu-taki 54 Kansai Area
Mitsua 80 Aizu, Inawashiro & Ura-bandai
Mitsubishi Ichigokan Museum 7 Imperial Palace
    & Tokyo Station
Mitsubishi Minatomirai Industrial Museum 24
    Yokohama
Mitsubishi Tokyo UFJ Bank Kahei Museum 37
    Central Nagoya
Mitsue 54 Kansai Area
Mitsui Memorial Museum 7 Imperial Palace &
    Tokyo Station
Mitsui Outlet Park Kurashiki 74 Kurashiki
Mitsuikecho 36 Central Nagoya
Mitsukaido 23 Mt. Fuji & Around Tokyo
Mitsuke 77 Northern Honshu
Mitsukejima Rock 39 Noto Peninsula
Mitsukuri 30 Izu Peninsula
Mitsumine-guchi 22 Mt. Fuji & Around Tokyo
Mitsumine-sancho 22 Mt. Fuji & Around Tokyo
Mitsunori Hot Spring 32 Nikko Area
Mitsuo Hot Spring 68 Hiroshima & Western
    Honshu
Mitsutoge 22 Mt. Fuji & Around Tokyo
Mitsutoge City 28 Mt. Fuji
Mitsuya-kita 56 Greater Osaka
Mitsuya-minami 56 Greater Osaka
Mitsuyanaka 56 Greater Osaka
Miura 22 Mt. Fuji & Around Tokyo
Miurakaigan 22 Mt. Fuji & Around Tokyo
Miwa 41 Nagano
Miwa Museum of History & Folklore 35 Nagoya
    Area
Miwatamachi 41 Nagano
Miya-mae 26 Kamakura
Miyachiyo 81 Sendai
Miyada 34 Central Honshu
Miyadamachi 72 Shimonoseki
Miyagahama Beach 67 Lake Biwa
Miyagakicho 43 Central & Eastern Kyoto
Miyagasakicho 41 Shizuoka
Miyagawa-cho Kaburenjo (Kyo-odori) 43
    Central & Eastern Kyoto
Miyagawacho 24 Yokohama
Miyagawasuji 44 Kawaramachi & Gion
Miyagi 95 Okinawa-honto
Miyagi Michio Memorial Museum 6 Imperial
    Palace & Tokyo Station
Miyagi Pref. 77 Northern Honshu
Miyagi Prefectural Art Museum 81 Sendai
Miyagino 29 Hakone Town
Miyagino 81 Sendai
Miyagino Hot Spring 29 Hakone Town
Miyahara 57 Greater Osaka
Miyaji 91 Aso Area
Miyajihama Beach 90 Kyusu
Miyajima Ropeway 73 Miyajima
Miyajimacho 73 Miyajima
Miyajiri 91 Yufuin
Miyakami 30 Izu Peninsula
Miyakawacho 43 Central & Eastern Kyoto
Miyake Hot Spring 30 Miyake-jima
Miyake Town 64 Around Nara
Miyake-jima Nature Center 30 Miyake-jima
Miyakecho 47 Northern Kyoto
Miyakitacho 46 Northern Kyoto
Miyako 77 Northern Honshu
Miyako 90 Kyusu
Miyako Airport 97 Miyako Islands
Miyako-jima City Museum 97 Miyako Islands
Miyako-jima Undersea Park 97 Miyako Islands
Miyako-odori 45 Kawaramachi & Gion
Miyako-taki 32 Nikko Area
Miyakocho 25 Kawasaki
Miyakojima Ward 57 Greater Osaka
Miyakojima-hon-dori 57 Greater Osaka
Miyakojima-minami-dori 57 Greater Osaka

Miyakojima-naka-dori 57 Greater Osaka
Miyakoma-kita-dori 57 Greater Osaka
Miyakomachi 70 Hiroshima
Miyakonojo 90 Kyusu
Miyama 90 Kyusu
Miyamachi 48 Western Kyoto
Miyamae 4 Greater Tokyo
Miyamaecho 25 Kawasaki
Miyamaecho 49 Western Kyoto
Miyamaecho 64 Nara
Miyamothocho 49 Western Kyoto
Miyamoto Saburo Memorial Art Museum 4
    Greater Tokyo
Miyamotocho 25 Kawasaki
Miyanishi 88 Matsuyama
Miyanishicho 46 Northern Kyoto
Miyanohama Beach 31 Chichi-jima
Miyanohigashicho 47 Northern Kyoto
Miyanojo Hot Spring 90 Kyusu
Miyanokamicho 49 Western Kyoto
Miyanokitacho 48 Western Kyoto
Miyanomachi 92 Shimabara
Miyanomae 47 Northern Kyoto
Miyanomae 73 Iwami Ginzan
Miyanomaecho 48 Western Kyoto
Miyanoshita 29 Hakone Town
Miyanoshita Hot Spring 29 Hakone Town
Miyanoshitacho 48 Western Kyoto
Miyanouchicho 43 Central & Eastern Kyoto
Miyanoura 97 Yakushima
Miyara Dounchi (Old House of Ryukyu Era) 96
    Ishigaki City
Miyasaka 4 Greater Tokyo
Miyasakacho 79 Hiraizumi & Ichinoseki
Miyashitacho 79 Hiraizumi & Ichinoseki
Miyashitamachi 32 Kawagoe-little Edo
Miyata 79 Hiraizumi & Ichinoseki
Miyatacho 91 Miyazaki
Miyatamachi 88 Matsuyama
Miyauchicho 56 Greater Osaka
Miyawaka 90 Kyusu
Miyawakicho 49 Western Kyoto
Miyawakicho 89 Takamatsu
Miyawakicho 91 Miyazaki
Miyazaki 90 Kyusu
Miyazaki Airport 90 Kyusu
Miyazaki Pref. 90 Kyusu
Miyazaki-eki-higashi 91 Miyazaki
Miyazakicho 24 Yokohama
Miyazakicho 47 Northern Kyoto
Miyazawa Kenji Dowa Mura Museum 79
    Hanamaki
Miyazawa Kenji Lihatobu Center 79 Hanamaki
Miyazawa Kenji Memorial Museum 79
    Hanamaki
Miyazawa Kenji Monument 79 Hanamaki
Miyazu 66 Amano Hashidate
Miyazuri Beach 90 Kyusu
Miyoshi 87 Iya Valley
Miyoshi City 35 Nagoya Area
Miyoshi-cho 87 Iya Valley
Miyoshicho 45 Kawaramachi & Gion
Miyuki 91 Kannawa Hells Area
Miyuki-taki 31 Hachijo-jima
Miyukicho 41 Shizuoka
Miyukicho 57 Greater Osaka
Miyukigahama Beach 90 Kyusu
Mizomaecho 49 Western Kyoto
Mizonokuchi 4 Greater Tokyo
Mizosakicho 49 Western Kyoto
Mizu-no-shiryokan Museum 94 Naha
Mizugakecho 47 Northern Kyoto
Mizugukicho 46 Northern Kyoto
Mizuha-no-yu Hot Spring 64 Around Nara
Mizuhashimachi 39 Noto Peninsula
Mizuho Highland Ski Area 68 Hiroshima &
    Western Honshu
Mizuho Park 35 Nagoya Area
Mizuho Ward 35 Nagoya Area
Mizuhocho 25 Yokohama
Mizuhocho 48 Western Kyoto
Mizukami 90 Kyusu
Mizuki Beach 77 Northern Honshu
Mizuki Shigeru Road 69 Hiroshima & Western
    Honshu
Mizuki-dori 62 Kobe
Mizunomaru Fureai Park 87 Iya Valley
Mizunoo 29 Hakone
Mizuochi-taki 96 Yaeyama Islands
Mizuochicho 41 Shizuoka
Mizutamemachi 38 Kanazawa
Moa Museum of Art 30 Izu Peninsula
Mobara 23 Mt. Fuji & Around Tokyo
Mochidamachi 89 Matsuyama
Mochikoshi 30 Izu Peninsula
Modern Art Museum 34 Central Honshu

Modern Art Museum 67 Lake Biwa
Modern Transportation Museum 56 Greater Osaka
Moegi-no-Yakata 63 Kobe
Mogamicho 50 Fushimi Area
Moguri-taki 80 Aizu, Inawashiro & Ura-Bandai
Mogushi Beach 90 Kyusu
Mohara Beach 34 Central Honshu
Moichan-daki 82 Sado-ga Island
Moji 73 Shimonoseki
Moka 23 Mt. Fuji & Around Tokyo
Momiji-daki 86 Shikoku
Momijigaoka 24 Yokohama
Momijigaokacho 31 Atami
Momijihodo Nature Walk 73 Miyajima
Momijimachi 89 Matsuyama
Momodani 57 Greater Osaka
Momofunecho 36 Central Nagoya
Momogaikecho 57 Greater Osaka
Momoi 4 Greater Tokyo
Momonokicho 36 Central Nagoya
Momoo-no-daki 64 Around Nara
Momoyama 46 Northern Kyoto
Momoyama 51 Southern Kyoto
Monbetsu 83 Hokaido
Monbetsu Airport 83 Hokaido
Mondacho 49 Western Kyoto
Mondenmachi 80 Aizu, Inawashiro & Ura-bandai
Monguchi 53 Uji Town
Monguchicho 62 Kobe
Monmae 53 Uji Town
Monomi-iwa Rock 76 Shirakami Mountains
Monument Moku-moku Waku-wakuYokohama Yo-yo 24 Yokohama
Monument of Himeyuri-no-to 95 Okinawa-Honto
Monyacho 49 Western Kyoto
Monzen 39 Noto Peninsula
Monzen-nakacho 9 Ginza, Tsukiji & Tokyo Tower
Monzencho 36 Central Nagoya
Monzenmachi-ogama 39 Noto Peninsula
Monzenmachi-taira 39 Noto Peninsula
Mooka 77 Northern Honshu
Moon Beach Beach 95 Okinawa-Honto
Moraihama-chuo Beach 82 Hokaido
Mori 42 Kyoto
Mori 82 Hokaido
Mori 92 Nagasaki
Mori Art Museum 13 Roppongi, Shibuya, Omotesando, Harajuku & Meiji Shrine
Mori Folk Museum 82 Sado-ga Island
Mori Ogai Memorial Museum 73 Tsuwano
Mori-ga-higashicho 49 Western Kyoto
Mori-ga-maecho 47 Northern Kyoto
Mori-ga-maecho 49 Western Kyoto
Mori-ga-nishicho 49 Western Kyoto
Moricho 50 Fushimi Area
Moridera Ruins 39 Noto Peninsula
Morigawachi-higashi 57 Greater Osaka
Morigawachi-nishi 57 Greater Osaka
Moriguchi 55 Osaka Area
Moriguchi City 64 Around Nara
Moriichi 73 Tsuwano
Morijuku Museum 73 Tsuwano
Morikamicho 48 Western Kyoto
Morimachi 49 Western Kyoto
Morimotocho 47 Northern Kyoto
Morimotocho 50 Southern Kyoto
Morini 73 Tsuwano
Morinoki-cho 46 Northern Kyoto
Morinomaecho 48 Western Kyoto
Morinomiya 57 Greater Osaka
Morinomiya-chuo 59 Osaka Station
Morioka 77 Northern Honshu
Morisan 73 Tsuwano
Morishita 79 Hiraizumi & Ichinoseki
Morishitacho 41 Shizuoka
Morishitacho 48 Western Kyoto
Morishitamachi 39 Takayama
Morishoji 57 Greater Osaka
Morito Beach 23 Yokohama Area
Moriya 23 Mt. Fuji & Around Tokyo
Moriyama 34 Central Honshu
Moriyama 38 Kanazawa
Moriyama 76 Shirakami Mountains
Moriyama City 67 Lake Biwa
Moriyama Ward 35 Nagoya Area
Moriyon 73 Tsuwano
Moriyoshizan National Park 77 Northern Honshu
Morning Market 39 Takayama
Morning Market 90 Kagoshima
Morokicho 47 Northern Kyoto
Morotsuka 90 Kyusu

Mosaic Garden Amusement Park 62 Kobe
Moseushi 83 Hokaido
Mosukegahara 88 Tokushima
Motegi 23 Mt. Fuji & Around Tokyo
Moto-akasaka 13 Roppongi, Shibuya, Omotesando, Harajuku & Meiji Shrine
Moto-asakusa 7 Imperial Palace & Tokyo Station
Moto-azabu 13 Roppongi, Shibuya, Omotesando, Harajuku & Meiji Shrine
Moto-daikumachi 76 Hirosaki
Moto-hakone 29 Hakone
Moto-hakone Hot Spring 29 Hakone
Moto-honnojicho 44 Kawaramachi & Gion
Moto-yoyogicho 12 Roppongi, Shibuya, Omotesando, Harajuku & Meiji Shrine
Motobu 95 Okinawa-honto
Motodate Ruins 76 Shirakami Mountains
Motofuna 92 Nagasaki
Motogi 25 Kawasaki
Motogikucho 38 Kanazawa
Motogumi 93 Takachiho
Motohamacho 24 Yokohama
Motohamacho 56 Greater Osaka
Motohara 92 Nagasaki
Motomachi 92 Nagasaki
Motomachi 25 Yokohama
Motomachi 32 Kawagoe-little Edo
Motomachi 38 Kanazawa
Motomachi 46 Northern Kyoto
Motomachi 60 Osaka Namba
Motomachi 66 Hikone Castle
Motomachi 70 Hiroshima
Motomachi 91 Central Beppu
Motomachi Naganehama Park 31 Oshima
Motomachi Shopping Area 25 Kawasaki
Motomachi-dori 62 Kobe
Motomachi-koka-dori 63 Kobe
Motomiya 80 Aizu, Inawashiro & Ura-bandai
Motomiyacho 91 Miyazaki
Motoo 92 Nagasaki
Motoshinmeicho 44 Kawaramachi & Gion
Motoshinzaikecho 43 Central & Eastern Kyoto
Motoshiomachi 66 Himeji Castle
Motosu 54 Kansai Area
Motosu Fuketsu (Wind Cave) 28 Mt. Fuji
Mototakedacho 44 Kawaramachi & Gion
Motouomachi 75 Tottori
Motoyama 69 Hiroshima & Western Honshu
Motoyama 87 Shikoku
Motsu-ji 79 Hiraizumi & Ichinoseki
Motsu-ji Garden 79 Hiraizumi & Ichinoseki
Motsu-ji Treasure House 79 Hiraizumi & Ichinoseki
Mourazaki Park 80 Sado-ga Island
Mozencho 49 Western Kyoto
Mozume-cho 42 Kyoto
Mt. Fuji 3776 m 28 Mt. Fuji
Mt. Fuji Children's World 28 Mt. Fuji
Mt. Gassan 81 Dewa Sanzen
Mt. Haguro 81 Dewa Sanzen
Mt. Hakkoda 77 Northern Honshu
Mt. Hiei-zan 848 m 52 Enryaku-ji & Mt. Hiei
Mt. Iozan 83 Akan National Park
Mt. Kinkei 79 Hiraizumi & Ichinoseki
Mt. Yoshino 65 Yoshina
Mt. Yudonosan 81 Dewa Sanzen
Mugi 87 Shikoku
Mugio 97 Yakushima
Muiga Cliff 97 Miyako Islands
Mujishi 76 Lake Towada
Mukadeyacho 44 Kawaramachi & Gion
Mukai-shima Orchid Center 86 Shimanami Kaido
Mukaibatacho 47 Northern Kyoto
Mukaihara 16 Ikebukuro
Mukaijima 42 Kyoto
Mukainawatecho 46 Northern Kyoto
Mukaishimacho 74 Onomichi
Mukaiumecho 46 Northern Kyoto
Mukaiyama 39 Gujo Hachiman
Mukaiyama 81 Sendai
Mukaiyamachi 81 Matsushima
Mukajima Marina 86 Shimanami Kaido
Mukashi Shimotsui Kaisendonya 87 Seto-ohasi Bridge
Mukata Beach 90 Kyusu
Mukawa 83 Hokaido
Mukawame Hot Spring 77 Northern Honshu
Mukogaoka 10 Asakusa, Ueno & Akihabara
Mukogawacho 56 Greater Osaka
Mukojima 11 Asakusa, Ueno & Akihabara
Mukojimacho 56 Greater Osaka
Mukojimacho 74 Matsue
Munakata 90 Kyusu

Munakata Hot Spring 68 Hiroshima & Western Honshu
Munakata Print Museum 26 Kamakura
Munakata Shiko Memorial Museum of Art 77 Aomori
Muncipal Museum 83 Rishiri-rebun-sarobetsu National Park
Municipal Bullfighting Ring 86 Uwajima
Municipal Museum of Art 45 Kawaramachi & Gion
Municipal Museum of Art 61 Osaka Namba
Municipal Museum of Art Annex 45 Kawaramachi & Gion
Municipal Museum of Modern Art 45 Kawaramachi & Gion
Municipal Museum of School History 44 Kawaramachi & Gion
Municipal Science Center for Youth 42 Kyoto
Municipal Ski Area 83 Hokaido
Municipal Zoo (Dobutsu-en) 45 Kawaramachi & Gion
Muraichi 76 Shirakami Mountains
Murakami 77 Northern Honshu
Muramatsu-cho 42 Kyoto
Muraoka Hot Spring 69 Hiroshima & Western Honshu
Muraoka-higashi 26 Kamakura
Murasakino 46 Northern Kyoto
Murata Antique Museum 29 Hakone
Murayama 77 Northern Honshu
Muro Saisei Memorial Museum 38 Kanazawa
Murodo 40 Nagano & Matsumoto Areas
Murodo Museum 28 Mt. Fuji
Muromachi 43 Central & Eastern Kyoto
Muromachi 89 Takamatsu
Muroran 82 Sado-ga Island
Muroran City Aquarium 82 Sado-ga Island
Muroran Sports Park 82 Sado-ga Island
Muroto 87 Shikoku
Murou 68 Shodo Island
Murozumi Beach 68 Hiroshima & Western Honshu
Musashikyuro Civic Park 22 Mt. Fuji & Around Tokyo
Musashimachi 38 Kanazawa
Musee Du Petit Prince de Saint-Exupery a Hakone 29 Hakone
Musee Hamaguchi Yozo 7 Imperial Palace & Tokyo Station
Museum of Abashiri Prison 83 Hokaido
Museum of Aeronautical Sciences 33 Narita
Museum of Agriculture 78 Hanamaki
Museum of Art 23 Yokohama Area
Museum of Fine Art of Gifu 35 Nagoya Area
Museum of Fishery Sciences 15 Meguro & Shinagawa
Museum of History & Culture 64 Around Nara
Museum of History & Culture 67 Lake Biwa
Museum of History & Folklore 30 Izu Peninsula
Museum of History & Folklore 31 Hachijo-jima
Museum of History & Folklore 4 Greater Tokyo
Museum of History & Folklore 41 Lake Suwa
Museum of History & Folklore 67 Lake Biwa
Museum of History & Folklore 73 Yamaguchi
Museum of History & Folklore 95 Okinawa & The Southwest Islands
Museum of History 88 Kotohira
Museum of Imperial Collections 6 Imperial Palace & Tokyo Station
Museum of Kura-zukuri 32 Kawagoe-Little Edo
Museum of Kyoto 44 Kawaramachi & Gion
Museum of Logistics 15 Meguro & Shinagawa
Museum of Maritime Science 21 Odaiba
Museum of Modern Japanese Literature 12 Roppongi, Shibuya, Omotesando, Harajuku & Meiji Shrine
Museum of Natural History 75 Kurashiki
Museum of Northern Peoples 84 Hakodate
Museum of Northern Peoples 85 Sapporo
Museum of Oriental Ceramics 59 Osaka Station
Museum of Photographic History 84 Hakodate
Museum of Snow & Ice 34 Central Honshu
Museum Tsuru 28 Mt. Fuji
Mushanokoji Saneatsu Memorial Museum 23 Yokohama Area
Musohiro-notaki 54 Kansai Area
Mutagahara 72 Hagi
Mutsu 77 Northern Honshu
Muza Symphony Hall 25 Kawasaki
Mydome Osaka 59 Osaka Station
Myo Daimonji Fire Festival Characters 47 Northern Kyoto
Myoban Hot Spring 91 Beppu Area
Myogi 22 Mt. Fuji & Around Tokyo
Myoho-ji 27 Kamakura

Myohoin-maekawacho 43 Central & Eastern Kyoto
Myohon-ji 27 Kamakura
Myojin 81 Matsushima
Myojocho 48 Western Kyoto
Myoken 53 Uji Town
Myokendo 46 Northern Kyoto
Myoku 34 Central Honshu
Myoraku 53 Uji Town
Myorenjimaecho 46 Northern Kyoto
Myoryu-ji 27 Kamakura
Myoshinjicho 49 Western Kyoto
Myoto-taki 67 Lake Biwa
Myozuicho 48 Western Kyoto
Nabana-no Sato Park 35 Nagoya Area
Nabarakyo Natural Park 68 Hiroshima & Western Honshu
Nabari 54 Kansai Area
Nabekura 78 Hanamaki
Nabeshimahanyo Park 90 Kyusu
Nabeyacho 44 Kawaramachi & Gion
Nabeyacho 65 Nara
Nachi-katsu'ura 54 Kansai Area
Nachi-otaki 54 Kansai Area
Nachi-otaki Nachi Primeval Forest 54 Kansai Area
Nada Ward 55 Osaka Area
Nadachi Beach 34 Central Honshu
Nadamachi 74 Matsue
Nadayama 68 Shodo Island
Naemachi 49 Western Kyoto
Nagadohe 38 Kanazawa
Nagae 74 Onomichi
Nagahama 29 Lake Kawaguchi
Nagahama 54 Kansai Area
Nagahama 68 Shodo Island
Nagahama 93 Fukuoka
Nagahama Beach 30 Izu Peninsula
Nagahama Beach 30 Kozu-shima & Nii-jima
Nagahama Beach 68 Hiroshima & Western Honshu
Nagahama Beach 73 Miyajima
Nagahama Beach 95 Okinawa-Honto
Nagahama Beach 97 Miyako Islands
Nagahama City 67 Lake Biwa
Nagahamacho 44 Kawaramachi & Gion
Nagahashi 60 Osaka Namba
Nagai 77 Northern Honshu
Nagai Takashi Memorial Museum 92 Nagasaki
Nagaikecho 57 Greater Osaka
Nagaiso Beach 68 Hiroshima & Western Honshu
Nagakimachi 88 Matsuyama
Nagakubo 97 Yakushima
Nagakute City 35 Nagoya Area
Nagamachi 38 Kanazawa
Nagamachi Samurai House Site 38 Kanazawa
Nagamachi Yuzen-kan 38 Kanazawa
Nagamine 97 Yakushima
Nagano 41 Nagano
Nagano 77 Northern Honshu
Nagano 81 Zao Onsen
Nagano Pref. 40 Nagano & Matsumoto Areas
Nagano-ojoji 41 Nagano
Naganohara 77 Northern Honshu
Nagaocho 49 Western Kyoto
Nagaoka 42 Kyoto
Nagaoka 77 Northern Honshu
Nagaokakyo 54 Kansai Area
Nagara-higashi 57 Greater Osaka
Nagara-naka 57 Greater Osaka
Nagara-nishi 57 Greater Osaka
Nagaracho 36 Central Nagoya
Nagaredacho 47 Northern Kyoto
Nagareyama 22 Mt. Fuji & Around Tokyo
Nagasaka 46 Northern Kyoto
Nagasakamachi 39 Takayama
Nagasaki 16 Ikebukuro
Nagasaki 68 Shodo Island
Nagasaki 90 Kyusu
Nagasaki 93 Takachiho
Nagasaki Airport 90 Kyusu
Nagasaki Atomic Bomb Museum 92 Nagasaki
Nagasaki Beach 77 Northern Honshu
Nagasaki Dento Geinokan Kunchi Museum 92 Nagasaki
Nagasaki Harbor Cruises 92 Nagasaki
Nagasaki History & Folk Museum 92 Nagasaki
Nagasaki Minami Yamate Art Museum 92 Nagasaki
Nagasaki Museum of History & Culture 92 Nagasaki
Nagasaki Peace Museum 92 Nagasaki
Nagasaki Peace Statue 92 Nagasaki
Nagasaki Pref. 90 Kyusu
Nagasaki Prefectural Art Museum 92 Nagasaki

Nagasaki-chuocho 72 Shimonoseki
Nagasakicho 72 Shimonoseki
Nagasecho 57 Greater Osaka
Nagashima 76 Aomori
Nagashima 79 Hiraizumi & Ichinoseki
Nagashima 90 Kyusu
Nagashima Spa Land 35 Nagoya Area
Nagashima Sports Land 35 Nagoya Area
Nagasu 90 Kyusu
Nagasu-higashi-dori 56 Greater Osaka
Nagasu-hondori 56 Greater Osaka
Nagasu-naka-dori 56 Greater Osaka
Nagasu-nishi-dori 56 Greater Osaka
Nagasucho 56 Greater Osaka
Nagata 33 Narita
Nagata 57 Greater Osaka
Nagata 94 Naha
Nagata 96 Yakushima
Nagata Inakahama Beach 96 Yakushima
Nagata Ward 55 Osaka Area
Nagata-honmachi 38 Kanazawa
Nagatacho 8 Ginza, Tsukiji & Tokyo Tower
Nagatamachi 38 Kanazawa
Nagatanicho 47 Northern Kyoto
Nagato 68 Hiroshima & Western Honshu
Nagatocho 49 Western Kyoto
Nagatoichi 36 Central Nagoya
Nagatomachi 72 Shimonoseki
Nagatoro 22 Mt. Fuji & Around Tokyo
Nagatoro Valley 22 Mt. Fuji & Around Tokyo
Nagatsura Beach 77 Northern Honshu
Nagawa Hot Spring 34 Central Honshu
Nagawa Hot Spring 40 Nagano & Matsumoto
   Areas
Nagawa Museum of History & Folklore 40
   Nagano & Matsumoto Areas
Nagi 69 Hiroshima & Western Honshu
Naginatazakacho 48 Western Kyoto
Nagisa 40 Matsumoto
Nagisa Koen Beach 67 Lake Biwa
Nagisacho 31 Atami
Nago 95 Okinawa-honto
Nago Shimin Beach 95 Okinawa-Honto
Nagomi 90 Kyusu
Nagono 36 Central Nagoya
Nagoya 34 Central Honshu
Nagoya Airport 35 Nagoya Area
Nagoya Castle 36 Central Nagoya
Nagoya City 35 Nagoya Area
Nagoya City Art Museum 36 Central Nagoya
Nagoya City Science Museum 36 Central
   Nagoya
Nagoya Peace Park 35 Nagoya Area
Nagushiyama Park 90 Kyusu
Naha Airport 95 Okinawa-Honto
Naie 83 Hokaido
Naito Museum 35 Nagoya Area
Naitomachi 15 Shinjuku
Naizencho 50 Fushimi Area
Naka 23 Yokohama Area
Naka 31 Shimoda
Naka 65 Yoshina
Naka 87 Shikoku
Naka Ward 35 Nagoya Area
Naka Ward 55 Osaka Area
Naka Ward 70 Hiroshima
Naka-adachicho 43 Central & Eastern Kyoto
Naka-biraki 57 Greater Osaka
Naka-dake Crater 91 Aso Area
Naka-dori 57 Greater Osaka
Naka-furano 82 Daisetsuzan National Park
Naka-goshomachi 41 Nagano
Naka-kashiwanocho 46 Northern Kyoto
Naka-kawamakicho 46 Northern Kyoto
Naka-kawayokemachi 38 Kanazawa
Naka-komatsu 80 Aizu, Inawashiro & Ura-
   bandai
Naka-koshima 92 Nagasaki
Naka-ku 69 Hiroshima & Western Honshu
Naka-maegawacho 88 Tokushima
Naka-meguro 18 Meguro & Shinagawa
Naka-mikadocho 65 Nara
Naka-no-hashi Bridge 65 Mt. Koya
Naka-nosakacho 46 Northern Kyoto
Naka-ochiai 16 Ikebukuro
Naka-ojicho 43 Central & Eastern Kyoto
Naka-saiwaicho 25 Kawasaki
Naka-shibetsu 83 Hokaido
Naka-shinmachi 92 Nagasaki
Naka-taki 76 Lake Towada
Naka-tonbetsu 83 Hokaido
Nakabaracho 74 Matsue
Nakabashimachi 38 Kanazawa
Nakabayashicho 47 Northern Kyoto
Nakabiraki 60 Osaka Namba

Nakabusa Hot Spring 40 Nagano & Matsumoto
   Areas
Nakacho 32 Kawagoe-little Edo
Nakacho 41 Shizuoka
Nakacho 6 Imperial Palace & Tokyo Station
Nakada 80 Aizu, Inawashiro & Ura-bandai
Nakadahama Beach 80 Aizu, Inawashiro &
   Ura-Bandai
Nakadai 33 Narita
Nakadake Hot Spring 82 Daisetsuzan National
   Park
Nakadera 57 Greater Osaka
Nakadomari 77 Northern Honshu
Nakadomari 95 Okinawa-honto
Nakadori 78 Akita
Nakadoricho 48 Western Kyoto
Nakae 81 Sendai
Nakae Toju Memorial Museum 67 Lake Biwa
Nakagawa 23 Mt. Fuji & Around Tokyo
Nakagawa 42 Kyoto
Nakagawa 57 Greater Osaka
Nakagawa 77 Northern Honshu
Nakagawa 83 Hokaido
Nakagawa 90 Kyusu
Nakagawa Funa Bansho Museum 5 Greater
   Tokyo
Nakagawa Ward 35 Nagoya Area
Nakagawa-higashi 57 Greater Osaka
Nakagawa-nishi 57 Greater Osaka
Nakagawacho 49 Western Kyoto
Nakagawara 73 Yamaguchi
Nakagawara 78 Kakunodate
Nakagawaracho 47 Northern Kyoto
Nakagawaunga 36 Central Nagoya
Nakagi 30 Izu Peninsula
Nakagosho 41 Nagano
Nakagusuku 95 Okinawa-honto
Nakahama 57 Greater Osaka
Nakahara 23 Yokohama Area
Nakahara Limestone 97 Miyako Islands
Nakaharamachi 32 Kawagoe-little Edo
Nakahiromachi 70 Hiroshima
Nakai 16 Ikebukuro
Nakai 39 Noto Peninsula
Nakaichicho 73 Yamaguchi
Nakaji 80 Aizu, Inawashiro & Ura-bandai
Nakajima 50 Southern Kyoto
Nakajima 56 Greater Osaka
Nakajima 79 Hiraizumi & Ichinoseki
Nakajima Park 85 Sapporo
Nakajimacho 36 Central Nagoya
Nakajimacho 48 Western Kyoto
Nakajimacho 70 Hiroshima
Nakajimagawaracho 46 Northern Kyoto
Nakajimamachiomaki 39 Noto Peninsula
Nakajo 41 Matsumoto
Nakajo 79 Hiraizumi & Ichinoseki
Nakakura 81 Sendai
Nakama 90 Kyusu
Nakama Gajumaru Banyan 96 Yakushima
Nakamachi 4 Greater Tokyo
Nakamachi 49 Western Kyoto
Nakamachi 50 Fushimi Area
Nakamachi 92 Nagasaki
Nakamachi-dori 62 Kobe
Nakamarucho 16 Ikebukuro
Nakamichi 37 Inuyama
Nakamichi 57 Greater Osaka
Nakamichi-dori 62 Kobe
Nakaminato 23 Mt. Fuji & Around Tokyo
Nakamiya 57 Greater Osaka
Nakamizocho 48 Western Kyoto
Nakamoto 57 Greater Osaka
Nakamura 4 Greater Tokyo
Nakamura 88 Matsuyama
Nakamura Memorial Museum 38 Kanazawa
Nakamura Ward 35 Nagoya Area
Nakamuracho 48 Western Kyoto
Nakamuramachi 38 Kanazawa
Nakanamacho 56 Greater Osaka
Nakane 4 Greater Tokyo
Nakano 14 Shinjuku
Nakano 22 Mt. Fuji & Around Tokyo
Nakano Ward 4 Greater Tokyo
Nakanocho 44 Kawaramachi & Gion
Nakanocho 50 Fushimi Area
Nakanocho 57 Greater Osaka
Nakanocho 89 Tokushima
Nakanodacho 47 Northern Kyoto
Nakanoharu 93 Takachiho
Nakanohashi 65 Mt. Koya
Nakanojo 22 Mt. Fuji & Around Tokyo
Nakanomiya 37 Inuyama
Nakanomiyashita 37 Inuyama
Nakanosawa Hot Spring 80 Aizu, Inawashiro &
   Ura-Bandai

Nakanoshima 59 Osaka Station
Nakanoshima 62 Kobe
Nakanoshima Beach 97 Miyako Islands
Nakanoshima Library 59 Osaka Station
Nakanotai 76 Lake Towada
Nakanotani 93 Takachiho
Nakanoura Beach 68 Hiroshima & Western
   Honshu
Nakanoyashirocho 46 Northern Kyoto
Nakanoyu 40 Nagano & Matsumoto Areas
Nakanoyu Hot Spring 80 Aizu, Inawashiro &
   Ura-Bandai
Nakaosagicho 47 Northern Kyoto
Nakaoshi 95 Okinawa-honto
Nakaoshitacho 48 Western Kyoto
Nakasange 75 Okamaya
Nakasato 22 Mt. Fuji & Around Tokyo
Nakasatsumai 83 Hokaido
Nakashima 91 Yufuin
Nakashimacho 91 Central Beppu
Nakasibetsu Airport 83 Hokaido
Nakasu 41 Lake Suwa
Nakasu 93 Fukuoka
Nakasuji 53 Uji Town
Nakasujicho 48 Western Kyoto
Nakasujicho 65 Nara
Nakata 37 Central Nagoya
Nakata Museum of Art 74 Onomichi
Nakataki 76 Lake Towada
Nakatokushimacho 89 Tokushima
Nakatorimachi 89 Tokushima
Nakatosa 86 Shikoku
Nakatsu 58 Osaka Station
Nakatsu 66 Amano Hashidate
Nakatsu Valley 22 Mt. Fuji & Around Tokyo
Nakatsubo 39 Gujo Hachiman
Nakatsugawa 34 Central Honshu
Nakatsukasacho 49 Western Kyoto
Nakatsukeikoku Natural Park 86 Shikoku
Nakatsusecho 91 Miyazaki
Nakayachi 78 Akita
Nakayama 68 Shodo Island
Nakayama Hot Spring 40 Nagano & Matsumoto
   Areas
Nakayama Kabuki Stage 68 Shodo Island
Nakayama Terraced Rice Fields 68 Shodo Island
Nakayamacho 37 Inuyama
Nakayamacho 48 Western Kyoto
Nakayamate-dori 63 Kobe
Nakayamatoge Ski Area 82 Sado-ga Island
Nakazaichi 73 Tsuwano
Nakazaikecho 56 Greater Osaka
Nakazaki 57 Greater Osaka
Nakazaki-nishi 59 Osaka Station
Nakazani 73 Tsuwano
Nakazato 5 Greater Tokyo
Nakazato Tropical Fruit Garden 97 Miyako
   Islands
Nakazatocho 6 Imperial Palace & Tokyo Station
Nakazawacho 49 Western Kyoto
Nakazucho 89 Tokushima
Nakijin 95 Okinawa-honto
Nakiriyamacho 56 Greater Osaka
Nakoshocho 48 Western Kyoto
Nakoso Beach 77 Northern Honshu
Nakuracho 49 Western Kyoto
Namaeda 79 Hiraizumi & Ichinoseki
Namariyama 76 Lake Towada
Namba 61 Osaka Namba
Namba Grand Kagetsu Theater 61 Osaka
   Namba
Namba Parks 61 Osaka Namba
Namba-sennichimae 61 Osaka Namba
Nambanaka 61 Osaka Namba
Nambo Paradise 22 Mt. Fuji & Around Tokyo
Nambu 22 Mt. Fuji & Around Tokyo
Nambu Central Wholesale Market 23 Yoko-
   hama Area
Namco City 59 Osaka Station
Namco Nanja Town 17 Ikebukuro
Namegawa Hot Spring 80 Aizu, Inawashiro &
   Ura-Bandai
Namerikawa 39 Noto Peninsula
Namie 77 Northern Honshu
Namihaya Dome 64 Around Nara
Namikicho 33 Narita
Namikimachi 38 Kanazawa
Naminohira 92 Nagasaki
Naminoue Shrine 94 Naha
Namiyotoyamacho 62 Kobe
Namiyoke 56 Greater Osaka
Nammoku 34 Central Honshu
Nana-taki 32 Nikko Area
Nanae 33 Narita
Nanae 82 Hokaido
Nanae Waterfall 90 Kyusu

Nanakai 23 Mt. Fuji & Around Tokyo
Nanamatsucho 56 Greater Osaka
Nanao 39 Noto Peninsula
Nanao Flower Park 39 Noto Peninsula
Nanao Ruins 39 Noto Peninsula
Nanase 41 Nagano
Nanatsu-daki Hot Spring 81 Dewa Sanzen
Nanatsuyama Beach 95 Okinawa & The South-
   west Islands
Nanatsuyamachi 38 Kanazawa
Nanbakana 57 Greater Osaka
Nanbu 69 Hiroshima & Western Honshu
Nanbumachi 50 Fushimi Area
Nandomachi 6 Imperial Palace & Tokyo Station
Nango 79 Hiraizumi & Ichinoseki
Naniwa Ward 57 Greater Osaka
Naniwa-higashi 60 Osaka Namba
Naniwa-nishi 60 Osaka Namba
Naniwacho 56 Greater Osaka
Naniwacho 59 Osaka Station
Naniwamachi 63 Kobe
Nanjo 30 Izu Peninsula
Nanjo 79 Hanamaki
Nanjo 95 Okinawa-honto
Nankan 90 Kyusu
Nanki Shirahama Airport 54 Kansai Area
Nankin-machi (China Town) 63 Kobe
Nanko Wild Bird Sanctuary 56 Greater Osaka
Nanko-kita 56 Greater Osaka
Nankoku 87 Shikoku
Nankonaka 56 Greater Osaka
Nanmoku 22 Mt. Fuji & Around Tokyo
Nanokamachi 78 Kakunodate
Nanokawa 93 Fukuoka
Nanotsu 93 Fukuoka
Nanpeidai 33 Narita
Nanpeidaicho 12 Roppongi, Shibuya, Omote-
   sando, Harajuku & Meiji Shrine
Nanpocho 49 Western Kyoto
Nanrinjicho 91 Kagoshima
Nanryocho 42 Kyoto
Nanso Museum 39 Noto Peninsula
Nantan 54 Kansai Area
Nanto Folk Museum 96 Ishigaki City
Nantocho 76 Hirosaki
Nanzenji 43 Central & Eastern Kyoto
Nanzenji Kusagawacho 45 Kawaramachi & Gion
Naoetsu Beach 77 Northern Honshu
Naoshima 69 Hiroshima & Western Honshu
Nara 65 Nara
Nara City 64 Around Nara
Nara City Museum of Photography 65 Nara
Nara National Museum Annex 65 Nara
Nara NationalMuseum 65 Nara
Nara Pref. 54 Kansai Area
Nara Prefecture Kashihara Archaeological
   Museum 64 Around Nara
Nara-machi (Nara Old Town) 65 Nara
Naraha 77 Northern Honshu
Narai 79 Hiraizumi & Ichinoseki
Naramachi Museum 65 Nara
Naramoto 30 Izu Peninsula
Narashino 23 Mt. Fuji & Around Tokyo
Nariaiji 66 Amano Hashidate
Narihira 11 Asakusa, Ueno & Akihabara
Narita 33 Narita
Narita 79 Hanamaki
Narita International Airport 33 Narita
Narita Park 33 Narita
Narita Town 33 Narita
Naru-daki 54 Kansai Area
Narude 34 Shirakawa-go & Gokayama
Narugami-no-taki 82 Hokaido
Narukawa Art Museum 29 Hakone
Narusawa Hyoketsu (Ice Cave) 28 Mt. Fuji
Narusawa Village 28 Mt. Fuji
Narutaki 49 Western Kyoto
Narutaki Ruins 86 Shimanami Kaido
Naruto 87 Shikoku
Naruwa 38 Kanazawa
Naruwadai 38 Kanazawa
Naruwamachi 38 Kanazawa
Nashiharacho 65 Nara
Nashimoto 30 Izu Peninsula
Nashitani 34 Shirakawa-go & Gokayama
Nasu-karasuyama 23 Mt. Fuji & Around Tokyo
Nasu-shiobara 77 Northern Honshu
Natadera 34 Central Honshu
National Art Center 13 Roppongi, Shibuya,
   Omotesando, Harajuku & Meiji Shrine
National Bunraku Theater 61 Osaka Namba
National Diet Building Kokkai Gijido 8 Ginza,
   Tsukiji & Tokyo Tower
National Film Center 9 Ginza, Tsukiji & Tokyo
   Tower
National Museum of Art 58 Osaka Station

National Museum of Emerging Science and Innovation 21 Odaiba
National Museum of Modern Art 43 Central & Eastern Kyoto
National Museum of Modern Art 6 Imperial Palace & Tokyo Station
National Museum of Western Art 10 Asakusa, Ueno & Akihabara
National Science Museum 10 Asakusa, Ueno & Akihabara
National Showa Memorial Museum 6 Imperial Palace & Tokyo Station
Natsui 81 Matsushima
Natural Science Museum 32 Nikko Area
Natural Zoo 5 Greater Tokyo
Nature Museum 23 Yokohama Area
Nawaji 30 Izu Peninsula
Nayacho 46 Northern Kyoto
Nayoro 83 Hokaido
Nebuta House Wa Rasse 76 Aomori
Negimachi 76 Hirosaki
Neginohata Hot Spring 30 Izu Peninsula
Negishi 10 Asakusa, Ueno & Akihabara
Neiraku Museum 65 Nara
Nejame Ruins 95 Okinawa-Honto
Nemuri-neko (Sleeping Cat) 32 Nikko Town
Nemuro 83 Hokaido
Nenegayama 47 Northern Kyoto
Nenokuchi 77 Lake Towada
Neo-taki 34 Central Honshu
Neputa-mura Museum 76 Hirosaki
Nerima 4 Greater Tokyo
Nerima Ward Art Museum 4 Greater Tokyo
New Century Industrial Arts 35 Nagoya Area
New Chitose Airport 83 Hokaido
New Kansai International Airport 55 Osaka Area
New Otani Art Museum 6 Imperial Palace & Tokyo Station
Nezu 10 Asakusa, Ueno & Akihabara
Nezu Museum 13 Roppongi, Shibuya, Omotesando, Harajuku & Meiji Shrine
NHK Broadcast Museum 8 Ginza, Tsukiji & Tokyo Tower
Ni-jo-ichiba Market 85 Sapporo
Ni'ida 79 Hiraizumi & Ichinoseki
Niban 53 Uji Town
Nibancho 6 Imperial Palace & Tokyo Station
Nibancho 88 Matsuyama
Nibukawa Hot Spring 86 Shikoku
Nibushi Hot Spring 83 Akan National Park
Nichinan 69 Hiroshima & Western Honshu
Nichinan 90 Kyusu
Nichinan Coast 90 Kyusu
Nichiren & The Kamakura Execution Grounds 26 Kamakura
Nichome 31 Shimoda
Nichome 45 Kawaramachi & Gion
Nichumae 94 Naha
Niemachi 39 Noto Peninsula
Nigatake 81 Sendai
Nigiwai-za Theater 24 Yokohama
Nigiwaimachi 92 Nagasaki
Nihom-bashi 7 Imperial Palace & Tokyo Station
Nihombashi-bakurocho 7 Imperial Palace & Tokyo Station
Nihombashi-hamacho 7 Imperial Palace & Tokyo Station
Nihombashi-hisamatsucho 7 Imperial Palace & Tokyo Station
Nihombashi-honcho 7 Imperial Palace & Tokyo Station
Nihombashi-hongokucho 7 Imperial Palace & Tokyo Station
Nihombashi-horidomecho 7 Imperial Palace & Tokyo Station
Nihombashi-kabutocho 7 Imperial Palace & Tokyo Station
Nihombashi-kakigaracho 7 Imperial Palace & Tokyo Station
Nihombashi-koamicho 7 Imperial Palace & Tokyo Station
Nihombashi-kobunacho 7 Imperial Palace & Tokyo Station
Nihombashi-kodenmacho 7 Imperial Palace & Tokyo Station
Nihombashi-muromachi 7 Imperial Palace & Tokyo Station
Nihombashi-nakasu 7 Imperial Palace & Tokyo Station
Nihombashi-ningyocho 7 Imperial Palace & Tokyo Station
Nihombashi-odenmacho 7 Imperial Palace & Tokyo Station
Nihombashi-tomizawacho 7 Imperial Palace & Tokyo Station

Nihombashi-yokoyamacho 7 Imperial Palace & Tokyo Station
Nihommatsu Beach 67 Lake Biwa
Nihon-odori 25 Yokohama
Nihonmatsu 77 Northern Honshu
Nii-jima Museum 30 Kozu-shima & Nii-jima
Niida 79 Hiraizumi & Ichinoseki
Niigata 77 Northern Honshu
Niigata Airport 77 Northern Honshu
Niigata Pref. 77 Northern Honshu
Niihama 86 Shikoku
Niihari 23 Mt. Fuji & Around Tokyo
Niikappu 83 Hokaido
Niimi 69 Hiroshima & Western Honshu
Niitaka 56 Greater Osaka
Niiza 22 Mt. Fuji & Around Tokyo
Nijigahama Beach 68 Hiroshima & Western Honshu
Nijo 30 Izu Peninsula
Nijo-jo Castle 49 Western Kyoto
Nijukkimachi 15 Shinjuku
Nikadori 97 Miyakojima
Nikaido 27 Kamakura
Nikaimachi 66 Himeji Castle
Nikenchaya 81 Sendai
Nikenyacho 46 Northern Kyoto
Niki 82 Hokaido
Nikko 33 Nikko Area
Nikko 33 Nikko Area
Nikko 77 Northern Honshu
Nikko Daiya River Park 33 Nikko Area
Nikko Flower Park 33 Nikko Area
Nikko Futarasan Shrine Treasure Museum 32 Nikko Area
Nikko Hanaichimomme 33 Nikko Area
Nikko Kirifuri Ice Arena 32 Nikko Town
Nikko National Park 22 Mt. Fuji & Around Tokyo
Nikko Saru Gundan (Monkey Entertainment) 33 Nikko Area
Nikko Takehisa Yumeji Art Museum 33 Nikko Area
Nikko Woodcarving Center 32 Nikko Town
Nikko Woodcarving Center Annex 32 Nikko Town
Nikko Yumoto Ski Area 32 Nikko Area
Nikolai Cathedral 7 Imperial Palace & Tokyo Station
Niku 86 Uwajima
Nimaibashi 78 Hanamaki
Ninen-zaka 45 Kawaramachi & Gion
Ningyo-cho (Doll Town) Pleasure District 7 Imperial Palace & Tokyo Station
Ningyo-no-museum Soleil 30 Izu Peninsula
Ninjinkata 74 Matsue
Ninna-ji 49 Western Kyoto
Ninoecho 5 Greater Tokyo
Ninohe 77 Northern Honshu
Ninohira Hot Spring 29 Hakone Town
Ninomaru 36 Central Nagoya
Ninomaru 93 Kumamoto
Ninomaru Historical Garden 88 Matsuyama
Ninomiya 23 Mt. Fuji & Around Tokyo
Ninomiyach 63 Kobe
Ninomori 81 Sendai
Ninosaka 46 Northern Kyoto
Ninotaira 29 Hakone Town
Ninpo Museum 40 Nagano & Matsumoto Areas
Nintozeiseki Stone Monument 97 Miyakojima
Nio-mon Gate 41 Nagano
Nioza Historical Street 90 Kyusu
Nippara Limestone Cave 22 Mt. Fuji & Around Tokyo
Nippon Yusen Navigation Museum 24 Yokohama
Nippon-bashi 61 Osaka Namba
Nippon-bashi-higashi 61 Osaka Namba
Nippon-bashi-nishi 61 Osaka Namba
Nippon-maru (Sail Training Ship) 24 Yokohama
Nirai Beach 95 Okinawa-Honto
Niraki 34 Central Honshu
Niseko 82 Sado-ga Island
Niseko Annupuri Ski Area 82 Sado-ga Island
Niseko Mt. Resort Grand Hirafu Ski Area 82 Sado-ga Island
Niseko Village Ski Area 82 Sado-ga Island
Nishi 56 Greater Osaka
Nishi Chaya Museum 38 Kanazawa
Nishi Kaigan Park 97 Miyako Islands
Nishi Ward 35 Nagoya Area
Nishi Ward 57 Greater Osaka
Nishi Ward 70 Hiroshima
Nishi-aizu 77 Northern Honshu
Nishi-asakusa 11 Asakusa, Ueno & Akihabara
Nishi-atami 31 Atami
Nishi-awakura 69 Hiroshima & Western Honshu

Nishi-azabu 13 Roppongi, Shibuya, Omotesando, Harajuku & Meiji Shrine
Nishi-babacho 46 Northern Kyoto
Nishi-birakicho 47 Northern Kyoto
Nishi-boramachi 39 Takayama
Nishi-daikumachi 88 Tokushima
Nishi-daimonshi 37 Inuyama
Nishi-futo 84 Hakodate
Nishi-gawaracho 47 Northern Kyoto
Nishi-godacho 47 Northern Kyoto
Nishi-gokencho 6 Imperial Palace & Tokyo Station
Nishi-gomoncho 44 Kawaramachi & Gion
Nishi-goshocho 74 Onomichi
Nishi-gotanda 18 Meguro & Shinagawa
Nishi-gotocho 46 Northern Kyoto
Nishi-hagiwara 46 Northern Kyoto
Nishi-hakubaicho 49 Western Kyoto
Nishi-hakushimacho 71 Hiroshima
Nishi-hashizumecho 43 Central & Eastern Kyoto
Nishi-hattandocho 49 Western Kyoto
Nishi-himurocho 47 Northern Kyoto
Nishi-hioki 36 Central Nagoya
Nishi-hirakicho 46 Northern Kyoto
Nishi-honji 75 Tottori
Nishi-honmachi 57 Greater Osaka
Nishi-horikawamachi 38 Kanazawa
Nishi-ichikawacho 48 Western Kyoto
Nishi-ichimanmachi 88 Matsuyama
Nishi-ikebukuro 16 Ikebukuro
Nishi-ikecho 91 Miyazaki
Nishi-inaba Natural Park 69 Hiroshima & Western Honshu
Nishi-ioricho 47 Northern Kyoto
Nishi-iriecho 72 Shimonoseki
Nishi-ishimatsu 91 Yufuin
Nishi-izu 30 Izu Peninsula
Nishi-jodocho 65 Nara
Nishi-kamakura 26 Kamakura
Nishi-kanda 6 Imperial Palace & Tokyo Station
Nishi-kanenagacho 65 Nara
Nishi-kaniya 71 Hiroshima
Nishi-kannonmachi 70 Hiroshima
Nishi-kasai 5 Greater Tokyo
Nishi-kasatori 42 Kyoto
Nishi-kasugai District 35 Nagoya Area
Nishi-kata 10 Asakusa, Ueno & Akihabara
Nishi-kata 22 Mt. Fuji & Around Tokyo
Nishi-katsura Town 28 Mt. Fuji
Nishi-kawacho 49 Western Kyoto
Nishi-kawaguchicho 70 Hiroshima
Nishi-kazariyacho 44 Kawaramachi & Gion
Nishi-kitano 78 Kakunodate
Nishi-kitsujicho 65 Nara
Nishi-kodocho 43 Central & Eastern Kyoto
Nishi-koen 93 Fukuoka
Nishi-komatsugawa-machi 5 Greater Tokyo
Nishi-kosenbamachi 32 Kawagoe-little Edo
Nishi-koshima 92 Nagasaki
Nishi-kubocho 49 Western Kyoto
Nishi-kubocho 74 Onomichi
Nishi-kujo 50 Southern Kyoto
Nishi-kujo 58 Osaka Station
Nishi-kusabukacho 41 Shizuoka
Nishi-kyogoku 49 Western Kyoto
Nishi-maecho 24 Yokohama
Nishi-mikado 27 Kamakura
Nishi-mikawa Gold Park 80 Sado-ga Island
Nishi-miyanome 79 Hanamaki
Nishi-miyatacho 47 Northern Kyoto
Nishi-miyauchicho 62 Kobe
Nishi-nagano 41 Nagano
Nishi-nagano-ojoji 41 Nagano
Nishi-naka'aicho 49 Western Kyoto
Nishi-nakacho 24 Yokohama
Nishi-nakajima 57 Greater Osaka
Nishi-nakamachi 62 Kobe
Nishi-nakanobu 4 Greater Tokyo
Nishi-nakasone 97 Miyakojima
Nishi-nikaimachi 66 Himeji Castle
Nishi-ninosaka 46 Northern Kyoto
Nishi-no-hama Beach 97 Miyako Islands
Nishi-no-isshikimachi 39 Takayama
Nishi-no-moncho 41 Nagano
Nishi-no-omote 95 Okinawa & The Southwest Islands
Nishi-noguchicho 91 Central Beppu
Nishi-odawara 64 Mt. Koya
Nishi-onoboricho 46 Northern Kyoto
Nishi-rendainocho 46 Northern Kyoto
Nishi-sanrizuka 33 Narita
Nishi-sasabokocho 65 Nara
Nishi-shichijo 49 Western Kyoto
Nishi-shigemori 76 Hirosaki
Nishi-shimbashi 8 Ginza, Tsukiji & Tokyo Tower
Nishi-shinagawa 15 Meguro & Shinagawa

Nishi-shinjuku 14 Shinjuku
Nishi-shinkoiwa 5 Greater Tokyo
Nishi-shinsaibashi 61 Osaka Namba
Nishi-shinzakikecho 65 Nara
Nishi-shiraishi 73 Yamaguchi
Nishi-somonguchicho 46 Northern Kyoto
Nishi-sugamo 17 Ikebukuro
Nishi-takadacho 49 Western Kyoto
Nishi-takaharacho 47 Northern Kyoto
Nishi-takamatsucho 91 Miyazaki
Nishi-takanawacho 46 Northern Kyoto
Nishi-takeyacho 44 Kawaramachi & Gion
Nishi-tamachi 72 Hagi
Nishi-tenma 57 Greater Osaka
Nishi-tennocho 43 Central & Eastern Kyoto
Nishi-teranomaecho 43 Central & Eastern Kyoto
Nishi-tobecho 24 Yokohama
Nishi-tokaichimachi 70 Hiroshima
Nishi-tomi 26 Kamakura
Nishi-tominakacho 49 Western Kyoto
Nishi-tsuda 74 Matsue
Nishi-tsurugamachi 41 Nagano
Nishi-uenodancho 46 Northern Kyoto
Nishi-uraenashi 30 Izu Peninsula
Nishi-uratachibo 30 Izu Peninsula
Nishi-waseda 17 Ikebukuro
Nishi-yamashita 37 Inuyama
Nishi-yanagiwaracho 62 Kobe
Nishi-yashirocho 46 Northern Kyoto
Nishi-yashirocho 66 Himeji Castle
Nishi-zawaValley 22 Mt. Fuji & Around Tokyo
Nishiamuro Beach 97 Amami Oshima
Nishiaraya Beach 34 Central Honshu
Nishicho 48 Western Kyoto
Nishicho-sanbancho 38 Kanazawa
Nishida 90 Kagoshima
Nishidacho 49 Western Kyoto
Nishidemachi 62 Kobe
Nishigamo 46 Northern Kyoto
Nishigocho 41 Nagano
Nishihama Beach 87 Shikoku
Nishihara 12 Roppongi, Shibuya, Omotesando, Harajuku & Meiji Shrine
Nishihara 90 Kyusu
Nishihara 95 Okinawa-honto
Nishihata 37 Inuyama
Nishihayashizaki 37 Inuyama
Nishihira 37 Inuyama
Nishihongo 31 Shimoda
Nishiicho 48 Western Kyoto
Nishijima 56 Greater Osaka
Nishijin 46 Northern Kyoto
Nishijin 92 Fukuoka
Nishijin Textile Center 42 Kyoto
Nishikami-fusacho 46 Northern Kyoto
Nishikawa 77 Northern Honshu
Nishiki 36 Central Nagoya
Nishikicho 41 Shizuoka
Nishikicho 59 Osaka Station
Nishikicho 81 Sendai
Nishikimachi 84 Otaru
Nishikimachi 89 Takamatsu
Nishikimachi 91 Miyazaki
Nishikionuma Park 82 Sado-ga Island
Nishimachi 39 Takayama
Nishimachi 41 Nagano
Nishimachi 49 Western Kyoto
Nishimachi 50 Fushimi Area
Nishimachi 63 Kobe
Nishimachi 75 Tottori
Nishimera 90 Kyusu
Nishimeya 76 Shirakami Mountains
Nishimoncho 41 Shizuoka
Nishimura 68 Shodo Island
Nishina 30 Izu Peninsula
Nishinaka 53 Uji Town
Nishinaka 88 Kotohira
Nishinakasu 93 Fukuoka
Nishinari Ward 57 Greater Osaka
Nishino 51 Southern Kyoto
Nishinocho 45 Kawaramachi & Gion
Nishinohama Beach 72 Hagi
Nishinoichi Hot Spring 68 Hiroshima & Western Honshu
Nishinokawara 78 Kakunodate
Nishinokyo 49 Western Kyoto
Nishinomiya 54 Kansai Area
Nishinomiya City 55 Osaka Area
Nishinomiya Museum 78 Kakunodate
Nishinomori 77 Lake Towada
Nishinoyama 51 Southern Kyoto
Nishinoyamacho 46 Northern Kyoto
Nishinoyu Hot Spring 95 Okinawa & The Southwest Islands
Nishio 34 Central Honshu
Nishiocho 74 Matsue

Nishiogi-kita 4 Greater Tokyo
Nishiokoppe 83 Hokaido
Nishionishicho 73 Miyajima
Nishiro Beach 95 Okinawa-Honto
Nishitaki 73 Yamaguchi
Nishiuracho 48 Western Kyoto
Nishiusuki 93 Takachiho
Nishiwaki 57 Greater Osaka
Nishiwaki Beach 69 Hiroshima & Western Honshu
Nishiwaki City Sundial Garden (Belly Button of Japan) 54 Kansai Area
Nishiyachi 78 Akita
Nishiyama 46 Northern Kyoto
Nishiyama-honmachi 92 Nagasaki
Nishiyamacho 31 Atami
Nishiyamada 53 Uji Town
Nishiyodogawa Ward 56 Greater Osaka
Nishizaka 92 Nagasaki
Nishizato 97 Miyakojima
Nisshin 35 Nagoya Area
Nisshincho 25 Kawasaki
Nisshoku Kansoku Monument 83 Rishiri-rebun-sarobetsu National Park
Nitanda 79 Hiraizumi & Ichinoseki
Nitayachi 81 Sendai
Nitta 30 Izu Peninsula
Niu-Kanshobu Shrine 64 Around Nara
Niwa District 35 Nagoya Area
Niyodogawa 86 Shikoku
Niyodogawa Odo Dam Park 86 Shikoku
Nobeoka 90 Kyusu
Noboribetsu 82 Sado-ga Island
Noboribetsu Bear Farm 82 Sado-ga Island
Noboribetsu Date Jidai Mura 82 Sado-ga Island
Noboribetsu Hot Spring 82 Sado-ga Island
Noboribetsu Marine Park Nixe 82 Sado-ga Island
Noboricho 48 Western Kyoto
Noboricho 86 Shimanami Kaido
Noboriojicho 65 Nara
Noda 56 Greater Osaka
Noda 76 Hirosaki
Noda 77 Northern Honshu
Nodayacho 75 Okamaya
Nodomaecho 48 Western Kyoto
Noge 4 Greater Tokyo
Nogecho 24 Yokohama
Nogedaira 33 Narita
Nogeyama Zoo 24 Yokohama
Nogi 22 Mt. Fuji & Around Tokyo
Noguchi 33 Nikko Area
Noguchi 65 Asuka
Noguchi Hideyo Memorial Hall 15 Shinjuku
Noguchi Hideyo Memorial Hall 80 Aizu, Inawashiro & Ura-Bandai
Noguchi Kenzo Memorial Museum 67 Lake Biwa
Noguchi Yataro Memorial Museum 92 Nagasaki
Noguchi-hara 91 Central Beppu
Noguro 37 Inuyama
Nogyo Fureai Park 78 Hanamaki
Noh Theater 24 Yokohama
Noheji 77 Northern Honshu
Nokatano 93 Takachiho
Nokikura-kogen 40 Nagano & Matsumoto Areas
Nokonoshima Island Park 90 Kyusu
Noma 68 Shodo Island
Nomachi 38 Kanazawa
Nomachi 39 Noto Peninsula
Nomashi Fureai-no-yu Hot Spring 31 Oshima
Nomi 34 Central Honshu
Nomine Ruins 34 Central Honshu
Nomotocho 49 Western Kyoto
Nomura Art Museum 43 Central & Eastern Kyoto
Nonaka 79 Hiraizumi & Ichinoseki
Nonaka-kita 56 Greater Osaka
Nonaka-minami 57 Greater Osaka
Noninbashi 59 Osaka Station
Nonomiyacho 48 Western Kyoto
Norikoshicho 36 Central Nagoya
Noritake 36 Central Nagoya
Noritake Museum, Craft Center 36 Central Nagoya
Noritake-hondori 36 Central Nagoya
Noritake-shinmachi 36 Central Nagoya
Noritakecho 36 Central Nagoya
Norman Rockwell Museum 91 Yufuin
Noroshi 39 Noto Peninsula
Noroshi Lighthouse 39 Noto Peninsula
North Canal 84 Otaru
North Palace 95 Shuri Castle

Northern History Museum 84 Hakodate
Nosato-higashi 57 Greater Osaka
Nose 54 Kansai Area
Nosegawa 54 Kansai Area
Nosegawa Hot Spring 64 Around Nara
Nosegawa Village 64 Around Nara
Noshappu-misaki 83 Rishiri-rebun-sarobetsu National Park
Noshichiri 27 Kamakura
Noshima Murakami Suigun Museum 86 Shimanami Kaido
Noshimizucho 48 Western Kyoto
Noshiro 76 Shirakami Mountains
Noshiro 76 Shirakami Mountains
Noshiro Energium Park 76 Shirakami Mountains
Noso 42 Kyoto
Notebai 79 Hiraizumi & Ichinoseki
Noto 59 Noto Peninsula
Noto Airport 34 Central Honshu
Notojima Aquarium 39 Noto Peninsula
Notojima-hachisakimachi 39 Noto Peninsula
Notojima-musekimachi 39 Noto Peninsula
Nounencho 66 Himeji Castle
Nozaki's Historical Museum 87 Seto-ohasi Bridge
Nozakicho 59 Osaka Station
Nozato 56 Greater Osaka
Nozawa 4 Greater Tokyo
Nozawa Onsen Ski Area 34 Central Honshu
Nukabira Gonsenkyo 83 Hokaido
Nukui 4 Greater Tokyo
Numajiri Ski Area 80 Aizu, Inawashiro & Ura-Bandai
Numata 77 Northern Honshu
Numata 83 Hokaido
Numazu 30 Izu Peninsula
Nunobiki-daki 96 Yakushima
Nunobikicho 63 Kobe
Nunobikime-daki 63 Kobe
Nunobikio-daki 63 Kobe
Nunobikiyama 63 Kobe
Nunobikiyuenchi 63 Kobe
Nunoura 39 Noto Peninsula
Nupuntomuraushi Hot Spring 82 Daisetsuzan National Park
Nushiyacho 43 Central & Eastern Kyoto
Nutacho 86 Shimanami Kaido
O 80 Aizu, Inawashiro & Ura-bandai
O Art Museum 15 Meguro & Shinagawa
O-daki 80 Aizu, Inawashiro & Ura-Bandai
O-daki 83 Shiretoko National Park
O-mon 88 Kotohira
O-taki 82 Daisetsuzan National Park
O-taki 82 Hokaido
O-taki 83 Hokaido
Oakicho 36 Central Nagoya
Oami 23 Mt. Fuji & Around Tokyo
Oarai 23 Mt. Fuji & Around Tokyo
Oarai Coast Beach 23 Mt. Fuji & Around Tokyo
Oarashi 29 Lake Kawaguchi
Oba-joshi Park 23 Yokohama Area
Obama 54 Kansai Area
Obanazawa 77 Northern Honshu
Obasecho 61 Osaka Namba
Obashi-higashi 88 Kotohira
Obashinishi 88 Kotohira
Obatake 91 Beppu Area
Obe 68 Shodo Island
Obihiro 83 Hokaido
Obira 83 Hokaido
Obiyacho 50 Fushimi Area
Oboke 87 Iya Valley
Oboke Gorge 87 Iya Valley
Observation Lighthouse 26 Kamakura
Observation Point Deck 83 Akan National Park
Obukecho 46 Northern Kyoto
Obukuro 33 Narita
Obuse 34 Central Honshu
Ocean Expo Park 95 Okinawa-Honto
Ochatsubo-dochu 43 Central & Eastern Kyoto
Ochatsubo-dochu/ Parade of Tea Jars 45 Kawaramachi & Gion
Ochi 86 Shikoku
Oda 68 Hiroshima & Western Honshu
Odai 54 Kansai Area
Odai Park 35 Nagoya Area
Odaiba 5 Greater Tokyo
Odaiba Hot Spring Theme Park (Oedo-onsen Monogatari Spa) 21 Odaiba
Odaira 76 Lake Towada
Odaira 79 Hiraizumi & Ichinoseki
Odaira 80 Aizu, Inawashiro & Ura-bandai

Odaira Hot Spring 80 Aizu, Inawashiro & Ura-Bandai
Odaka Park 35 Nagoya Area
Odake 39 Noto Peninsula
Odana-no-taki 28 Mt. Fuji
Odano Family Old House 78 Kakunodate
Odashirogahara Plateau 32 Nikko Area
Odate 77 Northern Honshu
Odate-Noshiro Airport 77 Northern Honshu
Odawa 29 Lake Kawaguchi
Odawara 29 Hakone
Odawara 39 Noto Peninsula
Odawara 81 Sendai
Odawara Flower Garden 29 Hakone
Odawara-yuminomachi 81 Sendai
Odawara's Castle & Folk Arts Museum 29 Hakone
Odawaracho 44 Kawaramachi & Gion
Odo Monkey Park 86 Shikoku
Odoguchicho 46 Northern Kyoto
Odoi Beach 30 Izu Peninsula
Odomari Beach 95 Okinawa-Honto
Odonooji 73 Yamaguchi
Odori Park 85 Sapporo
Odori-nishi 85 Sapporo
Odotsu Beach 90 Kyusu
Oe 42 Kyoto
Oe 68 Shodo Island
Oe 77 Northern Honshu
Oecho 44 Kawaramachi & Gion
Oeda-minamimachi 57 Greater Osaka
Oekita-kustuka-kecho 42 Kyoto
Oeminami-fukunishicho 42 Kyoto
Oeyama Ski Area 54 Kansai Area
Ofu City 35 Nagoya Area
Ofukacho 58 Osaka Station
Ofukaimaru Museum 36 Central Nagoya
Ofuna 27 Kamakura
Ofuna Botanical Garden 26 Kamakura
Ofunagura 92 Nagasaki
Ofunato 77 Northern Honshu
Ofune Hot Spring 82 Hokaido
Oga 77 Northern Honshu
Ogahara Kogen Ski Area 68 Hiroshima & Western Honshu
Ogaito 53 Uji Town
Ogaki 34 Central Honshu
Ogamachi 41 Shizuoka
Ogamo 30 Izu Peninsula
Ogano 22 Mt. Fuji & Around Tokyo
Ogara 76 Shirakami Mountains
Ogara-taki 76 Shirakami Mountains
Ogarucho 65 Asuka
Ogasawara Islands 22 Ogasawara Islands
Ogasawara National Park 22 Ogasawara Islands
Ogata 77 Northern Honshu
Ogata Folk Museum 28 Mt. Fuji
Ogawa 22 Mt. Fuji & Around Tokyo
Ogawa 40 Nagano & Matsumoto Areas
Ogawa Shu Museum 82 Sado-ga Island
Ogawa-dori 62 Kobe
Ogawa-no-taki 90 Kyusu
Ogawachimachi 70 Hiroshima
Ogawacho 25 Kawasaki
Ogawacho 65 Nara
Ogi 30 Izu Peninsula
Ogi 39 Noto Peninsula
Ogi 80 Sado-ga Island
Ogicho 24 Yokohama
Ogida 76 Shirakami Mountains
Ogidacho 48 Western Kyoto
Ogigayatsu 27 Kamakura
Ogikubo 4 Greater Tokyo
Ogimachi 38 Kanazawa
Ogimachi 59 Osaka Station
Ogimachi 80 Aizu, Inawashiro & Ura-bandai
Ogimachi 89 Takamatsu
Ogimachi Traditional Farmhouses 34 Shirakawa-go & Gokayama
Ogimi 95 Okinawa-honto
Ogino 79 Hiraizumi & Ichinoseki
Oginocho 49 Western Kyoto
Ogisakayacho 44 Kawaramachi & Gion
Ogishima Marina 80 Aizu, Inawashiro & Ura-Bandai
Ogito 68 Shodo Island
Ogo 22 Mt. Fuji & Around Tokyo
Ogori 68 Hiroshima & Western Honshu
Ogori 90 Kyusu
Oguchi Town 35 Nagoya Area
Oguiss Memorial Art Museum 35 Nagoya Area
Oguni 77 Northern Honshu
Oguni-numa March Plant Community 80 Aizu, Inawashiro & Ura-Bandai
Oguracho 48 Western Kyoto

Ogurami-jo Ruins 67 Lake Biwa
Ogurisu 51 Southern Kyoto
Ogushi Natural Park 87 Shikoku
Ogusu 93 Fukuoka
Oh Sadaharu Baseball Museum 92 Fukuoka
Ohama Beach 30 Izu Peninsula
Ohama Beach 86 Shimanami Kaido
Ohama Kaihin Park 97 Amami Oshima
Ohama Nobumoto Memorial Hall 96 Ishigaki City
Ohamacho 56 Greater Osaka
Ohamakaigan Beach 68 Hiroshima & Western Honshu
Ohanabeyama Viewpoint 76 Lake Towada
Ohanajaya 5 Greater Tokyo
Ohara 23 Mt. Fuji & Around Tokyo
Ohara 34 Shirakawa-go & Gokayama
Ohara 4 Greater Tokyo
Ohara 42 Kyoto
Ohara Home Village Museum 53 Ohara Village
Ohara Museum of Art 75 Kurashiki
Ohara Site 80 Aizu, Inawashiro & Ura-Bandai
Ohara-kusaocho 53 Ohara Village
Ohara-nokamizato 42 Kyoto
Ohara-nomuracho 53 Ohara Village
Ohara-onagasecho 53 Ohara Village
Ohara-raikoincho 53 Ohara Village
Ohara-shorin'incho 53 Ohara Village
Ohara-uenocho 53 Ohara Village
Oharaidecho 53 Ohara Village
Oharano 42 Kyoto
Ohashi 12 Roppongi, Shibuya, Omotesando, Harajuku & Meiji Shrine
Ohashi 91 Miyazaki
Ohata 53 Uji Town
Ohi Pottery Museum 38 Kanazawa
Ohigashi 29 Hakone Town
Ohigashicho 49 Western Kyoto
Ohimachi 38 Kanazawa
Ohira 22 Mt. Fuji & Around Tokyo
Ohiraki 56 Greater Osaka
Ohito 30 Izu Peninsula
Ohori 92 Fukuoka
Ohotsuku 83 Hokaido
Ohura Beach 96 Yakushima
Oi 4 Greater Tokyo
Oi 54 Kansai Area
Oi-dori 62 Kobe
Oiagecho 48 Western Kyoto
Oichicho 73 Yamaguchi
Oicho 37 Central Nagoya
Oicho 44 Kawaramachi & Gion
Oide 76 Lake Towada
Oide 92 Nagasaki
Oike Park 35 Nagoya Area
Oikecho 49 Western Kyoto
Oikenocho 44 Kawaramachi & Gion
Oil Lamp Museum 45 Kawaramachi & Gion
Oimatsu 91 Miyazaki
Oimatsucho 24 Yokohama
Oimatsucho 46 Northern Kyoto
Oimatsucho 74 Kurashiki
Oimazato 57 Greater Osaka
Oimazato-minami 57 Greater Osaka
Oimazato-nishi 57 Greater Osaka
Oinoue Memorial Museum 30 Izu Peninsula
Oirase 77 Northern Honshu
Oirase Stream 77 Lake Towada
Oirase Yusui-kan Museum 77 Lake Towada
Oisecho 36 Central Nagoya
Oishi 29 Lake Kawaguchi
Oishi 80 Aizu, Inawashiro & Ura-bandai
Oishikogen Natural Park 54 Kansai Area
Oiso Long Beach 22 Mt. Fuji & Around Tokyo
Oita 90 Kyusu
Oita Airport 90 Kyusu
Oita Pref. 90 Kyusu
Oiwa-miyashitacho 41 Shizuoka
Oiwake Hot Spring 86 Shimanami Kaido
Oiwakecho 49 Western Kyoto
Oizumi 22 Mt. Fuji & Around Tokyo
Oji 54 Kansai Area
Oji Town 64 Around Nara
Ojicho 57 Greater Osaka
Ojika-no-taki 83 Akan National Park
Ojima 22 Mt. Fuji & Around Tokyo
Ojima 5 Greater Tokyo
Ojiro Ski Area 69 Hiroshima & Western Honshu
Ojiya 77 Northern Honshu
Ojoincho 48 Western Kyoto
Oka 65 Asuka
Oka Masaharu Memorial Nagasaki Peace Museum 92 Nagasaki
Okabe 22 Mt. Fuji & Around Tokyo
Okadamachi 41 Nagano
Okadani 53 Uji Town

Okadohana 68 Shodo Island
Okagaki 90 Kyusu
Okagomi 88 Kotohira
Okaido 88 Matsuyama
Okaji 81 Sendai
Okamachi 92 Nagasaki
Okamedani 51 Southern Kyoto
Okamizawa 78 Hanamaki
Okamoto 27 Kamakura
Okamoto 4 Greater Tokyo
Okamoto Taro Memorial Museum 13 Roppongi, Shibuya, Omotesando, Harajuku & Meiji Shrine
Okamotocho 46 Northern Kyoto
Okamotoguchicho 47 Northern Kyoto
Okamotomachi 39 Takayama
Okano 24 Yokohama
Okata 22 Mt. Fuji & Around Tokyo
Okawa 30 Izu Peninsula
Okawa 86 Shikoku
Okawa 96 Ishigaki City
Okawa Museum of Modern Art 22 Mt. Fuji & Around Tokyo
Okawa-no-taki 96 Yakushima
Okawachi Hot Spring 68 Hiroshima & Western Honshu
Okawatai 76 Lake Towada
Okaya 40 Nagano & Matsumoto Areas
Okaya City 41 Lake Suwa
Okayacho 51 Southern Kyoto
Okayama 69 Hiroshima & Western Honshu
Okayama Airport 69 Hiroshima & Western Honshu
Okayama Castle 75 Okamaya
Okayama Karokuen Garden 75 Okamaya
Okayama Pref. 69 Hiroshima & Western Honshu
Okayama Prefectural Forest Park 69 Hiroshima & Western Honshu
Okazaki 43 Central & Eastern Kyoto
Okazaki Castle 35 Nagoya Area
Okazaki Higashi-tennocho 45 Kawaramachi & Gion
Okazaki Hoshojicho 45 Kawaramachi & Gion
Okazaki Iriecho 45 Kawaramachi & Gion
Okazaki Kita-goshocho 45 Kawaramachi & Gion
Okazaki Minami-goshocho 45 Kawaramachi & Gion
Okazaki Nishi-tennocho 45 Kawaramachi & Gion
Okazaki Tennocho 45 Kawaramachi & Gion
Okazaki-enshojicho 45 Kawaramachi & Gion
Okazaki-tokuseicho 45 Kawaramachi & Gion
Okazakicho 48 Western Kyoto
Oke-taki 39 Noto Peninsula
Oketo 83 Hokaido
Okeya 92 Nagasaki
Okeyamachi 76 Hirosaki
Okihamachi 93 Fukuoka
Okimicho 47 Northern Kyoto
Okinacho 24 Yokohama
Okinawa 95 Okinawa-honto
Okinawa Churaumi Aquarium 95 Okinawa-Honto
Okinawa Peace Memorial Museum 95 Okinawa-Honto
Okinawa Postal Museum 94 Naha
Okinawa World & Snake Park 95 Okinawa-Honto
Okinazawa 80 Aizu, Inawashiro & Ura-bandai
Okinomiyacho 5 Greater Tokyo
Okitayama 46 Northern Kyoto
Okiura Beach 86 Shimanami Kaido
Okochi Sanso 48 Western Kyoto
Okoppe 83 Hokaido
Oku 95 Okinawa-honto
Oku Hakone Yumoto Hot Spring 29 Hakone
Oku Iya Valley 87 Iya Valley
Oku-Iya Niju Kazurabashi (Double Vine Bridge) 87 Iya Valley
Oku-komoricho 65 Nara
Oku-Mino Omodaka-ke Mingei-kan 39 Gujo Hachiman
Oku-yuki Hot Spring 68 Hiroshima & Western Honshu
Okubo 15 Shinjuku
Okubo 34 Shirakawa-go & Gokayama
Okubo Iwaminokami Tomb 73 Iwami Ginzan
Okubo Machizukuri-kan 65 Asuka
Okubo Mine 73 Iwami Ginzan
Okubocho 47 Northern Kyoto
Okubocho 65 Asuka
Okubohama Beach 30 Miyake-jima
Okudanicho 74 Matsue
Okudo 5 Greater Tokyo
Okudonocho 48 Western Kyoto

Okuhino Prefectural Natural Park 69 Hiroshima & Western Honshu
Okuizumo 69 Hiroshima & Western Honshu
Okukahadakyo Hot Spring 54 Kansai Area
Okukaiinji 42 Kyoto
Okukoboke Hot Spring 87 Shikoku
Okukomoricho 47 Northern Kyoto
Okuma 95 Okinawa-honto
Okumizumai Hot Spring 55 Osaka Area
Okuniwa Nature Park 28 Mt. Fuji
Okunoike 53 Uji Town
Okura 4 Greater Tokyo
Okura Museum 8 Ginza, Tsukiji & Tokyo Tower
Okuricho 46 Northern Kyoto
Okusawa 4 Greater Tokyo
Okuse 76 Lake Towada
Okushibacho 65 Nara
Okushiga Kogen Ski Area 34 Central Honshu
Okushiri 82 Hokaido
Okushiri Airport 82 Hokaido
Okutamako 22 Mt. Fuji & Around Tokyo
Okutsu Hot Spring 69 Hiroshima & Western Honshu
Okuwamachi 33 Nikko Area
Old Amagi Tunnel 30 Izu Peninsula
Old Hagi Domain Boathouse 72 Hagi
Old Hong Kong Shanghai Bank Memorial Museum 92 Nagasaki
Old Hosokawa Gyobu-tei 92 Kumamoto
Old House of Mori Ogai 73 Tsuwano
Old House of Nishi Amane 73 Tsuwano
Old Jiyu-tei House 92 Nagasaki
Old Mekata Family House 73 Iwakuni
Old Ohara Family Residence 75 Kurashiki
Old Tachikawa Family Residence (Tachikawa Cafe) 84 Hakodate
Old UK Consular Office 92 Nagasaki
Olive Beach 68 Shodo Island
Olympic Stadium 40 Nagano & Matsumoto Areas
Oma 77 Northern Honshu
Omachi 27 Kamakura
Omachi 40 Nagano & Matsumoto Areas
Omachi 49 Western Kyoto
Omachi 73 Miyajima
Omachi 74 Matsue
Omachi 76 Hirosaki
Omachi 78 Akita
Omachi 81 Sendai
Omachi 84 Hakodate
Omachi 90 Kyusu
Omachi Hot Spring 40 Nagano & Matsumoto Areas
Omaezaki 34 Central Honshu
Omagoshi 76 Shirakami Mountains
Omatsucho 37 Central Nagoya
Omatsuzawa 78 Akita
Ombara Kogen Ski Area 69 Hiroshima & Western Honshu
Omi 40 Nagano & Matsumoto Areas
Omi 68 Shodo Island
Omi Shirahama Beach 67 Lake Biwa
Omi Shonin Folk 67 Lake Biwa
Omi-hachiman 54 Kansai Area
Omi-hachiman City 67 Lake Biwa
Omika 23 Mt. Fuji & Around Tokyo
Omishima Art Museum 86 Shimanami Kaido
Omitama 23 Mt. Fuji & Around Tokyo
Omiya 22 Mt. Fuji & Around Tokyo
Omiya 4 Greater Tokyo
Omiya 46 Northern Kyoto
Omiya 93 Fukuoka
Omiya Palace 43 Central & Eastern Kyoto
Omiya-dori 57 Greater Osaka
Omiyacho 25 Kawasaki
Omiyacho 42 Central & Eastern Kyoto
Omiyacho 64 Nara
Omiyacho 86 Uwajima
Omiyacho Nobutoshi 66 Amano Hashidate
Omiyadai 4 Greater Tokyo
Omogo Sangaku Museum 86 Shikoku
Omoikecho 62 Kobe
Omokagecho 48 Western Kyoto
Omori-nishimachi 64 Nara
Omoricho 65 Nara
Omoricho 73 Iwami Ginzan
Omoricho 84 Hakodate
Omoromachi 94 Naha
Omotecho 75 Okamaya
Omotesando 13 Roppongi, Shibuya, Omotesan-do, Harajuku & Meiji Shrine
Omotomachi 72 Hagi
Omron Sogyo Memorial Museum 48 Western Kyoto
Omu 83 Hokaido
Omura 90 Kyusu

Omura Art Museum 78 Kakunodate
Omura Bay Park 90 Kyusu
Omuro 49 Western Kyoto
Omuronohama Beach 86 Shikoku
Omuta 90 Kyusu
Onabe 30 Izu Peninsula
Onan 68 Hiroshima & Western Honshu
Onarimachi 27 Kamakura
Onaruto-bashi Kakyo Memorial Museum Edy 87 Shikoku
Onarutokyo Memorial Museum 87 Shikoku
Onashishi Beach 86 Shikoku
Onawabacho 48 Western Kyoto
Onawacho 84 Hakodate
Ondonoseto Park 68 Hiroshima & Western Honshu
Ondoyamacho 48 Western Kyoto
One Pillar Torii 92 Nagasaki
Onga 90 Kyusu
Ongonyu Hot Spring 40 Nagano & Matsumoto Areas
Oni-ishi Bozu Jigoku (Oni-ishi Monk's Hell) 91 Kannawa Hells Area
Oni-yama Jigoku (Demon Mountain Hell) 91 Kannawa Hells Area
Onigaiwaya Hot Spring 87 Shikoku
Onigatake Hot Spring 69 Hiroshima & Western Honshu
Onishi 22 Mt. Fuji & Around Tokyo
Onishi Seiemon Museum 44 Kawaramachi & Gion
Onishiyama 88 Kotohira
Oniwa Nature Park 28 Mt. Fuji
Onjuku 23 Mt. Fuji & Around Tokyo
Onmaedacho 49 Western Kyoto
Onna 95 Okinawa-honto
Onnadaiba (Women's Mound) 72 Hagi
Onnazaka Hot Spring 76 Shirakami Mountains
Ono 51 Southern Kyoto
Ono 56 Greater Osaka
Ono 68 Hiroshima & Western Honshu
Ono-game Rock 80 Sado-ga Island
Onoaida 97 Yakushima
Onoaida Onsen 97 Yakushima
Onobaru 93 Takachiho
Onocho 24 Yokohama
Onocho 47 Northern Kyoto
Onocho 48 Western Kyoto
Onoda 68 Hiroshima & Western Honshu
Onoe-dori 63 Kobe
Onoecho 24 Yokohama
Onohamacho 63 Kobe
Onokaigan 35 Nagoya Area
Onomichi 86 Shimanami Kaido
Onomichi Cinema Museum 74 Onomichi
Onomichi Historical Museum 74 Onomichi
Onoue 92 Nagasaki
Onoyamacho 94 Naha
Ontake Ski Area 34 Central Honshu
Ontocho 49 Western Kyoto
Onuma Quasi National Park 82 Hokaido
Ookubo Toshimichi statue 90 Kagoshima
Oomi 72 Hagi
Oranda-zaka (Dutch Hill) 92 Nagasaki
Orange Beach 69 Hiroshima & Western Honshu
Orient Museum 75 Okamaya
Origami Kaikan 7 Imperial Palace & Tokyo Station
Original Holand House 63 Kobe
Orii Beach 68 Hiroshima & Western Honshu
Oriinishie-no-Hama Beach 86 Shimanami Kaido
Orinasu-kan 49 Western Kyoto
Oritocho 48 Western Kyoto
Oriwara 93 Takachiho
Orofure Ski Area 82 Sado-ga Island
Oroshimachi 78 Hanamaki
Osa 79 Hiraizumi & Ichinoseki
Osabanai 76 Shirakami Mountains
Osacho 88 Kotohira
Osada 80 Aizu, Inawashiro & Ura-bandai
Osado Skyline Drive 80 Sado-ga Island
Osagicho 47 Northern Kyoto
Osaka 61 Osaka Namba
Osaka Aquarium (Kaiyukan) 56 Greater Osaka
Osaka Castle Main Tower (Castle Museum) 59 Osaka Station
Osaka Castle Stone Quarry Ruins 68 Shodo Island
Osaka Contemporary Art Center 59 Osaka Station
Osaka Historical Museum 59 Osaka Station
Osaka Human Rights Museum 60 Osaka Namba
Osaka Int'l Aipot (Itami Airport) 55 Osaka Area
Osaka International Peace Center 57 Greater Osaka

Osaka Nohgaku KaikanTheater 59 Osaka Station
Osaka Pref. 54 Kansai Area
Osaka Science Museum 58 Osaka Station
Osaka Shiki Theater 58 Osaka Station
Osakacho 43 Central & Eastern Kyoto
Osakacho 86 Shimanami Kaido
Osakajo 59 Osaka Station
Osakamachi 50 Fushimi Area
Osakasayama City 55 Osaka Area
Osaki 18 Meguro & Shinagawa
Osaki 77 Northern Honshu
Osakicho 39 Gujo Hachiman
Osakikamijima 69 Hiroshima & Western Honshu
Osakobaru 93 Takachiho
Osaragi Jiro Memorial Museum 25 Kawasaki
Osato 33 Narita
Osato 77 Northern Honshu
Osawa 30 Izu Peninsula
Osawa 76 Shirakami Mountains
Osawa 79 Hiraizumi & Ichinoseki
Osawa Family House 32 Kawagoe-Little Edo
Osawa Hot Spring 30 Izu Peninsula
Osawa Miizubasho Garden 79 Lake Tazawa
Osawa-ochikubocho 48 Western Kyoto
Osawa-yanagidecho 48 Western Kyoto
Ose Beach 30 Izu Peninsula
Oshamanbe 82 Hokaido
Oshiage 11 Asakusa, Ueno & Akihabara
Oshiagecho 65 Nara
Oshika-taki 32 Nikko Area
Oshikata 93 Takachiho
Oshikiri 36 Central Nagoya
Oshima 34 Shirakawa-go & Gokayama
Oshima 53 Uji Town
Oshima 56 Greater Osaka
Oshima Beach 39 Noto Peninsula
Oshima Park 31 Oshima
Oshima Park Zoo 31 Oshima
Oshimaco 56 Greater Osaka
Oshimizu 33 Narita
Oshino Village 28 Mt. Fuji
Oshio Hot Spring 40 Nagano & Matsumoto Areas
Oshioi 93 Takachiho
Oshirabu 80 Aizu, Inawashiro & Ura-bandai
Osho-kita 56 Greater Osaka
Osho-nishimachi 56 Greater Osaka
Oshokawatacho 56 Greater Osaka
Oshonaka-dori 56 Greater Osaka
Oshu 77 Northern Honshu
Osori 30 Izu Peninsula
Osozu Beach 86 Shikoku
OSTEC (Osaka Science & Technology Center) 58 Osaka Station
Osu 36 Central Nagoya
Osugacho 71 Hiroshima
Osugi 37 Central Nagoya
Osuke 76 Shirakami Mountains
Osuminanbu Natural Park 90 Kyusu
Ota 23 Yokohama Area
Ota 78 Hanamaki
Ota Museum of Ukiyo-e Prints 12 Roppongi, Shibuya, Omotesando, Harajuku & Meiji Shrine
Ota National Park 77 Northern Honshu
Otaine Monument 31 Oshima
Otakasucho 56 Greater Osaka
Otake 68 Hiroshima & Western Honshu
Otaki 23 Mt. Fuji & Around Tokyo
Otaki 82 Sado-ga Island
Otaki Daisen Prefectural Natural Park 87 Shikoku
Otakinaizawa 76 Lake Towada
Otakiyama 88 Tokushima
Otamachi 24 Yokohama
Otamachi 41 Shizuoka
Otamayashita 81 Sendai
Otani 47 Northern Kyoto
Otani 53 Uji Town
Otani 93 Takachiho
Otani Hot Spring 68 Hiroshima & Western Honshu
Otanimachi 39 Noto Peninsula
Otari 40 Nagano & Matsumoto Areas
Otari Hot Spring 40 Nagano & Matsumoto Areas
Otaru 82 Hokaido
Otaru Art Museum 84 Otaru
Otaru Canal 84 Otaru
Otaru City Noh Theater 84 Otaru
Otaru Museum Ungakan 84 Otaru
Otaru Rekishi-kan Museum 84 Otaru
Otawara 23 Mt. Fuji & Around Tokyo
Otawara 77 Northern Honshu

Ote 41 Matsumoto
Ote-dori 57 Greater Osaka
Otemachi 38 Kanazawa
Otemachi 39 Gujo Hachiman
Otemachi 41 Shizuoka
Otemachi 7 Imperial Palace & Tokyo Station
Otemachi 73 Yamaguchi
Otemachi 81 Sendai
Otemae 59 Osaka Station
Otemon 93 Fukuoka
Otesenbacho 74 Matsue
Oto Hot Spring 64 Around Nara
Otobe 82 Hokaido
Otofuke 83 Hokaido
Otoireppu 83 Hokaido
Otoko-daki 76 Lake Towada
Otokoyama 66 Amano Hashidate
Otokuni Oyamazakicho 42 Kyoto
Otomachi 80 Aizu, Inawashiro & Ura-bandai
OtomachiKami-miyoriOmameda 80 Aizu, Inawashiro & Ura-bandai
Otomarimachi 39 Noto Peninsula
Otomarumachi 38 Kanazawa
Otome-no-Zo Statue 76 Lake Towada
Otonotani Camp Site 93 Takachiho
Otori 92 Nagasaki
Otorii (Floating Torii) 73 Miyajima
Otorozawa 33 Nikko Area
Otowa 17 Ikebukuro
Otowa 42 Kyoto
Otowa-jo Ruins 67 Lake Biwa
Otowacho 41 Shizuoka
Otowadani 47 Northern Kyoto
Otoyo 87 Shikoku
Otsu 54 Kansai Area
Otsu City 67 Lake Biwa
Otsu City Museum of History 67 Lake Biwa
Otsubocho 41 Shizuoka
Otsuchi 77 Northern Honshu
Otsuka 17 Ikebukuro
Otsuka 42 Kyoto
Otsukata 53 Uji Town
Otsuki 22 Mt. Fuji & Around Tokyo
Otsuki 86 Shikoku
Otsuki City 28 Mt. Fuji
Otsumachi 39 Noto Peninsula
Otsusoba 29 Hakone Town
Ottate Hot Spring 80 Aizu, Inawashiro & Ura-Bandai
Ouchiyama Zoo 54 Kansai Area
Oura 92 Nagasaki
Oura Tenshu-do Cathedral 92 Nagasaki
Ouramachi 76 Hirosaki
Owa 33 Narita
Owa 41 Lake Suwa
Owada 56 Greater Osaka
Owakudani Hot Spring 29 Hakone
Owakudani Volcanic Site 29 Hakone
Owani 77 Northern Honshu
Owari-asahi City 35 Nagoya Area
Owaricho 38 Kanazawa
Owase 54 Kansai Area
Oya Magaibutsu 22 Mt. Fuji & Around Tokyo
Oyachi 78 Hanamaki
Oyaguchi 4 Greater Tokyo
Oyake 42 Kyoto
Oyakuen Garden 80 Aizu, Inawashiro & Ura-Bandai
Oyama 33 Narita
Oyama Hot Spring 77 Northern Honshu
Oyama Park 81 Dewa Sanzen
Oyama Ski Area 83 Hokaido
Oyama Town 28 Mt. Fuji
Oyamamachi 38 Kanazawa
Oyanagicho 46 Northern Kyoto
Oyashirazu Beach 34 Central Honshu
Oyashirazu Cliff 34 Central Honshu
Oyayubidake "Thumb Rock" 68 Shodo Island
Oyodo 54 Kansai Area
Oyodo City 64 Around Nara
Oyodo-kita 57 Greater Osaka
Oyodo-minami 58 Osaka Station
Oyodo-naka 58 Osaka Station
Oyu Hot Spring 77 Northern Honshu
Ozaki Shiro Memorial Museum 23 Yokohama Area
Ozaki-honmachi 74 Onomichi
Ozawa 31 Shimoda
Oze 34 Shirakawa-go & Gokayama
Oze National Park 77 Northern Honshu
Ozone 37 Central Nagoya
Ozora 83 Hokaido
Ozu 86 Shikoku
Ozu 90 Kyusu
Ozuna Beach 87 Shikoku

Palais-la-mer (Oshima Seashell Museum) 31 Oshima
Panaisara-no-taki 96 Yaeyama Islands
Panasonic Digital Network Museum (Risupia) 21 Odaiba
Panasonic Shiodome Museum 8 Ginza, Tsukiji & Tokyo Tower
Park Hill Valley Ski Area 82 Daisetsuzan National Park
Parliamentary Museum 8 Ginza, Tsukiji & Tokyo Tower
Pasadena Art Museum 30 Izu Peninsula
Path of Philosophy (Tetsugaku-no-Michi) 43 Central & Eastern Kyoto
Peace Memorial Museum 70 Hiroshima
Peace Memorial Park 70 Hiroshima
Peacock Garden 68 Shodo Island
Performing Square 38 Kanazawa
Perry Monument 31 Shimoda
Philatelic Museum 16 Ikebukuro
Photograph Gallery 40 Nagano & Matsumoto Areas
Pichipichi Beach 87 Shikoku
Picture Book Museum of Art 30 Izu Peninsula
Pile Orimono Museum 64 Around Nara
Pinagama Beach 97 Miyako Islands
Pinneshiri Hot Spring 83 Hokaido
Pippu 83 Hokaido
Pirika Ski Area 82 Hokaido
Pissiri-soryu-no-taki 83 Hokaido
Piste Japon Ibuki Ski Area 54 Kansai Area
Plasnow Gelaende Ski Area 77 Northern Honshu
Platon Decorative Art Museum 63 Kobe
Pola Museum 29 Hakone
Police Museum 9 Ginza, Tsukiji & Tokyo Tower
Ponto-cho Kaburenjo (Kamogawa-odori) 43 Central & Eastern Kyoto
Pontocho 44 Kawaramachi & Gion
Port Museum 62 Kobe
Port of Hiwasa 54 Kansai Area
Port of Nagoya Public Aquarium 35 Nagoya Area
Port Opening Square 25 Kawasaki
Port Tower 62 Kobe
Pref. Art Museum 93 Fukuoka
Pref. Historical Museum 66 Himeji Castle
Pref. Modern Art Museum Kamakura Annex 27 Kamakura
Prefectural Literary and Calligraphy Museum 89 Tokushima
Prefectural Museum & Art Museum 94 Naha
Prefectural Museum 65 Nara
Prefectural Museum 75 Okamaya
Prefectural Museum 91 Kagoshima
Prefectural Museum of Art 75 Okamaya
Prefectural Museum of Art 88 Matsuyama
Prince Beach 95 Okinawa & The Southwest Islands
Prince Chichibu Memorial Sports Museum 13 Roppongi, Shibuya, Omotesando, Harajuku & Meiji Shrine
Printing Museum 6 Imperial Palace & Tokyo Station
Public Museum 77 Aomori

Rai Sanyo Shiseki Museum 70 Hiroshima
Raiko-ji 27 Kamakura
Railway History Exhibition Hall 8 Ginza, Tsukiji & Tokyo Tower
Railway Memorial Museum 83 Hokaido
Railway Museum 35 Nagoya Area
Rakugeikan Gallery & Exhibition Hall 39 Gujo Hachiman
Rakusai Joka Center Park 42 Kyoto
Rakusai New Town 42 Kyoto
Rakushi Art Museum 37 Central Nagoya
Rakutenchi Amusement Park 91 Beppu Area
Ramen Museum 23 Yokohama Area
Ramen Yokocho (Ramen Street) 85 Sapporo
Ran-no-sato Dogashima Orchid Resort 30 Izu Peninsula
Ran-no-yakata Orchid Garden 37 Central Nagoya
Ranbaicho 79 Hiraizumi & Ichinoseki
Rankoshi 82 Sado-ga Island
Ranzan 22 Mt. Fuji & Around Tokyo
Ranzan Memorial Art Gallery 32 Kawagoe-Little Edo
Rarara Sun Beach 30 Izu Peninsula
Rausu 83 Shiretoko National Park
Rausu Hot Spring 83 Shiretoko National Park
Rebun Airport (closed) 83 Rishiri-rebun-sarobetsu National Park
Red Beach Beach 95 Okinawa-Honto
Red Brick Park 25 Kawasaki
Reihokan Museum 49 Western Kyoto

Reihoku 90 Kyusu
Reikokan Historical Museum 33 Narita
Reimeikan 91 Kagoshima
Reinincho 61 Osaka Namba
Reisencho 44 Kawaramachi & Gion
Rekishi-Densetsu-kan 80 Sado-ga Island
Rendaiji 30 Izu Peninsula
Renge 53 Uji Town
Rengejicho 49 Western Kyoto
Rengezocho 43 Central & Eastern Kyoto
Renjakucho 32 Kawagoe-little Edo
Rice Gallery 59 Osaka Station
Rikubama Beach 95 Okinawa & The Southwest Islands
Rikubetsu 83 Hokaido
Rikugi-en Garden 5 Greater Tokyo
Rikuzen-takata 77 Northern Honshu
Rinkacho 45 Kawaramachi & Gion
Rinkaicho 5 Greater Tokyo
Rinkocho 47 Northern Kyoto
Rinku Pleasure Town Seacle 55 Osaka Area
Rinno-ji 32 Nikko Town
Rinno-ji Homotsu-den (Treasure House) 32 Nikko Town
Rinzaiin 81 Sendai
Rishiri Airport 83 Rishiri-rebun-sarobetsu National Park
Rishiri Fuji Hot Spring 83 Rishiri-rebun-sarobet-su National Park
Rishiri Island Folk Museum 83 Rishiri-rebun-sarobetsu National Park
Rishiri Rebun Sarobetsu National Park 83 Rishiri-rebun-sarobetsu National Park
Ritsurin-koen East Gate 89 Takamatsu
Ritsurin-koen North Gate 89 Takamatsu
Ritsurincho 89 Takamatsu
Ritto 54 Kansai Area
Ritto City 67 Lake Biwa
Ritto Museum of History & Folklore 67 Lake Biwa
River Cruise, Himawari Pier 59 Osaka Station
Rokasu 92 Nagasaki
Rokkaku-aburanokojicho 44 Kawaramachi & Gion
Rokkasho 77 Northern Honshu
Rokkasho Hot Spring 77 Northern Honshu
Rokkenyacho 88 Matsuyama
Rokubancho 6 Imperial Palace & Tokyo Station
Rokuchome 44 Kawaramachi & Gion
Rokudaishibacho 48 Western Kyoto
Rokudandacho 46 Northern Kyoto
Rokudocho 48 Western Kyoto
Rokuhigashi 88 Kotohira
Rokumaimachi 38 Kanazawa
Rokumantaicho 61 Osaka Namba
Rokumei-no-taki 83 Hokaido
Rokunishi 88 Kotohira
Rokuon-ji (Kinkaku-ji) 46 Northern Kyoto
Rokuon-ji Garden 46 Northern Kyoto
Rokurocho 43 Central & Eastern Kyoto
Rokutancho 48 Western Kyoto
Rokutandacho 48 Western Kyoto
Rokuzan Art Museum 40 Nagano & Matsumoto Areas
Ropeway 84 Hakodate
Roppongi 13 Roppongi, Shibuya, Omotesando, Harajuku & Meiji Shrine
Roppongi Hills 4 Greater Tokyo
Rose Garden 59 Osaka Station
Rose Garden 78 Hanamaki
Rosoku-iwa (Candle Rock) 83 Rishiri-rebun-sarobetsu National Park
Rosu Memorial Museum 31 Haha-jima
Ruin of Daisoku 73 Miyajima
Ruin of Dutch Trading House 92 Nagasaki
Ruin of Former Kema Lock Gate 57 Greater Osaka
Ruin of Kanayama Castle 77 Northern Honshu
Ruin of Kanjizaio-In 79 Hiraizumi & Ichinoseki
Ruin of Katsuren Castle 95 Okinawa-Honto
Ruin of Muryoko 79 Hiraizumi & Ichinoseki
Ruin of Nakagusuku Castle 95 Okinawa-Honto
Ruin of Nakijin Castle 95 Okinawa-Honto
Ruin of Omagoshi Sekisho Barrier 76 Shirakami Mountains
Ruin of Rajo-mon Gate 50 Southern Kyoto
Ruin of Sohara Genko Historic Battlefield 92 Fukuoka
Ruin of Tsuwano Castle 73 Tsuwano
Ruin of Zakimi Castle 95 Okinawa-Honto
Ruins of Aoba (Sendai) Castle 81 Sendai
Ruins of Fujiwara Palace 65 Asuka
Ruins of Fukuoka Castle 93 Fukuoka
Ruins of Hagi Castle 72 Hagi
Ruins of Kameyama Castle 93 Takachiho
Ruins of Kubota Castle 78 Akita

Ruins of Maruoka Castle Park 81 Dewa Sanzen
Ruins of Mihara Castle 86 Shimanami Kaido
Ruins of Niitakayama Castle 86 Shimanami Kaido
Ruins of Shimabara-no-ran (Historic Battle Field) 90 Kyusu
Ruins of Sugisawadai 76 Shirakami Mountains
Ruins of Takamatsu Castle 89 Takamatsu
Ruins of Takayama Castle 86 Shimanami Kaido
Ruins of Takeyama Castle 90 Kyusu
Ruins of Toba Imperial Villa 50 Southern Kyoto
Ruins of Tobarikyu Park 50 Southern Kyoto
Ruins of Tokushima Castle 89 Tokushima
Ruins of Tottori Castle 75 Tottori
Ruins of Yamaguchi Castle 73 Yamaguchi
Rukorocho 45 Kawaramachi & Gion
Rumoi 82 Hokaido
Ruriko-ji 68 Hiroshima & Western Honshu
Rusutsu 82 Sado-ga Island
Ryoan-ji 46 Northern Kyoto
Ryoan-ji Hojo Stone Garden 46 Northern Kyoto
Ryoanji 49 Western Kyoto
Ryogaecho 41 Shizuoka
Ryogoku 11 Asakusa, Ueno & Akihabara
Ryokuchi-koen 57 Greater Osaka
Ryori Beach 77 Northern Honshu
Ryotsu 80 Sado-ga Island
Ryozancho 43 Central & Eastern Kyoto
Ryozen Historical Museum 45 Kawaramachi & Gion
Ryuei Museum 33 Nikko Area
Ryufuku-ji 73 Yamaguchi
Ryugasaka 79 Hiraizumi & Ichinoseki
Ryugasaki 23 Mt. Fuji & Around Tokyo
Ryugasawa Yusui Spring 80 Aizu, Inawashiro & Ura-Bandai
Ryugen-ji Mine 73 Iwami Ginzan
Ryugugake Park 87 Iya Valley
Ryujin Hot Spring 54 Kansai Area
Ryuko-ji 26 Kamakura
Ryukyu-mura 95 Okinawa-Honto
Ryuo 54 Kansai Area
Ryuo Town 67 Lake Biwa
Ryuo-no-taki 87 Shikoku
Ryuo-no-taki 96 Yakushima
Ryuocho 70 Hiroshima
Ryusei-no-taki 82 Daisetsuzan National Park
Ryusen 5 Greater Tokyo
Ryutan Pond 95 Shuri Castle
Ryuzojicho 61 Osaka Namba
Ryuzu-no-taki 32 Nikko Area
Ryuzuga-taki 69 Hiroshima & Western Honshu
Sabae 34 Central Honshu
Sabiecho 62 Kobe
Sabigahama Beach 30 Miyake-jima
Sacred Hill of Kinkeisan 79 Hiraizumi & Ichinoseki
Sado 80 Sado-ga Island
Sado Folk Museum 80 Sado-ga Island
Sado Kinzan (Gold Mine) 80 Sado-ga Island
Sado Museum 80 Sado-ga Island
Sadohara 91 Yufuin
Saeki-ku 68 Hiroshima & Western Honshu
Safro Hot Spring 85 Sapporo
Saga 48 Western Kyoto
Saga 9 Ginza, Tsukiji & Tokyo Tower
Saga 90 Kyusu
Saga Airport 90 Kyusu
Saga Pref. 90 Kyusu
Saga-daikakuji- Monzen 48 Western Kyoto
Saga-hirosawa 48 Western Kyoto
Saga-kamemo'ocho 48 Western Kyoto
Saga-kameyamacho 48 Western Kyoto
Saga-kankuji 48 Western Kyoto
Saga-nison'In- Monzen 48 Western Kyoto
Saga-ogurayamacho 48 Western Kyoto
Saga-osawacho 48 Western Kyoto
Saga-shakado-monzen 48 Western Kyoto
Saga-tenryuji 48 Western Kyoto
Saga-toriimoto 48 Western Kyoto
Sagamihara 22 Mt. Fuji & Around Tokyo
Sagamiko 22 Mt. Fuji & Around Tokyo
Sagano 48 Western Kyoto
Sagano Auto Camp 30 Izu Peninsula
Sagano-danmachi 48 Western Kyoto
Sagara 90 Kyusu
Sagara Sun Beach 34 Central Honshu
Sagawa Art Museum 67 Lake Biwa
Sagimachi 47 Northern Kyoto
Saginoyu Hot Spring 69 Hiroshima & Western Honshu
Sagisu 58 Osaka Station
Sai 77 Northern Honshu
Sai-to 64 Mt. Koya
Saifukuji Museum 30 Izu Peninsula
Saigo Takamori Statue 91 Kagoshima

Saigo-dori 57 Greater Osaka
Saigucho 49 Western Kyoto
Saiho-ji (Koke-dera) 48 Western Kyoto
Saiin 49 Western Kyoto
Saiincho 49 Western Kyoto
Saijo 86 Shikoku
Saikaihisaki 39 Noto Peninsula
Saikamachi 74 Matsue
Saikatacho 47 Northern Kyoto
Saiki 90 Kyusu
Saiko-iyashi-no-sato Nenba 28 Mt. Fuji
Saikumachi 6 Imperial Palace & Tokyo Station
Saikumachi 72 Hagi
Saimyojiyama 47 Northern Kyoto
Sainen 38 Kanazawa
Saitama 22 Mt. Fuji & Around Tokyo
Saitama Pref. 22 Mt. Fuji & Around Tokyo
Saitani 65 Yoshina
Saito 90 Kyusu
Saito Mokichi Monument 83 Hokaido
Saito Museum of Art 39 Gujo Hachiman
Saitocho 44 Kawaramachi & Gion
Saiwai 23 Yokohama Area
Saiwaicho 25 Kawasaki
Saiwaicho 32 Kawagoe-little Edo
Saiwaicho 57 Greater Osaka
Saiwaicho 75 Okamaya
Saiwaicho 75 Tottori
Saiwaicho 81 Sendai
Saiwaicho 89 Tokushima
Saiwaimachi 38 Kanazawa
Saiwaimachi 72 Shimonoseki
Saiwaimachi 74 Matsue
Saiwaimachi 91 Central Beppu
Saka 68 Hiroshima & Western Honshu
Saka-no-ue-no-kumo Museum 88 Matsuyama
Sakada 65 Asuka
Sakado 22 Mt. Fuji & Around Tokyo
Sakae 23 Yokohama Area
Sakae 36 Central Nagoya
Sakae Ski Area 77 Northern Honshu
Sakae Tsuboi Literature Museum 68 Shodo Island
Sakaecho 24 Yokohama
Sakaecho 41 Nagano
Sakaecho 41 Shizuoka
Sakaecho 49 Western Kyoto
Sakaecho 84 Hakodate
Sakaemachi 64 Nara
Sakaemachi 75 Tottori
Sakaemachi 88 Kotohira
Sakaemachi-dori 63 Kobe
Sakaguchicho 46 Northern Kyoto
Sakahogi Town 35 Nagoya Area
Sakai 34 Central Honshu
Sakai City 55 Osaka Area
Sakai Ward 55 Osaka Area
Sakai-minato 69 Hiroshima & Western Honshu
Sakai-tsutsuji 83 Hokaido
Sakaida 79 Hiraizumi & Ichinoseki
Sakaide 87 Shikoku
Sakaigawa 56 Greater Osaka
Sakaimachi 25 Kawasaki
Sakaimachi 66 Himeji Castle
Sakaimachi 84 Otaru
Sakainokami 79 Hiraizumi & Ichinoseki
Sakainotani 24 Yokohama
Sakaiura Beach 31 Chichi-jima
Sakaki 77 Northern Honshu
Sakakibara Hot Spring 54 Kansai Area
Sakamachi 15 Shinjuku
Sakamoto 92 Nagasaki
Sakamoto Hot Spring 95 Okinawa & The Southwest Islands
Sakamoto-honcho 42 Kyoto
Sakamoto-honmachi 52 Enryaku-ji & Mt. Hiei
Sakamotocho 44 Kawaramachi & Gion
Sakamotocho 76 Hirosaki
Sakana-to-mori-no Kansatsu-en Park 32 Nikko Area
Sakanamachi 39 Gujo Hachiman
Sakaneguchi Bansho-ato (Guard Station) 73 Iwami Ginzan
Sakanoshita 27 Kamakura
Sakanoshita Beach 83 Rishiri-rebun-sarobetsu National Park
Sakata 77 Northern Honshu
Sakatamachi 66 Himeji Castle
Sakate 68 Shodo Island
Sakawa 86 Shikoku
Sakazuki Maehama Beach 82 Hokaido
Sake Brewery Museum 42 Kyusu
Sakibaru Beach 97 Amami Oshima
Sakidencho 43 Central & Eastern Kyoto

Sakigakemachi 92 Shimabara
Sakikawahama Beach 80 Aizu, Inawashiro & Ura-Bandai
Sakimicho 31 Atami
Sakitama Old Tombs 22 Mt. Fuji & Around Tokyo
Sako Ichibancho 88 Tokushima
Sako Nibancho 88 Tokushima
Sakocho 36 Central Nagoya
Sakomaecho 36 Central Nagoya
Sakou 36 Central Nagoya
Saku 34 Central Honshu
Sakuda Gold Leaf Company 38 Kanazawa
Sakuho 34 Central Honshu
Sakura 23 Mt. Fuji & Around Tokyo
Sakura 4 Greater Tokyo
Sakura 77 Northern Honshu
Sakura-Chijin-kan 79 Hanamaki
Sakura-jima Volcano 90 Kyusu
Sakura-no-sato Athletic Park 90 Kyusu
Sakura-shinmachi 4 Greater Tokyo
Sakura-taki 39 Noto Peninsula
Sakuracho 31 Atami
Sakuradanicho 43 Central & Eastern Kyoto
Sakuradanicho 89 Matsuyama
Sakuraecho 41 Nagano
Sakuragaoka 4 Greater Tokyo
Sakuragaokacho 12 Roppongi, Shibuya, Omotesando, Harajuku & Meiji Shrine
Sakuragawa 57 Greater Osaka
Sakuragicho 24 Yokohama
Sakuragicho 31 Atami
Sakuragicho 47 Northern Kyoto
Sakuragicho 56 Greater Osaka
Sakuragimachi 81 Sendai
Sakurai 54 Kansai Area
Sakurai City 64 Around Nara
Sakurai Kaigan Beach 86 Shikoku
Sakurajima 56 Greater Osaka
Sakurajosui 4 Greater Tokyo
Sakuramachi 38 Kanazawa
Sakuramachi 39 Gujo Hachiman
Sakuramachi 39 Takayama
Sakuramachi 73 Miyajima
Sakuramachi 74 Onomichi
Sakurano Hot Spring 82 Hokaido
Sakuranocho 44 Kawaramachi & Gion
Sakuratanicho 48 Western Kyoto
Sakurazaka 93 Fukuoka
Sakuya Konohana Kan 57 Greater Osaka
Sakyo Ward 67 Lake Biwa
Salwal 92 Nagasaki
Samani 83 Hokaido
Samaryocho 49 Western Kyoto
Sambancho 6 Imperial Palace & Tokyo Station
Sambaseki-valley 22 Mt. Fuji & Around Tokyo
Sambon-daki 40 Nagano & Matsumoto Areas
Sambonyanagi Hot Spring 76 Shirakami Mountains
Samegaicho 38 Kanazawa
Sammyo 39 Noto Peninsula
Samoncho 15 Shinjuku
Sample Kobo 39 Gujo Hachiman
Sample Village Iwasaki 39 Gujo Hachiman
Samurai Residence Museum 78 Kakunodate
San Alpina Hukuba Sanosaka 40 Nagano & Matsumoto Areas
San-no-taki 68 Hiroshima & Western Honshu
San'eicho 15 Shinjuku
Sanadayamacho 57 Greater Osaka
Sanage Adventure Field 35 Nagoya Area
Sanagochi 69 Hiroshima & Western Honshu
Sanagouchi 87 Shikoku
Sanai-no-oka Observatory Park 82 Daisetsuzan National Park
Sanbancho 41 Shizuoka
Sanbancho 88 Matsuyama
Sanbongicho 44 Kawaramachi & Gion
Sanchome 31 Shimoda
Sanchome 45 Kawaramachi & Gion
Sanchujicho 45 Kawaramachi & Gion
Sand Ski 30 Izu Peninsula
Sanda 55 Osaka Area
Sandanosacho 47 Northern Kyoto
Saneku Beach 97 Amami Oshima
Sangai-taki 82 Sado-ga Island
Sangaku Museum 39 Takayama
Sangaku Museum 40 Nagano & Matsumoto Areas
Sangedatsu-mon Gate 8 Ginza, Tsukiji & Tokyo Tower
Sangencho 49 Western Kyoto
Sangenya-higashi 60 Osaka Namba
Sangenya-nishi 56 Greater Osaka
Sangenyacho 74 Onomichi
Sangi-daki 80 Aizu, Inawashiro & Ura-Bandai

Sango Town 64 Around Nara
Sango-no-hama Beach 96 Yakushima
Sanjamachi 38 Kanazawa
Sanjo 64 Nara
Sanjo 77 Northern Honshu
Sanjo Tenno Imperial Mausoleum (Kitayama-no-misasagi) 46 Northern Kyoto
Sanjocho 44 Kawaramachi & Gion
Sanjocho 89 Takamatsu
Sanjomachi 81 Sendai
Sanju-no-to (Three-story Pagoda) 64 Around Nara
Sankei-en Garden 23 Yokohama Area
Sanko Art Museum 35 Nagoya Area
Sankubocho 32 Kawagoe-little Edo
Sankyozawa 81 Sendai
Sanmeicho 57 Greater Osaka
Sanmon Gate 41 Nagano
Sanmonjicho 44 Kawaramachi & Gion
Sanmu 23 Mt. Fuji & Around Tokyo
Sannai 32 Nikko Town
Sanno 36 Central Nagoya
Sanno 53 Uji Town
Sanno 61 Osaka Namba
Sannocho 43 Central & Eastern Kyoto
Sannocho 62 Kobe
Sannocho 76 Hirosaki
Sannomaru 36 Central Nagoya
Sannomiyacho 48 Western Kyoto
Sannomiyacho 63 Kobe
Sannose 57 Greater Osaka
Sano 30 Izu Peninsula
Sano 79 Hiraizumi & Ichinoseki
Sanocho 48 Western Kyoto
Sanohama Beach 31 Oshima
Sanraiba Ski Area 82 Sado-ga Island
Sanrio Puro Land 22 Mt. Fuji & Around Tokyo
Sanrizuka 33 Narita
Sanrizuka-hikarigaoka 33 Narita
Sanrizuke-goryo 33 Narita
Sansodori 93 Fukuoka
Santa 79 Hiraizumi & Ichinoseki
Santa Claus Museum 28 Mt. Fuji
Santanda 37 Inuyama
Santonodai Archaeological Museum 23 Yokohama Area
Sanuki 87 Shikoku
Sanuki Folkcraft Museum 89 Takamatsu
Sanuki Hot Spring 87 Shikoku
Sanukicho 50 Fushimi Area
Sanwa 22 Mt. Fuji & Around Tokyo
Sanyo 68 Hiroshima & Western Honshu
Sanyo-onoda 68 Hiroshima & Western Honshu
Sanzaigaike Forest Park 23 Yokohama Area
Sapporo 82 Hokaido
Sapporo Art Park 82 Sado-ga Island
Sapporo Beer Garden 85 Sapporo
Sapporo Beer Museum 85 Sapporo
Sapporo Citizens Gallery 85 Sapporo
Sapporo Factory 85 Sapporo
Sapporo Museum 85 Sapporo
Sapporo Museum Activity Center 85 Sapporo
Sapporo Okadama Airport 82 Hokaido
Sarabetsu 83 Hokaido
Saraki 79 Hanamaki
Sarashina 80 Aizu, Inawashiro & Ura-bandai
Sari Hot Spring 90 Kyusu
Saroma 83 Hokaido
Sarubuchi-daki 87 Shikoku
Sarubushi 93 Takachiho
Sarue 5 Greater Tokyo
Sarufutsu 83 Hokaido
Sarufutsu Park 83 Hokaido
Sarugakucho 12 Roppongi, Shibuya, Omote-sando, Harajuku & Meiji Shrine
Sarugakyo Hot Spring 22 Mt. Fuji & Around Tokyo
Sarukura Ski Area 81 Zao Onsen
Sarunoyu 76 Shirakami Mountains
Sasagatani 47 Northern Kyoto
Sasagawa 23 Mt. Fuji & Around Tokyo
Sasago 22 Mt. Fuji & Around Tokyo
Sasamemachi 27 Kamakura
Sasamori Viewpoint 76 Lake Towada
Sasamoricho 76 Hirosaki
Sasashimacho 36 Central Nagoya
Sasaya 79 Hiraizumi & Ichinoseki
Sasayacho 49 Western Kyoto
Sasayama 54 Kansai Area
Sasayamacho 72 Shimonoseki
Sasebo 90 Kyusu
Sashiki 95 Okinawa-honto
Sashima 22 Mt. Fuji & Around Tokyo
Sasuke 27 Kamakura
Sasuke Inari Shrine 27 Kamakura
Satake Historical Museum 78 Akita

Satake History & Culture Museum 78 Kaku-nodate
Sato 79 Hiraizumi & Ichinoseki
Sato Kei Art Museum 91 Central Beppu
Satobama Beach 90 Kyusu
Satojiri 53 Uji Town
Satono Beach 54 Kansai Area
Satsuki-minamitori 36 Central Nagoya
Satsukitori 36 Central Nagoya
Satsuma 90 Kyusu
Satsuma-sendai 90 Kyusu
Satsutacho 47 Northern Kyoto
Satte 22 Mt. Fuji & Around Tokyo
Sawabuchicho 47 Northern Kyoto
Sawacho 66 Hikone Castle
Sawada 79 Hiraizumi & Ichinoseki
Sawada Beach 97 Miyako Islands
Sawada Hot Spring 80 Sado-ga Island
Sawada Seiko Memorial Museum 31 Atami
Sawadacho 30 Izu Peninsula
Sawaguchi 79 Hiraizumi & Ichinoseki
Sawajiri Beach 30 Kozu-shima & Nii-jima
Sawanotsuru Sake Museum 55 Osaka Area
Sawara 23 Mt. Fuji & Around Tokyo
Sawara Hot Spring 82 Sado-ga Island
Sawauchi 79 Hiraizumi & Ichinoseki
Sayama 22 Mt. Fuji & Around Tokyo
Sayo 54 Kansai Area
Sayo 69 Hiroshima & Western Honshu
Saza 90 Kyusu
Sazanamimachi 39 Noto Peninsula
Sazu Beach 54 Kansai Area
Scai The Bath House 10 Asakusa, Ueno & Akihabara
Scichiri 33 Nikko Area
Science Museum 6 Imperial Palace & Tokyo Station
Science Museum 91 Miyazaki
Science Museum for Youth 23 Yokohama Area
Science Museum for Youth 55 Osaka Area
Science Museum of Water Environment 67 Lake Biwa
Scmaglev and Railway Park 35 Nagoya Area
Sculptures Promenade 30 Kozu-shima & Nii-jima
Sea Train Land Amusement Park 35 Nagoya Area
Sea Turtle's Nesting Ground 96 Yakushima
Seabird Habitat 83 Hokaido
Sebahira 73 Iwami Ginzan
Sechibaru Museum 90 Kyusu
Sedake 95 Okinawa-honto
Sefautaki (Sacred Area) 95 Okinawa-Honto
Sefurihokusan Natural Park 90 Kyusu
Sega World 33 Narita
Segaraki Beach 95 Okinawa-Honto
Segashiracho 91 Miyazaki
Segire-daki 96 Yakushima
Seibu Rindo Forest Path 96 Yakushima
Seibu-en Amusement Park 22 Mt. Fuji & Around Tokyo
Seidocho 44 Kawaramachi & Gion
Seiganji Temple Cycads 68 Shodo Island
Seiganto-Ji Kumano Nachi-Taisha Shrine 54 Kansai Area
Seihokucho 46 Northern Kyoto
Seiiku 57 Greater Osaka
Seika 54 Kansai Area
Seika Theater 61 Osaka Namba
Seikado Bunko Art Museum 4 Greater Tokyo
Seikan Ferry Memorial Ship Hakkoda-maru 76 Aomori
Seikanji 43 Central & Eastern Kyoto
Seikanji Ryozancho 45 Kawaramachi & Gion
Seikanrenrakusen Memorial Ship Mashumaru 84 Hakodate
Seimei-dori 57 Greater Osaka
Seimeicho 44 Kawaramachi & Gion
Seinan Gakuin Univ. Museum 92 Fukuoka
Seinancho 46 Northern Kyoto
Seiro 77 Northern Honshu
Seiryocho 81 Sendai
Seiryucho 43 Central & Eastern Kyoto
Seishincho 5 Greater Tokyo
Seishohama Beach 80 Aizu, Inawashiro & Ura-Bandai
Seison-kaku Daimyo Residence 38 Kanazawa
Seitoku Memorial Picture Gallery 13 Roppongi, Shibuya, Omotesando, Harajuku & Meiji Shrine
Seiyo 86 Shikoku
Seki 34 Central Honshu
Seki Art Gallery 89 Matsuyama
Seki-no-ichi Sake Museum 79 Hiraizumi & Ichinoseki
Sekiba 80 Aizu, Inawashiro & Ura-bandai

Sekido 33 Narita
Sekigahara 54 Kansai Area
Sekigaoka 79 Hiraizumi & Ichinoseki
Sekiguchi 17 Ikebukuro
Sekijomachi 93 Fukuoka
Sekikawa 77 Northern Honshu
Sekiryucho 46 Northern Kyoto
Sekime 57 Greater Osaka
Sekinohana 39 Noto Peninsula
Sekitan-no-rekishimura Museum 83 Hokaido
Sekiyado 22 Mt. Fuji & Around Tokyo
Semi-ga-kakiuchicho 46 Northern Kyoto
Semmai Hot Spring 87 Shikoku
Sen-oku Hakuko-kan Art Museum 43 Central & Eastern Kyoto
Senauchicho 47 Northern Kyoto
Senba 57 Greater Osaka
Senba-chuo 59 Osaka Station
Senbamachi 32 Kawagoe-little Edo
Senbamachi 93 Kumamoto
Senbayashi 57 Greater Osaka
Senboku City 78 Lake Tazawa
Senbon-kita 57 Greater Osaka
Senbon-minami 57 Greater Osaka
Senbon-naka 57 Greater Osaka
Senda 5 Greater Tokyo
Sendagaya 13 Roppongi, Shibuya, Omotesando, Harajuku & Meiji Shrine
Sendagi 10 Asakusa, Ueno & Akihabara
Sendai 77 Northern Honshu
Sendai Airport 77 Northern Honshu
Sendai City Museum 81 Sendai
Sendai Hot Spring 90 Kyusu
Sendai Yagiyama Zoological Park 81 Sendai
Sendaigawa-ryokuchi Park 75 Tottori
Sendamachi 70 Hiroshima
Sendocho 46 Northern Kyoto
Senganmon Rock Gate 30 Izu Peninsula
Senge 68 Shodo Island
Sengen 36 Central Nagoya
Sengencho 41 Shizuoka
Sengoku 17 Ikebukuro
Sengokubara-kogen 29 Hakone
Sengokuhara 29 Hakone
Senhiro-no-taki 97 Yakushima
Senjogahara Monument 32 Nikko Area
Senjogahara Plateau 32 Nikko Area
Senjokei Prefectural Natural Park 68 Hiroshima & Western Honshu
Senju-akebonocho 5 Greater Tokyo
Senju-nakaicho 5 Greater Tokyo
Senjuga-hama Beach 32 Nikko Area
Senjugahara 32 Nikko Area
Senjuin 64 Mt. Koya
Senkawa 16 Ikebukuro
Senko-ji 74 Onomichi
Senmaida 39 Noto Peninsula
Senmaida Rice Fields 39 Noto Peninsula
Senmandacho 47 Northern Kyoto
Sennaritori 36 Central Nagoya
Sennencho 49 Western Kyoto
Sennichicho 91 Kagoshima
Sennichimachi 38 Kanazawa
Sennichimae 61 Osaka Namba
Senninyu Hot Spring 40 Nagano & Matsumoto Areas
Sennocho 48 Western Kyoto
Sennyuji 51 Southern Kyoto
Senoo 33 Nikko Area
Senshu-jokamachi 78 Akita
Senshu-kitanomachi 78 Akita
Senshu-koen 78 Akita
Senshu-kubotamachi 78 Akita
Senshu-meitokumachi 78 Akita
Senshu-nakajimamachi 78 Akita
Senshu-yadomemachi 78 Akita
Senso-ji 5 Greater Tokyo
Sensui Gorge 91 Aso Area
Sento Palace 43 Central & Eastern Kyoto
Senzokou 11 Asakusa, Ueno & Akihabara
Senzoku-ike Park 4 Greater Tokyo
Senzokucho 46 Northern Kyoto
Senzui 81 Matsushima
Sera 69 Hiroshima & Western Honshu
Serinuma 33 Nikko Area
Seseki Hot Spring 83 Shiretoko National Park
Seseki-no-taki 83 Shiretoko National Park
Session House Dance Studio 6 Imperial Palace & Tokyo Station
Sessokyo Hot Spring 34 Central Honshu
Seta 4 Greater Tokyo
Setagaya 23 Yokohama Area
Setagaya 4 Greater Tokyo
Setagaya Art Museum 4 Greater Tokyo
Setagaya Literary Museum 4 Greater Tokyo
Setagaya Ward Folk Museum 4 Greater Tokyo

Setana 82 Hokaido
Setaumi Beach 95 Okinawa & The Southwest Islands
Seto 39 Noto Peninsula
Seto City 35 Nagoya Area
Seto Ohashi Tower 87 Seto-ohasi Bridge
Setogawacho 48 Western Kyoto
Setohatacho 49 Western Kyoto
Setonaikai National Park 55 Osaka Area
Setouchi 69 Hiroshima & Western Honshu
Setouchi Hot Spring 68 Shodo Island
Seventh Station 82 Sado-ga Island
Sewara 79 Hiraizumi & Ichinoseki
Sgurigane Hot Spring 82 Daisetsuzan National Park
Shaboten Park 22 Mt. Fuji & Around Tokyo
Shadai-daki 82 Sado-ga Island
Shakadani 46 Northern Kyoto
Shakadocho 47 Northern Kyoto
Shakotan 82 Hokaido
Shakuji Park 4 Greater Tokyo
Shan Shan Festival 75 Tottori
Shandake Natural Park 83 Akan National Park
Shari 83 Hokaido
Sharidake National Park 83 Hokaido
Shariji 57 Greater Osaka
Shell Museum 87 Shikoku
Shiawasemura Park 35 Nagoya Area
Shiba 5 Ginza, Tsukiji & Tokyo Tower
Shiba Daimon 5 Greater Tokyo
Shiba Rikyu Garden 8 Ginza, Tsukiji & Tokyo Tower
Shiba- Daimon 8 Ginza, Tsukiji & Tokyo Tower
Shiba-koen 8 Ginza, Tsukiji & Tokyo Tower
Shibagaki Beach 39 Noto Peninsula
Shibamotocho 47 Northern Kyoto
Shibanocho 48 Western Kyoto
Shibanoshitacho 49 Western Kyoto
Shibaseki Hot Spring 91 Beppu Area
Shibata 57 Greater Osaka
Shibata 59 Osaka Station
Shibata 77 Northern Honshu
Shibatsujicho 64 Nara
Shibaura 15 Meguro & Shinagawa
Shibayama Mizube No Sato 33 Narita
Shibecha 83 Hokaido
Shibecha Hot Spring 83 Hokaido
Shibetsu 83 Hokaido
Shibo-horikawacho 44 Kawaramachi & Gion
Shibo-omiyacho 49 Western Kyoto
Shibukawa 77 Northern Honshu
Shibukawacho 57 Greater Osaka
Shibun-kaku Art Museum 43 Central & Eastern Kyoto
Shibusecho 43 Central & Eastern Kyoto
Shibushi 90 Kyusu
Shibuya 12 Roppongi, Shibuya, Omotesando, Harajuku & Meiji Shrine
Shibuya 23 Yokohama Area
Shibuya Shopping 12 Roppongi, Shibuya, Omotesando, Harajuku & Meiji Shrine
Shibuya Ward Museum 13 Roppongi, Shibuya, Omotesando, Harajuku & Meiji Shrine
Shichibancho 49 Western Kyoto
Shichijo Goshonouchi 49 Western Kyoto
Shichikama Hot Spring 69 Hiroshima & Western Honshu
Shichiku 46 Northern Kyoto
Shichimi 39 Noto Peninsula
Shichinohe 77 Northern Honshu
Shichinomiyacho 62 Kobe
Shidencho 49 Western Kyoto
Shiga Pref. 54 Kansai Area
Shigaraki 34 Central Honshu
Shigatani 53 Uji Town
Shige 30 Izu Peninsula
Shigemorimachi 76 Hirosaki
Shigenobu 69 Hiroshima & Western Honshu
Shigino-higashi 57 Greater Osaka
Shigino-nishi 57 Greater Osaka
Shigita 57 Greater Osaka
Shigita-higashi 57 Greater Osaka
Shiheimachi 81 Sendai
Shihoro 83 Hokaido
Shihozashi Scenic View Point 68 Shodo Island
Shiiba 90 Kyusu
Shiinocho 48 Western Kyoto
Shiinoki 92 Nagasaki
Shijima Beach 86 Shikoku
Shijo 88 Kotohira
Shijocho 44 Kawaramachi & Gion
Shijonawate City 64 Around Nara
Shijuhachi-taki 76 Shirakami Mountains
Shika 39 Noto Peninsula
Shikabe 82 Hokaido
Shikanjima 56 Greater Osaka

Shikaoi 83 Hokaido
Shiki District 64 Around Nara
Shiki Memorial Museum 89 Matsuyama
Shiki Theater Museum 40 Nagano & Matsumoto Areas
Shiki-do Museum 88 Matsuyama
Shikibucho 49 Western Kyoto
Shikina-En Garden 95 Okinawa-Honto
Shikine 31 Shimoda
Shikitsu-higashi 61 Osaka Namba
Shikitsu-nishi 60 Osaka Namba
Shikokuchuo 87 Shikoku
Shikotsu-Toya National Park 82 Sado-ga Island
Shikotsuko Hot Spring 82 Sado-ga Island
Shima 34 Shirakawa-go & Gokayama
Shima 55 Kansai
Shima Spain Village Parque Espana 55 Kansai
Shima-machi 59 Osaka Station
Shimabara 49 Western Kyoto
Shimabara 90 Kyusu
Shimabara Castle & Christian Museum 92 Shimabara
Shimada 34 Central Honshu
Shimada Hot Spring 83 Hokaido
Shimadani 39 Gujo Hachiman
Shimado 93 Takachiho
Shimado Beach 68 Hiroshima & Western Honshu
Shimagamicho 62 Kobe
Shimamaki 82 Hokaido
Shimamoto 42 Kyoto
Shimanami-kaido 86 Shimanami Kaido
Shimane Art Museum 74 Matsue
Shimane International Centre 74 Matsue
Shimane Pref. 69 Hiroshima & Western Honshu
Shimanouchi 57 Greater Osaka
Shimanto 86 Shikoku
Shimantogawa Gakuyu-kan Museum 86 Shikoku
Shimao Beach 39 Noto Peninsula
Shimasho 65 Asuka
Shimata 42 Kyoto
Shimaya 56 Greater Osaka
Shimazu Foundation Memorial Hall 44 Kawaramachi & Gion
Shimbashi 8 Ginza, Tsukiji & Tokyo Tower
Shimbashi Embujo Theater 9 Ginza, Tsukiji & Tokyo Tower
Shimbayashi Park 26 Kamakura
Shimeitei Viewpoint 76 Lake Towada
Shimizu 30 Izu Peninsula
Shimizu 4 Greater Tokyo
Shimizu 57 Greater Osaka
Shimizu 83 Hokaido
Shimizu 91 Miyazaki
Shimizu Beach 97 Amami Oshima
Shimizucho 31 Atami
Shimizucho 44 Kawaramachi & Gion
Shimizucho 62 Kobe
Shimizudani Smelter Site 73 Iwami Ginzan
Shimizudanicho 61 Osaka Namba
Shimizumachi 88 Matsuyama
Shimizunuma 81 Sendai
Shimmachi Beach 80 Sado-ga Island
Shimmaiko Beach 77 Northern Honshu
Shimo-adachicho 43 Central & Eastern Kyoto
Shimo-bentencho 45 Kawaramachi & Gion
Shimo-dera 61 Osaka Namba
Shimo-gawaracho 47 Northern Kyoto
Shimo-gioncho 62 Kobe
Shimo-gokenmachi 72 Hagi
Shimo-hakusancho 44 Kawaramachi & Gion
Shimo-haracho 91 Miyazaki
Shimo-hatsuishimachi 32 Nikko Town
Shimo-hiroicho 36 Central Nagoya
Shimo-hondamachi Gobancho 38 Kanazawa
Shimo-honnojimaecho 44 Kawaramachi & Gion
Shimo-ichinomachi 39 Takayama
Shimo-igusa 4 Greater Tokyo
Shimo-ikedacho 43 Central & Eastern Kyoto
Shimo-ishibikimachi 38 Kanazawa
Shimo-jimbaracho 46 Northern Kyoto
Shimo-kakinokibatake 38 Kanazawa
Shimo-kanayama 33 Narita
Shimo-kashiwamachi 46 Northern Kyoto
Shimo-komenocho 36 Central Nagoya
Shimo-kosaicho 46 Northern Kyoto
Shimo-meguro 18 Meguro & Shinagawa
Shimo-midoricho 46 Northern Kyoto
Shimo-mikadocho 65 Nara
Shimo-minamidacho 43 Central & Eastern Kyoto
Shimo-miyabicho 6 Imperial Palace & Tokyo Station
Shimo-nagamecho 46 Northern Kyoto
Shimo-nakacho 50 Fushimi Area

Shikaoi 83 Hokaido
Shimo-namiki 25 Kawasaki
Shimo-nishiyama 92 Nagasaki
Shimo-nita 72 Mt. Fuji & Around Tokyo
Shimo-ochiai 16 Ikebukuro
Shimo-ojicho 43 Central & Eastern Kyoto
Shimo-oshikata 93 Takachiho
Shimo-sairencho 73 Miyajima
Shimo-sanjocho 62 Kobe
Shimo-seizoguchicho 46 Northern Kyoto
Shimo-shakuji 4 Greater Tokyo
Shimo-shinsenencho 50 Fushimi Area
Shimo-shiroganecho 76 Hirosaki
Shimo-shodacho 46 Northern Kyoto
Shimo-suwa Hot Spring 41 Lake Suwa
Shimo-takaido 4 Greater Tokyo
Shimo-takayama 54 Kansai Area
Shimo-tatekami 73 Yamaguchi
Shimo-tokihazama 37 Inuyama
Shimo-tsubayashi 50 Southern Kyoto
Shimo-tsukiyamacho 46 Northern Kyoto
Shimo-tsutsumicho 45 Kawaramachi & Gion
Shimo-ueno 42 Kyoto
Shimo-umenokicho 46 Northern Kyoto
Shimo-yamada-chozukacho 48 Western Kyoto
Shimo-yamada-kami-sono'ocho 48 Western Kyoto
Shimo-yamate-dori 62 Kobe
Shimo-yanagicho 46 Northern Kyoto
Shimo-yatsuricho 65 Asuka
Shimo-yokocho 49 Western Kyoto
Shimo-yukawa 66 Hongu Onsens
Shimo-zaijicho 47 Northern Kyoto
Shimo-zaimokucho 44 Kawaramachi & Gion
Shimoaicho 49 Western Kyoto
Shimoda 30 Izu Peninsula
Shimoda Castle Museum 31 Shimoda
Shimoda Hot Spring 90 Kyusu
Shimoda Kaikoku Museum 31 Shimoda
Shimogamo 47 Northern Kyoto
Shimogamo Hot Spring 30 Izu Peninsula
Shimogamo Tropical Garden 30 Izu Peninsula
Shimogo 77 Northern Honshu
Shimoichi Town 64 Around Nara
Shimoishii 75 Okamaya
Shimoji-shima Airport 97 Miyako Islands
Shimojo 34 Central Honshu
Shimokawa 83 Hokaido
Shimokawara 78 Kakunodate
Shimokawaracho 45 Kawaramachi & Gion
Shimokita Shopping Town 4 Greater Tokyo
Shimoma 4 Greater Tokyo
Shimomaruyacho 44 Kawaramachi & Gion
Shimomisu 50 Southern Kyoto
Shimomizocho 49 Western Kyoto
Shimomura 78 Kakunodate
Shimonitanai 79 Hanamaki
Shimonocho 49 Western Kyoto
Shimonoseki 68 Hiroshima & Western Honshu
Shimonoseki Marin Hot Spring 68 Hiroshima & Western Honshu
Shimosawa-dori 62 Kobe
Shimosuketocho 89 Tokushima
Shimosuwa 40 Nagano & Matsumoto Areas
Shimotoba 50 Southern Kyoto
Shimotsui Hot Spring 86 Shikoku
Shimouma 4 Greater Tokyo
Shimoura Beach 69 Hiroshima & Western Honshu
Shimoyachi 79 Hiraizumi & Ichinoseki
Shimoyamacho 43 Central & Eastern Kyoto
Shimozato 97 Miyakojima
Shimozawacho 49 Western Kyoto
Shimukappu 83 Hokaido
Shin-beppu 91 Kannawa Hells Area
Shin-enoshima Aquarium 26 Kamakura
Shin-goryoguchicho 46 Northern Kyoto
Shin-honjicho 75 Tottori
Shin-Hotaka Hot Spring 40 Nagano & Matsumoto Areas
Shin-Hotaka Ropeway 40 Nagano & Matsumoto Areas
Shin-Kabukiza Theater 61 Osaka Namba
Shin-kiba 5 Greater Tokyo
Shin-kitano 56 Greater Osaka
Shin-Kobe Ropeway 63 Kobe
Shin-komaino 33 Narita
Shin-kyo 32 Nikko Town
Shin-kyusha (Holy Stable) 32 Nikko Town
Shin-maebashi 22 Mt. Fuji & Around Tokyo
Shin-maiko Beach 69 Hiroshima & Western Honshu
Shin-ogawamachi 6 Imperial Palace & Tokyo Station
Shin-omiya 42 Kyoto
Shin-onomecho 84 Otaru
Shin-onsen 54 Kansai Area

Shin-pontocho 45 Kawaramachi & Gion
Shin-saikamachi 74 Matsue
Shin-sakae 37 Central Nagoya
Shin-shigai 93 Kumamoto
Shin-shoincho 90 Kagoshima
Shin-teramachi 76 Hirosaki
Shin-yamashita 25 Yokohama
Shin-yashikicho 91 Kagoshima
Shinagawa 23 Yokohama Area
Shinagawa 5 Greater Tokyo
Shinagawa Aquarium 22 Mt. Fuji & Around Tokyo
Shinakawamachi 76 Hirosaki
Shinano 34 Central Honshu
Shinano Art Museum Higashiyama Kaii Gallery 41 Nagano
Shinano Education Museum 41 Nagano
Shinanomachi 15 Shinjuku
Shinchi 77 Northern Honshu
Shinchicho 72 Shimonoseki
Shincho 44 Kawaramachi & Gion
Shinchosha Memorial Literary Museum 78 Kakunodate
Shinco 80 Aizu, Inawashiro & Ura-bandai
Shindatecho 49 Western Kyoto
Shindeki 37 Central Nagoya
Shinden 33 Narita
Shinden 79 Hiraizumi & Ichinoseki
Shinden 81 Sendai
Shindencho 41 Nagano
Shindencho 48 Western Kyoto
Shindenmachi 92 Shimabara
Shineicho 96 Ishigaki City
Shingaihama Beach 67 Lake Biwa
Shingo 77 Northern Honshu
Shingo Dai-ichi Ski Area 69 Hiroshima & Western Honshu
Shingu 54 Kansai Area
Shingu 90 Kyusu
Shingu Hot Spring 39 Noto Peninsula
Shingucho 48 Western Kyoto
Shinhidaka 83 Hokaido
Shinichi 69 Hiroshima & Western Honshu
Shinimazato 57 Greater Osaka
Shinji-no-taki 67 Lake Biwa
Shinjo 69 Hiroshima & Western Honshu
Shinjo 77 Northern Honshu
Shinjuku 15 Shinjuku
Shinjuku 27 Kamakura
Shinjuku Skyscraper District 14 Shinjuku
Shinjuku-gyoen Garden 4 Greater Tokyo
ShinjukuHistorical Museum 15 Shinjuku
Shinkaichi 62 Kobe
Shinkawa 9 Ginza, Tsukiji & Tokyo Tower
Shinkawa-higashi 72 Hagi
Shinkawa-minami 72 Hagi
Shinkawadori 25 Kawasaki
Shinkawanishi 72 Hagi
Shinkazawa Hot Spring 22 Mt. Fuji & Around Tokyo
Shinkin Mine 73 Iwami Ginzan
Shinko 24 Yokohama
Shinko 68 Shodo Island
Shinkuracho 89 Tokushima
Shinmachi 33 Narita
Shinmachi 39 Gujo Hachiman
Shinmachi 4 Greater Tokyo
Shinmachi 41 Nagano
Shinmachi 58 Osaka Station
Shinmachi 60 Osaka Namba
Shinmachi 73 Miyajima
Shinmachi 74 Matsue
Shinmachi 77 Aomori
Shinmachi 86 Uwajima
Shinmachi 92 Kumamoto
Shinmeicho 25 Kawasaki
Shinmeicho 49 Western Kyoto
Shinmeicho 62 Kobe
Shinmeicho 88 Kotohira
Shinmichi 36 Central Nagoya
Shinmichi 73 Yamaguchi
Shinmichi 88 Kotohira
Shinmori 57 Greater Osaka
Shinnyocho 43 Central & Eastern Kyoto
Shinobumachi 66 Himeji Castle
Shinoda 76 Aomori
Shinodayama 55 Osaka Area
Shinohara-daki 64 Around Nara
Shinonome 21 Odaiba
Shinonome 71 Hiroshima
Shinonome-dori 62 Kobe
Shinonome-honmachi 71 Hiroshima
Shinotsubocho 48 Western Kyoto
Shinpoincho 61 Osaka Namba
Shinri 94 Okinawa & The Southwest Islands
Shinsaibashi 61 Osaka Namba

Shinsaibashi-suji 61 Osaka Namba
Shinseicho 49 Western Kyoto
Shinsencho 12 Roppongi, Shibuya, Omote-sando, Harajuku & Meiji Shrine
Shinshiro 34 Central Honshu
Shinsho-den Treasure House 51 Southern Kyoto
Shinso-ji Temple 33 Narita
Shintakayama 74 Onomichi
Shintera 81 Sendai
Shinto 22 Mt. Fuji & Around Tokyo
Shintoku 83 Hokaido
Shintomi 90 Kyusu
Shintomicho 44 Kawaramachi & Gion
Shinuchimachi 89 Tokushima
Shinwa Hot Spring 39 Noto Peninsula
Shinwanihama Beach 67 Lake Biwa
Shinyokoai Mine 73 Iwami Ginzan
Shio Sight 8 Ginza, Tsukiji & Tokyo Tower
Shiogamacho 44 Kawaramachi & Gion
Shiogamicho 89 Takamatsu
Shiohama 5 Greater Tokyo
Shiohama 76 Shirakami Mountains
Shioji 57 Greater Osaka
Shiojiri 40 Nagano & Matsumoto Areas
Shiokari Hot Spring 83 Hokaido
Shiokawa Beach 95 Okinawa-Honto
Shiokecho 36 Central Nagoya
Shiokusa 57 Greater Osaka
Shioma Beach 31 Hachijo-jima
Shiomachi 66 Himeji Castle
Shiomicho 74 Onomichi
Shiomicho 86 Shimanami Kaido
Shionoe Art Museum 87 Shikoku
Shionoe Hot Spring 69 Hiroshima & Western Honshu
Shionoha Hot Spring 54 Kansai Area
Shiosai Museum 23 Yokohama Area
Shiotsu Beach 39 Noto Peninsula
Shioya 22 Mt. Fuji & Around Tokyo
Shioyacho 72 Hagi
Shira-ike Jigoku (White Pond Hell) 91 Kannawa Hells Area
Shira-taki 22 Izu Islands
Shirabu Hot Spring 80 Aizu, Inawashiro & Ura-Bandai
Shirachimachi 92 Shimabara
Shirada 30 Izu Peninsula
Shirafuji-no-taki 83 Akan National Park
Shirafuji-taki 34 Central Honshu
Shiragikucho 38 Kanazawa
Shirahagimachi 81 Sendai
Shirahama 22 Mt. Fuji & Around Tokyo
Shirahama 54 Kansai Area
Shirahama Beach 77 Northern Honshu
Shirahama Beach 90 Kyusu
Shirahama Beach 97 Amami Oshima
Shirahama Chuo Beach 30 Izu Peninsula
Shirahama Flower Park 22 Mt. Fuji & Around Tokyo
Shirahama Limestone Cave 22 Mt. Fuji & Around Tokyo
Shirahama-ohama Beach 30 Izu Peninsula
Shirahata 26 Kamakura
Shirahone Hot Spring 40 Nagano & Matsumoto Areas
Shiraishi 73 Yamaguchi
Shiraishimachi 39 Noto Peninsula
Shiraita 40 Matsumoto
Shiraiti-no-daki 80 Aizu, Inawashiro & Ura-Bandai
Shiraito-no-taki 28 Mt. Fuji
Shiraito-no-taki 32 Nikko Town
Shiraito-no-taki 69 Hiroshima & Western Honshu
Shirakaba Art Museum 74 Onomichi
Shirakabe 37 Central Nagoya
Shirakami Sanchi Mountains 76 Shirakami Mountains
Shirakashicho 65 Asuka
Shirakata-honmachi 74 Matsue
Shirakawa 77 Northern Honshu
Shirakawa Sanchi Visitor Center 76 Shirakami Mountains
Shirakawa Tenno Imperial Mausoleum (Kasori-zuka) 46 Northern Kyoto
Shirakawa-go Historic Village 34 Shirakawa-go & Gokayama
Shiraki Beach 90 Kyusu
Shirako Beach 23 Mt. Fuji & Around Tokyo
Shirakocho 36 Central Nagoya
Shirakumo-no-taki 32 Nikko Area
Shiramizu Waterfall 90 Kyusu
Shiranuka 83 Hokaido
Shirao 55 Kansai
Shiraoi 82 Sado-ga Island

Shiraoi Ainu Museum 82 Sado-ga Island
Shiraoi Car Land 82 Sado-ga Island
Shiraoi-daki 82 Sado-ga Island
Shirasagi 4 Greater Tokyo
Shirasaki Kaiyo Park 54 Kansai Area
Shirasawa 76 Lake Towada
Shirasawa 76 Shirakami Mountains
Shirase Antarctic Expedition Memorial 77 Northern Honshu
Shirasugao Hot Spring 90 Kyusu
Shirasuna Beach 90 Kyusu
Shirataki Hot Spring 83 Hokaido
Shiratani-unsuikyo Starting Point 97 Yakushima
Shirataniso Folk Museum 67 Lake Biwa
Shiratsuchi Beach 68 Hiroshima & Western Honshu
Shirayama 34 Central Honshu
Shirayama Shrine Noh Stage 79 Hiraizumi & Ichinoseki
Shiretoko Five Lakes 83 Shiretoko National Park
Shiretoko Museum 83 Hokaido
Shiretoko National Park 83 Shiretoko National Park
Shiretoko Nature Center 83 Shiretoko National Park
Shirimizocho 48 Western Kyoto
Shiriuchi 82 Hokaido
Shiriuchi Hot Spring 82 Hokaido
Shiro-yama-zakura Wild Cherry Tree 79 Lake Tazawa
Shirogane 93 Fukuoka
Shiroganecho 24 Yokohama
Shiroganecho 6 Imperial Palace & Tokyo Station
Shiroganefudo-no-taki 82 Daisetsuzan National Park
Shiroi-no-taki 86 Shikoku
Shiroishi 77 Northern Honshu
Shiroiwa National Park 77 Northern Honshu
Shirokane 15 Meguro & Shinagawa
Shirokanedai 15 Meguro & Shinagawa
Shiromachi 66 Hikone Castle
Shiromama Cliff 30 Kozu-shima & Nii-jima
Shiromeguri 26 Kamakura
Shiromi 57 Greater Osaka
Shironosato 42 Kyoto
Shirotoritate 79 Hiraizumi & Ichinoseki
Shiroyama 39 Takayama
Shiroyama Lookout 91 Aso Area
Shiroyama Observatory 91 Kagoshima
Shiroyamacho 91 Kagoshima
Shisagasonocho 48 Western Kyoto
Shishi-kaikan Karakuri Museum 39 Takayama
Shishigatani 43 Central & Eastern Kyoto
Shishigatani Takagishicho 45 Kawaramachi & Gion
Shishizaki 66 Amano Hashidate
Shiso 54 Kansai Area
Shitadera-machi 61 Osaka Namba
Shitamachi 32 Kawagoe-little Edo
Shitamachi Museum 10 Asakusa, Ueno & Akihabara
Shitara 34 Central Honshu
Shitaru 30 Izu Peninsula
Shitaya 10 Asakusa, Ueno & Akihabara
Shitecho 43 Central & Eastern Kyoto
Shitenno-ji 61 Osaka Namba
Shitennoji 61 Osaka Namba
Shitoko Gajumaru-en Banyan Garden 96 Yakushima
Shiwa 77 Northern Honshu
Shiwaku Kimbansho Museum 87 Seto-ohasi Bridge
Shiwamachi 81 Sendai
Shizen Jimbun Museum 23 Yokohama Area
Shizenshi Hyohon-kan Museum 81 Sendai
Shizuichi 42 Kyoto
Shizukuishi 77 Northern Honshu
Shizuoka 30 Izu Peninsula
Shizuoka 34 Central Honshu
Shizuoka City Museum of Art 41 Shizuoka
Shizuoka Peace Museum 41 Shizuoka
Shizuoka Pref. 34 Central Honshu
Shobara 69 Hiroshima & Western Honshu
Shobo (Extinguishing Fire) Museum 15 Shinjuku
Shobu 75 Tottori
Shobu 81 Zao Onsen
Shobucho 65 Asuka
Shobuencho 46 Northern Kyoto
Shobuga-hama Beach 32 Nikko Area
Shobuikecho 65 Nara
Shochiku-za Theater 61 Osaka Namba
Shochu Museum 90 Kyusu

Shodai 92 Fukuoka
Shodencho 47 Northern Kyoto
Shodo-shima Giant Kannon 68 Shodo Island
Shodo-shima Olive Park & Sun Olive Onsen 68 Shodo Island
Shodoshima 68 Shodo Island
Shoeimachi 38 Kanazawa
Shofuku-ji 92 Nagasaki
Shogoin 43 Central & Eastern Kyoto
Shogoin Sannocho 45 Kawaramachi & Gion
Shogoin-nishimachi 43 Central & Eastern Kyoto
Shogoin-rengezocho 45 Kawaramachi & Gion
Shoin 88 Kotohira
Shoji 57 Greater Osaka
Shoji-higashi 57 Greater Osaka
Shoka Museum 28 Mt. Fuji
Shoke-daru 30 Izu Peninsula
Shokei Yashiki Residence 73 Miyajima
Shoken 37 Central Nagoya
Shokuninmachi 39 Gujo Hachiman
Shomutenno-ryo (Mausoleum) 65 Nara
Shonai 41 Matsumoto
Shonai 77 Northern Honshu
Shonai Eiga Mura Open Set 81 Dewa Sanzen
Shonin-ga-hama Park 91 Beppu Area
Shonin-ga-hama Sand Bath Hot Spring 91 Beppu Area
Shonin-no-taki 31 Oshima
Shoo 69 Hiroshima & Western Honshu
Shoojicho 45 Kawaramachi & Gion
Shopping Arcades 89 Takamatsu
Shoryu-no-taki 82 Daisetsuzan National Park
Shosanbetsu 83 Hokaido
Shosei-en Garden 43 Central & Eastern Kyoto
Shoshoicho 44 Kawaramachi & Gion
Shosuikaku 46 Northern Kyoto
Shotenshita 57 Greater Osaka
Shoto 12 Roppongi, Shibuya, Omotesando, Harajuku & Meiji Shrine
Shoto Art Museum 12 Roppongi, Shibuya, Omotesando, Harajuku & Meiji Shrine
Shotoku Memorial Picture Gallery 15 Shinjuku
Showa 75 Kurashiki
Showa 77 Northern Honshu
Showa Ward 35 Nagoya Area
Showa-dori 56 Greater Osaka
Showa-minamidori 56 Greater Osaka
Showa-no-mori Park 80 Aizu, Inawashiro & Ura-Bandai
Showacho 31 Atami
Showacho 91 Miyazaki
Showamachi 38 Kanazawa
Showamachi 39 Takayama
Showamachi 71 Hiroshima
Showmachi 88 Matsuyama
Shuba Beach 97 Amami Oshima
Shudokan (Martial Art Training Hall) 59 Osaka Station
Shugakuin 47 Northern Kyoto
Shugakuin Rikyu Imperial Villa 47 Northern Kyoto
Shuhoshiraio-no-taki 68 Hiroshima & Western Honshu
Shujakucho 49 Western Kyoto
Shukaen 74 Onomichi
Shukkei-en Garden 71 Hiroshima
Shukkei-en Path and Bridges 71 Hiroshima
Shuku 79 Hiraizumi & Ichinoseki
Shukuincho 65 Nara
Shukunegi 80 Sado-ga Island
Shunan 68 Hiroshima & Western Honshu
Shuneicho 49 Western Kyoto
Shuntokucho 57 Greater Osaka
Shuri Castle (Main Palace) 95 Shuri Castle
Shuri-akatacho 95 Shuri Castle
Shuri-ikehatacho 95 Shuri Castle
Shuri-mawashicho 95 Shuri Castle
Shuri-onakacho 95 Shuri Castle
Shuri-samukawacho 95 Shuri Castle
Shuri-tonokuracho 95 Shuri Castle
Shuzeicho 49 Western Kyoto
Shuzen-ji Niji-no-sato Amusement Park 30 Izu Peninsula
Shuzenan 47 Northern Kyoto
Shuzenji 30 Izu Peninsula
Shuzenji Hot Spring 30 Izu Peninsula
Sichirigahama 26 Kamakura
Sichirigahama Beach 26 Kamakura
Sichirigahama-higashi 26 Kamakura
Silk Center & Museum 25 Kawasaki
Silk, Art and Archeological Museum 41 Lake Suwa
Silver Beach 68 Shodo Island
Singonzaka Slope 61 Osaka Namba
Sintomi 9 Ginza, Tsukiji & Tokyo Tower
Sirahama 54 Kansai Area

Shiratsuruhama Beach 90 Kyusu
Ski Jam Katsuyama 34 Central Honshu
Ski Park Kambiki Ski Area 68 Hiroshima & Western Honshu
Sky Valley Ski Area 69 Hiroshima & Western Honshu
SL Yamaguchi Train 73 Yamaguchi
Snow Harp Ski Area 40 Nagano & Matsumoto Areas
Snow Town Yeti 28 Mt. Fuji
Sobama Beach 80 Sado-ga Island
Sobe 77 Lake Towada
Sobe 94 Naha
Sobetsu 82 Sado-ga Island
Sobokatamuki Natural Park 90 Kyusu
Sodayama Hot Spring 86 Shikoku
Sodayucho 73 Yamaguchi
Soekawacho 64 Nara
Soemoncho 61 Osaka Namba
Sofuku-ji 92 Nagasaki
Sogisui Spring 39 Gujo Hachiman
Sogo Museum of Art 24 Yokohama
Sohara 92 Fukuoka
Soja 69 Hiroshima & Western Honshu
Soka 22 Mt. Fuji & Around Tokyo
Sokei Beach 95 Okinawa-Honto
Sokokura 29 Hakone Town
Sokokura Hot Spring 29 Hakone Town
Sol-fa Oda Ski Area 86 Shikoku
Soma 76 Shirakami Mountains
Somedonocho 43 Central & Eastern Kyoto
Someikan Museum 41 Lake Suwa
Somon-cho 46 Northern Kyoto
Sonezaki 57 Greater Osaka
Sonezaki-shinchi 58 Osaka Station
Soni 54 Kansai Area
Sonohyan-Utaki Ishi-Mon Gate 95 Shuri Castle
Sonota 29 Lake Kawaguchi
Sonota 68 Shodo Island
Sony Historical Museum 15 Meguro & Shinagawa
Soo 90 Kyusu
Sorincho 44 Kawaramachi & Gion
Soryu-no-taki 77 Lake Towada
Sosa 37 Mt. Fuji & Around Tokyo
Sosakucho 47 Northern Kyoto
Sosei-taki 33 Nikko Area
Soshigaya 4 Greater Tokyo
Sosogi 39 Noto Peninsula
Sosogi-kagian Coast 39 Noto Peninsula
Sosu 95 Okinawa-honto
Sotetsu Honda Theater 24 Yokohama
Soto 53 Uji Town
Soto-kanda 7 Imperial Palace & Tokyo Station
Soto-nakabaracho 74 Matsue
Sotogaoka 31 Shimoda
Sotokaifu Beach 80 Sado-ga Island
Sotoura Beach 30 Izu Peninsula
Sotowa Beach 54 Kansai Area
Sotoyama 79 Hiraizumi & Ichinoseki
Souemoncho 57 Greater Osaka
Sounkyo Hot Spring 82 Daisetsuzan National Park
South Palace 95 Shuri Castle
Southern Park Nomozaki Botanical Garden 90 Kyusu
Souvenir Center 74 Matsue
Sowajiura Beach 39 Noto Peninsula
Soyujimachi 39 Takayama
Spa Azelea 21 91 Aso Area
Spa Beach 91 Central Beppu
Spa Rakan Hot Spring 68 Hiroshima & Western Honshu
Spa World 61 Osaka Namba
Spa Yume-tamatebako 91 Kannawa Hells Area
Sportology Gallery 56 Greater Osaka
St Francis Xavier Memorial Church 73 Yama-guchi
Stained Art Glass Museum 91 Yufuin
Stained Glass Museum 38 Kanazawa
Stationery Museum 41 Nagano
Statue of Date Masamune 81 Sendai
Statue of Ii Naosuke 66 Hikone Castle
Statue of Liberty 21 Odaiba
Statue of Mizube-no-momokun 75 Okamaya
Statue of the Girl in Red Shoes with Her Parents 84 Otaru
Statute of Tokugawa Ieyasu 41 Shizuoka
Straw Crafts Museum 66 Kinosaki
Strawberry Park 39 Noto Peninsula
Striped House Museum of Art 13 Roppongi, Shibuya, Omotesando, Harajuku & Meiji Shrine
Suda 76 Shirakami Mountains
Sudama Hot Spring 34 Central Honshu

Sueda Art Museum 91 Yufuin
Suehiro 79 Hiraizumi & Ichinoseki
Suehiro 91 Miyazaki
Suehiro Brewery 80 Aizu, Inawashiro & Ura-Bandai
Suehirocho 24 Yokohama
Suehirocho 56 Greater Osaka
Suehirocho 59 Osaka Station
Suehirocho 84 Hakodate
Suehiromachi 39 Takayama
Suehiromachi 88 Matsuyama
Suetomo 37 Inuyama
Suetsugucho 74 Matsue
Sueyoshicho 24 Yokohama
Sueyoshicho 44 Kawaramachi & Gion
Sugacho 15 Shinjuku
Sugaharacho 59 Osaka Station
Sugamo 17 Ikebukuro
Sugasawa 78 Kakunodate
Sugimoto-dera 27 Kamakura
Sugimotocho 45 Kawaramachi & Gion
Sugimura 37 Central Nagoya
Suginami 4 Greater Tokyo
Suginami Science Museum 4 Greater Tokyo
Suginami Ward Folk Museum 4 Greater Tokyo
Sugino Costume Museum 18 Meguro & Shinagawa
Suginoi Palace 91 Beppu Area
Suginoura 73 Miyajima
Sugioka Calligraphy Museum 65 Nara
Sugisaka 42 Kyoto
Sugiyacho 44 Kawaramachi & Gion
Suguhiramachi 39 Noto Peninsula
Suhara 30 Izu Peninsula
Suido 17 Ikebukuro
Suidocho 6 Imperial Palace & Tokyo Station
Suidocho 93 Kumamoto
Suigo Sawara Water Garden 23 Mt. Fuji & Around Tokyo
Suigo-tsukuba Q.N.P. 23 Mt. Fuji & Around Tokyo
Suimoncho 65 Nara
Suishacho 47 Northern Kyoto
Suishohama Beach 54 Kansai Area
Suita City 55 Osaka Area
Sujaku 49 Western Kyoto
Sujaku-hozocho 49 Western Kyoto
Sujikaibashicho 46 Northern Kyoto
Sujiyacho 44 Kawaramachi & Gion
Suka Gogodo Art Museum 92 Nagasaki
Sukadori 86 Uwajima
Sukagawa 80 Aizu, Inawashiro & Ura-bandai
Suketohoncho 89 Tokushima
Sukiyacho 36 Central Nagoya
Sukuji Beach 96 Yaeyama Islands
Sukumo 86 Shikoku
Sukumogawa 29 Hakone
Suma AqualifePark 55 Osaka Area
Sumatakyo Hot Spring 34 Central Honshu
Sumida 5 Greater Tokyo
Sumida City Museum 11 Asakusa, Ueno & Akihabara
Sumiikecho 36 Central Nagoya
Suminoe Ward 55 Osaka Area
Suminokuracho 48 Western Kyoto
Sumita 77 Northern Honshu
Sumiya Museum 49 Western Kyoto
Sumiyashirocho 46 Northern Kyoto
Sumiyo-shima Beach 90 Kyusu
Sumiyoshi 93 Fukuoka
Sumiyoshi Hot Spring 80 Sado-ga Island
Sumiyoshi Ward 55 Osaka Area
Sumiyoshicho 15 Shinjuku
Sumiyoshicho 70 Hiroshima
Sumiyoshicho 84 Otaru
Sumiyoshicho 91 Kagoshima
Sumo Stadium, Sumo Museum 11 Asakusa, Ueno & Akihabara
Sumoto 87 Shikoku
Sumoto Castle 54 Kansai Area
Sumoto Hot Spring 87 Shikoku
Sumpu Castle 41 Shizuoka
Sumpu Castle Park 41 Shizuoka
Sumpu Museum 41 Shizuoka
Sun 35 Nagoya Area
Sun Beach 87 Shikoku
Sun Kurino Museum 31 Atami
Sunagawa 83 Hokaido
Sunagocho 74 Matsue
Sunayama Beach 97 Miyako Islands
Sunayu Hot Spring 83 Akan National Park
Sunhine 60 4 Greater Tokyo
Sunkei-kaikan Museum 39 Takayama
Sunport Takamatsu 89 Takamatsu
Sunpucho 41 Shizuoka
Sunritz Hattori Museum of Art 41 Lake Suwa

Sunset Beach 82 Hokaido
Sunset Beach 86 Shimanami Kaido
Sunset Beach 95 Okinawa-Honto
Sunset Beach 96 Yaeyama Islands
Sunshine 60 17 Ikebukuro
Sunshine City 17 Ikebukuro
Sunto District 30 Izu Peninsula
Suntory Museum 56 Greater Osaka
Suntory Museum of Art 13 Roppongi, Shibuya, Omotesando, Harajuku & Meiji Shrine
Suntory Yamazaki Distillery 42 Kyoto
Suo-oshima 68 Hiroshima & Western Honshu
Suruga-machi 65 Nara
Surugacho 41 Shizuoka
Susaki 79 Hiraizumi & Ichinoseki
Susaki 86 Shikoku
Susakimachi 93 Fukuoka
Susami 54 Kansai Area
Susano-dori 62 Kobe
Susono 22 Mt. Fuji & Around Tokyo
Susono City 28 Mt. Fuji
Susuki-no-babacho 48 Western Kyoto
Sutokuin 56 Greater Osaka
Suttsu 82 Hokaido
Suwa 4 Greater Tokyo
Suwa 40 Nagano & Matsumoto Areas
Suwa 57 Greater Osaka
Suwa 92 Nagasaki
Suwa City 41 Lake Suwa
Suwa City Art Museum 41 Lake Suwa
Suwa Galass-no-sato 41 Lake Suwa
Suwa Museum 35 Nagoya Area
Suwa Shrine 92 Nagasaki
Suwacho 25 Yokohama
Suwacho 41 Nagano
Suwamae 80 Aizu, Inawashiro & Ura-bandai
Suwayamacho 63 Kobe
Suzaka 34 Central Honshu
Suzu 39 Noto Peninsula
Suzu 66 Amano Hashidate
Suzu Enden Mura 34 Central Honshu
Suzu Hot Spring 39 Noto Peninsula
Suzu Sea Salt Farm 39 Noto Peninsula
Suzuka 54 Kansai Area
Suzuka Circuit 54 Kansai Area
Suzukawacho 48 Western Kyoto
Suzuki Daisetsu Museum 38 Kanazawa
Suzumenomiya 22 Mt. Fuji & Around Tokyo
Suzusawa 79 Hiraizumi & Ichinoseki

Ta-taki 95 Okinawa-Honto
Tabata 5 Greater Tokyo
Tabata Bunshimura Memorial Museum 5 Greater Tokyo
Tabayama 22 Mt. Fuji & Around Tokyo
Tabi 30 Izu Peninsula
Tabuchiyamacho 48 Western Kyoto
Tabuse 68 Hiroshima & Western Honshu
Tachibana 36 Central Nagoya
Tachibana 5 Greater Tokyo
Tachibana 57 Greater Osaka
Tachibana 65 Asuka
Tachibana 68 Shodo Island
Tachibana-dori 62 Kobe
Tachibanacho 44 Kawaramachi & Gion
Tachibanacho 66 Hikone Castle
Tachibanadori- higashi 91 Miyazaki
Tachibanadori-nishi 91 Miyazaki
Tachibe 65 Asuka
Tachikara 79 Hanamaki
Tachikawacho 75 Tottori
Tachiurihigashicho 44 Kawaramachi & Gion
Tadakawa 53 Uji Town
Tadami 77 Northern Honshu
Tadaoka 55 Osaka Area
Tadeharacho 47 Northern Kyoto
Tadekuracho 47 Northern Kyoto
Tadotsu 87 Shikoku
Taen Beach 97 Amami Oshima
Taga 54 Kansai Area
Taga Shrine & Sex Museum 86 Uwajima
Taga Town 67 Lake Biwa
Tagaki 34 Central Honshu
Tagami 77 Northern Honshu
Tagata District 30 Izu Peninsula
Tagawa 56 Greater Osaka
Tagawa 90 Kyusu
Tagawa-kita 56 Greater Osaka
Tago 30 Izu Peninsula
Tagonoura Beach 22 Mt. Fuji & Around Tokyo
Tahara 34 Central Honshu
Taharano 30 Izu Peninsula
Taho-to Pagoda 73 Miyajima
Tai 68 Shodo Island
Taiaki 76 Shirakami Mountains
Taihaku Hot Spring 76 Shirakami Mountains
Taihakumachi 93 Fukuoka

Taihama Beach 68 Shodo Island
Taihei 11 Asakusa, Ueno & Akihabara
Taiheizan 79 Hiraizumi & Ichinoseki
Taiheji 57 Greater Osaka
Taiho 95 Okinawa-honto
Taiji Whale Museum 54 Kansai Area
Taiki 83 Hokaido
Taiko 36 Central Nagoya
Taiko Drum Museum 11 Asakusa, Ueno & Akihabara
Taimachi 38 Kanazawa
Taiminato Park 69 Hiroshima & Western Honshu
Tainai 77 Northern Honshu
Taisetsu Kogen Hot Spring 82 Daisetsuzan National Park
Taishi 54 Kansai Area
Taishi Town 64 Around Nara
Taishibashi 57 Greater Osaka
Taishido 4 Greater Tokyo
Taisho Hot Spring 86 Shikoku
Taisho Pond 40 Nagano & Matsumoto Areas
Taisho Ward 56 Greater Osaka
Taishocho 36 Central Nagoya
Taishocho 74 Matsue
Taishogun 49 Western Kyoto
Taishomachi 39 Gujo Hachiman
Taito 7 Imperial Palace & Tokyo Station
Taiyo 23 Mt. Fuji & Around Tokyo
Taiyujicho 59 Osaka Station
Tajima 57 Greater Osaka
Tajima Airport 54 Kansai Area
Tajima-sangaku Natural Park 69 Hiroshima & Western Honshu
Tajimi 34 Central Honshu
Tajimi City 35 Nagoya Area
Tajimi Mino Pottery Museum 35 Nagoya Area
Tajiri 55 Osaka Area
Tajiri Town 55 Osaka Area
Tajiricho 46 Northern Kyoto
Taka 54 Kansai Area
Takaban 4 Greater Tokyo
Takabatakecho 65 Nara
Takabyaku 33 Nikko Area
Takachiho Freshwater Aquarium 93 Takachiho
Takachiho Gorge 93 Takachiho
Takachiho Hot Spring 93 Takachiho
Takachihodori 91 Miyazaki
Takachihoso ShrineNight Kagura (Shinto Dance) 93 Takachiho
Takada 17 Ikebukuro
Takada 79 Hiraizumi & Ichinoseki
Takada Samurai House Site 38 Kanazawa
Takadacho 48 Western Kyoto
Takadai-nishi 42 Kyoto
Takadamae 79 Hiraizumi & Ichinoseki
Takadanobaba 16 Ikebukuro
Takadono 57 Greater Osaka
Takadoro (Lantern Tower) 88 Kotohira
Takagamine 46 Northern Kyoto
Takagi 81 Matsushima
Takagicho 47 Northern Kyoto
Takahagi 77 Northern Honshu
Takahama 54 Kansai Area
Takahama Beach 90 Kyusu
Takahama City 35 Nagoya Area
Takahana 76 Shirakami Mountains
Takaharu 90 Kyusu
Takahashi 69 Hiroshima & Western Honshu
Takahashi Yuichi Museum 88 Kotohira
Takahashicho 44 Kawaramachi & Gion
Takahata 65 Nara
Takahata 77 Northern Honshu
Takahicho 49 Western Kyoto
Takahira 92 Nagasaki
Takaichi District 64 Around Nara
Takaida 57 Greater Osaka
Takaida-motomachi 57 Greater Osaka
Takaida-nishi 57 Greater Osaka
Takaidahon-dori 57 Greater Osaka
Takaidanaka 57 Greater Osaka
Takaido-higashi 4 Greater Tokyo
Takaido-nishi 4 Greater Tokyo
Takaishi City 55 Osaka Area
Takajima 92 Shimabara
Takajo 41 Shizuoka
Takajomachi 66 Himeji Castle
Takajomachi 76 Hirosaki
Takaki 79 Hanamaki
Takakuracho 57 Greater Osaka
Takamagahara Hot Spring 34 Central Honshu
Takamagahara Hot Spring 40 Nagano & Matsumoto Areas
Takamaichicho 65 Nara
Takamatsu 16 Ikebukuro
Takamatsu 87 Shikoku

Takamatsu Airport 87 Shikoku
Takamatsu City Art Museum 89 Takamatsu
Takamatsu-jo Tenshu Tower Site 89 Takamatsu
Takamatsuzuka Hekiga-kan 65 Asuka
Takami 56 Greater Osaka
Takamicho 37 Inuyama
Takamine Hot Spring 22 Mt. Fuji & Around Tokyo
Takamori 34 Central Honshu
Takamori 80 Aizu, Inawashiro & Ura-bandai
Takamori 91 Aso Area
Takamori Onsenkan 91 Aso Area
Takanawa 15 Meguro & Shinagawa
Takanawacho 46 Northern Kyoto
Takanawatecho 46 Northern Kyoto
Takano 27 Kamakura
Takano 47 Northern Kyoto
Takano Kogen Ski Area 69 Hiroshima & Western Honshu
Takanodai 4 Greater Tokyo
Takanosu 76 Shirakami Mountains
Takao 92 Nagasaki
Takao 42 Kyoto
Takaodai 30 Izu Peninsula
Takaoka 39 Noto Peninsula
Takaoka 92 Nagasaki
Takaokamachi 38 Kanazawa
Takara 92 Nagasaki
Takaramachi 38 Kanazawa
Takaramachi 5 Greater Tokyo
Takaramachi 71 Hiroshima
Takarazuka 54 Kansai Area
Takarazuka City 55 Osaka Area
Takasago 54 Kansai Area
Takasago 93 Fukuoka
Takasago Shuzo Museum 73 Tsuwano
Takasagocho 42 Kyoto
Takasagomachi 88 Matsuyama
Takasaka 80 Aizu, Inawashiro & Ura-bandai
Takasaki 22 Mt. Fuji & Around Tokyo
Takase Canal 44 Kawaramachi & Gion
Takasecho 57 Greater Osaka
Takashi 90 Kagoshima
Takashiba 33 Nikko Area
Takashima 24 Yokohama
Takashima 54 Kansai Area
Takashima Castle 41 Lake Suwa
Takashima City 67 Lake Biwa
Takasu 82 Daisetsuzan National Park
Takasucho 56 Greater Osaka
Takatori Town 64 Around Nara
Takatsu 23 Yokohama Area
Takatsudo Valley 22 Mt. Fuji & Around Tokyo
Takatsuka Park 54 Kansai Area
Takatsukacho 49 Western Kyoto
Takatsuki 54 Kansai Area
Takaya 26 Kamakura
Takayama 34 Central Honshu
Takayama 47 Northern Kyoto
Takayama Castle Site 39 Takayama
Takayama Hikokuro Statue 45 Kawaramachi & Gion
Takayama Jinya 39 Takayama
Takayama Matsuri Yatai-kaikan Museum (Festival Floats Exhibition Hall) 39 Takayama
Takayama Showa-kan Museum 39 Takayama
Takayama-shita 81 Matsushima
Takazecho 49 Western Kyoto
Takebashicho 36 Central Nagoya
Takebe 39 Noto Peninsula
Takeda 39 Noto Peninsula
Takeda 50 Southern Kyoto
Takeda Botanical Garden 47 Northern Kyoto
Takedao Hot Spring 55 Osaka Area
Takegahama 31 Shimoda
Takehara 69 Hiroshima & Western Honshu
Takejima 56 Greater Osaka
Takekawa Folk Museum 34 Central Honshu
Takenokozawa Hot Spring 81 Dewa Sanzen
Takenokuchi Beach 87 Shikoku
Takenosako 93 Takachiho
Takenouchicho 47 Northern Kyoto
Takenoyu Ski Area 40 Nagano & Matsumoto Areas
Takeo 90 Kyusu
Takeshita-dori Shopping Street 12 Roppongi, Shibuya, Omotesando, Harajuku & Meiji Shrine
Taketa 90 Kyusu
Taketomi 96 Yaeyama Islands
Taketomi Mingei-kan 96 Yaeyama Islands
Takeura Hot Spring 82 Sado-ga Island
Takewaramachi 78 Kakunodate
Takewaramachi 88 Matsuyama
Takeyacho 44 Kawaramachi & Gion
Takeyacho 71 Hiroshima

Takezaki Beach 95 Okinawa & The Southwest Islands
Takezakicho 72 Shimonoseki
Takezawa Marsh 40 Nagano & Matsumoto Areas
Taki 54 Kansai Area
Takibe Hot Spring 68 Hiroshima & Western Honshu
Takigahanacho 47 Northern Kyoto
Takiguchi Undersea Park 86 Shikoku
Takihata Lake Park 55 Osaka Area
Takii-motomachi 57 Greater Osaka
Takii-nishimachi 57 Greater Osaka
Takikawa 83 Hokaido
Takimachi 73 Miyajima
Takino Suzuran Hillside Nat'l Park 82 Sado-ga Island
Takinogawa 4 Greater Tokyo
Takinomiya 68 Shodo Island
Takinosawa 76 Lake Towada
Takinosawa 79 Hiraizumi & Ichinoseki
Takinosawa Viewpoint 76 Lake Towada
Takinoue 83 Hokaido
Takinoyu 23 Mt. Fuji & Around Tokyo
Takiwacho 24 Yokohama
Takiyamacho 62 Kobe
Tako 23 Mt. Fuji & Around Tokyo
Takohama Beach 30 Kozu-shima & Nii-jima
Takojima 39 Noto Peninsula
Takoma 30 Izu Peninsula
Takoyakushicho 44 Kawaramachi & Gion
Taku 90 Kyusu
Takumicho 32 Nikko Town
Tama 23 Yokohama Area
Tamachi 33 Narita
Tamachi 41 Nagano
Tamachi 75 Okamaya
Tamadenaka 57 Greater Osaka
Tamae 72 Hagi
Tamaeura 72 Hagi
Tamagawa 4 Greater Tokyo
Tamagawa 56 Greater Osaka
Tamagawa-den'enchofu 4 Greater Tokyo
Tamagawa-dori 65 Mt. Koya
Tamagawacho 38 Kanazawa
Tamaki 54 Kansai Area
Tamamocho 89 Takamatsu
Tamana 90 Kyusu
Tamano 69 Hiroshima & Western Honshu
Tamanoura Beach 54 Kansai Area
Tamaokacho 47 Northern Kyoto
Tamari 23 Mt. Fuji & Around Tokyo
Tamatori-zaki Observatory 96 Yaeyama Islands
Tamatsu 57 Greater Osaka
Tamatsukuri 33 Narita
Tamatsukuri 57 Greater Osaka
Tamatsukuri Hot Spring 69 Hiroshima & Western Honshu
Tamatsukuri-motomachi 57 Greater Osaka
Tamatsushimacho 44 Kawaramachi & Gion
Tamaudun (Tomb of Ryukyu King) 95 Shuri Castle
Tamazawa 30 Izu Peninsula
Tamogimachi 76 Hirosaki
Tamon-dori 62 Kobe
Tamon-jo Castle Site 65 Nara
Tamoncho 45 Kawaramachi & Gion
Tamoncho 65 Nara
Tamugimata Hot Spring 81 Dewa Sanzen
Tamura 77 Northern Honshu
Tamura Memorial Museum 79 Hiraizumi & Ichinoseki
Tamurabizencho 49 Western Kyoto
Tanabata Festival 81 Sendai
Tanabe 54 Kansai Area
Tanabe 57 Greater Osaka
Tanabe Art Museum 74 Matsue
Tanagura 77 Northern Honshu
Tanaka 30 Izu Peninsula
Tanaka 43 Central & Eastern Kyoto
Tanaka 47 Northern Kyoto
Tanaka 53 Uji Town
Tanaka 56 Greater Osaka
Tanaka 91 Yufuin
Tanakacho 44 Kawaramachi & Gion
Tanakacho 65 Asuka
Tanakamachi 72 Shimonoseki
Tanamoricho 48 Western Kyoto
Tanashiro Swamp 76 Shirakami Mountains
Tanayu Hot Spring 91 Beppu Area
Tanba 54 Kansai Area
Tanbasayama Keikoku-no-mori Park 54 Kansai Area
Tancha 95 Okinawa-honto
Tanchozuru Nat'l Park 83 Hokaido
Tango Folk Museum 66 Amano Hashidate

Tani 93 Fukuoka
Tanidayama 48 Western Kyoto
Tanigamine 64 Mt. Koya
Tanigatsujikocho 48 Western Kyoto
Tanigawa 88 Kotohira
Tanigawacho 45 Kawaramachi & Gion
Taniguchi 49 Western Kyoto
Tanimachi 61 Osaka Namba
Tanisagari 53 Uji Town
Taniya 39 Noto Peninsula
Tanna Rift Park 30 Izu Peninsula
Tannojicho-kita 61 Osaka Namba
Tano 87 Shikoku
Tanohata 77 Northern Honshu
Tanoura 68 Shodo Island
Tanoura Beach 68 Hiroshima & Western Honshu
Tanouracho 86 Shimanami Kaido
Tanoyumachi 91 Central Beppu
Tansho 22 Mt. Fuji & Around Tokyo
Tansumachi 6 Imperial Palace & Tokyo Station
Tanzawa Oyama Q.N.P. 22 Mt. Fuji & Around Tokyo
Tao Ruins 87 Iya Valley
Tara 90 Kyusu
Taragi 90 Kyusu
Taraino 39 Noto Peninsula
Taranokidai Ski Area 81 Dewa Sanzen
Taro-daki 86 Shikoku
Tarui 54 Kansai Area
Tarui Southern Beach 55 Osaka Area
Tarumi 89 Matsuyama
Tarumi-taki 39 Noto Peninsula
Tarumiyamacho 48 Western Kyoto
Tarumizu 90 Kyusu
Tarutama & Jigoku Hot Spring 90 Aso Area
Taruyacho 72 Hagi
Tashima 75 Tottori
Tashiro 80 Aizu, Inawashiro & Ura-bandai
Tashiro Hot Spring 77 Northern Honshu
Tashirodake National Park 77 Northern Honshu
Tashirotai 77 Lake Towada
Tassa 80 Sado-ga Island
Tassha Beach 80 Sado-ga Island
Tatado Beach 30 Izu Peninsula
Tatara 23 Mt. Fuji & Around Tokyo
Tatara Hot Spring 86 Shimanami Kaido
Tateba 57 Greater Osaka
Tateishi 5 Greater Tokyo
Tatekawa 5 Greater Tokyo
Tatemachi 38 Kanazawa
Tatemachi 49 Western Kyoto
Tateshina Hot Spring 34 Central Honshu
Tatetsu Residence (Tomachi Museum) 78 Kakunodate
Tatewakimachi 80 Aizu, Inawashiro & Ura-bandai
Tateyacho 56 Greater Osaka
Tateyama 22 Mt. Fuji & Around Tokyo
Tateyama 92 Nagasaki
Tateyama Ropeway & Kurobe Cablecar 40 Nagano & Matsumoto Areas
Tateyama Sangaku Ski Area 40 Nagano & Matsumoto Areas
Tateyama Snow Corridor 40 Nagano & Matsumoto Areas
Tatsugaike 37 Inuyama
Tatsuko Statue 78 Lake Tazawa
Tatsumi-higashi 57 Greater Osaka
Tatsumi-kita 57 Greater Osaka
Tatsumi-minami 57 Greater Osaka
Tatsumi-naka 57 Greater Osaka
Tatsumi-nishi 57 Greater Osaka
Tatsumicho 45 Kawaramachi & Gion
Tatsuno 34 Central Honshu
Tatsuno 54 Kansai Area
Tatsunoo 65 Yoshina
Tatsusawa-fudo-daki 80 Aizu, Inawashiro & Ura-Bandai
Tatsutacho 91 Central Beppu
Tawara Hot Spring 68 Hiroshima & Western Honshu
Tawarahoncho 31 Atami
Tawaramoto Town 64 Around Nara
Tawarayacho 44 Kawaramachi & Gion
Tayabucho 48 Western Kyoto
Tazawa Hot Spring 40 Nagano & Matsumoto Areas
Tazawa-ko Swiss-mura 78 Lake Tazawa
Tazawako Herb Garden 79 Lake Tazawa
Tazawako Historical Museum 79 Lake Tazawa
Tazawako-kata 79 Lake Tazawa
Tazawako-obonai 79 Lake Tazawa
Tazawakokazawa 79 Lake Tazawa
Tebiro 26 Kamakura
Teein Art Museum 23 Yokohama Area

Tegaicho 65 Nara
Tegata 78 Akita
Tegata-gakuenmachi 78 Akita
Tegata-karamiden 78 Akita
Tegata-kyukamachi 78 Akita
Tegata-shinsakaemachi 78 Akita
Tegata-sumiyoshicho 78 Akita
Tegata-tanaka 78 Akita
Tegata-yamazakicho 78 Akita
Tegatayama- nishimachi 78 Akita
Teianmaenocho 44 Kawaramachi & Gion
Tempozan Big Ferris Wheel 56 Greater Osaka
Tenbincho 69 Western Kyoto
Tendo 77 Northern Honshu
Tengachaya 57 Greater Osaka
Tengachaya-higashi 57 Greater Osaka
Tengendai Kogen Ski Area 80 Aizu, Inawashiro & Ura-Bandai
Tengumori Museum 81 Dewa Sanzen
Tenjikusan-koen 65 Mt. Koya
Tenjimbara Botanical Garden 30 Izu Peninsula
Tenjin 92 Nagasaki
Tenjin 53 Uji Town
Tenjin-nishimachi 59 Osaka Station
Tenjinbashi 57 Greater Osaka
Tenjincho 37 Inuyama
Tenjincho 75 Okamaya
Tenjincho 75 Tottori
Tenjindai 53 Uji Town
Tenjindori 73 Yamaguchi
Tenjinmachi 38 Kanazawa
Tenjinmachi 74 Matsue
Tenjinmae 89 Takamatsu
Tenjinmine 33 Narita
Tenjinmoricho 46 Northern Kyoto
Tenjinyamacho 36 Central Nagoya
Tenkada 78 Hanamaki
Tenkawa 64 Around Nara
Tenma 59 Osaka Station
Tenma Tenjin Hanjo-tei Rakugo Theater 59 Osaka Station
Tenmabashi 57 Greater Osaka
Tenmabashi-kyomachi 59 Osaka Station
Tenmacho 41 Shizuoka
Tenmacho 70 Hiroshima
Tenmacho 74 Onomichi
Tenmancho 91 Central Beppu
Tenmanmachi 39 Takayama
Tenmayacho 49 Western Kyoto
Tennami 33 Narita
Tenninkyo Hot Spring 82 Daisetsuzan National Park
Tennocho 43 Central & Eastern Kyoto
Tennocho 62 Kobe
Tennodani-higashifuku 62 Kobe
Tennodani-higashifukuyama 62 Kobe
Tennoden 57 Greater Osaka
Tennogawa Park 35 Nagoya Area
Tennoji 61 Osaka Namba
Tennoji Ward 57 Greater Osaka
Tennoji Zoo 61 Osaka Namba
Tennojicho-kita 57 Greater Osaka
Tennojicho-minami 57 Greater Osaka
Tennokawa Hot Spring 64 Around Nara
Tennozaka 37 Inuyama
Tenpaku 37 Inuyama
Tenpaku Ward 35 Nagoya Area
Tenpaku-matsushita 37 Inuyama
Tenri 54 Kansai Area
Tenri City 64 Around Nara
Tenryu 34 Central Honshu
Tenryu-ji 48 Western Kyoto
Tensha Garden 86 Uwajima
Tenshukaku Ruins 72 Hagi
Tenyamachi 93 Fukuoka
Teppocho 88 Matsuyama
Teppomachi 39 Takayama
Teppomachi 76 Hirosaki
Teppomachi 81 Sendai
Tera 92 Nagasaki
Tera Machi 65 Nara
Terabun 27 Kamakura
Teradacho 61 Osaka Namba
Teradani 47 Northern Kyoto
Teradaya 50 Fushimi Area
Terahata 37 Inuyama
Teramachi 38 Kanazawa
Teramachi 70 Hiroshima
Teramachi 72 Hagi
Teramachi 74 Matsue
Teramachi 88 Kushima
Teramachi 92 Shimabara
Teramaecho 57 Greater Osaka
Terarura Hot Spring 90 Kyusu
Terasako 93 Takachiho

Terashita 37 Inuyama
Teruitate 79 Hiraizumi & Ichinoseki
Terukuni 93 Fukuoka
Terukuni Bunko 91 Kagoshima
Teshikaga (Mashu) Hot Spring 83 Akan National Park
Teshikaga 83 Hokaido
Teshio 83 Hokaido
Teshiogawa Hot Spring 83 Hokaido
Tessenkai Noh Theater 13 Roppongi, Shibuya, Omotesando, Harajuku & Meiji Shrine
The Bank of Japan Otaru Museum 84 Otaru
The Electricity Museum 36 Central Nagoya
The Five Mountain Peaks 76 Shirakami Mountains
The Former Hokkaido Government Building 85 Sapporo
The Hiroshima City Museum of Contemporary Art 71 Hiroshima
The Imperial Palace East Garden 6 Imperial Palace & Tokyo Station
The Instant Ramen Museum 55 Osaka Area
The Kagawa Museum 89 Takamatsu
The Kofuku-ji National Treasure Museum 65 Nara
The Memorial Hall of Yoko Gushiken 96 Ishigaki City
The Monument of Tennojimura 61 Osaka Namba
The Museum 12 Roppongi, Shibuya, Omotesando, Harajuku & Meiji Shrine
The Museum of Modern Art, Kamakura & Hayama 27 Kamakura
The Museum of Modern Japanese Literature Narita 33 Narita
The Nawa Insect Museum 35 Nagoya Area
The Northern End of Japan Monument 83 Hokaido
The Remaining Stone's of Osaka Castle Memorial Park Michi no Eki 68 Shodo Island
The Shin Nagoya Musical Theatre 36 Central Nagoya
The Sky Wheel 21 Odaiba
The Tale of Genji Museum 53 Uji Town
Theater Drama City 59 Osaka Station
Theater Museum 15 Shinjuku
Three Storied Pagoda 65 Nara
Tiara Koto Hall 5 Greater Tokyo
Tini 65 Yoshina
Toba 55 Kansai
Toba Aquarium 55 Kansai
Tobacco and Salt Museum 12 Roppongi, Shibuya, Omotesando, Harajuku & Meiji Shrine
Tobamachi 50 Fushimi Area
Tobata-ku 68 Hiroshima & Western Honshu
Tobe 86 Shikoku
Tobecho 24 Yokohama
Tobehoncho 24 Yokohama
Tobira Hot Spring 40 Nagano & Matsumoto Areas
Tobishima Village 35 Nagoya Area
Tobiumecho 38 Kanazawa
Tobu World Square 33 Nikko Area
Tobu Zoological Park 22 Mt. Fuji & Around Tokyo
Tobuhino 65 Nara
Tochigi 22 Mt. Fuji & Around Tokyo
Tochigi Pref. 22 Mt. Fuji & Around Tokyo
Tochikubo 77 Lake Towada
Tochikubo Hot Spring 77 Northern Honshu
Tochodai-Ji 64 Around Nara
Todagawa Kodomo Land 35 Nagoya Area
Todagawa Park 35 Nagoya Area
Todai 79 Hanamaki
Todai-Ji 65 Nara
Todo 53 Uji Town
Todoroki 4 Greater Tokyo
Todoroki-no-taki 87 Shikoku
Todoruki 33 Nikko Area
Todou 42 Kyoto
Toei Kyoto Studio Park 48 Western Kyoto
Toei Uzumasa Movie Village 42 Kyoto
Togakushi Ski Area 40 Nagano & Matsumoto Areas
Togane 23 Mt. Fuji & Around Tokyo
Toganocho 59 Osaka Station
Togendai 29 Hakone
Togi 39 Noto Peninsula
Togiyacho 41 Shizuoka
Togiyacho 75 Okamaya
Togo Beach 30 Izu Peninsula
Togo Hot Spring 69 Hiroshima & Western Honshu
Togo Seiji Art Museum 14 Shinjuku

Togoshi 18 Meguro & Shinagawa
Toguchi 95 Okinawa-honto
Toguchi Beach 97 Miyako Islands
Togura Kamiyamada Hot Spring 40 Nagano & Matsumoto Areas
Toguri Museum of Art 12 Roppongi, Shibuya, Omotesando, Harajuku & Meiji Shrine
Tohei 57 Greater Osaka
Toho 33 Narita
Tohoku 57 Northern Honshu
Toi 30 Izu Peninsula
Toi Hot Spring 30 Izu Peninsula
Toihama Beach 30 Izu Peninsula
Toin 54 Kansai Area
Toiyamachi 50 Fushimi Area
Toji Beach 30 Izu Peninsula
Tojiin 49 Western Kyoto
Tojijicho 44 Kawaramachi & Gion
Tojinbo Cliff 34 Central Honshu
Tojinmachi 92 Fukuoka
Tojocho 57 Greater Osaka
Tokachi-Obihiro Airport 83 Hokaido
Tokachidake Hot Spring 82 Daisetsuzan National Park
Tokai 35 Nagoya Area
Tokai 5 Greater Tokyo
Tokaichimachi 70 Hiroshima
Tokamachi 77 Northern Honshu
Tokei Museum 42 Kyoto
Tokei-ji 27 Kamakura
Toki 34 Central Honshu
Toki City 35 Nagoya Area
Toki-no-kane Bell Tower 32 Kawagoe-Little Edo
Tokikuni-ke & Kami-tokikuni-ke Old House 39 Noto Peninsula
Tokiwa 26 Kamakura
Tokiwa 49 Western Kyoto
Tokiwacho 41 Shizuoka
Tokiwadai 29 Lake Kawaguchi
Tokiwamachi 38 Kanazawa
Tokiwamachi 59 Osaka Station
Tokkarisho Beach 82 Sado-ga Island
Tokko 33 Narita
Tokocho 57 Greater Osaka
Tokoname 34 Central Honshu
Tokoro Museum 86 Shimanami Kaido
Tokorono 33 Nikko Area
Tokorozawa 22 Mt. Fuji & Around Tokyo
Tokoyo-no-taki 31 Chichi-jima
Tokuda Shusei Memorial Museum 38 Kanazawa
Tokudaiji-dangodencho 49 Western Kyoto
Tokudaijicho 48 Western Kyoto
Tokugawa 37 Central Nagoya
Tokugawa Art Museum 37 Central Nagoya
Tokugawacho 37 Central Nagoya
Tokuicho 57 Greater Osaka
Tokunaga 30 Izu Peninsula
Tokuro Memorial Art Museum 35 Nagoya Area
Tokushima 87 Shikoku
Tokushima Awa-odori Airport 87 Shikoku
Tokushima Botanical Garden 87 Shikoku
Tokushima Castle Museum 89 Tokushima
Tokushima Hanshu Hachisuka-ke Tomb 89 Tokushima
Tokushima Pref. 87 Shikoku
Tokushimacho 89 Tokushima
Tokyo Anime Center 7 Imperial Palace & Tokyo Station
Tokyo Anime Center Akiba Info 10 Asakusa, Ueno & Akihabara
Tokyo Big Site 22 Mt. Fuji & Around Tokyo
Tokyo Disney Land 22 Mt. Fuji & Around Tokyo
Tokyo Disney Sea 22 Mt. Fuji & Around Tokyo
Tokyo Dome (Big Egg) 5 Greater Tokyo
Tokyo Dome City 6 Imperial Palace & Tokyo Station
Tokyo Gas Science Museum 9 Ginza, Tsukiji & Tokyo Tower
Tokyo International (Haneda) Airport 22 Mt. Fuji & Around Tokyo
Tokyo International Exhibition Hall (Tokyo Big Sight) 21 Odaiba
Tokyo International Forum 8 Ginza, Tsukiji & Tokyo Tower
Tokyo Metro Museum of Photography 18 Meguro & Shinagawa
Tokyo Metro Teien Art Museum 18 Meguro & Shinagawa
Tokyo Metropolitan Art Museum 10 Asakusa, Ueno & Akihabara
Tokyo Metropolitan Museum of Modern Arts 5 Greater Tokyo
Tokyo National Museum Complex 10 Asakusa, Ueno & Akihabara
Tokyo Opera City 14 Shinjuku

Tokyo Pref. 22 Mt. Fuji & Around Tokyo
Tokyo Sky Tree 11 Asakusa, Ueno & Akihabara
Tokyo Some-monogatari Museum 17 Ikebukuro
Tokyo Station Gallery 7 Imperial Palace & Tokyo Station
Tokyo Summerland 22 Mt. Fuji & Around Tokyo
Tokyo Tower 8 Ginza, Tsukiji & Tokyo Tower
Tokyo Toy Museum 15 Shinjuku
Tokyo Univ. Museum 7 Imperial Palace & Tokyo Station
Tokyo University of the Arts Museum 10 Asakusa, Ueno & Akihabara
Tokyo Water Science Museum 21 Odaiba
Tokyo Waterworks History Museum 7 Imperial Palace & Tokyo Station
Tokyo Wonder Site Hongo 10 Asakusa, Ueno & Akihabara
Toma 82 Daisetsuzan National Park
Toma Calcareous Cave 82 Daisetsuzan National Park
Tomakomai 82 Hokaido
Tomamae 82 Hokaido
Tomari 82 Hokaido
Tomari 94 Naha
Tomari Beach 54 Kansai Area
Tomari Beach 87 Seto-ohasi Bridge
Tomari Fish Market 94 Naha
Tomb of Ishibutai 65 Asuka
Tomb of Marukoyama 65 Asuka
Tomb of Maruyama 65 Asuka
Tomb of Tenno-no-mori 42 Kyoto
Tome 77 Northern Honshu
Tomi 77 Northern Honshu
Tomigaya 12 Roppongi, Shibuya, Omotesando, Harajuku & Meiji Shrine
Tomigusuku 95 Okinawa-honto
Tomihisacho 15 Shinjuku
Tominagacho 45 Kawaramachi & Gion
Tomioka 22 Mt. Fuji & Around Tokyo
Tomioka 5 Greater Tokyo
Tomioka 77 Northern Honshu
Tomioka 84 Otaru
Tomiokashinmachi 37 Inuyama
Tomisato 33 Narita
Tomita Memorial Museum 40 Nagano & Matsumoto Areas
Tomiyama 22 Mt. Fuji & Around Tokyo
Tomizawa 30 Izu Peninsula
Tomoecho 41 Shizuoka
Tomori Beach 97 Amami Oshima
Tomuraushi Hot Spring 82 Daisetsuzan National Park
Tonahan Beach 95 Okinawa-Honto
Tondabayashi City 64 Around Nara
Tondacho 75 Okamaya
Tonden Kaitaku Memorial Museum 83 Hokaido
Tondocho 94 Naha
Tono 77 Northern Honshu
Tonodacho 50 Southern Kyoto
Tonode 65 Yoshina
Tonomachi 39 Gujo Hachiman
Tonomachi 74 Matsue
Tonomi Beach 68 Hiroshima & Western Honshu
Tonoshiro 96 Ishigaki City
Tonoshitacho 49 Western Kyoto
Tonosho 68 Shodo Island
Tonouchi 53 Uji Town
Tonoyama 78 Kakunodate
Toon 86 Shikoku
Torahime Jiyu-kan 67 Lake Biwa
Toranomon 8 Ginza, Tsukiji & Tokyo Tower
Tori-ike 94 Okinawa & The Southwest Islands
Toricho 81 Sendai
Torigoe 7 Imperial Palace & Tokyo Station
Torigoeyama Beach 77 Northern Honshu
Torii Beach 68 Hiroshima & Western Honshu
Toriicho 43 Central & Eastern Kyoto
Toriigata Daimonji Fire Festival Characters 48 Western Kyoto
Torikai 92 Fukuoka
Torikurumacho 41 Shizuoka
Torimachi 32 Kawagoe-little Edo
Torishima 56 Greater Osaka
Toro-do Hall 65 Mt. Koya
Torocho 44 Kawaramachi & Gion
Toroki-no-taki 97 Yakushima
Toroyamacho 44 Kawaramachi & Gion
Toryocho 50 Fushimi Area
Tosa 87 Shikoku
Tosa Iwahara 87 Iya Valley
Tosabori 57 Greater Osaka
Tosashimizu 86 Shikoku
Toshiba Science Museum 23 Yokohama Area
Toshima 4 Greater Tokyo
Toshima Mimizuku Museum 17 Ikebukuro
Toshima Ward Local Museum 16 Ikebukuro

Toshima-en Amusement Park 4 Greater Tokyo
Tosho-gu 32 Nikko Town
Tosho-gu Treasure House 32 Nikko Town
Toshogu 81 Sendai
Toshogu Museum 32 Nikko Town
Tosu 90 Kyusu
Totari 30 Izu Peninsula
Totsuka 23 Yokohama Area
Totsukamachi 15 Shinjuku
Totsukawa 54 Kansai Area
Tottori 69 Hiroshima & Western Honshu
Tottori Airport 69 Hiroshima & Western Honshu
Tottori City Historical Museum 75 Tottori
Tottori Hot Spring 75 Tottori
Tottori Pref. 69 Hiroshima & Western Honshu
Tottori Prefectural Museum 75 Tottori
Tottori Sand Dunes & Sand Museum 69 Hiroshima & Western Honshu
Towada 33 Narita
Towada 77 Northern Honshu
Towada Science Museum 76 Lake Towada
Towada-ko Oide Camping Ground 76 Lake Towada
Towadako 77 Lake Towada
Towaen 42 Kyoto
Towarida 76 Shirakami Mountains
Toya 30 Izu Peninsula
Toya 82 Sado-ga Island
Toya-ikoi-no-ie Hot Spring 82 Sado-ga Island
Toya-mizube-no-sato Camp Site 82 Sado-ga Island
Toyako 82 Sado-ga Island
Toyako Hot Spring 82 Sado-ga Island
Toyama 15 Shinjuku
Toyama 34 Central Honshu
Toyama Pref. 34 Central Honshu
Toyo 5 Greater Tokyo
Toyo 87 Shikoku
Toyo Ito Museum 86 Shimanami Kaido
Toyoake City 35 Nagoya Area
Toyoda 33 Nikko Area
Toyoda 41 Lake Suwa
Toyodacho 47 Northern Kyoto
Toyohashi 34 Central Honshu
Toyohidecho 57 Greater Osaka
Toyoiwa Site 83 Hokaido
Toyokan Asian Museum 10 Asakusa, Ueno & Akihabara
Toyokawa 34 Central Honshu
Toyokawacho 84 Hakodate
Toyokoro 83 Hokaido
Toyomaecho 37 Central Nagoya
Toyomicho 9 Ginza, Tsukiji & Tokyo Tower
Toyonaka 55 Osaka Area
Toyonaka City 55 Osaka Area
Toyono 54 Kansai Area
Toyooka 54 Kansai Area
Toyosaki 57 Greater Osaka
Toyosato Town 67 Lake Biwa
Toyosu 9 Ginza, Tsukiji & Tokyo Tower
Toyota 34 Central Honshu
Toyota Automobile Museum 35 Nagoya Area
Toyota Commemorative Museum of Industry and Technology 36 Central Nagoya
Toyota Kaikan Museum 35 Nagoya Area
Toyota Municipal Museum of Art 35 Nagoya Area
Toyotama 4 Greater Tokyo
Toyotama-kami 4 Greater Tokyo
Toyotomi 83 Hokaido
Toyoura 65 Asuka
Toyoura 68 Hiroshima & Western Honshu
Toyoura 82 Sado-ga Island
Toyozo Museum 35 Nagoya Area
Tozai-tawaracho 49 Western Kyoto
Tozawa 77 Northern Honshu
Traditional Arts & Crafts Center 94 Naha
Traditional Crafts Museum 45 Kawaramachi & Gion
Traditional Crafts Museum 93 Kumamoto
Transportation Museum 83 Hokaido
Treasure Museum 14 Shinjuku
Treasure Museum 64 Mt. Koya
Trick Art Museum 82 Daisetsuzan National Park
Trick Art Pia Nikko 33 Nikko Area
Tropical Beach Beach 95 Okinawa-honto
Tropical Garden 22 Mt. Fuji & Around Tokyo
Tropical Garden and Activity Center 97 Miyako Islands
Tsrunocho 57 Greater Osaka
Tsu 26 Kamakura
Tsu 54 Kansai Area
Tsu-nishi 26 Kamakura
Tsubaki 72 Hagi
Tsubaki Hot Spring 54 Kansai Area
Tsubaki Museum 31 Oshima

Tsubaki-no-you 89 Matsuyama
Tsubaki-no-yu-Onsen 89 Matsuyama
Tsubakiuchico 36 Central Nagoya
Tsubakihara 34 Shirakawa-go & Gokayama
Tsubakio Beach 80 Sado-ga Island
Tsubame 77 Northern Honshu
Tsubamesawa 81 Sendai
Tsubetsu Ski Area 83 Akan National Park
Tsubogawa 94 Naha
Tsuboya 94 Naha
Tsuboya Pottery Museum 94 Naha
Tsuboyo 80 Aizu, Inawashiro & Ura-bandai
Tsuchi Ruins 34 Central Honshu
Tsuchidocho 49 Western Kyoto
Tsuchikadocho 46 Northern Kyoto
Tsuchimotocho 48 Western Kyoto
Tsuchitenjocho 46 Northern Kyoto
Tsuchitoi 81 Sendai
Tsuchiura 23 Mt. Fuji & Around Tokyo
Tsuchiya 33 Narita
Tsuchiyacho 44 Kawaramachi & Gion
Tsuchiyuzawa Hot Spring 80 Aizu, Inawashiro & Ura-Bandai
Tsudacho 74 Matsue
Tsue 91 Yufuin
Tsuga 22 Mt. Fuji & Around Tokyo
Tsugaike Kogen Ski Area 40 Nagano & Matsumoto Areas
Tsugaike Natural Garden 40 Nagano & Matsumoto Areas
Tsuha 95 Okinawa-honto
Tsuhido 74 Onomichi
Tsuji 94 Naha
Tsujido-taiheidai 26 Kamakura
Tsujidocho 50 Fushimi Area
Tsujimachi 88 Matsuyama
Tsujimura Botanical Park 29 Hakone
Tsujinouchicho 65 Nara
Tsukamoto 56 Greater Osaka
Tsukamoto-dori 62 Kobe
Tsukamotocho 49 Western Kyoto
Tsuki-ga-hama Beach 96 Yaeyama Islands
Tsukidate 79 Hiraizumi & Ichinoseki
Tsukigata Daitobo Art Museum 35 Nagoya Area
Tsukiji 56 Greater Osaka
Tsukiji 9 Ginza, Tsukiji & Tokyo Tower
Tsukiji Central Wholesale Market 9 Ginza, Tsukiji & Tokyo Tower
Tsukiji Fish Market 5 Greater Tokyo
Tsukijicho 62 Kobe
Tsukijimachi 6 Imperial Palace & Tokyo Station
Tsukimachi 79 Hiraizumi & Ichinoseki
Tsukimachi 92 Nagasaki
Tsukimicho 44 Kawaramachi & Gion
Tsukishima 9 Ginza, Tsukiji & Tokyo Tower
Tsukishimacho 36 Central Nagoya
Tsukisocho 49 Western Kyoto
Tsukiyo 53 Uji Town
Tsukuba 23 Mt. Fuji & Around Tokyo
Tsukuba Wanwan Land 23 Mt. Fuji & Around Tokyo
Tsukuda 56 Greater Osaka
Tsukuda 9 Ginza, Tsukiji & Tokyo Tower
Tsukudacho 49 Western Kyoto
Tsukudo-hachimancho 6 Imperial Palace & Tokyo Station
Tsukudo 6 Imperial Palace & Tokyo Station
Tsukuihama 22 Mt. Fuji & Around Tokyo
Tsukumi 90 Kyusu
Tsukumicho 45 Kawaramachi & Gion
Tsukuno Hot Spring 68 Hiroshima & Western Honshu
Tsukurimachicho 48 Western Kyoto
Tsumagi Ruins 35 Nagoya Area
Tsumagoi 77 Northern Honshu
Tsumashima 41 Nagano
Tsumashoji 93 Fukuoka
Tsumemaru Ruins 72 Hagi
Tsumori 57 Greater Osaka
Tsumoricho 72 Hagi
Tsunabamachi 93 Fukuoka
Tsunagi 80 Aizu, Inawashiro & Ura-bandai
Tsunan 77 Northern Honshu
Tsunekawamori 76 Lake Towada
Tsuneyoshi 56 Greater Osaka
Tsuno 86 Shikoku
Tsuno 90 Kyusu
Tsunogoro 81 Sendai
Tsunokunicho 46 Northern Kyoto
Tsunoshima Todai Park 68 Hiroshima & Western Honshu
Tsuridonocho 48 Western Kyoto
Tsuriganecho 59 Osaka Station
Tsurihama Beach 31 Chichi-jima
Tsuru 22 Mt. Fuji & Around Tokyo

Tsuru City 28 Mt. Fuji
Tsurue 72 Hagi
Tsuruga 41 Nagano
Tsuruga 54 Kansai Area
Tsuruga Castle 80 Aizu, Inawashiro & Ura-Bandai
Tsurugaoka Hachiman-gu Shrine 27 Kamakura
Tsurugashima 22 Mt. Fuji & Around Tokyo
Tsurugata 75 Kurashiki
Tsurugaya 81 Sendai
Tsurugi 87 Shikoku
Tsurugusan Ski Area 87 Shikoku
Tsuruhashi 57 Greater Osaka
Tsurui 83 Hokaido
Tsuruma Park 35 Nagoya Area
Tsurumachi 56 Greater Osaka
Tsurumai 37 Central Nagoya
Tsurumaicho 37 Central Nagoya
Tsurumaki 4 Greater Tokyo
Tsurumi 57 Greater Osaka
Tsurumi Ward 64 Around Nara
Tsurumibashi 60 Osaka Namba
Tsurumicho 71 Hiroshima
Tsurumiryokuchi Expo '90 Commemorative Park 57 Greater Osaka
Tsurunocho 59 Osaka Station
Tsurunoshima 91 Miyazaki
Tsurunuma 80 Aizu, Inawashiro & Ura-bandai
Tsuruoka 77 Northern Honshu
Tsuruoka 81 Dewa Sanzen
Tsuruyacho 24 Yokohama
Tsushima 34 Central Honshu
Tsushima City 35 Nagoya Area
Tsushimaru Museum 94 Naha
Tsutenkaku Tower 61 Osaka Namba
Tsutsui 37 Central Nagoya
Tsutsuicho 37 Central Nagoya
Tsutsujigaoka Park 22 Mt. Fuji & Around Tokyo
Tsutsukihama Beach 90 Kyusu
Tsutsumi-dori 11 Asakusa, Ueno & Akihabara
Tsutsumicho 45 Kawaramachi & Gion
Tsutsumidanicho 43 Central & Eastern Kyoto
Tsutsumimachi 77 Aomori
Tsutsumimachi 81 Sendai
Tsutsumine 25 Kawasaki
Tsutsumisotocho 49 Western Kyoto
Tsutsuo Beach 68 Hiroshima & Western Honshu
Tsuwano 68 Hiroshima & Western Honshu
Tsuwano Folk Museum 73 Tsuwano
Tsuwanocho 73 Tsuwano
Tsuyama 69 Hiroshima & Western Honshu
Tsuyuhashicho 36 Central Nagoya
Tsuyunocho 62 Kobe
Tsuzuki 23 Yokohama Area
TV Tower 85 Sapporo
Twenty Four Eyes Movie Village 68 Shodo Island
Uayocho 44 Kawaramachi & Gion
Ubayu Hot Spring 80 Aizu, Inawashiro & Ura-Bandai
Ube 68 Hiroshima & Western Honshu
Ubuyama 91 Aso Area
UCC Coffee Museum 55 Osaka Area
Uchi-hiranomachi 59 Osaka Station
Uchi-honmachi 59 Osaka Station
Uchi-kanda 7 Imperial Palace & Tokyo Station
Uchi-kyuhojimachi 59 Osaka Station
Uchi-nakabaracho 74 Matsue
Uchi-tsuboimachi 93 Kumamoto
Uchiawajimachi 57 Greater Osaka
Uchida-higashimachi 37 Inuyama
Uchidacho 24 Yokohama
Uchidacho 48 Western Kyoto
Uchigato 34 Shirakawa-go & Gokayama
Uchihatacho 49 Western Kyoto
Uchiko 86 Shikoku
Uchiko Historical and Folk Museum 86 Shikoku
Uchimachi 88 Kotohira
Uchindaicho 57 Greater Osaka
Uchino-maki Hot Spring 90 Aso Area
Uchinomi 68 Shodo Island
Uchisaiwaicho 8 Ginza, Tsukiji & Tokyo Tower
Uchisange 75 Okamaya
Uchiuramito 30 Izu Peninsula
Uchiyama 37 Central Nagoya
Uchizaka 76 Shirakami Mountains
Uchizuma Beach 87 Shikoku
Uda 64 Around Nara
Uda Matsuyama Ruins 64 Around Nara
Udagawa-cho 12 Roppongi, Shibuya, Omotesando, Harajuku & Meiji Shrine
Udanotani 48 Western Kyoto
Ueda 40 Nagano & Matsumoto Areas
Ueda 92 Nagasaki
Uedacho 45 Kawaramachi & Gion

Uehara 12 Roppongi, Shibuya, Omotesando, Harajuku & Meiji Shrine
Uehara Museum of Buddhism Art 30 Izu Peninsula
Uehonmachi 61 Osaka Namba
Uehonmachi-nishi 61 Osaka Namba
Uejocho 72 Shimonoseki
Uemachi 57 Greater Osaka
Uemachi 75 Tottori
Uematsucho 44 Kawaramachi & Gion
Ueno 10 Asakusa, Ueno & Akihabara
Ueno 22 Mt. Fuji & Around Tokyo
Ueno 92 Nagasaki
Ueno German Culture Village 97 Miyako Islands
Ueno Park 5 Greater Tokyo
Ueno Royal Museum 10 Asakusa, Ueno & Akihabara
Ueno Zoo 10 Asakusa, Ueno & Akihabara
Ueno-dai 79 Hiraizumi & Ichinoseki
Ueno-koen 10 Asakusa, Ueno & Akihabara
Ueno-sakuragi 10 Asakusa, Ueno & Akihabara
Uenocho 46 Northern Kyoto
Uenocho 47 Northern Kyoto
Uenohara 22 Mt. Fuji & Around Tokyo
Uenomiyacho 61 Osaka Namba
Uenosonocho 91 Kagoshima
Uenoya 94 Naha
Uenoyamacho 48 Western Kyoto
Ueshio 57 Greater Osaka
Ugo 77 Northern Honshu
Uguisudani 64 Mt. Koya
Uguisudanicho 12 Roppongi, Shibuya, Omotesando, Harajuku & Meiji Shrine
Uguisuhodo Nature Walk 73 Miyajima
Uguisumachi 38 Kanazawa
Uingutsuchiya 33 Narita
Uita Hot Spring 69 Hiroshima & Western Honshu
Uji 54 Kansai Area
Ujigami Shrine 53 Uji Town
Ujo Park 75 Okamaya
Uka 95 Okinawa-honto
Ukedo Beach 77 Northern Honshu
Ukegahara 34 Shirakawa-go & Gokayama
Ukegawa 66 Hongu Onsens
Uken Beach 95 Okinawa-Honto
Uki 90 Kyusu
Ukida 57 Greater Osaka
Ukiha 90 Kyusu
Ukitacho 5 Greater Tokyo
Ukitsu Beach 86 Shikoku
Ukiyama Hot Spring 30 Izu Peninsula
Ukiyo-e Tokyo Museum 9 Ginza, Tsukiji & Tokyo Tower
Uku-no-Hama Beach 95 Okinawa-Honto
Ukuma Beach 95 Okinawa-Honto
Uma-no-yakata Museum 90 Kyusu
Umadome 63 Kobe
Umagoe 68 Shodo Island
Umaji 87 Shikoku
Umanomecho 46 Northern Kyoto
Umatate 88 Kotohira
Umazakacho 48 Western Kyoto
Umazukacho 49 Western Kyoto
Umeda 58 Osaka Station
Umedamachi 81 Sendai
Umegahata 42 Kyoto
Umegahata-takaocho 52 Takao Village
Umegahata-togano'ocho 52 Takao Village
Umegashima Hot Spring 34 Central Honshu
Umegatsujicho 46 Northern Kyoto
Umegi 30 Izu Peninsula
Umekoji 50 Southern Kyoto
Umekoji Park 50 Southern Kyoto
Umekoji Steam Locomotive Museum 50 Southern Kyoto
Umemachi 56 Greater Osaka
Umemiyacho 45 Kawaramachi & Gion
Umemotocho 45 Kawaramachi & Gion
Umemotocho 62 Kobe
Umenokicho 44 Kawaramachi & Gion
Umetsubo 37 Inuyama
Umeyacho 41 Shizuoka
Umeyacho 44 Kawaramachi & Gion
Umezawamachi 38 Kanazawa
Umezonocho 57 Greater Osaka
Umezu 48 Western Kyoto
Umi 90 Kyusu
Umi Jigoku (Sea/Ocean Hell) 91 Kannawa Hells Area
Umibe 5 Greater Tokyo
Umigame-kan 96 Yakushima
Umonji 53 Uji Town
Unane 4 Greater Tokyo
Unazaki Onsen 40 Nagano & Matsumoto Areas

Unazuki Hot Spring 40 Nagano & Matsumoto Areas
Underground Naval Headquarters 95 Okinawa-Honto
Unebicho 65 Asuka
Ungacho 36 Central Nagoya
Ungatori 36 Central Nagoya
Universal Studio Japan 56 Greater Osaka
University of Tokyo Museum Koishikawa Annex 17 Ikebukuro
Unnan 69 Hiroshima & Western Honshu
Unoura Beach 39 Noto Peninsula
Unouramachi 39 Noto Peninsula
Unpenji Ropeway 87 Iya Valley
Unrinincho 46 Northern Kyoto
Unryu-taki 32 Nikko Area
Unten 95 Okinawa-honto
Untsunomiya 77 Northern Honshu
Unuma-minamimachi 37 Inuyama
Unzen 90 Kyusu
Uodomari-no-taki 76 Shirakami Mountains
Uomachi 74 Matsue
Uono 92 Nagasaki
Uonotanacho 73 Miyajima
Uozu 34 Central Honshu
Uppama Beach 95 Okinawa-Honto
Ura-bandai Area 80 Aizu, Inawashiro & Ura-bandai
Ura-bandai Highland 80 Aizu, Inawashiro & Ura-Bandai
Ura-bandai Nekoma Ski Area 80 Aizu, Inawashiro & Ura-Bandai
Ura-bandai Ski Area 80 Aizu, Inawashiro & Ura-Bandai
Uraderacho 44 Kawaramachi & Gion
Uradome Beach 69 Hiroshima & Western Honshu
Urahoro 83 Hokaido
Urakami Tenshudo Cathedral 92 Nagasaki
Urakawa 83 Hokaido
Urakuen Garden 37 Inuyama
Urami-no-taki 32 Nikko Area
Uramachi 39 Takayama
Uramiga-taki 31 Hachijo-jima
Uranokawa 92 Shimabara
Urasenke Chado Research Center 46 Northern Kyoto
Urasoe 95 Okinawa-honto
Uratsukijicho 43 Central & Eastern Kyoto
Urauchi-gawa River Trip Pier 96 Yaeyama Islands
Urausu 83 Hokaido
Urawa 22 Mt. Fuji & Around Tokyo
UrayamaValley 22 Mt. Fuji & Around Tokyo
Urayanagicho 48 Western Kyoto
Urban Dock Lalaport Toyosu 9 Ginza, Tsukiji & Tokyo Tower
Urban History Museum 25 Kawasaki
Urizura 23 Mt. Fuji & Around Tokyo
Uroko-no-ie, Uroko Museum 63 Kobe
Urokomachi 38 Kanazawa
Urukami Hot Spring 39 Noto Peninsula
Uruma 95 Okinawa-honto
Uruma Culture of Ocean Museum 95 Okinawa-Honto
Urushi Museum 32 Nikko Town
Urushitani 34 Shirakawa-go & Gokayama
Uruya 80 Sado-ga Island
Uryuzancho 47 Northern Kyoto
US Naval Airbase Atsugi 22 Mt. Fuji & Around Tokyo
Usa 90 Kyusu
Usami 30 Izu Peninsula
Usami Beach 30 Izu Peninsula
Ushibori 23 Mt. Fuji & Around Tokyo
Ushigase 50 Southern Kyoto
Ushijimacho 36 Central Nagoya
Ushiku 23 Mt. Fuji & Around Tokyo
Ushikubi 34 Shirakawa-go & Gokayama
Ushimado Beach 69 Hiroshima & Western Honshu
Ushio Hot Spring 69 Hiroshima & Western Honshu
Ushiroda 73 Tsuwano
Ushirogawara 73 Yamaguchi
Ushita-higashi 71 Hiroshima
Ushita-honmachi 71 Hiroshima
Ushita-minami 71 Hiroshima
Ushita-naka 71 Hiroshima
Ushitayama 71 Hiroshima
Ushitoracho 48 Western Kyoto
Ushitsu 39 Noto Peninsula
Ushiwakacho 46 Northern Kyoto
Usu Beach 82 Sado-ga Island
Usubetsu Hot Spring 82 Hokaido
Usui Cave 29 Hakone Town

Usuiso Beach 77 Northern Honshu
Usuki 90 Kyusu
Usuki Sekibutsu (Stone Buddha) 90 Kyusu
Usuya Beach 82 Hokaido
Usuzan Ropeway 82 Sado-ga Island
Utajima 56 Greater Osaka
Utano 49 Western Kyoto
Utarube 77 Lake Towada
Utatsu Craft Workshop 38 Kanazawa
Utatsumachi 38 Kanazawa
Utena Beach 86 Shimanami Kaido
Uto 90 Kyusu
Utoro 83 Shiretoko National Park
Utoro Hot Spring 83 Shiretoko National Park
Utsubohonmachi 58 Osaka Station
Utsukushi-ga-hara Hot Spring 40 Nagano & Matsumoto Areas
Utsukushi-ga-hara Kogen Museum 40 Nagano & Matsumoto Areas
Utsukushigahara Hot Spring 34 Central Honshu
Utsunomiya 22 Mt. Fuji & Around Tokyo
Uwa 92 Nagasaki
Uwabukuro 79 Hiraizumi & Ichinoseki
Uwadana 39 Noto Peninsula
Uwajima 86 Shikoku
Uwajima Castle 86 Uwajima
Uzuhashi 41 Matsumoto
Uzumasa 48 Western Kyoto
Uzumasa-yasui 49 Western Kyoto
Uzunomichi (Whirling Waves) 87 Shikoku
Venetian Glass Museum 29 Hakone
Venus Bridge 63 Kobe
View Land Amusement Park 66 Amano Hashidate
Viewing Platform 74 Onomichi
Villa Museum 42 Yufuin
Visitor Center 6 Imperial Palace & Tokyo Station
Visitors Information Center 58 Osaka Station
Visitors Information Center Tennoji 61 Osaka Namba
Vita Italia 8 Ginza, Tsukiji & Tokyo Tower
Volcanic Science Museum 82 Sado-ga Island
Volcano Museum 31 Oshima
Wachigawara 91 Miyazaki
Wada 31 Shimoda
Wada 33 Narita
Wada 4 Greater Tokyo
Wadacho 31 Atami
Wadacho 65 Asuka
Wadahama Beach 30 Kozu-shima & Nii-jima
Wadahama Beach 54 Kansai Area
Wahha Kamigata 61 Osaka Namba
Wainai 76 Lake Towada
Wajima 39 Noto Peninsula
Wajima Urushi Art Museum 39 Noto Peninsula
Wakaba 15 Shinjuku
Wakabacho 24 Yokohama
Wakago Maehama Beach 30 Kozu-shima & Nii-jima
Wakakusacho 71 Hiroshima
Wakakusacho 91 Central Beppu
Wakamatsucho 15 Shinjuku
Wakamatsucho 45 Kawaramachi & Gion
Wakamatsucho 84 Hakodate
Wakamiya 79 Hiraizumi & Ichinoseki
Wakamiya 80 Aizu, Inawashiro & Ura-bandai
Wakamiyacho 36 Central Nagoya
Wakamiyacho 48 Western Kyoto
Wakamiyacho 6 Imperial Palace & Tokyo Station
Wakamori 53 Uji Town
Wakana-dori 63 Kobe
Wakasa 69 Hiroshima & Western Honshu
Wakasa 94 Naha
Wakasu 5 Greater Tokyo
Wakayama 54 Kansai Area
Wakayama Bokusui Memorial Museum 30 Izu Peninsula
Wakayama Pref. 54 Kansai Area
Wakaza 54 Kansai Area
Wakazuki Kogen Oya Ski Area 69 Hiroshima & Western Honshu
Wake 69 Hiroshima & Western Honshu
Waki 69 Hiroshima & Western Honshu
Wakicho 49 Western Kyoto
Wakinohama-kaigan-dori 63 Kobe
Wakita-honcho 32 Kawagoe-little Edo
Wakitamachi 32 Kawagoe-little Edo
Wakkanai 83 Rishiri-rebun-sarobetsu National Park
Wakkanai Airport 83 Hokaido
Wako 22 Mt. Fuji & Around Tokyo
Wakokucho 45 Kawaramachi & Gion
Wakoto Hot Spring 83 Akan National Park
Wakoto Museum 83 Akan National Park

Waku Waku-za History & Culture Museum 93 Kumamoto
Wakura Hot Spring 34 Central Honshu
Wakura-onsen 39 Noto Peninsula
Wakuya 77 Northern Honshu
Wakuyacho 44 Kawaramachi & Gion
Wanihama Beach 67 Lake Biwa
Wanouchi 54 Kansai Area
Wanza Ariake 21 Odaiba
Wappaichi 81 Matsushima
Wappani 81 Matsushima
Warabekan (Toy Museum) 75 Tottori
Warabo 30 Izu Peninsula
Warayacho 49 Western Kyoto
Warei 86 Uwajima
Waseda- Minami-icho 15 Shinjuku
Waseda- Tsurumakicho 15 Shinjuku
Wasedamachi 15 Shinjuku
Wasezawa Hot Spring 80 Aizu, Inawashiro & Ura-Bandai
Washibara-ni-kami 73 Tsuwano
Washibara-ni-shimo 73 Tsuwano
Washigatake Ski Area 34 Central Honshu
Washiminecho 46 Northern Kyoto
Washiocho 45 Kawaramachi & Gion
Washisaki 80 Sado-ga Island
Wassamu 83 Hokaido
Watakushi Art Museum 91 Yufuin
Watamachi 66 Himeji Castle
Watanabe Jun'ichi Museum of Literature 85 Sapporo
Watanabe-ke Old House 41 Lake Suwa
Watanabedori 93 Fukuoka
Watarai 54 Kansai Area
Watarase Hot Spring 66 Hongu Onsens
Watari 77 Northern Honshu
Watari-Um Museum 13 Roppongi, Shibuya, Omotesando, Harajuku & Meiji Shrine
Watarida 25 Kawasaki
Watarida-mukaincho 25 Kawasaki
Watarida-shincho 25 Kawasaki
Watauchi 26 Kamakura
Wataze 66 Hongu Onsens
Watch Tower 72 Hagi
Water & Life Museum 35 Nagoya Area
Waterfront Promenade 92 Nagasaki
Waterworks Memorial Hall 23 Yokohama Area
Watokumachi 76 Hirosaki
Wazuka 54 Kansai Area
Western Mura 33 Nikko Area
Western Precinct (Saito) 52 Enryaku-ji & Mt. Hiei
White Ring 40 Nagano & Matsumoto Areas
White Snake Museum 73 Iwakuni
White Valley Matsubara Ski Area 68 Hiroshima & Western Honshu
Wild Bird Society of Japan 82 Kushiro National Park
Windflower Garden Bluebonnet 35 Nagoya Area
Windsor Snow Village Ski Area 82 Sado-ga Island
Wine Museum 56 Greater Osaka
Woods Motor Land Shimoichi 64 Around Nara
World Glassware Hall 87 Seto-ohasi Bridge
WTC Cosmo Tower 56 Greater Osaka
Yabahitahikosan Quasi National Park 90 Kyusu
Yabase Beach 69 Hiroshima & Western Honshu
Yabecho 62 Kobe
Yabegawa Natural Park 90 Kyusu
Yabu 54 Kansai Area
Yabu 95 Okinawa-honto
Yabuki 77 Northern Honshu
Yabusato 53 Uji Town
Yabushita 37 Inuyama
Yabusoe 47 Northern Kyoto
Yabuzuka-honmachi 22 Mt. Fuji & Around Tokyo
Yachiyo 23 Mt. Fuji & Around Tokyo
Yachiyo 92 Nagasaki
Yachiyo-daki 69 Hiroshima & Western Honshu
Yachiyocho 41 Shizuoka
Yachiyodai 23 Mt. Fuji & Around Tokyo
Yada-minami 37 Central Nagoya
Yadon Beach 97 Amami Oshima
Yadorihama Beach 97 Amami Oshima
Yaese 95 Okinawa-honto
Yaesu 7 Imperial Palace & Tokyo Station
Yaeyama District 96 Yaeyama Islands
Yaeyama Peace Museum 96 Ishigaki City
Yaga 22 Mt. Fuji & Around Tokyo
Yagisawa 30 Izu Peninsula
Yagiyama Beny Land 81 Sendai
Yagiyama-midoricho 81 Sendai

Yaguma 30 Izu Peninsula
Yagumo Shrine 27 Kamakura
Yagumo-dori 63 Kobe
Yaguracho 50 Fushimi Area
Yahaba 77 Northern Honshu
Yahata 92 Nagasaki
Yahata 41 Shizuoka
Yahata 80 Aizu, Inawashiro & Ura-bandai
Yahataya 56 Greater Osaka
Yahiro 5 Greater Tokyo
Yaima-mura Folk Museum Yaima-mura 96 Yaeyama Islands
Yaita 77 Northern Honshu
Yaizu 34 Central Honshu
Yakage 69 Hiroshima & Western Honshu
Yakakecho 49 Western Kyoto
Yakako 79 Hiraizumi & Ichinoseki
Yakatazaki 68 Shodo Island
Yaku-sugi Land 97 Yakushima
Yaku-sugi Shizen-kan Museum 97 Yakushima
Yakuin 93 Fukuoka
Yakuin-fukumachi 93 Fukuoka
Yakuinodori 93 Fukuoka
Yakumo 4 Greater Tokyo
Yakumo 82 Hokaido
Yakumo Hot Spring 82 Hokaido
Yakuo-ji 27 Kamakura
Yakushi 37 Inuyama
Yakushi 90 Kagoshima
Yakushi-ji 64 Around Nara
Yakushicho 37 Inuyama
Yakushicho 44 Kawaramachi & Gion
Yakushima Airport 97 Yakushima
Yakushima Environment Culture Village Center 97 Yakushima
Yakushima Fruits Garden 96 Yakushima
Yakushima National Park 97 Yakushima
Yakushimachi 75 Tottori
Yakushishitacho 48 Western Kyoto
Yakushiyama-higashicho 46 Northern Kyoto
Yama Jigoku (Mountain Hell) 91 Kannawa Hells Area
Yama-no-Aquarium & Museum 83 Hokaido
Yama-to-Mizu-no-Seikatsu Museum 95 Okinawa-Honto
Yamabana 47 Northern Kyoto
Yamabuki Castle Ruins 73 Iwami Ginzan
Yamabukicho 15 Shinjuku
Yamacho 46 Northern Kyoto
Yamada 23 Mt. Fuji & Around Tokyo
Yamada 39 Noto Peninsula
Yamada 48 Western Kyoto
Yamada 53 Uji Town
Yamada 72 Hagi
Yamada 77 Northern Honshu
Yamada 95 Okinawa-honto
Yamada Hot Spring 82 Sado-ga Island
Yamada-minami-matsuoyama 48 Western Kyoto
Yamadacho 44 Kawaramachi & Gion
Yamadamachi 84 Otaru
Yamadera 37 Inuyama
Yamae 90 Kyusu
Yamaga 90 Kyusu
Yamagata 40 Nagano & Matsumoto Areas
Yamagata 77 Northern Honshu
Yamagata Aritomo Birthplace 72 Hagi
Yamagata Pref. 77 Northern Honshu
Yamagin Data Museum 72 Shimonoseki
Yamagoe 48 Western Kyoto
Yamagoemachi 88 Matsuyama
Yamaguchi 73 Yamaguchi
Yamaguchi 90 Kyusu
Yamaguchi Hoshun Memorial Museum 23 Yokohama Area
Yamaguchi Museum 73 Yamaguchi
Yamaguchi Pref. 68 Hiroshima & Western Honshu
Yamaguchi Prefectural Museum of Art 73 Yamaguchi
Yamaguchi Ube Airport 68 Hiroshima & Western Honshu
Yamaguchicho 37 Central Nagoya
Yamahana Kinen-kaikan Museum 85 Sapporo
Yamahana Onsen Tonden-yu Hot Spring 85 Sapporo
Yamakita 22 Mt. Fuji & Around Tokyo
Yamako Usuki Museum 90 Kyusu
Yamakurosawa 29 Hakone Town
Yamamoto-dori 63 Kobe
Yamamoto-tei Samurai Residence 92 Shimabara
Yamamotocho 48 Western Kyoto
Yamamura Museum 34 Central Honshu
Yamanaka 22 Mt. Fuji & Around Tokyo
Yamanaka 66 Amano Hashidate
Yamanaka Castle Ruins Park 30 Izu Peninsula

Yamanaka Family Old Residence 72 Hagi
Yamanakako 22 Mt. Fuji & Around Tokyo
Yamanakako Village 28 Mt. Fuji
Yamanashi 28 Mt. Fuji
Yamanashi Gem Museum 29 Lake Kawaguchi
Yamanashi Pref. 22 Mt. Fuji & Around Tokyo
Yamanohashicho 47 Northern Kyoto
Yamanokyo Natural Park 69 Hiroshima & Western Honshu
Yamanome 79 Hiraizumi & Ichinoseki
Yamanomemachi 79 Hiraizumi & Ichinoseki
Yamanomoricho 46 Northern Kyoto
Yamanone 27 Kamakura
Yamanoshitacho 49 Western Kyoto
Yamanouchi 27 Kamakura
Yamanouchi 49 Western Kyoto
Yamanouchicho 24 Yokohama
Yamanouchicho 43 Central & Eastern Kyoto
Yamanouemachi 38 Kanazawa
Yamasaki 69 Hiroshima & Western Honshu
Yamasaki 93 Takachiho
Yamashina Ward 67 Lake Biwa
Yamashiro-cho 87 Iya Valley
Yamashita Park 25 Kawasaki
Yamashitacho 43 Central & Eastern Kyoto
Yamasitacho 25 Yokohama
Yamasitacho 94 Naha
Yamatacho 49 Western Kyoto
Yamatane Museum of Art 13 Roppongi, Shibuya, Omotesando, Harajuku & Meiji Shrine
Yamate Museum 25 Kawasaki
Yamatecho 70 Hiroshima
Yamatecho 72 Shimonoseki
Yamatemachi 81 Sendai
Yamato 22 Mt. Fuji & Around Tokyo
Yamato 41 Shizuoka
Yamato Museum 68 Hiroshima & Western Honshu
Yamato-koriyama City 64 Around Nara
Yamato-takeda City 64 Around Nara
Yamatocho 4 Greater Tokyo
Yamatocho 45 Kawaramachi & Gion
Yamatocho 50 Fushimi Area
Yamatomachi 39 Noto Peninsula
Yamatomachi 73 Miyajima
Yamatomachi 81 Sendai
Yamatotakada 54 Kansai Area
Yamatsuri 23 Mt. Fuji & Around Tokyo
Yamazaki 27 Kamakura
Yamazaki 42 Kyoto
Yamazaki 78 Akita
Yamazaki Art Museum 32 Kawagoe-Little Edo
Yamazaki Mazak Art Museum 37 Central Nagoya
Yamazakicho 50 Fushimi Area
Yamazakicho 59 Osaka Station
Yamazoe 54 Kansai Area
Yamazoecho 48 Western Kyoto
Yanaba Snow & Green Park 40 Nagano & Matsumoto Areas
Yanagawa 90 Kyusu
Yanagawa 92 Nagasaki
Yanagi 68 Shodo Island
Yanagi-no-gosho Museum 79 Hiraizumi & Ichinoseki
Yanagi-yu 66 Kinosaki
Yanagibashi 7 Imperial Palace & Tokyo Station
Yanagiboricho 36 Central Nagoya
Yanagida Botanical Garden 39 Noto Peninsula
Yanagida Hot Spring 39 Noto Peninsula
Yanagihara 37 Central Nagoya
Yanagihara 5 Greater Tokyo
Yanagimachi 37 Inuyama
Yanagimachi 39 Gujo Hachiman
Yanagimachi 66 Himeji Castle
Yanagimachi 75 Okamaya
Yanaginohana 88 Kotohira
Yanagisawa 79 Hiraizumi & Ichinoseki
Yanagishimacho 36 Central Nagoya
Yanai 68 Hiroshima & Western Honshu
Yanaida 39 Noto Peninsula
Yanaimachi 88 Matsuyama
Yanaizu 77 Northern Honshu
Yanaka 10 Asakusa, Ueno & Akihabara
Yanaka Ginza 5 Greater Tokyo
Yanakawa 76 Aomori
Yanase Dam 87 Shikoku
Yanase Natural Park 87 Shikoku
Yano Hot Spring 69 Hiroshima & Western Honshu
Yao 54 Kansai Area
Yao Airport 64 Around Nara
Yao City 64 Around Nara
Yaochi 53 Uji Town
Yaoko Kawagoe Museum 32 Kawagoe-Little Edo

Yaoya 92 Nagasaki
Yaraicho 6 Imperial Palace & Tokyo Station
Yariyamachi 57 Greater Osaka
Yasaka Matsuri Festival 45 Kawaramachi & Gion
Yasaka-minamimachi 45 Kawaramachi & Gion
Yasaki 79 Hiraizumi & Ichinoseki
Yasashigaura Beach 23 Mt. Fuji & Around Tokyo
Yase 42 Kyoto
Yashiki 80 Aizu, Inawashiro & Ura-bandai
Yashikida 78 Akita
Yashimacho 96 Ishigaki City
Yashio 20 Odaiba
Yashiro-honcho 66 Himeji Castle
Yasio 22 Mt. Fuji & Around Tokyo
Yasu City 67 Lake Biwa
Yasuda 68 Shodo Island
Yasuda 87 Shikoku
Yasue Gold Leaf Museum 38 Kanazawa
Yasuecho 38 Kanazawa
Yasugi 69 Hiroshima & Western Honshu
Yasuicho 91 Kagoshima
Yasukata 77 Aomori
Yasukawacho 32 Nikko Town
Yasukuni Shrine 6 Imperial Palace & Tokyo Station
Yasumiishi Hot Spring 80 Aizu, Inawashiro & Ura-Bandai
Yasumiya 76 Lake Towada
Yasuoka 34 Central Honshu
Yasuoka Beach 68 Hiroshima & Western Honshu
Yasuzukacho 49 Western Kyoto
Yataro Iwasaki Birth Place 87 Shikoku
Yatate Hot Spring 77 Northern Honshu
Yatomi 54 Kansai Area
Yatomi City 35 Nagoya Area
Yatomi Historical Museum 35 Nagoya Area
Yatomi Yachoen Bird Sanctuary 35 Nagoya Area
Yatsubuchi-no-taki 67 Lake Biwa
Yatsuishi Ruins 87 Iya Valley
Yatsukuchicho 49 Western Kyoto
Yatsuri 65 Asuka
Yatsushiro 90 Kyusu
Yawara 66 Amano Hashidate
Yawata 42 Kyoto
Yawata 54 Kansai Area
Yawata Highland 191 Resort Ski Area 68 Hiroshima & Western Honshu
Yawatacho 44 Kawaramachi & Gion
Yawatahama 86 Shikoku
Yayoi 10 Asakusa, Ueno & Akihabara
Yayoi 38 Kanazawa
Yayoi Art Museum 10 Asakusa, Ueno & Akihabara
Yayoicho 14 Shinjuku
Yayoicho 24 Yokohama
Yayoicho 42 Kyoto
Yayoicho 75 Tottori
Yayoicho 84 Hakodate
Yazu 69 Hiroshima & Western Honshu
Yebisu Beer Museum 18 Meguro & Shinagawa
Yema-no-sachi Museum 78 Lake Tazawa
Yo Beach 97 Amami Oshima
Yo Shomei Museum 27 Kamakura
Yoancho 43 Central & Eastern Kyoto
Yobikaericho 47 Northern Kyoto
Yochomachi 15 Shinjuku
Yodo 42 Kyoto
Yodogabashi 41 Nagano
Yodogawa Starting Point 97 Yakushima
Yodogawa Ward 57 Greater Osaka
Yoga 4 Greater Tokyo
Yogai 79 Hiraizumi & Ichinoseki
Yogi 94 Naha
Yohicho 44 Kawaramachi & Gion
Yoichi 82 Hokaido
Yokaichiba 23 Mt. Fuji & Around Tokyo
Yokino Beach 95 Okinawa & The Southwest Islands
Yokinoura Beach 90 Kyusu
Yokizaki Beach 87 Shikoku
Yokkaichi 34 Central Honshu
Yoko-taki 82 Hokaido
Yokoami 11 Asakusa, Ueno & Akihabara
Yokobamacho 74 Matsue
Yokoboricho 36 Central Nagoya
Yokogawa-shinmachi 70 Hiroshima
Yokogawacho 70 Hiroshima
Yokohama 77 Northern Honshu
Yokohama Archives Of History 25 Kawasaki
Yokohama Cosmoworld 24 Yokohama
Yokohama Doll Museum 25 Kawasaki
Yokohama Hakkeijima Sea Paradise Amusement Park 23 Yokohama Area
Yokohama International Passenger Terminal

25 Kawasaki
Yokohama Museum of Art 24 Yokohama
Yokohama Port Museum 24 Yokohama
Yokohamakoen 24 Yokohama
Yokoiso 76 Shirakami Mountains
Yokokawa 11 Asakusa, Ueno & Akihabara
Yokokawa Hot Spring 30 Izu Peninsula
Yokomachi 41 Nagano
Yokooji 50 Southern Kyoto
Yokosawacho 41 Nagano
Yokosawahama Beach 80 Aizu, Inawashiro & Ura-Bandai
Yokosuka 23 Yokohama Area
Yokosuka Art Museum 23 Yokohama Area
Yokosuka Ruins 34 Central Honshu
Yokota Air Base 22 Mt. Fuji & Around Tokyo
Yokotamachi 41 Shizuoka
Yokote 77 Northern Honshu
Yokoteramachi 6 Imperial Palace & Tokyo Station
Yokouchicho 41 Shizuoka
Yokoyama 41 Nagano
Yokoyama 73 Iwakuni
Yokoyamamachi 38 Kanazawa
Yokoze 22 Mt. Fuji & Around Tokyo
Yokoze 88 Kotohira
Yokozutsumi 57 Greater Osaka
Yomei-mon Gate 32 Nikko Town
Yomitan 95 Okinawa-honto
Yomogawacho 56 Greater Osaka
Yomogawasoen 56 Greater Osaka
Yomogigadanicho 47 Northern Kyoto
Yomogita 77 Northern Honshu
Yona 95 Okinawa-honto
Yonabaru 95 Okinawa-honto
Yonago 69 Hiroshima & Western Honshu
Yonago Airport 69 Hiroshima & Western Honshu
Yonago City Museum of Art 69 Hiroshima & Western Honshu
Yonagomachi 74 Matsue
Yonaguni Submarine Ruins 94 Okinawa & The Southwest Islands
Yonagusuku 95 Okinawa-honto
Yonbancho 49 Western Kyoto
Yonbancho 6 Imperial Palace & Tokyo Station
Yonchome 31 Shimoda
Yonchome 44 Kawaramachi & Gion
Yonedacho 36 Central Nagoya
Yonehara Beach 96 Yaeyama Islands
Yoneno 33 Narita
Yonezawa 77 Northern Honshu
Yorikimachi 59 Osaka Station
Yorimiya 94 Naha
Yoro 54 Kansai Area
Yoronotaki Hot Spring 90 Kyusu
Yosano 66 Amano Hashidate
Yoshi 22 Mt. Fuji & Around Tokyo
Yoshida 30 Izu Peninsula
Yoshida 43 Central & Eastern Kyoto
Yoshida 68 Shodo Island
Yoshida 96 Yakushima
Yoshida Auto Camp Site 68 Shodo Island
Yoshida Hot Spring 90 Kyusu
Yoshida-ya Sake Shop Museum 10 Asakusa, Ueno & Akihabara
Yoshidacho 72 Hagi
Yoshidamachi 24 Yokohama
Yoshijima-ke House 39 Takayama
Yoshijimacho 70 Hiroshima
Yoshika 68 Hiroshima & Western Honshu
Yoshikata 75 Tottori
Yoshikawa 22 Mt. Fuji & Around Tokyo
Yoshikura 33 Narita
Yoshimi-hyakketsu 22 Mt. Fuji & Around Tokyo
Yoshimizu Shrine 65 Yoshina
Yoshimo Beach 68 Hiroshima & Western Honshu
Yoshimoto Aquarium 25 Kawasaki
Yoshina Hot Spring 30 Izu Peninsula
Yoshino 37 Central Nagoya
Yoshino 54 Kansai Area
Yoshino 58 Osaka Station
Yoshino 68 Shodo Island
Yoshino District 64 Around Nara
Yoshino-Mikuri Shrine 65 Yoshina
Yoshinocho 76 Hirosaki
Yoshinogawa 87 Shikoku
Yoshinoyama 65 Yoshina
Yoshioka 22 Mt. Fuji & Around Tokyo
Yoshioka Hot Spring 69 Hiroshima & Western Honshu
Yoshiumi Rose Park 86 Shimanami Kaido
Yoshiwara 22 Mt. Fuji & Around Tokyo
Yoshizuka 93 Fukuoka
Yoshono Town 64 Around Nara

Yoteizan Fukidashi Park 82 Sado-ga Island
Yoteizan Natural Park 82 Sado-ga Island
Yotsuya 15 Shinjuku
Yoyogi 12 Roppongi, Shibuya, Omotesando, Harajuku & Meiji Shrine
Yoyogi Park 4 Greater Tokyo
Yoyogi-kamizonocho 12 Roppongi, Shibuya, Omotesando, Harajuku & Meiji Shrine
Yozan Museum 91 Kagoshima
Yu Hot Spring 68 Hiroshima & Western Honshu
Yu-taki 32 Nikko Area
Yuba Hot Spring 31 Oshima
Yubae Hot Spring 34 Central Honshu
Yubara Hot Spring 69 Hiroshima & Western Honshu
Yubaraokutsu Prefectural Natural Park 69 Hiroshima & Western Honshu
Yubari 83 Hokaido
Yubetsu Hot Spring 82 Hokaido
Yubi-kan 72 Hagi
Yubuku-no-Satoyu Hot Spring 40 Nagano & Matsumoto Areas
Yuda Onsen 68 Hiroshima & Western Honshu
Yuda Sanso Hot Spring 69 Hiroshima & Western Honshu
Yudamakigari Hot Spring 90 Aso Area
Yudanaka Hot Spring 22 Mt. Fuji & Around Tokyo
Yudani Hot Spring 69 Hiroshima & Western Honshu
Yudoku Hot Spring 82 Daisetsuzan National Park
Yudomari 96 Yakushima
Yudomari Hot Spring 95 Okinawa & The Southwest Islands
Yudomari Hot Spring 96 Yakushima
Yudonosan Hot Spring 81 Dewa Sanzen
Yudonosan Ski Area 81 Dewa Sanzen
Yufu 90 Kyusu
Yufuin Yume Art Museum 91 Yufuin
Yugafu-kan 96 Yaeyama Islands
Yugakae Hot Spring 68 Hiroshima & Western Honshu
Yugashima 30 Izu Peninsula
Yugashima Hot Spring 30 Izu Peninsula
Yugawa 80 Aizu, Inawashiro & Ura-bandai
Yugawara 29 Hakone
Yugawara 30 Izu Peninsula
Yugawara Hot Spring 30 Izu Peninsula
Yugawara Yoshihama Beach 30 Izu Peninsula
Yugono-taki 96 Yakushima
Yuhigaokacho 61 Osaka Namba
Yuigahama 27 Kamakura
Yuigahama Beach 27 Kamakura
Yukawa Family Old Residence 72 Hagi
Yukawa Hot Spring 34 Central Honshu
Yuki Art Museum 59 Osaka Station
Yuki Hot Spring 68 Hiroshima & Western Honshu
Yuki-no-goshocho 62 Kobe
Yukinoshita 27 Kamakura
Yukishio Salt Museum 97 Miyako Islands
Yukuhashi 90 Kyusu
Yukyu-no-yu Hiraizumi Onsen 79 Hiraizumi & Ichinoseki
Yume Hot Spring 69 Hiroshima & Western Honshu
Yume-minato Park 69 Hiroshima & Western Honshu
Yume-no-yu Hot Spring 91 Aso Area
Yume-Yakata Oshu Fujiwara Rekishi-Monogatari 79 Hiraizumi & Ichinoseki
Yumeji Art Museum 75 Okamaya
Yumemigaoka Observatory 42 Kyoto
Yumenochi 62 Kobe
Yumenoshima 5 Greater Tokyo
Yumenoshima Tropical Greenhouse Dome 5 Greater Tokyo
Yumeori-no-sato 97 Amami Oshima
Yumeshima-higashi 56 Greater Osaka
Yumeshima-naka 56 Greater Osaka
Yumicho 88 Tokushima
Yumigahama Beach 30 Izu Peninsula
Yumigahara Beach 90 Kyusu
Yumiharidaira National Park 77 Northern Honshu
Yumiki 66 Amano Hashidate
Yuminocho 75 Okamaya
Yuminomachi 81 Sendai
Yumiyacho 45 Kawaramachi & Gion
Yumori 64 Around Nara
Yumori Hot Spring 34 Central Honshu
Yumoto 32 Nikko Area
Yumoto 32 Nikko Area
Yumoto 78 Hanamaki
Yumoto Hot Spring 68 Hiroshima & Western Honshu

Yumoto Hot Spring 82 Sado-ga Island
Yumugi Hot Spring 95 Okinawa & The Southwest Islands
Yumura Hot Spring 69 Hiroshima & Western Honshu
Yunagi 56 Greater Osaka
Yuni 83 Hokaido
Yuno Hot Spring 68 Hiroshima & Western Honshu
Yunodai Hot Spring 77 Northern Honshu
Yunohama Beach 30 Miyake-jima
Yunohama Beach 77 Northern Honshu
Yunohama Roten Hot Spring 30 Kozu-shima & Nii-jima
Yunohana Hot Spring 54 Kansai Area
Yunokicho 45 Kawaramachi & Gion
Yunomine 66 Hongu Onsens
Yunomine Hot Spring 66 Hongu Onsens
Yunomoto Hot Spring 90 Kyusu
Yunoo Hot Spring 90 Kyusu
Yunosawa Hot Spring 40 Nagano & Matsumoto Areas
Yunosawa Hot Spring 76 Shirakami Mountains
Yunosawa Hot Spring 81 Dewa Sanzen
Yunosawa Hot Spring 83 Hokaido
Yunose Hot Spring 69 Hiroshima & Western Honshu
Yunotai Hot Spring 82 Hokaido
Yunotaira Hot Spring 22 Mt. Fuji & Around Tokyo
Yunotani Hot Spring 86 Shikoku
Yunotsu Hot Spring 68 Hiroshima & Western Honshu
Yurakucho 8 Ginza, Tsukiji & Tokyo Tower
Yuriage Beach 77 Northern Honshu
Yurigamotocho 48 Western Kyoto
Yurihama 69 Hiroshima & Western Honshu
Yurinkan Museum 45 Kawaramachi & Gion
Yurugicho 65 Nara
Yusaka Hot Spring 69 Hiroshima & Western Honshu
Yushima 7 Imperial Palace & Tokyo Station
Yushukan War Museum 6 Imperial Palace & Tokyo Station
Yusuhara 86 Shikoku
Yusui 90 Kyusu
Yutagawa Hot Spring 81 Dewa Sanzen
Yutaka-kaikan 67 Lake Biwa
Yutakacho 4 Greater Tokyo
Yuwatarimachi 89 Matsuyama
Yuyama Hot Spring 34 Central Honshu
Yuza 77 Northern Honshu
Yuzawa 77 Northern Honshu
Yuzen Cultural Hall 49 Western Kyoto
Yuzuki-jo Museum 89 Matsuyama
YY Beach Beach 68 Hiroshima & Western Honshu

Zaifucho 76 Hirosaki
Zaimoku-cho 59 Osaka Station
Zaimokucho 38 Kanazawa
Zaimokucho 43 Central & Eastern Kyoto
Zaimokucho 75 Tottori
Zaimokumachi 66 Himeji Castle
Zaimokuza 27 Kamakura
Zaimokuza Beach 27 Kamakura
Zao Hot Spring 81 Zao Onsen
Zao Lisa World Ski Area 81 Zao Onsen
Zao Onsen Ski Resort 81 Zao Onsen
Zao-hotta 81 Zao Onsen
Zao-uwano 81 Zao Onsen
Zenami 79 Hiraizumi & Ichinoseki
Zengenjicho 57 Greater Osaka
Zengoro-no-taki & Ushidome Pond 40 Nagano & Matsumoto Areas
Zeniarai Benten Shrine 27 Kamakura
Zenkoji 37 Inuyama
Zentsuji 87 Shikoku
Zenza 92 Nagasaki
Zenzamachi 41 Shizuoka
Zo-iwa (Elephant Rock) 87 Seto-ohasi Bridge
Zojo-ji 8 Ginza, Tsukiji & Tokyo Tower
Zoshicho 65 Nara
Zoshigaya 17 Ikebukuro
Zoshigaya Missionary Museum 17 Ikebukuro
Zoshikicho 72 Hagi
Zuigan-ji 81 Matsushima
Zuiganji Art Museum 81 Matsushima
Zuihoden (Mausoleum of Date Masamune) 81 Sendai
Zuisen-ji 27 Kamakura
Zuisenji 37 Inuyama
Zushi 23 Yokohama Area
Zushigahama Beach 68 Hiroshima & Western Honshu
Zushioku 42 Kyoto
Zutsumihon-dori-nishi 57 Greater Osaka

Other books of interest from Tuttle Publishing

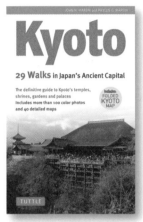

ISBN 978-4-8053-0918-6

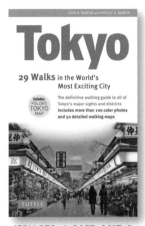

ISBN 978-4-8053-0917-9

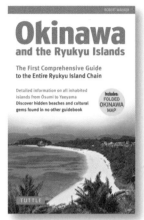

ISBN 978-4-8053-1233-9

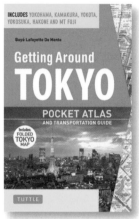

ISBN 978-4-8053-0965-0

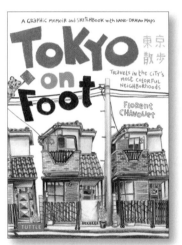

ISBN 978-4-8053-1137-0

ISBN 978-4-8053-1129-5

ISBN 978-4-8053-1285-8

ISBN 978-4-8053-1288-9

ISBN 978-4-8053-0978-0

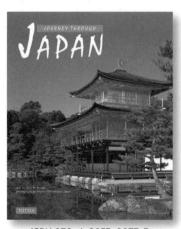

ISBN 978-4-8053-0977-3

tuttlepublishing.com